Współczesny herb m. Zgierza, wprowadzony
od 1921 roku.

Miasto Zgierz jest jednym z ważniejszych ośrodków przemysłowych Polski, położonym wśród wyniosłego płaskowzgórza piotrkowsko-łódzkiego nad rzeką Bzurą, która o 7 km na południowo-wschód od Zgierza bierze swój początek we wsi Rogi.

Składa się ono z 2 części: z tak zwanego Starego Miasta ze Starym Rynkiem i z Nowego Miasta z Rynkiem Kilińskiego (dawniej Nowym Rynkiem). Oprócz tego ma przedmieście, zwane Przybyłowem, oddzielone niegdyś od Zgierza gruntami wsi Zegrzanki, której granice długim językiem wrzynały się w posiadłości miejskie.

Jakże przedstawia się przeszłość tego miasta?

דף ראשון מספרו של ברוניסלב וכניק „זגירז'", שהופיע בפולנית, בהוצאת א. לאך
בזגירז', בשנת 1933.

ערשטע זייט פון בראָניסלאָוו וואָכניק'ס בוך „זגערזש" (היסטאָרישע סקיצע),
דערשינען אין פֿאַרלאָג פון א. לאַך אין זגערזש, 1933.

The first page of the book of Bronislaw Wiechnik, "Zgierz", which was printed in Polish. It was published by A. Lach in Zgierz, 1933.

The Book of Zgierz

An Eternal Memorial
for a
Jewish Community of Poland

By The Survivors

Edited by Jerrold Jacobs

Published by JewishGen, Inc.
An Affiliate of
The Museum of Jewish Heritage - A Living Memorial to the Holocaust

The Book of Zgierz

An Eternal Memorial for a Jewish Community of Poland

By The Survivors

Copyright ©2007 by JewishGen, Inc

Edited: Jerrold Jacobs
Translation: Jerrold Landau

JewishGen, Inc
2951 Marina Bay Drive, Suite 130-472
League City, TX 77573

Printed in the United States of America by Lightning Source, Inc.

Library of Congress Control Number (LCCN): 2007922624
ISBN: 978-0-9764759-2-7
(hard cover: 783 pages, alk. paper)

Dedication

This English Edition is dedicated to those who did not survive the Shoah. It is also dedicated to the descendants of the Jewish residents of Zgierz who reside throughout the world. In particular I would like to acknowledge my: Jakubowicz, Feldon, Kincler and Moskowitz ancestors.

Jerrold Jacobs, Editor
2007

Preface

The English translation of the Zgierz book was originally made available on the Internet by JewishGen's Yizkor Book Translation Project, fulfilling its mission of disseminating information about the Holocaust and destroyed Jewish communities. The release of a hard copy not withstanding, the online English translation remains on the internet. This translation is augmented by the translation of the Zgierz Chapter from *Pinkhas Hakelliot Polin* which was provided as a graciously shared service to JewishGen by Yad Vashem.

Today in 2007, some thirty two years after the initial efforts of the Organization of Zgierz Natives in Israel to memorialize their community, the story they envisioned has taken on a new life. We who have been involved in both the online Internet version and the hard copy publication of this book feel the story and the efforts of all involved at every step of the way should not be left out of the process. It was their initial efforts and accomplishment that fueled ours. Theirs began with the following letter in 1975:

The Organization of Zgierz Natives in Israel
Address: Halperin,
David Hamelech Street 51, Tel Aviv
Telephone 233870

Dear Friend!

We present you this book with deep feelings of the great moral obligation that fate has placed upon us -the remnants who survived the destruction of the holocaust. The purpose of this book is the perpetuation of the community of Zgierz, a community of 5,000 souls, which was ruined and destroyed by the Nazi Germans and their accomplices during the years 1939-1945. This book should serve as an eternal memorial and a warning to future generations:

Remember! Never Forget!

The Zgierz Yizkor Book Committee
Tel Aviv 5735 - 1975
{Title page}

The Book of Zgierz
An Eternal Memorial for a Jewish Community of Poland.

Memorial Book Zgierz
Edited by David Shtockfish
Vice-Editor: Y. A. Malchieli
Printed in Israel 5735 - 1975
Printed by "Lavav" Tel Aviv, Hamisgar Street 60.
Telephone-36564.

Write this as a memorial in a book

(Exodus 17, 14) [1]

Announcing the first publication, Zeev Wolf Fisher wrote:

With holy trepidation and deep spiritual satisfaction, we present this modest book to the honored readers, in particular to the natives of our town in Israel and in the Diaspora, in order to serve as a monument and memorial for the community of Zgierz, which was destroyed by the Nazi Germans and their murderous accomplices during the years of the holocaust (5700 - 5705, 1939 -1945).

We indeed realize that we did not complete the task. Despite the great efforts that we put into this holy work, we were only able to obtain that which was possible to obtain via the meager methods that we had at our disposal. The working conditions that prevailed in our time and the financial situation did not ease our task. The small amount of money that we raised through difficult efforts was quickly used up, and organized financial assistance from the Diaspora did not reach us. Nevertheless, through the publication of the Book of Zgierz, we can see that the efforts of a group of people, who gave of their means and time with generosity and great dedication, were not in vain. These efforts were expended in order to memorialize and perpetuate the memory of the community in our town - its rich and variegated past, its unique human landscape with feelings of love and respect to everything that is close and dear to our hearts.

We attempted to present to the future generations the story of the flourishing of the community of Zgierz through all of its stages of development; its tribulations and struggles with the earlier governing authorities and the specific conditions of the place and the region; the makeup of the community, its great activity and great stature in Torah, teaching, industry, business, the various crafts, the wisdom of the Jewish people and its literature. We attempted to present the communal vivaciousness of the Jews with regards to their outlook, goals, ways of life and human dedication (the communal, social, economic, cultural and ideological struggles). We particularly attempted to present echoes of the social life and the charitable and benevolent work which marked the epitome of communal life. All of these are accompanied by pictures and photographs that portray people and important communal events of our town.

There remains in our hands a significant amount of material which, for various reasons, technical and otherwise, were not included in this book. We hope that there will be people who follow after us, who will add in all those items that are fit to be published, and may they be blessed.

In general, the book does not follow a chronological order, and everything that is important is in its own place. Section by section, we attempted to merge a chronological order with an appropriate layout. We did this in a certain measure in order to provide continuity in family chains, to place in proximity members of the same family who are mentioned, and also to connect various organizations and factions with their appropriate ideologies. On the other hand, after the book had been printed in sections, some omissions came to light, and some items could not be put into their appropriate place. We express our regrets over this.

With the publication of this book, we believe that we have fulfilled a great moral obligation to the martyrs of our city, may they all be remembered for a blessing. With this recognition, we present the book with a silent prayer: May it be the will that this book should serve as an eternal memorial for all of those people, through whose efforts, steadfastness of heart, and vision (including those righteous and pure people who are hidden among the "general populace", the workers and simple folk) all together created the magnificent human mosaic of the community of Zgierz, which was destroyed along with the rest of the holy communities of Poland. May their souls be bound in the bonds of eternal life, and may their names be intertwined for all generations in the historical annals of the eternal people.

Our deep gratitude goes out to all of those who offered their assistance in any form; to those who gave us advice or support during difficult times of disappointment and weakness of resolve. We would particularly like to thank the directors of Yad Vashem of Jerusalem; the directors of YIVO of New York; the Jewish Historical Archives of Jerusalem; the "Shaarei Zion" library and its staff of Tel Aviv; Mr. Tzvi Shener, the director of the Yitzchak Katznelson Beit Lochmei Hagetaot (the memorial institute for the ghetto fighters); Mrs. David Davidowitz, the directory of the museum of ethnography and folklore of Tel Aviv; G. Kressel, the writer and bibliographer of Holon; and Mr. Moshe Chaim Morgenstern of Tel Aviv - for their unique and relevant material that they provided.

Our gratitude and esteem go out to Mr. David Shtockfish, the editor of the book, for all the patience that he exhibited during our long, drawn-out efforts, and for the wisdom that he displayed for our sublime task.

We should remember for a blessing the first editor of the book, Mr. A. Wolf-Jasni of blessed memory, who began this sacred task and did not merit to see its conclusion. May his memory be blessed.

In the name of the Committee of the Zgierz Book and the editorial committee

Zeev Wolf Fisher

Tel Aviv, Tevet-Shvat 5735 (January 1975)

Zeev Fisher's words are followed by those of Fabian Greenberg, a Zgierz Community Activist who emigrated to the United States:

With trembling and heartfelt emotion, I write the introduction to the Zgierz Yizkor Book. These few hundred pages are about an annihilated Jewish community, which was destroyed under terrible circumstances. The people were pursued and afflicted, robbed of their livelihood and their human means, at a time when onlookers cynically mocked them in their anguish; they were expelled from their homes into ghettoes where they suffered from hunger, their energy was drained; until the murderous Germans misled them with deceit and treachery, loaded them upon transports, and hauled them to the gas chambers and crematoria.

Upon us, the survivors, lies the holy duty to perpetuate the memory of the martyrs - and that is the purpose of this Yizkor book.

It is not sufficient to exclusively paint the tragic portrait of the destruction. The Jews lived and flourished in Zgierz throughout the course of hundreds of years. Therefore, this book presents significant material regarding the development of the Jewish community; the various streams of Polish Jewry throughout the previous century; the culture, political, religious and communal life - which had a strong effect on the Jewish people of our town. In this book, we will present detailed, interesting and instructive articles, memories and descriptions.

A few chapters were written by people who went through the Hitlerian concentration camps, work camps, ghettos, and wanderings during the years of the Second World War. Reading their stories, we all relive those bitter times.

Every town had its own characters and individualists. Zgierz was an industrial town. It was especially known for its textile industry, which employed a large number of Jewish and Christian workers. There were no members of the leisure class [2] there. Jewish entrepreneurs, initiators, and inventors passed through there, and the town took an honorable place in the economy of the country, a fact that will certainly be of interest to future historians.

Compiling such a book was a very difficult task, which took a great a great deal of time, energy and diligence. It required that everyone maintain a strong faith that we would be able to accomplish this task, that the Jewry of Zgierz would be memorialized by a monument, not of stone or of marble -but rather a spiritual, literary monument, enclosed between the two hard covers of this Yizkor book. This monument should be found in every home that has a connection to bygone Jewish Zgierz.

We owe thanks to all those who lent a hand to the production of this book - the committee members in Tel Aviv and New York. The highest gratitude goes to the initiator and actualizer, Wolf Fischer. Without him, the book of Zgierz would never have seen the light of day.

Fabian Greenberg, New York

Editor Jerrold Jacobs writes:

The idea of creating an English version of the Zgierz Memorial Book actually began in 1999 with a visit to my father's birthplace. The center of the City was still suggestive of the now lost community that existed at the time of his birth in 1898. I wanted to know more. I searched the listings of Communities that produced Yizkor Books and found that one had been written for Zgierz. The internet helped me to locate two used copies at a bookstore in Tel Aviv.

The translation which appears on the JewishGen website took three years to complete. It portrays a vibrantly diverse community. For much of its modern history, Zgierz was a diverse mix of Jewish, Polish and German citizens who found commercial reasons to coexist. This book concentrates on a lively, productive Jewish community obliterated by the Nazi invasion of Poland.

The story continues:

As a totally unanticipated result of placing the first chapters of an English translation of the Zgierz book online, the Yizkor Book Translation Project Manager received a surprising request. It came from a group in Zgierz explaining that their organization was made up of people who had no idea of the Jewish contribution to the history of their city.

About each chapter as it appeared, they wrote, "we read the text with baited breath for we had to face a completely new image of our city. We in Zgierz have very little knowledge of other nations that once lived here. Hardly anybody knows where was the synagogue and other Jewish communal buildings; people don't even remember of the Jewish cemetery, although it is fenced and there is a commemorating plate on it. The great majority of citizens have not the slightest idea how rich and varied the Jewish life in Zgierz was."

To reach out to this community and to extend the impact of our English translation, JewishGen granted permission for a Polish translation to be created. As each chapter is completed, it is put online and linked from the English version. Thus, what happened in Poland has come almost full circle, to be completed only when the final chapter can be read in their native language by the current and future residents of Zgierz. It is hoped that someday a complete Polish translation will be available as a book to be read by all with an interest in the contribution of a Jewish community to the history of a town in Poland.

To all those who combined their talents, their efforts and their will to accomplish a task, we are pleased and honored to be able to join with them and to present to the current readership and to those who will come after them, the English translation of The Book of Zgierz.

Joyce Field, JewishGen Vice President for Data Acquisitons, Manager Yizkor Book Translations Project; Jerrold L. Jacobs, Zgierz Project Coordinator and Editor; Jerrold Landau, English Translation; Joel Alpert, Layout and Production for Published by JewishGen Project; Carol W. Skydell, JewishGen Vice President for Special Projects, Manager of Published by JewishGen Project

Notes to the Reader

The online English translation of the Zgierz Yizkor Book is available at: *http://www.jewishgen.org/Yizkor/zgierz/zgierz.html*

The translation of the Zgierz Chapter from Pinkhas Hakelliot Polin, shared with JewishGen by Yad Vashem is available at: *http://www.jewishgen.org/Yizkor/pinkas_poland/pol1_00106.html*

Table of Contents

A. History of the City

Zgierz in Historical Sources   1
History of Jews in Zgierz until 1862
   by A. Wolfe Yasni   8
Jews in Zgierz in the Latter Half of the 19th and
   Beginning of the 20th Centuries by Avraham Wein   72
My Hometown at the End of the 19th
   Century by Leon Lifschitz   93
A View into Zgierz and the Life of its Jews
   From the Community Annals From the years 1915-1930
   Edited by Y. A. Malchieli   96

B. The Development of Jewish Zgierz

Zgierz through the Perspective of Passing
   Years by Yaakov Cohen   133
Zgierz and Kotzk by Yaakov Kirshenbaum   150
Zgierz Brings Honor to the Jewish
   Entrepreneurial Spirit by A. Litwin   153
The Synagogue and Study Hall of Zgierz
   by Rabbi Shimon Huberband   158
The Weaver   162
The Textile Industry in Zgierz in 1936
   by David Baum   163
From the Cloth Maker's Group Prior to
   The Handworker's Club by Y. L. Weinstein   169
Dyers in Zgierz by Chaya Sperling Halperin   171
Our Commissioners by Fabian Greenberg   172
The Struggle for Jewish Work and Jewish
   Manufacturing by Y. Sczaransky   174

About Jewish Employment in Zgierz by F   177

My Ten Years in Zgierz by
    Menachem (Manes) Angel   178

The Chant of a Generation by Pinchas Bizberg   179

My Old Good Home by Dov Grand   198

The First Charitable Fund by W. F   199

Two Important Jewish Institutions by Yaakov Cincinatus   201

The Jewish Orphanage of Zgierz by Chana Sczaransky   203

In the Presence of my Teacher and Rabbi,
    Rabbi Rafael Henech Blostein of
    Blessed memory by F. BenSrok   204

My Teachers and Educators in Zgierz by F. Ben-Sira   209

Reb Yaakov the son of Yaakov Milichovitzki of blessed
    Memory byY. A.Malchieli   212

Reb Wolf Lieb Haltrecht by W. Fisher   215

The Businessman's School of Zgierz by F.Greenberg.   217

In the Businessman's School of Zgierz by Dr. Jacob Eichner   217

Jewish Elementary Schools in Zgierz by Sara Katz   218

A Ruined Lag Baomer by Yitzchak Sczaransky   221

The David Frischman Jewish Library by W. Fisher   223

The Zamir Literary and Musical Club by W. F.   229

The Dramatic Circle by Abu-Arieh   233

The Symphonia Singing Group by W. F.   234

The Zionist Federation ("Agudat Hatzionim") in Zgierz
    by Yosef Katz and Yehuda Weinstein   235

The Young People's Group and Young Zionists
    by Yosef Katz   240

The Mizrachi Organization of Zgierz by Yehoshua Berliner   242

Agudas Yisrael and its Institutions by F. S   244

"Maccabee" by Y. Weinstein and D. Berger   252

The "Dvora" Zionist Women's Group by Rachel
    Sperling Shapira   258

The Jewish Scout Organization of Zgierz by L. Rubinstein   259

The Hashomer Hatzair Youth Organization of Zgierz
    by Chaya Sperling-Halperin and Rafael Katz   262

Hechalutz by Chaya Halperin and Yaakov Lewin   266

The Hitachdut Zionist Worker's Group by W. Fisher and
   David Berger   268
Gordonia by Y. Sh.   271
About Gordonia by Yisrael Chaimowitz   273
The Revisionist Faction of Zgierz by Mordechai
   the son of Reb Yaakov Glazer   273
The Borochov Group by Yitzchak Sczaransky   277
The Bund by Vove   280
The Communist Party in Zgierz by A.Y.   281

C. Personalities and Characters

Rabbi Shalom Tzvi Hakohen of blessed memory by
   Rabbi A. Y. Brumberg and other sources   283
The Second Rabbi of Zgierz, Rabbi Tzvi Hakohen of
   Blessed memory by Rabbi A. Y. Brumberg and other sources   296
Rabbi Shlomo Yehuda Leib Hakoen of blessed memory by
   Rabbi A. Y. Brumberg and other sources   299
The First Rabbi, Rabbi Shalom Tzvi Hakohen of blessed
   Memory by Rabbi A.Y. Brumberg and other sources   305
The Rabbi and Teacher Rabbi Yechiel Michel Elberg of
   Blessed memory and His Son Rabbi Avraham Natan of
   Blessed memory by Yehuda Elberg   309
Rabbi Yitzchak Mendel Hakohen of blessed memory
   by F. S.   314
The House of the Admor Rabbi Shmuel Bornstein of
   Sochaczew of blessed Memory   318
The House of the Admor Rabbi Menachem Mendel Landau
   of Strikow of blessed memory by F. Sirkes   322
Rabbi Avraham Yaakov Weisenfeld of blessed
   Memory by Y. A. M.   325
Reb Tovia Lifschitz of blessed memory by W. F.   330
Reb Tovia Lifschitz by Aryeh Lifschitz   335
The Writer and Poet David Frischman by Y. A. M.   336
My Father Yissachar Moshe Schwartz
   by Shmuel Schwartz   341
Reb Yissachar Moshe Schwartz of blessed
   Memory by Y. A. M.   350

Someone in a City by W. F. 355

The Poem of my Grandfather Yisachar Schwartz
"Tshaika" by Yeshayahu Spiegel 361

Shmuel Schwartz by A. Y. Brzezinski and other sources 364

The House of Shapira by A. Y. Sh. Hakohen 368

The Eiger Family by Engineer Avraham Eiger 372

The Industrialist – the Poet by Z. Fisher and Y. A. Malchieli 378

Akiva (Karol) Eiger by Y. L. Weinstein
   and W. Fisher 384

Reb Yaakov Binyamin and his Son Yitzchak Katznelson
   by Tzipora Katznelson Nachumov 387

The Poet and Writer Yaakov Cohen by Y. A. M. 390

The Poet Yaakov Cohen by Y. Avishuv 397

Reb Mordechai Shmuel Czudkowitz by Yaakov Cohen 400

The Sirkes Family by F. Abba 401

The Boaz Family by Avraham Boaz 411

The Greenberg Family by Fabian Greenberg 413

Fabian Greenberg-Green by Z. Fisher 415

The Reichert Family by Tamar Itinson-Reichert 418

My Grandfather Reb Fishel Bunim Hollander
   by David Wechsler 428

Rabbi Mendel Wechsler may his blood be avenged
   by David Wechsler and Other sources 431

Reb Aharon Yosef Berger by Z. Ben Shimon 434

Reb Fishel Rus by Yitzchak Sczaransky 437

Reb Avraham Klorfeld by Yoav Katz 438

Zalman Feldscher by Yitzchak Sczaransky 439

Yaakov Berliner-Baniel by Y. D. Beit-Halevi
   and other sources 440

Menachem Berliner by Yehoshua Manoach 443

Reb Henech Ehrsohn P. S. 454

Reb Yosef Bialystoczki by P. S. 454

Avraham Chaim Michelson by P. S. 454

AvrahamAvr Morganstern by Fabian Greenberg-Green 456

Reb Yehuda Leib Sczaransky by Hillel Zeidman
   From the book "Eileh Ezkera" 457

Rabbi Meir Sczaransky from the Newspapers 460

Reb Yitzchak Bornsztejn by David Eisenberg   462
Rabbi Moshe Goldberg of blessed memory by A. Bornstein   464
Chaya Bornstein Goldberg by Y. Lavie   465
Aharon Cincinatus of blessed memory by Shmuel Shachar   466
My Brother Aharon by Tala Cincinatus   468
Reb Yoshke Lewin by Y. Sh.   470
Machla Wransky (The Sky Gazer) by Vove   471
Chava-Itta by Yitzchak Sczaransky   472
Yisrael Veinik from the Lexicon of the New Yiddish
    Literature and the Lerer Yizkor Book   473
Pinchas Bizberg from the Lexicon of the New Yiddish
    Literature and other sources   474
Pinchas Bizberg – a Writer and a Mentsch
    by Yaakov Piloyovski   475
"Riches are not the Main Thing" by Pinchas Bizberg   477
Lazo Waszasz-Sczaransky by Ch. L. Fuchs   479
Shia Zaklikovski by Y. A.   479
Yaakov Aharon the Water Carrier   480
Yoav Katz of blessed memory   483
Menachem Mendel Zakon of blessed memory   486
Leon Rubinstein by Mordechai Shtrigler and Dr. Sh. Margoshes   487
Rabbi Yechiel Zeltzer by F. Zeev   490
Pinchas A. Sirkes from the Lexicon of the New Yiddish
    Literature and other sources   491
Yehuda Elberg from the Lexicon of the New Yiddish
    Literature and other sources   492

D. The Holocaust

A Dirge for my Nation! By Yoav Katz of blessed memory   494
In One Day by W. F.   495
Jews of Zgierz Under the German Occupation
    by Danuta Dombrowsky and Avraham Wein   496
Jews of Zgierz in the Warsaw Ghetto
    by Mary Fisher-Fishman   510
This City was also registered by W. Ben Shimon   512
The Way of Martyrdom for a Jew of Zgierz
    by Arash Rozenstrauch of Blessed memory   516

From Skiernewice to Monte Casino
   by Moshe Yaakov Grand   531
A Few Words about Yaakov Grand of blessed memory
   by W. Fisher   527
Herschel – One of the First Victims of the Nazi Murder
   by Abu Aryeh   538
Drops of Agony from the Sea of Destruction
   by Hela Goldberg-Finkelstein   539
The Destruction of Zgierz by Rabbi Shimon Huberband   541
The Germans of Zgierz Made Themselves Known
   by Yaakov   545
Jumping from the Death Wagon which was traveling to
   Treblinka by Mordechai Grand   546
My Child... My Child... by W. Ben Shimon   552
The Miracle with My Child by Tamar (Tala) Cincinatus   553
My Two Friends from Zgierz in the Warsaw Ghetto
   by Hirsch Wasser   554
Our Family and Other Jews Were Saved
   by Shalom Tzvi Lasker   556
With The Germans and Russians in Postwar Poland
   by Dov Grand   560
Encounters with Zgierzers in Russia by Yitzchak Gotthelf   565
Sad Memories by Esther Gotthelf   566
In My Destroyed Home by Fabian Greenberg   566
For My Hometown Zgierz by Y. A. Malchieli   578

E. Eternal Lights

A Memorial for the Souls   590
Of Our Neighbors and Those we Remember

F. The Survivors of Zgierz
Our Fellow Townsmen after the Holocaust by W. Fisher   711
Zgierz Natives in Israel by Zeev Fisher   725

Footnotes

Section A   737

Section B   741

Section C   748

Section D   758

Section E   762

Section F   762

A. History of the City

Zgierz in Historical Sources

In the book "Polish Cities throughout One Thousand Years" "*Miasta Polsky W Tysiacleciu*", published in 1965 in two volumes by the Osolinskich National foundation (Wroclaw - Warsaw - Krakow), we read the following details about the history of Zgierz.

Zgierz is a regional city belonging to the Lodz district. It is bounded on the south by Lodz, and is located on the Bzura River.

General View of Zgierz

The communication artery that runs from Piotrkow and Leczyca to Torun passes through Zgierz. During the early middle ages, Zgierz was the property of the noblemen. It is first mentioned in 1231. There used to be a palace there, and some remnants from the time of the breakup of the feudal system still exist.

In 1255, the sources mention Alexei the Kaplan of Zgierz, and in 1295, the Rector of Zgierz. The first mention of Zgierz as a city is in 1318. At that time, a tax office existed there. During the 13th century, the settlement of

1

Zgierz already was of a civic nature. In 1420, Zgierz was granted the rights of a city.

The growth of the city during the era prior to the beginning of industry began only during the 14th century and at the beginning of the 15th century. The main economic activities that sustained the civic population were agriculture, hunting, artisanship and trade - particularly after the city received the rights in 1505 to conduct weekly and annual fairs. The annual fairs took place three times a year.

In 1564, there were 129 homes, 7 guesthouses, and 33 workshops, including 6 butcher shops in Zgierz. It is possible to estimate that there were approximately 700 residents.

During the middle of the seventeenth century, there was a period of backsliding. In 1642, there were only approximately 142 people living there, not more. During the following 100 years, there was a marked improvement. In 1763, houses were built upon 56 lots. Among the citizens of the town who owned property there were the following artisans: 6 shoemakers, 7 potters, 21 manufacturers of wheels and wagons, 6 barrel makers, 3 hat makers, as well as butchers, smiths and others. There were also 6 salt merchants. To complete the portrait of the professional situation in Zgierz, we can add 1 miller, as well as some beer brewers and restaurant owners.

The fact of the transfer of the regional center of Brzeziny and Inowo Lodzki from Brzeziny, which was the town of the noblemen, to Zgierz, a city of the independent republic, in 1792, testifies to the rise of the prominence of Zgierz.

There was a synagogue in Zgierz. During the years of Prussian occupation, Zgierz was the seat of the regional government (from 1798). In 1802, there were already 77 houses and 463 residents of Zgierz.

Two Polish weavers, who began their efforts between 1817 and 1820, were the driving forces behind the establishment of the textile industry in Lodz, independent of government help. In 1819, there were about 60 weavers working there. The beginnings of Zgierz as a major industrial city was in the years 1820-1821, when, in accordance with a decision of the offices of the Polish governor, the agricultural / artisan oriented city changed its character, and took on the character of a diligent and progressive textile manufacturing city.

Representatives of the government of Congress Poland made the well known agreement with Zgierz, the most important agreement from the point of view of the development of the industrial city, which granted independent rights to the manufacturing in Lodz and the surrounding area. A new settlement sprouted up and developed next to the old city. This settlement started on the areas of the east bank of the Bzura.

The population of Zgierz quickly grew due to newcomers who were artisans, merchants and professionals: Poles, Germans, Jews and also Russians. The population grew from 994 in 1820 to more than 10,000 about ten years later. Favorable local conditions inspired the governing authorities to designate Zgierz as a manufacturing center. At the same time, various trades, organized into professional organizations, began to develop.

After 1822, the textile manufacturing industry became organized, and later on, the wool workshop did so as well. In addition, the manufacture of utensils and machines that were needed for the flourishing textile trade developed. The first steam operated felt factory was established in 1837.

Conflicts regarding status broke out already from the earliest time of the industrial development of Zgierz. A revolt of the workers against the artisans and the town government broke out in 1826. It was broken up by force with the assistance of an infantry unit that was called in from Leczyca after two days of street fights.

In 1829, Zgierz received rights and jurisdiction over other cities in the region, and the major was replaced with a council president. The first serious crisis in the history of the city took place after the failure of the November revolt. Despite the difficulties in manufacturing and marketing, the textile industry held its own during the difficult years between the two revolts, and even continued to progress. The number of workshops and factories increased. In 1866, there were already 11,341 residents of Zgierz, including 4,280 Poles, 4,346 Germans, and 2,633 Jews. 636 people were employed in the trades.

Zgierz was a city that was very concerned with its physical structure. This can be seen from the data in the lists of 1860: at that time there were 29 paved roads, public buildings, a town hall, a synagogue, a church, and manufacturing buildings. The people of Zgierz at that time lived in 317 wooden houses, 95 brick bungalows and 5 two-story buildings. Barter of merchandise took place on the two weekly market days, as well as during the six annual fairs that took place during the course of the years.

3

The population of Zgierz took part in the January revolt, and they participated in the various partisan organizations. The leader of the revolutionary movement and the demonstrations in the region of Zgierz was Kazimierz Wojciech Gadomski.

During the era of large scale manufacturing at the end of the 19th century, Zgierz took strong steps forward in its development. In 1891, the population was 17,743, and at the beginning of the 20th century, the population reached 21,034. There were 1,869 houses in the city, including 484 built of brick. There were 316 manufacturing enterprises functioning in the city. The 29 largest factories produced products with an annual value of 4,432,330 rubles, and employed 2,584 workers. The 12 next smallest factories had an annual production valued at 258,609 rubles and employed only 242 Zgierz natives. The local industry included the processing of wool. The German population was particularly prominent. It was progressive, active, and well organized into various organizations and factions. Various social and inter-factional disputes broke out. [3]

During the 1870s, the first social organizations began to function in Zgierz. The first widespread strikes began to take place in 1871-1874. In the years 1882-1885, Zgierz turned into a center of action of the "Proletariat" party of the Lodz district. The pride of the Zgierz "Proletariats" was a young weaver by the name of Jan Pietroszinski, who was killed on top of the Warsaw Citadel in 1886. The workers of Zgierz along with the workers of Lodz were particularly active during the battles of the revolt of 1905-1907.

The First World War impeded the economic development of the city. In independent Poland, the national conditions in the city changed: from among 21,129 residents, 16,232 were Poles. At the end of the 1920s, between the two world wars, the German population of Zgierz dropped to 2,358 souls.

The city boundaries encompassed the entire old and new cities, along with the fields and suburbs of Piaski, Wolki and Przybylow.

Starting from 1903, there was a railway connection from Zgierz to Lodz and Warsaw via the Kalisz railway line, and with the regional seat of government by electric tram. A few years later, a new tramline started that went from Lodz to Ozorkow, and passed through the western part of Zgierz. From 1923, there was a railway connection between Zgierz and Kutno. At the same time, the chemical industry weakened, and the textile industry increased.

4

After the First World War, cultural progression took place. Along with the government Staszic Gymnasium and the German Frau Gymnasium, in 1919 a government seminary for girls and a government business school opened up. In 1916, the newspaper "Gazeta Zgierska" started publication.

In 1927, the population of Zgierz was 23,130, and in 1931, it was 26,618. In 1938, the population was 27,853. Regarding the economic composition of the population, the percentage of the population that worked in industry reached 82%.

The era of German occupation made life very difficult in the city. A significant portion of the Polish population was transferred out of Zgierz. Much of the population was imprisoned in jail and in concentration camps. The Jewish population was completely destroyed. The cruelty of the Hitlerists reached its peak in the public murder on March 21, 1942 of more than one hundred prisoners in the area of the civic garbage dump who had been transferred from Radogoszcz.

From 1942, various military and citizen's organizations belonging to the Polish workers faction and the civil defense faction operated in Zgierz.

In 1945, a new era of Zgierz history began [4]. It was characterized by rebuilding and rapid development along the communist economic pattern. Along with the economic development, we should make note of the demographic situation. The population grew from 21,960 in 1946 to 37,647 at the end of 1961. The city occupied an area of 3,057 square kilometers.

Zgierz is an important center of the textile and chemical industries. The structure of the city improved, with multi story housing blocks, communal gardens, appropriate heating systems, and a complete health network with a modern civic hospital. There were 11 elementary schools, 13 trade schools, 2 high schools, and a school for teachers. The city had a fine swimming pool.

It is fitting to take note of the diligent protection of the antiquities of the city from the time of the beginning of the textile industry. There is a wooden church dating from the eighteenth century. The pride of the city was the above mentioned Jan Pietrusinski as well as Adolf Pawinski (1840-1896), the son of a soldier, who was a noted historian during that era.

Zgierz in "Yevreiska Encyclopedia" (St. Petersburg, 1908-1913)

In accordance to a decision of the Czarist government on December 21, 1824, this city imposed the same restrictions on the settlement of the Jews as existed in the city of Warsaw. In 1855, a residential quarter was set aside for the Jews, with various restrictions. These restrictions were cancelled in 1865.

In 1856, 6,690 Christians and 1,637 Jews lived in Zgierz. In 1897 the population was 19,108, of which 3,548 were Jews.

Zgierz, in the "Encyklopedia Powszechna" Of Orgelbrand- Warsaw, 1884.

Zgierz is a city on the Bzura River in the region of Piotrkow, in the district of Lodz. It was settled in ancient times, and received the rights of the Magdeburg Charter in 1420. It was destroyed completely during the first Swedish war, and was subsequently rebuilt. The serious growth of Zgierz began from the time that the textile factories were established. The population is 11,000.

The entrance to the Henryk Sznekiewicz Public Gardens

The town hall and the old market

History of Jews in Zgierz until 1862 by A. Wolf-Yasni of blessed memory

The Ancient History of the City and its Development

According to the historical development of the economic organizations that comprised the Lodzer textile region, Zgierz was one of the oldest Polish settlements, much older than the metropolis of that area itself - Lodz.

It is not known when Zgierz changed from a town to a city, and what type of role it played during the first century of the Polish kingdom. Evidence of the ancient settlement of the city can be found from the objects that were found in the nineteenth century in the sandy areas along the way to Konstantynow: knives and arrows made of flint [9] that belong to an early epoch when the inhabitants of what later became the Polish kingdom did not yet use metal. Trenches were also found in the same area. They were dug out in the southwestern area of the city, and are called the "Swedish Trenches" by the residents of Zgierz.

These archeological artifacts tell, albeit in a clouded manner, about the beginning of the settlement that later took on the name Zgierz. We do not know about the origins of the name. In old documents, the settlement is referred to as: Zguyr, Sguyr, Segey and Shegrz.

The first document that mentions the settlement of Zgierz informs us that in the year 1231, at Easter [10] the following people arrived: Konrad the leader of Mazowia in the company of the great Polish Duke Wladyslaw Odonic, the Bishop of Wloclawek Michael, and others. In a decree of Kazimierz the Duke of Leczyca and Kujawy, issued in Zgierz in 1248, the local taxes are designated to the Wachock Church, which then must cede them to Duke Wladyslaw Lokietek. In a deed of exchange of land, Zgierz was called a city belonging to a duke. In the year 1345, Duke Wladyslaw of Dobrzyn and Leczyca granted Zgierz the right of regional administration (wojewodztwo). The following belonged to the regional administration: two mills with their lakes, pasturelands, meadows, forests, beehives, and other such things. It is also evident that at that time, there were already artisans in Zgierz, for the same document establishes the taxes that each artisan must pay.

8

Later documents, from 1388 and 1391, describe controversies that Zgierz residents had with surrounding peasants. These controversies were adjudicated through the civic court of Leczyca.

The Polish King Aleksander (1501-1526), a former Lithuanian Grand Duke, recognized Zgierz as a municipal settlement and assigned to it one annual fair as well as weekly market days, which transformed Zgierz into an economic center of the area. Lodz was then a small town that did not appear in any documents from that time.

In later years, Zgierz strengthened its civic appearance. The tax ledgers show that in the year 1576, the town had 17 artisans, 3 taverns, 3 liquor stills, 6 merchants, and a few rural enterprises that also belonged to Zgierz.

The population records of 1661 report that the city had 10 owned houses [11], 3 breweries, and 2 shoemakers. Of the 21 potters, only one remained, who worked for the court. Due to war and disturbances, business almost ground to a halt, and the three annual fairs were discontinued. Only one annual market day remained. From the records, we know also that the Zgierz residents paid most of their taxes in a natural fashion [12], although they could have paid with money. Several rural enterprises belonged to the city as well.

About one hundred years later, in 1765, Zgierz already had 56 houses and a greater number of artisans: 7 potters, 6 shoemakers, 5 coopers, 13 wheelwrights, 6 carpenters, and other artisans.

A population record (lustracza) from 1789 records 65 houses and the same number of artisans as in 1765. By the end of the eighteenth century, no great changes had taken place in the town.

When Did Jews Settle in Zgierz?

According to the Slavonic Geographical Dictionary, number 14, book 164, titled Zgierz, published in Warsaw in the year 1894, Zgierz had a population of 500 individuals in 1807. No Jews were mentioned. Zgierz was at that time a regional center (pawiat) [13]. Lodz also belonged to that region, which at that time had a population of 434 individuals, including 58 Jews. It is hard to understand why in the last two decades of the eighteenth century, Jews already lived in the small town of Lodz, while they were not found in Zgierz, which had already been a city for centuries. We must surmise that, among the artisans that were mentioned in the lustraczas of 1765 and 1789, there would have been some Jews. The first mention of Jews in Zgierz is in a document from February 1822, which contains a declaration of the elders of the Zgierz community - Leizer Moszkowicz and Moshe Goldberg - given to the regional commissar Adjunct Zawadski, regarding the rights and privileges of the Jews that lived in Zgierz.

The Jews answered the query of Zawadski as follows: "As far as we remember, during the time of the former Polish regime, there were five or six Jewish families living in Zgierz. During the time of the Prussian regime, more arrived. Every Old Believer [14] looked for a livelihood. Seeing that there were no businessmen or artisans in this city, such as tailors, etc., the Old Believers approached the civic authorities (that is to say the *burmistrz* [15] with the request to be allowed to become involved n this city. After a meeting with the citizens, who had permitted the believers to live there, a formal decree of migration was made. They owned property, and were able to continue owning property."

The first official documents from the city of Zgierz that mention Jews are from the year 1813. These documents include a letter of exchange between the vice president of the Zgierz pawiat and the *burmistrz* (bergermeister) of Zgierz regarding the right of the Old Believers to purchase houses there.

In the first letter, dated May 10, 1813, the vice president writes:

"According to the prescript of the all-powerful, illuminated president, delivered here on April 28th, supported by a message of direction from the ministers responsible for these matters, containing the directives for formalizing the protocols of qualifications of the Old Believers who wish to own land in the city, I divide it up in this manner (the directives for formalizing the protocols) - -"

"The honorable *burmistrz*s (bergermeisters) of the cities recommend that the protocols be adopted, in the event that such should take place."

The document dated May 10th 1813 (unsigned) relates to the beginning of the activities of the Polish authorities in Warsaw to substantiate the rights of the Jews who lived in the Polish cities. In a second letter from October of that same year, the vice president of Leczyca clarified to the *burmistrz* of

10

Zgierz, that he will make efforts to investigate which Old Believers possess various agreements and contracts. That is to say, that someone sold houses and land to Jews. Such purchases must be reported within 48 hours to the vice president, and immediately thereafter to the president.

The local priest, who appeared before the vice president of the Zgierz pawiat with an accusation against the citizen Skilski who wished to lease his house to a Jew, also took part in the activities to restrict the rights of residents of Jews in Zgierz. The above mentioned house was "a house that stands in very close proximity to the church, right near the great altar".

The vice president who wrote about this to the Zgierz magistrate made mention that this was against the monarchy and against the religion, and requested from the magistrate to strictly forbid Jews from living there without the permission of the government.

In September of the same year, the representative of the *burmistrz* of Zgierz sent an application to the vice president of the Zgierz-Leczyca area requesting that he certify a deed of sale for a house that the citizen Jan Hejna, who lived in the city of Zgierz, sold to the Old Believer Rafael Dobrzynski [16].

In later documents, it is not mentioned whether the purchase of the house from Rafael Dobrzynski actually took place, but this was the first official document regarding the purchase of a house by a Jew of Zgierz. That purchase, which was certainly not the first, was the beginning of the struggle for the rights of Jews to settle in Zgierz. This was similar to the struggle in nearby Lodz, which at that time had a population of 58 Jews (13.4% of the general population).

In later years, the struggle increased. The Vienna Congress of 1815, which established the new order in Europe after Napoleon's downfall, liquidated the Duchy of Warsaw and established the Kingdom of Poland, which was later called Congress Poland, and had a semblance of autonomy from the Czarist regime. A provisional government was established in Warsaw, under the auspices of Czar Alexander I. In the new Polish constitution there was a clause stating: "The Israelite people are granted all rights of citizenship, which are certified by the present assembly. Laws must be passed to enable the Jews to fully participate in the rights of citizenship."

Relying on this point, the "Commission for Improvement", founded in Warsaw in 1815 and headed by the liberal Polish duke Adam Czartoryski, began to work for the "improvement" of the lives of the Jews in Congress Poland. After lengthy discussions, the Commission reached a consensus with the anti-Semites led by the priest Staszicz, in association with anti-Jewish tendencies from the Czarist regime. The "Improvement of the Jews" finally was able to begin a project to create Jewish ghettos in Polish cities.

Those above mentioned forces that were hostile to the Jews began their actions with a letter to the Warsaw regime on November 5, 1816, regarding a plan to enumerate the Jews who live in cities. The letter was also sent to the wojewodzkis (regional heads) who were requested to submit their enumerations to the various commissioners. They were to transmit the request to the various commissioners. The commissar of the Leczycza region submitted the following written request to the Zgierz *burmistrz* on November 5, 1816:

"With respect to the recent prescript from the important committee from the Mazowia wojewodztwo, which requested the action of the *burmistrz* of the city of Zgierz that he should in four days present a list of the Old Believers (Starozakonny) who live in the market area of the city of Zgierz- This list must include the following items:

1. The number of the house in the market.
2. The name and family name of the owner.
3. The date of the lease agreement that was set with the Old Believer.
4. The expiration date of the current lease.
5. An accounting of the rooms in the house and areas that are rented by the Old Believer.
6. A description of how the resident (Old Believer) makes use of the space, and what he does with each room in the dwelling.

The results of this recommendation from the regional committee are eagerly awaited." From Leczyca, November 5, 1816 Signed (not legible)

That letter to the *burmistrz* of Zgierz, later translated into Yiddish, faithful to the Polish chancellery style of that time - demonstrates clearly that

12

the first Jews came to settle in that city, which, along with Lodz, became a center of work, business and livelihood. From that letter to the *burmistrz* it is clear that: 1) Jews already lived in Zgierz in 1816, and 2) Just as in Lodz and other cities of Congress Poland - the Polish authorities of that time began activities to distance Jews from the market, which was the most important location of livelihood. They were to be pushed into a ghetto, which was designated as a "Jewish precinct".

It can also be seen that the few Jewish families in Zgierz of the time, just like Jews in other Polish towns, fought a legal battle, supported by the law, against being wedged into a ghetto. For two years later, on October 2, 1818, the Commissar of the Leczyca area approached the *burmistrz* of Zgierz with a request to "transmit the privileges of the city, with respect to the setting up of a separate precinct for Jews".

This letter mentions the "privileges" that existed in certain old cities in Poland, where Polish kings or dukes of that time did not permit Jews to settle in their areas, or enclosed them in their own neighborhoods by means of setting up a precinct for Jews.

The First "Project" Regarding a Jewish Precinct in Zgierz

As an answer to all of the requests that came from the government in Warsaw and from the regional committee, the *burmistrz* of Zgierz set up a project to "remove the Old Believers from amongst the Christians in the city of Zgierz".

Regarding this project, the historical number of residents of Zgierz from the year 1818 was submitted as 400, including 198 Jews (49.7 % of the Zgierz population), which seems like an unbelievable exaggeration. We can see from this that false data was submitted into this project. A correct statistic from the year 1827 set the Zgierz population from that time as 3,162 residents, and Jews made up only 7.8% of the total population of Zgierz (Dr. F. Friedman - "Dzezi Zydi Lodzi, number 41, "Slavonic Geography", B).

There are other unintelligible facts available in this document, which is kept in the archives of the city of Zgierz. As is recorded there, in the "privilege", the inability of Jews to settle in Zgierz stems from the year 1038, from the Mazowian Duke Ziemowit, when in fact, that duke actually lived in the 15th century. The "project" also answers the question: From when and

13

under whose authority were Jews allowed to settle in the city? According to the privileges from the year 1589, this was granted by the Polish King Zygmunt III and confirmed by the Sejm Conferences of 1768. From that time on, according to the document, Jews began to settle in Zgierz.

The conclusion of the project was: the market in the center of the city was heavily populated, and Jews had already taken 40 places. Jews were not supposed to be permitted to live there. They were only allowed to live on Sowia Street, which was vacant, and a distance from the center. According to the document, Jews already had 16 places there (among 13 Christians).

As can be seen, this project of the Zgierz *burmistrz* presented several incorrect facts regarding the Jews of Zgierz. With this project began the difficult struggle of the Jews for their rights to live in the town. A few Jewish families purchased houses in Zgierz and settled there. These include the aforementioned Leizer Moszkowicz, Jachim Leizerowicz, Lewka Stoma and Berek Zelnik. As is mentioned in one of the documents, Leizer Moszkowicz, the Old Believer, purchased a place in the city of Zgierz already in 1812, and built liquor still there. The other Jews most likely also established their affairs there, which aroused the wrath of the Polish authorities.

The committee or of the Mazowia Wojewodztwo ordered the *burmistrz* of Zgierz, in a document dated July 12, 1820, to call upon the Old Believers (whose names were previously given) to officially declare: 1) The places where they (the Jews) occupied, acknowledged as being illegal by the Wojewodztwo committee. 2) The houses and the places where Jews lived, which they were obligated to sell to Christians. 3) That the *burmistrz* is setting up a six month period during which the Jews must sell their houses, and if, during this period, they are not working towards a sale, all of the income from these places and houses will be sequestered, or the houses will be sold and all of the proceeds "will go toward the accounts of the hospital".

The drastic decree of the Mazowian Wojewodztwo committee, which demanded that the Jews leave their places in Zgierz for which they did not hold a concession, was signed by the vice president of the committee (name not legible), and by the General Secretary Filipecki.

The first Jews of Zgierz were not able to act upon their rights to settle in the city, and they brought the issue to the authorities by means of petitions and requests. When the "overseer of the city", who at that time served as the central municipal authority, signed for the brewery of Leizer Moszkowicz, he entered into a dispute with the Wojewodztwo committee, the answer was as follows: "The Old Believer had already purchased a place in the city of Zegsza (an old name of Zgierz) from the citizen Koranski and built a brewery there, without having a concession to purchase such a place from a Christian." Further, in the answer of the Wojewodztwo committee regarding the ordinance to sell Jewish property to Christians, if such were not to take place, the income was to be sequestered and given over to the hospital. The accusation against Leizer Moszkowicz was ultimately thrown out.

The *burmistrz* of Zgierz carried out the instructions of the Wojewodztwo committee and informed the Old Believers that they must sell their houses and properties to the Christians, "in order that the *burmistrz* will be able to give the required report to the Wojewodztwo committee". Once the Jews were informed that they must sell their houses, the *burmistrz* of Zgierz informed the Wojewodztwo committee.

The first Jews of Zgierz - Leizer Moszkowicz, Jachim Leizerowicz, Rafael Dobrzynski, Lewek Sloma and Berek Zelnik - did not rush to carry out the orders of the Mazowia Wojewodztwo committee, and their houses were not sold to Christians.

Liberal Rights for Immigrating Germans, and Restrictions for Jews

In the year 1820, Rajmund Rembielinski, chairman of the Mazowia Wojewodztwo committee, visited the Leczyca region, to which Zgierz belonged, and wrote about the city in a report, as follows:

"Near to the city of Ozorkow and its current colony of Aleksandrow, one can find the city of Zgierz. It is a settlement on the highway that runs Leczyca to Piotrkow, between thick forests and the dark countryside, but with a fruitful soil, on the Bzura River. The local residents are either farmers or Jews. The appearance of the city is not orderly: separated houses in poor condition. It does not have any fairs or yearly market days, since it is lacking any privileges. Indeed, in general, the settlement of Zgierz does not warrant the designation of city."

Rembelinski continues with his report: "In the past year, there was evidence of 60 manufacturers who came from various places, including from outside of the country, and requested places to set up their businesses. Since there were no municipal places for them to buy, they went to the ministry of the interior and police, who granted them the farms that lay across the Zegrzanki. It was hard to acquire lumber with which to build, and the manufacturers were left with their desires unfulfilled. They had to live off groszys [17]. No more than fifteen manufacturers lived in Zgierz. The remainder moved on after a few months of waiting emptily. Most of them went to Ozorkow or Aleksandrow."

From that segment of the report that Rajmund Rembielinski sent to the Duke Naniestnik, one can comprehend the situation of Zgierz during the first 20 years of the nineteenth century, when the town and the entire region began to be built up as a center for the textile industry.

The manufacturers who visited Zgierz were German weavers from Silesia, where the textile manufacturers were undergoing a crisis during that time. The German manufacturers were in the area of the Bzura River, which was sparsely populated, with many empty areas. They found appropriate grounds upon which to get settled there. Rembelinski took note of the immigration of those German weavers, and set forth a plan to create a textile center in the Leczyca region. The plan was adopted by the leaders of the Polish regime of the time, the priest Staszicz and Mostowski. With the approval of the Czarist authorities of Petersburg, the Silesian German manufacturers were granted privileges to acquire land and to set up factories in the empty areas around Zgierz.

Between the years 1818 and 1820, there are unfortunately no statistics about the number of Jews who lived in Zgierz. However, their number was certainly significant, as is shown by a later section of Rembelinski's report, where he expresses an inimical attitude toward the Jews who already lived in Zgierz, or who were making efforts to settle there. Rembelinski wrote to the town accountant regarding "giving over territory to the manufacturers who wish to establish factories in Zgierz".

"If one desires to bring about a positive result regarding the entrepreneurs, one must firstly insure that the territory of the entire city is designated, and that the plan must be duly executed. Regarding this, I recommend that the rights of rental of premises for the citizens of the town, which are exploitatively abused by the sickening Jews, be given via an auction for three year terms." This will be good for the city, and good for the public."

Later Rembelinski points out that there is an elementary school Zgierz. The parish priest does not teach religion there. The teachers are not especially capable "and in the schools the Jews (Zydki") [18] manifest their expertise in teaching".

As a result of that report, the minister and the regional commissioner for internal affairs and police - Mostowski and the Priest Staszic -adopted Rembelinski's plan. The obstacles were removed, and the German weavers and manufacturers were granted the possibility of arranging their affairs in Zgierz. Jews came upon a fresh shift of enemies, who waged a stubborn battle against the rights of Jews to live in Zgierz, including in the Neistadt section of town where the manufacturing center was being built.

At the same time, when the German immigrants, who were longstanding enemies of Poland, were granted special privileges of residency in Zgierz, the Polish authorities strengthened their battle to restrict the rights of Jews to settle in the town, with the exception of the ghetto, and they did not allow the number of Jewish residents to increase.

On January 25, 1819, Poniatowski, the overseer of the cities of the Mazowian Wojewodztwo, requested that the Leczyca *burmistrz* remind the Zgierz *burmistrz* regarding the need to separate the Old Believers from the Christian population. During the succeeding two years, the negotiations took place regarding the creation of a Jewish quarter. It is also evident that the Zgierz municipality did not rush to carry out the anti-Semitic decision of the Warsaw regime and the instructions of its own regional commissioners. The semi-rural Zgierz was in need of Jewish artisans and businessmen. However, new ordinances from the regional commissioners arrived in succession. Thanks to Zawadski who made a request from the commissioner of the Leczyca region, as of October 1821, Jews were forbidden by the Zgierz municipal authorities to live on the larger streets, since the issue of the Jewish quarter had not been resolved.

On account of an intervention by the Zgierz *burmistrz* to the Mazowian Wojewodztwo authorities, the ordinance that required to Jews to sell their homes in places that they had acquired through a legal concession was postponed, since the area for the Jewish quarter had not yet been prepared. In that manner, the *burmistrz* made sure that the Old Believers would no longer be allowed to acquire houses in the quarters of Zgierz. Relying on that attitude, the Wojewodztwo commissioner rejected the request of Rafael Dobrzynski to be permitted to build a house in the Forstadt near the mill, and to be granted a concession. The rejection notice mentioned that one must wait until the rights of Jews to live in Zgierz are clarified.

As can be seen from documents, the Zgierz municipal authorities made no efforts to set up the Jewish quarter. The Polish regime in Warsaw, which was ostensibly autonomous, independently acted upon the situation by confirming the rights of Jews to live in the cities. The commissars of the regions took the chance of acting upon their anti-Semitic ordinances. Since the Zgierz municipal authorities did nothing in this respect, the all-powerful commissioner Adjunkt Zawadski, the overseer of the cities of the region of Leczyca region, came to town to conduct an investigation regarding the rights and privileges of Jews to live in Zgierz. Zawadski interrogated the three senior Poles in the town and four Jews "the elders of the community), and inquired of them regarding the rights and privileges of Jews to live in Zgierz.

"It took place on the land of the city of Zgierz, on February 10, 1822" - thus begins the protocol regarding the statement given by the eldest citizens: Wiecszorek, the former *burmistrz* in the days of the Polish regime and, prior to that, a civic councilor under the Prussian regime; Kazimierz Radzinski and Pawel Domanski. They answered the queries of Adjunkt Zawadski as follows:

"In previous times, as far as we remember, two (Jewish) tailors came to Zgierz, and lived in rented premises with appropriate rights. In a tavern that is called the Starosztyner, a Jew, by virtue of a signed contract with the Starosta (town official) of Zgierz, took possession of a tavern that is known to this day as the Folwark Zegrzanki. At first, during the time of the Prussian regime, Jews were able to make their living arrangements in the city. The elder Wolf was granted a lease to the Propynacia.

No agreements existed between citizens of the city and the Jews. There were also no court injunctions. The Old Believers never had any rental rights in the city. At first, prior to the time of the Prussian regime, when the citizens were given the duty of providing drinks to the military, the city

18

would have been glad to grant Jews the right of rental. However, later, the Old Believers came upon the rights of rental in other businesses via auctions.

Regarding the leasing of the Propynacia by the Old Believers, the city had no reason to prevent the Jews from earning their livelihood, provided it was arranged through an appropriate contract. The city did not sign any agreements with the Old Believers. There was no reason to move the Jews into a separate quarter.

Prior to the time of the Warsaw Duchy, a few Jews purchased immovable property from Christians. Regarding the acquisition of such objects, the Jews neglected the appropriate permits."

This protocol with the signature of the Polish elders from the investigation of Zawadski shows that the simple Zgierz folk had little interest in sequestering the Jews into a separate Jewish quarter in town. The arrival of Jews and their economic activity was regarded a natural occurrence for the local Poles. It was only the Polish authorities in Warsaw along with their regional commissars who were insistent that Jews be separated from the Christian population by means of a ghetto.

The declaration that was presented by the four communal elders - Leizer Moszkowicz, Jakob Kalski, Lewek Solomonowicz and Moszek Goldberg - presented to Zawadski for the most part confirmed the facts that were presented by the Polish elders. The overseer of the cities in the Leczyca region, Adjunkt Zawadski, concluded his inquiry regarding the rights of the Jews to live in Zgierz. Similar investigations were also conducted in other cities of Poland. The accumulated material was presented to the Warsaw regime, and, after considering it, instructions were issued by the commissar of internal affairs on July 14th, 1822.

The instructions included in the first ordinance, in accordance with article 3 of the decision of February 14th, 1818, stated that "Any Jew who did not have a concession for a tavern in the previous year cannot be issued a new one".

The second point of the instructions repeated the "De non tolerandes" privilege of the middle Ages, which stated that the cities had the right to refuse to admit Jews. The Jews who already held concessions and rights to own a tavern can remain in the city. The following points made the following additional statement: "Jews who live in the city without a concession and do not own any immovable property in the first year (of their settlement in the city), must leave the city". The Jews who "own immovable property and concessions" must (with brief period of time) sell their property and leave the city.

Full rights of residence in the city, that is to say in Zgierz, were given only to those Jews who owned immovable property by rights of government concessions. The rights to immovable property can be transferred to an heir until the end of the family (when there are no longer any heirs).

The instructions end with the following announcement: "These orders must be followed precisely and accurately". Approved by the acting minister -representative of the royal committee

(Signed by Staszic and General Secretary Skalski).

These instructions (actually ordinances) from the authorities in Warsaw, which were also sent to all the cities of Congress Poland, apparently also to Zgierz, defined the limitations upon the rights of Jews to live in the larger Polish cities. However those cities which were first beginning to develop and expand at that time could not manage without Jews as a factor in business and labor. Those cities that were in the process of development took the initiative to deviate somewhat from the anti-Semitic ordinances that came from Warsaw, and gave the possibility to Jews - in the first place to wealthy Jews such as merchants and artisans - to settle in the cities.

The Jews at Poland at that time, who were considered to be residents of the country, struggled with all their might for their rights to live in the cities of Congress Poland, as well as in the new settlements that were being developed as centers of manufacturing, labor and business. Zgierz was such a settlement, which was being set up as a manufacturing town even prior to Lodz. For a historical reason, the development of Zgierz slowed down, and Lodz overtook it.

When Jews took note of the ordinances from Warsaw affected their settlement in Zgierz, as can be seen from the documents that were brought down; they found themselves engaged in only a mild struggle against the local citizens during the second decade of the 1800s. All of the ordinances against Jews settling in Zgierz, which were preserved in the archives, indeed originated from the regime in Warsaw and were sent to the *burmistrz* of Zgierz via the regional commissars. Under the threat of punishment, they required him to carry out the anti-Jewish ordinances. No documents show any evidence that the Zgierz municipal authorities did anything to carry out the ordinances against the Jews.

Jews settled in Zgierz, as they did in Lodz and other cities. The Jew haters in the allegedly autonomous Polish regime in Warsaw (in fact - a puppet of the Czarist reactionary authorities) forced through the project of restricting the Jewish population in the cities by setting up a ghetto, or in official language - a Jewish quarter. That project was strongly supported by the priests.

The Economic Situation of the Jews of Zgierz in the Year 1822 and the Ongoing Struggle for the Rights to Settle in the City

In the year 1822, the Jews of Zgierz were already playing important roles in the local economy. In the list of Jewish families, which is preserved in the Zgierz archives, the number of Jews in various professions is listed:

1 shochet (ritual slaughterer), 2 tenant innkeepers (one of them was Mendel Pachtasz), 4 butchers, 5 restaurateurs (two of them were also involved in business, the third was Rafael Dobrzynski), 4 shopkeepers, 1 merchant, 1 glassmaker who was called Moshe Glezer [19], 7 day workers, 1 shoemaker, 1 judge, 1 miner, 1 attendant, 1 barber and 1 director.

The same document also gives the net worth of the wealthy Jews of Zgierz: Hirsch Walstok, with a family of 7 people, a butcher by trade, born in Zgierz in 1770, was worth 3,000 Polish Zloty. Joskowa Weinstein, a woman shopkeeper, arrived in Zgierz in 1797 with the permission from the Leczyca regional authorities, was worth 2,300 Polish Zloty. Moshe Werfel (Wirfel?) is also mentioned. He was a day worker, born in 1790. He came to Zgierz with a permit from the *burmistrz* of Kutno.

Seventeen other persons, earning their livelihoods from various professions, were mentioned in the list of Jewish families. It is difficult to estimate the number of people in the families mentioned. Only with regard to Hirsch Walstok is it mentioned that he had a 7-member family. However, it is indeed certain that the 17 people mentioned in the document did have 17 families. According to the custom of the time, only the head of the family worked. The Polish authorities, who wished to restrict the Jews into a ghetto by establishing a Jewish quarter, conducted a campaign against those Jews.

21

With respect to the restriction of the rights of residence of Jews, which was instituted by the royal regime of Poland with the approval of the Czarist regime who in fact ruled over the land of the Vistula - the small town of Zgierz plays an important historical role. On March 30, 1821 in Zgierz, the anti-Semitic agreement was signed between the Commissar Witowski who was the representative of the Mazowian Wojewodztwo committee, and the German textile manufacturers who came to settle in Zgierz, regarding the founding of an industrial textile center. The anti-Semitic points in the agreement are as follows:

Point 38: No Jew shall have the right to live or to own property in the new colony.

Point 39: In the future, no Jew in the city of Zgierz shall be allowed to begin to earn his living from a saloon, or to do business with strong drink. Only those Jews who are already earning their livelihood in that manner shall be permitted to continue to do so. No new permits (concessions) will be given to Jews.

Those anti-Semitic points in the "Zgierz agreement", as it was always called by the German entrepreneurs who began to build the Lodz manufacturing center in the third decade of the 1800s, had no application in Zgierz. This was simply due to the fact that the newly arrived German manufacturers did not succeed in setting up an industrial center in Zgierz, as is known from the aforementioned report of Rembelinski. Nevertheless, the Polish authorities did not have to legally rely on the "Zgierz agreement" in order to restrict the rights of residence to Jews. The regime in Warsaw already had their own ordinances, upon which they could rely to create a Jewish quarter.

The first document that deals with a Jewish quarter in Zgierz, is titled "Methods and means of establishing a Jewish quarter", and is dated January 18, 1823. That document, signed by commissar Zawadski, mentions that on May 7, 1822, in the official "Dzenin Wojewodski" number 337 the decree was issued "to arrange living accommodations for the Jews in the city in regions that I (i.e. Zawadski) designate". In his document, Zawadski laments that only the *burmistrz* of Dabie (at that time an insignificant settlement) has "vigorously taken the appropriate steps" to set up a Jewish quarter. The commissar threatens a fine of 10 Zloty if steps are not taken within 14 days to set up a Jewish quarter.

The Mazowian Wojewodztwo committee busied himself with the question of creating Jewish quarters in the newly arisen Polish settlements as well in the already existing cities. The royal commissar R. Rembelinski had a more liberal attitude about the issue of Jewish residency rights in the cities. He felt that Jews, as a well-to-do element, would contribute to the development of Polish cities. Rembelinski brought his point of view to print in his directive regarding the development of the city of Zgierz, sent to the city council on February 2, 1823. Rembelinski recommends that the "Old Believers" (Jews) build houses on the Blotene [20] Street that runs into the projected Lodzer Street. The houses must only be built according to plans that are approved by the Wojewodztwo committee.

As we can presume from Rembelinski's directives, the priest of Zgierz was against allowing Jews to build houses on the designated area, since he, the priest, had his fields there. Therefore, the representative of the Wojewodztwo committee recommended that the priest sign a perpetual agreement, mediated by the Wojewodztwo committee, which would be approved by the royal commissioner of religion and enlightenment. Rembelinski rejected this recommendation with the following statement:

"In order to encourage the Old Believers, they should be allowed to build around the Lodzer Highway and to build upon the street with the same name, the civic committee should follow the designated plans and build a bridge. The Old Believers can build along the highway, until the bridge, by the Bzura River." Signed by the Royal Representative R. Rembelinski.

Rembelinski's instructions to permit the Jews of Zgierz to acquire land and build houses on a designated area of the city was in fact the beginning of the creation of the Jewish quarter. That is how Adjunkt Zawadski, the commissar of the Leczyca area, interpreted the instructions. In his message to the *burmistrz* of Zgierz on March 24, 1823, Zawadski reviewed the instructions of Rembelinski to encourage the Jews to build houses on Lodzer Street near the banks of the Bzura River. Zawodski wanted to have the assurance that the Jews who wished to settle there would indeed build buildings, and therefore he requested that the "Starozakonny" (Old Believers) place a deposit into the civic bank and present a declaration which include a building plan, that must be approved by the regional committee. In the declaration, the Jews were also to state their intended occupation in Zgierz. They were permitted to deal with wool, textile merchandise, and minerals.

When the Jews found out about the possibility of settling in Zgierz, they quickly began, in accordance with Zawadski's instructions, to present declarations with building plans. In one such declaration, "signed" with circles since they did not know how to write, Nachum Michael Feldman and Rachel Weinstein assert in their declaration that they intend to follow all of the instructions. He guarantees his assurance with his moveable possessions, as well as those of his mother Rachel, who lives in Zgierz. He requests in his application that he be designated a place on the designated street, so that he can quickly begin to build.

The aforementioned royal representative Rembelinski further took the trouble to insure that Jews would cause no disturbances in their efforts to settle in Zgierz in the area that he designated. Rembelinski issued a decree on January 7, 1824, that the *burmistrz* of Zgierz should immediately provide the wood and appropriate tolls that are necessary to build a brick house on the Szeradzer -Lodzer Road.

At the same time as Jews began to build houses on the designated street in Zgierz, the Polish authorities in Warsaw made further endeavors to enclose the Jews in ghettos in the cities and towns. A correspondence took place between Zgierz and Warsaw regarding this issue.

The royal commissioner for internal and police affairs, at a meeting in Warsaw on June 28, 1824, issued a declaration that "the project in Zgierz to set up a quarter for the Jews in Zgierz differs from the report, and differs from the situation plan in the city. Regarding the plans to set up a Jewish quarter, this should include the Szeradzer Street as well as a street that is projected in the plan and does not as yet have a name. The document that discusses this subject is signed by the priest Staszic, as well as Karski, the acting minister and representatives of the royal ministers and general secretary.

In the ongoing negotiations toward ultimately setting up a Jewish quarter, the regional commissar Zawadski came forward with complaints against the *burmistrz* of Zgierz as to why he had not made sure that the Lodzer Street, which was designated for the Jewish quarter, be demarcated by posts. Zawadski threatened the *burmistrz* with a punishment if he does not demarcate the boundary of the Jewish quarter with 120 posts.

In the end, after long negotiations between various Wojewodztwo commissioners, the Polish regime in Warsaw and the Czarist regime in Petersburg (Leningrad), issued a supreme decree regarding instituting a Jewish quarter in Zgierz. As it turned out, this small town in the Leczyca region had the privilege of being the first [21] to confine the Jewish population. Following the pattern of the Zgierz decree, which was instigated by the commissar of the Leczyca region, within the next few years decrees were issued to establish Jewish quarters in thirty cities in Poland, including Lodz, which had a population of 342 Jews in 1825, comprising 24% of the general population.

The original decree to Zgierz, regarding the Jewish quarter in the town, issued on December 21, 1824, begins with the following words:

"In the name of His Highness Alexander I, Czar of all of Russia and King of Poland

The royal duke Namiestnik and the royal council, who wish to designate separate living quarters for Jews in the city of Zgierz in the Mazowian Wojewodztwo as well as in other cities in royal Poland -already have their assurances based on article 9 of the directives issued by His Highness dated April 25th and May 7th of the year that is about to conclude, regarding the suggestion of the royal committee for internal affairs and police. We have made the following decision: Jews are permitted to live in Zgierz, and to acquire empty places and houses - on one side of Szeradzer Street, which lies in the south, and on both sides of Lodzer Street. Beginning on July 1, 1825, Jews of Zgierz will not be permitted to live in any other places in the city, with the exception of the designated quarter." The ordinance continues:

"In order to persuade the Old Believers that the regime does not want them to curtail the other residents of the place, so that the brothers of that people will have the same level of participation [22], I permit two families of the Old Believers to live in any street of Zgierz as an exception, with the following condition: that they must possess 20,000 Polish Zloty, without debts and without having made loans; they must be bankers or those who conduct a steady and open business; they must know how to read and write Polish, French or at least German; they must send their children after the 7th year to a public school; and they must bear no unusual marks, that is to say those clothes that distinguish Jews from all other citizens.

Aside from the aforementioned two Jewish families, other Jews can live on any street in Zgierz if they establish needed factories, purchase empty plots in order to build houses - as well as scholars, doctors, artists and large scale merchants. They must know how to read and right foreign languages, they must send their children to school, and they must not wear Jewish garb."

The further articles in this ordinance - 4, 5, 6 and 7 - deal with administrative instructions, as well as insuring that this directive is observed and fulfilled, so that Jews should not transgress it. It specified the police fines that are to be imposed for breaking the ordinance regarding the Jewish quarter. Article 8 states that Jews who purchased or leased wooden houses in the market area prior to the publication of the directive may live in them for five years. During the course of these five years, Jews were not permitted to rent to Jewish tenants in those houses. Therefore, they could only rent or lease to Christians. After the five years, the Jews must dispose of their houses by selling them to Christians. An exception was made for Jews who were willing to tear down their wooden houses and erect brick houses in their place.

The 9th article states: Jewish owners of brick houses on the streets outside the quarter are permitted to remain living there. All Jews who take advantage of the above mentioned "privileges" must be able to read and write foreign languages, as has been already mentioned.

The last line of the directive is as follows:

This was authorized in Warsaw, at a meeting of the administrative council on December 21, 1824.

Minister of Internal and Police Affairs - Zajaczek, Representative of the Royal Secretary - Mostowski.

As can be seen, the decree setting up a Jewish quarter was directed primarily toward the lower classes. For Jews with capital, the town of Zgierz as well as other cities in Poland were open and free for settlement. Polish cities, large and small, which were beginning to develop at the time, and were in need of capital, as well as of business and industrial class, who, via the creation of factories, would employ the growing population. For that reason, there was goodwill toward the Old Believers who had capital and the means to build houses, factories, and business enterprises.

Jews who immigrated to Zgierz, or to the region in general, where a textile manufacturing center was developing, had only one goal: to set up their lives on the basis of work and business. Regardless of all the restrictions and inimical decrees originating from the Polish bourgeois class, the clergy and the Czarist authorities, Jews settled where they found it necessary. Relying on the directive regarding a Jewish quarter, the civic authorities in Zgierz began a program to clear the Jews off of the streets upon which they were not permitted to live.

26

The decree regarding the creation of a Jewish quarter was signed on December 21, 1824. One month later, on January 27th, 1825, R. Rembelinski, the representative of the Mazowian committee, gave instructions to the county committee to publish the decree regarding the Jewish quarter of Zgierz in "Dziennik Wojewodzki", so that the residents should know that "according to article 2 of the decree, the Old Believers must move to the Jewish quarter by June 1, 1826." The county committee was obligated, twice a year, in April and in September, to "personally implement controls in the city" so as to insure that the ordinances of the regime regarding the Jewish living quarter are being fulfilled. Any Old Believer who does not follow the ordinances is to be evicted from his home.

Rembelinski also requested that the Zgierz municipality compose ledgers regarding these issues. The ledgers must include the following information: where the Jewish families who live outside the quarter live; on which streets they have houses; whether the houses are of brick or wood; whether they are owned or rented; whether the lease is for a set time or permanent; what types of livelihood do those families have; and whether they house foreign people in their living quarters "as is the custom of the Old Believers".

Relying on these instructions, the municipal authorities of Zgierz took up the battle against the Jews who did not want to move into the ghetto. The Jews of Zgierz were faced with a stubborn, repressive, reactionary anti-Semitic council, who wished to confine them into a ghetto consisting of one and a half muddy streets at the edge of the town. Jews were not willing to leave their houses in the town. The Zgierz municipal authorities had to impose punishments in order to compel the Jews to enter the ghetto.

On June 13, 1825, the Zgierz municipal authorities issued a decree to the local Christian citizens who were homeowners, that they would be punished with a fine if they permit Jews to live in their houses after the deadline of July 1, 1826. The police will evict Jewish families who live in such houses outside of the quarter. The decree concludes with the following statement: "This ordinance is directed toward all of the homeowners as well as the Old Believers who are tenants". As testimony to the authenticity of the ordinance, it is signed by the two citizens: Pawel Domanski and Jan

Walencinski, and by the following members of the municipal authorities: Grzegorzewski, the *burmistrz*, Raszynski and Dombrowski, councilors.

The Christian homeowners who were making profits from their Jewish tenants were not willing to evict their tenants. The Zgierz municipal office demanded that the Jews abandon their homes and residences in which they were living without the appropriate official permission (concession). Such notices, signed by the officials Raszynski and Dombrowski, were issued to: Jachim (Nechemia?) Lazarowicz, Tewek Slam and Szymon Garborski. The notice demanded that the Jews sell their homes to Christians by June 1, 1826 and move to the Jewish quarter. If the Jews do not wish to follow the ordinance, they will be evicted by the police, and furthermore, they will be required to pay a fine.

Regardless of all the ordinances and notices issued by the municipal council, Jews did not hurry to give up their houses and residences in Zgierz and move to the Jewish quarter, which in the interim remained open and vacant. At the end of 1825, an ordinance from the Leczyca regional county commissar Zawadski was issued regarding the demarcation of the Jewish quarter with posts. The commissar demanded that this ordinance be carried out immediately.

The Organized Jewish Community of Zgierz

During the era of living restrictions for Jews in Zgierz, the town achieved the pinnacle of its industrial development. Zgierz became a center for the production of woolen textiles. According to the testimony of General Kasecki, the secretary of the administrative committee of royal Poland, in 1825, the following quantities of textile merchandise were exported to Russia: from Zgierz, 209 units of 10 piece cloth; from Ozorkow, 106 units of 12 piece cloth; from Aleksander, 560 units of 4 piece cloth; from Lodz, 334 units of cloth. According to the measures of that time, a piece of cloth was between 20-30 Polish ells (an ell is 56 centimeters).

The above mentioned accounting does not imply that Zgierz played a greater role in textile production than Lodz. That city, which later became the largest textile center in Poland, was occupied in that period with wool manufacturing and small-scale business. At that time, commerce was better developed in Zgierz. Understandably, that town attracted Jewish families, who, regardless of all of the living restrictions, settled in Zgierz, purchased and built houses.

Obviously, the Jews were most comfortable in houses that were near to the places where the textile enterprises were being built. The Zgierz archives contain no statistics that show how many Jews lived in the designated, demarcated quarter on Lodzer Street and part of Szeradzer Street. However, outside of the quarter, by 1826 there were already 79 Jewish families. Including the residents of the quarter, there must have been at least 400 Jewish people in Zgierz.

According to a non-precise accounting, the professional structure of the working Jews in Zgierz at that time was as follows: 19 tailors; monczaszes (?) [23]; 14 day workers, 2 tavern owners - one of them being Ruda Dobrzynski; 3 balbires [24]; 5 directors; 15 merchants of wool and textiles; 1 merchant of wool, cloth and iron; 2 salt merchant; 2 hat makers; 1 shoemaker; 2 bakers, 2 glazers; 2 kreiczaszes (?) [25]; 2 tanners - Zelnik and Slama; 1 salaried tanner; 1 school overseer; 1 leather merchant; 1 hotel owner; 1 iron merchant; 1 metal sheet maker; 1 lace maker; 1 bailiff (Komornik); 1 comb maker; 1 artist; 2 shochtim (ritual slaughterers); 1 merchant of edible oils; 1 tea merchant; 1 rabbi.

Obviously, those above-mentioned individuals who had specific professions were the heads of families. As was the custom among Jews of that time, only the head of the family was employed and brought in the livelihood. That is how one can estimate the number of Jewish people who lived in Zgierz at that time was approximately 400. By 1824, the Jews already had an organized community and a *"Dozor* Shtibel"*, which was called *"Dozor* Buzniczy"* (religious institution) in the official Polish archival documents. From there came the Yiddish expression *"Dozors"* as the term for the leaders of the community. According to the documents in the Zgierz archives, the committee of *Dozors* was exchanged every three years. The archives do not mention why and how the exchange of office took place.

The first communal leadership committee is mentioned in the year 1824. The following names are mentioned: Leizer Bornstein, Baruch Steinbok, and Meir Blumenthal. In the years 1828-1830, only one name was mentioned on the committee - Moshe Steinbok. In the following years (1831-1833); Jozef Weiland, Niecki, and Baruch Warwaser. 1834-1836: Elias Majdan and Chaim Liberzuker. 1840-1842: Chaim Lubraniecki, Hillel Berlinski, and Menashe Blawat. 1843-1845: Menashe Blawat, Shimon Waldberg, and

Shimon Lewin. 1846-1848: Yisrael Litauer and Chaim Walko Zonnenfeld. During the aforementioned term, Shimon Waldberg left the communal committee, and Henech Librach took his place. The aforementioned *dozor*s were also served a further term, until 1855. After them, by the year 1857, the following people stood at the helm of the Zgierz community   Yerucham Berliner, Gershon Blum, and Walek Zonnenfeld.

The First Rabbi in Zgierz

The organized Jewish community of Zgierz, which began in 1824 according to official documents, shortly took the steps to engage a rabbi for the Jews of Zgierz.

In a statement to the municipal commissar who dealt with religions affairs, the *dozor*s Baruch Steinbok and Meir Blumenthal asked to be permitted to appoint the Old Believer Rabbi Shalom Hirsch Kahn (Cohen?) as rabbi of Zgierz, in accordance with the wishes of the entire "parish". In their statement to the authorities, the *dozor*s praised the rabbinical candidate as a man who is exemplary in his moral conduct, and, no less significant, in his heartfelt manner of conducting prayers. Therefore, the communal leaders ("*Dozor* Buzniczy") request to give approval for the appointment of Rabbi Shalom Hirsch Kahn. They enclosed 60 Polish Zloty as official payment. The statement concludes with the request to expedite the consideration of this matter. The "parish", which usually refers to the regional leadership of the Catholic Church, here refers to the Jewish community of Zgierz, which was dealing with this matter.

The approval of Rabbi Shalom Hirsch Kahn as rabbi of the community did not come easily. The municipal authorities did not reject the recommendation of the *dozor*s, but rather demanded confirmations and recommendations regarding the rabbi's rabbinical qualifications and personal stature. Manes Skalski and Abba Dorembus presented such recommendations. In their declarations, they asserted that Shalom Hirsch Kahn, rabbi of the synagogue of the city of Zgierz, had already served in such an office from 1823, when he fulfilled the role as rabbi in the town of Grabow, in the region of Leczyca.

Over and above the above mentioned recommendations, Rabbi Kahn appeared himself in person at the administrative office of the Zgierz *burmistrz*, and presented his document of rabbinical ordination, which he had obtained from the rabbi of Leczyca. The document states the following:

Shalom Hirsch Aronowicz Kahn, the popular rabbi of the city of Zgierz, is noted to be a person who is very intelligent, learned in piety, and extremely competent regarding religious ceremonies. I am familiar with his fine manner of speech, and his saturation in Talmud as well as early and latter Jewish law. In my discussions with him, I have found him to be full of wisdom and piety. All of his deeds are proper and exceptional. Therefore, I have in an honorable manner placed my hands upon him, saying: he should learn and judge, so that things should be decided in accordance with his opinion. As a further token, he (Rabbi Shalom Hirsch Kahn) possesses a token of approval from the eminent Strikower Rebbe, Moshe Aharon. Two are better than one (referring to tokens of approval), and these two testify to the stability of this upright person. These words are spoken in honor of his knowledge and piety. In Leczyca, Monday January 24, 1827. (Signed by) Chaim Itzkowicz Orbach of Leszno.

In confirmation of the authenticity, I issue my approval in Zgierz, January 27, 1827. Y. Zimski, the judicial translator.

The final document is a confirmation of a concession to Rabbi Shalom Hirsch Kahn in the office of the rabbi. The document states:

"...executed in the city of Zgierz in February, 1827.

The Old Believer Shalom Hirsch Kahn presented himself in the bureau of the *burmistrz* of the city of Zgierz, and as a rabbi, issued the following declaration: Seeing that I am qualified as a rabbi, as is shown by the qualifying examination given the rabbi of the Leczyca community, which I have taken; as well as by the fact that I have taken on the duties of rabbi at the local (Zgierz) house of prayer; and by the enclosed certificate from the communal leadership, I feel that I am fit to take this office - and I request from you that I be granted a concession for this office.

This declaration is signed by Shalom Hirsch Kahn."

The signature at the end is from Grzegorzewski - the representative of the secretary of the bureau of the *burmistrz* of the city of Zgierz.

At that period, the Zgierz community specified the payment for kosher meat. The income from the special Jewish tax was overseen by Jakob Jedlicki. His position was mentioned in a statement to the authorities on August 12, 1825, asking for permission for him to build a house outside of the quarter.

The Persistent Struggle of the Jews for the Right to Live in all of the Streets of Zgierz

In accordance with the ordinance of the duke, the representative of the king on the royal council, dated December 21, 1824, which defined the Jewish quarter in Zgierz, the Jews who lived outside of the specified streets - Lodzer Street and a part of Szeradzer - were required to sell their homes by July 1, 1826, or to forfeit their dwellings. They were to move into the specified streets, which were neither paved nor lined with sidewalks.

The Jews of Zgierz did not hurry to fulfill the instructions of the directive, and they remained in their dwellings and houses. The municipal authorities, assisted by the police, were to proceed to forcefully evict the Jews from their dwellings or homes. That is to say, they were simply going to toss out into the street 79 Jewish families that lived in Zgierz outside the designated quarter. When the evictions notices were delivered in June 1826, the forlorn Jewish families approached the Zgierz community for assistance (as is mentioned in the archival documents). Berek Grynberg "the junior official of the religious organization" ("Najnizszy sluga *Dozor* Buzniczy") came to their defense. According to the ordinance that he signed that is found in the archival documents, it is not clear what role Berek Grynberg played in Zgierz communal life of that time. The aforementioned list of *dozor*s does not mention his name. Apparently, he was the communal intercessor, who presented Jewish matters before the Polish authorities.

On June 25, 1826, Berek Grynberg issued a plea from the communal leadership (*Dozor* Buzniczy) to the "all powerful Wojewodztwo commissar, delegated to the Leczyca region", that he temporarily extend the deadline of moving the 79 families to the designated quarter. In the request, the communal authorities of Zgierz as well as the representative of the 79 Jewish families ask for a delay in the evictions, since the eminent regional commissar for internal and police affairs had agreed, based on a prior request from the communal leadership, to delay the settling in the quarter of the 79 families for another year. The agreement would have to be approved by the Wojewodztwo committee. No confirmation from for Wojewodztwo committee was forthcoming. The Zgierz *burmistrz* kept to the original

32

deadline of eviction of the 79 Jewish families.

"In the name of the poor 79 families, the communal leadership begs the important regional commissar to delay the evictions, until a decision arrives from Wojewodztwo committee. I await the results of my modest request, and a merciful reply.

With the deepest respect for the all-powerful regional commissar- the junior servant of the religious committee - Berek Grynberg."

On the margin of the request, a copy of which is held in the Zgierz archives, the following is written: "Relying on the enclosed decision of the royal committee on June 15, the regional committee suspended the movement of Old Believers into the new quarter". This was concerning the cessation of activity that was recommended by the *burmistrz*. This entire matter is to be written up in a report.

Leczyca, June 25, 1826. Signed- Krolewski.

In his report to the commissar of the Leczyca region that was sent on June 26, 1825, the Zgierz *burmistrz* lashes out very sharply against Berek Grynberg, whose request to push off the eviction of the 79 Jewish families reached the highest authorities. He accused him of telling lies for which he should be punished.

The *burmistrz* accused Berek Grynberg of falsifying the title of religious overseer "*Dozor* Buzniczy") and employing a fabricated authorization from the Zgierz community, which deserves "an appropriate punishment".

The *burmistrz* states in his report that the members of the religious committee (communal leaders): Leizer Bornstein, Binyamin Steinbach and Meir Blumenthal, the "Old Believers", did not oppose the authorities and speedily moved into the Jewish quarter. "Bornstein already has his own house there, and Blumenthal and Steinbach have dwellings".

The *burmistrz* informed the higher authorities that from among the 79 families, there are some who are objecting, and the objectors do not wish to move into the quarter, and "there are others who have been hindered from living there, even though they already have places there. They wish to move only into those new houses which can be obtained from the newly arrived textile manufacturers."

In that report of the Zgierz *burmistrz* to the higher authorities, he reflects upon the persistent struggle of the Zgierz Jews in a non-organized fashion during the first 20 years of the 1800s against being forced into a ghetto. As is usual in such struggles against the authorities, the more energetic and

33

determined people pushed themselves into the foreground, and led the struggle, while the weaker ones made peace with the anti-Semitic decision of the authorities and moved into the ghetto.

The struggle of the Jews of Zgierz for their unlimited rights of residency in the town also brought a disagreement between the Leczyca region and the *burmistrz* of Zgierz. This was not only a struggle regarding better or worse relations with the Jews, but also regarding the competency of the authorities. The commissar reproved the *burmistrz*, complaining that he mixed his private viewpoint into the deliberations. At first, one week previously, he helped Grynberg to obtain a certificate, and now he accuses him in his report. "For such disreputable behavior, the *burmistrz* must be held responsible and is to be punished, by an ordinance of His Eminence the royal councilor." The result of this situation is that the *burmistrz* was to act upon the ordinance of eviction of the 79 Jewish families into a defined quarter by enforcing the existing ordinance.

As a final result of these deliberations, the Mazowian Wojewodztwo committee decided to fine the religious committee (the communal leadership), since "they illegally became involved in such matters that do not pertain to their duties, and authorized Berek Grynberg to issue a plea from all of the 'Old Believers' that live in Zgierz to extend the deadline of settling into the designated quarter." Regarding this, the Wojewodztwo committee told the regional commissar to fine each of the *dozor*s with a fine of 10 Zloty. If such a situation occurs again, they will be punished more harshly.

According the instructions of the Wojewodztwo committee, the *burmistrz* was fined with 25 Zlotys [26], and issued a warning that if such a matter were to occur again, he (the *burmistrz*) would be forced to resign. He was accused of various improprieties: intermixing a private side to the deliberations, dealing with a matter that belonged to the jurisdiction of the police administrative office, and making mention of a synagogue that did not exist [27].

In the archival documents, there is no mention of the final decision of the authorities regarding whether the 79 Jewish families must settle in the Jewish quarter. However, from the fine that was imposed upon the various members of the Zgierz communal leaders for intermingling in the matter of the evictions, one can surmise that the authorities compelled the 79 families to move into the quarter.

On November 2, 1826, the *burmistrz* of Zgierz informed the community that they must pay of fine of 84 Zloty. If the fine is not paid by the appropriate time, the matter will be turned over to administrative authorities. As well, the intercessor Grynberg (or Grynbaum) was fined with a payment of 40 Zloty. It is not clear whether this was a portion of the total fine that the community was required to pay, or a separate monetary fine for his personal intercession on behalf of the 79 families.

Berek Grynbaum-Grynberg presented a request "to the all-powerful Wojewodztwo commissar, to overlook the sum that he, Grynberg, was required to pay as a fine, since the investigation, which is being conducted by the commissar regarding the unjust evictions, has not yet concluded."

The following was written by the commissar on the margin of that request: "The *burmistrz* is required to adjust the fine for the guilty as is commanded by the prescript of the regional commissar. However the collection of the sum cannot be enforced in this manner, and I ask that the execution of this matter be carried out immediately."

The following is appended in a different handwriting: "The sum has already been collected".

Zgierz, December 18, 1826. Signed by Wratnowski.

With the monetary fine, which was paid by the Zgierz community also on behalf of the intercessor Berek Grynberg, the archival documents conclude the matter of the 79 Jewish families, who were evicted from their residences by an order from the Polish authorities and settled into the Jewish quarter.

The Struggle to Expand the Jewish Quarter

As soon as the authorities designated certain streets and houses for the Jewish quarter, the Jews began a struggle to expand it into the adjacent areas. In July 1825, Mrs. Roda Rafaelowa Dobrzynska filed a request to be permitted to continue living in her house, which was on the section of Szeradzer Street that was not part of the Jewish quarter.

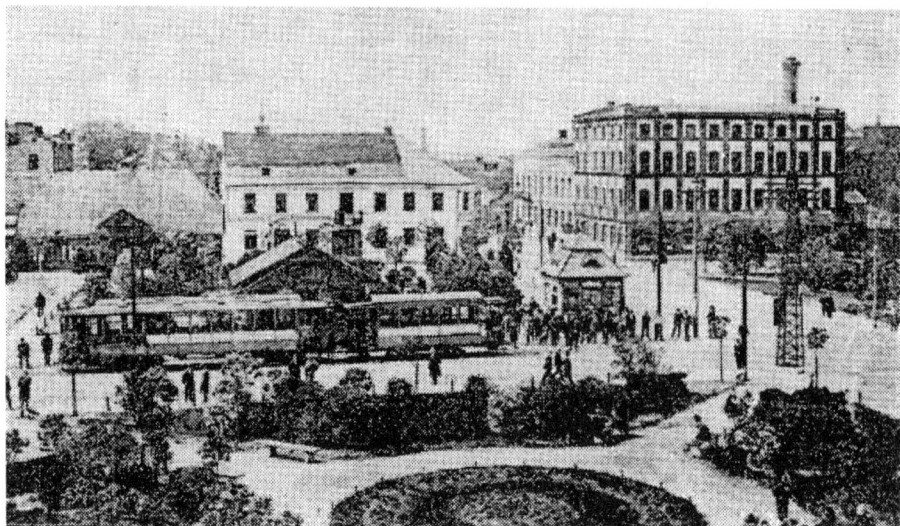

The new marketplace (on the right, the factory of Sirkes and Eiger, in the center, the station for the electric train to Lodz)

The following answer to the request came from the Zgierz managing committee, signed by the lawyers Raszynski and Dombrowski: "The Old Believer Roda Rafaelowa Dobrzynska has permission to live in her house that is not part of the Jewish quarter, but only until the year 1832. The residents must fulfill the following condition: they are not permitted to permit any other Old Believer to live in the house. Only Mrs. Dobrzynska and her unmarried children are permitted to be dwell in the house. People who illegally move into the house will be evicted, and the residents will be fined with a monetary penalty. Mrs. Dobrzynska has the right to rent portions of her house to Christians.

The answer continues, and states that prior to the expiry of the designated term (1832), Mrs. Dobrzynska must sell her house and move into the quarter with her entire family. She can continue to live outside of the quarter if she replaces her wooden house with a brick house. She must follow the conditions that are specified in article 3 of the ordinance regarding Jewish residency rights, that is to say, she must be able to read and write a foreign language, and the children must be sent to school, etc.

The following comment was written on the request of Roda Rafaelowa Dobrzynska: "She cannot write".

As can be seen from her second request, Roda Dobrzynska was a well-to-do proprietor of an enterprise that employed "craftsmen" and she took the trouble to expand her enterprise outside of the Jewish quarter. After the arrival of the above mentioned response from the Zgierz city council, Dobrzynska, who owned two houses outside of the quarter, undertook to construct a brick "fancy house". Therefore, she submitted a request to be permitted to move the wooden houses, which serve as living quarters for her and the craftsmen, from Szeradzer Street to Lodzer Street.

This request, which was sent to the Wojewodztwo committee, was responded to in writing with the agreement of Commissar Zawadski, with the condition that the newly built house must be especially beautiful.

In August 1826, Jakob Jedlicki presented a request to the representative of the Mazowian Wojewodztwo committee to be permitted to build a house on the field of the priest, which is outside of the Jewish quarter. That request, which is preserved in the Zgierz civic archives, gives a clear picture of the persistent struggle that Zgierz Jews conducted against the living restrictions during the first two decades of the 19th century.

The "Old Believer" Jakob Jedlicki, as is evident from the aforementioned request, was one of the prominent Jews of Zgierz at that time. He was one of the eldest Jewish residents of the town, and he held the lease for the income from kosher meat. On account of his prominence, the priest of the entire region ("Proboszcz") agreed to sell one of his lots to Jedlicki, where the Jew would build a house - an act which violated the ordinance that forbade Jews from living outside of the designated quarter.

In his request to the representative of the Mazowian Wojewodztwo committee, Jedlicki wrote:

"The undersigned, a resident of 35 years duration in this city of Zgierz, has lost his entire fortune due to ill luck during the time of war, and to the marching through of the military. I hold the lease for the income from kosher meat, and I lived with my wife and children on Tilne Street, which is also called Ogrodowa. I have been evicted from my dwelling. Having lived for a given time out of doors, I have not opposed the will of the higher authorities, and I have made efforts, in a provisional manner, to obtain a dwelling. To that end, I have received permission from the local priest to build a small house on the priest's fields behind the city, with the assurance from the priest that nobody would prohibit me from living there. The house will be located behind the city, and will not be in anyone's way. I have paid several scores of ducats to purchase lumber. I have paid the craftsmen, and have arranged all matters, up to the covering of the roof. Today unexpectedly, the regional authorities and the police magistrate took down the house.

In an unfortunate state, as I am again living with my family behind the fence, I modestly come to request the kindness of the eminent, all-powerful royal councilor and representative, to permit the rebuilding of the torn down house on the priest's fields. This house does not violate any police ordinances, nor does it interfere with any public and royal ordinance. Otherwise, please suggest to me another place behind the city where I can build a house, for I am unable to build a house on the Lodzer Street, or to build a house in accordance with the plans of the regime.

With the deepest respect for Your Eminence, the all-powerful royal councilor, representative of the Mazowian Wojewodztwo committee.

The junior servant, Jakob Jedlicki

Rembelinski, the representative of the Mazowian Wojewodztwo committee, wrote the following on Jedlicki's request: places for Jews can only be on the Lodzer Street; in consideration of the priest of Zgierz, he should conform to the ordinance with respect to distributing property, and he is personally responsible for disorder. The local *burmistrz* should impose a fine of 10 Zloty for permitting a Jew to put up a booth. The commissar's agents and the regional authorities are ordered to take it down.

The Living Restrictions of the Jews of Zgierz

Due to various legal reasons, the economic development of Zgierz lagged behind that of Lodz. This eased the struggle of the Zgierz Jews for their living rights. The leadership of the town was interested in its economic development. Therefore, they paid close attention when Jews took up residence in the forbidden streets of Zgierz. The most important thing that the municipality concerned itself with was that Jews should build brick houses. The living restrictions affected the lower class primarily, mainly Orthodox Jews, who settled in the quarter very quickly. If one wanted to live outside the quarter, one had to wear gentile garb and to send their children to Christian schools, conditions to which no Orthodox Jew would agree.

According to the ordinance regarding the Jewish quarter, the Jewish home dwellers were allowed the right to live in their homes for five years following the beginning of the ordinance. During the course of that time period, the houses had to be sold to Christians. Jews did not hurry to fulfill the ordinance. In the meantime, the Polish revolution took place in the year 1831. The progressive Polish royal leadership succeeded in the November revolution. Members of the undercover revolutionary regime stood at the head of the royal committee responsible for internal affairs, which was responsible for deciding upon Jewish living rights. The committee decided that the Jewish quarter impedes the acculturation of the Jews to European civilization. No visible changes in the Jewish quarter took place. It was not abolished. However, fewer Jews were driven into the quarter. Jews became bolder, and presented petitions to be allowed to live outside of the quarter, where Germans had built factories and enterprises. Some even acquired dwellings there without special permission.

In the revolution of 1831, Zawadski, the commissar of the Leczyca region, who certainly did not have any special love for Jews, became gentler. Regarding the request of Elias Majdan (Mirdan?) for permission to live outside the quarter, Zawadski issued the following directive to the president of the city of Zgierz:

"Regarding the necessity of expanding the living place of the Old Believers in the city of Zgierz, and the need to inhibit the spread of the cholera epidemic, and also regarding the declaration of the Old Believer Elias Mirdan that he intends to follow the ordinances" (dressing in European fashion, sending his children to school, and knowing a language), "and the Old Believer wishes to live outside the (Jewish) quarter". "Therefore, the regional commissar permits the Old Believer Elias Mirdan to live on Szeradzer Street." (This is obviously referring to the portion of the street that did not belong to the quarter). "Elias Mirdan is also permitted to conduct a leather business, and to build houses."

A very short time after the November uprising, when the royal regions of Congress Poland began to display liberal inclinations toward the "Old Believers", Jews of Zgierz, as can be seen from the archival documents, began to settle outside the quarter. These liberal tendencies did not last for long. After the uprising died down, the anti-Semites again began to drive the Jews into a ghetto ("quarter") and to expel them from their dwellings outside of the quarter. Alas, this also affected the Jewish homeowners in the quarter.

In the Zgierz archives, there is a document of a request "to the all-powerful commissar of the Leczyca region", dated January 12, 1832, and written by Avraham Kaliski.

In the name of Jews, owners of immovable property on Lodzer Street (in the quarter), Kaliski requested that the commissar prohibit Jews to live in Zgierz outside the quarter, since they, the owners of places and houses "have assurances from the regime that Szeradzer Street is designated as the quarter (for Jews), and have built houses on the muddy terrain that remain vacant. The ordinance was signed by the monarch (referring to the Russian Czar), and was broken by lower officials" - thus did Avraham Kaliski complain in his request to the all-powerful commissar of the Leczyca region.

The commissar of the Leczyca region, who quickly became affiliated with the anti-Semitic royal reactionaries after the failed revolution, made reference to this request of Avraham Kaliski when he reproved the president of Zgierz for not only failing to fulfill the order of the commissar to evict the Jews who lived outside of the quarter with the help of the police, but also for overlooking with indifference the fact that more Old Believers were taking ownership of residences outside of the quarter. The commissar demanded that the president immediately evict Jews who illegally "infiltrated the area outside the quarter".

The president of Zgierz was greatly frightened by the warning, and ordered the secretary of the local police to immediately evict the Jews from the areas outside the quarter. No special arrangements would be made for Elias Majdan, since he had no intention of remaining as a resident of the city.

Economic factors played a role in all of these struggles regarding the residency rights of the Jews of Zgierz. Jews took the risk of living outside of the quarter, where the center of business and manufacturing was being built up. It was developing very poorly, since the German manufacturers preferred to settle in Lodz, which had special conditions favorable to a large textile center. The Zgierz municipality, which was interested in the growth of the city, recognized the Jewish entrepreneurial expertise in business and manufacturing, and therefore permitted Jews to live outside the quarter, in the center of the city, in violation of the ordinances of the anti-Semitic Leczyca regional commissariat.

The well-to-do Jews who purchased places and built houses in the Jewish quarter, with the hope that there would be an influx due to the ordinances of the regime and that they would be able to obtain good rent money, were disappointed in that Jews did not wish to move into the ghetto, and they had to pay high taxes for their empty houses. This was indeed evident from the above-mentioned "request" of Avraham Kaliski. As well, a Christian element was interested in Jewish living rights in all of the streets. There were some Christians who rented dwellings to Jews, and would have to evict them. The owners of these dwellings did not wish to forgo their rent that was being paid by the Jews, and interceded for them.

The commissar of the Leczyca region did not cease demanding from the president of Zgierz that he evict the Jews from outside the quarter. The deputy of the higher authorities threatened the president with disciplinary fines if he does not submit a report indicating that he has evicted those Jews who live outside the quarter without appropriate residency permits.

In the spring of 1832, the Zgierz *burmistrz* informed the commissar of the Leczyca region that all of the Jews have been evicted from their places outside the quarter. In a second letter the *burmistrz* declared to the commissar that he has informed all of the citizens of the old city of Zgierz as well as the Old Believers, that as of July 1, 1832, nobody would be permitted to live in a place that has not been designated for that person. Police fines would be imposed for violation of the ordinance. The elder Rafaelowa Dobrszinska was informed that she can remain in her house outside of the Jewish quarter even after July 1, 1832, but with the restriction that she must not rent dwellings to any Jew, and she must sell her ownership to a Christian.

In the letter from the *burmistrz* to the commissar it is written that this ordinance excludes those Jewish homeowners who have a concession from the regime regarding their ownership. They are allowed to remain in their homes following July 1, 1832.

On that date, the first stage of the struggle of Zgierz Jewry for their living rights in all streets of the city ended.

The Development of the Jewish Quarter and the Situation in the City

After overcoming a variety of economic challenges, Zgierz began to develop as an industrial city in the Lodzer textile region. By 1825, the city already had cobblestone streets, two marketplaces, 300 houses (mainly brick) in which lived merchants and manufacturers. Such a report was written by the Polish statesmen of that time, the priest Stanislaw Staszic. The number of

41

Jewish merchants and manufacturers is not brought down in Staszic' report. However, from the constant accusations that were made against Jews for building houses in the industrial center, it is clear that Jews were penetrating in that area, and they conducted their businesses and enterprises.

Jews would generally come to Zgierz without having any other means, so they would settle in the Jewish quarter and eventually build dwellings there, which were not in accordance with the building codes of the civic authorities. The representative of the industrial section of Zgierz complained to the Mazowian Wojewodztwo commission that in the old city as well as in the Jewish quarters, houses were being built, "more accurately - huts", that do not have architectural approval. On the streets, uncleanness prevails, and the residents hang dirty laundry outside. Wood is lying everywhere, and broken ditches impede the outflow of water.

This report illustrates of picture as to how the Jewish quarter was built in Zgierz. The newly arriving Jews set themselves up, plunked down their belongings, procured wood and proceeded to build dwellings. The local authorities even assisted the Jews in building houses, but only in the Jewish quarter.

Regarding the request of Daniel Diwan to the Zgierz civic authorities for lumber to build a dwelling on Lodzer Street #6 (in the quarter), the *burmistrz* of the city of Zgierz wrote to the Leczyca regional commissar that one must be given a permit to be allowed to obtain wood from the local forests, as well as to build a house. The regional commissar from his side sent a notice to the Zgierz forestry office, asking them to give Daniel Diwan the needed lumber for building.

At the same time when Jews were being crowded into the ghetto, there were empty lots in the new city (Neistadt), not needed by the German manufacturer immigrants who were building the new industrial center in Zgierz. The "artisans" as they were known in official documents, only set up covered wagons in the lots that they obtained, and then they moved on to nearby Lodz, where the new textile center was developing in earnest.

We have already mentioned the case of the Christian homeowner Kaszochowska, who submitted a request in 1832 to the Mazowian Wojewodztwo commission to not be required to evict a Jew who rented a dwelling in her house, which was located outside the quarter.

A second citizen of Zgierz, Bartolomiej Nikel, went further in his request to the Warsaw royal committee in 1836, and made a request on behalf of the residents "that they be granted all rights for living freely and conducting business in the entire city of Zgierz". In justification of his request, Nikel wrote: "The city has fallen greatly in the realm of industry, so that the manufacturers and homeowners do not have the means of livelihood, for the rental income from their own homes has been taken away, while a significant segment of the population is unfortunately not able to lease dwellings."

In his request, Nikel did not mention which portion of the population did not have the rights to rent houses. Therefore, the homeowners who had their properties in the Jewish quarter, Bonifacy Witkowski, Kruszewski, and others, quickly wrote a request. In their request to the royal commission, they asked that the Jewish quarter be left as is, along with all of its ordinances and agreements. These included the agreement between the regime and the Germans in 1821, which forbade Jews from living and purchasing property in the new industrial quarter, as well as the ordinance of 1824 regarding the creation of the Jewish quarter.

The request from the Christian homeowners in the quarter was supported by the Zgierz municipality. The royal committee, which handled both requests, gave preference to the homeowners in the quarter, and confirmed that Jews have no rights to settle in all of the streets of Zgierz. The royal committee expressed its conclusion that "Only because they wished to charge a higher rent from the tenants, there was a need for some manufacturers and homeowners to enter into a partnership with Old Believers, and therefore permit them to become tenants in houses that are found in the center of the city."

The royal committee finally rejected the unjustified request of Bartolomiej Nikel, which he made in the name of the manufacturers, and recommended to the Wojewodztwo committee that they uphold the details of the aforementioned agreement.

The decision of the royal committee in answer to Nikel's request was also sent as a prescript to the commissar of the Leczyca region, and from there to the president of the city of Zgierz. He informed Bartolomiej Nikel that "the royal committee for spiritual and internal affairs and societal development" has rejected his request regarding permitting Jews to live in all of the streets of Zgierz. The city president advised Mr. Nikel that not only must he not make any request which are against the status quo, but also that he should come to his office where the prescript of the royal committee would be read to him.

The Struggle of the Zgierz committee with the Local Authorities for a Place to Erect the First Synagogue

In the 1830s, the Jews of Zgierz, despite all of the restrictions of residency rights, felt quite secure in their new settlement. As has been mentioned, the town had an organized community (*Dozor* Buzniczy) already in 1824. In 1836, the community proceeded to build a synagogue. The first efforts in that direction involved acquiring a permit from the local authorities to place a synagogue leader (szkolnik) in the community. From the available documents, it is not clear what sort of function this would have had. They only explain as follows:

In the beginning of the year 1836, the Zgierz communal leadership endeavored to ask the local city president to appoint David Torunczyk as synagogue leader. In the request to the city president, signed by the *dozor*s Berek Warmwasser, Elias Majdan and Chaim Lubraniecki, they asserted that the community decided to pay from its coffers for a synagogue leader with a salary of 100 Polish Zloty a year. "The synagogue is in need of a synagogue leader, and we have appointed the Old Believer Torunczyk for this purpose. He is a local resident, is capable, settled in his personal affairs, holding his calm, is moral, and nobody has any suspicions regarding him."

Along with the request ("declaration") the communal leadership enclosed 60 Polish Zloty as official payment for the concession which was to be given to the synagogue leader. Thereby, the *dozor*s confirmed that prior to David Torunczyk, the Zgierz community had no synagogue leader.

The synagogue leader, which was in actuality an official office, had to take an oath of allegiance to the Russian Czar prior to assuming his post. David Torunczyk took such an oath in December 1832.

The application from the communal leaders, which received the confirmation of the Zgierz city president, was sent to the commissar of the Leczyca region, and from there to the Mazowian Wojewodztwo committee, which in June 1836 issued a nomination to the Old Believer David Torunczyk as the synagogue leader of the Zgierz house of prayer.

At the same time, the Zgierz community purchased a lot upon which to build a synagogue. A notice regarding the purchase was presented to the city president, and was then forwarded to the Leczyca regional commissar, who in turn requested the city president to conduct an investigation about the land transaction. The investigation revealed that the lot was noted by mortgage number 244, and was situated on Lodzer Street, that is to say in the Jewish quarter. It had previously belonged to the local priest. Samuel Grzegorzewski, a Christian, purchased the lot that was sold by the priest for an appropriate price. The place was swampy, and Grzegorzewski conducted ameliorations, and sold the lot to the community for 600 Zloty. According to the declaration, Grzegorzewski also paid the priest for watching over the lot. Someone issued an accusation against Grzegorzewski for selling church land to Jews, upon which a synagogue is to be built.

The commissar of the Leczyca region requested outright that the Zgierz city president should send in documents that demonstrate that the lot that the communal leadership purchased from Grzegorzewski was indeed his own. On November 25 1838, the commissar, under the threat of a fine, repeated his request to send in proof within eight days regarding the purchase of the lot upon which the community wishes to build a synagogue.

The further handling of this affair is not known, due to the lack of authentic documents.

The Activity of English Missionaries during that Time

At the same time that the Jews of Zgierz, with great effort and despite all of the decrees, established a religious communal life in the town, the Leczyca region sent in English evangelical missionaries, and charged them with the sad task of converting Jews. In accordance with the dangerous activities that were taking place within the royal Polish Catholic religious authorities, the Leczyca regional commissar issued a request to the bergermeisters of the region that they should supervise the activity of the missionaries "who have permission to occupy themselves with inviting Jews to the Christian faith".

The missionaries were boundless in their efforts to convert Jews. However, they were not noted for their success with the Zgierz Jews. They found only three dissidents who endeavored to adopt the Christian faith: Lewin Winkler, Maria Pinkus and Jakob Dombrowski. All three came from outside of the Zgierz vicinity, and probably had little connection to Judaism. Dombrowski served for two and a half years with the Franciscan priests in the village of Lagiewniki, between Zgierz and Lodz. There, he studied the catechism. The priests of the Franciscan order did not pay their servant for his work. He left Zgierz so as to convert in the village - thus did the apostate

45

claim in his petition to the commissar of the Leczyza region, requesting permission to adopt the Christian faith.

Those apostates made no impression upon the Jewish people of Zgierz. There remains no trace of them, neither in folklore nor in memory, contrary to what is usually the case in families who tragically suffer from apostasy. Fortunately, those apostates had no effect upon the Jewish community of Zgierz, whose members remained faithful to the traditional observant Jewish lifestyle, as is reflected in the Zgierz archival documents.

The Ban against Erecting "Posts with Taught Wire" in the Jewish Quarter

Two documents exist in the archives, which describe a severe ban against the Old Believers erecting posts with taught wire or chains near their houses. This ban was issued by the Mazowian Wojewodztwo commission on September 4, 1834, and is published in "Dziennik Wojewodzki" number 168.

From the stringency of the ban, and from the demand of the regional commissar to the *burmistrz* of Zgierz and of other cities to uphold the ban rigorously, it can be understood that this was not meant to refer to ordinary posts, chains and wire near Jewish houses, but rather to the "eruv" [28] which was made around Jewish homes, so that one could carry on the Sabbath. The eruv, poles with chains around Jewish homes, caught the eye of the Polish authorities in such a major fashion that the Leczyca regional commissar obligated the *burmistrz* of Zgierz and the civic authorities of other towns to announce the ban against erecting posts and chains near Jewish houses three times in the synagogue. After that, Jews who do not follow the ban would be severely arraigned.

The struggle to erect an eruv lasted for over a year. Firstly, in January 1836, in the "Dziennik Wojewodzki" number 202 a permit was published for the Old Believers: "In the streets which are populated by the people of that faith, it is permitted to put up posts of a specified height and connect them with chains of wire or iron". The permit was sent by the secretary of the Leczyca regional commissar to the *burmistrz* of Zgierz and to the civic authorities of other towns with the following warning: "It must be strictly observed that the chains should be made of thin wire or iron". Those who put up thick chains "which irritate the eye and make the street ugly, must immediately replace them with other ones."

The Zgierz Civic Committee for Expanding the Jewish Quarter

Following the Polish revolt against the Russian occupational regime in 1831, Zgierz and other cities that were developed industrially entered into an economic crisis. As a punishment for the revolt, the Czarist authorities imposed a toll-boundary between Poland and Russia. The wool-working enterprises in Zgierz, which were primarily conducted by the Russian Mark, were shut down. The textile manufacturers, who immigrated and settled in Zgierz, therefore moved their enterprises to nearby Lodz.

Jews played a very important role in the commerce with the Lodzer textile merchants. Lodz also had a Jewish quarter, and the Jews of Lodz, as the Jews of Zgierz, struggled greatly for their rights to live in the entire city.

The anti-Semitic attitude of the secretary of the Leczyca region, as was the case in general with the administrative council in royal Poland, which was the central authority in Poland established by the Czarist regime of Nikolai I - did nothing to improve the economic situation in Zgierz, which had taken a sharp turn for the worse.

"Following the ill-fated revolution (the November Uprising of 1831)" - states a document from 1838 - "the manufacturers moved away from the city. The houses were empty on Strikowska and Szeradzka Streets. A few of these houses are not yet completed, and stand as testimony to the devastation in the city."

The municipal leadership of the town, along with the president who bore the non-Polish name Blumenfeld, came together for a meeting in the president's chancellery. The protocol of the meeting, which took place in March 1838, depicted Jewish life in the involuntary Jewish ghetto:

"The population of the quarter is growing in a reasonable fashion due to the immigration of families from other cities, as well as natural growth. No new houses can be built. Three or four families, of reasonable size, live in one room, even in small rooms. Such living conditions violate the police rules for health reasons."

On account of the situation, the meeting with the city president decided that they should agree to the aforementioned "request from the Old Believers" and expand the quarter by including the nearby Strykowska and Szeradzka Streets. Thus, the empty houses will be filled up, the unfinished

47

houses will be completed, and the empty lots will have structures built upon them. The population will find themselves in a better health situation, and thereby, the bad conditions that can endanger also the health of the Christians will be removed...

The protocol was forwarded to the commissar of the Leczyca region, along with the request to enlarge the quarter in accordance with a submitted plan and a list of the Jewish families who live there. The reply came in due course from the regional commissar, indicating that, in
accordance with the respect of the royal committee for inner and spiritual affairs and general health, after April 1836 - he can not agree to the request of the municipal authorities to enlarge the Jewish quarter.

The Supervisory Authorities Struggle Against the Jews who settled Outside of the Quarter in Zgierz

Due to the dearth of authentic documents, it is impossible to determine the growth of the Jewish population in Zgierz in general, and in Jewish quarter specifically, during the time frame that is being written about. However, it is clear that Jews immigrated to Zgierz from other town, and this increased the crowding in the Jewish quarter.

Despite the ban, Jews settled outside the quarter. The Zgierz civic authorities did not take the matter seriously, and allowed Jews to live in the new areas. Regarding the territory, a sharp struggle broke out between the supervisory authorities and the Zgierz municipality, as we can surmise from the archival documents: the president of Zgierz was fired by the authorities for tolerating the settling of Jews outside the quarter.

In June 1844, the Leczyca regional commissar requested the municipal authorities of Zgierz to strictly uphold the ban that forbade Jews to settle outside the quarter. The Jews, who, under the protection of the former city president Borodiszcz, illegally encroached on other quarters, should immediately be evicted. They must be informed of this.

The newly appointed Zgierz city president, whose name does not appear in the documents, immediately began to implement the request of the supervisory committee, and demanded that the following Jews leave the areas that are outside the quarter within 48 hours and move into the original quarter that was designated for the Old Believers: Daniel Zlotnik, the widow Cymber with her son-in-law, Walik Makowski, Walk Rubensztejn, the widow Dobrzynska, David Dawidowicz, and David Kaliski.

From among the aforementioned, only the widow Rafaelka Dobrzynska (her husband was Rafael), issued an accusation to the Leczyca commissar against being evicted from outside the quarter. She had already lived there for thirteen years, and owned a tavern. In her accusation, she wrote: "now, I would have to move the tavern to the middle of the Jewish quarter, I would be left without means of livelihood. I am a poor widow, quite old, without the means to a livelihood. The wretched tavern gives me my only means of livelihood." The widow requested "the all-powerful commissar" to allow her to remain in her dwelling.

The Leczyca regional commissar wrote the following on the request: "The decision of the Mazowian gubernatorial authorities must be executed precisely, and the instructions must be followed immediately" (that is to say, the widow must settle in the Jewish quarter, and sell her house to a Christian). On May 13, 1941, a second Jew, Avraham Pinkus Kaliski, submitted a request to the royal committee in Warsaw regarding the expansion of the Jewish quarter in Zgierz. The documents provide no details about the person of Avraham Pinkus Kaliski (one document is signed by Chaim Pinkus Koliski). From his "signature" (thee circles), it is obvious that he was unable to read or write. His request regarding the expansion of the Jewish quarter made its way through all of the levels of authority, namely: the royal committee in Warsaw, the Mazowian gubernatorial authorities (that is what the previous Wojewodztwo was referred to in documents from the year 1841 and onward), the Leczyca regional commissar, and finally - the municipal authorities of Zgierz. All of those levels of authority considered Kaliski's request regarding the expansion of the Jewish quarter, and the request was finally rejected. All documents from the above mentioned levels of authority were copied to the Zgierz civic authorities.

On May 2, 1842, a few years after he submitted the request for expanding the Jewish quarter, Avraham Chaim Pinkus Kaliski was summoned to the Zgierz civic authorities. There, he was told that "his request regarding the expansion of the quarter for the Old Believers can not succeed appropriately, since the motives to justify it are not that clear. There are still available places in the quarter for Old Believers that can be built up and one can find there many dwellings for rental."

A protocol was written up regarding the entire matter, which Kaliski signed with three circles, as one who was not able to write.

In all of the prescripts from the royal committee regarding Kaliski's request that were sent to the Zgierz civic authorities, it was stressed that the municipal authorities must evict from outside the quarter "the Old Believers who have settled there in the year 1833. They must unconditionally settle in the Jewish quarter."

The Struggle for Rights of Residency outside (Extra) the Quarter

In the 1850s, Jews who immigrated to Zgierz strengthened their struggle for living rights outside the quarter. Those who submitted various requests were for the most part Jews of means or those who had vocations that were desirable for the town. These included the assistant barber-surgeon [29] Zygmunt Rszepkowicz, the barber-surgeon Meir Jakubowicz, the merchant Wolf Glicksman, and the manufacturers Jozef Weiland, Shimon Waldberg, the Librach brothers and others. The requests of those Jews to live outside the quarter were the cause of a lengthy correspondence between the Zgierz city president, the municipal authorities, the regional authorities, and the central regime in Warsaw.

It is interesting to see the motives that were given by the various petitioners for living rights outside of the quarter. The assistant barber-surgeon Zygmunt Rszepkowicz wrote in his request (April 1839) that he lived in Zgierz from 1821, he was the first barber-surgeon in town, and is needed by the local doctors Funkensztejn and Tuczinski, as well as many other people who have faith in him. Rszepkowicz complains in his request that if he does not live in the center of town, the town will not be able to make appropriate use of his services. On account of this motive, he requests the city president obtain a permit for him to live "in one of the streets that is settled by Catholics".

In Rszepkowicz' request, the following is written: "He is permitted to live with Rafaelski, in the house of the Old Believer Josek Brzezinski". This house was indeed outside of the Jewish quarter; however it is not in the "extra quarter" where Jews were permitted to live only with special permits.

A second barber-surgeon with appropriate qualifications, Meir Jakubowicz, who lived in Zgierz from 1826 and made a request to live in the "extra quarter", conducted a correspondence with the various municipal offices and the central authorities in Warsaw between March 1843 and September 1844. Jakubowicz also stressed in his position his needed work for the city, and he requested the president of the city of Zgierz to consider the various motives that justify a Jewish barber-surgeon to live outside (extra) of the quarter:

1. My service as a barber-surgeon.
2. I wear different garb than is usually worn by the Old Believers.
3. I took the barber-surgeon exams in the Kielce and Sandomierz gubernias, and I possess a diploma from doctor's offices in those gubernias testifying to my qualifications as a barber-surgeon.

The Zgierz magistrate dealt with the matter in a special meeting. The protocols testify strongly to Jakubowicz' good deeds as a barber-surgeon for the city: "When the cholera epidemic and other illnesses spread in the city, Jakubowicz always was available to serve the sick from various walks of life. His activities were conducted without reward." He also performs small operations under the supervision of doctors.

The protocol from the magistrate's meeting, which dealt with the request of Jakubowicz to live outside of the quarter, was sent to the police chief of the Leczyca region (powiat). The official wrote on the document that he found no reason to justify Jakubowicz to live outside of the quarter.

The Zgierz civic authorities were not satisfied with the answer, and they sent the request to higher authorities, asking for permission for Jakubowicz to live provisionally outside of the quarter. In this request of April 1844, the beneficial activities of the Jewish barber-surgeon among the Zgierz population was even more clearly described. The request states the following:

"The city of Zgierz has a population of over 7,000, excluding the temporary residents of the city. Various illnesses would not be taken care of without the help of the medical and barber-surgical arts. The latter has been conducted recently in the city by Meir Jakubowicz, the qualified barber-surgeon."

The request from the magistrate to the higher authorities, signed by the Zgierz city president and councilors, made mention of the above-mentioned decision of the police authorities, and requested the higher authorities to issue at their discretion a provisional permit for Jakubowicz allowing him to live outside of the quarter, for if he is found far from the center of town "in the quarter of the Old Believers", there would be the danger of a delay in treatment for those people who require his help.

The magistrate of Zgierz added several confirmations to this request: Meir Jakubowicz is fluent in the Polish and German languages, both orally and in writing, and his two children, Aharon and Jakob, between the ages of 8 and 10 years old, are registered in the Catholic elementary school where they attend regularly. They conduct themselves well, and display exemplary diligence in their studies, which earns them recognition.

The confirmation from the school was signed by the teacher Traborski, the supervisor of the Catholic elementary schools in the Zgierz parish. It was also confirmed by Father S. Hirszberger.

All of these requests and confirmation were obviously intended to encourage the police chief of the Leczyca region to request from the Mazowian gubernatorial authorities to permit Jakubowicz to live outside the Jewish quarter. The regional police chief appended his recommendation for the Jewish barber-surgeon onto the documents that were sent by the Zgierz magistrate and police authorities.

On September 3, 1844, Jakubowicz received the decision of the authorities of the Mazowian gubernia, which granted him provisional permission to live outside the quarter in the city of Zgierz.

The Zgierz Civic Committee for the Rights of Jews of Means to Live Outside (Extra) the Quarter

In the following years, the Zgierz municipality strongly interceded for the rights of Jews who possessed means and who were needed to live outside the quarter. The head of the city kept in mind the economic development of the city, which severely lagged behind the development of its younger sister - Lodz. The gubernatorial and central supervisory authorities in Warsaw, with their anti-Semitic politics, barely took into account the economic conditions of Zgierz, and did not permit Jews of means to live outside the quarter.

During the years 1846-1848, a correspondence took place regarding permitting Shimon Waldberg to open a textile factory for the production of "kort" and "cashmere" cloth outside the quarter. Waldberg was already operating the factory and 20 workshops. In the opinion of the magistrate, he had fulfilled all of the obligations that were required of the Old Believers.

The police authorities of the Leczyca region held the same opinion as the Zgierz municipality, and the Waldman's request was sent on to the governing authorities in Warsaw.

The request was rejected by the governing authorities in Warsaw, with the justification that Zgierz already had the well-known Maues factory that produces the same textiles that Waldberg mentioned in his request.

Shimon Waldberg appealed to the governor, and made mention of the ordinance of Duke Namjestnik of 1824, which "permitted Old Believers to live outside the quarter if they establish factories". In his request to the governor, Waldberg demonstrated that his factory was one of the most significant in Zgierz, and that it employed 70 people who would have no means of living if the development of the enterprise is hampered.

The Jewish manufacturer also disproved the claim that there was already such a factory in Zgierz. One could not hope for a better one. He further claimed that "our factories will soon be at the level of those outside the country. The regime must support the development of new factories, , for the factories of Malts and Maues (Germans) do not possess exclusive patents for manufacture."

Finally Waldberg asked, in his request to the governor, to be permitted to maintain his factory outside the quarter without the rights to live there. The Jewish manufacturer received such permission from the governing authorities on February 27, 1847.

In the same time period (1846-1848) similar things took place with two Jewish manufacturers, the brothers Feivish and Henech Librach. They belonged to the Librach family who were textile manufacturers in Ozorkow and Lodz. No financial connection existed between the family members.

The Zgierz magistrate strongly interceded to allow the Librachs to conduct a textile factory with 20 workshops outside the quarter, and to allow them to live there. In his request to the supervisory authorities, he listed several of his possessions.

As he did with the case of Waldbergs, in his report to the gubernatorial authorities in Warsaw, the official of the Leczyca region supported Librach's request to be granted a concession to live and conduct a textile factory outside of the quarter, in the house of the Metner heirs on Blotene (Muddy) Street number 191. The governing authorities in Warsaw requested that the Leczyca regional authorities clarify: whether the Librachs are the entrepreneurs who own a textile factory in Ozorkow, whether they are the

53

owners of such a factory in the Jewish quarter, and whether their enterprise has neglected the manufacturing trademark of the cloth professionals that is authorized by the governing authorities. After receiving the answer from the Leczyca regional official that the Librachs do not own any other factory other than what they have established in Zgierz, that they are in compliance with the manufacturing trademark, as that all of the residents in their homes have declared that they would not wear Jewish garb, and that they would send their children to Catholic schools -in October 1849, the Warsaw governing authorities permitted the Librach brothers to conduct a factory and to live outside of the quarter in Zgierz.

The two Librach brothers, the first large scale Jewish manufacturers who set up textile enterprises in Zgierz, were the heads of two large families, as can be seen in the declaration that they gave on July 1847 regarding receiving living rights for all family members.

In the Zgierz archives, there are no statistics regarding the number of Jewish manufacturers, merchants and artisans who already lived outside of the quarter in the 1850s. We do know that the number was growing, as can be seen from the petitions of Jews who requested living rights in that part of the city, in order to set up factories or businesses there. The governing authorities took interest in how many Jews already lived in the extra quarter, and they asked the official of the Leczyca region about this at the time that he brought in the request of Chaim Lubraniecki [30] for a permit to live outside the quarter, and to open up a store for both locally and externally manufactured goods. In response to the query, the magistrate of Zgierz presented a list of the Jews who lived outside of the quarter: Jozef Weiland who built a two story house in the old city, and the barber-surgeon Meir Jakubowicz who lived there provisionally with a concession from the Mazowian gubernatorial authorities. That list, signed by the city president and the councilors Jesse and Zigler, dated July 10, 1848, was not exact, since it is clear from the aforementioned documents that there were already more Jews living outside the quarter. The Zgierz civic authorities, who were interested in having more Jews settle there, did not give an accurate number to the governing authorities.

The royal committee dealt with the issue of Lubraniecki. The Jewish manufacturer-merchant obtained the permit to live outside of the quarter, and to conduct his business there. He had to submit the following documents.

1. A statement from the financial office regarding the financial reserves of his business, and regarding his financial status.
2. A statement from the magistrate of Zgierz regarding the good moral conduct of the petitioner.
3. A confirmation from the "cloth guild" that he conducts his business affairs with honesty, and that, in 1831, at the time of the crisis of the cloth weavers, he helped and supported them.

During the course of five months, a correspondence took place between the Zgierz municipality and the central authorities regarding permission for the Jew Blum to live in the Christian area of Zgierz. In August 1849, Gershon Blum was unfortunately ordered for a second time to abandon his home outside of the quarter, and he was informed that he would be evicted within four hours by the police.

Blum reacted to this with a request to the civil governor of Warsaw. The request was supported by the magistrate of Zgierz and the official of the Leczyca region. The city president of Zgierz remarked in his request to the supervisory authorities that outside of the quarter, there are no Christian businesses dealing with fashion merchandise of the type that Gershon Blum intends to deal with. In due course, an answer arrived from the Warsaw regime that due to the situation with Blum's wife, he is provisionally permitted to live outside the quarter with his family until the end of September, 1849. After Mrs. Blum gives birth, the family must immediately settle in the ghetto. The Zgierz city president will be reproved sharply if he allows the Blum family to remain in a dwelling outside of the quarter. The governing authorities threatened the president with dismissal if he purposefully disobeys the statutes regarding the Jewish quarter.

In the years 1850-1851, the documents record only three requests of Jews to live outside of the quarter. Each one of those requests had its own manner of being dealt with, and resolution. All three were supported by the Zgierz municipality and the Leczyca regional official.

The Zgierz Magistrate is in Favor of Expanding the Jewish Quarter

At the end of the 1850s, the struggle between the Zgierz magistrate and the supervisory authorities regarding the living rights of the Jews in the city intensified. The Jewish population increased naturally. According to the magistrate's accounts, there were already 1,590 Jewish residents of Zgierz in August 1848. The ghetto was overfilled. Jews had already rented dwellings, purchased lots, built houses, and opened stores and business enterprises outside (extra) the quarter. The Zgierz magistrate "looked through his fingers" at the expansion of the Jewish business element in the city. A reaction came from two sides: from the anti-Semitic supervisory authorities - the Lodz city president Treiger who influenced the Warsaw governing authorities with his anti-Semitic reports; and the homeowners in the Jewish quarter, both Jews and Christian, who were afraid that the expansion of the quarter would depress the established prices in the restricted living area. There was also a third group that fought against the rights of Jews to live in the entire city: the German and Polish manufacturers in the extra quarter.

In August 1848, the Zgierz magistrate (city president Blumenfeld, and councilors Jarani, Esse and A. Lebelt) undertook a project to expand the Jewish quarter. The project began with the words: "On account of the complaints of the Old Believers in our city that their living accommodations are crowded in their restricted quarter, and on account of the complaints of the homeowners of the Jewish quarter that their homes apparently are empty as the Old Believers push themselves outside the quarter - the magistrate and his entourage will visit the Jewish quarter in order to determine who is correct".

The Lustracia (population registry) of the magistrate from that time regarding the Jewish quarter presents a sad picture of the Jewish living conditions. It was determined that the empty houses were in such a state that nobody could live there. The rents were so high that the poorer classes did not have the means to rent even a one-room dwelling. Two, three or four families live in such dwellings, which causes uncleanness, discomfort and illness.

According to this, the Zgierz magistrate believes that the quarter must be expanded, for the streets that were designated in December 1824 as part of the Jewish quarter are now too small for the Jewish population. The Jewish population of Zgierz was 345 people when the quarter was established, and today (1848) there area already has 1,590 Jewish people. Due to this situation, Jews are pushing themselves outside the quarter, and the living accommodations are becoming more difficult there.

The project of the magistrate contained no indication as to how to expand the quarter. However, all of the opponents to granting Jews living rights in all of the streets of the city of Zgierz reacted to the project.

Franciszek Zalewski, a homeowner in the Jewish quarter, issued a request in the name of all of the homeowners of the area to the governing authorities in Warsaw to evict the Jews from outside the quarter. Zalewski made mention of the ordinance of December 1824, which restricted the Jews to Lodzer Street and a half of Szeradzer Street, due to the fact that the Old Believers had made various efforts to enter into the marketplace and live in the streets outside the quarter.

Zalewski ended his request to the governing authorities in the name of all of the homeowners of the Jewish quarters with the request that a delegate be sent to determine the truth regarding the submitted facts. "The aforementioned Old Believers, who have pushed themselves into areas outside the quarter, must be evicted. Also in the future, such transgressions must be halted." He requested that the Lodz city president Treiger, well known for his anti-Semitism, be sent to Zgierz as a delegate to adjudicate on the matters that are dealt with in the request to the governing authorities.

In answer to the request of Zalewski and the other Christian manufacturers and homeowners, the governing authorities ordered the official of the Leczyca region to conduct an investigation regarding the justification of the request to ban the frequent encroachment of Old Believers outside the quarter, and the need to evict those Jews who live there illegally. The official of the Leczyca region sent the Lodz city president Treiger to Zgierz in order to adjudicate on all the issues that were mentioned in Zalewski's request and to demand a clarification from the Zgierz magistrate.

Treiger came to Zgierz in July 1849, held a meeting with the Zgierz magistrate, and posed the following questions: a) On what authority did they rely to allow the following Jews to settle outside of the quarter: Gershon Blum, Chaim Lubraniecki, Elisha Fein, Menashe Beril, the widow Blima, Eva Goldsztejn, and A. Shafir -when they did not have any permits from the regime; and why were they not immediately removed from outside the quarter? b) What type of disturbances took place that did not permit the

57

fulfillment of the ordinance of the regional official regarding evicting the Old Believers from outside the quarter, and the submission of a protocol to the appropriate authorities?

The Zgierz magistrate gave the following characteristic answer to the questions of the Lodz city president, and to the accusation of Zalewski and his people:

"The people who made the accusation do not have the general welfare in mind, only their own personal goals. A careful investigation into their complaints will show that the owners of houses in the Jewish quarter do not want to be forced to pay for the burden of their houses, or to absorb the cost of repairs when the Old Believers would be permitted to live outside the quarter." The magistrate continued on: "In addition, the owners of houses outside the Jewish quarter surmise that they will be able to benefit themselves by increasing their income." (This is a reference to the fixed rents in the Jewish quarter, which the local homeowners maintained by means of the restriction of the living rights of Jews).

One month after hearing the declaration of the Zgierz magistrate, the anti-Semitic city president of Lodz went with the police to the homes of Elisha Fein, Menashe Beril, the widow Blima and Eva Goldsztejn, and evicted them from their homes, since they were not willing to leave on their own. Gershon Blum was not evicted from his home by the president, for his wife was in her ninth month of pregnancy. In order to insure that Blum would be forced to later leave his home outside the quarter, Treiger sealed Blum's textile shop and informed the civic authorities that they must act on the eviction of Gershon Blum at the appropriate time.

The magistrate of Zgierz did not give up his plan to expand the Jewish quarter, and he continued to tolerate Jews living outside the quarter. The leaders of the city continued to make requests to the official of the Leczyca region, and submitted the previously mentioned statistics regarding the number of Jewish residents in Zgierz, the difficulties of living in the Jewish quarter, and crowding that could have an ill effect on the health of the population. The regional official brought the reasons for expanding the quarter to the governing authorities. Therefore, in the year 1849, the Lodz city president Treiger was delegated to verify the situation in the Jewish quarter and the living rights of Jews outside the quarter, and bring his findings to the supervisory authorities.

From his Lustracia of the Jewish quarter, Treiger pointed out in his report that the Jews live 23 families per room, and that people live in cellars, attics and unheated rooms. However, the Jew hater felt that there was no danger of epidemic diseases, for the Jews live there in their usual thrifty and exceptionally economical fashion. That is their lifestyle.

In his report, Treiger denied that there was the fixing off rents in the Jewish quarter, which hinders the poorer classes from settling there. There are empty places and rooms available that Jews do not wish to rent, for they would rather push themselves into the marketplace of the old city and the extra quarter. Jews are willing to pay 25-30% more in rent, so long as they do not have to live in the Jewish quarter. The city president of Lodz also made mention of the losses that would be suffered by the homeowners of the Jewish quarter if Jews would be permitted to live outside the quarter, and decried the attempts of the Zgierz magistrate to expand the Jewish quarter. One can simply round it out by lengthening Szeradzer Street. In the latter part of his report, the anti-Semite accuses the Jews of wishing to encroach upon the Christian streets for reasons of financial gain, for the Christians would not be able to withstand the Jewish competition in their enterprises, business and speculation.

Treiger also suggested an "improvement" to the already existing ordinances that gave Jews of means rights to settle outside the quarter; namely: "Not to permit the Old Believers any rights of choice of dwelling places, but rather to make it dependent on the opinions of the higher authorities, so that Jews would not be able to become concentrated in the most important areas of the city."

The report of the Lodzer city president regarding Jewish living rights in Zgierz was in complete accordance with the anti-Semitic reactionary leanings of the Polish ruling authorities of that time, who ruled due to the goodwill of the anti-Semitic, reactionary Czarist despots of Petersburg. The determinations of the Lodzer city president regarding Jewish living rights in Zgierz were in contradiction to the leanings of the local civic authorities who regarded the Jews as a necessary element for the economic development of the city. With respect to the conflict between the municipality and the authorities, during the 1860s there were three groups in Zgierz who had their various economic interests regarding the living rights of Jews in the city; namely: the homeowners of the Jewish quarter, both Christians and Jews, supported by the Christian manufacturers outside the quarter, who were in favor of maintaining the already designated ghetto for the Jews; the Jewish residents of Zgierz in both quarters, who struggled for free living rights in the entire city; the third group was the municipality, which had an interest in the economic development of the city, who were in favor of expanding the Jewish quarter and not permitting Jews to settle in the extra quarter.

The struggle between those groups grew stronger after the report of the Lodz city president regarding the population records (Lustracia) of the Jewish quarter was submitted to the supervisory authorities. The official of the Leczyca region affixed his own report to Treiger's Lustracia report, clarifying why Jews were permitted to live in the extra quarter.

As can be seen, the Zgierz magistrate did not hasten to evict the aforementioned seven Jewish families from outside the quarter, even though the governing authorities in Warsaw issued a strong order to the regional official regarding this matter.

The homeowners of the Jewish quarter soon made mention of the orders of the supervisory authorities to the Zgierz magistrate and city president. In 1851, Franciszek Zalewski again presented a request to the governing regime in Warsaw to not permit Jews to live outside the quarter. This time, his request also had the signatures of the Jewish homeowners in the Jewish quarter - Nathan Goldberg and David Sadokerski.

In the request, the signers complained about the Zgierz magistrate, pointing out that instead of scrupulously carrying out the ordinances of the higher authorities (to restrict the Jewish living rights), he gave matters an opposite direction. "The Zgierz city president did not issue any ordinances to evict the Jews from outside the quarter." Later, the request mentions the aforementioned reason that "there are many empty places in the Jewish quarter that are not built up, and many dwellings that are not rented, which harms the local homeowners."

Regarding the inimical attitudes to Jewish living rights in Zgierz, the local Jews presented their own characteristic and significant request to the Zgierz city president. The author of the request, Yisrael Litauer, wrote the following in his name, and in the name of all of the Old Believers who are residents of that city:

1. When the quarter for the Old Believers of the city was set up a few decades ago, their number was 300 families, or 2,000 people. There were only 24 houses available for them – and these were bungalows.

2. The increase in the population of the Old Believers in the quarter has brought great pressure upon the poorer classes of locals, who have large families. Regarding the rental rates, which are fixed very high by the homeowners, the residents become even poorer. Regarding the crowding in the dwellings, even the smallest attic rooms are occupied by several families.

3. On account of the situation, there is great poverty, oppression, and foul air, which will eventually expose the entire population with various diseases and fatal illnesses. It is not secret to Mr. President that the first outbreak of an epidemic was in the quarter (referring to cholera). This took place in 1848 in Zgierz, and was confirmed by the qualified city doctor.

The latter points of the earlier mentioned request, claiming that there were vacant places in the Jewish quarter that should be built up by residents who possess the means, were denied by Litauer.

It was the wish of all the residents, not only Jews, to be able to rent dwellings in the entire old city, to be "permitted to expand the business and industry there, as is shown by the enclosed declaration". (The declaration by the Christian residents of the Zgierz old city, mentioned by Litauer, is not found in the archives.)

In his further justifications, the author of the request, who knew that the German manufacturers left Zgierz and went to Lodz, stressed the painful point that, given the current situation, the Jews would be forced to leave Zgierz. Therefore, the increase in the Jewish population is a great boon for the city. For in addition to the loss of the business and work that is conducted y the Old Believers, the civic coffers will be emptier, which is certainly not the wish of the regime and others, as is known by Mr. city president.

A few months later, in November 1851, a second Jew, Shlomo Placki, presented a request to the official of the Leczyca region "in the name of the residents of the same faith" to expand the Jewish quarter, for on account of

61

the cramped living conditions in the quarter, there is the threat of epidemic illnesses.

In the same period of time, several individual Jews requested from the supervisory authorities to be permitted to settle in the extra quarter of Zgierz. In his request to the regional official, Jozef Rzorkowski made mention of his wealth, which permitted him to live in the extra quarter in accordance with the ordinances. Aside from that "he is a broker, who is needed by the cloth manufacturers".

The official of the Leczyca region sent the request to the ruling authorities of the Warsaw Gubernia with his note that dismiss the request of the cloth weaver's guild and the Zgierz magistrate to permit the Old Believer Rzorkowski to live in the extra quarter. A confirmation from the guild and the protocol of the Zgierz magistrate, giving their approval to Rzorkowski's request, were attached to the request.

The ruling authorities of the Warsaw Gubernia did not permit Rzorkowski to live in the extra quarter, for according to the high command of 1848, a Jew can only obtain such permission if he has a net worth of 1,500 rubles, and if he agrees to the ordinances regarding garb, and to sent his children to Christian schools, etc. "Rzorkowski does not have the qualifications". The regional official warned him that he should not again make such requests that go against the authorized ordinances.

The Warsaw governing authorities displayed a different attitude to the request of the elder barber-surgeon Shmuel Szerpinski. They were not able to deny him living rights in the extra quarter, for there were no Christian barber-surgeons who could administer medical care to the population at the time of the spread of the cholera epidemic. The governing authorities presented this justification to the royal committee for internal and spiritual affairs to permit Szerpinski to settle in the extra quarter, which will be for the benefit of the entire population.

The royal committee for internal and spiritual affairs permitted the Jewish elder barber-surgeon, with his wife and unmarried children, to live in a house in the Christian streets, with the restriction that he must not become involved in manufacturing or with the sale of national drinks.

The salt merchant Wolf Glicksman submitted a request to the Zgierz city president that he intercede to the higher authorities for a permit for him to live on the non-designated streets and conduct business there. Glicksman pointed out that he fulfilled all the required qualifications, as is certified by the documents that should give him the rights to live in the extra quarter.

We can assume that Wolf Glicksman received this permission, even though there are no official confirmations in the archives.

A different complicated matter that is not sufficiently clarified in the archival documents was the question of the residency rights for Hersch Ber Szwarc, the father of the Zgierz writer and social activist Yissachar Szwarc. His struggle to live in the extra quarter lasted twelve years. His struggle started in 1849 and ended in 1861, near the time of the end of residency restrictions for Jews in royal Poland.

It is not stated from where Hersch Ber Szwarc came before coming to Zgierz. In an archive document from 1849, his name appears in a lease agreement that was agreed upon between the Old Believer merchant Hersch Ber Szwarc who lived in the city with Yisrael Litauer, leasing eight stores from the civic "Oisteria" (?) [31]. According to the agreement, Hirsch Ber Szwarc rented a store from Litauer for 40 silver rubles a year.

It is not known what Hersch Ber Szwarc did in Zgierz during the two year period of 1849-1851 that his name suddenly began to appear in all of the requests regarding the rights of Jews to live in the extra quarter, as well as in all of the ordinances that came from the supervisory authorities during that timeframe.

In the aforementioned request from Franciszek Zalewski and his support from the Warsaw governing authorities regarding not permitting Jews to live in the extra quarter - the Old Believer Hersch Ber Szwarc played a very important place. There, it is related about him that he occupies himself with small-scale business, and he is at liberty to live in the extra quarter. Even though he does not have the appropriate qualifications for this, the Zgierz city president supported Szwarc' declaration regarding his rights to live in the extra quarter. The reasons that Zalewski lists against the rights of residency of Hersch Ber Szwarc are typical: he does not know how to write, and he does not know a foreign language, which disqualifies his rights to live in the extra quarter. Regardless of this, the councilor Antony Lebelt purchased a house in his name on the market, on the Street of the Representatives, for the sum of 900 silver rubles. Through an act of the Zgierz Court of the Peace, it was shown that Lebelt purchased this home for the Old Believer Hersch Ber Szwarc, so that he will be able to live in the extra quarter.

In his request, Zalewski accused the Zgierz city president of supporting Szwarc. Regarding the fact that he cannot write and does not know a foreign language, the city president defended Szwarc by claiming that his hand was injured in an accident. In fact, he understands a foreign European language, and possesses the appropriate means, which gives him the right to dwell in the extra quarter. The defender of the owners in the Jewish quarter was not lazy, and uncovered the court deeds of the above mentioned lease agreement between Litauer and Szwarc with his signature "in Hebrew". Zalewski attached this document to his request to the governing authorities of Warsaw and posed the questions: If his (Szwarc) handicapped hand permits him to write in Hebrew, why would it not permit him to write in Polish or in another foreign language?

In addition, the cringing Jew Sadokerski "the Old Believer who owns a home in Zgierz" who cosigned Zalewski's request to the governing authorities in Warsaw to not allow Jews to live in the extra quarter, also submitted a different request, requesting "from the royal committee for internal and spiritual affairs, to forbid Hersch Ber Szwarc from moving out of the Jewish quarter". That request bore the characteristics of a denunciation of a "wonderful" Jew against his brethren in Zgierz who were leaving the Jewish quarter in order to settle in the streets that had been designated for the manufacturers. The denunciator wrote in his request that such business is not only a damaging influence on the Old Believers, but it will also cause a .loss to the royal treasury, for the homeowners in the Jewish quarter who have to pay higher fees will lose their tenants who move into the extra quarter.

In his request, Sadokerski asserted that he is making his request on behalf of the entire community of Old Believers. There are no confirmations available that the Zgierz community authorized him to do this. As is known from a previous description, the community interceded strongly for Jewish living rights in the entire city. The name Sadokerski [32] is also not mentioned on the list of dozors, and we can surmise that the Zgierz communal leadership had no connection to the denunciation.

On all the requests and submissions regarding Jewish living rights, the Warsaw governing authorities alerted the official of the Leczyca region regarding the repeated complaints from the Zgierz citizens who lament the indifference of the magistrate "to the encroaching of Old Believers onto certain streets". The ordinances were not being upheld, and the meetings of the magistrate did not place blame in the situation regarding the six Jewish families who did not have the appropriate qualifications, and who were not evicted despite the fact that it has now been over a year since the ordinance was issued. Similarly, the governing authorities wrote in 1851 to the regional official regarding the illegal granting of living rights to Hersch Ber Szwarc, who was accused of slyly obtaining a house on the specified streets, and living in it.

Relying on a report from the governing authorities of Warsaw to the royal committee for internal affairs, the Lodz city president Treiger was again delegated to go to Zgierz. This time (January 1852), he issued a public defense for the Jews who wish to settle in the streets that were forbidden to them, and a defense of Hersch Ber Szwarc against the homeowners in the extra quarter, who "came together and accused Szwarc in order to remove from him and others the will to make efforts to obtain permission to settle in the extra quarter." Those people, driven by personal hatred and even more by the intention to insure that the Old Believers remain in the quarter, had only one aim: to assure the rental income at very high fixed rates" - this is what Treiger wrote in his report to the official of the Leczyca region.

At the same time as the supervisory authorities were already prepared to expand the Jewish quarter, and the Zgierz magistrate and the president Blumenfeld pushed strongly for an expansion, they also with the same strength opposed the Jews who wished to settle in the extra quarter without the proper qualifications.

In February 1852, the governing authorities issued a plan for the city, which defined the Jewish quarter and designated which streets would be included in the expansion. The homeowners in the Jewish quarter again issued a request against expansion. The Warsaw governing authorities reacted with a letter to the regional committee for internal and spiritual affairs. In that letter, the usual arguments against the homeowners were mentioned, that they only wish to insure their own income, and that the crowding in the Jewish quarter brings the threat of illness.

In July of the same year, the regional committee for internal and spiritual affairs answered the letter from the Warsaw governing authorities. In the answer, it was mentioned that the Jewish quarter was created in Zgierz in 1824, and included only Lodzer Street and the south portion of Szeradzer Street.

The committee criticized the plan to expand the quarter with the rented parts of the following streets: Strykowska, and the second side of Szeradzer

Street. They left in the plan a small lane in that area, which had no name and without mentioning how many houses and empty lots are there. In its answer, the committee also expressed wonder at the growth of the Jewish population of Zgierz, which grew from 343 people in 1848 to 2,400 in 1852. It was for this reason that the dwellings were crowded. The answer brought down complaints against the local authorities, as to why they did not mention how many Jews were permanent and temporary residents, and why they did not insure that all of the Jews who settled there have the appropriate documents… It could possibly be that some are hiding from military registration. Further on, a typical question comes from the regional committee: "Why did the local authorities not take notice of the rapid influx of Jews from other places?"

Further documents regarding Jewish living rights in Zgierz are not available in the archives.

The Project of the Zgierz Magistrate to Enlarge the Jewish Quarter

In his letter and request to the supervisory authorities regarding the enlargement of the Jewish quarter, the Zgierz magistrate submitted his project, signed by president Blumenfeld, regarding which streets should be given over to the extra quarter.

In his draft, the city president gave an answer to the following question to the royal committee: "From where did such a large increase in the Jewish population come?" The answer presented a clear picture of the development of the Jewish settlement in Zgierz. President Blumenfeld wrote the following:

"Since the city of Zgierz has expanded in manufacturing, the population, both Christian and Jews, increased. Since the Jews have many factories that require employees for their work, they brought in workers from other cities that possessed passports or formal permits of residency. For this reason, the number of families increased, that is to say the number of married couples. Due to this, many families would live in a single dwelling, for in order to purchase houses or lease factories, the working families would have to band together. This is the main reason for the growth in the city, due to the cloth and textile business. That quarter (the Jewish quarter) has become far too small."

In accordance with the bureaucratic attitude of the officials of the ruling authorities in Congress Poland of the time, with all of their subordinate sectors, who were dependent on the Czarist regime and the supreme command of Czar Alexander II - it was not so easy to proceed with the enlargement of the Jewish quarter. The entire matter remained "frozen". Jews from the crowded quarter as well as recent arrivals continued to settle in the extra quarter and continued to make requests and submissions to the supervisory authorities, and even to His Excellency Duke Namiestnik, regarding the permission of Jews to settle in the extra quarter. Such requests were made through the civic councilor and merchant August Kriger, "in his name and in the name of the citizens", to Duke Namiestnik regarding 50 Jewish families who "are away from their quarter and left behind unoccupied houses". In that same request, Kriger together with Jan Pawinski requested from the Warsaw governing authorities to permit Jews to live in the extra quarter. The supervisory authorities again made a request to the official of the Leczyca region regarding the evicting of Jews to live in the extra quarter, as has been confirmed by the governing authorities. Jews who lived illegally in the non-permitted streets should be evicted from there.

Relying on the report of the official, the Warsaw governing authorities answered the request of Jan Pawinski and August Kriger as follows: The Jews who are living illegally must be evicted, and newly arrived Jews who continue to settle on the non-permitted streets must also be evicted. Those Jews who have the required qualifications, giving them the right to live there, need not be evicted from the extra quarter.

In April 1853, Hersch Fogel, in the name of the Jewish residents of Zgierz, requested from the Warsaw civilian governor regarding not evicting 40 families from their dwellings. In his request, Fogel made reference to the visit of the civilian governor to Zgierz, "where he saw with his own eyes the crowding (in the Jewish quarter) and the need to enlarge it. I wish that a resolution to my request be given by the month of Mach in the coming year, which will permit the Old Believers to settle in places and streets outside of the Jewish quarter. Relying on this, over 40 families found dwellings in those places, and they live there until today, however a portion of the Old Believers have met with opposition."

Hersch Fogel requested from the civilian governor that in accordance with the resolution, the 40 Jewish families should be permitted to remain in their places that they rented or purchased without disturbance. Relying on the documents, the magistrate of Zgierz permitted a few Jewish families to settle on Blotene (Muddy) and Strikower streets, "taking into account the cholera that prevailed at that time, and spread due to the crowding in the Jewish quarter". Blumenfeld made a new point in his answer: The leaders of the Jewish community (*Dozor* Buzniczy) came with a request to the Warsaw governor as he was passing through Zgierz to not evict the Jewish families from the streets outside the Jewish quarter. The governor, relying on his prescript, recommended to the city president to hold back on the eviction of the Jews who settled in the extra quarter.

The title page of the ledger book of the Jewish community of Zgierz from the year 5679 (1919).

The artist was Mark Schwartz, the son of Yissachar Schwartz

The Ordinance of Czar Alexander II Regarding the Expansion of the Jewish Quarter

At the beginning of the 1840s, the Jews of Zgierz made up approximately 20% of the general population, and numbered 1,934 souls. Of them, 226 resided there provisionally. The reason for the provisional situation was that it was not possible to find any dwellings in the crowded Jewish quarter. Those 226 Jews, who resided in Zgierz only provisionally, were traveling merchants who were needed by the city.

Zgierz had not succeeded in becoming a large industrial center, as had Lodz, which was only 10 kilometers away.

The leaders of the city, as has already been mentioned, made efforts to expand the Jewish quarter, so that Jewish merchants and manufacturers would settle in the city and cause the industry to flourish. In 1853, the city council prepared a plan that specified the streets that should be added to the Jewish living area.

The official of the Leczyca region, who in general struggled against the expansion of the quarter, sent a report in June 1843 to the Warsaw governing commission, which stated the following in point 4:

"The growth of the population of Old Believers in the city of Zgierz caused an influx of temporary residents into the city, which is a manufacturing region that lies on a paved highway, and has developed in business and industry. --- Among the general population of the city of Zgierz, there are 1,934 Old Believers, of whom 225 are provisional residents. - - - Regarding the expansion of the Jewish quarter in the city of Zgierz, requests have been presented to Your All-Powerful Eminence the Governor, in private, to add some streets onto the Jewish quarter in order to accommodate the newcomers."

From the report, we can also see that the 1,934 permanent Jewish residents of Zgierz occupy 467 dwellings, which consist of one room for the most part. This translates to four persons per room. The dwellings are not all spacious. Some of them are very small, and the families that live there are large. They also contain workshops. Therefore, they require larger dwellings. There is also a need for extra dwellings for the people who come provisionally for business. The ratio of people to the number of houses translates to a great crowding.

In the summer months of 1855, negotiations were conducted with the Polish authorities regarding the expansion of the Jewish quarter in Zgierz. Regarding this matter, a report was made to the highest authorities in Petersburg, and in October 1855, the following answer was received:

"In the name of His Majesty Alexander II, the Czar of all Russia, and the King of Poland.

To the administrative authority of Royal Poland.

The quarter for the Old Believers in Zgierz, established by the decision of the royal representative on December 21, 1824, requires an expansion in order to accommodate the growth of the local population of Old Believers. Regarding this, the royal administrative council has decided the following: First article.

The following are to be added to the Jewish quarter in the city of Zgierz: the north side of Szeradzer Street, the north side of the Piaskowa -- - both sides of the Strikower Street, between Szeradzer and Blotene. Both side of the Blotene, between the Lodzer and Strikowr Streets, both side of the Konstantiner Street, between Lodzer and the Konstantine Highway, both side of Szlachthaus (Slaughterhouse) Street between Piaskowa and the Bzura River. Those streets are designated for Jews, and from now they are permitted to live there. The second article of the ordinance is directed to the Jews who settled in the extra quarter without permits. The Jews who acquired houses or dwellings there were given a term of one year to leave their places of residents.

The high decree was signed by the following: The representative General Field marshal, the Warsaw Duke (signature not legible).

The high director of the presidium of the royal committee for spiritual and internal affairs, General Lieutenant Wikinski.
The secretary of the royal committee - Lebron. There are three more signatures of the high office of the regime, certifying the authenticity of the original.

The Continuing Struggle of Jews for Full Rights of Residency in the City of Zgierz

The above-mentioned ordinance regarding the expansion of the Jewish quarter, confirmed by the Czar himself, did not satisfy the Jewish population of Zgierz. As can be seen by the accusations from Christians, the Jews did not wish to follow "article two" of the ordinance, and did not leave their houses in the extra quarter, where only Christians were permitted to live. The Jews continued to acquire dwellings in streets that were outside of the Jewish quarter. There, they established stores near the Christian Neistadt, where commerce in the city was being greatly developed.

The market, the Town Hall and the church of Zgierz.

Regarding this movement of Jews "toward the new town", Y. Bretschneider, in the name of the Zgierz citizens, sent a request in January 1856 to the following authorities: the governing regime of Warsaw, the official of the Leczyca region, and the Zgierz city president. In his request, Bretschneider accused the Jews of "penetrating into the extra quarter, and setting up businesses there".

The struggle of the Jews for full rights of residency in the city of Zgierz continued in later years. Not paying attention to the existing ordinances and restrictions of the Old Believers from living on the streets where business and manufacturing were developing, Jews would settle in the new quarters, in dwellings and houses outside of the Jewish quarter. This would cause

71

protests by Jew haters, lead by the Christian merchants who were afraid of the competition due to the rise of Jewish business.

The aforementioned Franciszek Zalewski made a request in 1858 to the governing authorities in Warsaw with the accusation that Jews had settled in the extra quarter without permission, in the houses numbered 1, 61, 62, 70, 72, 73, and 91. The governing authorities in Warsaw sent the request to the regional official, requesting that he investigate whether the accusation against the Jews is correct, and if so, for how long they have lived there without permission.

The further correspondence between the Warsaw authorities and the official of the Leczyca region regarding this matter is not available to us. There is only a copy of an instruction from the Warsaw governing authorities, dated September 30, 1858. The instructions made reference to the already known stipulations (regarding means and education) that gave Jews the rights to live in the extra quarter.

From the document, it can be seen that a stringent attitude was taken toward Jews who acquired dwellings outside the Jewish quarter. There are no indications of forceful eviction. In Poland, new winds were beginning to blow at that time. Jews took part in the demonstrations in Warsaw against the Czarist regime. In the Polish liberal circles, there were discussions about giving Jews full rights, conducted by the Markgraf [33] Wielopolski, who was appointed by the civilian administrator (governor) of Congress Poland. Through his ordinance, on July 5, 1862, full rights were granted to Jews.

For the Jews in the city of Zgierz, as in all other cities in Congress Poland, a new epoch began. The Jewish population of that time was 1,637 souls. —

Jews in Zgierz in the Latter Half of the 19th and Beginning of the 20th Centuries by Avraham Wein of Jerusalem

The fate of the Jewish settlement in Zgierz in the second half of the 19th century and the beginning of the 20th century (until the First World War, 1914-1918) does not differ from that which prevailed in all of the Jewish settlements in Congress Poland of that era. However, there were aspects that were specific to the character of the industrial city of Zgierz.

In order to appropriately portray the picture and evaluate the era of

72

"stabilization" and "positivism" in Jewish Zgierz of that time, it is necessary to often return back to the earlier years, when the settlement conducted a bitter struggle for its existence, for living rights in the Jewish quarter and in the extra quarter, and - prior to being freed from the oppression of the Czarist authorities and their local Polish "stooges" - for civic and economic rights.

The relative stability was a result of the persistent struggle during the first half of the 19th century between the nobility in Congress Poland, who were the conservative-feudal powers and wished to preserve their privileged status; and the new powers -the representatives of the ascendant industrialization and urbanization processes in the country.

The final victory came immediately upon the release of the new powers of the workers by removing the oppression of the peasants [35], and was also caused by the removal of some of the restrictions upon business, craftsmanship, and the investment of money in land and building enterprises of the Jews. The decree by Czar and his "followers" on June 6th 1862 (in which some of the feudal restrictions against the Jews were removed) sealed, perforce, the partial victory for the new ways. This brought about - in accordance with the needs of the new era and as a result of the prolonged struggle of the Jews for their rights - a demonstration of their capabilities to conform to the new and display their vitality, despite the unfavorable restrictions that had been placed upon them for many generations.

The situation of the Jewish community of Zgierz stood out in the following area: the growth of the Jewish population during the 19th century and the beginning of the 20th century. Later, we will present a table illustrating the growth of the population of Zgierz, which shows that the greatest growth occurred during the years of the restriction on residency rights and other restrictions on the Jews (1827-1857). The growth was almost five-fold. During the following forty years, the Jewish population grew two-fold, at a time when the growth of the non-Jewish population stagnated.

Year	1808	1827	1857	1897	1921
Entire Population	506	4,527	8,337	19,103	21,129
Jewish Population	27	356	1,637	3,543	3,828
Percent of Jews	5.3	7.9	19.6	18.6	18.2

The Vocational Structure of the Jews in the 19th Century

Even though we are lacking exact data from the second half of the 19th century, we can derive analogies from the court cases that took place about the vocational structure from the 1850s and through the later years. We note a growth in the numbers of artisans, workers, and manufacturers. There were groups of manufacturers, textile and confectionery [36] - clear signs of the productivity of the newer times.

In the 1840s, there was already specialization in the fields of manufacturing. Together with the population growth and development of industry, the number of Jewish textile workers also grew. In 1828, there were a few trades that were not found among the Jews of Zgierz.

The following is the list of the number of Jews involved in various textile trades in Zgierz in 1848: 1 'drelich' worker [37], 1 weaver, 1 dyer, 1 cotton worker, 1 'grempler', 1 ribbon maker.

In Zgierz, as in other places, the number of Jews in the clothing industry grew quickly. In the first half of the 19th century, there was only a small group of Jews working in these vocations, as can be seen from the following table regarding the number of Jews in the clothing industry in the years 1828-1848.

	1828	1848
Hat makers	3	10
Tailors	15	46
Shoemakers	1	3
Total	19	59

The population growth also caused an increase in the number of other artisans including the food industries.

	1828	1848
Oil makers	0	1
Bakers	2	1
Pastry bakers	0	2
Butchers	4	6
Vinegar makers	0	1
Total	6	11

Jews engaged in other trades, in the years 1828-1848:

	1828	1848
Sheet metal manufacturers	1	0
Tanners	2	0
Comb makers	1	2
Book binders	0	0
Jewelers	0	3
Blacksmiths	0	2
Painters	1	0
Glazers	1	5
Lace makers	1	3
Turners	0	2
Various others	6	4
Total	13	21

Jewish business also attained a new situation. Already by the year 1828, a large number of Jews merchants were involved in the textile branch. Some of them marketed wool for the manufacturers and weavers who worked in their own homes. Others dealt directly with wool and cloth, and a few with other merchandise. Those merchants were also involved with organizing the production of textiles. They would give wool to the weavers, take the cloth from them, supervise the manufacturing, and then sell it to wholesales, or sell it in their own stores. It is known that the first Jewish manufacturers in Zgierz, such as Chanoch Librach, Yisael Litauer and Shimon Waldenberg, began their careers in that fashion. Thereafter, as their capital increased and they gained experience in the textile industry, they established their own factories. Instead of having the wool woven by home manufacturers, they organized the production in their own workshop.

The following is a list of Jewish merchants in Zgierz in 1828:

Wool, textile and iron dealers [38]	1
Wool and textile dealers	3
Wool merchants	9
Textile merchants	1
Fashion merchants	2
Spice merchants	1
Flour merchants	1
Oil merchants	1
Salt merchants	1
Tobacco merchants	1
Iron merchants	1
Saloon keepers	2
Total	24

Already in the 1850s, the number of merchants, shopkeepers and country-goers [39] was smaller than the number of artisans and workers (employees). Only a portion of the merchants (wholesale and retail) had stores. Others owned shops in the market, and some transported their merchandise and sold it in the surrounding villages.

Jews in business in Zgierz in the years 1828-1848:

	1828	1848
Dealers and merchants	24	37
Shopkeepers	1	5
Saloon keepers [40]	2	1
Total	27	43

Besides the already mentioned trades, the number of Jewish workers also increased. This formed a new vocational structure among Zgierz Jews at that time.

	1828	1848
Hairdressers	3	0
Doctors	0	3
Feldschers	0	1
Wagon Drivers	0	5
Workers	17	46
Total	20	55

The complete vocational structure of Zgierz Jews in the years 1828-1848:

	1828	1848
Manufacturers	0	5
Workers connected with textile production	0	6
Craftsmen	38	92
Dealers and merchants	27	43
Workers	17	46
Others	3	11
Total	85	203

The First Commissioners

It is assumed that the vocational structure and its proportional statistics did not change greatly until the end of the period that we are dealing with. The changes that took place were the increase in the number of workers towards the end of the 19th century, including the proletariat, agents of the semi-proletariat, and home manufacturers. For example, the number of

Jewish wagon drives and coachmen reached approximately 100 at the beginning of the 20th century. They served the Zgierz-Lodz route. The construction of a tramway line along that route took away their livelihood.

To our regret, we do not have available any numbers; however, there was a large group of brokers and commissioners in Zgierz at the end of the 19th century. They oversaw the staff in the factories, and the marketing of the particular type of merchandise. They played an honorable role in the economic life, and gained the trust of the Jewish merchants who had come from Russia (known as Litvaks). The better known commissioners included: Ozer Cohen, Tzvi Hirsch Cohen, Tovia Lipschitz, Beinish Cohen, Yehoshua Kaufman, and Leib Paizer. They all excelled as maskilim and general activists.

The First Jewish Manufacturers in Zgierz

In Zgierz, as a center of the textile industry, the manufacturers were smaller in scale than those of neighboring Lodz, which had first of all developed in the beinvol [41] industry. At first, in the 1840s, the first Jewish manufacturers came to Zgierz. One of them established the first factory for beinvol production. There were such factories in Zgierz, however the main role was played by the textile manufacturers. The participation of Jewish in industry in Zgierz began after the conclusion of the crisis in the textile productivity during the 1830s.

The first Jews who established factories in Zgierz were: Henech Librach, who together with his brother Feivish set up a factory with 20 weaving workbenches; and later Yisrael Litauer. Two large factories were founded around the year 1845. They belonged to Shimon Waldberg and Marcus (Mordechai) Rubinstein. Shimon Waldberg encountered great difficulties in obtaining the rights to live outside of the Jewish quarter. They also refused to grant him a concession to establish the factory, which was to be outside of the quarter, in a house rented from a Pole. The reason given by the person in charge for rejecting the request was that he must insure that there would be no complaints from the eminent Zgierz manufacturers, the brothers Maues and Malc, and for this reason, the governing authorities see no need to permit the Old Believer (starozakonny) Shimon Waldberg to establish a new factory and to live in the extra quarter. After a great deal of negotiation and intercession, the Old Believer Waldberg succeeded in obtaining a concession. A bit later, he purchased the house, where the factory was established and enlarged.

It is not clear for how long the first Jewish factories existed. In all likelihood, they met the same fate as other factories that were founded at that time - they existed until the 1880s.

Internal Jewish Life

The so-called synagogue leaders ("*Dozor* Boznicki") became active in the year 1824, in the community office that had already existed there for about two decades. The Zgierz community was not left with large debts and other difficult problems, as was the case with other Jewish settlements that had a longer history. Nevertheless, within the first decades, the synagogue *dozor*s already faced many problems. The *dozor*s had no small amount of problems due to the deadly epidemic.

In the 1820s and 1830s, an active missionary campaign was directed toward the Jews by the monks of the Franciscan monastery of the neighboring town of Lagiewniki, and also by the Protestant ministers who served the German colonists. Through many means, the *dozor*s were successful in averting the missionizing activity.

Until the 1860s, the *dozor*s had to deal with ongoing problems regarding the difficult living conditions within the Jewish quarter, and with efforts to enlarge the area. The *dozor*s also attempted to help Jews who wished to obtain a permit to live outside the quarter. Very often, it was a member of the *dozor*s who did this; for they were members of the richer strata of Zgierz Jews. Some of them, such as Hillel Berlinski or Chaim Lubraniecki, conducted an extensive battle during the 1830s and 1840s for the right to continue living in their own houses in the extra quarter or in rented houses in the market or on neighboring streets.

For the most part, the representatives of the *dozor*s conducted their work over a set term. From their documents we can find the names of the first Jewish manufacturers. It is clear that, in the industrialized city, they were among the wealthiest and most honorable citizens, the foremost speakers of the Jewish community. The first manufacturer who was registered as a *Dozor* was Shimon Waldenberg. His term was during the years of 1843-1851. In 1846-1848, the manufacturer Yisrael Litauer wished to be recognized as a *dozor*. He also played a significant role in the struggle of the Jewish community to enlarge the quarter. Chaim Librach as well was one of the first Jewish industrialists. He became a *dozor* in the years 1849-1851.

In the later years, the stature and importance of the *dozor* function in the eyes of the Jewish community diminished. In his letter to Yitzchak Mizes, the well-known Maskil from Krakow Avraham Yaakov Weisenfeld (who settled in Zgierz in the year 1860) characterized the parnasim*dozor*s of Zgierz with sarcastic words. According to him, "they do not occupy themselves with communal matters, for there are a bunch of ignoramuses who occupy themselves with communal needs. For here, it is considered an embarrassment to lead the people." It is possible that there is a great deal of exaggeration within these satirical words; however that is how a prominent maskil reacted to the social and cultural situation of the Jewish community of Zgierz.

Certainly the work of a synagogue *dozor* was not easy, for with every step, he would run into restrictions and anti-Semitic decrees. In 1837, the Jews of Zgierz attempted to obtain a permit to build a synagogue. The houses of prayer and shtibels that were available at that time were too small for the growing community. The synagogue would have to be built in the Jewish quarter, on a lot that was purchased from a Pole. The commissar of the Leczyca region did not wish to grant his approval, with the pretext that the Jews must not erect a building on that lot, for it belongs to the regime, and the previous owner did not have the rights to sell it to the Jews. The eventual agreement of the commissar cost no small amount of trouble and money.

The synagogue was built on that lot on Lodzer Street. It was a small, wooden building. During the 1850s, the Jews of Zgierz first began to collect money to build a brick synagogue. The building cost a great deal of money. At the time of the sale of the synagogue by the "city" (1853) [42], they had collected 9,930 rubles. By around 1860, they were already able to inaugurate the new, brick synagogue.

In the middle of the 19th century, the synagogue *dozor*s had a wooden communal building. In the 1850s, the *dozor*s built a new building. There was also a mikva (ritual bath) in that building. The poorhouse was also moved to the new communal building. It is worthwhile to point out that the number of elderly and ill in the poorhouse was not very large. In 1841, for example, there was only one resident.

In the middle of the 19th century, all of the traditional, religious and communal institutions already existed in Zgierz, and the *dozor*s were responsible for providing them with buildings. The building was too crowded for their needs, and in the latter half of the eighteenth century, new and better buildings were built for them.

In 1879, they began to collect money for a new mikva and bathhouse, for the old one was ruined. After receiving approval from the authorities, they build a new, brick mikva. The building cost 5,314 rubles. At approximately the same time, they also built a new, brick building for the Beis Midrash.

In the later half of the 19th century, the *dozor*s attempted to acquire a permit from the authorities to purchase a field in order to enlarge the cemetery. This issue dragged on for years. At first, the city physician and the architectural supervisor of the magistrate refused to grant a permit. Later, after they succeeded in overcoming those difficulties, a new decree was issued: the authorities did not permit collecting money for that purpose. Indeed, the money was collected in an illegal manner. The authorities claimed that the money stemmed from foundations to which a few rich Jews of Zgierz contributed. The cemetery was expanded in the year 1885.

We can conceive of the amount of "silencing" money each action cost [43]. As in all towns, the Jewish community of Zgierz had to deal with the question of the "eruv" [44], which was deliberated upon for several years. The authorities (the Leczyca commissar or the magistrate of Zgierz) would order the dismantling of the eruv, or would impose new demands (how high the posts can be, the thickness of the wire, etc.). The Jews would pay bribes in order to have the decree annulled. This situation repeated itself in the years 1834, 1857, and later.

In the second half of the 19th century, the *dozor*s had to deal with new specific problems regarding the status of an industrial city, and also with the growth of the Jewish population. Due to the economic circumstances, the following issues arose: the impoverishment of the employed workers, the Sabbath peace, and the work in larger factories, etc.

The Decree against the Wearing of Jewish Garb

The struggle of the Jews of Zgierz against the clothing decrees forms a chapter unto itself. In 1844, the Czar issued a decree that the Jews in his empire must exchange their clothing for that of Russian citizens. They were prohibited from having peyos (sidecurls), and they were required to cut their beards. In 1846, the deputy of the Zgierz city president came to the synagogue five times, read out the new decree, and threatened fines for not obeying it. The results were negligible, and the Jews continued to dress in their traditional garb. In February 1847, the city president himself came to a Hassidic shtibel on a Sabbath morning during the time of the prayers, in order to investigate why they were not following the directive. He saw that the Jews were wearing their kapotes, and many of them were fined.

The secretary of the magistrate came to the synagogue a second time. They did not let him enter the synagogue. In his report, he wrote: "The representatives of the synagogue *dozor*s, in particular Yisrael Litauer and Hersch Horowitz, met him in the synagogue and impeded him. He was afraid of trouble from the Jews, as is often encountered in Jewish Beis Midrashes, and he had to leave empty handed."

There were other forms of opposition to the decree. A characteristic occurrence took place in the year 1846. After the speech of the city president, in which he clarified the question of wearing Jewish garb and having a beard and peyos, the rabbi of the city, Shalom Tzvi Hakohen, turned to the worshippers with a few words regarding the relations with the city president: "The peyos can be a little shorter and the beard a little trimmed. However, if the beard is shaved off and if short cloaks are worn, a person will no longer be considered part of the Jewish community. If one has already cut off the beard, one has already been cut off, and if not - he will soon be cut off." Later, the rabbi summoned the gabbaim of the charitable organization and the burial society (Chevra Kadisha) and warned them of his decision.

The administrative authorities demanded from the synagogue *dozor*s and the rabbi that they convince the Jews to obey the directive. However, neither the rabbi nor the parnassim would allow themselves to be overseers of the fulfillment of anti-Semitic decrees.

Yisrael Litauer, in the name of the synagogue *dozor*s, gave over a declaration to the city president, in which he writes as follows: "I believe that it is not appropriate to control the Jews at the synagogue during the times of prayers. I am not able to guarantee whether or not all of the Jews who do not hold a permit to wear Jewish garb have indeed changed their clothes, for I do not even know all of the Jews…".

The tactic of the *dozor* changed completely the persecutions of the authorities. When they demanded that the *dozor* compile a list of Jews who are not following the directive, he beat around the bush and answered that "the Jews of Zgierz no longer wear illegal cloaks. Some of them have received permits to wear Jewish garb, and some have paid, in accordance to the law."

This answer was far from the truth. In the years 1848-1850, only a few changed their cloaks, and shortened their beard and peyos. The issue of paying for the rights to wear Jewish garb only later came into effect.

The situation of the poverty, in particular among the Jews who lacked means, was even more difficult. They did not have money to purchase or to pay the fines in order to wear Jewish garb and to maintain their beard and peyos. They tried to rescue themselves with various excuses, claiming that they could not cut off their beard and peyos due to various illnesses. However, it was more difficult to find an excuse regarding the Jewish garb.

Shmuel Senderowicz attempted to find a workaround even in that area. When an official of the magistrate detained him, he declared that "The Jewish garb is much warmer". However, this excuse did not help him - he was required to shorten his beard and peyos, and to pay a fine.

Many other Jews found themselves with the same fate. It was also to no avail when a few of them attempted to save their beards by shortening their kapotes slightly, claiming that their cloaks are of "the Russian style".

Without paying attention to the persecution, many Zgierz Jews, in particular the Hassidim, did not change their clothing, and did not attempt to pay the fines. The Hassid Yosef Zhurkowsky was a characteristically stubborn example of that type. The city president wrote the following regarding him: "Zhurkowsky did not pay attention to any of the warnings, he laughed at them, and he instigated the Old Believers to speak out against the authorities… We can see Zhurkowsky on Sabbaths and festivals parading about in Jewish garb." They recognized Zhurkowsky as the chief rebel who instigated the Jews to disobey the ordinance, and they imposed a large monetary fine upon him. The cholera epidemic (1848) deflected the attention of the authorities from this question, and in the 1850s, the Jews were already

83

permitted, in exchange for a large sum of money, to wear various types of garb, not only in accordance with the "Russian style".

Cultural Life and Education

The aforementioned maskil Avraham Yaakov Weisenfeld wrote in 1860, in dark colors, about the cultural situation of the Zgierz community. From his words, we can create an image of a backward town, with a traditional way of life and set of customs. It is clear that such a maskil who came from such a large Jewish center as Krakow, which was full with teachers, Torah giants, and maskilim, felt that Zgierz, with its restricted horizons, Hassidic ways and toiling masses - and that indeed describes the majority - was in complete contrast to Krakow. In fact, during the second half of the 19th century, Zgierz became known in the region as a place of Torah. The city acquired a name for itself with its rabbis, Yeshiva, and ordinary studiers of the Beis Midrash. The first rabbi, Rabbi Shlomo Tzvi Hakohen (died in 1877) occupied the rabbinical seat for 52 years. He was lauded in the rabbinical literature as "a Gaon and Tzadik, who presided over a great Yeshiva". Hundreds of students, and approximately fifty rabbis, graduated from his Yeshiva. After him, Rabbi Tzvi the son of Eliezer Hakohen occupied the rabbinical seat. He had previously been a rabbi in Sochaczew and Pultusk (he was a grandson of the well-known Rabbi Yaakov of Lissa). In 1898, his son-in-law Rabbi Shlomo Yehuda Leib Hakohen, the son of the first rabbi, Rabbi Shalom Tzvi of holy blessed memory, became the rabbi of Zgierz. He was the author of Neveh Shalom. He was known as an expert in Torah and wisdom. Rabbi Shlomo Yehuda also took an interest in worldly matters. He boldly advocated with the city president on behalf of Jewish workers and Jewish factories. In his speech at the inauguration of the Machzikei Hadas organization (1912), aside from his words regarding the mater at hand, he also lectured the Jewish manufacturers and reminded them of the importance of solidarity with their fellow Jews.

A deed for the purchase of a plot of land to enlarge the Jewish cemetery of Zgierz, March 3, 1885.

It is clear that almost until the end of the 19th century, the Jewish cultural life centered on the cheder, Yeshiva, Beis Midrash, and Hassidic shtibels: Kotzker, Gerer, Aleksandrower, Sochaczewer, Strykower, and others.

However, the new winds already blew in with the creation of the "Cheder Metukan" (1891) under the leadership of the scholar and writer Yaakov Binyamin Katzenelson (Y. Ben-Yamini), the father of the poet and later the eulogizer of the Holocaust Yitzchak Katzenelson may G-d avenge his death. The leaning toward a worldly education can be seen by the participation of Jewish children of Zgierz in the elementary school.

At the beginning of the 19th century, a significant number of Jewish children attended the local elementary school, where they studied alongside Polish children. This fact stood out in comparison with other Jewish settlements. Incidentally, the synagogue was very characteristic. The provost of the diocese did not wish to engage in didactics, so he did not teach the children the Christian religion. The teacher also did not take the initiative in this situation. Thus, the school had a worldly character. In a report from the chairman of the Wojewodztwo Commission of Mazowia (1820), we read the following: "An elementary school existed in Zgierz. The teacher is not overly capable, however he comes from a good stock." The chairman talked much better about the Jewish children in that school: "Among the school children, the Jews especially exhibit their abilities in study."

However, the unfavorable situation of Jews in the Kingdom of Poland, and the continuing restrictions regarding Jewish life described in the "Zgierz agreement" [45], as well as the restrictions upon the Jewish quarter - restricted the participation of Jewish children in the local, general elementary schools.

The first acknowledgement by the authorities of the Jewish elementary school took place on July 1st, 1885. From among the synagogue *dozor*s [46], the guardian of the school (which consisted of one class!) was Avraham Weiss. The school was located in rented premises on Lodzer Street. The first teacher was Isidor Jakubowicz. He received an official nomination from the city president. Jakubowicz possessed the appropriate pedagogical qualifications; however in 1890, he moved to Lodz. Shimshon Schnepper, a graduate of the teachers' seminary of Leczyca, took his place.

The Jewish elementary school in Zgierz was under the strict supervision of the Lodzer school directors. On more that one occasion, that fact was the cause of various forms of friction. For example, the directors demanded the observance of the regulation that Jewish teachers should not teach in schools or institutions over which the directors were not in control. In 1890, the teacher David Karelicki was fired from his work in a school for violating that regulation by teaching children in a cheder. In 1912, the inspector demanded that another teacher be expelled, with the motive that his teaching results were not good even though he possessed the required qualifications - he was a graduate of the teacher's institute of Vilna. The *dozor*s attempted to protest to the Lodz school directors when they ordered the transfer of Karelicki to Sulejow. The *dozor*s claimed that the poor results of his teaching was not a result of poor teaching methods, but rather was caused by the style of language that was not understood by the students. This was a much clearer hint of the strict ordinance to teach only in the Russian language. In 1890, when Cecilia Holland became the principal of the elementary school, at the time of her nomination she wrote an instruction against strictly upholding the principal of teaching in the Russian language at school.

Only a small percentage of the children attended the elementary school. The majority of children obtained their elementary worldly education from other schools or from private tutors. The cheders continued to play the dominant role in the life of the Jewish children of Zgierz.

The following table shows the number of students of the Jewish elementary school in Zgierz from the years 1886-1912.

Year	Number of students
1886	38
1891	64
1910	54
1912	34

In the first elementary school, there was a co-educational system in place. The majority of the students were girls.

The absenteeism rate among the students was large: 30% among the boys and 13% among the girls. The reason for this was, first and foremost, the inconvenient location. The classroom was crowded, the air was stale, and the children often suffered from headaches. In 1894, the school principal Avraham Wachtel attempted to obtain money and a permit to rent an additional location. This took place shortly thereafter.

The budget of the school was obtained from two sources: the parents of the children paid specific sums, and a tax was collected from the Jewish residents of the city. Approximately 250 citizens paid between 50 kopecks and 5 rubles annually to that end.

In the year 1913, the school was split into two classes. In the same year, a one classroom school was opened for girls.

After the outbreak of the First World War, a few preschools and elementary schools for Jewish children opened. They played an important role in the cultural and social life of the Jewish settlement. In the schools, they organized performances with the participation of the children. As with other events, they were organized around the Jewish holidays and important nationalistic occasions. In 1917, for example, in the school that was directed by Perl Bergholtz, they organized a Chanuka evening, and the income went towards the building of a childrens' home.

In 1918, there were five Jewish elementary schools in Zgierz, and the city council planned for a subsidy in that year to build a Jewish middle school. Until the year 1914, the Jewish youth enrolled in significant numbers to the business school that was well-known in Zgierz and the area. A large percentage of the Jewish intelligentsia of Zgierz was connected with that well-known learning institution.

In 1912, a Yagdil Torah society was founded in Zgierz. The following people belonged to the management committee: Shlomo Sirkes, Eliezer Sirkes, Mordechai Shmuel Cudkowicz, Gedalyahu Yedidyah Zwiekelski, Yisrael Moshe Rozenowicz, Avraham Natan Elberg, Mendel Wechsler and Yitzchak Niekricz. The purpose of the organization was to enable students to learn for free. The organization oversaw the building of Cheders, Yeshivas and Beis Midrashes, as well as libraries and dormitories. They concerned themselves with the material wellbeing of the students and teachers. In 1912, the Talmud Torah and Yeshiva were founded, which continued in existence until the outbreak of the Second World War.

The development of synagogue organizations and groups, as well as the scholarly atmosphere from the Yeshivas and Beis Midrashes created a general climate that was able to give rise to the first groups of maskilim and social activists with a worldly outlook; later this current increased, and encompassed larger segments of the youth and the adults.

In the 1880s, the maskilim, in addition to the circles of professional intelligentsia such as doctors and others, concentrated around Avraham Yaakov Weisenfeld. His house served as the gathering place of the wise. It became a sort of a "salon" for students, scholars and poets; there, one discussed problems of "Torah and wisdom". As Nachum Sokolow lamented in his eulogy (in Hatzefira, 1897): "He belonged to the last of the old generation of wise men of Galicia [47]". In his eulogy, he also summarized Weisenfeld's cultural activities in Zgierz.

The following people were prominent among the group of maskilim: Tuvia Lipschitz (his rich library was donated to the national library in Jerusalem by his heirs); Yissachar Moshe Szwarc (he published scientific treatises in various periodicals, and was published with the pseudonym "Black Sea" [48]); Yaakov Berliner (Baniel), a well-known Zionist activist in Zgierz and in Israel (from the year 1926), as was Moshel Eiger.

The great writer David Frischman and the well-known writer and poet Yaakov Cohen were born and raised in Zgierz. At the end of the 19th century and the beginning of the 20th century.

The Revolution of 1905; Political Life

Already in the first years of the development of industry in Zgierz, rebellions [49] by the factory workers took place. In 1826, the first rebellion of employees and textile workers in the kingdom took place. That tradition of struggle workers movement in the city, and its influence was still noted in the 1880s. The first Polish workers' party, called Proletariat, conducted broad-based activity in the Zgierz. We cannot state the exact participation of Zgierz Jews in the activities of Proletariat. However, it is known that many Jewish families, especially workers and artisans, who lived in need, did create the foundation for Jewish participation in the actions of Proletariat.

It is interesting to see the various observations of Dr. A. Zonnenberg in his brochure about Zgierz (printed in 1890). Various educational forums were organized for workers, artisans, business employees, and groups of youth who did not have the means to study in the middle schools. The initiators of those courses were groups and organizations that were founded with the purpose of spreading culture and education among the youth and the broad masses. This started with the Hazamir organization (at first, this organization bore the name Muza). The initiators of Hazamir were: Yeshayahu Shapiro, Ber Kon and Aharon Kaltgrad, who were also members of the first managing committee.

According to its charter, Hazamir [50] was first and foremost an organization for music, song, drama and literature; spreading musical and literary culture, and assisting talented youth. They created a choir, an orchestra and a dramatic group. Hazamir organized concerts and literary evenings, and popularized the best music and books, in particular Yiddish ones. They organized speakers and popular lectures. Well-known writers, artists and scholars would appear as lecturers, including ones from the large centers of Jewish culture (Hillel Zeitlin, Yitzchak Katzenelson, etc.) In 1913, Hazamir also took on the role of a sports club.

In 1913, Michael Shimon Zaltzwasser (a dentist), Avraham Morgenstern (a craftsman) and the weaver Leib Miller created the Jewish handworkers union, with the aim of spreading culture, science, tourism and geographical knowledge among the Jewish workers and artisans. The union had a library and a club, where various events took place. It also was also a soup kitchen, which played an important role during the time of the First World War. The organization ran vocational courses for the youth, and in 1915, it conducted a course for weavers.

From 1910, Zgierz had a very large Jewish library. The Lodzer Volksblatt of July 18, 1915 wrote that the library contained over 1,000 books, and had more than 150 members.

The author lived in Zgierz and was known as a Jewish doctor and general activist. He writes: "The average dwelling of a Jewish resident of Zgierz was a room of 25-30 square meters, with, for the most part, one window that let in a small amount of light. The walls were not of limestone, the ceiling was low, and there were holes in the floor. In the summer, particularly in the hot months, the heat was unbearable. Winter was even worse. The small ovens did not give off sufficient warmth, the walls were wet, there were drafts from the windows, and there were holes all over, which the dweller could not patch up themselves or ask the landlord to do so, since he was owing in rent. This all created a difficult atmosphere, and not infrequently, I myself witnessed the lowly state, when I was called in as a doctor."

In the beginning of the 20th century, the participation of Zgierz Jews in the workers and revolutionary movements, especially among the youth, became significant. The influence of the S.D.K.P.L. (Social Democratic party of Royal Poland and Lithuania) became quite large among the Jewish workers. At that time, The Bund did not have a local branch in Zgierz. The local agitators helped lead the Lodzer committee of that organization. After the revolution of 1905, a local Bund organization was first created.

The Jewish students of the business school formed an important base for the activities of the S.D.K.P.L. and played a visible role during the time of the revolutionary events. Josef Bierzenzweig stood out in the front rows of the revolutionaries, not only in Zgierz but also in the entire Mazowia area. He was arrested for the first time in 1901. At that time, he was 20 years old, and a student in the fifth class of the business school of Zgierz. The police conducted a search at his home, and found a great deal of revolutionary and Marxist literature, originating both from within the country and from the outside. In 1903, he was sentenced to three years of exile in eastern Siberia. At that time, the police discovered new material regarding his activities and leadership in the Zgierz organization. They ordered a new investigation, and jailed him in the famous 10th pavilion of the Warsaw citadel. There, he became ill with tuberculosis and died. His funeral in Warsaw on May 6, 1904 turned into a gigantic manifesto. It turned into a confrontation with the police. Many participants in the funeral were arrested by the police including some Jewish young people from Zgierz.

The revolutionary events strengthened in Zgierz in particular in January, 1905. Under the influence of agitators who came from Lodz, a general strike was proclaimed on January 28th. A gigantic meeting took place on that day. Three thousand Jews, Poles and Germans participated. During May and June of 1905, there were strikes in the factory and smaller workshops. New demonstrations took place on October 18th. The students of the business school were in the lead. The demonstrators waved a red flag. A Cossack charged in and dispersed the demonstrators; a number of them were wounded and arrested. Two Jewish students, Max Szreiner and Moshe Zeidman were among those arrested.

Organized Zionistic activity took place in Zgierz during the first years of the 20th century. Zionist circles were formed, which conducted broad-based publicity and cultural activities. In 1911, during the era when the Zionist organizations were declared illegal by the authorities, a youth movement by the name of Tzeirei Zion was created in Zgierz. It was officially called "The Youth Union". It was forbidden from conducting political activities, so only cultural events were mentioned in its program. In that group, they discussed the spreading and propagating of the study of Hebrew, strengthening the Hebrew press, and creating a library for Hebrew books.

The members of Tzeirei Zion were numbered among the Zionist activists of Zgierz during the later years.

Composition of the Communal Leadership (*Dozor* **Boznicki**) of Zgierz in the years 1824

In the years 1824, 1826, 1827: Leizer Bornstein, Baruch Steinbok, and Meir Blumenthal. They were elected on January 19th, 1825.

In the years 1828, 1829, 1830: Moshe Steinbok, Meir Blumenthal, and Leizer Bornstein. They were elected on December 3rd, 1827.

In the years 1831, 1832, 1833: Yosef Weilandt, Yisrael Frakenberg, and Berl Warmwasser.

In the years 1834, 1835, 1836: Eli Mogden, Chaim Lubraniecki, and Baruch Warmwasser.

In the years 1837, 1838, 1839: Chaim Klimentowski, Yaakov Poznanski, and Rafael Zucker.

In the years 1840, 1841, 1842: Chaim Lubraniecki, Hillel Berlinski, and Menashe Blawat.

In the years 1843, 1844, 1845: Menashe Blawat, Shimon Waldberg, and Shimon Lewin.

In the years 1846, 1847, 1848: Yisrael Litauer, Chaim Meir Horowitz, and Rafael Zucker.

In the years 1849, 1850, 1851: Chaim Lubraniecki, Shimon Waldberg, and Wolko Zonnenfeld. During the term, Henech Librach replaced Shimon Waldberg.

In the years 1852, 1853, 1854: The same representatives as in the previous term was elected again.

In the years 1855, 1856, 1857: Yerucham Berliner, Gershon Blum, and Wolf Zonnenfeld.

(From the protocols of the general archive in Lodz and from the archives of the Pietrikower governing authorities, number 2581.)

My Hometown at the End of the 19th Century by Leon Lipschitz of Gan Shlomo, Petach Tikva.

Zgierz had a German character approximately 80 years ago. The streets with German residents bore the names "Heren Strasse", "Meierhoff Strasse", etc. The Germans employed various means not to let the Jews enter into the new forms of livelihood in the textile industry, in which the following German industrialists dominated: Barst, Lorentz, Binder, Dlugoshevski, Ernst, Cerent, Meierhoff, Schultz, Hoffman (Masshinen), etc. The first Jewish industrialist in Zgierz was Reb Yossel Rubinstein, a deeply pious Orthodox Jew. He studied the weaving trade, and set up future generations of weavers who remained weavers in Zgierz or in the surrounding towns. These weavers included: Reb Moshe Eiger (both a Torah scholar and a maskil), Fuchs, Zucker, Szaransky, Glicksman, and Zilbershatz.

After difficult tribulations and discrimination that was perpetrated by the Germans upon the Jews via various intrigues with the regime, they began to deal in all areas of the textile industry. Such industrialists included the father the well-known weaver David Frischman, Fogel, and others.

At that time, Jews from Latvia began to arrive in Poland. They knew how to communicate with the Germans very well, thanks to their worldly outlook and business activities. They became the confidantes of the large-scale German industrialists.

At that time, a new element could be seen among the textile industrialists - the commissioners. The first commissioners of the textile industry in Zgierz, who introduced the use of the Russian Mark in the Zgierz production, were Jews. All of the participants in business gradually became wealthier, and earned good livelihoods. The well-known commissioners of the textile industry in Zgierz were: Shlomo Horowitz (from Byelorussia), who was a fine Jew, and used to blow the shofar on Rosh Hashanah; Tuvia Lipschitz, a great scholar who was familiar with worldly languages; a writer who enriched Hebrew literature of the haskalah generation and helped develop new young talent; David Frischman; Yaakov Cohen, Yehuda Leib Lewin, Berkowicz, and others.

I remember Zgierz very well from my childhood - the last years of the 1800s. The Germans babbled about town. The councilors of the Zgierz magistrate were Germans. The civic garden, between Pienkowska and Leczyca Streets, was adorned with a wooden stand and a musical band that played every Sunday. The city president was Pienkowski, a patriarchal warrior with a German wife. He rose to his position as a loyal citizen in the Czarist authorities, and became president of Lodz, distinguishing himself in the higher rungs of the Czarist regime. The president of the magistrate in Zgierz was a drunk by the name of Sluszewski. The civic cashier was Malinowski, also a man with a German wife. The doctor was Banda, an old German who loved his patients. He knew all of the children by their names. Polonized Germans included Drs. Hesner and Neubauer (the later changes his name to Nowomieski). The first opticians were Gebel and Eisenschmidt, and later also Patek, a Pole.

Little by little, with great effort, Jews in Zgierz also were numbered among the doctors. They also were Polonized and assimilated. These included Drs. Krowkowski, Schreier, and the Jewish national spokesman Dr. Zilberstram, the brother of the deputy of the Russian Duma and the Zionist leader Dr. Zilberstram.

I also remember the name of other Jewish intellectuals: Kahanstam, who graduated from the rabbinical school in Warsaw (under the leadership of the assimilated Dr. Eisenstat) [51]; Yaakov Jakubowicz, an old feldscher; and Baruch Botshe Grynfarb - both graduates of the feldscher school of Warsaw. They were both well mannered and very popular with the Jewish masses.

The largest segment of the Jewish community consisted of long-cloaked Orthodox Jews. As in other cities, most of them opposed the establishment of a Jewish elementary public school with Russian as the language of instruction. Prior to the establishment of the school, the authorities appointed teachers for the cheders and for the Jewish Metukan school, which was lead by Binyamin Katzenelson, a great scholar who was the author of "Olelot Efraim". He was the father of the poet and martyr Yitzchak Katzenelson.

With the founding of the elementary school, the great Wachtel arrived as the principal. He was a graduate of a teaching seminary, and he led the school without nonsense, as he established generations of students, including from the poorer strata. The students completed school able to understand Russian reasonably well, and knowing a little German. It was forbidden to teach Polish.

Young people with peyos and long cloaks would secretly "steal into" the teacher in the class, having come from the Beis Midrash to learn Russian and arithmetic very secretly.

The center of haskalah and the study of Hebrew literature were built up in Zgierz by the following people: Yissachar Szwarc, Moshel Eiger, and Reb Tuvia Lipschitz. Their work for the Jewish national renaissance in our city was with the greatest meaning. They were the shapers of the Chovevei Zion group in Zgierz, and later, the founders of the Zionist union. Under their influence, in cooperation with the young intelligentsia, Zgierz became a center of Zionist work and pioneering.

Greetings of Congratulations marking a donation to the Keren Kayemet (Jewish National Fund) in honor of the young couple Glika and Aharon Sperling. Signed by Yissachar Szwarc and his wife, 1912.

A View into Zgierz and the Life of its Jews from the Community Annals of the Years 1915-1930 by Y. A. Malchieli

It is possible to look upon the community of Zgierz during the fifteen-year period spanning from 1915 to 1930 through the lens of the Annals of the Communal Council. By briefly studying the 416 protocols listed there, we learn that the Communal Council was deeply integrated into the life of the community, and its influence upon the communal institutions and activities was great.

As is known, matters of ritual slaughter (shechita), schools, prayers, bathhouses, cemeteries, the various assistance and support organizations serving the needy, religious affairs and other matters were in the hands of the Communal Council. As well, it served as the official representative body of the Jewish community to the various governments and other causes. The Communal Council oversaw a staff of workers and a variety of institutions and funds. To support its activities, it imposed taxes upon the community, and its manner was for the most part straightforward and fixed.

Four committees fulfilling various tasks worked constantly at the side of the Communal Council. These committees included the finance committee, which took care of the allocations, collection and expenditures; the educational committee; the support committee; and the general committee, which oversaw matters of shechita, the mikva (ritual bath), eruv (Sabbath boundary [52]), etc.

With the development of the town, we see the first protocol dated August 1, 1915, written in German. [53]. This protocol relates that, at a meeting of the Communal Council under the directorship of the rabbi of the town, the financial and education committees were selected, consisting of the following people:

For the financial committee: T. Lipschitz, N. Ader, L. Posnersohn, Y. Strykowski, B. Cohn,
A. Y. Berger, Y. Schwartz, M. Eiger, M. Y. Margolies. [54]

The signatories of the protocol include two additional names as chairmen of the meeting: M. Naftali, and Sh. Ring.

The next meeting took place about three weeks later, on August 24, 1914. We see a different list of delegates this time: T. Lipschitz as chairman, Eiger,

Ring, Naftali, L. Sirkes, A. Y. Berger, Margolies, Ader, and Strykowski.

The protocol only mentions that a decision was made to prepare a budget and collect taxes for 1915. At the next meeting, about two months later on October 30, 1915, a prepared budget, including revenue and expenditures, was already presented to the forum.

The budget documents an income of 4,259 marks, which is to be collected from 254 taxpayers, leaving a surplus of 319 marks after a list of twelve expenditures that total 3,940 marks.

The detailed expenditures include: salary and rent for the rabbi -- 800 marks; for the judge 510 marks; for the cantor - 200 marks; for the two shamashes (sextons), one for the synagogue and one for the Beis Midrash - 50 marks each; watchmen for the synagogues - 75 marks; heating and lighting for the synagogues - 100 marks; staff for three months (October - December 1915) 75 marks; office supplies - 30 marks; repairs for the synagogues - 300 marks; a new fence for the cemetery - 650 marks; maintenance of the Talmud Torah school - 900 marks; heating and lighting for the Talmud Torah - 20 marks.

The surplus of 319 marks will be given for the benefit of the poor who require support.

The beginning was quite modest.

In the following meetings, which took place on March 3, 4, and 5, 1916, a representative committee of ten people were chosen by fifty taxpayers. This committee was composed of: M. Kaltzowski, M. Klowinski, G. D. Zwykielski, Sh. Boaz, Y. M. Bialostocki, Sh. Zelmanowicz, Sh. Wronski, M. Prinz, H. Gelkopf, and H. Luftman. The first task of these people was to prepare a methodology for tax collection, as well as a budgetary committee for the Communal Council.

The meetings of the council were headed by the chairman Naftali and Michaelson as the secretary and recorder.

In accordance with a request of the mayor, the Communal Council met on July 17, 1916 to prepare a budget for 1916. This budget was not very different from the previous year's budget. It was based on estimated revenue of 4,492 marks. The expenditures included: the rabbi 1,020 marks; Judge Elberg - 510 marks, Cantor Berish Gad - 200 marks; the Shamash Feldon 50 marks; the Shamash Moshe Gelbard - 50 marks; Zelnik the watchman - 100 marks; the allocation for the Talmud Torah - 600 marks; rent - 16 marks; security - 39.65; lighting and heat -300 marks; repairs - 300 marks; tax arrears from the previous year - 500 marks. The total was 3829.65 marks.

In September, the elected taxpayers' committee crystallized. After a period of preparation, meetings, and taking advice on various methodologies, the order of electing the delegates was set at one delegate per twenty taxpayers. The delegates who became part of the Communal Council in this manner included: Sh. Sirkes, L. Parizer, D. Sirkes, Sh. Boaz, Sh. Sribnik, N. Mendelsohn, G. D. Zwykielski, L. Posnersohn, Sh. Wronski, M. H. Eiger, A. Y. Berger, N. Trotsky, W. Reichert.

From those elected at the meeting of September 20, 1916, four committees were chosen: for taxes, education, assistance, and miscellaneous (shechita, mikva, eruv, etc.). The names Naftali, L. Sirkes, and Ring continue to appear constantly in following meetings, where Eliezer Sirkes served as the chairman.

Belt Tightening and the Struggle for Existence

February 24, 1917

The continuing war and occupation shook up the economic situation in the city. The number of poor increased, and income diminished. On the other hand, inflation was growing. In order to strengthen the communal institutions, the income would have to at least double. The situation of collection of taxes was particularly bad. Therefore, they decided to raise the fees for shechita. For cattle - from 3 marks to 10; for calves, chickens and ducks - from 1 mark to 3. The price rose by a factor of three. The budget for communal expenditures was set at 8,169 marks, divided up among the different branches according to the set allocation. This amount was double the amount of the previous year.

From that time on, a long and painful struggle took place between the Communal Council and its staff of workers, rabbis, and shochtim (ritual slaughterers). The cost of living rose, and everyone found themselves in a perplexing, desperate situation. They were fighting with each other, whether for their own personal livelihood or for providing for the needs of the community.

The provision of matzos and other festival needs to the poor is a story unto itself. Similarly, there was always the pressure of the various needs of the sick that were in need of healing, brides who did not have money for their wedding, and people who lost their livelihood.

For example, we see that that there was a certain well-known young woman who requested support for the learning of a trade. She was answered. Another person received 2,000 marks for the purchase of eyeglasses. So and so receive support for mute son in an appropriate institution. There is almost no protocol that does not mention a request for support for various reasons, for marriage, healing, travel to a healing institution, or simply for livelihood. As well, support was given in various amounts, to all who made aliya to the Land. There were many people who made aliya during the fifteen-year period. There were also requests by various Admorim (Hassidic leaders) and various institutions in town and external to the town. Some were answered positively, and others were shown the empty coffers of the community.

As Passover approached in 5678 (1918), the community distributed matzos, potatoes, as well as monetary stipends to 1,500 people. The value of the stipends was about 9,000 marks, and was collected by the Passover appeal. We have previously seen that the budget of the community in 1917 was about 8,000 marks. The budget for 1918 approached 21,000 marks. In an effort to balance the communal budget as much as possible, and to instill order in all areas of communal affairs, the Chevra Kadisha (Burial Society) was placed under communal supervision, and attempts were made to strengthen the supervision of shechita, where there had been many breeches. This was no simple matter, and the opposition was great, both from the shochtim and the butchers. Order was also imposed on the communal offices and the accounting ledgers, and an inventory of the communal assets was taken, including as well the Torah scrolls in the synagogues. As the salaries rose, the shechita fees rose, as did the communal tax rates. This caused strong protests from several of the taxpayers. One of the taxpayers grabbed hold of the list of expenditures of the Communal Council and tore it up in his wrath, as he uttered curses.

In order to understand the communal life with greater clarity, and to understand the various events which shed light on the image of the makeup of the community of Zgierz, it is fitting to make note of several of the events which took place and were noted in the protocols of the Communal Council. We will bring these down in chronological order.

June 30, 1918: Daniel Sirkes was chosen as the chairman of the Communal Council. The vice chair was Yissachar Schwartz, and the rabbi of the city was the honorary chairman. The members of the council were Yisrael Frugal, Yosef Miechowski, Eliezer Landau, Leibush Szarkowiak, Y. Rosenzweig, B. Cohn, Zeev Eliahu Reichert, Aharon Yosef Berger, Chaim Posnersohn, Moshe Zigler, and A. Schwartzbart.

July 7, 1918: The protocols are to be taken in Hebrew from this point.

July 15, 1918: For the committee in charge of allocation the money received from America, one person each from the Orthodox union, the Zionists, Mizrachi, Beit Haam, the artisans' club, and the orphanage, and two from the Communal Council were chosen. The rabbi was to be the chairman.

July 16, 1918: A decision was made to support a Hebrew kindergarten, on the condition that it was to be conducted in a religious spirit, and that the students would learn prayers, blessings, etc.

January 29, 1918: There were to be elections for the Jewish community, according to the election statutes of April 23, 1917.

From that time, the Communal Council was composed of four administrators (parnasim) along with the rabbi of the city. They would appoint people to perform the various roles. There were four other people chosen as back-ups. They also had the right to present an opinion, however their say was only worth half, two of them having the weight of one of the main elected officials. The administrators were as follows: Aharon Yosef Berger, Yissachar Schwartz, Daniel Sirkes, and Wolf Reichert. The replacements were Chaim Posnersohn, Moshe Zigler, Yisrael Frugal, and Eliahu Schwartzbard.

We see that the council concerning itself with the acquisition of a plot of land for the new cemetery, and the establishment of a communal committee of the various organizations in the town - "The American Committee". The members of this committee were as follows: the representative of the Communal Council -the rabbi, Schwartz and Berger; from the Jewish faction in the Sejm - Eliezer Sirkes; from the Orthodox union - Ch. Boaz; from the Zionists Berliner; from the Mizrachi - Michel Kuperman; from the tailors - Menashe Schwartzbard; from the Jewish orphanage - F. Greenberg; from the artisans - M. Librach; from the old age home Ch. Segal.

This council was established to oversee the soup kitchen that was established in the city for poor children. It obtained 75 pair of shoes for poor children. It gained assistance from the bakers to fix up the ovens that stopped working. It hired a teacher for Hebrew and religion for the public schools, Cytrynowski from Lodz. It provided singers for the holidays to assist the cantor. It distributed various types of support, to private individuals and institutions. After a period of difficulties, a committee for the soup kitchen was appointed, consisting of: Yisrael Moshe Rozenowicz, Avraham Morgenstern, Moshe Librach, Binyamin Sczaransky, Yisrael Preshker, Moshe Zigler, and one person from the Communal Council. The backups included Michael Zeev Reichert, Nathan Ader, and Manis Engel.

From among the various protocols which deal with day to day issues, such as the synagogue, the mikva, monuments, support, protests, boring correspondence with the institutions and the government, provisions for the soup kitchen, requests from the cantor, shochtim, etc., we find one protocol which is exceptional:

Protocol 33, November 1, 1918, from a meeting of the Communal Council on Friday, the eve of the Sabbath of Chaye Sarah [55]. A special meeting: It is a day of memorial for us today, today is exactly one year since we received notification from Minister Balfour that the Government of England promised Palestine to the Jewish people. This will be a redemption for us.

In honor of this anniversary, we, the members of the Jewish Communal Council have gathered together, and we are publicizing this day, and we have decided to celebrate this anniversary day with a public gathering in holy splendor.

We will send out invitations and invite all of the leaders of the different groups from all the different factions to come and participate in the celebration.

All members of the Communal Council will come to worship tomorrow in the synagogue.

We request that the rabbi deliver a sermon in the synagogue on the events of the day.

Signed by Secretary Michaelson, Daniel Sirkes, Aharon Yosef Berger, Yissachar Moshe Schwartz, and Zeev Eliahu Reichert.

And on the other hand, we have the following protocol:

A Deep Mourning for the Jews!!

On Monday of the week of the Torah portion of Miketz 5679 [A footnote at the bottom of the page notes: December 2, 1918, appearing on a protocol surrounded by a black border, the content of which is full of mourning and grief, with the note "Yizkor" ("Let us remember").] a) A special meting of all the members of the Communal Council was called, headed by the rabbi.

The order of the day was: a) a strong protest against the pogroms in Poland and Galicia, primarily in Lvov. b) Support and help to the victims of the pogrom.

It was decided: a) that a memorial for the souls of our holy brethren who were killed and slaughtered in Lvov and other cities should be inscribed in the communal ledgers in order to publicize the matter to the generation. We also issue a strong protest against the perpetrators of the evil who plan and execute pogroms against Jews. b) We invite two members from each of the various factions and groups in our city, including the Jewish party, the artisans' club, the Mizrachi, the Zionist union, the tailors' union, the merchants union, Young Zion, the old age home, the "Maccabee", the Orthodox union, the Hebrew Library, the Gideon group, to come together next Wednesday at 10:00 am in order to plan a large scale assistance effort for our brothers who were victims of the pogroms, and in order to organize how to take part in the general mourning of the Jews in Poland for the terrible pogroms that is planned for Monday of the week of Vayigash [56].
Signed by Secretary Michaelson, Daniel Sirkes, Yissachar Schwartz, and Aharon Yosef Berger.

In the following protocols, we see special activities to organize the assistance committee for the victims of the pogroms; conflict between various factions, especially from the orthodox factions, regarding representation in the communal council, as if they had been pushed aside on account of the painful problems that affect the entire people; and a request from the rabbi for a significant amount of support on the occasion of the marriage of his son. The latter request was filled immediately, without being pushed off.

At the general meeting that was called with representatives from all of the organizations, and was chaired by Mr. Yissachar Schwartz and officially conducted by Mr. Morgenstern, an action committee was chosen and asked to join forces with a similar women's action committee. The following people were chosen for the committee: Yissachar Schwartz, A. Y. Berger, L. Sirkes, D. Sirkes, A. Sokosowski, Y. Librach, and Ch. Segal. Later, A. Eiger and L. Posnersohn were added to it.

The committee was asked to send one of its members to the national committee in order to receive direction as to how to undertake the required activity. In accordance with a recommendation by L. Sirkes, a collection of funds was declared already on the spot, from among those gathered. 2,182 marks and 27 rubles were gathered on the spot.

The chairman turned to the gathering with warm and emotional words, and expressed his hope that this mourning would inspire a true unity among all segments of the community, and that with G-d's help, better days should come.

In accordance with the advice of the rabbi of the city, they declared that the Monday of Torah portion Vayigash should be a day of mourning and a public fast day.

December 12, 1918: Daniel Sirkes was chosen as a the delegate to the national council in Warsaw, with instructions to request equal national rights for the Jewish people in the lands of the Diaspora, as well as a safe haven in the Land of Israel for the people of Israel.

June 15, 1919: Due to the growing numbers of people making aliya to the Land, the chairman Daniel Sirkes advised the creation of a special fund to support those making aliya, and to allocate a certain percentage of the budget for that purpose.

Furthermore, due to concern about the price of wheat, the rising price of matzo, the rising of taxes, shechita fees, requests for support, other budgetary allocations, and all other problems, complaints, judgements, and threats from the communal workers against various shochtim, a new protocol appears which includes "old tunes": happenings in the midst of the city of Zgierz.

July 14, 1919: It was decided to gather any information available about incidents against the Jews in our city, and to send it to the national council in Warsaw, on the condition that these incidents not be published in newspapers under the name of the Communal Council.

A request was also received from those burned in Chervetsov for help and support.

August 22, 1919: The member of the council Yissachar Schwartz traveled to Warsaw to meet with Morgenthau. Mr. Schwartz greeted him in the name of the Jews of Zgierz, and presented before him a report of the tribulations of the city, the economic situation, relations with the gentiles, communal concerns, etc.

In the following protocols during the latter half of 1919, we see that the tribulations increased in the city Opinions were heard in the Communal Council not to impose taxes that year due to the dimness of the economy and the tribulations in livelihood. The chairman presented the bare truth about the communal coffers: the coffers were empty, and the Communal Council was already in debt by about 10,000 mark, and if taxes were not collected, everything would have to be shut down.

In the meantime, there were problems regarding the Talmud Torah, which was in need of reorganization and an increase in allocations for its maintenance, in order to hire teachers and purchase an honorable building. In addition, communal workers, rabbis, shochtim, and shamashim all placed request for their needs, that is to say an increased in salary to offset the increased cost of living. There were also all types of requests for support that could not be overlooked. The Communal Council wept and gave, bargained and apologized, debated, but paid in the end. Of course, they raised the shechita fees, for, what choice was there, those who eat meat would pay, for what would they do, eat non-kosher meat?

However, the enemies did not let up. In Ukraine, there were further pogroms against the Jews.

The Communal Council prepared a protest. The Sejm prepared to declare Sunday as a rest day, a law that would also affect the Jews. This of course required a protest, for if it would not help, it certainly would not hurt.

With all this, the Talmud Torah developed with proper teachers also for secular subject and a full curriculum that included Hebrew, Torah, prophets, Talmud, etc. A supervisory committee for the Talmud Torah was set up by the community, with wide representation from various communal bodies. The legalization of the merchants' union in Zgierz also took place. They attempted to obtain etrogs, wheat for Passover, etc. They sent a letter of thanks and appreciation to the representative Grynbaum for his strong battle against the law of the day of rest on Sunday.

Thus, the Communal Council was occupied with both holy and secular matters, with trivial matters such as disputes and conflicts regarding the bathhouse, shechita, the sale of meat, etc., and important matters in the Jewish world. Schwartz was sent to various places to search for wheat and to receive permits for such. Intercession was made to factories so that Jews would be employed. So and so received 500 marks to help marry of his daughter for otherwise... The flour millers requested support, but the communal council was not able to fill the request... etc. etc.

And suddenly, there was another ray of light... The peace conference of San Remo: Friday, Iyar 13, 5680 (April 30, 1920)

A Special Meeting

Which was called on the occasion of the good news that reached us that the peace conference gave authorization to the rights of the Jewish people in the Land of Israel.

The chairman Mr. D. Sirkes spoke about the significance of the day and expressed the happiness of the members of the council regarding this good news.

After a discussion, it was decided:

To arrange prayers of thanks in the synagogue and the Beis Midrash, when the rabbi of the city will speak about the value and greatness of the day; to distribute an announcement among all the Jews of our town regarding this matter; to invite all members of the various organizations and schools in our city to come to the synagogue, and also to send a telegram of greeting to the central Zionist organization in Poland, and to the central Mizrachi organization in Warsaw.

Signed by all members of the committee, and a number of guests.

The Joy of the Jews and the Anger of Esau

With the rise of the spiritual status of the Jewish masses, there was a desire to express some of the joy. What better day than Lag Baomer, the holiday which symbolizes freedom and liberty for Jewish children.

It was therefore decided to arrange a lovely celebration for the school children and the youth on lag Baomer. After a lunch for the children, they would gather in the garden of the Sirkes brothers on 98 Dombrowski St., and from there set out on a parade to the Konstantynowski Forest.

The organizing committee included Morgenstern, Weisenfreund, Lipowicz (from the Maccabee), and two members of "Hatzofim" and "Gideon." The Communal Council would obtain the permit for the parade. Psiakrew Zydki!! (Damn Jews!!)

The mounted police suddenly overtook the parade as it was going out. They trampled and injured the youth and older people, calling out "Psiakrew Zydki!!." Avraham Leib Sluma, 70 years old, was pushed down by the police and his leg as injured. Yisrael Horen was also trampled by the police, and he was injured in his arms and legs. Several of the students were injured, including Jozef Cohn who was a student of the gymnasia, Ignia Cohn and Y.

105

Katz. The latter was revived with difficulty. Finally, several of the students and adults were imprisoned.

Of course, a harsh protest was issued…

Fishel Feldon complained that the neighboring gentiles were damaging the cemetery, breaking the monuments and the fence. The appeal of the Communal Council to Father Stefanski, asking him to influence his congregation, did not bear fruit. Therefore it was decided that the rabbi, along with Yissachar Schwartz, would attempt to deal with the matter.

The Budget of 1920

After lengthy deliberations and bitter arguments with several dozen taxpayers, the Communal Council finally compiled the budget for the year 1920:   Revenue:

Shechita	80,000 marks
External Aid	15,000
Various	5,000
Communal Tax	328,000
Total	428,000 marks

Disbursements:

Rabbi of the City	50,000 marks
Rabbi Ichal	30,000
Shochtim (30,000 each)	60,000
Cantor and Trustee B. Gad	30,000
Shamash F. Feldon	10,000
Shamash Moshe Gelbard	5,000
Secretary	30,000
Disbursements for the Synagogue and Beis Midrash	5,000
Bikur Cholim (Care of the Sick)	12,000
Support for the Poor	90,000
Mikva	10,000
Miscellaneous (Cohn, Bennet, The office, etc.)	18,000
Debts from Previous Year	13,000
Education	100,000
Total	428,000 marks

The sum of the columns adds up to 428,000 marks; however, the budget was nullified due to the opposition presented in the form of a written petition signed by 93 taxpayers. The deliberations began anew, and the budget was lowered to 357,000 marks by reducing the revenue of taxes from 328,000 to 160,000, and increasing the revenue from shechita from 80,000 to 182,000.

However, this was still not the end of the story.

After a bitter struggle over each entry, and through reasoning and pressure, the elected council arrived at a different budget. There were further complaints about the new budget, from the Communal Council and also from the outside - from the community of taxpayers, who still saw their burden as too heavy.

After weeks of debates and struggles accompanied by troubling events, they arrived at a drastically reduced budget, totaling 205,000 marks, of which only 85,000 was to come from taxes. Several of the opponents protested the claims of the members of the council with exceptional bitterness and even threats of slander and imprisonment.

The council battled and struggled, issued a proclamation to the residents, and appealed to the worshippers in the synagogue. However as the storm abated, it gave in and returned to its activities of adjudication without any budgetary direction. From that time, life was from hand to mouth. It can easily be understood that the shechita fees rose drastically, since one way or another, the money had to be found.

Without doubt, education at that time suffe from great difficulties, and other activities were also affected. In the meantime, flour, matzos, Passover allocation and other collections that were made for various immediate needs occupied the attention of the Communal Council significantly. However, no matter what, it was impossible live without a budget, and therefore at the end of May 1921, they salaries and disbursements of the Communal Council were set according to the weekly need, without any connection to a set budget, for in any cases, there would be the need for constant changes almost every week, due to the severe inflation.

Among the protocols, we enter into the boiling cauldron of interpersonal relations, poverty, good deeds, meanness from some people and sacrifice from others, private and public disputes, the struggle for existence, and various issues regarding deviations by delegations responsible for local needs, such as a protest against Agudas Yisrael in Vienna when it got involved with England in opposition to Zionism, and a protest and a day of mourning in memory of the victims of the incidents in Jaffa. There was no shortage of tribulations and worry. Locally, there were concerns about increases of salary, and to counteract that, increases in taxes, the rising price of shechita came around again. The secretary of the community protested and wished to resign, so they had to find another. The local shamashim (sextons) made use of the communal coffers as if it was their own money. The trustee Shalom Zelmanowicz complained about the lack of obedience. The magistrate, the police, the mayor (starosta), the interior minister and others, all had their own request from the unfortunate members of the council.

And again: the synagogue, the mikva, an ill person who needed an operation and requested support, and he was not the only one. There were also poor mothers giving birth, orphans, foundlings, and others, and others... And the census that was requested by the government...why did it have to be specifically on the Sabbath?

There was a need to add to the allocation for the mikva, since there was no fuel or coal for heating. There was a need to order etrogim early, since without doubt the price would rise.

And what about the soup kitchen? And the children's orphanage? And the academics, they also have their requests.

The civic government requested a payment of 10,000 marks for the Jewish sick. From where would this come? From the granary or the vineyard? Reb Ichal is also requesting a raise, as are the rabbi and the shochtim. Moshe Gelbard requests damages, and a Jewish child is housed in a Christian orphanage and must be rescued. Again, there were matzos, Passover funds, seriously ill people, a renewal of the agreement with the mikva, a raise for the shochtim, and along with all this...

There was a sharp protest against Agudas Yisrael and its delegation, which traveled to Lord Notcliffe protesting against Zionism (protocol 141 from March 5, 1922).

The Satanic Dance of the Mark

The rabbi of the community received a weekly salary in 1920 of 4,000 marks and the Shamash received 400; however in 1922, one year later, the rabbi's salary reached 55,000 and the Shamash's salary 6,000. A half-year later, the salary of the rabbi had jumped to 150,000 marks, and one month later to a quarter of a million, and one week later than that to 325,000. Within the next month, the salary reached one half a million. Of course, the shechita fees rose proportionately: 5,000 marks for a chicken and 50,000 for a head of cattle. As the shechita fees rose, the salary of the rabbi rose to 650,000, and two weeks later it rose to 900,000 marks per week. In November, his salary had already reached 1,214,000, and then it jumped to 1,494,000 and to 1,748,000. Cantor Konwisser received 1,000,000 marks. The situation with Cantor Konwisser is a story unto itself.

The community requested that a new cantor be appointed to replace B. Gad. After various deliberations and pressure from a group of worshippers that became more severe and reached the point of threats, it was decided to fire Gad from his duties and pay him 3,000,000 marks as reparations. Cantor Konwisser took his place, and the worshippers in the synagogue worked on his behalf and created a special fund to support him. On account of a minor incident, complaints rose against him, and disputes arose from the Great Synagogue, which caused perplexity for the community, and the Communal Council. Since the shamash of the synagogue, Mr. Feldon, was also involved in this incident, he aroused the ire of several worshippers. When Mr. Fishel Feldon was cruelly murdered in his home along with his entire family, the government did not hesitate to accuse five worshippers of being involved in the murder, and they were imprisoned. Later, it became clear that the family was murdered by Polish criminals who hid out in the cemetery, and suspected that Feldon would inform on them. Therefore, they took their revenge upon him and his family. This internecine struggle regarding the cantor and the murder, and the communal embarrassment that ensued caused a black mark, which darkened life in the city, and had a varying effect at different times.

It is sad that during the fifteen-year period that we are studying from this important ledger, the shadows are larger than the light, and the sadness is greater than the spiritual highs. Here and there, various events came across the scene, dim rays of light regarding local or foreign notables, which brought a semblance of a smile onto the weary and darkened face of the

Jewish community. These included the festivities surrounding the authorization of the mandate at the Geneva peace conference, the telegram from the Communal Council on that occasion along with the prayers of thanksgiving in the synagogues, the opening of the Hebrew University in Jerusalem, the opening of a new institution or school when the representatives of the Communal Council would speak at the opening ceremonies. In March 1927, a Beis Yaakov girls' school opened. Aharon Hirsch Kompel spoke at the opening festivities. Noach Trotsky came to the jubilee celebration of the Maccabee. However these were dim rays over a constant cloud, darkness and grayness. The daily reality was - a battle for existence and a struggle for a peace of bread, which naturally caused conflicts, fear as well as personal and social tension. There were cases where the Satan held the opinion of "not by bread alone does man live", and also became involved in pure spiritual matters, such as with the prayer leader and the cantor, regarding either salary or wishing to have control over the cantor. However, we can take comfort that only in a Jewish community can one see a spirit of mutual concern and responsibility. In critical situations, they did not worry only about local matters, but also about any call from help from afar. Great efforts were made to collect Passover funds for the poor of the city, however when a call came from the central communal organization to collect funds for the Jews of Russia who had no matzos, people would immediately add 20% to their personal donations. Jews would be asked and would give. Dr. Fishel took it upon himself to take care of the indigent sick for free, in return for a small favor - being freed from the communal tax. Miss F. was about to get married and there was a "blight" in the home. The Communal Council gave her 5,000 marks. Rabbi Cantorczik arrived from the refugees of Ukraine (August 13, 1922), and was given 25,000 marks. The Jewish community of Lutamirsk issued a call for help, and was given 25,000 marks. The wife of Yerachmiel Podlowski was in need of an operation. Who would pay for the operation? The Communal Council. They made an appeal to the authorities on behalf of Mrs. Lipschitz for a permit to open a wine store so she would be able to earn a livelihood.

There were also warm relationships with proper communal formality and politeness, according to established tradition. On the thirtieth anniversary of the appointment of the rabbi, they gave him as a gift a fur coat worth 3,000 guilder. The communal coffers were low, so the Communal Council contributed 800 guilder, and the rest was collected from the residents. An additional 75 guilder were necessary as tailoring fees, for the gift had to be proper and a perfect fit.

When the rabbi was in need of the theraputical baths of Germany, they gave him 500 guilder (June 10, 1928).

When Cantor Yisrael Yitzchak Gad went to a summer home in Dombrowska, they gave him 150 guilder without delay. When the shochet Dov Gad married off his daughter, would he not receive 500 guilder? Without any doubt he would. Even when the secretary moved to his new home, he was given a significant gift.

Thus, in any situation and with all the tribulations, they would give money out for marriages, for the study of a trade for unemployed workers, for baking of bread for the poor, for the healing of the sick, for mourners, for the deaf and mute, for those who made aliya to the Land, for those who lost their livelihood, for any need and to anyone who stuck out a hand.

What about the institutions? Praised be G-d, there was no shortage of these. There was the Yesodei Hatorah Cheder, Beis Yaakov, the orphanage, the charitable fund, Talmud Torah, Yavneh, Keren Hayesod, Keren Kayemet (The Jewish National Fund), the Frischman library, the fund for evening classes in the Beis Midrash, the fund for Mizrachi pioneers, the fund for the settlers of Israel, the fund for poor mothers, the Agudas Yisrael girls' library, and many others.

In order to complete the picture presented by the book, we will bring down a few other facts:

In June 1922, the communal officials (rabbis, cantors, shochtim, shamashim, communal servants, etc.) received only 50% of their salary, for the shechita produced a loss, and there was no money. The salaried workers refused to accept this.

In May, a committee was appointed to maintain the Beis Midrash, and 20,000 marks were collected for this purpose. The committee consisted of Zwykielski, Ader, Goldstein, Gibralter, Siedlawski, and Kompel.

In June, a committee was established to aid the Jews of Ukraine, headed by Mr. Eiger.

In July of that year, the shochet Fishel Bunim Hollander was fired from his duties on account of his age. He received a six-week stipend as reparations, and his son-in-law Eisenstadt took his place.

About three months later, in October 1922, Fishel Bunim was fired as well from his position of cantor. He requested reparations of 200,000, but was given half that until a final decision. In the meantime, he was given 8,000 marks per week. His place was given to Cantor D. Gad.

In January 1923, the position of selling shechita cards was given to the widow Genia Weitzman. This position was originally in the hands of the widow Gad.

In May, the Communal Council decided to issue a protest against the Minister of Religion who made things difficult for the community and restricted its activities.

In September, A. Morgenstern was chosen as the representative of the community to the public school council of the Lodz region.

By the end of the year, salaries had increased to such heights that the secretary received 7,000,000 marks per week, and everyone else according to the same proportion.

In November, Naftali Moshe Rosenes was hired as a shochet to replace Shlomowicz who died. His heirs receive support of 70,000,000 marks aside from the money that was collected in a special campaign to benefit the widow, so that she would be able to move to a different place. Those who took care of this collection included Reb Shlomo Sirkes, Noach Trotsky and Aharon The committee that worked on behalf of Cantor Konwisser set up a special fund to firm up his livelihood.

In May 1924 an assistant was hired for the communal secretary, the widow Nekritz. At that time, the communal budget reached the level of milliards [57]. However at the end of the month the currency changed to Polish guilder, even though on occasion prices were still registered in the millions of marks for various needs.

In August 1924 the situation became more difficult. They presented the head of the region with a memorandum of the difficulties. The shechita fees rose by 50%. The butchers protested. A delegation of them came for a demonstration. That delegation included Avigdor Roszaloski, Avraham Grand, Avraham Dov Grand, Yitzchak Trauanowski, Shaul Trauanowski, Ziskind Trauanowski, Yisrael Grand, Zanwil Sochaczewski, A Y. Sperling, and Wolf Szmietanski.

In June 1924, a new council was elected headed by Eliezer Sirkes. The vice-chairman was Leib Goldberg, the treasurer was Noach Trotsky, and A. H. Kompel was a member.

In December 1924, a budgetary committee for the year 1925 was appointed, with participants from all the groups, as follows:

From the synagogue: Avraham Morgenstern and Moshe Reznik.

From the Beis Midrash: Shalom Zelmanowicz and Yoel Spiwak.

From the first Gur Hassidim shtibel: Yitzchak Nekritz, Yosef Hirsch Shapira.

From the second Gur Hassidim shtibel: Leibish Rosenberg, Menachem Frohman.

From the Alexander Hassidim shtibel: Moshe Itzkowicz and Michael Kuperman.

From the Sochaczew Hassidim shtibel: Wolf Kojawski.

From the Zyradrow Hassidim shtibel: Avraham Mandel and Shlomo Cincinatus.

From the Strykow Hassidim shtibel: Yisrael Mordechai Preshker, Nathan David Katz.

From the Mizrachi prayer hall: Yitzchak Meir Halpern and Avraham Finkelstein.

From the Parizer prayer hall: Yitzchak Meir Zilberberg, Kasriel Ginzberg, Pinchas Wand, David Wand, Shmuel Bennet and David Honigstock.

At the first meeting, the members of the committee removed themselves from common effort with the Communal Council regarding to the preparation of the budget, for according to their opinion: "in these pressing times, the Communal Council cannot produce a budget of 35,000 guilder per year with us being able to state that our hands did not spill this blood" [58], as expressed by the committee member Morgenstein.

When the Communal Council ran into difficulties in preparing the budget in subsequent meetings, they decided to appoint a new committee, consisting of the following people:

From the industrialists: Yaakov Meir Kuper, Shmuel Kuper, Noach Boaz, and Avigdor Kaufman, from the householders: Shalom Zelmanowicz, Moshe Skosowski, Yaakov Leib Rosenzweig, Yisrael Yitzchak Finkelstein and Moshe Blanket.

From the tailors: Getzel Schwartzbard. From the shoemakers: Nachum Kaminski. From the butchers: Avraham Grand and Shaul Trauanowski. This time, the committee succeeded in arriving at an authorized budget.

However, in March 1925, the situation became more critical. Kompel and Trotsky lent money to the Communal Council to enable it to meet its most urgent expenditures. There was a desire to open a civic butcher shop under the direction of the Communal Council in order to sell meat for

113

cheaper, since the butchers had been raising their prices more than in any other sector.

In June 1926, a popular bank was opened in Zgierz. Mr. Leib Goldberg participated in the opening celebrations as a representative of the council.

As the time approached for preparing the 1926 budget, the customary show took place again. The appointed committee could not reach agreement on various clauses. The budget that was prepared by the council itself was not authorized by the government, due to complaints that were directed at the committee itself.

This committee consisted of:

From citizens of the town: Shlomo Sirkes, Yosef Hirsch Shapira, Mendel Warshawski, Hershel Itzkowicz, Meir Schwartz, Eliezer Posnersohn, Gedalia Yedidya Zwykielski, Yaakov Meir Kuper, Shmuel Kuper, Yissachar Schwartz, Yitzchak Brahn, Eliezer Shlomowicz, Isadore Strykowski, Noach Mendelsohn, Aharon Kaltgrad, Chaim Boaz and Yitzchak Nekritz.

From the industrialists: Avraham Morgenstern

From the merchants: Yosef Blaustein, Binyamin Krishtal, Michael Radgowski.

From the artisans: Getzel Schwartzbard, Gershon Petrowicz.

The following people participated in the 1928 budgetary committee: Nathan Ader, Moshe Aronson, Shalom Boaz, Avraham Boaz, Noach Boaz, Aharon Yosef Berger, Yaakov Meir Kuper, Shmuel Bennet, Tovia Koppel Bumes, Ezriek Zucker, Shimon Cznichowski, Pinchas Davidowicz, Shmuel Davidowicz, Moshe Eiger, Yisrael Yitzchak Finkelstein, Moshe Glowinski, Fabian Greenberg, Leibel Halpern, Yosef Meir Horen, Moshe Itzkowicz, Hersch Itzkowicz, Shabtai Itzkowicz, Mordechai Jakubowicz, Yisrael Jakubowicz, Leon Krikus, Wolf Koyawski, Shmuel Kuper, Yissachar Lerner, Wolf Lipschitz, Yitzchak Nekritz, Chaim Posnersohn, Eliezer Posnersohn, Moshe Posnersohn, Moshe Preshker, Moshe Reznik, Avraham Meir Rubinson, Yaakov Rosenstrauch, Yeshaya Henech Segal, Shlomo Sirkes, Nathan David Shabshowicz, Eliezer Shlomowicz, Avraham Shlumiel, Yosef Hirsch Shapira, Meir Schwartz, Anshel Waldman, Wolf Wronski, Shalom Zelmanowicz, Yitzchak Meir Zilberberg, Yaakov Glazer, and Gedalya Zwykielski.

A Few Interesting Details

In November 1926, a stormy debate broke out among the members of the Communal Council regarding whether or not the dedication of a new fence surrounding the synagogue is an event worthy of celebration, and whether or not the town notables should be invited to such a dedication.

In May 1928, a tender was issued for painting the fence and gate of the synagogue. Henech Schleser won the tender. Friestadt's proposal was rejected, as it was too expensive. In July 1928, The Maccabee received a permit to erect a monument for the late Eliezer Mendelowicz, on the condition that they not go to the cemetery with a flag and white trousers.

Finally, there were the elections for the town council. In June 1927, a joint coalition of the Jewish organizations entered a party, with the objection of putting together a Jewish block that would be able to receive five mandates, which would represent 350 voters. Without joining together, they would perhaps be able to obtain three seats, with difficulty.

The participants of this party included:

From the Zionist Union: Fabian Greenberg, Yosef Katz, and L. Weinstein.

From Mizrachi: Y. M. Halperin, Avraham Finkelstein.

From the Shlomei Emunei Yisrael (Those at Peace with the Faith of Israel): Shlomo Sirkes, Ch., Y. Eisenschmidt.

From the Union: David Gahm, Shmuel Feldon, David Preshker.

From Young Mizrachi: Avraham Bornstein, Shmuel Jakubowicz.

From the Young of the Faithful of Israel: Meir Sczaransky, Avigdor Rosenblatt.

From the Merchant's Union: Michael Kuperman, Yechiel Kompel.

From the factories: Yitzchak Meir Zilberberg, A. Morgenstern.

From the artisans: A. Wald, Sh. Rotenberg, and Woidaslawsky.

From the workers (Professional Union): P. Lipschitz, M. Gross.

From the butchers: Moshe Hirsch Grand, David Grand

From the Bund: Chaim Wolkowicz, Z. Skoroka.

From the tailors' guild: Sh. M. Lewkowicz, Ch. N. Srowka, and Cincinatus.

The debates in this party were very vibrant. Every organization wished to take the first place in the list of candidates, or at least to be guaranteed a mandate for its representatives. Finally, a small committee was selected to set the mandates.

This was a world filled with life and energy, activity and work; a multi-faceted struggle regarding religion and behavior, desires and vision; composed of many souls from all edges of the spectrum in morality, thought and deeds. Woe to the fact that this community has passed from the world, as it was uprooted from its place by the cruel storm of the Holocaust.

The Communal Council. From right to left: L. Rosenberg, Warshawski, A. H. Kompel, Rabbi Shlomo Yehuda Leib Cohn, B. Bechler, Kihen, G. Korczej (the secretary), Weisbrott.

A page from the Book of minutes of the Zgierz community.
Translator's note: This is titled protocol 96, and is apparently a portion of the budget of 1920,which is discussed in the text above

March 9, 1918: Chairman of the meeting - Yissachar Schwartz: Committees were set up for the provision of matzos, for encouraging people to contribute to the Passover fund, for inviting Jewish soldiers for Passover. The chief nurse of the hospital was requested to announce every death to the community. Secretary -Michaelson. The distribution to the offices of the Communal Council: the treasurer A. Y. Berger. He will record the expenditures and income with status. Messrs. Miechowski, Morgenstern and Sender Landau were requested to record the status. The secretary is required to travel to Lodz in order to obtain from the police a permit to bake matzos in the near future. Messrs. Alexander Landau, Wolf Reichert, Mordechai Shmuel Zudkowicz, Gedalyahu Yedidya Zwykielski and Yisrael Frugal were asked to help in organizing the baking of matzos.

The synagogue and the Beis Midrash will no longer receive support. They will have to fend for themselves. The Chevra Kadisha (burial society) will come under the supervision of the community. The request by the rabbi and the shochtim for a raise was turned down until such time as shechita comes under the supervision of the community.

It was requested that the entire shechita enterprise come under the supervision of the community. The rabbi and both shochtim, Fishel Bunem

117

Hollander and Yisrael Yitzchak Gad will receive 80 marks a week. Three times a year, at Pesach, Rosh Hashanah and Sukkot, they will receive a double payment. Yisrael Yitzchak did not agree with these conditions - it is forbidden for him to practice shechita since he did not sign the agreement.

After discussions and the hearing of various opinions from the residents, it was decided that shechita should be supervised by the community, and not be overseen by the opponents of the Shochtim.

The price of shechita was set as follows: 20 marks for a large animal, and 7 marks for a small animal. Daniel Sirkes is responsible for actualizing the decision. The teacher Reb Michel Elberg will receive 50 marks per week, Cantor Berish Gad - 50, the widow of Reb Moshe Bennet will receive support of 15 marks, Reb Yitzchak Mendel - 5 marks and an addition teaching Ein Yaakov in the Beis Midrash (if he neglects to teach Ein Yaakov to the group, he will not receive the 10 marks). The shamashim Gelbard and Fishel Feldon - 16 marks, the watchman Reb Berl Zelnik - 8 marks a week. The shamashim are forbidden from charging money themselves to the householders. They will receive a double salary for the festivals.

Reb Moshe the Shamash must arrive every day an hour before the beginning of the morning services (shacharit) and before the afternoon and evening services (mincha and maariv) and maintain the cleanliness. The secretary Michaelson will receive 70 marks per week.

It was decided to maintain the books and ledgers in an organized fashion. An agreement was reached with the Chevra Kadisha to register all of the Torah scrolls in the town and to put them under their supervision. Each month, the secretary is required to prepare an accounting report.

May 29, 1918: The shechita fees were raised and the rabbi's salary was increased by 1,000 marks.

July 6, 1918: The 1918 budget was presented. The rabbi -3,040, Elberg - 1,520, Cantor Gad - 750, Shamash Feldon - 200, Gelbard - 200, the Talmud Torah - 4,000, the Talmud Torah building - 500, heating and lighting for the synagogue and the Beis Midrash - 500, insurance and property - 275, care of the sick (Bikur Cholim) - 2,565, support for the poor - 4,000, payment of the debt to the town council - 3,400. The total, 20,850 marks.

June 12, 1918: The family B. is making a scandal in the Communal Council regarding taxes. Noach B. grabbed the budget ledgers and tore them up with great anger.

June 13: A year later, B. repeated the same behavior in the community. A fine of 500 marks was imposed upon him by the onlookers (the rabbi and communal leaders). If he does not pay, he will be accused in court (he used various insults and derogatory names).

June 30: Daniel Sirkes was appointed as chairman of the Communal Council; Yissachar Schwartz - vice chairman; the rabbi of the town - the honorary Chairman.

July 5: Items were purchased for the youth of the community.

{At this point on, the Yiddish version matches up with the Hebrew - starting with the entry of July 7.}

**The decision of the Communal Council after the pogrom
in Lvov and Galicia in 1918.**

33

34

Photocopy of a page from the book of protocols.
Translator's note: This page includes protocol 33 and a portion of protocol 34. Protocol 33, regarding the anniversary of the Balfour Declaration, is brought down in full in the text

Am heutigen Tage unter Vorsitz unserer Gemeindemitglieder
Anwesenheit der Kaltberns ... der Gemeindevorsteher sind eine Finanzsteuer
Schulcommission gegründet worden zu welchen folgende Herren gewählt
wurden.

zur Finanz u. Steuer

1, J. Lipowitz
2, N. Adler
3, L. Pernersohn
4, J. Strykowski
5, B. Cohn
6, A. J. Berger
7, J. ...
8, M. Eiger.
9, M. J. Margolies

zur Schulcommission

1, G. d. Zaykielski
2, J. Strykowski
3, J. Michowski

Davon durch schriftliche Anzeige davon in Kenntnis
gesetzt wurden u. Ihre Wahl bestätigt haben.

Znin 1 August 1915

Rabbiner

Vorstand   M. Softeli S. Ring
Mitglieder
J. Strykowski
A. J. Berger
G. L. Zaykielski
N. Adler
J. Lipowitz
M. Eiger
L. Pernersohn

The first protocol of the protocol book of the Jewish community,
August 1, 1915. It is in German

121

Members of the Chevra Kadisha (Burial Society), Trustees and Workers

Reb Lipa Zelczer-Berliner, Ber Zucker (Bezshe), Chaim Mendel Herzog, Berl Zelnik, Shalom Zandberg, Gedalya-Yedidya Zwykielski, Meirl Kaloski, Eliahu Tennenbaum, Mendel Finkelstein, Berl Weisbaum, Yankel Rosenstrauch (Chanas), Mendel Warshawski, Henech Bonde, Avraham Kuperman, Anshel Waldman, Leibel Goldberg, Izak Szerodzkii

Cantorial Committee that Sang and Recited
By Wolf Fisher of Tel Aviv

At the beginning of the 1920s, after the long-time cantor Berish Gad left his job and became a shochet in place of his father, the old Hassid and scholar Reb Yisrael Yitzchak, the Communal Council announced that it was looking for a candidate for the cantor of the synagogue. Soon, a competition began for the job. Cantors would come to lead the services on Sabbaths, in particular on "Shabbat Mevarchim" [59], and the congregants were supposed to choose the best candidate. Finally, a special committee was chosen, consisting of distinguished congregants, as well as a few people who were familiar with singing and the cantorial arts, some of whom remembered the sweet, soft prayers of Reb Beinish Cahan (the father of the eminent poet Yaakov Cohen). After hearing a succession of cantors, the cantorial committee took council with a larger group of congregants. This strongly favored the well-known director and cantor of the Choral Synagogue of Dvinsk, H. Konwisser, who captivated the congregation with his lovely and talented prayers. In accordance with the speech of Leib Gelbard (today a cantor in Los Angeles), the cantorial committee decided to solicit the opinion of the manufacturer and Zionist activist Noach Trotsky, himself a lover of fine chazzanut.

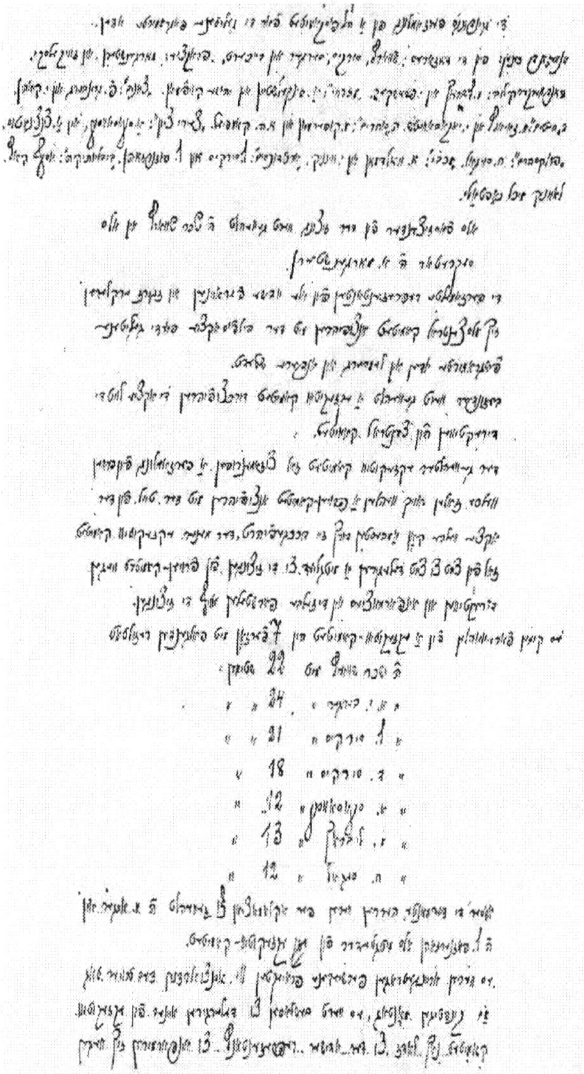

```
          24
          21
          18
          12
          13
          12
```

החלטות ועד הקהילה על הקמת ועדה לעזרת קורבנות הפרעות בלבוב (1918).

Protocol 43. A decision by the Communal Council regarding the establishment of a committee to assist the victims of the pogrom of Lvov, 1918

The independent Cantorial Committee

Due to the various opinions, for the next few months, there were disputes, struggles and invective in the synagogue on the Sabbaths. Everyone had their own excited opinion for the cantorial committee. The committee could not tolerate the open taking of sides by the Shamash and undertaker Fishel Feldon, who, according to them, should not give his opinion and get mixed up in these matters - neither on their side nor on the other side...

The matter would surely conclude, as did all synagogue disputes in cities and towns, with a drink (lechayim), some cake, and making peace. However, this time, a sudden tragic event took place, which neither side of the cantorial dispute wished to happen:

On one summer morning in 1925, terrible news spread through the town - the undertaker Fishel Feldon and his family, consisting of five people, was found murdered in their home.

The police officer came to Zgierz from Lodz with an entire staff of detectives. His aim was to find the murderer. When he heard something about Fishel Feldon becoming involved in an argument in the synagogue, he arrested the first five members of the cantorial committee. They were shackled and taken to a prison in Lodz, where they were beaten so that they would confess that the murder was their doing...

After a week of investigation and torture, and after the energetic efforts of the head of the Communal Council Reb Eliezer Sirkes who worked for their freedom, the five were freed - "for no evidence was found against them."

The Yeshiva Yagdil Torah of Zgierz

Included among the institutions that Zgierz was blessed with in the days prior to the First World War was the Yagdil Torah yeshiva, which educated the youth from both inside and outside of Zgierz in Torah and religion. Many people streamed to it from far off places. This institution was registered officially, and it is appropriate to present a memorial to it in this book by copying a few chapters from its charter, from which we can learn about the character of the institution, its tasks and its manner of funding. {The Hebrew footnote here reads as follows: The Jewish institution Yagdil Torah of Zgierz was officially registered in the list of institutions and organizations of the Piotrkow Gubernia as number 524, with the official approval of the Piotrkow Gubernia, on July 9.}

The charter includes 37 paragraphs and covers many pages. Here, we will present only a few of them:

1. The Jewish Yagdil Torah organization in Zgierz, Piotrkow Gubernia, for the purpose of arranging for the children of poor Jews to study for free. The sphere of activity of this institution will be in the city of Zgierz.
2. To realize this objective, the organization will open and maintain, with official government permission, schools such as cheders which will not charge tuition, as well as yeshivas, Beis Midrashes, etc. as educational institutions, libraries, and dormitories for students and teachers. Similarly, the organization will pay for students who are studying in their private homes.
3. While the students are studying in the institutions of this organization, they will not pay tuition, and they will benefit from the physical and spiritual protection of the organization. If there will be a need to collect some payment from the students in order to maintain the organization, the amount must be set by a general meeting of the organization.

    Note: The organization will abide by currently existing laws and regulations, as well as those that will be set in the future.

4. Children of permanent residents of Zgierz will be the first to be eligible for admission to the institutions of the organization.

5. The organization will concern itself with its students after the conclusion of their studies by granting them the means to continue in the development of their education.

6. In order to realize these objectives, the organization has the right to collect donations, to distribute collection boxes with the permission of the government, and to receive gifts and grants from individuals and organizations. Details are provided in paragraph 12 of this charter. In addition, the organization has the right to acquire and dispose of property, to sign various contracts and documents, to take on loans and pay off loans, and to protect its interests in courts of law and in front of other government institutions. It can do so by granting power of attorney to its delegates regarding any matter that might come from t his charter.

In the second chapter, where it discusses the income of the organization, we read the following paragraphs.

10. The income of the organization consists of: membership dues, donations from individuals and institutions, interest, periodic or regular grants, funds collected from the charity boxes, and other income.

11. The financial assets of the organization are divided into disposable cash, a contingency fund, and a perpetual fund.

12. The contingency fund will be made up from budget surpluses and savings. The perpetual fund will be made up of grants and dividends donated to the organization, and will be insured by interest bearing shares that will be kept in financial institutions.

In the third chapter, regarding members of the organization, there is the following paragraph.

13. The members of the organization must be adults, of the Mosaic faith, male or female, who pay membership fees of three rubles a year.

Note: People who have had legal proceedings or investigations initiated against them will not be accepted as members, nor will soldiers serving in a regular army.

Most of the paragraphs of the charter deal, as is customary, with the rights and obligations of the committee, the means of operation, general meetings, rights of members, means of reaching and executing decisions, as well as the means of operation of the auditing committee and the rights of its members. The signatories of the charter are registered as "founding members, residents of the city of Zgierz." They are:

Shlomo the son of Eliezer Sirkes, Mordechai Shmuel the son of Yisrael Zudkowicz, Gedalyahu Yedidya the son of Avraham Moshe Zwykielski, Yisrael Moshe the son of Avraham Rosowicz, Nathan the son of Yechiel Elberg, Eliezer the son of Shlomo Sirkes, Yaakov Mendel the son of Yitzchak Wechsler, Yitzchak the son of Avraham Nekritz.

The charter is signed by the Gubernator and vice Gubernator in Piotrkow, July 16, 1912.

These paragraphs were translated from Russian by A. Wien. The Russian text is stored in the government archives of the city of Lodz, Poland in section 108. A microfilm of this charter can be found in the general archives of the historical society in Jerusalem.

Part of the first page of the one time publication of "The Young Faithful of Israel", 1924.

127

Do mieszkańców miasta Zgierza.

Prezydent miasta Zgierza i Komitet milicyi upraszają wszystkich mieszkańców naszego miasta, ażeby w razie spodziewanego wkroczenia do Zgierza wojsk Cesarsko-niemieckich lub Austryackich, zachowali zupełny spokój i nie dali powodu do żadnych nieporozumień.

Wszelkie wystąpienia niezgodne z prawami stanu wojennego mogą sprowadzić na ludność i miasto największe nieszczęście.

Jednocześnie prosimy rodziców i opiekunów zwracać uwagę na młodzież i dzieci, ażeby takowe przez swą nieświadomość lub swawolę nie wywołały surowych kar ze strony wojska.

Zachowajmy rozwagę, spokój i porządek.

Zgierz, dnia 11 Sierpnia 1914 roku.

Prezydent miasta.

Komitet milicyi miejskiej.

A decree of the mayor from August 11, 1914 to the residents of Zgierz, as they entered into army service for Germany and Austria.
{Translator's note -- this decree is in Polish.}

„Zgierzer Blat" № 1. פרייז 50 גראשן.

זגערזשער בלאט

אונפארטייאיש · געזעלשאפטליך · ליטעראריש צווייי · וואכענבלאט.

Zgierz, 24 maja 1924.	ערשטער יארגאנג.	זגערזש, 24 מאי 1924.

אנאנסן-פרייז			אבאנאמענטס-פרייז	
א נאנצע דים 75 זל.		אדרעס פון רעדאקציע און אדמיניסטראציע :	א יאר 12 זל.	
„ האלבע „ 40 „			א האלב יאר 6 „	
„ פערטל „ 20 „	ŻYD. TOW. GIM. „MAKABI" w ZGIERZU.	א פערטל 3 „	
א. אז. וו.			אין אויגנעל פארקויף 50 גר.	

צו אונזערע לעזער !

אנגעפאנגען/גוט צוב זוויינן זאלצען מיר זיין בית איצם, מ'האָם אונז געסקולם אירנער סון די וויכטינסטע לעבצב'ס-פראגדן, יאקם יעל אונז געבן די לעבן.

חלק מן העמוד הראשון של „זגערזשער בלאט", דו-שבועון חברותי-ספרותי בלתי-מפלגתי (1924).

A portion of the first page of "Zgierzer Blat", edited by Yisrael Weinik, a bi-weekly, non-factional, sporting-social publication (1924).

The murder of Fishel Feldon on June 1, 1925.

{The text of the Mourning notice from the communal council (in Hebrew and Polish) regarding notice is as follows: (line breaks are not exact, due to word order differences in English and Hebrew):The Hebrew Community Council of Zgierz / expresses from the depths of its heart / the heavy mourning / over what happened in our town, that suddenly / a complete family from amongst our people was killed and slaughtered, in a / very cruel fashion, that had not occurred in such a manner from the time of the founding of our town / that the lives of five people should be cut off and exterminated / for no fault or sin of their own. / Alas! How great is this terrible tragedy! / Oh Land, Oh Land! Do not hide the blood that was spilled in this place / until the blood of those murdered / to the sorrow of our hearts and pain of our souls is avenged. / On Tuesday, the following were murdered. They were brought to their eternal rest / on Wednesday the 25th of Sivan, 5685. / Efraim Fishel the son of Yosef Feldon, 70 years old. / His wife Esther Malka Feldon, 68 years old. /Their daughter Perel Yehudit, a widow, 36 years old. / Their son Yerucham Feldon, 20 years old. / Avraham, 10 years.

The regulations of the "Yagdil Torah" organization (in Russian), which
was authorized by the governor in 1912. The heads of the Yagdil Torah
Yeshiva were Rabbi Mendel Noach Koren and Rabbi Chanoch
Ozorkower.

הילפֿס-קאָמיטעט פֿאַר איד. פּליטים פֿון דײַטשלאַנד
אין זגערזש

צו דער אידישער
באַפֿעלקערונג אין זגערזש!

זײַט עטליכע וואָכען געפֿונען זיך אין זגערזש די פּליטים, וועלכע
זענען אױסגעטוויזען געוואָרען פֿון דײַטשלאַנד. די דאָזיגע אומגליקליכע
זענען פּלוצלונג און אונבאַרמהאַרטע אַרױסגעריסען געוואָרען פֿון זײַערע
הײמען, דערוואַיַטערט פֿון זײַערע פֿאַטערס, מוטערס און קינדער און
געפֿונען זיך איצט אין אַ טראַגישער לאַגע.

אױף דעם ערשטען רוף פֿון דעם זגערזשער הילפֿס-קאָמיטעט האָט
די אידישע באַפֿעלקערונג אָבגעענטפֿערט אין אַ נישט גענינגענדער מאָס.

די הילפֿס-אַקציע פֿאַר די פּליטים, וועלכע געפֿינען זיך אין פֿאַר-
שידענע פֿונקטען פֿון לאַנד פֿאָדערט ריזיגע סומען, וועלכע דערגעהען
ביז 25,000 זל. טעגליך.

טויזענדער פֿון אונזערע ברידער, וועלכע זענען מאַראַליש און פֿיזיש
פֿאַרניכטעט געוואָרען, געפֿינען זיך צווישען אונז און וואַרטען אױף
אונזער הילף. מיר קענען זיך נישט באַענגעניצען מיט לאָקאַלער הילף.
אַ גרױסען טײל פֿון אונזער פֿאָנד מוזען מיר איבערווײַזען דעם צענט-
ראַלען הילפֿס-קאָמיטעטס פֿאַר אידישע פּליטים פֿון דײַטשלאַנד אין פֿוילען
וועלכער געפֿינט זיך אין וואַרשאַ.

די לאַגע פֿון טױזענדער מענשען, וועלכע האַבען פֿאַרלױרען דעם
דאַך איבער'ן קאָפּ, איז אַזוי טראַגיש, אַז אױב מיר וועלען נישט אָנ-
שטרענגען אַלע אונזערע כחות בכדי זײ צו האַלטפֿען, דראָהט זײ נױט
און הונגער.

מיר ווענדען זיך דעריבער צום צווייטען מאָל צו דער אידישער
באַפֿעלקערונג אין זגערזש מיט דעם הײסען אַפּעל: צאָהלט אײַן
מינדעסטענס אזוי פֿיל וויפֿיל עס מאַכט אױס אײַער קהלה-עסאַט.

די אַקציע פֿאָדערט ריזיגע געלד-מיטלען.
קײנער טאָר זיך נישט אָבזאָגען פֿון געבען הילף!
פֿאַרגעסט נישט. די הײמלאָזע!

דער הילפֿס-קאָמיטעט

12/23 1938

A decree of the Committee for Assistance of the Jewish refugees of
Germany, who were expelled by the Nazis to Zabonszyn in Poland. The
committee was set up in Zgierz in December, 1938, as it was in the other
cities of Poland.

B. The Development of Jewish Zgierz

Zgierz through the Perspective of Passing Years
(From the memoirs of the poet Yaakov Cohen)

(From "Netiv Chayay" "The Paths of my Life" - published by "Haboker", 5713 - 1953.)

{The note at the bottom of the page reads as follows :} The faithful description presented by the poet of his childhood in the city of Zgierz accurately portrays the nobility of the events in the life of a Jewish child of that era. This view on life, which depicts like a film the way of life in a traditional Jewish home saturated with religious nationalism, is fitting to take its place in the scroll of tribulations that seals the coffin on that life, which was suddenly swept away from the world by the sudden Holocaust. Therefore, we allot a significant space to present these stories of life, written by the author, a Zgierz native, who uses his literary style with realistic colors and especially enchanting spices. This section is fascinating, and will captivate the heart, as it presents an image of Zgierz.

"It seems that I do not remember anything of what I should truthfully call my city of birth, and if it were not related to me by faithful witnesses, I would not have imagined that I could see that town near Lodz as my birthplace, that house and those small rooms where I first found myself, and from where I first looked out and saw the world with its creations and breadth before me, the blue sky and the stars which moved above me.

I remember myself sitting in a highchair, with a wax bib tied to me lying on my waist, as my mother was feeding me. I remember cuddling up with my mother, hugging her neck with my two hands and asking: "Mother, will you love me forever?" I was already praised for my "wisdom." I remember how mother taught me to recite Modeh Ani [1], and how she sang various songs to me, with my head in her bosom. These songs included the well-known song "The White Goat." She sung to me even though my younger sister had already taken my place in the cradle. It is amazing that from all my memories, only this song is etched in my memory."

An Event on Purim

"I remember one event that is worthwhile to present, due to its essence. It was Purim, the time of the large Purim feast. The table was full and sparkling. The entire family was seated, as well as the guests. I was already

133

sitting in my customary seat, still near to mother, for I would certainly require her supervision, and perhaps even her assistance during the meal. Suddenly, a group of Purim players entered, wearing all sorts of funny clothing, and with masks covering their faces. One of them was wearing a white shroud, with his deep gray eyes looking out. The sight was so frightening that I fainted from fear. I heard mother chastising the players, and asking them to leave quickly. From that time, mother was very insistent that the Purim players not wear such frightening masks, so that they will not frighten the children." [2]

The House

"Our house looked out upon a small plaza that was known as the "old marketplace", as opposed to the "new marketplace", which was larger, and located in the upper portion of the city that was developing on the east side. This plaza was surrounded on three sides by blocks of old houses, most of them three stories high. The tower was on the fourth side, which was the west side opposite the town hall. The large town clock was on top of this tower. This clock chimed every hour, and all clocks in the city were set by it. In the basement of the tower, with closed shutters, was the prison. The plaza widened near the southwestern corner and became triangular. The Catholic Church jutted out from its depths. Its heavy bells rang with cold peals at set times, inspiring trepidation throughout the city. Our house was in the middle of the southern edge of the plaza. Our residence was on the middle floor. What more can I add about the feeling of this central square, which rose up from the place to the heart of a child.

Seven roads spread out from the plaza, each one leading through spotted fields into the deep forest. Behind the northern block of buildings was the small civic garden, with its modest meadows and heavy shade trees. Not far from it, toward the east, was the calm pond. It was quite wide, and its sparkling vapors danced over its dark, dangerous depths. In the winter it froze over completely, and turned into a play area for the youth, who would skate on it. It gained some of its water from a small river, the Bzura, which passed through the outskirts of the city. The Jewish women would go to the river to immerse their new dishes and utensils in its flowing waters, in order to make them fit for use [3].

The entrance to our house was through a wide, arched gate, which led to the courtyard. A small gate opened up on the left side, and led to the ground floor dwellings. A curved staircase led to the second floor, where our dwelling was. Our dwelling had four rooms. All of the windows, except for the kitchen window, faced the plaza. This small child stood for long periods of time next to the windows, absorbing the wonders of the expansive sky, with it clouds taking on forms, all sorts of stars twinkling in the evenings, sparkling and giving hints of their secrets to the gray world. The silent plaza spread out below, paved with large and small stones. Life continued silently next to the blocks of houses, disturbed at times with noisy wagons passing by. Two wells stood in the plaza, at some distance from each other. They were available for anyone who required their waters. After some time, the water of one of the wells dried up, and another well was dug in a different place, which gave very good and tasty water that only the wells in the mountains of Switzerland, with their taste of Genesis, reminded me after so many yeas of their very pure life giving sustenance. Four thick leafed trees decorated the side of the town hall. Each pair was planted in a large, deep, metal planter. Young chestnut trees, in a straight line, lined the tarred sidewalks on the other three sides of the plaza. Every Tuesday and Friday, the "small market" took place on the two opposite sides of the plaza, with baskets of splendid fruit and vegetables. Every Friday, there were also wagons and handcarts of the neighboring farmers, who brought foul, eggs, potatoes, and other produce from their fields. Every four months, on a Wednesday, the "fair" came, and the plaza was filled to the brim with all types of merchandise, vessels, furniture, clothing, jewelry, delicacies and toys - an entire world of wonders to curious youthful eyes.

In the depths of the courtyard, there was a horse stable, which was used by the Russian captains, who lived alone one after the other on the third floor of our house. They were of varying characters, but they all carried themselves with a kind of silent haughtiness, as if they were taking pride in their polished army fatigues and their thin, well-kept forms that differentiated them from the rest of humanity. I remember my surprise when I learned that they wore a corset under their fatigues, exactly as do women."

After he describes in detail the courtyard, the garden and the sukka that his father built for himself, in accordance with Jewish law, made of smoothed wooden planks, replete with a wooden floor, windows and a retractable roof set upon small wheels [4], he begins to describe the dwelling itself. He begins:

"If I attempt to describe the rooms in our dwelling and everything in them in accordance with the size of the place that they take in my heart, I would not be able to do so sufficiently. For there was no wall, corner, oven, door, shelf or window blind, not even any piece of furniture or any vessel, natural or man-made item, which was not an integral part of my existence. I will therefore have to satisfy myself with the smallest of the small in order to present some memories of them, which will only be symbolic."

With exactness and a display of exceptional memory, he describes each room with its furniture, vessels and decorations. The pictures hanging on the wall in the dining room were, first of all, of his father, and his paternal grandmother. Later there were pictures of Moses Montefiore and the famous benefactor Baron Rothschild. There were two other pictures, one of the Gaon Rabbi Naftali Tzvi Berlin the head of the Yeshiva of Volozhin [5], who as, according to father, a relative; and the second one of Rabbi Yitzchak Elchanan, the Rabbi of Kovno. When he comes to describe the bookcase, he writes:

"A special feeling of awe came upon me slowly with regard to the bookcase, even though it never changed its place, especially after the splendid volumes of the Reem edition of the Babylonian Talmud, occupying an entire shelf, took their place upon it. The golden letters on the spines of the giant books looked out through the upper glass doors and instilled wonder into the child due to their great mystique."

The Father - Reb Binyamin Hirsch Cohen

"My father was distinguished by the glory of his visage and his height. The blue of his handsome eyes and the softness of his shining skin peered over his well combed reddish-brown beard. His tall and erect stature befitted his long cloak, which only reached to his knees, and distinguished him and set him apart from the thousands of people around him. His appearance exuded grandeur, and his stately and independent look had something in it of a ruler exalted over people, instilling awe, and not only in the heart of a young person. His image is engraved upon my heat for all my days, as the image of 'the' father with the definitive article, as a sign and symbol for all fathers in the world.

136

Father also had a deep, sweet baritone voice, with a rich key, and his singing filled the house with the glory of the Temple. As well, the sweetness of the humming of his voice as he was studying Talmud carried with it latent majesty, and pervaded all rooms with a festive spirit. His style of educating his children was of the old style, with strictness. However, it was very broadminded. He never laid a hand upon a child. His warnings were sufficient. The commandment of honoring one's father stood in its full strength, and the awe of the father was upon the entire house. He governed with strict politeness. When my father rested in the afternoon, it was forbidden even to raise a voice in the third room. "Father is sleeping!"

My father was religiously orthodox, and very careful with all of the commandments. However, he also was enthusiastic with modern knowledge, and he respected every ability and trade. He was a staunch misnaged [6]. He ignored Hassidism. His opinion of the abilities of the all-powerful "Tzadik", and of their stories of wonders was not that far from the opinion of extreme maskilim on these matters.

He was very charitable, and not a day passed where he did not fulfill that commandment. On Sabbaths and festivals there were always two poor people dining at our table. On weekdays, there was a Yeshiva student, a soldier on a meal rotation, or just an ordinary needy person. My father was regarded as a well-to-do person in the family, and people certainly exaggerated about his wealth. He always answered, and he never turned away a poor person. He also gave tithes from his income.

One of my father's fundamental traits was a love of cleanliness and order. His clothes were always like new, and everything in the house had to be in its correct place. No spot of dust escaped his discerning eye. When the children got undressed, they had to fold their clothes nicely and lay them on the appropriate chair. Books had to be treated with respect, and even the fraying of the edge of a page in them was considered improper. Any spot of ink on a notebook, and certainly on a finger, was greeted with a stern rebuke.

This was certainly a result of his well-developed sense of esthetics. It can be assumed that any beautification that he made with holy objects, for the sake of glorifying the commandment, was also to satisfy his esthetic needs.

Above anything, he loved song. A beautiful melody could make him forget the world around him. If a cantor would visit the city, he would stay with us. My father's love of music was certainly an inheritance from his forbears. His eldest brother was a cantor, and his second brother used to lead

137

services on the High Holydays. Even his father, as I have heard from several people, loved song, and was attached to music in an exceptional manner. The lineage of musical ability also came to him from his maternal grandmother, who played the violin."

The Mother

Yaakov Cohen speaks about his mother with emotion. Her exact facial expressions are engraved in his memory. From a small, faded photograph, he remembers her "standing at full height, with her left hand resting on her half-page sized engraved title, and her right hand holding onto an umbrella propped up on the floor. The hem of her dress reaches the floor. The edges of the dress are fringed, and the dress has many buttons. She wore a fur pelt draped over her shoulders, flowing down over her chest."

"My mother was like a silent light to me", explains Yaakov Cohen with love and reverence, "a light that sustained my soul with the light of love and purity of heart. She was also a refuge of safety where I could be protected at times of danger and fear."

"As evening descended on the Sabbath day, as the dark shadows fell upon the house and the voice of my father and his two poor guests could be heard as they were singing Sabbath hymns at the third Sabbath meal as the Sabbath was departing, and there was a feeling of sadness an mystery in the air, I would join my mother and cling to her as she would look out the windowat the darkening sky and whisper chapters of Psalms by heart. The darkness increased, and my father finished the grace after meals and got up with his guests to go to the synagogue. Fear overtook me, and I grabbed hold of my mother who embraced me with her arms and placed me under her warm shawl. I closed my eyes and listened to the voice of my mother singing to me, full of sadness for the world, which could not be assuaged. However, the sweet voice of my mother's song, coming from the source of eternal love, comforted me somewhat."

The poet asks his soul: "At that time, did not the cold wing of the anguish of the world touch me, and my soul desired song and comfort, refuge through song?"

He continues describing his memories:

"One more pain, a stormy pain that burned and gnawed at me for my entire life, came to me for the first time through the mouth of mother."

138

"Evening fell. Father went to the synagogue, and the lights were not on in the rooms. Turned to and fro and saw: mother had lit a small candle; she sat on a hassock in front of the chair, placed the candle upon the chair, and began to read from a small book with the voice of stifled weeping. Startled, I looked at her from afar. I listened to her voice, and I was also close to weeping. Later, I strengthened myself and approached her. She hugged me with her arm, and continued reading.

"What are you reading, mother", I asked. She read and read, and when she stopped she began to tell me of a far off land that is ours, the Land of Israel. A cruel enemy came, destroyed it and murdered, and stole it from our hands. Rivers of blood were spilled. The enemy had no mercy upon the elderly or the women. He slaughtered thousands of children... On this day, Tisha Beav, he set fire to the great, splendid Holy Temple, and it was burnt.

What did I understand from her words? I saw slaughtered children, rivers of blood flowing, and the leaping flames, and it seemed that the blade of the sword also affected me, injuring me with an incurable wound. One spark of those flames took hold of my heart, and can never be extinguished."

My Maternal Grandparents

"I met my maternal grandfather, Reb Chaim the son of Reb Tzvi Hirsch Wandrowski, when I was a fourteen year old boy. He was already old and weak, and he made an impression upon me as a "righteous and upright man." He was a ritual slaughterer (shochet). He was soft and placid apparently the religious aspect of kosher shechita softened the cruelty of that line of work. The job of judge, his second job, better characterized him.

Grandmother Zelda, from the Wigodski family, was an intelligent and sharp woman. She ran a soap factory and a soap store. She gave birth too many children, of whom four sons and four daughters survived. Grandmother herself had nine brothers. One of them, Uncle Getzel, was a grain merchant who had nineteen children from two wives. The intelligence and acuity of grandmother, along with her kind heart, was passed down to most of her descendents. Her eldest child, Moshe, was considered to be a genius in his youth. His parents and teachers saw him as a future rabbi. However, he became a maskil, and chose a different path. He followed in the path of his Uncle Getzel as a grain merchant, and settled in Konotop, a suburb of Chernikhov, Russia.

139

Another son, Zalman, was the writer Z. Wandroff, who became well known in the world of Yiddish literature, with his humorous stories. Some of his stories were translated into Russian. Once, Shalom Aleichem visited him and then wrote about a new writer who imitated him without shame. This was my uncle.

My father, who generally liked Uncle Moshe, my mother's brother, and spoke of him with praise, did not hesitate on one occasion to denigrate him for the sparks of "apikorsut" ("apostasy") in him, in that he would treat lightly the sages of past generations. For example, when discussing that a certain Talmudic sage said such and such, he would comment: "If I was around in those days, I would also be a Talmudic sage…" Comments such as this, which father brought down in his name, made a dent in my heart and opened up a door to bold thoughts."

In the Old Cheder

"In the spring of 5647 (1887), as I was completing my sixth year, an old teacher came to town. He was Lithuanian, and his name was Reb Kasriel. He was older than seventy, and he took pride in that he had served as a teacher for one hundred terms."

"For three years the shadow of the Old Cheder oppressed me. It repeatedly oppressed my soul and my tender emotions. This cheder-prison forced me to come each morning and spend the majority of my day."

"I will not deny this hard old man his appropriate dues, and I will not deny him the recognition of the benefits that came to me via him, even though it was through a somewhat substandard manner. After all, I gleaned my first knowledge of the Hebrew language from him, as well as the ability to read the splendid books of the Bible that gave wings to my imagination and fed my soul with waters of life from the ancient roots of our nation.

Reb Kasriel was short in height and awkward in appearance. His face was bloated and puffy, somewhat red, and covered with the flowing hairs of his white beard that reached to his jaws. He had thick, white, slightly unruly eyebrows and small watchful eyes. He only had a place to sleep and the permission to use one room for his teaching in one small, two-room house that belonged to a young couple. His wife stood behind the curtain, taking care of her pots.

140

I began my studies with the book of Leviticus. From that era, I have one of the most pleasant memories of my life.

It was Friday, and I was sitting in front of the Rebbe reading Chumash (Pentateuch). The door opened and my mother entered. From under her shawl, she brought forth a bowl of fresh aromatic carrot pudding, cooked in fat.

She said: "I did not know exactly where the cheder was, and behold I heard a wonderful voice, the voice was the voice of Jacob [7]."

The Rebbe gave me permission to interrupt my studies. I sat and ate my carrots, and the eyes of my mother were glowing and joyous. From that time, I never remember an occasion when I was served carrot pudding, and I did not remember the taste of those carrots and the glowing loving eyes of my mother.

I only began to taste the true flavor of the Old Cheder during the following year, when the Rebbe found a small dwelling in an attic. The cheder had two windows, and there was a small dark bedroom next to it. The cheder was run according to tradition, with the students remaining all day, from 9:00 a.m. until 7:00 or 8:00 p.m., with an hour and a half break for lunch.

We studied Chumash with the commentary of Rashi. The stories of the Bible enthralled me, and I studied diligently. We also studied the musical trope of the Torah and the Haftarah (prophetic readings).

The situation changed completely when we began to study Talmud. The first Mishnah was "He who rides on the back of an animal" from tractate Baba Metzia. From the Mishnah with its strange logic, we immediately moved to Gemara [8]. Nothing stuck in my mind. I did not understand anything, and I made no effort to understand.

I and my friend Yaakov Meir (the youngest son of our relative Reb Shlomo Horowitz) sat at the narrow end of the table and studied from the same book. Across us on the other side, crouching like and old bear, was the Rebbe, without a coat. His giant tallit katan [9] covered his entire torso, and its fringes extended below his knees. His yarmulka stood up prominently on his head, and beside the Talmud volume in front of him was his symbol of authority - his threefold strap. His watchful eyes were piercing. His lips were constantly moving, as he asked questions and repeated his questions. He would wait as an animal waiting to pounce on its prey. On occasions, he would move his place and draw near, stand close to a student, and repeat a question over and over again. He would pinch his ear or slap his cheek, once and then a second time or he would order the young child to stand up and prepare himself to receive a whipping.

One of my friends, Woltek (Wolf), the son of Yissachar Schwartz, knew how to tell all sorts of frightening stories about demons and evil spirits that are found in all sorts of dark, unclean places. It was difficult for a child with an imagination as I had to hide his fear of these frightening spirits as I returned home alone on winter nights from the cheder without even a flashlight in my hand, with the dark shadows jumping from all directions. This Woltek had a twin brother in the cheder, named Simcha. The two of them were a group unto themselves. He was the sharper of them. One day Simcha came alone, for his brother was ill. Not even ten days later, the frightful news arrived that Woltek was no longer with us. I feel as if I am discharging and obligation as I erect a monument in writing for a beloved friend, who possessed a "spark", that was just about to be ignited as it was extinguished."

In the Cheder Hametukan [10] and outside it

After Y. Cohen had concluded three years of study in the cheder of Kasriel, he transferred to the Cheder Hametukan of Yaakov Binyamin Katznelson.

The author writes: "A new spirit pervaded in the new cheder, a freer spirit with a new and free light, and I absorbed the light with all of my youthful senses and with all the desire for knowledge and life that I possessed. Nevertheless, some shadows of the old cheder still drifted around, and stifled the young soul. The attachment to the school bench for the entire day with the exception of a recess for lunch was one of the weighty legacies of that cheder that my young heart had hoped would change. However, I was interested in the new studies, and the relationship with the teacher was entirely different.

I brought with me the repository of knowledge from my previous studies. Nevertheless, it seemed as if we were starting everything from the beginning. Along with the Early Prophets [11], we studied the book of Bereshit (Genesis) with a German translation and the commentary of Mendelsohn. This might sound curious, but the fact is that I learned more German than Hebrew by studying this translation, for I already had a proper knowledge of Hebrew.

142

Indeed, it was only at that time, through the study of grammar, that I began to acquire a correct understanding of the Hebrew language, with the beauty of its various forms. The teacher wrote down the roots of the verbs. Each root was used as a sample, and the seven forms of conjugation were written down on paper, which was then pasted on cardboard tablets. From there, I copied them all into my notebook. It did not take very long before all the root forms of the verbs were familiar to me. Then we moved on to different areas of grammar. I became enthralled with the internal grammatical rules of the language, which were similar to the rules of any other natural object, plant, animal, or inanimate object, along with all the exceptions to the rule, which seemed as if they were necessary from their sources.

A special teacher came to teach us Russian, arithmetic, and other elementary subjects. I already had some knowledge of these subjects, brought from my home, and my thirst for knowledge along with my diligence helped me to progress quickly, leaving all of my friends behind. There, I reached such a stature that required special consideration and treatment from the teacher.

Father took great pleasure in my progress. As a native of Lithuania, he had no toleration for the reading style of Polish Jews, who pronounce a kametz like a shuruk, a shuruk like a chirik, and a tzerei like a patach followed by a yod [12]. I learned the proper grammatical inflections of words, which later on eased my integration into the community in Israel.

My feelings of deep reverence for my father became stronger when he began to take me with him to the synagogue on Sabbaths and festivals. His seat was in the right corner of the eastern wall. In the left corner was the seat of Reb Shlomo Horowitz, our relative, who was at that time the gabbai (trustee) of the Beis Midrash. He was impressive in appearance, and it seemed that the two of them were the pillars upon which the house stood.

It goes without saying that the sources and texts in the synagogue, where my father took an active part at all times, enthralled my heart. The entire atmosphere in our home was one of tradition, holiness and nobility. The complete Sabbath rest with its purity of thought, the splendor and glory of the festivals, in particular of Passover, the regal Seder night, the new dishes, the new clothing, the four questions, the mysterious visit of Elijah the Prophet, all of these accompanied by the glorious visage of father and his melodious singing, father's caresses, mother's special delicacies, all of these will never be erased from my heart.

143

My teacher had me learn by heart the poem "Yonah Homia" by Meir Halevi Latris, and he later taught me the tune to it. I brought the song home, and my sister Rachel quickly added it to her rich repertoire, which included songs in Hebrew, Yiddish, Polish, Russian, German, and even Ukrainian. Song was an inseparable part of our home life. Even my mother from time to time would hum a popular song, and infuse it with the extra spirit of her intimate warmth. Sabbath evenings were almost entirely dedicated to song. Father would repeat the old and new tunes that he had learned. On warm nights, his voice would waft out of the open windows into the outside silence, and on occasion, groups of people would gather below to listen to his "concert."

Singing in our household received a new and strong impetus when my father answered the request of the honorable men of the congregation who worshipped in the Beis Midrash to lead the Musaf services on the High Holy Days. He agreed on the condition that he be given four or five singers to assist him. My father, of course, did not request any payment for his prayers, but his assistants received their payment. I would absorb most of the melodies and review them after the holidays. One year, when my father approached the prayer leader's lectern, surrounded by his singers to the right and left of him upon the steps that lead up to the Holy Ark, I took my place among them to their surprise, and sung with them to the best of my ability. I continued singing with them for the remainder of the Musaf services for that set of High Holy days, but I did not do so in subsequent years.

In his choir of assistants, once my father discovered a youth who had a great theoretical knowledge of music. He knew how to read and write musical notes, and he had a large collection from the famous cantors: Zultzer, Libendowski and others. He had already served with several cantors, and he came to our town as an assistant to our old cantor, who had taken ill. His family name was Kadish, and he was small and thin. He had the voice of a second tenor, very sweet and well trained. My father retained him and took him as his teacher, giving him a special room, so that he would teach him the cantorial compositions that he was familiar with. For some reason, this singer had to leave town after about three months.

One of the greatest joys in my young life was the trip to Lodz. There was not yet a train or the inter-city electric tram, so the connection between Zgierz and Lodz was with horse drawn wagons. These wagons did not move from their parking places until they were filled to capacity. When my father was in a hurry, he would hire a special wagon. At such times, I would have the opportunity to accompany him. I enjoyed the journey, which passed through open fields, flower patches, wondrous expanses of forests that excited me with their dark mystery, and again through expanses of fields and vineyards. The journey was long, and I was very impatient to see the big city, which was in the eyes of a child from a small, quiet town like a mighty city filled with noise and wondrous things. I was very jealous of the wagon drivers who traveled their daily and saw all of these sights.

My Bar Mitzvah

When I reached the thirteenth year of my life, like all the Jewish boys in the area who kept the traditions, I waited with silent joy for the day that was considered for many generations as the passage into adulthood.

I already had a repertoire of poems, or more precisely, attempts at poetry, in which I attempted to express the powers of the pure emotions of my soul in various forms.

Our Cheder Hametukan became more and more progressive in its ways, and it followed the modern teaching methodologies. At the beginning of 5654 (1894), our teacher rented a larger premises, and he brought his family from Karelitz. In one room, the largest, he set up the benches and arranged them at the various sides of the room. Every side was like a class unto itself. A different teacher was responsible for the lower grades. Class time was set from the hours of 9:00 1:00, and 3:00 - 7:00. The time devoted to secular subjects increased significantly. We also had a half-hour for relaxation, when the students went out to the yard to get fresh air and to play.

In those days, Y. B. Katznelson did not yet have the patriarchal appearance, with a long flowing white beard, which was made famous by the book written by his daughter. His bear was reddish brown and not full. His face was thin and his entire body was skinny. He wore a coat that reached to his knees, and he wore a hard felt hat upon his head, which gave him the appearance of a maskil, but one who had not yet left the influence of orthodoxy. He was not comfortable in his speech, and when he wanted to explain something, he would stutter, repeat, stumble, and reach the end of his statement with difficulty.

My father saw this as a deficiency in him; however mother related to him with trust and friendship. She also took care of him while he was ill and in

145

need of help and care. For about two or three weeks after that, he would come to us every day at noon, and my mother would prepare for him special light food, until he felt himself to be healthy and whole. For a long time after that he would remember this, and elaborate on her fine character.

One the second floor of the house, where our cheder was located, the Rebbe of the Hassidim lived. Apparently, he was not one of the famous ones, for not too many people came to consult him. However, once I saw a sick man lying on the Rebbe's steps. He had apparently been possessed by a demon ("dybbuk"), and he was brought from a nearby town so that the Rebbe could tend to him. The sick man himself was middle-aged, with an unkempt beard and a distorted face. He was lying on his back on the steps, and a melody was coming out of his mouth
- the tune of the prayers of the High Holy Days. It was as if melody after melody was arising from his belly. The hallway and stairs below were filled with people."

Yaakov Cohen describes: "It seemed very strange that from the vernacular languages, we studied Russian and German rather than Polish. The Russian government was certainly not concerned with this, and in the merchant circles, the knowledge of this language was not considered critical. This is one more indication as to how tied up business was at that time in the hands of the Jews and Germans."

Yaakov Cohen describes the great advancement in his Hebrew and Bible studies: "The eyes were in the book, but the head far off. Nevertheless, there were many chapters that were not only on the tip of my tongue, but that I also knew their exact place on the page of the book. I was already expert in all aspects of grammar, and I knew by heart many of the poems of Adam HaCohen and of Michel (Micha Yosef Cohen Lebensohn). However, father refused to purchase for me the poems of Yehuda Leib Gordon, lest this "apostate" have a bad influence upon me.

I do not remember what caused this; however one day we, the students of the highest class in Hebrew, took it upon ourselves, along with our teacher, to only speak Hebrew among ourselves. The beginning was difficult, however we got used to the language, and we slowly became able to express our thoughts with an appropriate speed. Thus did the speaking of the Hebrew language overtake me while I was still sitting on the school bench.

In those days, Ben Avigdor published his "Sefer HaAgora". A pleasant spirit blew from the pages, as a refreshing spring breeze."

146

The Luster of First Love

"She was the daughter of the landlord of our school" here: The landlord, Reb Binyamin Greenberg, was one of the town notables. He had a large stockpile of wood and planks for building in his yard. His house was at the corner of Lecicka and Parzenciwska Streets.) "We had numerous opportunities to meet. These chance meetings later turned into secret planned ideas almost daily. Utza (Eva-Chava) was a beautiful girl, thin with a straight neck, and in her gray eyes there was a delightful intelligence. She was approximately a half a year older than I was, and she seemed to be slightly taller than I was. She attended the Polish school as did all the girls, and she was top in her grade. It is possible that this fact was one of the first things that attracted us to each other. We chatted about everything, but we never said a word about the feelings in our heart. We were too young and shy. However, the fact that we met daily in secret places said a great deal. Every day, I eagerly waited for this meeting, and my heart was singing when I was with her, enjoying the splendor of her eyes, as her face was smiling love to me. When father and my teacher found out about this, we were forced to stop these meetings. The interruption lasted longer than we had at first imagined.

However, I did not forget her. In the year 5660 (1900), when I was already an adult, and given over to different worlds and horizons, there awakened in my heart a longing for her, as is testified in my poem "In A Summer Night". After several decades, the desire was reawakened again. This was also expressed in a poem, which described the idealism of this magic time, the time of the first blossoming of the heart."

In the chapter "Years from the Past", Cohen explains that "the pains of growing up often express themselves in different areas of behavior." He describes his deep feeling of loneliness, and "the longing pain of the youth that expanded and became the pain of the world." He continues:

"How wondrous is it that on frequent occasions I sought refuge in the garden, field or forest. For a long time, I would go out daily in the morning to the small civic garden, sit in a shady corner, and study the books of "Langsheid" in order to learn French. I received these from Yissachar Schwartz after his eldest son Shmuel traveled to Paris to study in an

147

engineering school. He also learned French from those books. The paths of the garden were empty at that time, and I was able to devote myself to my studies without interruption - until the garden itself with its heavenly silence interrupted me from the frozen letters. I accepted its mastery, and I willingly gave myself over to my younger and older brothers, who were standing and secretly weaving the fabric of their youthful lives, each in accordance to his inclination. A wooden stage of the military band was still standing in the middle of the garden. For some reason, the concerts had ceased for quite some time, and I remembered with sadness the days when I would come as a young child with my mother to the garden, and it would be like a joyous festival, with melodious trumpets. Everything was brilliant, sparkling and bustling, with numerous mothers and children, wearing variegated clothing, walking and filling the benches so that there was no place left. Now, there is no band, no mother…

In the afternoon, as the day was declining, I would go out the forest, often with a book in my hands, however I would never actually come to read it in actuality. The mighty images of the forest swept me away and left no room for other images. What could a book written by a human do when the book of G-d was open with its thousands of secrets and wonders of life, with its exalted secrets and whispers."

A few words about the city of Zgierz.

The population of Zgierz numbered about 20,000 souls, of which only about 3,000 were Jews.

Nevertheless, there were many who esteemed Zgierz (next to the Germans, who had even a smaller population) as the premier industrial city in the Lodz district, and came to dwell there. Zgierz excelled in the manufacture of heavy and expensive textiles for suits, garments, and summer and winter coats. Textile manufacturers competed to design the best patterns, and numerous looms and steam driven devices clanked away during the day, and some of them at night, marking the passage of time. The looms were used mainly by the Jews, and the steam driven devices in the larger factories were mainly operated by Christian workers. It would be an exaggeration to state as is written in another book, that the entire city was immersed in this factory, and was immersed in the smoke of the chimneys. The atmosphere of this small town, from which in ten minutes one could travel from the center of town to the lush fields and forests surrounding it, was clear, healthy and good, in opposition to the difficult and polluted atmosphere of several sections of crowded, overpopulated Lodz.

In Lodz as in Zgierz, the textile manufactures were mainly Germans and Jews. The workers and merchant assistants were only Jews. In the year 5652 (1892), when the Jews of Moscow were expelled, many of them came to settle in Lodz, and caused business in the city to flourish greatly. The neighboring communities benefited as well. There were two seasons during the year, autumn and spring, when the merchants would come to Lodz to display their wares. Many of them also came to Zgierz to complete their inventory with expensive textiles. The workers from Zgierz were in touch with their fellow workers in Lodz, and drew on their vast experience regarding the valuation of merchandise and the granting of credit.

I had a special relationship with the porters who came to pack up the merchandise for export. There were three partners in this enterprise: Yonis (Yonatan), Abba Yankel, and Shalom Mechel (Michael). The three of them were in their sixties, and their strength was still in its prime. On several occasions I was surprised to see Yonis, the oldest of them, small in stature, thin and white haired, carrying two heavy rolls of cloth on his back, walking straight and carefully, without any difficulties. He was extremely quiet, and humbly accepted the commands, and even their rebukes, of his peers. Abba Yankel was entirely different. He was hefty, and most of his hair was still brown. He was quite verbose and loved to tell jokes and hum tunes.

Shalom Mechel was the most diligent of them and also the youngest. He conducted the financial aspect of the business. He was tall, with bright, intelligent eyes. Not even one white hair could be seen on his black beard. He was also the biggest tippler of the three of them, and outlived the others. Brought to print by Z. F. and Y. A. M.

Zgierz and Kotzk by Yaakov Kirshenbaum of Kiryat Bialystok

The writer of these lines, a native of Zgierz, is the scion of a family that goes back sixteen generations, and was active in the Jewish world for a period of 400 years. The first generation came to Jerusalem in the 16th century. The second generation left Jerusalem to go to the Lithuanian Yeshivas. The last six generations lived in Zgierz and cemented the ties between their birthplace and the Kotzk Hassidic dynasty. A young woman of Zgierz became the Kotzker rebbetzin, and an Admor (Hassidic master) of Kotzk became a partner in the textile factory of Zgierz.

In the first half of the previous century, Reb Yaakov Moshe Poizner lived in Zgierz. He was a dedicated Hassid of Rabbi Mendele Morgenstern of holy blessed memory, the first Admor of Kotzk. Aside from this, he was a pioneer of the textile industry of Zgierz. He competed bitterly against the Germany manufacturers who set up in our city and succeeded in receiving an edict from Commissar Witkowski, the governor of the Mazowiecki area, dated March 30, 1821, forbidding Jews to acquire immovable objects and working in the textile industry. (From this we learn that 150 years ago, the German manufacturers were concerned about the competition from the Jewish manufacturers, and took steps to make their steps difficult.)

Reb Yaakov Moshe Poizner's wife, Rachel, was the daughter of Reb Leibish Berliner of Piotrkow, a well-known man and a descendent of the Gaon Reb Tzvi Ashkenazi of holy blessed memory, the author of the "Chacham Tzvi". Reb Leibish refused to accept the yoke of the rabbinate upon him, and occupied himself with business. Reb Leibish's grandfather was the Gaon Reb Hershel Lewin, the Rabbi of the Kollel of Berlin and Prussia for approximately thirty years. It was because of this that his grandchildren and great-grandchildren took on the name Berliner.

The products of Reb Yaakov Moshe Poizner's factory reached to the far off places of the Russian Empire of that time. Of course, his home was open for any Rabbi and Hassid who passed through our town. He was looked upon as the father of his Jewish workers, who included some Hassidim as well. He participated in their joy and sorrow. They traveled to Kotzk together, and the hall of the factory was often turned into a shtibel. Rosh

150

Chodesh festive meals [14] or festive meals for other occasions would take place there. Reb Yaakov Moshe even made the Kotzker Rebbe a partner of the factory, for good luck and blessing.

The son-in-law of Reb Yaakov Moshe Poizner was Reb Yitzchak Zelig Frankel, an enthusiastic Kotzker Hassid. He took over the directorship of the factory after his father-in-law's passing. Reb Yitzchak Zelig spent more time with his Rebbe in Kotzk than he did in his own town. He succeeded in marrying one of his children into the Kotzker dynasty. The middleman was Reb David Morgenstern of holy blessed memory (the eldest son of Reb Mendele of Kotzk). His daughter Yocheved married Rabbi Chaim Yisrael Morgenstern, the future Admor of Kotzk-Pilawa. The wedding took place in the year 5617 (1857) in Kotzk, and the grandfather Reb Mendele was present at the wedding.

The Admor Reb Chaim Yisrael, who was a partner in his father-in-law's factory, moved to Pilawa, and after the death of his father, Reb David he was crowned as the Admor of the Hassidim of Kotzk Pilawa. In the year 5645 (1886), he published his book "Shalom Yerushalayim", in which he requested that the Orthodox Jews of Poland settle in the Land of Israel, "They should purchase land and settle there, work the land, and bring out bread from the land with their own toil in agriculture and other occupations." In his book he brought proofs from Jewish law (Halacha), lore (aggada), and mysticism (kabbalah), that there was a holy duty incumbent upon every Jew to participate in the redemption of the soil of the Land of Israel.

In another place he writes: "When the government will give permission for thousands of Jews to make aliya to the Land of Israel, it will certainly be a mitzvah and a duty according to all opinions, even in this time...." "For if the land will go out from their hands and come into Jewish hands, our redemption will be soon in coming, and our re-establishment for good will come speedily in our days."

The Admor Reb Chaim Yisrael died in the year 5665 (1905). His children were the Admorim Reb Tzvi of Lukow, Reb Moshe Mordechai of Pilawa, Reb Yitzchak Zelig of Sokolow, and Reb Yosef of Kotzk. They were all of Zgierz descent from the side of their mother Yocheved, and took interest in their family from Zgierz.

151

The second son-in-law of Reb Yitzchak Zelig Frankel was Reb Avraham Hirsch Glicksman, a Kotzker Hassid, the son of Reb Baruch Bendet Glicksman, the Rabbi of Lusk and the author of many books. After his father-in-law's death, he inherited the textile factory, and moved it to Lodz in the year 5625 (1865). Reb Avraham Hirsch's son, Bendet Glicksman - also a Zgierz native - turned it into a limited company that issued shares. The shares remained in the hands of the family, and the products of this factory were well known even outside the borders of Poland.

Incidentally, it is fitting to note that Mr. Shinar, one of the grandchildren of Reb Avraham Hirsch Glicksman, was one of the founders of the "Beit Lochmei Hagetaot" museum ("The Museum of the Fighters of the Ghetto") named for Yitzchak Katznelson. He served as its first director.

The Kirshbaum family was also connected to the Poizner, Frankel and Glicksman families.

Reb Hirsch Kirshbaum married Leah, the daughter of Reb Yaakov Moshe Poizner. He lived in Zgierz. One of his children, Reb Noach Kirshbaum - the father of the writer of these lines - left Zgierz together with the factory, and moved to Lodz. He was active in the factory for many years. He was a Hassid of Pilawa-Sokolow, the heir of Kotzk Hassidism.

The brother of Bendet Glicksman, the last owner of the factory prior to the outbreak of the war, was the well-known historian Reb Pinchas Zelig Glicksman, who was famous for his great research into the spiritual life of Polish Jewry. He perished during the years of destruction of 1940-1945.

Zgierz Brings Honor to the Jewish Entrepreneurial Spirit by A. Litwin

From Brzeziny to Zgierz is very close: only a few stops. But what a difference, what a gulf lies between those two cities!

A heavy black pall falls over the soul when one enters into the dirty Jewish shantytown in the midst of the clean town with a full fledged European appearance and rich industry.

Zgierz and Tomaszow are two important points in Polish textile manufacturing. Higher class people of Zgierz stand taller than those of Lodz. Zgierz is not second to Lodz regarding a customer [15]. It does not push out merchandise to anybody; it does not build its existence upon "packages", that is upon yellow promissory notes.

Zgierz was at the peak of its power. The merchant who wishes to have a good piece of merchandise must come to it. He must come himself, and he must do so with hard cash. Only people with a steady company, with an impeccable reputation of many years duration would be permitted to come to Zgierz without ready cash.

Brzeziny's gloom lies on the heart, its pride is vacant for the Jewish "productivity", which is an ugly caricature of true productivity - it feels as its national self feelings are strongly raised up in Zgierz.

Zgierz is not Brzeziny. Zgierz has nothing to be ashamed of. She works precisely on such fine material, like a gentile from Bialystok. Zgierz is, like Bialystok , a Jewish manufacturing town. In Zgierz, the heart rejoices about the Jewish capital, about the Jewish entrepreneurial spirit.

And a few more words about its pride. It was only about 5-6 years earlier when the Jewish capital played a very peripheral role in Zgierz manufacturing. Only 10% of Zgierz factories belonged to Jews. The other manufacturers were all - Germans.

Now, Jews take the most prominent role in Zgierz industry. The German manufacturers slowly immigrated to Germany. Jewish manufacturers are now 70%.

And you have what to be happy about with respect to Jewish capital. Zgierz is not Brzeziny. Zgierz does honor to the Jewish entrepreneurial spirit. Zgierz is one of the most important points in Polish textile productions. And Zgierz is - a Jewish city...

However... Where are the Jews?

153

You go through the streets of Zgierz. It is appropriate to go through the streets of Zgierz. Here, the smokestacks are not in the middle of the city, as they are in Lodz. Here, one does not sense with the eyes the contrast between rich and dark ruins, as one usually sees in Lodz and in Warsaw.

Zgierz was above all a working city. Aside from a few large brick houses in the center where the electric tramway from Lodz stopped; most everywhere else there were small, clean workers houses. These houses were of a different type: one story with a room for two or three families. They had massive doors of the old German style, and a wide porch in the front with benches upon which to spend time after work. The streets were peaceful, quiet, and clean.

One goes further, and the few shadows disappear. Throughout there are either large factories or small brick houses; on the street, one encounters at every step German and Polish workers.

Off by the side, a little farther on, is a half collapsed, lowly shtibel [16]. In the window, you can notice a shadow from which comes to your ears the familiar "tic a toc" ... "tic a toc"... You go closer and make out the known portrait of the Lodzer Baluty; from Zdunska Wolia ... This is the last Mohawk.

Around an old, half destroyed armchair, and old, half wasted Jewish weaver is occupied ... the list of the Mohawk...

There, behind the synagogue, I tell you, the rabbi lives. The rabbi looks out from the window into the desolate street. It seems to be that aside from the Jewish woman with the old, tattered dress, with the wrinkled hands and face, sitting by her broken, empty closet and basket, and aside from the bent, sexagenarian weaver with the possibly hundred year old armchair, it is empty and desolate all around.

The rabbi is sitting there, deep in his thoughts, melancholy thoughts. He was the rabbi here for fourteen years. This is not a lot - fourteen years. He himself is not a particularly old man. And what has taken place around him during these fourteen years, above all during the last five or six years.

He will have to give a reckoning in the subversive world around him, in the jumble of questions that bring his thoughts and drive away his sleep; he searches for an answer to those questions in his bookcase. He ruminates in the Gemaras, and the early and latter commentators, as he searches for a way out of the tangle of new, difficult questions. He searches but does not find.

154

A remarkable thing takes place! Such a thing that never took place with any rabbi in any town or village. The rabbi of Zgierz began to occupy himself with completely different books. He reads and writes... reads and writes...

He does not write questions and responsa about the laws of divorces or marriages; he does not write novel ideas and commentaries about some sage or another. He writes page after page about... the national and economic desolation of the Jewish people.

He does not write theories or research ideas in books. He writes only what his eyes see, what he himself has experienced in the last five or six years. He writes with the agony of a prophet, with the blood of his heart... I am the man who witnessed agony [17].

He writes page after page, and comes to a sad, terrible conclusion:

The Jewish people are marching with hasty steps toward national and economic bankruptcy...

This presents iron clad facts about life. And the books, the new books demonstrate and declare that this is what has to be, this is what must be.

Nine or ten years previously, Jews lived here and nothing was bad. A hundred Jewish coachmen earned fine livelihoods. Then came the electric tramway from Lodz, and the next morning, the existence of all hundred coachmen was terminated.

Zgierz is a workers' town. The workers do not earn a bad living. The local German and Polish workers are not crude people. They eat, drink, and carry on respectably. Hundreds of Jewish families earn their livelihood from them. Then came the revolution with its new ideas. The workers learnt how to organize "spulkes" cooperatives. They learnt all of the commercial wisdom from the Jews, and were intelligent themselves - they had no more need of the Jews.

And the Mariowites [18], for example, completely killed off the Jewish existence. They had the opportunity to look well into their activity. Where else could they have as much power, as much influence, as much success as here. There was no anti-Semitism here in their section. Since they were here, the Polish workers were somewhat ideal; they conducted an empty life, the look with open eyes upon you and upon the world.

They learnt how do without the Jews completely. The Mariowites, if they wanted to embrace the Polish masses, which was indeed the main point of their doctrine - continued on and formed "spulkes". Everything in the life of the Polish workers was through their cooperatives. They did not have any bad thoughts against Jews; they snatched away their livelihood, and completely destroyed the foundation of their means of support.

Worse that everything, one cannot fault the strangers. What comes out of it: the present situation was worse than death. The situation grew worse from day to day.

A ruin was made of the Jews of Zgierz before their eyes. The situation grew sparser and sparser each day. Young and old had to pick up their walking sticks in order not to die from hunger.

Artisans were ruined in all of the stores. Only a few small stores and stalls remained, as a remembrance to the destruction [19]. However, that was for today - tomorrow they would be deceived.

Only one Jew remained here, who was not pushed out and removed or robbed of his human and civil rights by the electric tramway, the "spulke" or the Mariowites.

This is the weaver. He, who had a part in the building up, in the creation of Zgierz capital, of Zgierz riches, might and power, would not leave here under any circumstances.

The Jewish manufacturer came here and drove out the last Jew, who had full rights in Zgierz, his own brother…

And here, the questions for the rabbi of Zgierz were so muddled. As rabbi, he had to search for a merit for the Jewish people. As a Jew, he had to rejoice that Zgierz would once again be a Jewish city; where Jewish manufacturers had such a strong part in Zgierz industry.

However, how can there be a Jewish city without Jews? How can one rejoice over the good fortune of those who were the misfortune of their Jewish brothers? From then, who were cruel to their poor brethren, like the Mariowites, the "spulke", the priests?

And all of the muddled questions were merged together into one strong, terrible question in the rabbi's mind:

Will there still be a Jewish people?

From the new books in which the rabbi browses from time to time in order to find an answer to the new questions as the spiritual leader of the people, he felt obligated to answer. He knew that in every people, there were classes whose interests contradict each other. However, there are also interests that unite them, the opposing classes and parties.

He indeed sees, for example, how the lot of the Polish people is almost entirely different than that of the Jewish people. The struggles between them:

156

Naradowcy (Nationalist Party members), Postepowcy (Progress Party members), Ksieza (Clergy Party members), Socialists. In the competition with each other, each side wants to attract to it the people, the masses. That means that every side appreciates the people for their powers, shows them respect, has need of them, due to politics, or perhaps for the purpose of acting straight with the people and doing something for them. They educate them, they endeavor to organize them into some domain, and they show them new forms of living.

The people live somewhat, they begin the show culture, their economic situation strengthens, bridges are built between different portions of the people, and they unite.

The rabbi attempts to look for traces of such unity within the Jewish people. But there are none! It is exactly the opposite! Everyone for himself. Everyone is tearing farther from the other. Everyone is running from the other. If anything unites them, it is the general indifference to the lot of the Jewish masses. And there is no greater example of this than Zgierz.

The rabbi's glance turns to the invitation card that he had just received. He reads the card over again, and a deep pain twitches through his entire viscera.

They are inviting him. He must deliver a sermon on the topic of "strengthening the faith". They have chosen him to conduct the "dedication of the group". A group "of upholders of the faith" was founded by the Orthodox Jewish manufacturers of Zgierz. They have founded a Yeshiva in Zgierz. They are supporting a few dozen Yeshiva youth. They are concerned about the faith… that the religion should not, G-d forbid, go down.

He went to the dedication of their group, and he delivered a sermon to them. However it was not about strengthening the religion! No! He read a document of accusation. He demonstrated to them a greater destruction than the destruction of the religion. He showed them about the destruction of the nation. Dark, terrible colors did he portray to them. He wished to awaken sparks of love and pity for their people in their hearts…

When he concluded, a cold, angry murmur spread through the hall.

His ears distinctly heard: "The rabbi is becoming involved in matters that are not his business"; "A rabbi must speak about 'upholding the faith'"; "why is he getting involved into strange matters?."

From them on, the rabbi no longer spoke. Rather, on lonely nights, he would often sit down with new books and write. He wrote, the Jeremiah of

157

Zgierz, a new "Eicha", a new "I am the man" [20] - regarding the destruction of the Jewish nation.

(From the book, "Jewish Souls", volume 4, "Poland".)

The Zgierz Synagogue and Beis Midrash by Rabbi Shimon Huberband [21]

When the Jewish community of Zgierz was still very small and consisted of only a meager quantity of Jews, Zgierz was affiliated with the community of Leczyca. Later, it belonged to the old community of Parzencow, between Zgierz and Ozorkow. The Zgierz Jews buried their dead in Parzencow before a cemetery was founded in their own city.

The Jewish cemetery in Zgierz was founded in the year 5586 (1826). The ledgers of the Chevra Kadisha were kept from that year. The first monuments of the Zgierz cemetery are also from that year.

Formerly, the Jewish settlement in Zgierz was concentrated around the "Piaskes". There, there was a small, wooden synagogue. Later, the gentile guardian of the cemetery lived there.

Approximately one hundred years ago, thanks to the efforts of the local priests, the Jews had to leave the "Piaskes" and settle on the Jewish street (called Lodzer Street). At that time, the small wooden synagogue building became the residence of the gentile cemetery guard.

: **The Zgierz synagogue**

158

A wooden synagogue was constructed as well on the Jewish Street. It was not very large in size.

On one occasion on Yom Kippur at Kol Nidre, a Jew who was standing at the edge of the synagogue overheard a racket from the eastern wall of the synagogue. On account of the excitement and nervousness that the moment of Kol Nidre awakened in Orthodox Jews, he did not pay attention to what was taking place at the eastern wall. Shouts broke out: "It's burning! It's burning!" A forceful panic broke out in the women's section. Women started trampling one over the other, and a few women were thereby killed. Legend relates that one month later, the synagogue suddenly collapsed, and Zgierz was left without a synagogue.

At that time, the rabbi, Rabbi Shalom Tzvi HaKohen was offered the rabbinate of Kalisz. The rabbi of Zgierz decided to accept the rabbinate of Kalisz. At the same time, 85 years ago, that is in the year 5617 (1856), a guest rabbi, Rabbi Yechiel Meir, came to Zgierz for a Sabbath. The people of the community approached the guest with a complaint as to why their rabbi wishes to leave. The guest rabbi visited the rabbi, and asked him why he wants to leave the city.

The rabbi answered him: "How can I be in a city in which there is no synagogue?" The rabbi admitted that the local rabbi had a point, and promised him that if he does not leave Zgierz, he would see to it that they immediately commence building a fine synagogue.

The guest rabbi called a meeting of the local householders and told them of the rabbi's desire. It was immediately decided to begin building a synagogue. At that same meeting, 3,000 rubles were collected. The next day, a plot was purchased in the center of the city, and they immediately began to build a superb synagogue.

The work of building the synagogue lasted for several years. The synagogue building was a wonderful combination of architecture; from the outside, the synagogue was symmetrical; on the inside, it had a stately dome that appeared like the sun, moon, and stars. There were four very tall, thick wooden columns in the four corners of the synagogue, patterned after the balcony of the Holy temple. There were seventy Torah scrolls and many silver holy vessels in the synagogue. There was a stately reading desk in the middle of the synagogue - which according to its inscription was donated by the woman Chana, the wife of Reb David Hendlisz. There were many expensive ark covers and curtains. One silk curtain from the year 5626 (1866) was woven with some gold and silver threads. There was a tablecloth on the reader's lectern that is almost 200 years old, from the year 5532 (1772). That tablecloth is made of silk and velvet, adorned with an ample amount of pure gold and silver stripes. That tablecloth had its origins in a curtain that a community sent as a gift to the Zgierz synagogue at its founding.

A few years ago, the Zgierz community, as one of the richest in Poland, succeeded in installing 50 eight-branched electric chandeliers in the synagogue. During the time of the First World War, the Russians and later the Germans took very good care of the synagogue. The German officers, who used to often search the synagogue, did not have sufficient words to describe its beauty.

The Beis Midrash was also very beautiful and large. The Beis Midrash could hold over 2,000 people. Reb David the son of the rabbi of Brzeziny (the uncle of the writer David Frischman) donated 2,000 rubles for the construction of the synagogue. There was a special inscription in Polish regarding this in the Beis Midrash. There were 30 Torah scrolls there, and an unknown number of books, including many items of significance. The mikva was in the same courtyard as the synagogue and Beis Midrash.

The cemetery in Zgierz Drawing by Zeev Fisher

The cemetery was founded in the year 5686 (1826) as has been stated. In the Zgierz cemetery, one could find the resting place of the mother of the Ciechanower Rebbe Reb Avrahamele; the first rabbi Reb Shalom Tzvi; the second rabbi Reb Hirsch, and also the rabbis of Brzeziny and Zyrardow.

Jewish young men on a Sabbath stroll: M. Bomes, A. Boaz, Y. Elberg, A. Poznerson

The Weaver

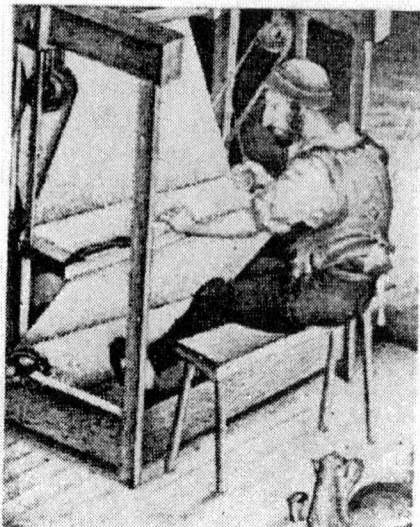

A fragment from "Kaluszer Statute", the work of the famous artist Arthur Szyk

... From the loaded weaver's machine
He pulls it now together, and everything
He glances through the combs;
He steps industriously on the shaft
Trip-Trap! Trip-Trap! On the shaft
The bars shoot together
According to what one sees with the eyes
The ship is running; an arrow from the boy
The weaving ship runs:
Nimbly here and nimbly there,
Chik-Chak! Chik-Chak! Nimbly here
And one does not see how much. - - -

(From David Frischman's "Before the Messiah")

The Jewish hand weaver - the pioneer and builder of the Jewish textile industry in Poland, made his first appearance; he who with his hard effort and diligence, from morning to night often hungry - at the loom, contributed the most to the immense growth of the general Polish textile industry.

The remnants of those who remained were murdered by the German murderers; their creative existence was completely obliterated from the history of the "new" Poland. May our modest words memorialize him, the Jewish hand weaver, with an eternal remembrance!

The Textile Industry in Zgierz in the year 1936 by David Baum

From the monthly journal "The Jewish Economic", June-July 1937. Published by the economic statistical section of Yivo, under the editorship of Yaakov Leczinski.

Prior to the First World War, Zgierz employed a smaller number of Jewish manufacturers than today, perhaps around 30 people. Their means were, however, greater than today. Many of them were requested to found their manufacturing enterprises with greater capital; others were veteran professionals of many years duration. Travelers traveled throughout Russia to procure material for their work from the residue market. A few Jewish textile enterprises became million-firms [22] with time. Socially, the pre-war Jewish manufacturers stemmed either from a half assimilated and Maskil environment, or from a Hasidic-aristocratic environment. It is remarkable that the large pre-war firms had for the most part existed for two generations. They could not uphold themselves for longer. Thereby, they made place for up and coming firms. There were several dozen German manufacturers before the war. There were very rich German manufacturers, with their own weavers, spinners, operators [23], and mid-sized factories with several looms. The rest worked for others. Today, two well-known, large German enterprises exist, who work with Jewish employees. In comparison to the role that they played in former years, they today lead a paltry existence.

Today, we find 61 Jewish manufacturers in Zgierz. We must add to the number 20 manufacturers from Lodz who give out work to the home manufacturers of Zgierz. From among that number of Zgierz manufacturers, there were 14 partnership enterprises, composing 36 families. In total, more than 80 Jewish families earn their living from manufacturing in Zgierz. The 61 manufacturers can be placed into three categories. Large textile firms, which own a large number of their own looms, spinning machines power cutting machines, etc., can be placed into the first category. These number approximately 16. To the next category belong manufacturers who run large scale enterprises, possess open stockrooms for merchandise, and employ hired shearers, stuffers, etc. However, they do not own their own factories, and give out the work to hired weavers and home manufacturers. In this category are also included those who used to own their own looms, but rented them out or sold them due to the high cost. This group numbers about 25 people. The last group consists of manufacturers who conduct their manufacturing on a small scale and do not own open warehouses, but rather hold their merchandise in their private dwelling. A portion of these manufacturers do not even employ shearers, but rather do the work themselves like the shearers of former times. A few of these small manufacturers own one or two looms, in which they give off their own woof [24]. These manufacturers employ their own children or family members to work those looms. This category includes about 20 people.

There are only very few textile firms that existed before the war. Presently, we only find in Zgierz six such Jewish firms. Of them, four enterprises were given as an inheritance to the present owners from their parents, and two were founded by their current owners. The current manufacturers are different in many ways from the pre-war ones. Most of them recruit from known master craftsmen, employees, brokers, weavers, tailors, garbage collectors, and regular merchants. The Hassidic manufacturers form a group among themselves. In general, they primarily engage employees, weavers, and other workers from amongst their own, from the shtibel. They give out work to home manufacturers from among the same group. Their first row consists of people from among their own. One Hassidic manufacturer rented out his workstations for very small rates. During the course of a few years, those formerly idle Gerrer Hassidic young men became owners of their own workshops, in which they themselves worked as weavers.

In Zgierz, there is one Jewish kamgarn spinning shop, whose owner can be counted among the richest Jews in the city. There are also large thread spinning shops in Lodz and in other cities. There Jewish firms in Lodz purchase from the thread spinning shops, who procure thread for their factories. Five Jews of Zgierz are employed in this commodity. They serve as middlemen, presenting the thread to the manufacturers of the large Lodzer firms.

164

A group of Jewish textile experts in Zgierz during their Sabbath rest. Sitting: L. Gelbard, Sh.Glowinski, B. Srkowowski, B. Sribnik, Y. Kaminsky. Standing - L. Tenenbaum, Y. Fisher, L.Sribnik

The suppliers of yarn to the industry in Zgierz are local Jewish spinners, who purchase used cloth [25] and sorted it out. Chalutzim (Zionist pioneers) from the local kibbutzim [26] are employed at that work Those spinners do not own their own spinning wheels, but rather give out the material to spin on rented spinning wheels that were found in Zgierz. Twelve Zgierz Jewish families (aside from Lodzers) earn their living from that branch of industry directly as spinners. As well, five families earn their living indirectly as deliverers of raw material and rags.   There are seven yarn spinning enterprises in Zgierz: one Jewish, one Polish, and five German. The only Jewish spinning enterprise in Zgierz belongs to a Jew from Lodz, and employed about 100 gentile workers. The hired people include two Jews one gentile. The firm own five spinning machines.

All of the Zgierz yarn spinning enterprises employ 650 gentile workers and 29 hired workers, including 2 Jews. One does not need any special qualifications to work in a yarn spinning factories. Experienced workers can earn up to twenty something guilder a week.

In Zgierz, there are two yarn dying workshops, Jewish enterprises, which provide for the Zgierz industry. One firm was in existence from before the war, and was given over as an inheritance. This enterprise grew greatly after the war and became one of the richest industrial enterprises in the city. Today, the firm employs 32 workers, including 13 Jews and 4 Jewish hired people. The second dying workshop is considerably smaller, and does not possess all of the modern machines. They work there in a more primitive fashion. That enterprise is a partnership of three people: one is the master dyer and the other two occupy themselves with the business side. There are 16 workers employed in the enterprise, including 11 Jews. Most of the Jewish employees are Hassidim, former shopkeepers who liquidated their business and became involved in physical labor.

The silk for effects is obtained from out of the country via Jewish firms in Lodz. Two Zgierz Jews occupy themselves with taking orders and delivering the various silks to the Zgierz factories.

There are seven hired tzvernereien [27] in Zgierz. Five of them are Jewish. The five Jewish enterprises employ 42 people, of whom 4 are Jewish (3 women workers and 1 porter), and 4 Jewish hired people. We find very few Jewish women workers employed in the Jewish tzverneriens, because until recently there were almost no Jewish tzvernerins. Today, a few Jewish girls study tzvernerei.

In Zgierz the woof are mostly sheared by hand. A shearer can shear one woof a day. Since there were eighty shearers today in Zgierz, it is obvious that the majority of them do not have a constant supply of work.

Aside from the hand shearers, there are also a small number of power shearers who work in factories that possess mechanical shearing machines. There are eight of these people. Six shearers run contract shearing workshops, and occupy themselves with spooling and shearing at other factories. Two contract shearers own power shearing machines. The shearing profession is exclusively in Jewish hands. Special rigging experts were needed to rig the woof. Two Jewish families occupy themselves with this, and employ a large number of gentiles. Six Jews and a large number of gentiles occupy themselves as special purchasers and winders.

The weaving trade is the most widespread and popular within the textile industry. Jewish weavers were hired at non-Jewish factories, and formed large percentage with respect to gentile weavers. During the last seven years, the situation radically changed for the benefit of the Jewish weavers. In the last few years, a new element of Jewish workers came, who set themselves up in factories as shearers, weavers, woof spoolers and stuffers. These are poor relatives of the manufacturer.

The wages of a weaver are paid according to the number of thousands of threads that one has put through the woof. A weaver can put 30,000 threads through a good woof in an eight hour working day. According to the agreement that has been in force since the last strike, the manufacturer must pay his weavers 25 Groszy for a thousand warps. In the majority of weaving enterprises, the Jewish workers do not work on the Sabbath, so they are missing one working day. In a few factories, however they do work on the Sabbath. In 1929, the manufacturers employed approximately 350 workers as shearers, weavers, and woof and warp spoolers. This number included 150 Jews. If you subtract 40 shearers from this number, you are left with 110 Jewish weavers and spoolers. In 1932, there were 400-410 workers, including about 200 Jews; the latter number includes approximately 50 shearers. In 1935, more Jews than non-Jews were employed in the factories. The total number of employed workers in 1936, excluding the shearers(212) was 351, consisting of 179 Jews and 172 non-Jews. Above this, there were 80 Jewish shearers.

The number of employed industrial workers include, spoolers of the woof and warp. In the last years, a larger number of Jewish women began to work in this trade. Jewish girls entered this trade from other trades. We can often encounter Jewish women who are former tailors, vesterins [28], rope makers, and stuffers working at the power spooling machines, spooling yarn in the woof or warp. They transferred over to this trade where they were able to work, and find regular employment. The salary for a woof and warp spooler is 3.50 - 5 guilder (Zloty) [29] a week.

Master weavers, who were employed in a steady fashion in textile enterprises in Zgierz, number over twenty. From that number we can subtract 8-9 masters who were children of or close family members of the manufacturers. All of the employed weaving masters in Zgierz at this point are Jews. The master weaver is the virtual director of the factory. All of them - the shearer, spooler, weaver, loom master, home manufacturer, stuffer, etc. come to him for instructions. The master weaver must undergo a long training period. Master weavers in small enterprises can earn 25-50 guilder (Zloty) a week. In larger enterprises, they can earn 45-70 guilder a week. There are about 22 loom masters employed in the factories, including 12-15 non-Jews and about 7 Jews. Often, the hiring of workers in the factory is dependent on the goodwill of the loom master. In those factories where there is a Jewish loom master, there work mainly Jewish weavers and spoolers. The training of Jews for the loom master qualification brought great profit.

Approximately 52 hired workers are employed in Jewish factories in Zgierz. Of them, 48 are Jews and 4 are non-Jews. From the number of 48, 15 are hired in enterprises that have workshops in Lodz.

The manufacturers give out a great amount of their work to home manufacturers and contract weavers. In Zgierz, there are approximately 130 Jewish home manufacturers and contract weavers. Factoring in the Jewish manufacturers who work alone, the number of Jews who work in this branch of industry is estimated to be greater than 270. Non-Jewish weavers hire approximately 300 Jewish home manufacturers and contract weavers. In 1929, the Zgierz manufacturers gave out work to 250 home manufacturers and contract weavers. Of these 90 were Jewish, comprising 36 percent. In 1936, work was given out to 355 home manufacturers, of whom 159 were Jewish, making 45 percent of the total.

These numbers that have been brought down here cannot be regarded as the absolute truth. Home manufacturers who work for more than one factory were doubly recorded. Aside from this, the gentile home manufacturer earned a greater salary than the Jewish ones. The manufacturers distribute the gentiles the working quantity of five looms, and to the Jewish home manufacturers, 1-2.

Approximately three Jewish families are occupied with the delivery of accessories to the looms. Approximately 10 Jewish families are occupied with junk purchasing. Stuffers - this trade is mainly occupied by Jewish women, and this is one of the most widespread in the city. The stuffers belong mainly to three groups: the first group includes the masters who obtain the merchandise for the factory. They hire girls as intakers [30] in the homes, who are paid for short stints of work. Most of the masters work on their own -we reckon that this is approximately 60 people. The girl intakers who work away from home at the place of the woman masters belong to the second group. There are approximately 160 such people. The third group consists of approximately 30 intakes who are employed by the factories themselves, who often send out an operator to cover the merchandise properly.

From the intaker, the merchandise goes to an operator, where it makes its final stop before completion. There, the merchandise is washed, trimmed and pressed. The smooth, white merchandise is also dyed there. There are currently five operator enterprises in Zgierz: two Jewish and three German. 106 workers are employed in one Jewish operator. Of them one is a foreman and the other is a night watchman. At that place, there are also three gentile dyers and master operators. There are six hired workers in that enterprise, including three Jews. 130 workers, all gentiles, are employed at the second Jewish operator. There are also three dyers and master operators, also gentile, and seven hired workers, of whom two are Jews. In the last few weeks, three Jewish women were hired as stuffers and intakers.

Two kibbutzim [31] have existed in Zgierz for several years. The largest one, Kibbutz Borochov, consists of 50 people, and the smaller one, Kibbutz Bilu, of 30. These chalutzim (Zionist pioneers) occupy themselves with various work, even with household work, with which the females are employed. They also involve themselves with industry. They take on the hardest and dirtiest jobs. Approximately fifty percent of all of the members of these kibbutzim are occupied in one way or another by the textile industry. We have not included here the travelers and commissioners, the porters and wagon drivers, the expediters and the merchants of the textile line of business. We come to the conclusion that approximately 1,000 Jewish families in Zgierz earn their livelihood from the textile line of business - eighty percent of all of the Jews.

From the Cloth Makers' Union (Textile Makers) Until the Handworkers' Club by Y. L.Weinstein

In the second half of the 19th century, when Zgierz had already taken on the prominent characteristic of a growing textile city, many Jews began to study the weaving trade with diligence - and became textile makers. In general, each one strove to become independent that is to set up their own handlooms in order to take on work for hire from the larger manufacturers from Zgierz and Lodz.

Just as at one time, the weaver at the loom required an assistant to throw back to him the protector [32] (as one called them: brashirer), the Jewish young people who worked as brashirer for the German weavers quickly learnt this trade, and later succeeded in becoming independent owners of one, two, or even three hand looms.

Setting up a hand loom was not easy. Only with the assistance of the family and an assistance organization could one set up a loom in a room. Quickly, the well-known, monotonous knocking began. Of course, the entire family was employed around the loom: the husband worked at the loom, the wife did the spooling, and the children served as the "brashirers".

Wage earning weavers with initiative, or those who had the means and possibility, set themselves up to "make a little bit of merchandise" with their own hands. Years later, they went out from their family to the factories. The influence of Yossel Rubensztejn, along with others, was evident here. He was the educator of a generation of weaving professionals and master weavers. A recognizable number of Zgierz cloth makers came out of his factory, such as: Emanuel and Henech Ber, Nachman Yechiel Zaonc, Meir and Avraham Temerzon, Shalom Weinstein, shalom Ber Michawicz, Meir Fogel and others. They were also the conspicuous activists of the "Cloth Makers' Union", which was founded in the 1890s.

This organization had various tasks. First and foremost, they had to protect the interest of the wage earning weavers from the large factories; to help their members with the professional council, to make loans when there was need, and other problems. The organization also concerned themselves with the "Jewish soul" of the weavers, for their spiritual sustenance. They used to gather together each Sabbath and festival to worship in their own minyan on the Jewish Street, where during the week an incessant sound If looms could be heard. There they would talk from the heart if there was some sort of pain. There, they would decide who they need to help.

At the end of the 1890s, the group wrote its own Torah scroll, which expressed its spiritual independence in a significant manner. On Fridays, Slotkowicz would drive around with his wagon, pick up the finished "pieces" from the hand weavers and took them to the factories. Thus went the business until the power looms began to appear more and more, which slowly but surely pushed aside the handlooms.

The mechanical looms initiated a new era in the development of the textile industry. The Jewish weavers and hired weavers had to enter into the new time. After a few years, they even became the leaders.

With the outbreak of the First World War (1914), the organization was liquidated. Its place in the Jewish weavers' family was taken in 1913 by the newly created modern and constructive handworkers union. That union, known by the name Handworkers' Club, drew into its ranks craftsmen from the different professions, but mainly -weavers and masters from the textile profession.

The presidium of the union consisted of: dentist Dr. Michael Zalcwaser, Master Avraham Morgensztern, and weaver Leib Miler. These people set the statutes for the society at the request of the Russian authorities. We still remember the following from among those most active in the Handworkers' Club: Moshe Lirach, Avraham Skosowski, Baruch Gibralter, Yisrael Praszker, Baruch Gelbard, and others. According to paragraph number 1 from its statutes, the union was created to help its members in their legal, material, cultural and physical development. The "Lodz Folksblatt" (August 16, 1915) mentions that the Handworkers' Club gave courses for weavers - "and in this way, a group of the young people will study the weaving profession".

During the time of the First World War, the Handworkers' Club conducted widespread activities to mitigate the need of the impoverished Jewish population. After the war, they injected organizational and professional consciousness into the ranks of the Jewish artisans. They helped them to stand on their own feet with council and deeds.

In 1925, a bank for the small businessmen and handworkers was founded under the directorship of M. Kwikzylber. The secretary was Yitzchak Tendowski. It is worthwhile to make note of the activity and dedication of the secretary of the union, Sczupak, who greatly assisted the handworkers in becoming an important factor in the Jewish economic life in the city.

Dyers in Zgierz by Chaya Sperling-Halprin

Reb Avraham Konski (1823-1905) was among the first manufacturers in Zgierz. He established a wool dying workshop in the first half of the 19th century, and thereby laid the foundations of a new branch of textile manufacturing in the city. His descendents, the Konski and Harun families, worked in this field until the outbreak of the Second World War. The dye house was located in the yard of his house on Piontkowska Street. There was a well of pure water, without minerals, on the premises.

The founder of the dynasty, Reb Avraham Konski was a learned man, apparently gifted with unusual technical abilities. Many legends circulate in the family regarding his inventions and powers of improvisation. He designed and built himself the equipment of the dye house, developed the dying processes, and made use of plant dies. He employed only Polish workers.

His son Yosef Konski expanded the enterprise, and began to make use of indigo dyes that had been invented in that era. He set up a steam boiler. During his time, Jewish workers began to work along with the Poles. After his death in 1920, the dye house transferred to his heirs. The members of the family that continued to be employed in this area included: Yehoshua Konski, Yitzchak Meir Zylberberg, Mordechai Nisan Kuperstoch, and Leibel Goldberg. Most of them continued to work until the outbreak of the Second World War.

In 1908, Leibel Harun, the son-in-law of Avraham Konski, founded a new dye house in partnership with his son Yosef Meir Harun.

Reb Leibel Harun was a wise Jew, knowledgeable in Torah. He acquired general knowledge with his own powers. He studied the dyeing profession at the dye house of Itzel Orbach, and worked for many years an expert (master) in the Kleczobski-Orbach dye house. He constantly excelled at his work and became a great expert in the profession. At first, his dye house was on Pilsudski Street in the yard of Gibralter's house, on the other side of the Bzura River. There, they dyed wool, kamgarn, and cotton.

During the First World War, the Germans confiscated the equipment of the dye house, and thereby destroyed it. The activity of the dye house was renewed after the First World War, and with time, it moved to a new, large building on Dombrowski Street in the yard of Reichert called "Palestynka". Then, they further expanded and established the enterprise, which employed modern dyeing processes, and was the largest in the city and area. The

172

enterprise was run by the son, Yosef Meir Harun until the day of the expulsion. Jewish and Polish employees worked in the dye house.

The era between the two world wars was an era of growth in the textile industry of Zgierz. The dye houses, in particular that of Leibel and Yosef Meir Harun, played no small role in promoting the fame of the wool that was processed in the factories of the Jews of Zgierz.

Our Commissioners by Fabian Grynberg

It is appropriate to make note of the role that as played by the Jewish commissioners in the development of the textile industry in our city. These were intelligent, capable people who developed relationships with textile merchants in the entire broad regions of Russia and the Far East. The Zgierz manufacturers did not know these merchants, and did not want to extend any credit to them. The commissioner offered guarantees, thereby helped distributed Zgierz merchandise, and broadened the market of our textile industry. They were indeed able to grow the factories through the German bourse [33] and the largest Jewish firms such as Sirkes and Eiger, Brothers Sirkes, Shimon Ring, Boaz, brothers Naftali, and others.

In the time before the First World War, the activity of the commissioners was entirely different than that of the dozens of small middlemen and even smaller brokers who stood near the tramway, waited for a merchant to come from Lodz, pulled him by his garment and told him that they will take him to a door, where he could buy a piece of kamgarn cheaply.

Every member of this category of commissioners was an institution, a much needed middleman between the large scale textile merchants in Poland, Lithuania, Russia, and even in the orient. They were financially responsible for the debts of the purchasers from the manufacturers. This enabled the Zgierz manufacturer to spread his wings, distribute more merchandise, employ more workers, and thereby improve the material situation in our city. He, the manufacturer, did not know the financial status of each merchant. That was the responsibility of the commissioner. Often the commissioner (who had given his guarantees) suffered great losses. Even when the merchant went into bankruptcy, the commissioner had to issue a promissory note, which he guaranteed.

The manufacturer had to place great trust in such people who guaranteed the duties of the merchant. The commissioner had to be honorable, honest and exact. Bankruptcy was a common occurrence.

I remember the following people from among the first commissioners: Yosef Rzurkowski, Avraham Nekricz, Beinish Kohen, Tovia Lipszicz, Y. A. Rusinow, Ozer Kohen, Hershel Kohen, Leib Pariser, Yehoshua Kaufman, Kiczinski, Leibish Rozenerg (White Leibish), and Avraham Berliner, Moshe Reznik, Hershel Merinski, Baruch Bizberg and others.

The Struggle for Jewish Labor in Jewish Factories by Y. Sczaransky

Zgierz, aside from its Jewish residents, suffered a great deal of pain and agony from the Germans in those years, according to A. G. "Zgierz Contract". They fought against them in the year 1821.

Among the many paragraphs (approximately 50) that this "Zgierz Contract" contained, the Germans enacted that an additional two (political) "hanachot" (enactments) must be placed before the "Good of the entire matter", which based itself upon expressing the lowest racism against Jews - literally a sort of "Nuremberg Laws", albeit earlier by more than one hundred years.

No Jew would be permitted to live in a resident in the "New Quarter", and neither could they acquire any immovable goods there.

Jewish were prohibited from occupying themselves with textile work. (Avraham Tenenbaum-Arzi in the book "Lodz in those Days", published in Buenos Aires, 1956).

First in 1862, when the regime enacted the reform statutes, and the life of the Jews in Congress Poland improved a little bit, new winds began to blow in Zgierz as well, just as they blew in Lodz, Tomaszow and other cities in Congress Poland. The Jews of Zgierz as well began to create hand weaving enterprises.

My present task is only to tell about the struggle for the right to work for Jewish workers in Jewish factories in Zgierz at that time, when Jews were already permitted to become involved in textile work, alongside the Germans and Poles.

With the development of the textile industry in Zgierz, thanks to Jewish energy and diligence, the Jewish hand weavers had employment, and improved their livelihoods. With the passage of time, the textile industry in Zgierz, as in other Polish cities, changed over from hand weaving to mechanical looms. Hand weaving enterprises ceased to be a source of livelihood for dozens of Zgierz hand weavers.

Despite the fact that many mechanical textile factories were owned by Jewish manufacturers, Jewish weavers were did not find employment there - for three reasons.

From one side, Jewish manufacturers in Zgierz, as opposed to Jewish manufacturers in Tomaszow and Bialystok, did not believe that Jews were capable of working with mechanical weaving machines. The second reason (and this is the main one), the Christian workers did not permit Jewish workers to gain a foothold in the Jewish mechanical weaving factories.

The time when Jewish workers still found livelihood from hand weaving enterprises had disappeared. The problem of finding employment and sustenance for those who had been ejected was very difficult, almost insolvable.

The rabbi of Zgierz, Rabbi Shlomo Yehuda Leib HaKohen literally screamed out to the Jewish manufacturers, and demanded that they use all means available to employ Jewish workers in their factories.

The energetic rabbi did not satisfy himself with his first call. He called the Jewish manufacturers together to a conference in 1911. He called the first meeting of all the Jewish manufacturers in Zgierz, and issued an appeal: Jewish manufacturers must employ Jewish weavers.

A committee was formed at the first meeting consisting of the rabbi, Reb Moshe Eiger, and Reb Aharon Yosef Berger. After a few meetings of the committee, the aforementioned Moshel Eiger and Aharon Yosef Berger took it upon themselves to employ two hand weavers from Zgierz. They would send them to Tomaszow on their accounts in order to qualify to work at mechanical looms.

Messrs. Eiger and Berger did not only take the support of the two weavers upon themselves, but also agreed to support the wives and children of the two weavers until they would return from Tomaszow with their new profession.

They choose two of the best Jewish hand weavers: Shalom Kaza and Uma Wicocki, who were sent to study with the Jewish manufacturer David Bernsztejn in Tomaszow.

When the two Jewish weavers returned from Tomaszow, they had to

175

educate other Jews in Zgierz to qualify for that profession.

When these two weavers returned from Tomaszow as professionals, the struggle with the Christian weavers began. They did not permit them to be employed in the factories that were owned by Jewish manufacturers.

After many conferences between the Jewish manufacturers and their Christian workers, they came to the following agreement:

"No more than 2-3% of workers in the Jewish factories may be Jews".

Even though the agreement was confirmed by the Christians, it fell apart when the Jewish weavers were beaten by their Christian friends.

Uma Wicocki, an active weaver, related the following to me:

On the first day that I began to work as a power weaver in the Sirkes and Eiger firm, I descended the steps of the factory in the evening after work together with the Christian workers. Suddenly, the Christian workers began to beat me, and then they threw me off the steps - I barely made it out alive. I was laid up in bed for a long time from the injuries.

The story with Uma Wicocki was the first such step by the Christian workers. Afterwards, other Jewish workers in Jewish factories suffered many blows upon their emaciated bodies from Poles.

The first person who reacted against the terror perpetrated by the Christian weavers against Jewish workers was the manufacturer Moshe Hendeles, who must be especially mentioned with honor. He dismissed all of the workers in his factory, and replaced them with Jewish textile workers only, beginning with the loom masters Chaim Itche Segal and Gershon Bennet, to the Jewish women spoolers. It seems to me that this was the first Jewish factory in Zgierz before the First World War that closed on the Sabbath. That bold step, taken without concern of financial loss and other consequences, raised the esteem of the Jewish workers in the city, and simultaneously encouraged them in their battle for full rights as fully valued textile workers in the mechanized Jewish factories.

Due to his authority in Jewish national business, Hendler became an example for other Jewish manufacturers, such as: Eliezer Shumiel, Nathan Ader, Aharon Yosef Berger, and others.

The boldness of those few Jewish manufacturers in employing solely Jewish workers was a cold knock on the heated heads of the Christian workers in the city. They desisted from their terror against the Jewish workers with whom they worked.

Incidentally, it is appropriate to mention on this occasion that one of the masters, Avraham Frenkel, who worked in the Hendeles firm, was hanged along with his friend Melech Zandberg (both from Zgierz) by the Russians in the city of Lewicz in 1914. This was as a result of a false accusation that they were German spies.

About Jewish Employment in Zgierz by F.

Aside from the large majority of the Jewish population who were employed in the textile industry and its various branches and related professions - a major portion of the Jews of Zgierz earned their living from craftsmanship and business. Most of them were organized into the small-scale businessmen's union or in the handworkers' union, which defended their interests before the authorities, and helped with interest-free loans and judicial advice.

There were also Jews who created or directed specific branches of work or enterprises that had not existed in Zgierz until then. Of those, we know of the following:

Yehuda (Yudel) Szapszowicz and his sons Nathan David and Shlomo, their chicory factories had a name in Poland, and their products often excelled at exhibitions.

Shimon Fiszer had an enterprise (until the outbreak of the First World War) that paved the streets of the city and the inter-city roads and highways. That work, after the appropriate designs, changed the appearance and character of the city. He also had held the concession for illuminating the city with kerosene lanterns, until the introduction of electric light in Zgierz (approximately 1909-1910).

Engineer Teitelbaum -His paper factory, organized in modern fashion, provided work for many people.

The printing presses of David Gothejner and Tzirel Gutsztat contributed greatly to the development and the reverberation of the cultural and social activity in our city.

Mendel Gibralter was the first Jewish construction undertaker in Zgierz.

"Expeditia" was the collective for shipping merchandise (with it own automobiles) along the Zgierz-Warsaw route. The partners were Sh. Wicocki, Sh. Buzin and Waldman. Gross, Wrona and others were also expediters.

There were also the soda water factories of Yaakov Glicksman and A. Rubin-Brzezinski.

Without doubt, the plywood factory and mill of Braun and Ginsberg was worthy of note. Jews were also employed there.

The electric cereal mill of Abe Baum (Abele Kashemacher) was of significantly small scope, but the noise of the mill traveled far over the Jewish street... A portion of this enterprise provided stable employment for a large number of Christian workers. [34]

My Ten Years in Zgierz by Menachem (Manis) Angel of Pardes Chana

I moved to Zgierz in the year 5670 (1910), when I married the daughter of the Hassid Reb Avraham Kuperman of blessed memory. I also was supported at his table. I worshiped, of course, in the shtibel of the Hassidim of Gur, in the house of Reb David Bandkowski. Reb Yitzchak Mendel HaKohen, the brother of the rabbi of the city, also worshipped there. He separated from his wife and lived like a "hermit" in poverty, as is the way of the Torah [35]. He sustained himself from the class in Ein Yaakov [36] that he gave to laymen in the Beis Midrash. He drew me near and enlightened my eyes with Torah and wisdom. In his house I found the "Kuzari", Moreh Nevuchim, Sefer Haikarim [37], and other books of depth and research, which broadened my horizons in my world of thought, and enriched my spirit. Reb Yitzchak Mendel himself was a Gaon, sharp and expert in Talmud and halachic decisors. He researched and studied opinions.

I became friendly with Reb Leibel Harun (nicknamed Leibel Farber [38]), an upright, levelheaded and liberal man who set aside times to study Torah. I also got to know Reb Tovia Kopel Bumes, the son-in-law of Reb Aharon Parizer, and Binem David Pszytik, a man full of energy and life, who was my friend in the community of Hassidim.

Of course, the Hassidic young men did not look favorably upon my distancing myself from them, and coming close to those of whom they did not approve. To my good fortune, my brother-in-law Reb Yosef Mandelman (Yosele Baluter [39]) protected me. Even though he was a staunch Hassid, a good musician with a voice that drew near the hearts (he led Musaf in the shtibel), he had other good traits: he was always in a good mood, and he always had a joke on his tongue.

The First World War (1914-1918) introduced a great change in the lives of the residents of the city, including the Hassidim. The sprouting of Zionism and the Balfour Declaration stirred up many echoes within the midst of the Jews of the city, who saw this as the dawn of the redemption. I myself did not ignore the situation, and I went with the times. At that time, a son was born to me. I called him Yechiel Meir, named after Dr. Czolnow of blessed memory, who died at that time.

I joined the Mizrachi movement, which was established in our city. I was one of the activists, along with Rabbi Yechiel Yitzchak Rappaport, the son-in-law of Reb Michael Mendel; the son of Reb Leibish Rozenberg (nicknamed the White Leibish). He was later appointed as the rabbi of Zychlin, and from there he moved to serve in the rabbinate of Janiszow. He was a first class preacher. He visited all of the towns in the region, and performed many great deeds wherever he went.

The following were numbered among the activists of Mizrachi: the aforementioned Binem David Pszytik, Reb Yisrael Frugel, Reb Michel Kuperman from among the Hassidim of Aleksandrow, and Reb Itche Meir Halperin of the Hassidim of Sochaczew.

In addition to Reb Daniel Sirkes who was chosen as the chairman of the organization until he made aliya to the Land, Reb Yehoshua Kaufman, the uncle of Reb Daniel Sirkes, joined Mizrachi. He was a Jew who was involved in Torah all of his life. His home was a gathering place for the nationalistic youth of the city, and many other city notables.

In the year 5680 (1920) I merited to make aliya to the Holy Land, and to strike down roots there with the help of G-d.

The Chant of a Generation by Pinchas Bizberg

Introduction:
Excerpts from the book "Sabbath and Festival Jews" - the Chant of a Generation. The author, a Jew of Zgierz, describes his hometown and its Jews, replacing the name Zgierz with Miechow.

"Sabbath and Festival Jews" was published and issued by the Central Organization of Polish Jews in Argentina, Buenos Aires, 1949, as part of the "Polish Jewry" series of books, volume 55.

The titles (captions) of the various segments are for the most part our own, not from P. Bizberg.

Simchat Torah in the Gerrer Shtibel

... Today is Simchat Beit Shoeva [40], and whoever did not witness the Simchat Beit Shoeva has not seen joy in his life... how light it is, and how calm is the festival peace in the Shtibel of the Hassidim. The clear, golden flashing lights, the light near the reader's podium, the white knitted ark cover; they light up the copper sink, the hand towels on the hangers, the book chests; they light up the group of Hassidim who are singing and dancing shoulder to shoulder. One tune flows into another tune, and nobody gets tired, for all are so fresh. From when it was still day, the sharp youth imbibed drinks at the home of Reb Shlomo Sirkes. At Reb Shlomo Sirkes' there was such refreshing Hungarian wine, such old sharp mead, another glass, another tune, and again a glass, again a tune. Like the sea, the Gerrer tunes do not run out... and whoever did not witness the joy at the water drawing in Jerusalem has never seen greater joy in his life... therefore Jews, shoulder to shoulder, dance and dance to express the joy. Then Chaim Hirsch, a deliberate Jew, bangs very seriously on the Torah reading platform: Jews, it is time for Maariv (the evening prayer)! --then Shabtai Nachums breaks out in the most joyous melody of Ger; and an old Warker [41], and an old Kotzker, and the tune of Reb Henech, and as the circle gets wider and larger, the young and old clap together; what do we pray, to whom do we pray, we must dance, serve the Blessed G-d from joy. And whoever did not witness the joy at the water drawing has never witnessed joy in his life... The circle got even larger, and it spread even further, people were already dancing in the yard of the Hassidic shtibel; the candles in the lads' hands dance, the full moon dances, the stars dance. Be happy, brothers, and dance! What's with Maariv, when is Maariv! Shabtai Nachums dances a Kozaczak again in Hassidic ecstasy, and Reb Yosele Baluter dances opposite him...

And who remembers the peak of Simchat Torah, when they climbed onto the roof of Reb Lipe's home and on the roofs of the Shpeichlers and Kammers, which border on the "Koze", in order to dance before the entire community, so that the entire world will know that Jews are rejoicing with the Torah, so that the firemen Maciej and Maczek, and Wacek the prison guard should know that the Jews have a Torah! The stony Yozel [42] and his crowned mother on both columns of the church should know this! The priest's orchard with the stone fence should know this!... Shabtai Nachums is the first one to creep up to the flimsy roof and he begins to flutter. Then they break out into a joyous Simchat Torah melody, and dance until the soul is filled with devotion and arousal, as they peer out into the wide open space [43] of the blue, cool, autumn, end of festival world...

And who was commanded to rip out the heavy, bulky sink of the Gerrer shtibel, and bring pails from the neighboring houses to the market pump, so as to fill the long Gerrer Shtibel with so much water so that the Hasidim can dance on the seventh night of Passover [44] with pulled up pants, bound kapotes and silk gartels, in order to fulfill the custom: to cross the sea on dry land? Shabtai Nachums fulfilled this custom, and his soul was full of joy when the time of song came, summertime was approaching, the yoke of livelihood would ease for the Jews, there would be no more worries about coal, no more worries about warm clothes, and fruit would be cheap.

Always-Shabtai Nachums, he advised the sharp youth to go on the night of Shmini Atzeret [45] to the homes of the rich people in order to empty out all that the ladies of the house had saved from the kingly foods: gefilte fish, stuffed cabbage, bags of sugar, semi-roasted turkeys, the pair of stuffed, roasted ducks and fatty geese. He advised the spirited, half drunk youths to go down into cellars and seek out bottles of wine that were stashed away, to drain out bottles of aromatic old mead and pour out black coffee.

And someone pushes the pock-marked fireman Maczej into the circle: [46] "Hey, those Jews, they want a masquerade show... Hey, those Jews... into the circle for a half a day, oh well, what can you do, it's Jews, and you must pay for the show..." Shabtai Nachums is paying for his joy. For the sake of Heaven.

Would it be that the day of eternal goodness would take hold [47], so many weekdays until a bit of Sabbath comes! And from every corner of the store, so much sadness comes! From the yellow plum, from the eight smoky lamps, from the herring cask, from the dirty barley sack, from the packages of tallow candles, from the mezuzos on the doorposts, from the gloomy glances after zlotys, from the dreadful night skies of the shtetl, from the pious sighs at daybreak from the Beis Midrashes and Hassidic shtibels, from the mumbling of Psalms by the Ein Yaakov Jews [48].

Master of the World, when will we be free of sadness!

The Fifth Year

Shifra from Miechow was not afraid of sticking the emblem consisting of the red piece of linen with the workers hands choking the two-headed eagle, just as Hershel the blacksmith was not afraid of wearing the badge of the tip of a bayonet.

We were not afraid, although in Lodz, General Kaznakow had conducted twenty hangings, and they were hanging men like a wash set out to dry. The united youth had no fear of robbing the post office, as long as the party was in need of money... And who was the chief spokesman of the demonstration in Miechow: Vove with the poor fitting suit and the forelocks.

The revolution of 1905 was drowned in blood. Everywhere, the gendarmes administered beatings with clubs over heads, over stomachs. Volleys mowed down everywhere.

In Shabtai Nachums' Miechow, Cossacks suddenly raced forth from the forest with their spades on their horses. An entire regiment of Cossacks with swords and rifles broke into their demonstration, trampling with their various hooves, stabbing, beating, and splitting heads with heavy sticks. The area in front of the magistrate was emptied. A little while later one could find the revolutionaries, accompanied by infantry solders of the Cossacks and goaded on by their knouts. The united youth went on like drunks, with bloody and injured faces, disheveled clothes; going, stopping, a bit resigned, a bit weary, with raised heads.

Russia shook from one end to the other. Hangings, hangings, and mothers weeping for children who were offered on the altar of freedom...

New Winds in the Shtetl

Typhus and other illnesses spread around in the town; women miscarried, freaks were born, bizarre things happened. Chava-Ita, Shalom-Henech the coal dealer's wife, forgot to put on her apron when she went at 12:00 midnight to buy vegetables from the farmer's wagons that were going to Lodz - some sort of a white thing floated out of the church ... and she fainted. Young children died; Wigder, the tall, yellow undertaker, had his hands full with work. The rabbi of the city Reb Yalke was afflicted with melancholy: he does not know what to do first to suspend the bitter decree: whether to mandate a fast, to conduct a strong moral discourse against heresy Heaven forbid in the large Beis Midrash, or to fervently recite the special chapters of Psalms.

The youths interrupted their studies in the Beis Midrash; often a disheveled Jewess tore forth like a blind person with a wild gait to the Holy Ark, a scream burst forth with a strange voice: I need help, help! She shook, her cheeks wrinkled, she lamented, she repeated over the name and the mother's name of the ill person, she pulled out one or two coins for the group of studiers - and now an agile Jew with a fine singing voice stood by the lectern, and conducted the group of Psalm reciters: "Happy is the man who did not walk in the company of evildoers..." [49]. It was good times for those who studied Gemara: those who were reciting Psalms for the seriously ill were literally a bounty of sweet drinks, egg biscuits and herring for the youths with rugged peyos and thin necks.

After the cucumber season, after Shavuot, the typhus ceased. During Tammuz [50] there was pickled fruit, out of season green pears, sour apples, hard plums, gooseberries without stems, children cannot restrain themselves, -- the town's cemetery behind the sandy area was enriched from the dysentery. Burial provided a good livelihood.

Observant Jews, and Jewesses with their hair covered, asked for advice. They wished to understand the reasons for the tribulations, Heaven forbid. People whispered, people told private secrets, that all of the tragedies are coming because the world is becoming wanton, unbound, people ceased to put on Tefillin, no longer recited prayers, people go around with girls and with shikses [51] Heaven forbid...with "men", that refers to the fine young men, sons-in-law who are supported, people who used to learn have now become involved in a bad crowd. Instead of studying in the shtibel and praying, they go into the forests, the pleasure gardens, and the back streets. They do not even show up in the shtibel on the Sabbath. A certain diligent learner started to talk to a girl, a second Yeshiva student is found behind the factories with a certain brazen girl. If a girl had the gall to go around and hide with a certain lowlife, then she would be considered a brazen girl by all opinions, and perhaps even worse. The Orthodox wives insisted that the only remedy for such a thing was to shave off the hair and put on a veil. Indeed, for the other lowlifes, the meat-cutters, the fish-sellers, the children of the shavers [52], the tailors and shoemakers, of them the community had no opinion. The vegetable Jews, those who walk around in gaiters, weavers, stuffers and servant girls, they listen to both the judge and the pious hair-covered women like the Purim rabbi. Oy, oy, what is going on, such wantonness in the shtetl! They bathe together in the pond, in public, boys and girls, they boat around precisely on Sabbath afternoons, and they smoke cigarettes and sing frivolous songs. And the problems with the unity-youth, for whom the world is entirely free: aside from the fact that they want to free themselves from being Jews, they irritate the regime with the red flags, with the revolutionary songs: woe, woe, what type of tragedy can they bring upon respectable people if the regime becomes angry.

In general, everything in Miechow was somewhat bewildering. The rabbi's son-in-law Gedalia began to shorten his jackets, going around like a shtshogel [53]. It seemed also that the beard became thinner and they said of him that he spoke Hebrew with Zanwil the Feldsher, who sold stamps with Dr. Herzl's picture and who claimed to everyone:

"In Bialystok, in Kishinev, I answer the murderers by building our own land, where they will not perpetrate pogroms upon us, for we will be in our own home…"

Everyone knows that Gedalia's nephew is a guard there in the Land of Israel. The relatives of the rabbi's son-in-law had not merely once seen the photograph of the guard with the Arab garb and the gun on the shoulder, and they dreamt of the daring jackals on the hills of the Galilee and of heroism. Bar Mitzvah boys consider it to be a great merit to help purchase the stamps from the Land of Israel, and to consider themselves as guards in the vineyards against the foxes and wild Arabs.

It is said that the rabbi's son-in-law is himself preparing to travel to the land of "our hopes". The proof is that he is also collecting money for the Land of Israel.'

Adult Jews believe that a spirit of folly has penetrated to none other than the spoiled Hassidic youth… how else can one declare that which the teachers say about him, that even though he is diligent in learning across from the rabbi, he has become an apikorus (heretic)! This confounds the mind! Paper collars, stiff starched collars, "noodle boards", cuffs, laced gaiters, out with; out with Jewish garb, woe, woe, Jews follow the customs of the gentiles.

The Gerrer shtibel was in ferment. Monsters, not me, not you, a young G-d fearing man goes away to Lodz, throws off the cloth hat, the Jewish kapote, the pointed soft collar, and comes back as a veritable "German", with a paper collar, long pants and a short jacket. And who is it? Michel the judge's son-in-law! Wolf Reichman still wears the silk kapote on the Sabbath, a new one, without a tiny rip as must be with a Hassidic kapote. Indeed, Wolf Reichman, a wealthy Jew, a large-scale manufacturer, who sat at the table of Ger, already had a reputation of wearing a stiff collar with a necktie. But to be so brazen as to come to the shtibel on the eve of Shavuot during the night with yellow gaiters and laces, with a trimmed bears - having the appearance

184

of a comedian - and placing himself near Zalman Skerniewiczer, this is more than brazen! Even the sharp youth could not tolerate this type of brazenness. Everything has a boundary. And when the tall Elya removed a staple from Wolf's new kapote and straightened it out. Yitzchak Ek, a Hassid who strapped his students with a wide belt from the pants, grabbed Wolf Reichman's necktie and played with it; and a pair of left leaning young men with soft silken beards snuck underneath Wolf and removed his gaiters, which sparkled to the bright lights with their glamorous pride. That Shavuot eve was very joyous in the Gerrer shtibel. Slaps flew around, torn collars and even neckties, and bans. Quiet, Quiet, shkotzim! A desecration of G-d's name! A terrible shame!

And who was called a "German with the yellow gaiters, who interceded in favor of Wolf Reichman, and who made a "pledge" to dare to come to the shtibel on the Festival of the giving of the Torah with such gentile garb? -- None other than the sharp young man, Shabtai Nachums.

This was indeed a great innovation. Farsighted Hasidim believed that something was the matter with Shabtai Nachums. Who knows if he was also involved in the deed. The temptation is great, from all corners the Satan lies in wait for pure souls...

The Eve of Passover

Spring winds blow over the country of Poland; the sun is already warm, relief already comes strongly from the harsh winter snow, which naws with its pranks for a day longer, gnaws, and melts into water, which flows noisily, noisily to the rivers, which rise and overflow the winter dikes; the refreshing end-of-March winds overtake the cold north winds, and are antithetical to the deathly winter white. First of all: let us see earth and then there will be sprouts of grass, we will kiss their heads so let them grow already, let the buds of the lilac trees sprout, soon there will be a green, singing world. The refreshing winds blow over the Polish villages, and the birds quack in the farms, spreading eggs around the world, laying eggs before the Jewish Passover so that the housewives will have the wherewithal to make kneidlach, kremzelech, and matzo brei [54]. The refreshing winds permit beets to grow from the ground, which the farmers of Piantkow bring to Miechow so that the housewives should have with what to make the Passover red borscht. Wagons travel carrying eggs, beets, garlands of onions, red radishes. The first swallows fly in the winds. Soon the wild ducks and the storks will come in beautiful flying formations. The nightingales nest in blind Shmuel's orchard, and there will be a twitter and a song during the day and the night... The refreshing winds make the Miechow housewives considerably more agile, who with kerchief covered heads, take makeshift brushes, brooms and scraping tools, to scrape, and dust. They bend over the pot of goose fat, kashering [55] the borscht pots, grind, change over the cupboards, make requests, look over the Passover dishes, purchase new goblets for a new goblet-drinker [56]... The refreshing winds bring the pre-Passover spirit to the town. Tailors are very busy, shoemakers stitch and mend boots, and hat makers make new Szykorno hats out of velvet and cloth. The chant of the matzo puncturers, rollers and kneaders comes forth from the bakeries:

I am Goliath, the great hero
The whole world must tremble before me
I am someone and not no-one,
Ten or twenty, or thirty pairs of oxen,
Are for me like a plate of noodles...

And Shikele the Warsawer permits himself to utter another chant regarding the new winds in Kalman Mendel's cheder - the chant over all chants; Kalman Mendel with the voice of a lion's roar conducts himself towards the cheder children like a general with his soldiers, like Zanwil Reib with his musicians and band who joyously sing the chant of the community of Israel and the Divine Presence, because we are free from the double darkness, from the jail of winter, free, free, and summertime is at the doorstep.

Mandelbaum the traveling salesman finds himself on his far off journeys with the chests filled with samples of Lodzer merchandise in Vladikovkhoz, somewhere near the Volga. He does business and trades with various long cloaked "shviles", with the broad shouldered and broad chinned Andreis and Ivans, and in his nose he still carries the aromas of the Passover of Miechow, carried by the nimble soft wings of the refreshing spring winds. He rushes speedily, quickly wrapping up his business in order to be able to help with the holy work of preparing for the Festival of Freedom in a timely fashion. He did something from afar. He sent to Miechow via a purchaser from Kishinev a hundred-quart cask of strong, sweet Bessarabian wine, which Moshel will siphon off into bottles with a rubber hose. As soon as the refreshing winds begin to arrive in the strange place, the traveling salesman makes great haste to seal up the accounts. There will be fewer purchasers, for it is before Passover, and the world is in action; homeward, homeward to Jewish Miechow, to see again the Jew Shabtai Nachums, to dust off the books, to prepare the matzo shmura [57], the raisin wine, to give the Maos Chittin [58] to the rabbi; he makes haste, the traveling salesman, from far off deep Russia to celebrate Passover appropriately...

On the eve of Passover during the day, Shabtai Nachums is ready with many tasks, to burn the chometz [59], to purchase coach tickets for two coins; to help prepare the matzo shmura, to himself bring the pitchers of matzo water from the pump in the market, to himself knead, roll, pierce and shape. All of the holy tasks connected with the commandment of matzo; he already distilled the raisin wine, he already sweetened the Passover liquor. At Shabtai Nachums there must be different types of wine in honor of Passover, whether for the four cups [60], or to make a benediction. The first wines of the Land of Israel came from Rishon Letzion in slender bottles, Carmel wine [61] with the label of the two bearded Jews carrying heavy, dark, plum colored clusters of grapes on a stick [62] - and Shabtai Nachums was among the first purchasers.

Passover was already being conducted in comfort. One must now sample the festive foods. Even though at his father's of blessed memory, one would be very stringent and eat very little that day, Shabtai was more lenient [63]: the children who are already going around in their new Passover wardrobe, Moshel in a fine cut jacket, were permitted to sample of soup with pancakes, noodles, and borscht with potatoes. The mother shouted out that the children should not stain their new clothing, so that they would still retain their new status on the first days of Passover.

Shabtai Nachums returned from the mikva (ritual bath), tasted a noodle and a small bowl of borscht, not too much, for the law is that one must approach the Passover meal with an appetite. He studied the laws of Passover in "Orach Chaim" [64], chanting it in a loud voice with a special Passover melody that his late father used when he studied the tractate of Pesachim [65], so that his father soul should be elevated - on the same page... Shalom Henech and Kaczmarek

Not even a small portion of the bounty of the Lodzer high society and upper class reached Shalom Henech. He indeed moved around among wealthy Hassidim who were able to take him in to the proper business world, but Shalom Henech's head was not into it; for of what worth is the portion of riches in the world, the prime thing is that riches must be collected for the World to Come. When they answered him by stating: The heavens are the heavens of G-d, but the land was given to human beings [66], meaning that one should derive benefit from this world, he would answer that the Chidushei Harim [67] would interpret this verse as follows: the earth is given to people in order to reach the heights of the heavens, so why must one accumulate riches to which one will become enslaved. And he, Shalom Henech does not want to become a Canaanite servant [68] to money [69], for it would not permit him to learn, and it would prevent him from worshipping G-d in a pure manner. He would become a haughty person, for he would be given over to the lust of money, that means that he would be bound to objects, to houses, factories, and money, and this is similar to idolatry. The main thing is that there should be sustenance for the soul for the ultimate future. The body is subordinate: for to serve G-d one does not need to be a rich man. When a rich man is happy, when he dances a little dance, it is not for its own sake. He rejoices that he and his family have a lot to eat and drink, and a lot of nice days; but this is not from love of the Creator of the World. But a Jew without wealth can worship the Creator of all Worlds without ulterior motives, with proper desire, with complete love and joy. It is better that Shalom Henech have a blackened livelihood, providing Jews with coal throughout the year.

Indeed, during the summer the livelihood was very scarce. During the summer, one cooks with woodchips. One does not cook much; sorrel soup, new potatoes, cherry soup, one generally eats dairy, the three weeks [70]... who needs coal? Therefore, when the Elul winds begin to blow, and the windowpanes and homes are damaged, the women of Miechow begin to keep Shalom Henech and Kaczmarek in mind [71]. During the High Holy Day season, when orchard keepers begin to harvest the winter apples, when the plum dryers are ready with their merchandise, when one hears the despairing Haazinu Hashamayim and Kohelet melodies from the cheders [72], Shalom Henech and Kaczmarek load up the coal sacks, for the housewives already need quantities of coal. A slender horse carries the coal wagon; the horse was no fatter than its owners are. They both have the same blackened faces and curves shoulders. Shalom Henech is the owner, but he shares the work with Kaczmarek, the gentile of Piontk, and they work very quickly. Kaczmarek was devoted to him with his heart and soul. He would even go through fire for Shalom Henech and his Chava Ita. When the season that the entire city is concerned about coal for the winter arrives, they divide up their work. Kaczmarek has consideration for Shalom Henech, who is a bit rabin [73]. Shalom Henech pours out the coal with a shovel, opens up the sacks, and lifts them underneath. Kaczmarek places them on his shoulders to bring them into the cellars or the rooms where the housewives wish to have heat. Then Friday comes, one can already smell the gefilte fish, and Jews are already coming with wet beards and peyos from the mikva [74]. Then Kaczmarek

shouts to his boss, he almost issues a command: -- Now Shlomke, the mikva! Go to the mikva!

As bright as in Lodz...

In those years, 1908-1910, Miechow was calm. The weaving looms hum their own monotonous melody. Merchants unwind the rolls of material with their hands, brokers make deals, Jewish householders erect brick houses, daughters and sons get married, large dowries are given, and summertime is spent in the spas or in summer dwellings in the dark Wysznagorer forests. Miechow had ample livelihood. It was light on the streets and alleys of Miechow, for on one bright day, Germans with green uniforms arrived. They dug deep pits, erected tall posts, decorated them with some type of porcelain objects, and put up polished, golden twisted wires and observant Jews said with astonishment: He who created the light of the fire [75], and rejoiced that there will be no more pitiful gloomy kerosene streetlights, but rather electric lamps that are as bright as the sun. Miechow will be as bright as Lodz. One could also see in Miechow "Zywe Obrazy" (Live Pictures) the merry pictures that look exactly like the Jews who are building up colonies in the Land of Israel; the people of the "Zywe Obrazy", for whom one must pay 10 kopecks in admission, were so quick that they appeared as squirmy people. The trees, the palms, the Western Wall, Mother Rachel's tomb, the mountains and hills of the Land of Israel, were so sunny and bright green; and they awakened in the youngsters and Yeshiva boys the desire to travel and see the world.

The First World War

It was 1914! Far away there was a city called Sarajevo in Bosnia Herzegovina. Moshel knows that country from the postage stamps that he collects, beautiful large postage stamps with mountains and valleys. A beautiful land. Some sort of a crown prince was murdered there. And therefore, on a certain hot day during the nine days, small white signs in

189

Russian were seen on the street corners: "Germany declared war against us..." What a commotion those small, unimpressive signs caused in Miechow! Mobilization! Daddies were taken from their children without being able to kiss the teary cheeks of their wives. Brides could not be pried loose from their grooms [76]. Sons were torn away from their parents! Mobilization!

It smelled like mint, like the strong smell of pitch, like Tisha Beov needles, like thin milk soup, like sour apples, like plums that were not left to ripen. Idle youths hung around in the unguarded orchards with unripe fruit. Everything was wanton. There were no more firemen, the "Koze" was empty, and the clock on the magistrate building sometimes worked and sometimes did not. The bells of the church chime so unwillingly; the village gentiles were afraid to come to town with their heavy wagons laden with carrots, cabbages, kohlrabi, sticks of butter, piglets, and fat birds. After a while, the stores had nothing to sell... Mobilization! War overtook the world.

It smelled like mowed fields, like arid burial sands, like the silence before a cloudburst, like the warm breath of someone seriously ill - A fine young German in a grayish green uniform traveled speedily through Miechow on a bicycle. On his back hung a gun and a sparkling, shiny bayonet. Behind him were ten Germans with guns, all of them smiling, all dressed the same, all spiffy. It was literally a pleasure to look at them. Descending from their bicycles, standing up by the magistrate, doing, doing nothing, appearing like good Germans. Abele the cereal maker jokes as follows: tall Germans with long whips [77]. Moshel stands himself before the Germans of the Grim brothers, of Friedrich Hauf who writes such good natured stories for children, the same Germans of Bad Kissingen where father and mother travel every year and send such happy colorful postcards with spring wells, sculptures of naked people, and rose gardens. The same Germans of the Kourerter, from where one brings souvenir knives with mother of pearl, purses with tricky keys, quills with large pebbles through which one can see beautiful scenery [78]... green Germans who smile foolishly: Ja, ja, jawohl, mein herr, jawohl, mein bursch... Tall Elya says: "Yeke the fool, yeke the dummy [79]... They stand by the city hall and smile: - Do you understand German, mein Bursch? Green young Germans, a delight to look at them. They came straight here from Germany, so that the children of Miechow can look at them with their shiny guns, their gray-green uniforms, and their pointy helmets...

Who can intercede with the Germans better than Shabtai Mandelbaum,

190

who is the representative of Kreitke and Company of Kottbus. It is probably the same Germans, the chairmen of these firms, with their round, solid hats, who always say: "Gruss Gott, Herr Mandelbaum". They always treat him to malt beer and cheese; for they know that he does not eat sausages because of the "religion". Moshel knows that the German cities are neat and tidy, and that with festive clothes one can lie down in Kottbus in the middle of the street and not get dirty... And now they are here, they came to bring culture to replace the Russian "barbarism". The green, good Germans laugh, and pay for everything: "Jawohl mein Herr, was kost?" Moshel surmised that every Germans knows at least entire segments of Goethe's works, of the Schiller's poems, that all are proficient in Kant's philosophy... Good Germans who came here to study the geography of Poland.

The Cossacks, who suddenly appeared from the forest, carried the Germans off to somewhere far away... A pity, such smiling good...

That was the end of the summer of 1914. The month of Av had one summer day after another, until Elul intruded with its terror; Elul with its shofar blasts, Elul with its cold, dewy mornings, Elul with its empty fields, Elul with its repentance [80]. Artillery cannons thundered when night covered Miechow. For eight days and eight nights, Nikolai Nikoleivich had a million Siberians, Turkmens, Groznians, Kalmyks and Kazaps from Nizhniy-Novogrod, Tambov and Arkhangelsk marched through Miechow, sixteen in a row, with their platoons. And cannons, cannons...

Of the million soldiers, few returned. They made their way back from East Prussia hungry and tired, with leggings instead of shoes. In Miechow, a battle took place with the persecuted Germans, which ended with a bayonet battle. The Germans were victorious, took Warsaw, and persecuted the Russians near the Bialeweszer Forests. Miechow also became an occupied area.

Those good, green Germans from Kottbus, who knew segments of Goethe by heart, were no longer there. These were a different type of Germans, German warriors, with typical, hard steel helmets. They were serious, sinister Saxons; impolite, thick skinned Berliners with their kreutzdonnerwerter! "Wehr sind ja im krieg, kreutzaperlot!"[81].

Moshel heard such an wicked scream, when with his text book German he attempted to understand a bearded Bavarian stating that the books which he uses to heat the oven, were his beloved story books. It pained him that Hedin's travel stories should warm his requisitioned home. Karl Plenchka, a corporal From East Prussia, broke the remnants of Shabtai Mandelbaum's book shop with his knee, and uttered a curse: "Leave it alone, you filthy [82] Jewish-Pole!"

At that moment, Moshele saw the Gothic characters in the Germans books as marching soldiers with pointed bonnets, spears, and pointed, military, unbecoming chins...

The green, good Germans had become sinister, threatening, haughty, yunkers [83], with sharp rods, who got drunk and stuffed themselves in the canteens, who confiscated things, set up guard on all the routes, and issued threats about smuggling ("The Poles should eat less, for the homeland is in need of the means of nourishment"), conscripted people into compulsory labor. Thus did Moshel's beautiful, bright world turn into a world of smuggling, theft by the guards, and a world of endless weeks...

A new era began for Miechow. A new vacant generation grew up during the time of the 1915-1918 occupation

Poland is Freed

It is November, 1918. It was the end of the war in the town of Miechow.

Outside it is late autumn, with snow mixed with rain. In the "Free Library", it is as calm as in a beehive. People are going in and out, going through the mud into the wide but not overly large hall in which on account of the smoke, one cannot see at all even over the doorstep - exactly as one might go around in a narrow, foggy street of London. As much as one can see, one sees on both sides, with a pathway in the middle, massive tailor's tables with long benches. At the eastern wall is the book case, a low writing table with a bespectacled librarian, who extends his hand to the readers with papers upon which is written the numbers of the catalogues. Where there is a little free place, pictures of great people hang - writers and party leaders who are content with all the rights of the non-partisan library: Karl Marx and his neighbors with Ussishkin; Katiski with Achad Haam, Borochov with Grosser; Hirsch Lekert across from Dr. Herzl. There are slogans: "The proletariat from all the lands must unite"! "With the Basle Program"! "Religion is the opiate of the masses" - along with a picture of an Orthodox Jewish woman making the blessing on the candles...

People discuss, debate, and throw about difficult, foreign words, complicated prose, and theories. "The dialectics of world supervision", "Tomorrow following the Socialist revolution", "Stychic Process"[84], 'Auto Builder", "Reverse Reformist", "Economic reasons which drive the

192

revolutionary movement", "The Land of Israel" , "Territory", "International Service"...

It was arranged as if on plates. People analyze the previous day's lecture delivered by a Bundist speaker, who was retorted by his opponent from the right leaning Poale Zion. He had the audacity to claim that we could continue on without a national home. Modern servile people! - And there you will live in a wild land, fighting with the wild Arabs! - You will remain forever bent in a strange land! - What is strange, when is it strange? One has to struggle for rights in this place!

People shout until they become hoarse, everyone is speaking together, nobody intends to digress even to a small degree. People listen to each other's opinions with a half an ear, and from the outset discounts the proofs, citations and verses that the opponent brings down.

- Socialism does not claim that one should not have one's own nation, with its own characteristics...
- With beard and peyos, with metzitza and chalitza, with a four cornered garment [85].
- And you are international suckers; you seek rosy birds in the air...
- And you are fantasizers regarding a Palestine with swamps and malaria...
- And you are blind fools, who do not understand the Stychic process...
- We do not rely on Stychic processes, for us there is only logical reason...

The debate that started ended in the street, for the manager of the library shut off the electric switch. They discuss endlessly, and without convincing each other, as they killed time. For the youth of Miechow have enough time. In the meantime, they have nothing to occupy themselves with. They had made it through the war, survived until November 1918. The German occupation, which had sucked the marrow out of the bones of the population, assured the youth that they were not needed, like flesh in front of a cannon [86]. Hindenberg as amiable to his "beloved Jews", even though he issued orders to take the bread, meat, milk, potatoes, fruit, butter, vegetables ("Let them burst those lousy Poles", thundered the commandant of the representative of the community of inhabitants, when they realized that the typhus epidemic was spreading due to hunger); they are good to occupied areas, even though seal up the ways with all sorts of prohibitions, ordinances, and identification passes; although they punished by correctional institutions, by conscription to forced labor, sending people to the coal mines, ammunition factories of the Ruhr and Uber-Silesia - many young men wandered around, and were spared. Who did not smuggle silk, linen, thread, meat, sugar, and rice? Who did not deal with dollars, Swiss franks, and who did not smuggle through various tricks soap, liquor, gold, etc.? They went around empty, thinking about world revolutions, new times, moonbeams… In Miechow many youths wandered around who grew up without a designated profession, with empty thoughts, filling their brains with modernist ideas, ideals, theories, projects and plans. The surroundings were narrow. People dreamed of lands, of the other side of the border. People looked with jealousy on a foreign post card that brought greetings from other cultures and climates, a different, perhaps better life. These defined a better life, not so monotonous, with an aim and a purpose. In the new lands and neighborhoods, one would be different. One would work, earn a living, and be productive. Away, far, far. Here one can do nothing, but there, on the other side of the border - if one can only leave, one can breathe, the hands can do something, for oneself and for the other.

In the meantime, here in Miechow people are sickened, in the meantime people only talk, talk talk; in the meantime people build up bizarre theories, in the meantime people devour books, and dream over colorful maps. In the meantime people argue with opponents who do not agree with their own version of truths…

The news was true that in Germany they were thankful to the Kaiser, and that he rules there with a revolutionary "spartacus". Here in Miechow the gendarmes are milder than the Wilhelm-Wanses. They almost never conduct searches near the town gates. The streets are full of extra-telegrams that are feverishly distributed by the Lodzer newspaper vendors. The war ended. Happiness is in everyone's hearts. There is no more oppression. The world is open, free, free. Everyone's wishes will now be fulfilled. No more stop lights requisitions, ration cards… There will now be a sunny, blue world. If you want you can travel to America. If you want you can travel to the land of Israel, Lord Balfour permits it. A new world, a good world.

But what is this? The awaited joy is not taken in by either Jews or gentiles, for it is after a world war in which ten million lives were lost.

People do not celebrate or rejoice. Various people go around in civilian clothes, and in army cloaks with guns on their backs. They appear familiar. Kaczmarek's son Janek, the gentile from Prowyzor, Wladek the slaughterer's [87] pock-marked gymnasia student son, Broniecki Shabtai Nachum's best friend. In the event that one needed a favor from the magistrate, they went only to Broniecki… And now he drives the people out of the streets: -

194

Ordinance! Ordinance! Do not remain! Go home!

Hey, what is this? Again not free? Again forbidden, forbidden!

Poland's dream was realized, a dream of the generations. Poland was liberated. However, from where came the personages with cornered caps, with eagles that look like hens, angry, scolding, ripping off the epaulets of the pushed aside Germans, beating Jews. Broniecki speaks with a strange language: - a few too many Jews in Poland, too many Jews on our own piece of land... All business, all factories, all doctors, all merchants - Jews... Poland has to many sloppy Jews, too many...

Moshel wonders to himself and asks his father: - this means that a people is free, we must embrace them and kiss them with joy. Shabtai Nachums answers him: - I am afraid that we have no connection to the joyous wedding...

Shabtai Nachums was correct. There was no new world. The atmosphere was saturated with venomous hatred. The hatred comes from those freed, from the people with the army cloaks, with the colorful ribbons, with the emblems of patriotism, who constantly sing the anthems, all the time the wonderful happy melody of "God, why did you wrong Poland for all these generations?", and "Jews, take off the caps"! - A vicious voice cries out from some old maid in a confederation with a Jew, who rushes home to her hungry children with a sack of potatoes.

The cap lies already on the cobblestone, trodden upon by the wild patriots. The exposed head of the Jew was pressed among the mob that had become like beasts. An unfortunate Jew among mauling and biting wolves, feels naked. His head is cold, the air of the end of November day is ice cold, and he hears mocking voices: - sing, sing, loathsome Jew, Boze cos [88] Polske!.. And the terrified man who carries the sack of potatoes with his weak, cramping hands is drenched with blood, that flows from his nose and mouth... forgotten blood from a Jew in honor of the liberation of Poland.

Poland is liberated. At night, guns peal out through the empty streets. Wladeks, Janeks and Jedrzejs play with instruments of murder, like children with toys, exactly like that, shooting for enjoyment...

Poland is liberated, and instead of building up the destroyed land, the Bronieckis, Wladeks, Barlickis sew up brand new military uniforms and request: Let us play in battle, let us shoot...

This free Poland quickly found whom to hate. This was a land which itself went through a terrible operation, an immense land that was bloodied and festering. The priests gave their clerical blessing, generals held patriotic lectures, rich countries lent out the remainder of their weapons, and the new soldier was thrown into the immense land with bloody wounds, and he wished to rip off the bandages.

Soldier's boots once again stomped upon the cobblestone. The head of the county office conscripted recruits, the farmers had to once again leave their fields empty. Weeds overran the fields, the potatoes were not planted on time, the bread in the small houses had to last until spring. Trains were once again filled with soldiers going to the front, and with the wounded coming from the front; the civilians again needed identity passes, again the gendarmes with the pointy moustaches demanded documents, again people were conscripted like dogcatchers catch suspicious dogs. Again people were suspected of espionage. Somewhere someone's life was taken away by rope as he crossed himself. Again the thunder of cannons, the wild piping of gunshots, the sounds of machine gun fire were heard through the night. Again young people hid and informers turned them over. Again smuggling flourished...

Miechower Nests Empty Themselves Out...

Shabtai Nachums hummed a tune: Certainly, rabbi, every adult belongs to his town, to his country; however there is no livelihood... They place us on a narrow rope. And who knows what the kettle of hell has in store for us next... For us alone... I was wealthy, but now I must begin everything anew. Everything collapsed, just like then after the wedding... Woe, woe, rabbi, the thought came to me that perhaps the youth in Russia are correct, they want to rebuild the world on the principal that there will be no poverty, no riches.. a pity, a pity, their "Miracle by the Vistula"...

The rabbi muses: -- They say that in Russia there is no faith... How can there be a world without a G-d? Shabtai, if not for this, I would also have fallen, one time before the next time, a world without jealousy and hatred, without beggars, without privileged people...

Shabtai once again spins his thoughts: -- Something is cooking here which the world has not yet seen... And if here there is faith, does that mean it is good? The tied a rope around our necks, a choking rope that causes children to desire to leave for far off places, I cannot oppose it, I cannot...

Thus did the Miechower nests begin to empty. In every home people discussed traveling, one to South Africa, another to France, to Brazil, and still another to Argentina. Here one packs his bags, there one prepares his documents, and they set out to the border by wagon, by foot, by train, by ship. Youths, marriageable girls, young men before marriage, a fever to travel, travel...

Zlata's home was not spared from emptying. On a certain night, Moshel packed a small valise, and put in it two shirts and some underwear. Father bade him to take along Tefillin, a small prayer book, a bible, and he caressed him as he took leave, so warmly, just like on the eve of Yom Kippur after the Grace after Meals [89]. They had to wait for a long time at the train that was to take them to the border. Shabtai had tears in his voice: - You are leaving, traveling away, Moshel? Go, and it should be with god fortune... Your first journey... You have a bible with you, look into it... Stay in Germany for a time.. I wrote to the Kreitke and Company with a recommendation... Learn something. I will send you something, in accordance with my means. The main thing, remember, is to preserve the purity of the body and the purity of the soul, which is even more important... The world is strange and generally cold, one must preserve the Sabbath and festival spirit, the main thing is to keep the Sabbath and festivals in the heart, so as not to become a boor, so as not to become drunk with mere physical matters. A person must have a stronghold and a meaning; and you, who are my firstborn, I want to see you immersed in the warm Judaism that you saw in your home...

The train let out such a mournful whistle, and Moshel set out for the border.

The situation was repeated shortly, first with the brothers and later with the sisters and their husbands. Zlata remained alone, while Shabtai was rarely at home. Business and searching for a place to live generally dragged him out of the empty nest. When he would return to Miechow for a while, he would also not be at home, for he was involved in the community, and took part in various societies involved in the founding of towns and colonies in the Land of Israel. He used to always state: - Jews in Poland are like vulcans, who slowly but surely will begin to spit fire...

My Old Good Home by Dov Grand of Jerusalem

Moshe Hirsch Grand

My town of Zgierz, as I remember it, my home, the childhood years that were so terribly frustrating to us, the youngsters thrust into the world of cruelty - will accompany me for my entire life.

My father Moshe Hirsch Grand of blessed memory, the son of Avraham the "Old Stanik" as they called him, was a Jew with a national consciousness, a dear man, a loving father and an enlightened man who bore dreams of improving the world.

He had a butcher shop on Pilsudski Street, and later - also a sausage factory. The sausages were produced in the factory in the courtyard of my uncle Avigdor Rozalski, may G-d avenge his blood, also a butcher. He was my father's partner.

We lived peacefully and happily. We children had a worry free world.

The anti-Semitic incitement began to grow during the 1930s. There were pickets and anti-Jewish decrees, such as the restrictions on ritual slaughter. My father organized all of the Jewish butchers in Zgierz and created a cooperative. He was chosen as chairman. My father served a representative in the Jewish communal council for a long period of time.

My mother, the daughter of Adam Szperling (also a butcher) was very devoted to her husband and children. She was always ready to sacrifice for us. She was a dear balabusta [90]. She would also stand in the butcher shop and sell meat. Mother was very refined and gentle. When she had a little time, she would read Yiddish books.

We were five children. My only sister was the eldest. I, Berl and my brother Mordechai were the only survivors of the family. Adam and Shimon were 9 and 11 years old at the outbreak of the war.

The First Charitable Fund by W. F.

The charitable fund was one of the most important and active philanthropic institutions in Zgierz.

It was officially founded and authorized by the Russian authorities in the year 1900, but already from several years earlier, it conducted widespread activity among the disadvantaged and impoverished segments of the Jewish community in the city.

The protocol of foundation ("Statutes") was undersigned by 64 Zgierz Jews, representatives of all strata, social organization and religious groups. The creation of such an important institution demonstrates the unity of the Zgierz community.

Paragraph 1 of the founding protocol states:

"The society has the purpose of creating the means to improve the material and moral situation of the impoverished Jews of Zgierz and vicinity, without differentiating between sex, profession, and status.

It is worthwhile to mention here that in the year 1900, the electric tramway began to travel between Lodz and Zgierz, and many wagon drivers and horse drawn carriage drivers of Zgierz thereby lost their livelihoods. This increased the number of poor and unemployed. The creation of such an assistance fund was an urgent necessity at that time. The protocol (of which we bring here a photocopy of its last page), ended with the names of Chanan Rozenstrauch, David Kanel, A. M. Weiss, and F. Margolies (?). The under-signers come in two straight columns, divided lengthwise.

First row (signatures not legible): Ozer Kohn, M. Krynski, T. Lipszicz (unclear), Y. A. Rosinow, B. (?) Szapiro, B. Zucker, A. Z. Borensztejn, A. Y. Kuperman, Sh. Z. Gelbart, B. Bentkowski, Izaak Nekricz, G. Szer, D.

199

Szapszowicz, M. Glowinski (unclear), B. Szaranski, M. L. Widowski (unclear), M. W. Berman, Sh. Landau, P. Kalmerski, Yosef Poznerzon, M. Rozenberg, M. Lerner, E. (?) Sztikgold (unclear), H. Kohn, Izidor Strikowski (unclear), Shalom Zandberg, Moshe Skosowski.

Second row from he top: Isuchar Szwarc, A. Y. Lis, Y. Szidlowski, Sh. Sirkis, N. Heinsdorf, D. Berliner, E.Praszker, M. sh. Dawidkowiz, Y. A. Gelbart, Y. D. Gerszon, W. Reichert, Y. Y. Blosztejn, Y. B. Lewkowicz, Izer. Bawes, Shia Kofman (unclear), Jakow Gricehendleer, Z. Bornsztejn, Y. B. Berman, F. Gorner, L. Lenczyski, L. Rozenberg, D. Bendkowski, M. H. Hanower, Abe Baum, A. Wachtel, A. Bozyn, M. N. Rubensztejn.

A segment of the signatures on the founding protocol of the Gemilat Chasadim organization in 1900

200

Two Important Jewish Institutions by Yaakov Cincinatus

A. The Jewish Tailor Guild of Zgierz

Regarding the activity of the Zgierz Jewish Tailor Guild, I remember a few important moments:

The unveiling of the flag came at the time when my father was the guild master and Feivish Moszkowicz was the vice guild master.

In fact, there was no management committee. If a craftsman wanted to obtain a master diploma, he had to present a request to the guild master. After that, he had to be officially examined by a committee consisting of the guild master, vice guild master, and two members of the guild, as well as a representative of the authorities who was called an assessor. The assessor was Rewerski, a Pole who worked in the evidence office of the Zgierz magistrate. He in fact received 50 Zloty for a master diploma, even though legally he was only entitles to 5 Zloty for undersigning the protocol.

Dov Cincinatus of blessed memory

The guild had the rights to issue a diploma from any tailor from Zgierz and from anywhere in Poland who was [91] able to demonstrate his knowledge of the profession. These diplomas, called "Master letters", had a great significance for the Jewish craftsman. This was especially so after the war, when the Polish authorities began to chicane the Jews.

In the time of my father's term as guild master, very many master letters were issued. I recall that my brother Aharon of blessed memory, who at that time lived in Vilna, wrote to my father: "Father, you do not realize the importance of your work that you do. Through your efforts, more Jewish craftsmen can obtain Master letters." I remember well all of the problems of the tailor's guild, for I was my father's secretary. I took care of all technical mattes that were connected to the guild.

I want to note here that all of the issued diplomas were 100% legal, and the authorities could not discredit them. During the 1930s, I do not remember the exact date, the Polish authorities made a decision that all guilds should be transferred over to the handworkers-branch ("Izba Rzemieslnicza"). This was a pretext to liquidate the Zgierz guild.

The "Izba Rzsemieszlanicza" in fact had the rights to permit the activity of the guild, for all other guilds remained, and they did not interfere with their activity.

On a certain day, my father and Moszkowicz went to the regional office (Wojewodszta) in Lodz. They declared to them without offering a reason that the Wojewodszta office and the "Izba Rzemieslnicza" decided to liquidate the tailors' guild. They were told that they must give over the books of protocols and cease activity. Fortunately, the speaker was a Pole from Zgierz, Gonszarowski, who was the Wojewodszta speaker for matters of the handworkers' industry. When my father tried to persuade him that the guild has an important significance for the craftsmen, and that the other guilds continue to exist, he answered with the following words.

"Mr. Cincinatus, I understand you very well, but this is the decision of the Wojewodszta and the handworkers' branch - and I cannot change it."

Thus ended the "Jewish Tailors' Guild in Zgierz" with its blue and white banner.

B. Hachnasat Orchim

The "Hachnasat Orchim" (Society for ensuring the wellbeing of wayfarers) was found on Narutowicza Street, in premises that were approximately 12 meters long and 4 meters wide. The manager and his family lived in a small portion of those premises. He was a shoemaker by trade. I do not remember his name.

Every Jewish stranger could spend the night there. Officially, they had rights for two nights. Unofficially, Jews would stay there for entire weeks.

The manager had the duty to maintain cleanliness and order. During the winter, he would cook a warm meal for the guests.

The guests consisted primarily of poor people who wandered about from city to city.

As I recall, Anshel Waldman and other Jews were also involved the Hachnasat Orchim.

Money would be collected from the Jewish population of Zgierz for the purchase of equipment and the maintenance of that institution.

The Jewish Orphanage in Zgierz by Chana Szaranski.

The Jewish orphanage in our city was founded in 1915. For its 24 years of existence, it was also known by the names "Ochronka", "Dom Sierot" [92], and Children's Home. The initiators of the effort to build up that institution were A. Morgensztern, Chama Sirkis and Sh. Ring.

The house was located on Pilsudskiego number 30. It consisted of 1 large room, 2 smaller rooms, and 1 small room for the educators. There was also a large kitchen where they would cook lunch for the children every day. The director of the institution was Morgensztern. The expenses were covered by the community, city council and Joint [93]. There were almost no private contributors. Children between the ages of 3 and 8, who were full or half orphans or were from poor homes, were taken into the orphanage. The children received food, upbringing and education (only arithmetic) at the institution. The younger children had several playthings at their disposition. There were performances four times a year, prepared and performed by the children.

The orphans did not sleep in the "Ochronka", but only came there to spend the day. They received bread with marmalade and milk at 8:00 a.m. At noon, they received soup with bread, after which they took a nap.

The institution moved to a different location in the year 1922. The greatest number of children that the institution could take in was - 7 [94].

The staff consisted of a teacher from Lodz, the director Chana Szaranski, and one cook. The medical supervision of the children was taken care of by the civic authorities, a Christian Doctor.

The Jewish orphanage (1921).
In the middle, the teacher A. Morgensztern and Chana Szaranski

In the Presence of my Teacher, Rabbi Rafael Henech Blosztejn of blessed memory by F. Ben-Srok

Reb Rafael Henech Blosztejn of blessed memory

On one of the days of Elul in 5677 (1917), between classes, our rabbi Reb Rafael Henech had a gloomy smile on his face that was adorned with a broad, black beard. He turned to us with a heavy heart:

"I can tell you pleasant news. After the upcoming holidays, we will be parting, for good fortune."

This came to us as a surprise. Exams took place only one month previously, and three of the best students received prizes. Through the year, we became accustomed to our revered rabbi, and we loved him very much. Why has the misfortune come that he was being taken from our midst? When we pushed him for the reasons for this parting, he pulled his broad, round shoulders and did not say anything.

When we asked him who would be replacing him, he smiled and said: "Don't worry! ... The person replacing me is a superb scholar, although his methodology is different with regard to the sharpness and the simple explanations.".....

A few days later we found out that our new rabbi who was replacing Reb Rafael Henech was Reb Mendel Wechsler, the son-in-law of Reb Fishel Binem the shochet, or as he was called in short, "Mendel Fishel Binem's".

The First World War that took place between the years of 1914-1918 obviously did not pass over our city. The Germans conquered the city, and conquered it again from the Russians during the battles that kept on returning. They then held it for four years. During this era, the troops of the German Kaiser were better than their children and grandchildren of the time of Hitler, may his bones be ground up. If they damaged the conquered population, they damaged their property, not their bodies.

In general, the occupying authorities did not mix into the private lives of the Jewish citizens. They only organized them into communities, and took great precautions regarding cleanliness out of fear of epidemics of typhus and other communicable diseases, that were caused from malnutrition and prolonged suffering. Their first task was to drag the children of the cheders and the schools to the city hospital on a weekly basis for washing and delousing.

The children of cheders indeed were not disappointed with this decree. Their fathers, the Orthodox men of the city, did not sit silently. They tried, pushed, requested and received deferment after deferment. When they had exhausted all ends, they founded a modern school under the name "House of

Learning of Torah and the Ways of the World". The modern cheder that had opened one year previously in nearby Lodz served as an example.

The "Cheder Metukan" (Modern Cheder) opened in our city in Tishrei 5677 (1917). The first teachers were Reb Yaakov Milichewicki (Reb Yaakov the son of Yaakov, with his popular nickname) who taught Bible and Hebrew, and Reb Rafael Henech Blosztejn who taught grade 4.

Reb Rafael Henech, the son of the rabbi of Lutomiersk and the son-in-law of Reb Shmuel Yechezkel Torenberg, was numbered among the expert scholars of our city. He did some work at home for the weaving factory, and in his free time, he educated older children, as well as grooms and young adults after their marriage. His sources of income dried up during the war years, and due to the financial pressure, Reb Rafael Henech agreed to accept a position of teacher at the school.

He was childless. He loved his students very much and they loved him. The children of the cheder, who were previously used to beatings with a strap, very much enjoyed the reprieve with their new Rebbe. They took advantage of his good heart, and disrupted the order of his day a times. The "whip" in his hand was the ledger of marks. Just as the school in Lodz, the school in Zgierz issued grades for each subject (Torah, Talmud, Bible, grammar, etc. and also for manners, politeness, diligence, attention, industriousness, etc.) The teacher kept a lined notebook with the names of the students, and whoever was impolite or did not pay attention received a dot, which meant a "minus". The best mark was a 5 (he). One dot lowered the mark, and two dots already lowered the 5 to a 4 (daled), etc. There were students who were bothered by the marks, and argued about them. Then, after they behaved properly, Reb Rafael Henech would forgive them.
There were also those who were not like "the bones of Joseph" (an exhaustive commentary on the tractate of Kiddushin).

That year, we studied the chapter of "Haisha Niknet" [95]. We succeeded in learning less than ten folios during the entire winter. The methodology of Reb Rafael Henech was to study "everything in its place", and to analyze the entire matter with all of the commentaries, including Tosafot, Maharsha, etc. The book "Atzamot Yosef" ("The bones of Joseph") (an exhaustive commentary on the tractate of Kiddushin) did not leave our hands.

Reb Rafael Henech also trained us in commandments. That year, several of the students, including the writer of these lines, reached the age of commandments. Reb Rafael Henech woke up early with us during the cold months of Tevet and Shvat, and taught us the laws of tefillin, and especially he helped us prepare the discourse ("pshetl") for the Bar Mitzvah. The pshetl was a finely interwoven work, and learning it by heart was not the easiest of tasks.

He once caught me in my error. During the time of studies, I looked into the book of the stories of Hassidim (The Saba from Shpoile - Portents of Rabbi Aryeh of Shpoile). I was very attracted to these books, and I brought the book from home to continue reading it from where I had left off. I placed the book on my lap and read it with lowered eyes in an attempt to hide my transgression from Reb Rafael Henech, who was immersed in the Talmudic discussion. However, he noticed my confusion, approached me and removed the book after a struggle. Of course, he looked into it, and immediately put a dot under attention. He returned me the book during recess, with a warning not to bring any more books to school.

He added: "If you enjoy reading books, why do you waste your time on the books of old tobacco chewers. I will give you a list of good and interesting reading books."

He gave me a list of European writers of that era, and the next day he even brought me the book "Secrets of Paris" by Izen Siv to read at home. This book was translated by Kalman Shulman. After I devoured all parts of that book in several evenings, he gave me another book.

However, he did not forego the dot that he jotted down regarding my first sin. He refused to forego.

I later found out that Reb Rafael Henech was involved with philosophy and research. It is no wonder, indeed, that storybooks were considered a waste of time for a youth who was growing up.

We never found out the reason why he left our school. Various rumors spread. One rumor stated that the committee of the school did not approve of his teaching methodology. The parents of the students demanded that the number of pages of Gemara studied be maximized, and not be satisfied with the less than 20 folios that we succeeded in learning throughout a year. Another version was that he was too weak and good for the children of the cheder, who were used to a stronger hand.

The true reason, as became clear later, was that the majority of the school committee, who were Hassidic, were concerned that his influence might "damage" Reb Rafael Henech. It was no secret that Reb Rafael

Henech, despite his Orthodoxy and milling about in Hassidic circles, had no small tendency toward Haskala and Zionism. These grew wings during the years of the world war. He supported Mizrachi, the new movement that had recently sprouted in our city. Many Orthodox people, including no small number of Hassidim, adhered to it. His critical stance to various manifestations of Hassidism and its practitioners was also well known. In his younger days, he would travel to the "Sfat Emet" and was numbered among those who revered him. After the death of the Sfat Emet, he did not continue to visit his son, the Rebbe. The Hassidim looked disapprovingly upon a Hassid who worshiped in the shtibel, wore Hassidic garb, and in addition was a scholar, but who kept away from the Rebbe even on the festivals.

It later become known that the school in Lodz that served as the model for ours began to bring forth "spoiled fruit". It was said that students abandoned the school and transferred to the gymnasia. They immediately decided to erase the "disgraceful name", and changed the name of the school to "Yesodei Hatorah". It was enlarged, and its scope expanded. They even brought in some more "traditional" teachers, who were considered to be fitting with regard to the tradition of studies. The sun of Reb Yitzchak Eksztejn (Reb Yitzchak Ek) shone once again in this group of teachers. He attained a great stature in the school in its new form. Moshe Zeida, the son of Kalman Mendel and others were also involved. The crowning glory of this school was Reb Mendel Wechsler, who took over the place of Reb Rafael Henech. Reb Mendel was a former Hassid of Sochaczew, the student of Reb Avrahamele who was the son-in-law of Rebbe Mendel of Kock. Once, he was enticed by his father to accompany him to visit the Sfat Emet, and from then on, he continued to travel to Gur.

Reb Rafael Henech continued on with his private work after he left our school. He occupied himself in this manner until the outbreak of the war. His influence was recognizable in our city. He educated and raised many fine Jews, observant and non-observant, all of them deeply rooted in Judaism and perfumed with enlightenment and Zionism. Reb Rafael Henech saw these attributes as the "interwoven thread" in the belt of a complete Jew. May his memory be a blessing.

My Teachers and Educators in Zgierz by F. Ben-Sira

With the guidance of the Shulchan Aruch, which (Code of Jewish Law) encompasses the paths of the life of every religious Jew from the day of his birth until the day of his death; our parents and grandparents concerned themselves with their children, to educate them as proper Jews from the age of earliest childhood until they left the home at the time of their marriage.

When I was five years old, I met my first teacher, Fishel the Lame. Our home, which was blessed with many children, "breathed a breath of air" when one of us went out to spend the majority of the hours of the day in the cheder.

Fishel hired an assistant (Belfer), who would bring the children to the cheder and take them back home again. Fishel himself did not budge from his table in his deep, dark cheder, where he was surrounded by his students who were being introduced to the Alef Beit. The children were obedient and calm. When he encountered a stubborn or obstinate child, Fishel did not waste any time - "he who withholds the rod hates the child". Without hesitation, he would pull down his pants, lay him over his knees, and count out the appropriate number. After such a "softening", this child would be as soft as butter.

His wife Perl would bake challas every Sabbath eve. From among these challas, there would be one small challa in the shape of a bird, with which she honored the child who excelled in his behavior during that week. The distribution of the prize awakened great interest in the children every Friday, and occupied their thoughts and yearning.

Shimshon Wolf, who inherited the cheder from his father, was short in stature and thick bearded. He had fine penmanship and good grammar. He was a slight reformist with regard to teaching methodology. He minimized corporal punishment, and maximized pleasant words.

My second teacher was Reb Shabtai Hoizszpigiel. I studied Chumash and Rashi from him. He had a splendid countenance and a good disposition. He raised his had against his students infrequently. He was missing teeth, and false teeth were not known to people of his status (wealthy people were able to afford such luxuries). Therefore, he used to divide his bread with his favorite students. He took the soft piece for himself, and gave the crusts to them. On the other hand, his wife Golda was always bitter. Whenever something improper happened with one of the students, she would lay her heavy hand upon him, and her husband would hurry to protect him. She also ruled with anger and wrath over her older children. They hid underneath the table from her hand when she chased them with a broom, spatula or rolling pin.

Shabtai took ill with paralysis in the middle of the semester, and died in the year 5676 - 1916.

From there, I transferred to Mendel Lunczycer (from the city of Leczyca). He was an idle Hassid, with a scraggly beard, who used to hit his students in his own fashion, with only three fingers. His two middle fingers were always bent inward. It was said that he had this injury inflicted upon himself by the medic at the time of his draft to the Russian army, so that he would be able to free himself from the yoke of the government that was so feared by the young Jews. What Jewish youth who was faithful to his religion would be willing to defile himself with treif foods and pork? He hated any thing new that took hold within the community, saying that "new is forbidden from the Torah" [96]. He taught us Gemara, and drew near the weaker students with extra love. He saw the visage of Esau in spoiled and pampered children. When the smell of fine soap from one of the children reached his nose, he would sneeze and complain: "Who brought her the smell of rosewater".

He had older sons and daughters with him in the house. Moshele, one of his sons, studied with us.

Reb Mendel became ill with paralysis [97] in the middle of the year in the year 5672 (1912). His students dispersed to other cheders.

My last cheder teacher was Reb Yitzchak Eksztejn. His was known as "Yitzchak Ek". He was a solid man, thick with a fat, red neck. The students received "the real thing" in his cheder, which was missing from the earlier cheders. He had a stricter mode of discipline, almost military. The workday was twelve hours, and the work was very difficult. The days passed by without change, in the summer and winter. With the exception of the vacations that we received on Friday afternoons, Sabbaths and festivals, we worked day and night, in the long summer days as in the tiresome winter nights. On Chanukah we were let out earlier than usual, but in lieu of this, we had to study without the afternoon break

Reb Yitzchak did not recognize the vacations that the other teachers were accustomed to, such as the time between terms [98], the evenings after the Torah portion of Vayakhel-Pikudei [99], etc. We had no such "idle time"!

Reb Yitzchak Ek was lacking in the trait of mercy with respect to his students. He would dispense slaps and serious thrashings from every small matter, and he paid no attention to the protests of the parents. When a parent complained to him about marks found on the body of a student who had received a beating, he replied decisively without any sign of regret: "Your son was given over to me, and for the time that he is with me in cheder, you have no control over him. He belongs to me!"

He did not desist from his duties even during the time that he was sitting Shiva in his house after the death of his brother. The students were forced to sit under his supervision and review their lessons. He did not regard his profession of teaching as a yoke of livelihood, but rather as a duty to teach.

His wife Reizel, on the other hand, was goodhearted. She frequently came to aid of the children who were forced to lie with their rears upward in order to receive the punishment. Such a punishment was degrading and oppressive for ten your old boys. She would also tell the children all soft of stories between Mincha and Maariv, during the brief period with Reb Yitzchak would go to worship with a Minyan (a formal prayer quorum), and the children were able to relax.

It was told that his father, Reb Berl Munish was even stricter and harsher than the son, and that he would beat his students with a sailor's staff.

At the conclusion of the war, when the period of the cheders ended, Reb Yitzchak transferred to the Yesodei Hatorah school. This was a modern cheder with classes and divisions that was founded by Agudas Yisroel. However, he did not pay attention to the new winds, and he continued with his methodology. The parents of the students did not let him go this time, and from time to time a scandal broke out. They even threatened to hit him. The fear of this teacher was so ingrained and rooted in his students, that even after they had graduated and left his cheder, they would tremble if they ran into him for some reason. His appearance instilled fear in them.

Reb Yitzchak died in the 1930s, a few years before the outbreak of the war.

The cheder of Reb Yitzchak was my final cheder. From there, I transferred to the Beis Midrash, where the rabbi of the city gave a class to the boys. Why did he teach specifically the tractate of Zevachim [100], which was generally not well studied? Perhaps because he was a Kohen, and the topic was close to him.

211

The sons of the wealthy people continued to study with Reb Bendet Frenkel. He was a scholarly Jew, and the number of his students was small. He would dish out beatings with his elbow. He used to say regularly, "Oh, the heart attracts, attracts!..."

Prior to the First World War (1914), there was a Yeshiva in Zgierz called Yagdil Torah. The students of the Yeshiva were called "Yagdilach" [101]. Students came to this Yeshiva from all corners of Poland. The Yeshiva students took their meals in rotation (Yamim) from residents of the city. Some of them ate fine food themselves, but distributed "bread and water" to the Yeshiva students.

Married youths, who would show off the gold watches that they received from their fathers-in-law, studied with Reb Ichel. They would go to him for a number of hours during the day and study Yoreh Deah [102] and halachic decisors. On occasion, the door would open and a woman would enter with a question regarding a needle found in the gizzard [103], or milk that dripped into a pot of meat. The elder rebbetzin (the second wife of the wife of the old rabbi, Reb Shalom Tzvi, who married him in his old age and bore two sons to him: the rabbi of the city and Reb Yitzchak Mendel, after he died she married Reb Ichel) would come and go, and when Ichel would go into the second room to deal with a question of matters of women [104], she would accompany him.

Reb Yaakov the son of Yaakov Milichewicki of blessed memory by Y. A. Malchieli

Reb Yaakov

My revered father Reb Yaakov Milichewicki arrived in Zgierz during the first decade of the 1900s from Karlitz, Lithuania. He was accepted in the city as a teacher and educator for good students.

His wife Hadassa Rachel was the daughter of Reb Eliezer Reuven Marishinski, a pious and noble man, the brother-in-law of Reb Reuven Halevi, the great rabbi of Dineburg (Dvinsk) (he was the brother of my maternal grandmother), and a descendent of the Gra [105] of blessed memory.

I remember that it was related at home that my father wished to dedicate his time to Torah and study immediately after his marriage, and my mother accepted upon herself the yoke of livelihood. She opened a small grocery store. The turnover was large but the customers were poor. When it came time to pay their debts, my mother did not wish to be a creditor to them. "How can I demand money from them", she would say, "they don't have any!..." Therefore, the store closed after a brief period. Then my father accepted the advice of Binyamin Katznelson (the father of the poet Yitzchak Katznelson) to travel to Zgierz and take his place in the field of education. B. Katznelson was attracted to educational work in Zgierz by Isuchar Szwarc of blessed memory, who became friendly with him in Warsaw.

It is strange that if one came to Zgierz and asked for the dwelling place of Michilewicki, it would be doubtful if they would receive an answer. However, the name of Reb Yaakov ben Yaakov was known to everybody in the city, from young to old.

This was because Reb Yaakov was one of the personalities who imprinted his mark upon Hebrew education in our city during the first third of the 1900s. He educated two generations, and had hundreds of students from all segments of the community. These students left his modern school as Jews with both traditional and national education.

In his cheder, students learned to worship in accordance with the law and they also learned to delve into the meaning of the prayers. They studied Torah and prophets with topical explanations and clear understanding of the words, as well as the lyrical and unique attributes. The students also learned Talmud, commentaries and halachic decisions, with full explanation of the material. They studied the Hebrew language and grammar in a fundamental manner, using modern books that were published in that era by the best authors and writers.

Not only did the children from homes whose parents had already become involved with Zionism and the signs of the times stream to the cheder; but also the children of Hassidim and Jews who were attached to the old ways, who were not able to resist the enticement of the acquisition of the complete Torah and a serious Jewish education for their children.

There were occasions when he was called to places outside of Zgierz, such as the cities of Nowe Radomsko, Zychlin and other such cities. He answered the call, and remained in each place for a few months to impart his teaching methodology.

As a preacher and educator to the ideas of the redemption, he actualized the desire for Zion in a real sense. He himself fulfilled the mitzvah of making aliya to the Holy land. He made aliya in 5686 (1926) and settled in Petach Tikva. There, he continued to impart Torah to the masses, and was honored and beloved by everybody, especially by those who took hold of and taught Torah.

When Reb Yaakov took leave of his many friends and students on the eve of his aliya from Zgierz, everybody raised their voices in weeping. Among those gathered was Reb Isuchar Szwarc of blessed memory, who was a friend and brother to Reb Yaakov for all the years. The parting was difficult for them.

One of the images that is deeply ingrained in my memory from the days of my youth was the image that repeated itself every Sabbath and festival, when these two friends paced together in the synagogue for a long time after the end of the service, exchanging novel ideas of Torah and words of the sages; Their tallises were still upon their shoulders, and their faces shone from the joy of the new ideas as people who have found a great treasure. They drew pearls discretely from the depths of Torah, and exchanged them with each other with a willing soul, and with a heart full of spiritual delights.

His eldest son was educated as an older lad in the Yeshivas of Lithuania. He made aliya even before his father, where he continued with his studies. His daughter Ita, who was educated in the Beis Yaakov Seminary in Krakow, and later served as a teacher in a Beis Yaakov school, made aliya later. She continued teaching here in the Beis Yaakov system. She died after her marriage. The youngest son Reuven also lives in Israel. The two sons live in Petach Tikva.

Reb Yaakov was called to his eternal world on the 3rd of Kislev 5723 (1963), and was buried in Kiryat Meir in Bnei Brak, where he lived during his final year. May his soul be bound in the bonds of eternal life.

Reb Wolf Leib Haltrecht (Ohev Tzedek) by W. Fiszer

Reb Wolf Leib Haltrecht

Reb Wolf Leib the teacher was without doubt one of the popular personalities of Zgierz. He was a Jew with a splendid countenance and a fine patriarchal beard. He was somewhat taller than average. He appeared both in the synagogue, where he served as the Torah reader and shofar blower, and on the street in clean clothes and with his unique, self-confident gait.

He was a teacher (melamed), but not only a teacher, but also an intelligent, knowledgeable Jew. His cheder also qualified as a modern cheder. His students came mainly from sophisticated, well-to-do homes. Wolf Leib did not only teach Gemara and Tosafot [106]. They also studied the verses (Bible) in a fundamental fashion, not restricted to the weekly Torah portion, as well as Hebrew and grammar. Separately, he made sure to teach the Haftorah [107] reading with the proper cantillation. Hassidim suspected him of teaching with Moshe Deser's commentary [108] and therefore did not permit their children to enter into close friendships with his

215

students, even though he himself was a warm, national-religious Jew.He could often be found with a select group of householders on summer Sabbath afternoons, studying the Torah portion of the week or a chapter of the Book of Proverbs (Mishlei). His face shone with satisfaction as he presented to them familiar and understandable explanations. His lectures were accompanied with examples from day to day life. It was literally sweet to hear.

Aside from teaching, he was also a bit of a handyman or a craftsman, as it is called. He would paint "shivitis" [109] and make various woodcuttings for the reader's desk, the Holy Ark and the like; or inscribe a "kegavna" and "brich shmei" [110] to hang upon the walls of the synagogues.

His prime source of livelihood, nevertheless, was from clock making. He even had his own little shop on the Long Street, where clocks, running and stopped, were lying in a glass case, as well as rings, earrings, hairpins, broaches and bracelets of all types and from all times. His wife and daughter would help him in his shop on market days.

He was also known in town as the best mohel. He conducted the circumcision fast and professionally while being strict about hygienic matters, just like a big city mohel from the new era. This made him very popular among the population. Therefore, he was able to proudly state, regarding half of the town: "These are my Jews".

The well-known writer Chaim Leib Fuchs in his article "Jewish Literary Lodz" ("From the Recent Past", volume 3, pp. 256-257, New York, 1957) makes mention of several Maskilim and writers from Zgierz: "The well-known Zgierz Maskil Reb Wolf Leib Haltrecht had a definite influence upon the Lodzer Jewish intelligentsia, even though he did not write himself. They used to bring to him, like to an editor, almost everything that the writers wrote during their first years."

Wolf Leib met his sad fate together with the entire community of Zgierz, in which he participated as a lively member, as a man well versed in interpersonal relations, and also as a communal activist. He was never heard from again after the expulsion from Zgierz.

May G-d avenge his blood! May his soul be bound in the bonds of eternal life.

The Businessman's School of Zgierz by F. Grynberg

Here are a few words about the Zgierz Businessman's School, as it was known throughout Russia.

The number of Jewish students there was very large. A diploma from that school gave one the right to live anywhere in Russia that is in the areas where Jews did not have the rights to live.

On "Galovka" as it was called at that time, the birthday of the Czar Nikolai II, or the days of other Czarist holidays, it was the duty of all students to go to the houses of prayer - each in accordance to his religion. We Jewish students went to the synagogue, two in a row. When the head of our procession reached Margolies' house, the last rows were still by the German Church. This demonstrates how large the number of Jewish students was.

The Jewish and Christian teachers entered the synagogue and stood at the pulpit. The students surrounded them. One of the teachers delivered a speech about the importance of the day. The proceedings concluded with the singing of the hymn "Boze Czaria Chrani" (God Save the Czar). Then the students had to stand like soldiers and salute.

The school was founded around 1892 by the Zgierz manufacturers and merchants, led by the well-known Borst firm.

All of the students from outside the city had to find homes. The found accommodations in the homes of members of the Jewish intelligentsia such as Isuchar Szwarc, Mrs. Feigele Margolies, Menashe Cohen and others.

The school existed until the revolution of 1905. The school strike then ended with the granting of permission to the Poles to have schools with the Polish language of instruction. Therefore, the schools lost all of the privileges that the Russian schools had. Zgierz was free of Russian schools.

General knowledge was complemented with Jewish knowledge in a number of Pensions [111], thanks to well-known teachers who taught the students. Among others was H. D. Nomberg, who as the educator in Isuchar Szwarc's Pension.

In the Zgierz Businessman's School by Dr. Jakob Eichner.

I entered the school in 1898. The Jewish students came mainly from White Russia, Kiev, Poltava, etc. Without being precise, approximately 40% of the students were Jewish. The students from out of town were put up in special Pensions. In 1901, I became friendly with Sasha Danzig, a gymnasia student who came from Riga. Sasha already knew about Socialism, and introduced me to Marxist literature, which I had to learn. I joined the library at the mutual benefit organization for business workers, and I borrowed books from there.

A student group was formed in the school. We read books together, spent time together at outings, and discussed politics. The heads of the group were David Mazor, today in the Soviet Union, and Leib Kolecki, today a doctor in the Soviet Union. Those two students and I were active Bundists. By 1903, the students group was no longer occupied solely with self-education, but also with creating assistance for revolutionary organizations. The Bund had the strongest influence on the students group.

Quoted from the book "History of the Jewish Workers' Movement in Lodz" by A. Wolf-Jasni, printed in Lodz, 1937.

Jewish Elementary Schools in Zgierz
by Sara Katz, principal of the Jewish Public School in Zgierz

A class in the Jewish Pubic School with the Polish principal Kuszmirk

The Jewish Public School was housed in the small house of the Zurkowski family on Blotene Street until the First World War. Mrs. Ela Tenenbaum was the principal. The language of education was Russian. The sanitary conditions were inferior, and impoverished students studied there. The children of the wealthier parents studied in private non-Jewish schools (such as Mrs. Tydlaska). At the end of the period of German occupation, the school moved to a larger building, and several classes were added to it, with the assistance of the representatives of the communal council, headed by Messrs. Naftali and Handelis.

The sanitary conditions improved in the new school, and the children stemmed from a variety of strata of society. The teachers were young Jewesses who had studied in teacher's seminaries The language of instruction was obviously German.

When the Germans left in 1918, the supervision of the schools transferred to the Polish authorities. The Jewish school became affiliated with the general educational network in the city as Public School number 6. The relationship of the authorities to the institution and to the teachers, most of whom were Jewish, was liberal. I was appointed as principal of the school, a position that I retained until 1927. During this era, the Endekes [112] had already taken control of the government. They imposed a Christian staff upon the Jewish school. The atmosphere became thick and oppressive. The staff slowly emptied of Jews, and became composed primarily of Polish teachers who openly spoke of the praises of Hitler. At the end of 1938, only very few Jews remained in the ranks of the teaching staff.

During the time of my work in this school, the following people served as teachers: Henka Cohen, Gita Rozenman, Leon Rusak, Jadzia Gutjehner, Eugenia Cohen and Pola Dawidowicz. Their relationship to the students was warm and enthusiastic. They offered their constant support during times of oppression, which were not infrequent in those days. They stood at their sides, literally as parents, and tried to ease their burden, and to strengthen them in soul and spirit.

With the exception of the teacher Guthejner who lives today in Israel, all of them, teachers and students, perished in the furnaces along with their parents and siblings. May these lines serve as a monument to all of the teachers in Zgierz who endured difficult conditions and dedicated their lives to the education of the Jewish children, and to forge their personalities and beings. May their memories be a blessing.

A class in the Jewish public school, with the teachers Henka Cohen, Gutzia Rozenman, Genia Dhan, Eugenia Rozenberg, Sara Katz, Jadzia Guthejner, unidentified, Leon Rusak

An excursion of the Zgierz public school to the salt pits of Wieliczka

A class in the Jewish public school of Zgierz, with the teachers H. Cohen, S .Katz, A. Rozenberg, L. Rusak, G. Rozenman, the principal Koszmirk, and Plasmonowa

A Ruined Lag Baomer by Yitzchak Sczaransky of Ramat Gan

After the Lame Fishel (Reb Fishel Glicksman), the teacher, with whom studied ninety percent of the children of Zgierz, and later his son Shimshon Wolf who taught trope (Torah cantillation) to the children, sixteen children including myself began to study with the teacher Kalman Mendel.

Kalman Mendel's cheder was located in a small house near the fish market, not far from the Catholic Church. We had to pass by the church every day when we went to cheder, and we never forgot to recite "thou shalt surely abhor it" [113]…

We commenced studying with the teacher Kalman Mendel immediately after Sukkot. We studied from 8 in the morning until 8 in the evening, with a recess of two hours in the afternoon.

We studied Chumash and Rashi, and later also Gemara. The worst was going home at 8:00 p.m. from the cheder, for fear that a sheigetz [114] might come upon us and extinguish the lanterns that each child carried. The streets were not lit, with the exception of Dluga Street.

The lanterns were made for the most part of colored paper. A few of the

221

children had glazed, well marked lanterns with tallow candles inside. It would happen on occasion that a sheigetz would come along the way and take the greatest pleasure in throwing the child into the snow. The lantern would immediately burn out.

At the beginning of the second term (a term was counted from Passover until Sukkot, and from Sukkot until Passover) with Kalman Mendel, he told us that if we would not forget to count Sefira [115], he would take us into the forest for Lag Baomer.

Nobody could imagine what it meant to us young chaps to go out into the forest on Lag Baomer. Every child began to acquire a branch with string in order to make a bow and arrow for Lag Baomer. Together, we collected shooting materials for the bows and arrows.

The preparations lasted for two weeks. Every child boasted about how much shooting material he had collected.

Everybody was jealous of the yellow Yaakov. He collected more than all of the others in the first weeks, for a tree grew in his courtyard, from which he broke off the "shooting material".

Our days and nights were tense with waiting for Lag Baomer.
{Photo page 217: Grade 5 of the Jewish Public School with Polish teachers. Translator's note: the inscription says, Zgierz, 28.6.37.}

The awaited day finally came. All 16 students arrived to cheder happy and in a festive mood. Each had his bow and arrow in hand, with full sacks of shooting material and a white bag with food for the entire day.

We were not led by our teacher Kalman Mendel, but rather by his son who was already an older lad. We went out from the Fish Market on the Jewish Street with exceptional joy. Every one of us was proud with his own bow and arrow.

We had already passed through "Kurak", a considerable distance, perhaps a kilometer from the Lodzer forest. Suddenly, our guide stopped. He looked straight ahead and shouted: "Let us quickly flee back. I see that a sheigetz is coming." We began to run back to the cheder in a wild panic. That Lag Baomer was ruined.

The David Friszman Jewish Library by W. Fisher of Tel Aviv

The Jewish Library was founded in the year 1907. It went through several incarnations under various social and political sponsors. However, it survived until the outbreak of the Second World War as the only, most important general Jewish cultural institution in our city.

It was founded (illegally, according tot he Czarist decrees) in the studio of the painter and later well-known metal sculptor Marek Szwarc. Its founders were a group of intelligent, young cultural activists and proponents of self education. Among them were also those who still wore the traditional Jewish garb, and who in their homes had already a book that was not from among the holy books - called a "treifa pasul" [116]. Hassidic parents would often give spankings for bringing such books into the home. Nevertheless, this could not stop the awakening of the intellectual current that began to surge strongly and boldly through the Jewish street and take hold among wide circles of the knowledge-thirsty youth.

Mr. Fabian Grynberg, who himself was one of its founders, writes in the same spirit, as follows: "The Jewish library was named for our fellow native, the writer David Friszman. It played an important role in Zgierz, raising the cultural level of the Jewish population, especially of the youth. Among the founders of the library was also our friend Menashe Szwarcbard. He was a popular man with a fine sense of humor, and near to the Jewish masses. Like a former Beis Midrash student, he used the opportunity to influence the youth from religious homes to join the library circles. He often conducted readings for those youth. Aharon Cincinatus had a separate reason to found the library."

We must emphasize here that the Jewish Library was initially created as a self-sufficient educational institution. Its goal was to raise the cultural level of all domains of national-societal life. The main thing was to awaken the interest for education and knowledge in all strata of the Jewish population.

With the development of the library and the simultaneous increase of its collection of books, the need for a permanent location grew stronger, so that it would be able to conduct its activities, which were widening and branching out, in an undisturbed fashion. When the library first obtained a location of two large rooms (one for books, and the other a reading hall) in the well-known house of the Reichters (as it was called "Palestine Court"), its work took on a surer form and more stable character. Bookshelves were made. The books were segregated into special sections, and the book catalogues were modernized. Within a short period of time, courses were arranged for languages and general subjects. There were groups for the study of Hebrew and elementary mathematics ("Lodzer Folksblatt", July 4, 1915).

After it obtained its own premises, the library became like a second home for a large segment of the youth, for there they were able to derive satisfaction from their lives in an unhindered fashion, according to their ideological principals, in a friendly environment. There they could give expression to their feelings, desires and hopes with words and song.

With the legalization of the Jewish Library in 1917 by the German occupation authorities ("Lodzer Tagblatt", August 15, 1917) its activities broadened. They were able to publicize on the streets of the city their cultural undertakings, such as: readings, literary evenings, mourning gatherings for writers and artists, formal academic events in honor of important historical events, etc. At the same time, a great deal was done to popularize the Yiddish and Hebrew book and increase the number of readers. In short, the library was an educational factor in cultural and communal life. Its popularity increased and widened, especially among the youth.

With the strengthened cultural activity, its monetary intake increased. There was little to wait for from the fund for the needy of the Jewish communal council, especially after the leadership of the council had been taken over by representatives of Agudas Yisroel. Therefore, it was fortunate that the chairman of the budget committee of the first Zgierz city council in liberated Poland, the communal activist Mr. Avraham Morgansztern, succeeded in securing a subsidy for the Jewish Library ("Lodzer Folksblatt", May 31, 1918).

In the later years, the burden of financial assistance for the library fell almost entirely upon Mr. F. Grynberg. He succeeded on occasion in obtaining a large or small subsidy for the library from the city council or the Jewish communal council.

In the year 1919, there was a large book purchase. A memorial notice was pasted upon the first purchased books "The Complete Works of David Friszman", dedicated to the memory of the young, late, active communal representative, Necha the daughter of Reb David Kac, as an expression of thanks for her dedicated work on behalf of the library. I wish to also mention here Leibel Sirkis, a dedicated worker for the library.

During the following three or four years, a noticeable stagnation took place in the cultural activity of the library on account f the Polish-Bolshevik

224

war. A portion of the Jewish youth were mobilized and sent to the fronts. Another segment fled over the borders into the neighboring countries. A significant portion went to the Land of Israel. Zgierz was almost emptied of its creative Jewish youth.

In the year 1923, the mourning academy that was set up by the Jewish Library for the first yahrzeit of David Friszman of blessed memory, decided to perpetuated the memory of our great townsman by calling the library after the name of their renowned deceased.

Its activity was further infused with life that could be felt in the air during the 1920s. The prime cultural and literary ascent, with all of its ideological and artistic streams that swept through the Jewish intelligentsia in Poland and also through broad segments of the masses of people, had a strong and enthusiastic reverberation in our city. The fresh committee, which adopted anything that was new with youthful ardor, found a free and wide field for educational and cultural work. Thanks to the proximity of the large city of Lodz, which with time became a well-known cultural center, literary or dramatic-musical forces were never lacking at every turn of the library.

A new managing committee of the library was elected at the general meeting in 1926. The writer of these lines gladly became its director. It was a difficult time then for the Jews of Poland. Hatred went through the circles of Jewish art and literature. However, the Jewish workers and business market deeply felt the effects of Grabski's anti-Jewish economic and taxation policies. Zgierz, as a textile city, felt this even more deeply.

In order to flow with the reverberations of the new era, the Jewish library did not only renovate itself with people who had aspirations and dedication to these matters, but also with fresh sources of material, for the old sources slowly dried up. On more than one occasion, our activists and representatives banged on the table of the communal council, demanding a subsidy for the sole Jewish cultural institution in the city. However, they almost always came across a hard, laconic refusal: "There is no money in the treasury!". The Jewish representatives on the city council also felt the negative anti-Semitic influence in an increasing fashion. Having no option, we had to turn to the "Jewish sack" [117]. The existence of the library hung on the balance.

Finally, we succeeded in acquiring a few friends who were smaller or larger money spenders (such as, for example, the manufacturer Moshe Kuperberg - himself a knowledgeable man and connoisseur of Yiddish books - who made an annual contribution) to restore the old book collection and purchase a fresh supply. We arranged various events for that purpose. We also went out into the street to collect money through what was called "flower days". We were generally successful, and in a short time, our book orders arrived. All of the books that were currently purchased stemmed from the best-known literary creations - originals or translations of world literature. The Hebrew readers were especially pleased with the books from the "Shtibel" publisher. In order to satisfy the Jewish-Polish readers, who were always enticed by the neighboring Polish "Wiedza Library", we enriched our library with a number of new Polish books.

Festive program for the 20th anniversary of the David Friszman Jewish Library in Zgierz.

The translation of the Yiddish is as follows:
1927 Program Of the twentieth anniversary Of the David Friszman Jewish Library April 24, 1927, Zgierz [118]

I

Opening: Mr. V. Fiszer Emergence and Development: Mr. F. Grynberg

Lectures: Mr. Y. Unger (Lodz)

Mr. Marek Szwarc (Paris)

II

Compositions of Achrona Chefetz and others: with a violin solo by Mr. D Jeselson of Lodz

A Shterendl (A Little Star) by Y. Kacenelson
Elend Song by Moshe Kulboka
Der Fadem (The Thread) by Y. L. Peretz
The above sung by the soloist of the Lodzer Hazamir Choir, Mr. H. Altman
Pianist: Mr. J. Fiszer
Recitations and Declamations: Mr. Szumacher (Lodz)
Dancing Attractions Buffet
Music under the direction of Mr. Gomberg}

Thus did the Friszman Library once again gain great esteem in the broad Jewish circles. The formal literary and artistic events, and the intimate artistic evenings were the best attended. They awakened interest in the actual cultural problems of that era.

I wish to end this survey with the crowning event of those years. I refer to the formal celebration of the twenty years of activity of the Jewish Library in Zgierz that took place in 1927 in the large hall of the tourist union. According to the photocopy of the program (sent in by F. Grynberg of America), the evening was chock-full of literary and artistic treats. Special attention was given to the witty insights into Yiddish culture, literature and art by the renowned writer and editor of the Lodzer Tagblatt, Yeshayahu Unger, and from the artist and founder of the library -Marek Szwarc and F. Grynberg. The conspicuous cultural activist in the city, the scholarly Isuchar Szwarc was present as honorary chairman. After the literary and artistic program, in which the young artist Yisrael Szumacher appeared, the crowd rejoiced until late in the night. As far as I remember, this was the most successful Jewish cultural event in Zgierz, organized by the David Friszman Library.

A remarkable curiosity: when I arrived in Zgierz shortly after the liberation and saw the desolation and destruction of my Jewish home, I conducted searches and rummages through the destroyed houses, perhaps I might find a sign, a memory of the Jewish life that used to brew here a few years previously - but I could find none. The Germans, together with their assistants, did everything so that such things would not remain. I asked Polish acquaintances about this, but without success. A short time later,

227

somebody stopped me in the street and handed me a book, asking me if it was interesting to me. I gave a glance - a Jewish book! I cast a glance at the title page and saw: The Complete Works of David Friszman - with the stamp of the Zgierz Jewish Library that was so familiar to me…

When I made aliya to the Land of Israel, I obviously took that book with me - like a remnant and rare treasure from the once so rich book treasury of Jewish Zgierz.

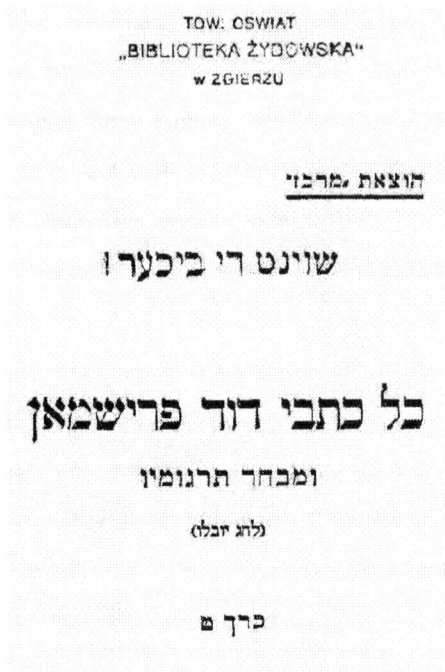

TOW: OSWIAT
„BIBLIOTEKA ŻYDOWSKA"
w ZGIERZU

הוצאת ,מרכז'

שוינט די ביכער!

כל כתבי דוד פרישמאן

ומבחר תרגומיו

(לתג יובלו)

כרך ם

Translator's Note: The entire text of the title page is as follows:

Tow: Oswiat
"Biblioteka Zydowska"
w Zgierzu
Published by "Merkaz"
Take good care of the books!
The Complete Works of David Friszman
And a Choice Selection of his Translations
(Celebrating his jubilee)
Volume 9}

The Zamir Literary and Musical Club by V. F.

It is possible that Hazamir was the first secular general Jewish cultural institution that was permitted in our city by the Russian government official. Its founders were part of a group of cultural activists from the national Jewish intelligentsia. Its heads were certainly included Messrs. Yeshayahu Szapiro, Beirech Kohn and Aharon Kaltgrad.

In order to understand the tasks and objectives of the organization, I will bring down a few of the most important paragraphs of its statutes that are included in the request to the authorities to register the "Zgierz Literary Musical Dramatic Organization 'Muza'" (the name was later changed to Hazamir). The request was signed by the three aforementioned people and was dated November 2, 1909.

The aims and rights of the society:

Muza has the aim of developing and spreading literature and music among the Jewish population in Zgierz and environs, and familiarizing its members with the best Jewish literary creations by means of the following:

1) Studying primary Jewish composers on Jewish themes.

2) Conducting open Jewish concerts with recitals and declamations.

3) Providing material help to those who wish to dedicate themselves to literary or musical study.

4) Organizing contests on better literary, musical or dramatic Jewish creations.

5) Organizing free discussions for our members. And

6) Giving the members of the society opportunities to spend their free time together.

The activity in Zgierz and environs.

The society has the rights to open a library and reading hall for its members.

Members of the society can be people of either sex, of Jewish origin, with appropriate parents, who agree with the aims of the society. The number of members is not limited.

The members of the society consist of: a) honorary members, b) true members, c) sympathizers (sorewnowateli).

1) Honorary members are elected at a general meeting with a majority of 2/3 of the ballots. They are people who play an important role in Jewish music, science or who have served in various services for the society.

2) True members of the society are those who take part in singing, the

orchestra of the society, in readings and declamations.

3) Sympathizers (sorewnowateli) of the society are those who support the activities of the society, and help the intellectual and material existence of the society in accordance with their ability.

Regarding the income of the society: distribution of the work to the various committees: for literature, music, library, secretary, finance; organizing evenings in order to develop the various fields of art; concern about the material wellbeing of the society; forging contact with other similar societies, etc.

In 1913, the society was already known as Hazamir. As we can see from these paragraphs, the aims were of broad horizon and deeply rooted in national, Jewish folk creativity, with the clear will to emphasize, live and enrich our spiritual treasures. We also, in Hazamir, took on a popular character, and had the primary goal of introducing our youth to the best of our folk creations.

ЕГО ПРЕВОСХОДИТЕЛЬСТВУ

Господину Петроковскому Губернатору

Учредителей Згерскаго еврейскаго
литературно-драматическо-музыкальнаго
Общества "МУЗА", жителей гор.Згержа,
Абеля Яковлева Шапиро, Береско Хаймови
Коне и Арона Хаимова Кильтграда

ПРОШЕНІЕ.

Представляя при семъ уставъ, учреждаемаго нами Общества
"МУЗА" во двухъ экземплярахъ и квитанціи во внесеніи нами
денегъ на публикацію, имѣемъ честь покорнѣйше просить ВАШЕ
ПРЕВОСХОДИТЕЛЬСТВО: соблаговолить распорядиться о регистраціи
онаго Общества подвѣдомственнымъ ВАШЕМУ ПРЕВОСХОДИТЕЛЬСТВУ
Присутствіемъ по дѣламъ объ Обществахъ.

Гор.Згержъ,

Ноября 8 дня 1909 г.

The request to the governor ("Gubernator") for authorization of the
Hazamir organization in Zgierz, 1909.

231

The Hazamir mandolin band

**A group of children of the sports organization (1916) with the counselors
P. Leczycki, K Eiger, and G. Lipowicz**

Fabian Grynberg, who was certainly very familiar with the activity of Hazamir, writes to us.

"Hazamir conducted very lively activities for a certain time. The choir sung Hebrew and Yiddish songs. There were readings with the participation of well-known writers - Hillel Cytlin, Yitzchak Kacenelson, Dr. Mokdoni, the editor Oger, and others."

With time, Hazamir became a noticeable factor in the cultural and educational life of the Zgierz community. It had a library at its disposition, and there were even filing devices in the spacious rooms of its own location in Bretsznejder's house on Dluga Street.

Almost all of the creative powers with a national conscience of the sophisticated Jewish population grouped around Hazamir. These especially included: Naftali, Michowski, Hendeles, M. Szidlowski, Avraham Szlumiel, Dr. Zalcwasser, Dr. Weicman, Herman Szwarc, Pesach Kempinski and others.

Dramatic Circle by Even-Aryeh

The dramatic group performing "Al Saf Haosher" ("On the Threshold of Happiness"). Participating are Z. Fogel, B. Fogel, Hanower, H. Gross, S. Frejberg, W. Klejnman, Korczej

Without considering the fact that Zgierz is situation close to Lodz and that the Zgierz Jewish population had the possibility of visiting the Lodz

Jewish theater, they had the ambition of creating their own Jewish dramatic circle.

At the People's-House, which was founded in 1916 by Shlomo Praszker, Chaim Itche Segal, Hirsch Gross, and Moshe Librach - the Jewish dramatic circle was founded in 1917, thanks to the following active members: Hirsch Gross, Zelig Fogel, Moshe, Yitzchak and Mordechai Grand.

After the first three months of rehearsals, the Zgierz Jews watched the opening performance of the dramatic circle: "Chasha the Orphan Girl" by Yaakov Gordon.

After the first performance, the dramatic group enlarged. New amateurs came in. At the home of Zelig Fogel, with the participation of his wife Bella (who already had a great deal of experience in an actor in the dramatic circle of Pultusk, where she had played for a few years) regular rehearsals took place. Later, they performed the following theatrical pieces in the large Lutnia hall: King Lear, the Stepmother, God of Vengeance, The Empty Tavern, The Yeshiva Student, and others. The director was the actor Nathan Reichenberg.

The dramatic circle brought a great deal of life into Zgierz. It was very popular and beloved by the Jewish population.

The entire income from the performances went to voluntary causes [119]. A symphony orchestra of over twenty men was also created by the dramatic circle.

The Symphonia Singing Group by V. F.

In the year 1934, the Symphonia singing group was founded by a youth group of the worker's circle. Its task was to develop the feeling for singing and acting among the working youth. A choir and an orchestra were founded under the direction of Rubin, the well-known director of the Lodzer Old City School. They developed in their own location, in the house of Szymanski on Pilsudskega Street, and conducted daily practices.

The choir, accompanied by the orchestra, put on performances in the same location. These performances were received by the audience with applause and appreciation.

The initiators and founders were Leib Sczupak (son-in-law of Gedalyahu Roizenman), Eliahu Finkelsztejn, Leib Gelbard, Rotkop, and others. Symphonia was a place of cultural life for a portion of our working youth.

The Zionist Federation ("Agudat Hatzionim") in Zgierz by Yosef Kac and Yehuda Wajnsztejn

Yosef Meir Harun, one of the founders of the group "Chovevei Sfat Ever" ("Lovers of the Hebrew Language"), and the final chairman of the Zionist Federation

Already at the beginning of the 20th century, immediately after the death of the Zionist seer Dr. Herzl of blessed memory, a group of Maskilim in our city - people immersed in Judaism and the wisdom of Israel - and founded "The Organization of the Lovers of the Hebrew Language". The organization was headed by Isuchar Szwarc, Tovia Lifszitz, Moshe Eiger, Yosef Meir Harun, Avraham Klorfeld, Y. A. Rosinow, the two brothers-in-law Zeev Eliahu and Zeev Michael Reichert, and others. These were from among the Maskilim and notables of the city, who were committed to the idea of the renaissance of the nation and the Hebrew language. This group acted strongly and diligently within the Jewish community in order to spread Zionism and its objective to establish the Jewish nation. They did their work in the Beis Midrash, the Great Synagogue, and the Hassidic shtibels. Afterward, they turned themselves toward the secular studying youth, and also to those who occupied the benches of the Beis Midrash. These included: Chaim Pinchas Poznerson, Menashe Szwarcbard, Mordechai Szapszowicz, Avraham Skosowski, Menachem (Mendel) Berliner, Tovia Grynfarb, Yosef Krasnopolski, Yaakov Nekricz, Yitzchak Berliner, Fabian Grynberg, Yosef Kac, and others.

As the group grew, it work branched out and it broadened its field of activity. They occupied themselves with distributing publications of the Zionist movement and Hebrew newspapers such as Hatzefira, arranging collections and systematic contributions to the Keren Kayemet (Jewish National Fund), and with games and performances whose intake was dedicated to the Keren Kayemet. They also arranged memorial evenings for Dr. Herzl, and conducted every task that a Zionist organization was expected to do. Of course, they did this in place of a Zionist organization, whose existence was not permitted by law during the time of the Czarist rule. They conducted their work without excess publicity, for fear of the government.

The first of the members of this group to make aliya was Menachem Berliner, who made aliya in 1909. After him, Asher Klorfeld, his sister Lea, and their family followed.

A reception in honor of Mr. Yitzchak Grynbaum, at the Zionist Federation of Zgierz. Sitting from right to left: P. Grynberg, M. Eiger, Y. Grynbaum, Isuchar Szwarc, A. Morgensztern.

Chalutzim (pioneers) from Zgierz on the occasion of their making aliya to the Land of Israel in 1920: A. Kuperman, A. Gotsztadt, L. Gotsztadt, Sh. Gorner, W. Kac

In the year 5676 (1916) towards the end of the First World War, a branch of the Zionist movement was officially founded in Zgierz. It was called "Agudat Hatzionim" (The Federation of Zionists). This organization spread out broadly with the uplifting of Zionism and great activity. The head of the Zionist Federation and its activists included Tovia Lipszicz, Isuchar Szwarc, the brothers-in-law / cousins Reichert [120], Moshe Glicksman, Yosef Kac, Leon Rosinow, and Moshe Siedlowski. Some of the youth joined them: L. Wajnsztejn, R. Szapszowicz, Y. L. Gotsztadt, Yaakov Gotsztadt, Shlomo Gorner, Herman Garzon, Leibel Sirkis, Wolf Fiszer, Moshe Landau and others from amongst the Hassidim and town residents.

In December, 1929, the Zionist Federation organized an enthusiastic reception for the leader of Polish Jewry and one of the heads of Zionism, Mr. Yitzchak Grynbaum. This was a spontaneous demonstration, in which the city notables and representatives of all local factions of Zionism participated. In a lecture full of content, he described the situation in the land of Israel with respect to the events that were taking place at that time. At this opportunity, a warm appreciation was extended to two veteran Zionist leaders in Zgierz, who were among the founders of the Zionist Federation -the late Tovia

Lipszicz and Isuchar Szwarc of blessed memories. At that meeting, they decided to recognize both of them in the Golden Book [121].

The library that was founded by Chovevei Zion and transferred to the Zionist Federation in the house of the Reichert family broadened, and turned into a cultural and educational center for the local youth. The library was tended and conducted by Fabian Grynberg, Menashe Szarcbard, Aharon Cincinatus, and others. It served the Zionist Federation in a blessed fashion. It supplied reading material and also served as a venue for lectures and Zionist meetings, especially for the youth who saw it as the center of their spiritual world. Evening classes, friendly conversations, conventions, and festive gatherings took place there.

The library also served as a venue for speakers who came from outside Zgierz, from Lodz and Warsaw. It was called by the name of the writer David Friszman on the anniversary of the death of this writer, who was a native of our city.

The Zionist camp branched off at this point, and strengthened itself. It performed its role strongly and with many branches in its Zionist work. The numbers of members of the Zionist Federation reached approximately 500. Its members came from all strata of society.

Representatives of the Zionist factions on the Keren Kayemet (Jewish National Fund) committee.Standing are D. Baum, H. Cincinatus, Brzowski, M. Glezer. Sitting are P. Szapszowicz, L.Gotstadt, D. Berger, A. Bornsztejn, S. Tamerzon

238

The committee for the arranging celebration of the opening of the Hebrew University of Jerusalem. Standing: Y. M. Harun, A. Reichert, A. Ch. Michelson, Y. Wajsbaum. Sitting: Y. Kac, N. Troczki, A. Morgensztern, F. Grynberg, N. Fajnngold, and L. Wajnsztejn

The Zionist Federation penetrated to all realms of life in the city, and it had representatives on the communal council and city council, including Morgansztern, Isuchar Szwarc, Fabian Grynberg, Noach Troczki, and Wolf Reichert, who served terms on these institutions. Yosef Kac was the representative on the council for the building of cities. He was diligent in Zionist activity already from the days of participation in the group of Menachem Berliner. He continued on until he made aliya to the land of Israel in the year 1935.

Fabian Grynberg served as chairman also on the committee for the Land of Israel, the Zionist founds, and other public institutions that had representation in the federation. The members of the federation penetrated into all public institutions that existed in the city, in the sport organizations, the orphanages, the soup kitchen that distributed meals and assistance to the poor and children, and to the charitable fund that was run by Moshe Eiger, Noach Troczki and Leibush Wajnsztejn. The latter was active in the Zionist Federation until he founded the Revisionist Zionist movement, and transferred his activities there.

The Zionist Federation gathered into its ranks a recognizable segment of the youth of Zgierz. It also was active in the public and Jewish realms in our city. The final chairman of the federation was Reb Yosef Meir Harun, who was active in it and its committees until the Holocaust, when the grave was covered upon all expressions of organized Jewish life.

The Young People's Organization (Agudat Tzeirim) and Young Zionists (Tzeirei Zion) by Yosef Kac

The "Zionist winds" already began to blow through Zgierz at the beginning of the 20th century, and a number of youths dreamed about formalizing an organization around their nationalistic outlook and tendencies. The awakening of the youth began to take form. Avraham Skosowski, Menashe Szwarcbard, Leon Rusinow, Chaim Pinchas Poznerson, Menachem Berliner, Fabian Grynberg, Marek Szwarc, Asher Klorfeld, Wajsbaum, Szapsowicz, Tovia Grynfarb, Aharon Cincinatus, Yitzchak Glicksman, and the writer of these lines - decided to found "Agudat Tzeirim" (The Young People's Organization) and to design a clear agenda for the activities of the organization: to study the Hebrew language, to spread the Jewish book and the Hatzefira newspaper, to understand all of the problems surrounding and within the Land of Israel, to maintain a connection with the Zionist organization, to assist the Keren Kayemet (Jewish National Fund), and to organize interest groups.

In later years, the number of members reached 100. Michael Siedlowski was very active. The frequent lectures, with the assistance of local powers [122] as well as those from Lodz and Warsaw, drew a large crowd.

The members of Tzeirei Zion distributed shekalim (tokens of membership in the Zionist organization) prior to Zionist congresses, collected monetary pledges to the Keren Kayemet from the houses of the city, and educated the youth in the spirit of pioneering Zionism - towards actualization and aliya.

The influence of this organization in our city was particularly strong due to the multiple relationships of its members. We worked together with Maccabee, the Dvora women's Zionist organization, Hazamir, and others.

240

Several founders and activists of the organizations excelled during that timeframe. They had great influence upon us with their speeches, their spirit, and their dedication to the issue. These included Menachem Berliner, Yehoshua Ru (known in Israel as a writer and one of the founders of Degania Aleph, known there as Yehoshua Manoach [123], Leon Rusinow, Asher Klorfeld, and others.

Members of "Tzeirei Zion" ("Young Zion") with Menachem Berliner prior to his aliya to the Land in 1910.

From right, in the upper row: G. Lipowicz, Yakir, Y. Kac, T. Grynfarb, A.Klorfeld, Y. Wajsbaum, and Y. H. Waldman. In the middle row: P. Leczyski, F. Grynberg, G.Wajsbaum, Y. Glicksman, A. Skosowski, Wajsberg, and L. Rusinow. Sitting: M. Szwarcberg, M.Szapszowicz, M. Berliner, Dawidowicz, and Y. Krasnopolski

The Mizrachi Organization in Zgierz by Yehoshua Berliner (Baniel)

Reb Nathan David Kac, one of the founders of Mizrachi in Zgierz (L)
Reb Yisrael Frugel, one of the heads of Mizrachi of Zgierz. (R)

The Mizrachi organization was founded in Zgierz in 1915, during the time of the German occupation, after an arousal by the religious preacher Rabbi Yechiel Rappaport of blessed memory (who was later appointed as the rabbi of Jadziow [124]). Reb Gedalya Yedidya Zwiklowski was elected as chairman of the interim committee. The members of the committee were Reb Yitzchak Meir Halperin, Reb Yisrael Frugel, Reb Nathan David Kac, Reb Yosel Cohen, Reb Eliahu Wronoski, and the writer of these lines.

Reb Daniel Sirkis joined Mizrachi in 1917. He was immediately elected as head of the faction. During the elections to the communal council in 1918, the national block (Zionists, Mizrachi, and religious householders) attained a great majority. Reb Daniel Sirkis was chosen as chairman of the communal council, which was run with inspiration of religious Zionism.

242

Reb Kalman Rosenblat, one of the Mizrachi activists in Zgierz

Activists of Young Mizrachi. Standing: L Trajanowski, Y. Wajndler, Rubin, A. Cohen, and A. Zajdel. Sitting: Z. Cohen, Rozenfeld, M. Zakon, Ch. Zakon, Pantel, and Klaski. In the front row: Rozenshein, Niszkowski, A. Konski, and B. Blank.

Many Hassidim and other townsfolk joined Mizrachi as time went on. These included: Reb Yehoshua Kaufman (the uncle of Daniel Sirkis) who was a scholarly Jew and a Hasid of Czortkow, who sat all of his days with Torah. His house was open to the nationalist religious youth thanks to his valiant wife Reizel; Reb Yitzchak Mendel HaKohen, the brother of the rabbi of the city and an Admor of his own right; Reb Aharon Parizer one of the veterans of Zionism in Russia; Reb Kalman Rozenblatt, a Hassid of Sokolow, Reb Meir Wajnik, Reb Michel Kuperman (an Aleksandrow Hassid, who was known by the name of Michel Endzis); Reb Chaim Cohen and others.

The Mizrachi organization, which reached 170 members with the passage of time, at first was headquartered in the home of Reb Isuchar Szwarc. The rabbi of the city would visit us on occasion. From there, we moved to the home of Reichert, where we had two spacious rooms. One of the activists was Reb Mendel Zakon, who died in the Land. We founded our own Beis Midrash, and we gathered together our members who worshipped in all of the shtibels of the city. The Torah reader was Reb Nathan Domnakowicz (who made aliya). We arranged evening classes and were active in all areas of communal life in our city.

A branch of Young Mizrachi was founded in Zgierz. It was one of the active forces in the city.

Agudas Yisroel and its founders

With the organization of Orthodox Jewry in Poland under the name of "Agudas Haorthodoxim" a branch of the Aguda was also founded in Zgierz. Its founders included: Reb Shlomo Sirkis and his son Eliezer, Reb Yosef Hirsch Szapiro, Reb Noach Mendelson, Reb Binyamin Szaranski, Reb Nathan Elberg, Reb Eliahu Tenenbaum, Reb Chaim Boaz, Reb Yisrael Moshe Rabinowicz, Reb Ezriel Cuker, and others.

The Aguda was founded in the year 5676 (1916). With time, it changed its name. Earlier, it was known as "Shlomei Emunei Yisroel" (The whole believers of Israel), and later Agudas Yisroel. Reb Eliezer Sirkis served as the president from the day of its founded until the year 5685 (1934). He was the living spirit of all its activities. After he made aliya, the following people filled his position: Reb Berish Bechler, Reb Aharon Hirsch Kompel, and the final one (until the outbreak of the world war) Reb Leibel Wyszogrodski. Reb Shimshon Wolf Glicksman served as secretary during the final years. Its active members included Reb Yitzchak Aryeh Minc, Reb Yechiel Meir Mankita, Reb Eliahu Tenenbaum, and others.

Agudas Yisroel also had a delegate to the city council. Reb Eliezer Sirkis served this role from the year 5676 (1925). From the year 5695 (1935) Reb Leibel Wyszogrodski served.

A youth faction called "Tzeirei Agudas Yisroel" (Youth of Agudas Yisroel) existed alongside Agudas Yisroel. It was very active in our city. It assisted Agudas Yisroel with its national activities, and also organized Torah study classes. The classes were given in the Beis Midrash by the rabbi of the city, and in the 1930s by Reb Mendel Wechsler and others. For a certain period of time, it also published a monthly in hectograph called "Unzer Vort" ("Our Word") (5686 1926). Its founders included Rabbi David Szapiro, Pinchas Sirkis, Meir Sczaranski, Feivel Mendel Cuker, Avraham Aharonson, Shlomo Bialostocki, Avigdor Rozenblat, Mordechai Sirkis, Leibel Librach, Leibel Bomes and others. From the late 1920s until the outbreak of the war, the following people were active in it: Shlomo David Przeworski (who was chosen as chairman in 5691 -1931), Sender Poznerson (who served as treasurer, and supported the activities of the Aguda from his pocket), Yosef Korczej, Moshe Rozenblat, David Wechsler, Avraham Ajzenszmidt, Mendel Boaz, Meir Boaz, Avraham Boaz, Binyamin Sztechelberg, Yechiel Yosef Zeida, Yaakov Banda, Nota Bomes, Mendel Mankita, Eliahu Feivel Przeworski, Shlomo Glicksman, Shmuel Ajzenszmidt, Avraham Kompel, Shalom Kompel, Yehuda Leib Zeida, Chaim Eliezer Domnakowicz, Mordechai Meir Krol, Yitzchak Przeworski, Avraham Bakerszpigiel, Feivel Szatszowicz and others.

The young people also were involved in economic activity. They established a committee called "Shomrei Shabbas" (Sabbath observers) whose members included also members of Agudas Yisroel. The members of the committee were: Reb Yosef Bialostocki (who was nicknamed Reb Yosef Shmuel Chasides), Daniel Lenczyski, Wolf Zelmanowicz, Leibel Wyszogrodski, Shlomo David Przeworski, Meir Boaz, Mendel Niszkowski, Chaim Eliezer Domnakowicz, Hershel Tenenbaum, Chaim Zeev Hoizszpigiel, and Shalom Kompel.

The committee for Israel affairs of the Agudas Yisrael movement of
Zgierz, including the founders and activists of the "Keren Hayishuv"
("The fund for the settlement").   Standing: Kompel, Bandkowski,
Bomes, Niszkowski. Sitting: Glicksman, Hollander, Y. M. Zylberberg,
A. Mankita, Rozenzweig, Kompel

Agudas Yisrael Youth in Zgierz.   Top row: Domnakowicz, Sh.
Glicksman. Sh. Kompel. Second row: Kotek, L. Wechsler, A. Frankel,
Y. Adler, Y. Tenenbaum, P. Glicksman, N. Mendelson. Third row:
Praszker, M. Boaz, Frankel, A. Bekershpigel, Y. Przeworski, P.
Szapszowicz, P. Mendelman, M. Mankita. Sitting: A. Ajsensczmidt,
Boaz, M. Rosznblat, Sh. Przeworski, and Domnakowicz

Children of the Talmud Torah Cheder with the teacher
Hershele Wajlsenfelner

Students and teachers of the Yesod Hatorah Cheder

The tasks of the committee were not restricted to matters of Sabbath observance, but also included the putting of pressure on the Orthodox manufacturers in our city to cancel the "document of sale" for work on Sabbaths [125] and to employ Jewish and observant employees. They delayed the reading of the Torah in the Hassidic shtibels [126], and at the end, they succeeded.

The following people were appointed to the committee for the "Keren Hayishuv" ("Settlement Fund"): Yechiel Meir Mankita (chairman), Shalom Kompel (secretary), Shlomo Glicksman, Shmuel Ajzenszmidt, Yosef Bendekowski, Avraham Kompel, Hillel Moshe Bomes, and Mendel Niszkowski. The founders of a branch of the benefit organization for the Chachmei Lublin Yeshiva included Meir Sczaranski, David Wechsler, and Avraham Ajzenszmidt.

An Agudas Yisroel Women's organization existed alongside Agudas Yisroel. It was engaged primarily in philanthropic activities. It was headed by the following women: Chaya Sirkis (the wife of Reb Eliezer), and Chana Szlaser (the daughter of Reb Binyamin Sczaranski). The Orthodox girls were organized into a Batya organization for young religious girls.

Agudas Yisroel was represented by the following people on the communal council: Reb Eliezer Sirkis (who served as chairman until 5693 - 1933), Reb Chaim Boaz, Reb Aharon Hirsch Kompel, Reb Berish Bechler and others.

a) Beit Ulpana (House of Learning)

The first institution that was established by the Orthodox group in our city (with the participation of observant householders) was "Beit Ulpana LeTorah Vederech Eretz" ("The House of Learning for Torah and the Ways of the World).

On account of the closing of the cheders in the year 5676 (1916) by the German occupation government, a modern cheder was founded in Lodz, called "Beit Ulpana LeTorah Vederech Eretz". It included secular studies as well. A modern cheder, patterned after that one, was founded in our city with that name in 5676 (1916). Several rooms were rented on Blotene Street for that purpose.

The following people were chosen for the first committee of the institution: Reb Daniel Sirkis as chairman, Reb Avraham Nathan Elberg as secretary, and Reb Aharon Yosef Berger, Reb Chaim Boaz, Reb Henech Ehrzon, Reb Noach Mendelson, and Reb Yisrael Moshe Rabinowicz as members of the committee.

There were five classes in the Beit Ulpana for students of ages 7 - 13. The first educators included Reb Rafael Henech Blausztejn (who taught the upper class), Reb Yaakov the son of Yaakov Milichewicki who taught Hebrew and grammar in all of the classes, Reb Yitzchak Eksztejn, Reb Shimshon Wolf Glicksman (the son of Reb Fishel the teacher), Reb Moshe

248

Zeida and others.

They studied primarily religious studies, but they dedicated about two hours of the day to secular education. German language, which was a requirement, was also taught.

When the Germans left the State of Poland, the name of the institution was changed to Yesodei Hatorah. The patrons of the institution were Reb Shlomo Sirkis, Reb Moshe Aharonson, and Reb Shalom Henech Bomes. New leaders became involved, such as Reb Mendel Wechsler and others, and the institution continued to develop from year to year. Hundreds of students studied there. It continued to exist until the outbreak of the final war in 5699 (1939), when destruction overtook the institution.

b) Beis Yaakov

The second institution that was established by Agudas Yisroel during the 1920s was a school for Orthodox girls called Bais Yaakov. It was established in the year 5686 (1926). Among others, Reb Shlomo Sirkis and his son Reb Eliezer Sirkis worked for its establishment. The first principal was Reb Meir Sczaranski. After him, Reb Yaakov Angel and Reb Leibel Wyszogrodski served in this position. The teachers included Mrs. Chajmowicz, who was helped by the following members of the Batya organization: Esther Rus and Gittel Goldwasser, the daughters of Reb Avraham Przeworski. This school graduated hundreds of Orthodox girls during the era of its existence, and developed well. It also existed until the outbreak of the war in 1939.

c) Miscellaneous

In addition to the Yagdil Torah Yeshiva that was founded and directed by the Hassidim before the First World War (it ceased its activities in the year 1914, with the outbreak of the world war), a Yeshiva existed in Zgierz alongside the Beis Midrash of the Admor of Strykow. Aside from the older youths of the city who completed their studies at Yesodei Hatorah, students from outside the city studied there. The Jews of our town supported them and fed them at their tables on a rotation system.

In the evenings, Reb Hershel Klejnman and Reb Yaakov Meir Torczinski, the son of Reb Zisha Glazer, taught Ein Yaakov to the lay people.

Teachers of the Beis Yaakov girl's school. Standing: Mrs. Bialostocki, unidentified, Tuchman, Zaszlichowski. Sitting: A. Milichewicki, Zaszlichowski, Tuchman, and Banda.

The Yesod Hatorah Cheder [127] of Agudas Yisroel (1935) with the activists Reb Shalom Chanoch Bomes and Reb Eliahu Tenenbaum

The following people represented Agudas Yisroel on the Chevra Kadisha: Reb Meir Klaski, Reb Eli Tenenbaum Reb Yaakov Rosenstrauch, and Reb Shalom Henech Bomes. The following women were active: Chana (the wife of Reb Mendel) Wechsler, Chava Ita (the wife of Reb Shalom Henech) Bomes, Chana Rachel (the mother-in-law of Reb Shimshon Wolf Glicksman) Birnsztock, and the veteran from among them, Machla Woronski (who was called in our town as Machla the Heaven's Gazer), who merited to make aliya to the Land and to be buried in its soil.

"Maccabee" by Y. Weinstein and D. Berger

(The Maccabee Hebrew organization for exercise and sport in Zgierz)

The Jewish touring organization of Zgierz, which was the oldest, largest, most popular and active youth organization in the city, was founded in the year 1913 - 5673.

The Maccabee sport organization at its tenth anniversary festivities.

The prime motivation and concern for the physical development of the Jewish youth began already in the 1880s and 1890s, with a need to learn how to defend oneself against pogroms that were organized by the Czarist authorities. In this manner, Jewish self-defense (Sabmoobrona) arose in many cities and towns, in the form of training and physical development in youth groups. These groups heroically repulsed every attack of the hooligans. At first with the call of Dr. Max Nordau at the First Zionist Congress to the

251

new generation of Jews that stand on the threshold of important national tasks, that they must first straighten out their crooked backs and carry their responsibility to the Jewish people with honor and pride; that they must not only develop their spirit, but also their muscles. When he repeated classic motto, "A healthy spirit and a healthy body", it impressed the studying youth and inspired national-idealist young people to move in that direction with dedication and enthusiasm. The idea of sports then took on a deeper being and wider character.

One of the Zgierz enthusiasts of that idea was certainly the young and fiery Zionist Leon Rusinow. The idea did not let him rest until he influenced his friend Akiva Eiger (a son of the manufacturer and Zionist activist Reb Moshel Eiger) to create in Zgierz - patterned after Tomaszow - a touring and sports club for the physical development of our youth.

Since creating an independent Jewish institution of that type was difficult under Czarist rule, perhaps even forbidden, the initiators found an alternative: to create a sports section within the already legalized Hazamir culture organization, with the assistance of the founders of Hazamir: Dr.Kaltgrad, Berek Cohen and Yeshaya Szapira.

Members of the Maccabee sport organization of Zgierz on a Lag Baomer excursion

Among the aforementioned initiators and founders, one must also count the sport activist, the temperamental social activist Abraham Morgensztern, who was later the founder and editor of the "Jewish Sports Newspaper" in

252

Poland; the brothers Yisrael and Fisherl Leczyszki, Yaakov Hirsch Waldman; Getzi Lipowicz and others who began to make use of Hazamir for sports needs. As can be understood, in those years and in the framework in which they had to act - their activity was quite bounded, and they did not have the possibility to fulfill all of the objectives that they had taken on. Shortly thereafter, the First World War broke out (1914) and the work that had been begun had to be interrupted. First in 1915, the German authorities permitted the Jewish population in the occupied Polish cities to found sports clubs and similar cultural institutions. The first open information about the Zgierz touring organization was brought to us by the Lodzer Folksblatt number 179 (August 16, 1915) in a correspondence from the province:

In Zgierz the Jewish touring organization began activity. A second newspaper correspondent from Zgierz writes to us as follows: "The library united with the Jewish Touring Organization in order to concentrate the energies and cooperative work. The Touring Organization developed an energetic activity, and arranged systematic events four times per week. As well, the Touring Organization had a choir and mandolin orchestra. At its last meeting, it was decided to conduct a wide-ranging activity in the cultural realm. It was decided to organize a large Peretz evening on the First Yahrzeit of Y. L. Peretz on Wednesday, the second day of Passover."

The Maccabee committee (1932). Y. Grand, A. Pietrowicz, L. Rozenberg, L. Gottstadt, K. Eiger, D. Berger, D. Praszker, M. Dzaloszynski, M. Szrowko

Members of the Maccabee sport organization on a parade to the
synagogue

The directors of the Maccabee sport organization. Standing: Flam, B.
Skosowski, L. Waldman, Sh. Feldman, K. Eiger, Y. Goldenberg, Y.
Lenczyki, Sh. Wichocki, Y. Waldman. Y. Rosenzweig, Frida. Sitting:
Mrs. Bomes, Sh. Katz, Chaikin, H. Waldman, R. Greenberg, P.
Greenberg, Tz.Goldberg, Lenczyki, Frida.

First in liberated Poland (around 1919), the Touring Organization undertook a significant and organization activity, with zest and tempo, in almost all areas of sport and culture.

The reasons that the popularity and esteem of that group, which encompassed almost all of the strata of the Zgierz youth, grew so quickly, were various. However, one of the most import reasons was certainly the attitude of volunteerism among the young and nationalistically inclined forces who took important leadership positions in the organization. They displayed energy and initiative, each according to his domain. Among others, these included Akiva Goldberg, Leibish Weinstein, David Berger (vice president until he left Poland in 1935), Yosef Leib Gottstadt, Reuven Szapszowicz, Leibish Waldman, Leibek Zylberberg, Moshe Yaakov Grand (secretary), Feivel Rozenman, and David Praszker. It must be emphasized that even though the organization included people with various political leanings, full harmony prevailed in their common work, under the fatherly direction of the good-natured yet energetic Karel (Akiva) Eiger, to whom the sports organization was his life's work.

In 1924, the Zgierz Touring Organization joined the world Maccabee organization, which was found in Karlsbad in 1921 and included almost all of the Jewish sports clubs in the Diaspora.

There were active and passive memberships. The active members participated in all of the activities under the supervision of experienced instructors. These included Zeida and Segal of the Lodzer Jewish Gymnasium, among others. There were also various sections, such as a children's and women's section directed by Fishel Lenczyki; a section for light athletics directed by Gezi Lipowicz, Yosef Leib Gottstadt, Mendelowicz, and Leibek Zylberberg; a festival section led by Bolek Trocki, Sewer Czernikowski, and Rotapel. The football players also played in inter-city matches. There was also a ping-pong group. In general the sporting standard of the Zgierz Touring Organization was at a significantly high level; so much so that our sports people were often requested to appear in other cities, to participate in significant Jewish events.

A festive reception of Maccabee in Zgierz in honor of the visiting sportsmen from the Land of Israel. In the center (in the foreground) sitting: A. Morgensztern, Isucher Szwarc, and the vice-mayor H. Zawinckowski

A group of girls of the Maccabee sport organization. From left: chairman Karel Eiger, and Y. L.Gottstadt

Members of Maccabee with their new flag

The dedication of the flag on the tenth anniversary of the founding of the Touring Organization was a festive occasion that left a strong imprint upon the city. The flag was lovely, with white-blue colors, ribbons and emblems. It was carried with great solemnity, and brought honor and pride to the Jewish population. On days of government nationalistic solemn ceremonies, the Jewish Touring Organization took part in full. The special march and formal procession used to start from the large practice area that used to be Grynberg's lumber warehouse. It marched toward the main street (Pilsudskiego), and went toward the Old City, accompanied by its own orchestra and headed by the flag group. Jews stood along the sidewalks on both sides of the long procession, and looked on with delight. People threw flowers from Jewish balconies, and Jewish children happily and playfully ran along. Alas, the processions were not always proud and festive. Often, the flag was decorated with black mourning bands, and was carried to the synagogue for a memorial to Herzl or Bialik, or - to a protest and mourning demonstration against pogroms and anti-Jewish discrimination in Poland or in Hitler's Germany. Thus did Jewish Zgierz demonstrate its joy or sorrow, its goodwill or protest.

The "Dvora" Women's Zionist Group by Rachel Szperling Szapira

The Jewish kindergarten and its leaders - In the center: Mrs. Roiza Haron, Tania Reichert, the kindergarten teachers Tamerzon and Glicka Szperling

During the years 1918-22, a women's Zionist organization called "Dvora" was active in Zgierz. Its purpose was to spread the Zionist idea among the women of the city.

The most important activity of this group was the Hebrew kindergarten "Prawlowka" in which approximately 40 students studies from all segments of the Jewish population. They sang and spoke Hebrew. The directors of the kindergarten were the following women: M. Reichert, G. Szperling, R. Haron and others, who concerned themselves with all the needs of the kindergarten. The kindergarten teachers were local and from the city of Lodz. These included Mrs. Rozenblum, Tamerzon and Ostrowski. The kindergarten was located in the home of the Reichert family.

The Dvora organization maintained a meeting place for its members. It conducted evening Hebrew classes, presentations, and a dramatic club. It worked on behalf of the Jewish National fund (Keren Kayemet), distributed Shkalim (Zionist membership tokens) and participated in all Zionist activities in the city. The founders and life force of the organization were Misses A. and M. Reichert.

258

The Jewish Scout Organization of Zgierz by L. Rubinstein of New York

A short time after the outbreak of the First World War in 1914, the German army took Lodz and the entire area. The occupation authority permitted Jews to conduct and organized, national and societal life, which had not been permitted under the Russian regime. Various Jewish parties legalized their activities, and Jewish youth organizations were founded in all cities and towns of occupied Poland.

In Zgierz in 1915, a small group of Jewish students from the local business school and the Jewish Gymnasium in Lodz thought of founding a youth organization. The group consisted of Zelig Reichert, Yoav Kac, Joszek Kohn, Leon Rubinsztejn, Yisrael Weinik and others. They would get together a few evenings a week in a roof in Wolf Reichert's factory and carefully study the programs of the Jewish youth movements throughout the world. They also learned about the Land of Israel. Later, when they had crystallized the program, they decided to found a Jewish scouting organization. Aside from scouting, the program would include Jewish history, Palestinography, pioneering living in the Land of Israel, and the personalities of the Second Aliya. They would also install in the members a striving for personal aliya to the Land of Israel.

The Scouting organization on an excursion with their counselors

After a short time, the group succeeded in recruiting a significant number of boys and girls, who were divided in groups according to their ages. Each group had a leader who conducted the program with them. The organization continued to grow. Shortly it was evident that there was a shortage of counselors. They attempted to attract older members. Yaakov Skosowski (who later became the head of the organization), Aharon Cincinatus, Nathan Spiwak, Yosef Kac and others joined the organization.

The Scouting organization with their counselors- A. Cincinatus (on the right) and Y. Weinik.

A number of the leading members of Zgierz were members of the Lodz higher leadership of the Jewish scouting organization.

From 1918, the scouting organization in Poland united with the Austrian Hashomer Hatzair to form one organization, under the name "Hashomer Hatzair". After the proclamation of the Balfour Declaration, the desire to make aliya to the Land of Israel increased. The leader of the organization decided that when the war ends, they would fulfill the dream of aliya.

Immediately after the armistice, a group of leaders of Hashomer Hatzair from Lodz and Zgierz was organized, who would leave Poland and make aliya. They departed from Vienna on December 3, 1918. The following people from Zgierz were included in this group: Yaakov Skosowski, Zelig Reichert, Nathan Spiwak and Leon Rubinsztejn. From Vienna, the group had to travel to Italy in order to board a ship to the Land of Israel. When we arrived in Vienna, the group met with the doctor-rabbi Zvi Chajes, who strongly urged us to abandon the journey on account of the great risk, for conditions of war still prevailed. However we found out that a train of evacuating soldiers was leaving Vienna for Trieste, and we set out on that train.

The Gideon Scouting group with Yaakov Skosowski (in the center)

The first group of Hashomer Hatzair- Front row: Sh. Cincinatus, L. Kohn, Y. Cohen, P.Goldstein, E. Reichert. Second row: A. Reichert, Tz. Lipszicz, G. Rozman, S.Nakrice, P.Zylberberg. Third row: H. Cohen, S. Grynwald, G.Kohn, Y. Reichert

They held us as suspects at the border with Italy, but through the endeavors of a Jew, Dr. Freund, who was passing through the station by chance - they let us continue on. We realized that in Trieste, there were no ships that were traveling to Egypt or the Land of Israel. Thanks to the Zionist leader Dlugacz and the rabbi of Trieste, Dr. Zaler, we received free transportation to Rome, where we obtained visas from the British consul to travel to the Land of Israel.

We were stuck in Rome for almost two months. During that time, other groups came from various places in Poland. Among these groups was another one from Zgierz, which included M. A. Kuperman, Yoav Kac, Klarfeld, Moshe Herszkowicz, and others. After that time, the entire group consisted of 105 people making aliya. It became known in the history of the Third Aliya as the "105". We finally obtained visas after two months. We traveled to Naples and took a ship to Alexandria. The first group arrived in Israel around the time of Passover, 1919.

The Hashomer Hatzair Youth Organization of Zgierz by Chaya Szperling-Halpern and Rafael Katz

The "Scouting" was founded in Zgierz in 1916. Its founders were Yisrael Weinik, Yaakov Skosowski, Leon Rubinsztejn, and others.

In 1918, after the "Scouting" movement merged with a group of Jewish students, the Zionist youth movement "Hashomer Hatzair" was founded.

This was a Jewish, Zionist youth movement whose purpose was to educate the Jewish youth toward the actualization of Zionism. The idea of "Hashomer Hatzair" spread among the studying and working youth throughout all the cities of Poland. They studied scouting, Hebrew, Bible, the history of the Jewish people in the Diaspora and the Land of Israel, and knowledge about the Land of Israel (Palestinography) in order to instill in the youth the Zionist idea and love of the native Land. Various conventions, meetings and excursions took place together with youth from chapters in other cities. The first location of the Hashomer Hatzair group in Zgierz was in a room in the home of the Reichert family, where the other Zionist organizations were also gathered. The Hashomer Hatzair youth for the most part came from petite-bourgeois families, who mostly spoke Polish. The

262

work of the group was conducted in that language.

There were also groups that were conducted in Hebrew (the students of the Hebrew school). The first head of the chapter was Yaakov Skosowski, followed by Joszek Kohn, Peretz Goldsztejn and Shaya Cincinatus.

A chapter of Hashomer Hatzair in Zgierz in 1932 in Grepsz's yard

With the growth of aliya to the Land of Israel, the Hashomer Hatzair chapter served as the largest gathering place of Jewish youth who saw their future in the actualization of aliya. The parents looked positively upon the movement as a preparation for aliya.

In 1932, a football sporting team called Shomria was established by the local chapter, similar to what was established in other cities of Poland. The Zgierz team took an honorable role among the other teams. In 1924, the local group organized their first summer camp in the city of Niedzwiedz, directed by Shaya Cincinatus, Peretz Goldsztejn, Fishek Zylberberg, Tovka Nakrice, Yisrael Weisman, Ruth Sirkes, Tovka Poznerzon, Janka Kac and others.

In the years 1924-1925, there was a crisis among the leadership of the chapter. Some of the leaders made aliya (Janka Kac, Peretz Goldsztejn, Ruth Sirkes, and others), and others left to continue their studies. In 1926, the leadership of the chapter was placed upon much younger people who were helped by counselors from the city of Lodz. During this period, the region of Lodz-Kalize prepared a joint plan of action, which served as material that

263

helped conduct the work of the group. From that time, the summer camps were arranged in common for all cities of the regions on a class basis. The counselors were Rafael Kac, Yaakov Albersztejn, Avraham Haron, Muniek Zelgow, Motel Rozman, Genia and Chana Gorner, Paula Ickowicz, and Esther Kac.

The period between the years 1923 and 1929 was a bright period for the local chapter of Hashomer Hatzair, which had up to 350 members. It was housed in a large, fine hall in the Grepsz home on Narutowicza Street, and had a stage for performances. The chapter occupied itself with all Zionist activities, and was a faithful participant in anything that took place in Zionist life in the city, such as Keren Kayemet, publicity activity and actions on behalf of the Zionist idea (lectures, presentations, parades, excursions, etc.). It was among the finest chapters in the region of Lodz-Kalisz.

During this period, Jewish youth started to come from the homes of the craftsmen and workers. On account of this, Yiddish began to penetrate, along with the Polish and Hebrew languages. In 1927, through the efforts of the youth group of the Working Land of Israel, a Hechalutz organization was founded. The chapter played an active role in the activities of the organization, leadership, and preparation for aliya to the land. After the disturbances of 5689 (1929), members of the eldest section of this group made aliya: including Rafael Kac, Mordechai Roizman, Avraham Haron, Paula Ickowicz, Genia and Chana Gorner, and Esther Kac.

Once again, the younger layer came to the directorship of the chapter, including Rivka Kac, Franka Szapszowicz and Aharon Abramowicz, who led the chapter for only a short time until the made aliya.

The chapter continued with its activities, and remained in constant communication with the head leadership, from which it received newspapers. It participated in worldwide and national conventions in such places as Danzig, Rotki-Czechia, and Warsaw. It was involved and alert to whatever took place in the movement.

When the younger segments took over leadership of the chapters, the activists included: Tzila Zelnik, Dova Kac, Batya Ickowicz, Chaya Szperling, Shalom Praszker, Chana Kirszstejn, Yosef Woronski, Achwa Lewin and others. Most of them made aliya. Due to the interruption in aliya, the members who had gone on Hachsharah returned home and searched for means to make aliya. Some of them indeed succeeded.

A group of Hashomer Hatzair in 1925- First row standing: T. Nakrice, Sh. Cincinatus, unidentified, Y. Weinbaum, P. Goldsztejn, Y. Kac, Zylberberg, R. Sirkes, T. Poznerzon. Second row: Ruth Sirkes, Y. A. Cincinatus, Z. Szkosowski, R. Rozenman. Third row: Sh. Rabinowicz, M. Sirkes, R. Cincinatus, Sh. Hochman, N. Gottheiner, P. Sibirsia. Fourth row: R. Kac, A. Szidlowski, M. Fiszer

The Aviv group of Hashomer Hatzair with their counselors- First row: Tz. Zelnik, A. Haron, B.Ickowicz, Sh. Finkelsztejn, Y. Albersztejn, Ch. Groner, A. Kac, P. Kac, P. Ickowicz- Sitting: R.Szperling, B. Jakubowicz, A. Lewin, A. Goldberg, and D. Kac.

265

The activities of the chapter indeed continued until the outbreak of the war, albeit with a smaller number of members. Those that lead the chapter through this period until the outbreak of the war included: Moshe Ickowicz, Binyamin Szirdski, Yitzchak Bornsztejn, Yoshia Kimelfeld, Shalom Bibersztejn, Yedidya Melinerski, Esther Praszker, Asher Gornicki, Rozka Radogowska, Miriam Widislowska, and others. Only a few of them survived the Holocaust, and very few made arrived in the land.

For many years, Hashomer Hatzair was the largest and most popular Zionist youth movement in Zgierz.

Hechalutz by Chaya Halpern and Yaakov Lewin

A branch of Hechalutz in Zgierz at the farewell for members who are going on Hachsharah (training in preparation for aliya) (1929)- First row: P. Szrakowiak, Y. Flink, Y. Chaimowicz, Fisher, B. Szeinholtz, Y. Woronski. Second row: Ch. Cesner, P. Sar, A. Trajanowski, R. Kac, G. Gorner, Sh. Szrakowiak, A. Haron, Z. Zalmanowicz, Ch. Gorner, A. Abramowicz, Y. Korczej, M. Rozman, G. Kirszsztejn. Third row: Y. Michowicz, Ch Cesner, H. L. Ickowicz, Y. Lewin, M. Gambicki, D. Zeidenwurm, Y. Wazonski, P. Ickowicz-Forth row: Y. Zalgow, A. Bornsztejn. M. Poznanski, Y. Wajnkranc, Sh. Skosowski

Hechalutz was founded in 1927 through the efforts of the Working Land of Israel Zionist youth movement. Its founders were Rafael Kac, Avraham Haron, Mordechai Rozman, Paula Ickowicz, Chana Gorner, Yisrael Chaimowicz, Mordechai Szewach, Yechezkel Wazonski and others.

Every member of a Zionist youth movement who wished to actualize their Zionism and make aliya to the Land had to go on Hachsharah through Hechalutz in order to receive a permit for aliya. Aside from members of the organized Zionist youth movements, Hechalutz also accepted into its ranks Jewish working youth who desired aliya. The counselors were members of Hashomer Hatzair and Gordonia in the city. Lectures took place on various themes, such as the history of the Land and the Jewish settlement, knowledge of Israel - Palestinography, and other topics. Evening classes in Hebrew were arranged under the direction of Yitzchak Pilcki, who was one of the teachers in the children's institution in Helenowek near Zgierz (and later a leader in Ben Shemen and a member of Kibbutz Ramat Rachel). There were joint meetings and excursions for the youth under the sponsorship of Hechalutz.

The meeting place was in the Hashomer Hatzair hall on Narotwicsza Street. The first who went on Hachsharah through Hechalutz in the summer of 1929 to the Klosowo mine worked and lived under difficult conditions. These members were Lipman Flam, Yitzchak Abramowicz, Yisrael Chaimowicz and Yechezkel Wazonski.

The second group went out to Suchedniow in 1929. This group included Yaakov Lewin, Mordechai Gembicki, Katriel Cesner, and Hirsh Leib Ickowicz. They were followed by Yosef Woronski, Avraham Bornsztejn, Yitzchak Goldberg, and Shlomo Wisznia.

There was no aliya in the years 1931-1932. The members who had received permits for aliya were sent home. Some of them enlisted in the Polish army. There was an interruption in the activities of Hechalutz, which continued until the establishment of the Borochov Hachsharah kibbutz.

267

The Hitachdut Zionist Worker's Group by W. Fisher and David Berger

A party marking the aliya of members of Hitachdut to the Land of Israel, 1925

The Hitachdut Zionist Workers party was founded in Prague in 1920 through a union of the Worker's party in Israel with the Diaspora radical Zionist Zeiri Zion youth movement.

A chapter of Hitachdut in Zgierz was established in 1920, with the active assistance of representatives of that movement in Lodz, Dr. Yosef Szweig and Dr. Aryeh Tratkower. They were present at the founding meeting, at which the first committee was chosen. The members of the committee were Wolf Fiszer, David Berger, David Tevil Elberg - secretary, and the members: Michel Szidlowski, Yaakov Szapira, Berish Librach, Betzalel Frugel, Yitzchak Sczaransky, and David Baum. After the aliya of Elberg to the Land of Israel, Yaakov Szapira replaced him in the secretariat.

The committee immediately entered into organized activity, and began to recruit members from the youth of Zgierz. This endeavor was crowned with success, for the Hitachdut found this field to be like a ploughed field waiting for seeding. From 1920, when the Tzeirei Zion movement disbanded on its own accord on the heels of the unification, and due to the fact that many of its most active members left, mainly to make aliya to the land, and others were uprooted to the battlefronts of the Russian-Polish war, the young

268

generation coming of age was left perplexed and searching for its way. It was seeking for a solution to its unique social and cultural issues. The existing Zionist organizations were burdened, and were not able to serve as a secure home for that segment of the youth in whom the streams of the new times began to take hold.

It is easy to understand that many of the youth answered the call to join with Hitachdut, for there, in the confines of a working, active, dynamic Zionist movement; they found an opening of hope to fulfil their Zionist desires and aspirations, and a paved road toward a more secure future.

During the first period, the Hitachdut activities were mainly involved in spreading the fundamental ideals of the movement: a desire to establish a new, working, free community in the Land of Israel without exploiters and the exploited; a renewal of the Hebrew language and culture, a renewal of the life of the nation in the exile on the basis of productive and independent work, etc. Above all - the aim was to awaken the national Jewish consciousness in the heart of the youth.

Particular attention was give to publicity to encourage the youth to productive work, in particular to the Jewish youth of the middle class, to whom work with the hands was a foreign idea. Already in its first year of existence, the Zgierz chapter took an honorable place in Zgierz life. At the festive gathering on the occasion of the opening of the Hebrew University of Jerusalem in April 1925 that took place in the Luna theater, Hitachdut presented an honorable presentation to the Zgierz community. This was its first appearance as a new political-communal body in the city.

One year later, when Hitachdut received the custodianship of the Friszman Library, its activities broadened, for the library hall was given over to cultural work during its free times. This activity included Hebrew classes that were conducted by the elder, well-known teacher Weinik; discussions among friends; readings about political, literary and general topics in which, aside from the members of the movement, members of the working youth also participated, including Yisrael Weinik, Yaakov Gottstadt and others. Special times were set aside, especially on Sabbaths and festivals, for communal singing, in which the youth expressed the desires of their hearts and their Zionist aspirations in music and song.

With the passage of time, Hitachdut broadened its activity in all aspects of cultural life of the Jewish community of Zgierz. Aside from its constant growth, it attained recognizable social and political power in the city. Its representatives penetrated and took honorable positions in all communal institutions. Especially prominent was its participation in Zionist conventions on behalf of the Land of Israel, on the committee for the league of Working Israel, etc.

One of our representatives, David Berger, was chosen as the chairman of the Keren Kayemet LeYisrael in Zgierz. He was also one of the chief activists of Keren Hayesod. Along with others, Berger represented Hitachdut in factional conventions, and joined together with them in fitting committees.

During the time of elections for the Zionist institutions or local civic institutions, Hitachdut was an important factor. David Baum, Shmuel Feldon and David Praszker (as is known from the book of protocols of the community council) participated with the support of the communal council in the preparation of lists of Jewish candidates for the city council in 1927. During the early 1930s, David Berger entered into the communal council on the united Zionist list.

At this occasion, I want to single out the most faithful and dedicated member of Hitachdut in Zgierz during all of its years of existence - David Baum who received the job of secretary from Yaakov Szapira. He filled his task with the attention to detail, seriousness and dedication in which he excelled.

A farewell party for members of Hitachdut who are making aliya to the Land of Israel- With the participation of representatives of the various Zionist groups (1925)

270

We should also mention here a number of members who joined the committee later. Each one gave their best ability to the work of the chapter. These included Moshe Landau, Avraham Zelgow, Yona Kirszbaum, Zanwil Librach, Moshe Akerman, Moshe Yaakov Grand, Moshe Yaakov Srebnik, Avraham Szewach, Kaszikac, and others whom I do not recall at this moment.

It is fitting to especially point out one of the aims of Hitachdut in the realm of Zionist work in the field of education. This was the creation of the Gordonia organization for pioneering Zionist youth. With the assistance of other local factors, this youth group grew to become a fruitful and flourishing branch of Hitachdut.

As we glance backward to that time, we can see that we should not feel bad about the effort and work that we invested to raise the level of Hebrew culture, and to awaken the Jewish goals within a portion of our youth who were motivate by the same goals that united and forged our camp. There is much heartache and agony over those young lives who pined and waited with longing eyes for that far off Land, who were full of hope and faith to find their enchanting, fine future there - and their path to that Land was cut off in such a cruel fashion during the days of murder and extermination. The hangman put an end to their lives and desires.

Their honor and memory shall be guarded along with all those who dedicated their souls upon the altars of the nation of Israel on the way to the liberation and establishment of our Land.

Gordonia by Y. Sz.

In the year 1928, David Baum, Yitzchak Sczaransky and Berish Librach, with the help of the leader of the central Gordonia organization Pinchas Lubianiker (Lavon), created the Gordonia youth organization within Hitachdut.

Thanks to the untiring, dedicated work of these three, Gordonia grew within a short time to become one of the most active youth organizations in our city.

Lecturers and representatives from the Lodzer Gordonia often came to us. Among them were the young artist Yisrael Szumacher, and Mrs. Zylberszac. They would study Hebrew and Yiddish songs with us, in the spirit of the Jewish workers movement.

271

Each week, new members arrived. We already had approximately 130 members a year after the founding. They received an education in the spirit of A. D. Gordon's teachings.

The older members later went out on Hachsharah. Fresh, younger members came into our ranks in their place.

The active members of Gordonia included the following: Simcha Szarkowiak, Zvulun Opozdower, Menachem Blank, Chana Rubin, Yisrael Chaimowicz, Shaul Blanket, Yaakov Korciasz, Zeev Blazer, Chava Zelgow, Hadasa Blanket, Chava Bocinski, Yechezkel Jazonski, and others.

Unfortunately not everyone was able to make aliya, on account of the certificate allocations of the English Mandate authorities in the Land of Israel during that time. Many of them were murdered by the German murderers. Their memory should be mentioned for good.

Group of Gordonia members prior to going out on an excursion- In the front row: Y. Wazinski, Blazer, Ch. Rozlaska, unidentified, A. Szrowko, A. Szewach, Y. Korwazow, A. Waller. In the second row: Ch. Wisoczka, R. Lewin, Szarkowiak, Ch. Bozinska, Ch. Gelbard, A. Moszkowicz, G. Weinkrancz. In the third row: Sh. Szrowko, C. Zalgow, M. Blank. Ch. Ickowicz. In the fourth row: Szeinholtz, Sh. Blanket, M. Zinamon, Wisocki

About Gordonia by Yisrael Chaimowitz of Ramat Gan

The events in the Land of Israel caused an awakening of the pioneering movement throughout Poland. The Gordonia movement arose with the assistance of the political Hitachdut movement. The branch of Hitachdut in our city was alert and active in this direction. It correctly saw in Gordonia a pioneering youth movement that educated its members toward communal life in the land, and actualized the vision of independent work without relying on others. I remember that when I went for the first time to Gordonia, which was situated in "Palestine Courtyard" on Dombrowska Street, I felt an uplifting of my spirit. I knew that I am changing the order of the life that I was used to from the home of my grandparents and parents, a life of cleaving to Hassidic faith, which was for many years the source of Jewish existence, whether it was the Hassidim of Ger, of the Rebbe of Aleksandrow, or any other Hassidic group. All of them had one aim, to guard the Jewish spark that it should not extinguish. I saw in the pioneering movement an extension and continuation of the guarding of the Jewish ember, and the first action toward the return to Zion. To our dismay and pain, only a few survived the Hell of the Holocaust and were able to actualize their Zionistic desires.

The Revisionist Movement in Zgierz by Mordechai the son of Yaakov Glazer

The Revisionist Movement in our city crystallized within the Zionist movements in the middle of the 1920s, with the call of Jabotinsky to the Zionist youth to gird themselves for the great endeavor of the redemption of our Land with the force and energy required by the times.

I absorbed a great deal of the love of the land and the Zionist vision during my youth by constantly listening to the enthusiastic chiselers of the Zionist cedars in Zgierz, such as Isuchar Szwarc, Moshel Eiger of blessed memories and others. Later, when I was already active in the Zionist movement, I was easily swayed by the warm speeches of Jabotinsky, for the Zionist work was being conducted with excessive slowness, and was missing the energy that the Jewish youth were awaiting.

273

A group of Beitar members and officials- Standing in the top row: M. Cohen, Jakubowicz, P. Davidowicz, Ch. Gincburg, R. Malchieli, L. Sribnik- Standing in the second row: Kaszibinus, M. Podmaski, and Sh. Zisman- Sitting: Szapir, Sh. Gottfreund, and M. Himmelfarb. A. Librach. Sitting in the bottom row: S. Szidlowski, Ch. Kaufman, Hirszberg

On account of this, when Jabotinsky founded Revisionist Zionism, my friends and I were attracted to the new movement with bonds of enchantment. A youth group of the new style was organized in our town at that time. Its ranks included Yehuda L. Weinsztejn who served as chairman; Reuven Malchieli and I who were young; and Leib Sribnik was the secretary. We immediately began our significant work. We called publicity meetings and conducted wide-ranging activity on behalf of the idea. We implemented new Zionist activities that were required by the times. It is possible to state that this young movement did a great deal to increase the Zionist mission within the youth. It dedicated itself to the education of the youth, and preparing them for pioneering and aliya. Hachsharah locations were set up near the city of Aleksandrow. Yitzchak Hameiri was appointed as the head of the Hachsharah camp. He succeeded greatly at his task, and raised the Zionist idea at all times and in every place.

Later, the Beitar movement was founded, that excelled in its appearances and parades at festive occasions and national events. It demonstrated the

Zionist flame by raising the national flag in the Jewish and gentile communal circles. The leader of Beitar was Avraham Teichner, and the vice-leaders were Moshe Zakon and Reuven Malchieli.

Brit Hachayil (The Covenant of the Soldiers) was founded later, during the 1930s. Youth who had been freed from the Polish army participated in this organization. The movements of Revisionist Zionism, Beitar and Brit Hachayil received additional power at that time. They strengthened until they succeeded in entering their representative Yehuda Leib Rozenberg to the Jewish communal council. Moshe Lewkowicz was the leader of Brit Hachayil. The members of the leadership who served with him were Yehuda Leib Szwarcbard, Finkelsztejn, Michael Cohen and others.

In the year 5698 (1938) the Revisionist Zionist movement dedicated itself to the Second Aliya with full strength. The impetus for this activity came for the most part from the dearth of certificates, which, as is known, was impeded by the relations between the various factions of the Zionist camp, and the lack of organization by those who controlled the quotas of certificates. The Revisionist Zionists were forced to gather crumbs from the tables of others, if it was indeed possible to obtain anything at all. The Second Aliya was the natural result of the pressure for aliya among the members of Beitar. The first of those who made aliya in this movement were Ozer Cohen, Epsztejn and others from the movement.

The Revisionist Movement always played an active role in the activities of Keren Hayesod and Keren Kayemet. The member of the Keren Hayesod committee from the Revisionist Zionists was our chairman Leibish Weinsztejn. Leib Sribnik of blessed memory served as our representative to the Keren Kayemet committee. The movement did a great deal of work in educating the youth, and all of those who were numbered under its flags were in agreement with the Zionist idea without bounds or limits.

The last of the activists before the Holocaust were Meir Leib Rozenberg who served as the chairman of the movement, Yosef Leib Gottstadt, Pinchas Dawidowicz, Elazar Zakon who dedicated himself to the work of the movement with diligence of heart and soul, Feivel Librach, the Finkelsztejn brothers, Michael Cohen, and others. The leader of Beitar was Elazar Zakon, who was assisted by his friends Michael Cohen and Menachem Gincberg.

The Jabotinsky faithful who hailed from Zgierz continued in their path after they made aliya to the land. During the time of the great revolt of the Jewish settlement against the British Mandatory government during the years

5704-5705 (1944-1945), when myriads of British army soldiers and officers spread themselves out to all places in the Hebrew settlement to track down the men of the underground, and particularly tried to hunt for the head of the

A party in Zgierz on the occasion of the freeing of Avraham Stowski from guilt of the murder of Dr. Chaim Arlozorov of blessed memory

A group of Beitar members

Etzel underground by placing pacing a price on his head, the underground leader Mr. Begin found a safe refuge in the home of a Beitar man who was a native of our city, Reuven Malchieli of Petach Tikva. From that house, the leadership of the underground conducted its work under the nose of the Mandatory police, in a heroic struggle against he forces that worked with all their might to thwart the development of the Jewish state while it was still in its infancy (M. Begin - "The Revolt", page 169).

Zgierz was blessed with an excited youth that was full of the Zionist flame. The pain and anguish is great regarding those who did not merit attaining the realization of their youthful longings and dreams, and waited for actualization. May their memories be blessed.

The Borochov Kibbutz by Yitzchak Sczaransky

Members of the Borochov Kibbutz in Zgierz (1933)

The Borochov Kibbutz in Zgierz was founded in 1932 with the assistance of the members Yaakov Lewin, Hirsch Ickowicz, Katriel Cesner and Mordechai Gembicki. At the outset, the kibbutz had 15 members who were accommodated in a small dwelling on the Jewish street. The first 15 members had no difficulty in finding work in the city. Therefore, several of them became members of trades, such as tailors, hat makers, and also carpenters.

The members of the kibbutz lived in a commune. There were indeed times where instead of supper, the group arranged themselves in a circle, shoulder to shoulder, danced a Hora, sang songs, and... went to sleep hungry.

They all held together thanks to the dedication of the members to the pioneering ideal. Ignoring the fact that some of the members were unemployed, they took in more and more members in order to expand the kibbutz.

A double problem came with the arrival of new members. First, the dwelling was too crowded, and they had to have special rooms for the girls. Second, there was a question about how to employ the 20 new members, while the first 15 were not fully employed.

The Zgierz resident Baruch Skosowski, who knew about the difficult conditions of the Borochov Kibbutz, procured a large dwelling on Dombrowska Street and began to concern himself about with employment for the kibbutz members. Thanks to him, almost all of the members found employment - a portion of the m in the wool workshop of Leizer Poznerzon and others in the factories of Brancher, Horowicz, and Skosowski, as well as in a wood workshop. Thanks to the fact that Baruch Skosowski found employment for 30 people, the kibbutz lived on, and new members came in. Baruch found employment for some of the new members as well. He did not rest during the day or night until he succeeded in finding new places of work.

After some time, the kibbutz was enriched with its own workshop that employed six members. Later, they set up a fowl farm with dozens of hens, geese and ducks. However, their greatestjoy was when theypurchased a cow that gave milk. The fowl and the milk cow greatly assisted the kibbutz in its livelihood and development.

There were times, nevertheless, when the kibbutz had a bit of a crisis. In concert with the general unemployment in the city, many kibbutz members also lost their stable employment. This occurred at the time when the kibbutz had close to a hundred members.

However, things work out in the end. The food merchants, Lifszitz on Piontker Street and Rozenstreich on Pilsudski Street, two Gerrer Hassidim, provided the kibbutz with products on credit until the members would find employment. The baker Eliezer Korczej must be singled out for praise, for he gave the kibbutz as much bread as was needed every day, without even writing it down. He said that he trusts them to keep accounts and to pay him. He would say, "People who hold the Land of Israel as an ideal will not deceive a fellow Jew monetarily".

A party at the Borochov Kibbutz in Zgierz - In the center are seated Mr. Fabian Grynberg and his wife

The kibbutz brought a revival of life to the Jewish street. The members took part in various Zionist activities, and also in professional movements.

It was indeed a wonder how young people came from different areas of Poland, with different ways of life and characters - and they conducted themselves like a family, thanks to the pioneering ideal.

It is worthwhile to mention the kibbutz member Yisrael Lifszitz who created the "Freiheit" in Zgierz. He would often speak on various subjects at the kibbutz. As well, the kibbutz members Yocheved Bogen and Simcha Ber were of those who helped create the spiritual life in the kibbutz through their efforts. The members Charna and Tzviek came from Kibbutz Gesher in Israel, and reported about kibbutz life in the Land of Israel.

From time to time, the city doctor Kaltgrad visited the kibbutz, and lectured on medical topics.

When the doctor Kaltgrad went to check on a sick person in the kibbutz, he took no money for his visit.

A festive joy pervaded in the kibbutz when members were approved for aliya.

The joy pervaded among all members without exception, so that it was impossible to discern which ones were certified for aliya, and which ones had to wait their turn to be certified.

There were some who were certified who did not have enough funds for the journey. In such cases, the situation was entrusted to the aforementioned Baruch Skosowski. Within a few days, he would arrange the funds for the journey for the aliya candidate, with some amount in addition. It was no secret that the largest sum of money was given out of his pocket.

There were also times when a feeling of despair prevailed among the members of the kibbutz who were not able to make aliya, for the British Mandatory authorities only gave out few certificates. It was characteristic that nobody left the kibbutz even in times of despair. The despair passed with a tune and a dance of "Am Yisrael Chai" (The Nation of Israel Lives), and "Unizke Lirot" (We will Merit to Witness).

The kibbutz moved to Lodz at the end of 1937. It was located on Leszna Street, where it was the central location of the Borochov Kibbutz for the Lodz region.

Many of the members of the Zgierz kibbutz can be found in the kibbutzim of Dafna, Ramat Rachel and others.

The Bund by Vove

The leaders of the Bund in Zgierz were known to use from the years 1905-1906, with their revolutionary, underground activity. They took part in the workers demonstrations against the Czar. They frequently issued proclamations to call upon the masses to struggle and uprising. They organized strikes, hung red flags from the factories and sung the "Czerwony Sztandar" ("Red flag")... They also conducted covert agitation among the Jewish students of the business school, to encourage them toward the Socialist idea. Several of them were arrested and exiled, while others left for America after the revolution failed. What is certain is that they stirred up the Jewish street, and new, strange songs were heard in the weaving factories and workshops.

During the years of the First World War, a portion of the Bund intelligentsia was very active in communal affairs, taking an active role in the general Jewish rescue committee for social assistance. Also during the years between the world wars, the Bund conducted a lively activity, particularly in the professional realm, in protecting the interests of the workers.

It was especially active in the time of the elections for the city council, the community or the Sejm. They conducted wide ranged activities for their desired candidates, with the agitation from the Lodz Bund. The Bund had one of their representatives, Moshe Gross, on the communal council.

A demonstration of members of the trade union against the concentration camp of Kartoz-Beroza in 1937

They had a large number of members and a significant influence in the Zgierz professional union, as well as in the old folk's home. A large group of Bund youth, called Zukunft, was active.

From among the most important activists, it is appropriate to mention Moshe Gross, B Crystal, H. Skurka, Yitzchak Grand, and others.

The Communist Party in Zgierz by A. Y.

Zgierz was an industrial city in pre-war Poland. Thousands of Polish, Jewish and German workers worked in the various factories, mainly in the textile industry. A noticeable number of workers and also of the intelligentsia belonged to the illegal Communist Party of Poland (K. P. P.)

Since the party was illegal, the number of its members was unknown, however, the existence of the party was perceived in the city. From time to time, especially on workers holidays such as the First of May and the anniversary of the October Revolution and others, red banners even hung

281

from the telephone wires. One could hear their slogans during economic strikes. They often conducted discussions in the professional union. They raised money for the political arrests "Red Help" (M. O P. R - International Organization for Help of the Revolutionaries).

No special Jewish section existed. The following were known from among the members who belong to the movement: Juszek Horowicz (He was arrested and spent some time in jail); Shlomo Szerman who was arrested from time to time and subsequently freed, for the police could not often find any compromising material in his house, and therefore could not keep him in prison prior to a trial.

At the time of the last elections for the Jewish community, the Comparty wished to present its own list. They united with left-leaning parties, and the united list succeeded in receiving a mandate. Shlomo Szerman was elected as a communal representative from that list.

C. Personalities and Characters

The Three Who Occupied the Rabbinical Seat of Zgierz

Rabbi Shalom Tzvi Hakohen of holy blessed memory
the first rabbi of the community of Zgierz

The first rabbi of the young community of Zgierz was the rabbi, Gaon and righteous man Reb Shalom Tzvi Hakohen, who was nicknamed by the people of his city "Der Alter Tzadik" - The Elder Tzadik. He was a Hassid of Pshishcha (Przysucha), Kock, Gur, and Aleksandrow. He spent a great deal of time at the table of his Rebbes, despite the strong opposition of his father-in-law.

Reb Shalom Tzvi was born in Piotrkow in the year 5553 (1793) to an illustrious family. In his youth, he excelled in his intellect, grasp, and also his diligence. While he was still studying in cheder, he would often continue his studies until the candle by which he was studying melted. In that era, there was no gas or electricity in Poland. People only used candles, and as long as the candle was burning, the child Shalom Tzvi sat in the cheder and studied. When the melamed (teacher) went out from the cheder for a few minutes, the young genius would exchange the remnants of the candle with a new candle, so that he could continue studying further.

At first, his parents would worry about him and they would come to search for him. Slowly but surely, they got used to the idea that their young son would return from cheder at a late hour in the night.

Aside from his diligence, the young Reb Shalom Tzvi also excelled in his sharpness. When he was thirteen years old, his name went out in a praiseworthy fashion as a young genius, the expert student of Reb Leibish Tablis of Piotrkow. At age fifteen, the learned wealthy man Reb Yaakov Aharon HaKohen Szatan of Lutomiersk, the grandfather of the Admor Reb Chanoch Henech HaKohen of Aleksandrow, set eyes upon him and took him as a husband for his daughter.

Reb Shalom Tzvi was supported at his father-in-law's table for several years. He occupied himself with Torah diligently in that home, which was a combination of Torah and greatness in one place. Aside from his father-in-law Reb Yaakov Aharon, in that group the following people were found, his brother-in-law Reb Pinchas Hakohen and his young son, the genius Reb Chanoch Henech the Kohen, who became the Admor of Aleksandrow after the death of the Rim of Gur in the year 5626 (1866). As well, the son-in-law of Reb Pinchas, the Gaon Reb Yechezkel Nomberg, who later became the rabbi the community of Lodz, was also supported at the table of his father-in-law as he occupied himself with Torah. This group would often sit closed together in one room in the home of Reb Yaakov Aharon for several hours in a day as they discussed topics regarding novel ideas in the Talmud and responsa among themselves. They did not have to worry about sustenance, and they were able to dedicate themselves, and create a group of great scholars.

Reb Yaakov Aharon was a strong Misnaged, and he did not permit the few Hassidim in the town of Lutomiersk to pass through the entrance to his house. However, the times did their work. The Hassidic movement quickly spread through Poland, and in almost all communities, many joined the movement. The students of the Besht [1], and the students of his students such as the "Chozeh" of Lublin [2] and the Magid of Kozienice, did a great deal to spread Torah and Hassidism among the masses. Reb Shalom Tzvi, even though he was supported at the table of his father-in-law who was a Misnaged, clung to the Hassidic movement. On occasions when his father-in-law was out of the country on business, he hastened to pack his suitcase and travel to Przysucha [3] to the "Holy Jew". He remained with the Rebbe for a number of months.

As is known, the "Jew" of Przysucha was one of the greats of Torah in his time, and he presented an intensive class in Talmud and halachic decisions every day before his students. Reb Shalom Tzvi, who came daily to hear the class, became not only an enthusiastic Hassid, but also a literal student of the "Jew".

When Reb Shalom Tzvi returned from this long journey, his Misnaged father-in-law was already in his home, and he knew all that his son-in-law did. When Reb Yaakov Aharon saw him approaching the home from afar, he got up and closed the doors of his home before him, and did not allow him to enter. Reb Shalom Tzvi decided then to go to the home of the Hassidim. There he met the grandson of Reb Yaakov Aharon, the young genius Chanoch Henech, who was already then close to Hassidic ideology, which helped him set himself up with seven Hassidim in that community. Each of

284

them volunteered to support the son-in-law of the wealthy Misnaged one day a week.

When Reb Yaakov Aharon heard from his grandson that Shalom Tzvi was eating on a daily rotation basis with Hassidim, he decided to change his relations with his son-in-law and invited him to return home. He made up with him, and finally made peace with the idea that Hassidim had penetrated his family.

Even after he made peace with Hassidism, Reb Shalom Tzvi did not change his behavior and his path. He continued studying diligently as he was supported at the table of his father-in-law. As well, when he traveled to Przysucha, he sat all day in the Beis Midrash bound to the Gemara. Hassidism imbued in him a spirit of joy, and he was always happy and glad to greet his Hassidic friends.

After the death of the "Holy Jew" of Przysucha in the year 5574 (1814), and the Chozeh of Lublin in the year 5575 (1815), Reb Shalom Tzvi moved to stand on the threshold of Reb Simcha Bunim of Przysucha. When he came to him for the first time, the Rebbe said to him "Shalom Hirsch! ... I made for you a name like one of the great people of the land..." The Hassidim saw in this an agreement that Reb Shalom Tzvi should take upon himself the mantle of the rabbinate.

In the year 5583 (1823) when he ceased to be supported at the table of his father-in-law, he was accepted as the rabbi of the community of Grabowo in the vicinity of Leczyca. He served in this rabbinate for four years, until he was asked to take on the rabbinate of Zgierz, in the year 5587 (1827). From that time, Reb Shalom Tzvi served as the rabbi of Zgierz until the day of his death in the year 5637 (1877) at the age of 84.

The appointment as the rabbi of Zgierz did not come easily to him. The community of Zgierz indeed invited him to occupy the rabbinical chair, but an agreement of the civic government was also needed, who demanded certificates and approbations from well-known ordained rabbis. Reb Shalom Tzvi brought out his first certificate of ordination from the rabbi and Gaon Reb Moshe Aharon, the head of the Beis Din (rabbinical court) of Strykow, and a second certificate with the approbation of the Gaon Reb Chaim Auerbach the head of the Beis Din and rabbi in Leczyca. In it was written: "I see in Reb Shalom Tzvi HaKohen a man wise in Torah and the fear of G-d. He is involved with all aspects of the worship of G-d. He is a fine speaker, and he is full and overflowing with Talmud and Jewish law. In

my discussions with him, I have found him to be full of wisdom. All of his deeds are measured and weighed. Therefore I have taken it upon myself to speak good of him, to support him, and to say of him, he shall surely teach, he shall surely judge [4]. Aside from this, he is already ordained from the prominent rabbi Reb Moshe Aharon of Strykow, and two are better than one. These are the words that were spoken in honor and awe of the Torah."
Leczyca, Monday 22 Shvat, 5587 (1827)
Chaim the son of Yitzchak Itzik Auerbach of Lissa

When Reb Shalom Tzvi was first appointed as rabbi of Zgierz, his first activity was to establish a Yeshiva in the city, and people came to him from all the reaches of Poland to study Torah. Since he was a diligent studier on his own, he would present his class in the Yeshiva from

4:00 a.m. until 8:00 a.m. Hundreds of students affiliated themselves with this Yeshiva, and many of the rabbis of Poland were among its students. His Hassidic Rebbes, the elder Rebbe of Kock (Kotzk) and the Chidushei Harim of Gur would send every find lad to his Yeshiva, and thus, the cream of the crop of Hassidic Jewry of Poland were centered in Zgierz.

Regarding his student the rabbi and Gaon Reb Shaul Moshe Zylberman of blessed memory of Wieruszow (died in Tel Aviv), his son Rabbi Yehoshua Zylberman writes in his preface to the book of his father "Responsa of Reb Shaul Moshe" (Tel Aviv 5719 - 1959), that his father Reb Shaul Moshe was already considered a renown genius when he was a Bar Mitzvah, and traveled with his father to the "Chidushei Harim" [5] of Gur. The Rim examined him and discussed Torah matters with him for three hours. When he realized that he was destined for greatness, he advised him to travel to Zgierz to the Yeshiva of Reb Shalom Tzvi.

The community of Zgierz was at the time, the time of Reb Shalom Tzvi, one of the youngest communities of Poland. Textile production was established there, and Jews came to settle there from all corners of Poland in order to find a good livelihood. Reb Shalom Tzvi found there a wide vista for his activities. The young community became a place of Torah because of his Yeshiva and his activities among the householders. Reb Shalom Tzvi sat for most of the day with his students, and gave them classes in Talmud and Halacha. He occupied himself with communal matters during the intermissions between lessons. At night he sat by candlelight and studied Torah. On Sabbath eves in particular, he prepared a candle by which to study.

The Gaonim of the generation valued Reb Shalom Tzvi as a Gaon and a Tzadik. The Gaon Reb Yitzchak Feigenbaum, who was the head of the Beis Din of Warsaw, a student of the Chidushei Harim and a Hassid of Kock, was also one of those who revered Reb Shalom Tzvi. His son Rabbi Yisrael Isser wrote in his book "Or Pnei Yitzchak" (Warsaw, 5699 - 1939): "I heard from the holy mouth of the Admor of holy blessed memory, who told of the Gaon and Hasid Reb Shalom Tzvi HaKohen of holy blessed memory, the head of the rabbinical court of Zgierz, that when he studied with his students and erred in a difficult matter, he would open the Holy Ark, and supplicate and pray as one would do for a dangerously ill person.

The Rabbi of Zgierz was famous for being lenient in matters of Halacha, especially with regards to fasts. It is told that on one occasion, one of the residents of Zgierz, the grandson of the Gaon Reb Bendet of Lask, came to him on a fast day, and complained that his hunger was great, his thirst was strong, and he was feeling weak. Reb Shalom Tzvi advised him to break his fast, and added: "Once I was sitting in Lutomiersk during a fast day, and studying together with my nephew Reb Henech of Aleksandrow and my brother-in-law's son-in-law the Gaon Reb Yechezkel Nomberg (who was later appointed rabbi of Lodz). Your grandfather Reb Bendet of Lask came in to us with various foods in his hands, and requested us to taste a bit and break our fast, saying: "I am certain that you will become teachers of law among Israel, therefore I want you to learn to be lenient with fasts."

"And now", added Reb Shalom Tzvi, "When his grandson comes to me with this matter, it is certainly my duty to decide leniently."

When a matter of forbiddingness or permissibility [6] was presented to him, and he found that the Taz was lenient and the Shach [7] stringent, he would decide like the opinion of the former, saying: "How great is the Taz, and it is fitting to rely on his words." If the situation were the opposite, he would praise the Shach, and decide like him. Thus was his methodology of decision to decide in the manner of the lenient decisor. The ritual slaughterers (shochtim) of the city knew about this.

One of his decisions is fitting to record for eternity: On the eve of Passover, Reb David Handelisz (known as Reb Dovidshe), a wealthy, wise householder, entered into the pharmacy that was owned by a certain gentile. They debated the characteristics of the Jewish people. The pharmacist spoke disparagingly: they are friends of thieves, who only have monetary gain before their eyes. Reb Dovidshe contradicted him, proving that if you pay a

Jew, the lowest of the low in Zgierz, any amount of money, he would not drink a drink of whiskey that day [8], which is forbidden according to his religion. Therefore the money is not the desire of the soul of the Jews. The pharmacist retorted that he was willing to guarantee that any Jew would drink whiskey in his home. Reb David accepted the guarantee and they bet a sum of eight ducats (the Jews of Poland called ducats: tukatn). The pharmacist sent for the Jewish barber to give him a haircut, and Reb David entered one of the rooms. After the barber did his job, the pharmacist paid him well, and honored him with a glass of whiskey. The barber declined, saying that it was the eve of Passover today. The pharmacist offered him one full ducat, two, three, until eight ducats. The barber did not agree, and left his house. Then Reb David left the room and received the money of his bet. On his way home, he entered the house of the rabbi and told him about this. The rabbi informed him that, in accordance with the law of the Torah, he must give over the money to the barber. Reb David accepted this decision with love.

A deed of purchase of a fixed seat in the synagogue of Zgierz, signed by the elder Rabbi Shalom Tzvi Hakohen, as well as the trustees A. H. Glicksman and Z. Bornsztejn

It is told that when they complained to Rabbi of Brzezina, the Gaon Reb Sinai Sapir the author of "Olat Chadash" about his tendency to be stringent in halachic decisions, while in the neighboring city of Zgierz, Reb Shalom Tzvi tended to be lenient he answered: "It is fitting and appropriate for him to be lenient in halachic decisions, for he has broad shoulders. He is a Gaon in

Torah and a pure Tzadik".

The livelihood of Rabbi Shalom Tzvi was meager, but he made do with what he had. He even donated a large portion of his meager salary to charity. He was offered the rabbinate in larger communities, but the grace of the place was upon him, and he declined the various offers.

In the year 5617 (1857) he was offered the rabbinate in Kalisz. After that position had been abandoned by Rabbi Tzvi Chayes, and he agreed. At that time, Rabbi Yechiel Meir, the "Tehillim Yid" [9], who had been the rabbi in Gostynin, arrived in Zgierz. He was a Hassid of Kock, and was the friend of Reb Shalom Tzvi. The householders in Zgierz complained before Rabbi Yechiel Meir that their rabbi wished to leave them. When he later came before Reb Shalom Tzvi, he asked him why he wanted to leave. Reb Shalom Tzvi answered him that he was not satisfied being in a city that does not have a synagogue that is fitting for its name. Reb Yechiel Meir promised him that if he to remain in Zgierz, they would build for him a fine synagogue. That week, Reb Yechiel Meir called a meeting of the important householders of the city, and gave over to them the words of Rabbi Shalom Tzvi. Those attending the meeting immediately gathered on the spot 3,000 rubles, and a few days later they purchased a lot in the center of the city, and began the building of the synagogue.

In the book "Tiferet Adam", a different version was found regarding the rabbinate of Kalisz, as follows: Reb Shalom Hirsch was called a few times to be the head of the rabbinical court in communities that were larger than Zgierz, such as Piotrkow and Kalisz, but he did not want to leave his city, where he had peace and quiet and was able to occupy himself with Torah and maintain a Yeshiva, for this was the entire desire of his soul. Once, the notables of the city of Kalisz came to him and asked him to accept the rabbinate of their city. He agreed to them. However, the matter became known to the heads of the community of Zgierz, who hurried to him and asked him: "Are you prepared to leave us, and what are you lacking here?" The rabbi answered them: "Indeed it is true that I am in debt". The heads of the community asked him: "How much do you owe?" He answered that his debt is several hundred rubles. At that meeting, the wealthy notables who were gathered took upon themselves the obligation to give him the required sum, and they also took council and agreed to increase his salary. The rabbi retracted his promise to the people of Kalisz. They later asked him why he did not inform them earlier about his tight situation. He answered them simply: "I cannot make myself so valuable)...

From his youth, Reb Shalom Tzvi loved his fellow man and brought them near to Torah. At the time when Reb Shalom Tzvi reached the age of eighty, the researcher of Hassidism Dr. Aharon Marcus visited Zgierz. In his book "Hassidism" (page 244), he wrote of him: "One of the dedicated elder rabbis, Reb Shalom Hirsch, the rabbi of Zgierz. I met him when he was eighty years old, and he is a man worthy of reverence".

When Reb Shalom Tzvi saw that there were breaches in the wall of Judaism, he was not afraid before any person. It is told that once a factory owner wished to open his business on the Sabbath. Reb Shalom Tzvi sent a message to him: "If you are stubborn in this matter and you violate the Sabbath in your business, I will be forced to pray that your entire business be "destructive", for in accordance with the law, only "someone who destroys on the Sabbath is exempt"[10]". The prayer of the rabbi was accepted, for the quality of the merchandise of that factory declined, and the manufacturer lost all of his money. He was forced to close his factory.

During the time he lived in Zgierz, Reb Shalom Tzvi endeared himself to the masses of people as a Gaon and a Tzadik. Hundreds of people came to him to take counsel with him on various matters, and he answered everybody. However, he did not wish to be a "rabbi".

It is told that when his first born son, Reb Yitzchak Mendel, was born, Reb Shalom Tzvi commanded to issue a declaration in his Beis Midrash that anyone who is in need of salvation should come to the circumcision ceremony, and he would assure them that they would be helped. One of the prominent men of the city, was Reb Yitzchak Zylberberg, the father-in-law of Reb Falik Kunsztam who had an only son who was mute. He brought his grandson with him and presented him before the rabbi. The rabbi gave the child a pear, and told him: "This is a pear, take it and make the "borei pri haeitz" [11] benediction on it. The child took the pear, made the benediction and from then on began to speak.

By nature, Reb Shalom Tzvi was moderate and calm and all of his steps were refined and measured. However, within his heart there was a fire locked up. When he was once asked by a Misnaged why he joined the Hassidim of Kock, he answered: "the truth is like a nail that penetrates every place. The heat is the wall, and not a soft wall but a very solid wall. The stronger the hammer, the more powerful its blows, the better the nail penetrates the wall".

In the era of Kock, Reb Shalom Tzvi was already known as one of the greats of generation. On account of his influenced, many joined Kocker Hassidism, and Zgierz became a Hassidic community. Many of the Hassidim of Poland were opposed to the ways and the viewpoint of the Hassidim of Kock, and Reb Shalom Tzvi was the defender of that brand of Hassidism. Once, one of the Misnagdim asked him: "If indeed the viewpoint of Kock is so important, what is the reason that many oppose it?" Reb Shalom Tzvi answered: "If the many would value the truth and only oppose the viewpoint of Kock, your question would have merit, but since the many also oppose the truth even more than they oppose the viewpoint of Kock, what can I answer you?"…

It is told that prior to the time that the Rebbe of Kock was closeted up in his home in the year 5600 (1840), he once turned to the rabbi of Zgierz and said: "See Shalom Tzvi, to where I have come! The masses rule over me, this one wants money, this one wants a cure, etc., is this the reason why I am living here?" Reb Shalom Tzvi answered him: "To where should they turn if not to their rabbi?" The Rabbi of Kock pointed out: "Did you forget what is written: 'that make a man an offender by words, and lay a trap for him that reproves in the gate, and turn aside the just with nothingness' (Isaiah 29, 21). Those who go with nothingness do not wish to have something of substance, and are liable to cause even the Tzadik to stumble and become mislead!"

After the Rebbe of Kock was closeted, Reb Shalom Tzvi groaned and said: "I was silent when the Rebbe spoke to me, and I did not answer him because of fear of his glory, and it is too bad that I did not say to him what I thought about answering. What does the prophet say in the following verses: "For when he sees his children, the work of My hands in his midst, that they sanctify My name, Indeed they shall sanctify the Holy One of Jacob, and shall revere the G-d of Israel". That is to say in their midst, in the midst of the community, you can find those that sanctify G-d's name, and they will no longer mislead a Tzadik with naught, but rather: "Those who err in spirit will know wisdom, and they that murmur should know instruction."

Reb Shalom Tzvi was one of the first and most important Hassidim of Kock, and Reb Shalom Tzvi was invited to the wedding of the grandson of Reb Chaim Yisrael of Pilawa with the daughter of the Hassid Reb Zelig Frenkel of Zgierz, that took place in Kock. While he was traveling to the wedding, he caught a cold, and ran a high fever. When he arrived in Kock, they brought a doctor who wrote him a prescription for pills. The Rebbe was concerned about the sick man, and commanded that the pills that the doctor prescribed be brought to him. When the Rebbe saw the pills, he pointed out to the men who were standing before him: "Does the doctor know that the sick man is already 66 years old?" When the doctor heard this, he apologized and prescribed different pills. The Rebbe was right.

In the year 5625 (1865), his first wife died, and he was left with no male children. Reb Shalom Tzvi was 72 years old at the time. Reb Henech of Aleksandrow advised him to marry a young woman whom was suggested to him, and promised him that he would have sons from him. After the death of the Rim of Gur on the 23rd of Adar 5626 (1826), Reb Shalom Tzvi accepted the mastery of Reb Henech [12], listened to his advice and married a young woman. A few months later he took ill, and the doctors gave up on him. When the young wife saw that her husband was dying, she hurried to the Rebbe of Aleksandrow, crying out that she had promised her children, and where are they? Behold her husband was now lying on his deathbed, from which he would never arise according to the doctors. Reb Henech arose and traveled immediately to Zgierz to visit the sick man. As he entered the room in which the sick man was lying, contravening the advise of the Chevra Kadisha, who tried to prevent him from doing so as he was a Cohen [13], Reb Henech called out: "This Jew spread Torah to the masses!". He repeated these words a number of times, and then returned to the prayer room in which the sick man would always join himself with his Creator. He remained there for about three hours, and then returned to the room of the sick man. A change had taken place in the complexion of the sick man. He opened up his eyes and said: "Oy! The Rebbe of Aleksandrow is here!" The Rebbe answered him calmly, "When you return to your strength, you will come to me in Aleksandrow".

Reb Shalom Tzvi regained his health and lived another eleven years. During this time, two sons were born to him. The elder was Rabbi Yitzchak Menachem, who was coronated as Rebbe after the death of the Admor of Zyrardow. The second was Reb Shlomo Leib, who was the rabbi of Zgierz after the death of his father-in-law Reb Tzvi HaKohen.

Reb Shalom Tzvi continued to travel to the son of his brother-in-law the Rebbe of Aleksandrow, even though he was older than he was. He was always surprised that the Rebbe of Aleksandrow conducted himself in a different manner than was customary among the Admorim of the Beis

Midrash of Reb Bunim of Przysucha. In Przysucha, Kock and Gur, they did not permit women to enter to the Rebbe, and in Aleksandrow, they entered the Rebbe with their requests. Once, Reb Shalom Tzvi asked his Rebbe why he differed from the custom of his Rebbes. Reb Henech answered him: "Being a Rebbe is a punishment, and we have already learned in the Talmud 'The Torah specifies that a woman is equivalent to a man with regard to all of the punishments in the Torah'".

In the year 5630 (1870), the Rebbe of Aleksandrow died, and there were those from among his Hassidim who wished to coronate Reb Shalom Hirsch to fill his place. Reb Shalom Hirsch refused them, saying: "Just as I knew that after the death of the Rim of Gur, we should turn only to the Rebbe of Aleksandrow, similarly I know now that we have no other Rebbe other than Reb Leibele of Gur." At the age of 77, he moved over to the young Rebbe from Gur, 23 years old, the author of the "Sfat Emet". He cleaved to the Sfat Emet until his death in the year 5637 (1877). Even in his last years he did not change from his custom, he was always happy, he slept little, he remained wonderfully studious, and he spread Torah to his students in the Yeshiva.

Reb Shalom Tzvi served as the rabbi of Zgierz for 54 years. He was beloved by his community, but he never took any benefit from any person. His friends and admirers wished to bestow benefit upon him, and purchased a lottery ticket in his name. Once it won, and the prize was several hundred rubles. He wrote in his will: "With regard to my wife Dvora, may she live, I promised her in her marriage contract the sum of 500 silver rubles, aside from all of the jewelry and clothing, if G-d grants me a male child from her. With G-d's help, when Yitzchak Mendel, may he live long and well, was born to me, I wondered from where I would be able to fulfil this promise, from where will it come, since the rabbinate does not provide enough for a livelihood. However, later the mercies of G-d were great for me, and the salvation came from a lottery, for which my friends purchased a ticket in my name, which won several hundred rubles several times. As well, several important people honored me on occasion with a large gift, may they be blessed by G-d. As well, some people of our town gave me gifts of money, may they be blessed by G-d, and I succeeded in collecting more than 400 silver rubles. I put them in a soft wallet that is resting in a box covered with iron. The box and what is in it should be for my wife on account of the money of the marriage contract, aside from all the jewelry and the clothing.

The bed, bedding, and all household utensils should also all be hers, without taking into account the marriage contract. In the hard wallet there is a promissory note worth 1,000 gold coins. This should be for my son Yitzchak Mendel may he live. The wallet also has more silver coins from the money that I received from the redemption of firstborns, may they live [14]. This should go to pay for the teacher who will learn with them. I am warning that nobody should dispute all of the above, and that matters should stand as stated in the will. Aside from this, there is another wallet in the box containing the sum of 1,000 gold coins. This should belong to my son Shlomo Leib, may his light shine. I sign this on the Sunday of the week of the Torah portion of Reeh [15] 5634 (1874) in the holy city of Zgierz. Shalom Tzvi HaKohen, the head of the rabbinical court of Zgierz.

When Reb Shalom Tzvi returned his soul to the Above on the 6th of Tevet 5637 (1877), masses of Jews came from all of the surrounding cities and towns to participate in the funeral. The rabbi of Ozorkow eulogized him as follows: "And the entire nation raised their voices in weeping, and rivers of tears, for a cedar from the cedars of Lebanon, the mighty ones of Torah, has fallen…" (From the eulogy that was written about him in "Hamagid" by the Maskil Avraham Yaakov Weisenfeld)- (Hamagid, 5637 - 1877).

The members of his community erected a canopy over his grave. People turned there at all times of tribulation to beseech him to pray on their behalf.

Reb Shalom Tzvi did not leave any books behind. During his youth, he authored a book "Chanoch Lanaar" ("Educate the Lad") regarding matters of education, and used this book for the education of his two sons. However this book and other of novel ideas of Torah of his that were written were lost with the passage of time.

In the eulogy of Mr. Weisenfeld in "Hamagid" under the title "The Tzadik is Lost" said among other things: "The Gaon and Hassid who was a Cohen was coronated with three crowns, the crown of the priesthood, the crown of Torah, and the crown of a good name. The crown of Torah, because he spread Torah publicly during the 54 years that he served in the rabbinate in our community. Fine young men streamed to him from all corners of the country, to study in his large Yeshiva. The crown of priesthood, because he was a priest (Cohen) of the supreme G-d, of the students of Aaron, who love peace, pursued peace, loved his fellowmen and

294

brought them near to Torah [16]. With the spirit of G-d that dwelled within him and with the spirit of grace that came from his lips, he drew near those who were far and returned their hearts to their father in heaven. However, the highest of them all was the crown of a good name, his great modesty, the holy Torah with which he occupied himself for its own sake, which is what merited him to be coronated with this crown, covered with graceful precious gems. He never exerted his leadership with a high hand, and he never told people to accept his will. He fled from honor. Despite the fact that honor was his lot in life, and the greatest of rabbis gave honor to his name, the honor did not affect his pure heart at all. With his great patience, his door was always open day and night to anyone who was in need, from the wealthy people to the cutters of trees and the drawers of water. The dew of his statements always was dispensed with calm, to penetrate the heart of his listeners..."

Reb Shalom Tzvi left behind two young sons who were born to him in his old age by his second wife - the Admor Reb Yitzchak Mendel and Rabbi Shlomo Yehuda Leib. From his first wife he had only daughters: Chaya and Breina.

The Second Rabbi of Zgierz, Reb Tzvi HaKohen of holy blessed memory 5638 - 5678 (1878-1898)

After the death of Reb Shalom Tzvi in the year 5637 (1877), the community of Zgierz was left without a rabbi, until finally they found a fitting rabbi to take the place of Reb Shalom Tzvi, who was beloved and accepted by all segments of the community of Zgierz. They chose the rabbi and Gaon Reb Tzvi Hirsch HaKohen, who was the son of the famous rabbi and Gaon Reb Elazar of Pultusk, one of the important Hassidim of Kock, and the grandson of the light of the exile, Reb Yaakov of Lissa, the author of "Chavat Daat" and "Netivot Hamishpat".

Reb Tzvi HaKohen was born and educated in the home of his father, the Gaon and Hassid Reb Elazar of Pultusk. When he attained the age of majority, he married the daughter of the Hassid Reb Leib Kahana of Cekeanow. He was supported at the table of his father-in-law for many years, and he occupied himself with Torah and Hassidism. Reb Tzvi was the right hand man of his father, the Gaon Reb Elazar, and he often accompanied his father on his journeys. In the year 5616 (1856) his father Reb Elazar was offered the rabbinate of Plock. Reb Elazar traveled to Plock, accompanied by his son, to accept the rabbinate there. Reb Elazar lived in Plock for several years, and then moved to Pultusk.

In the year 5630 (1870), when his father Reb Elazar left the rabbinate in Pultusk and move to Sochaczew, the people of Pultusk accepted Reb Tzvi as their rabbi. There, he became known as a Gaon and a Tzadik, with a very dedicated personality. He had a great influence on the members of his community.

Reb Tzvi occupied the rabbinical seat in Pultusk for approximately eight years (5630-5638 / 1870-1878). In the year 5638, about one year after the death of Reb Shalom Hirsch the head of the rabbinical court of Zgierz, Reb Tzvi HaKohen was coronated in his stead as the rabbi of Zgierz. There are those who did not easily agree to his being chosen as the rabbi of Zgierz. They still remembered their first rabbi, Reb Shalom Tzvi, and were not able to get used to Reb Tzvi. However, he influenced them, saying: "You still want your first rabbi, Reb Shalom Tzvi. I, my name is Tzvi, and if you make 'peace' ('shalom') with me, they I will be to you 'Shalom Tzvi'…" . And thus it was.

As he had done in Pultusk, he endeared himself to the members of the community. There was an incident of one of the members of the community in Zgierz who built his house on Chol Hamoed [17]. Reb Tzvi asked them to desist from their work on Chol Hamoed due to the holiness of the festival. The householder said to him: "How can I desist from my work, given that I have already paid the workers for their work on Chol Hamoed?" Reb Tzvi did not think a great deal, he removed the sum of money from his pocket and gave it to him so that he would desist from the work.

Reb Tzvi was known as a great diligent learner, and he was always sitting with a Gemara in front of him, occupying himself with Torah. However, he did not ignore the issues of the world, and he had a sense of humor. It is told that once a tailor sewed a new garment for him. When the tailor brought him the garment, Reb Tzvi noticed that the garment was too short for his height. He turned to the tailor with the melody of the Gemara [18] and said: "Tailor, tailor, why did you sew the garment only with threads, why did you not sew the garment also with wisdom?"

For his daughter Tzipora, he took as a groom the young genius Reb Shlomo Yehuda Leib HaKohen, the son of the first rabbi of Zgierz Reb Shalom Tzvi. Reb Shlomo Yehuda Leib was supported at the table of his father-in-law the rabbi Reb Tzvi for ten years.

Reb Tzvi served in the rabbinate of Zgierz for twenty years, and as his son-in-law testified about him, he was a righteous and modest man.

Reb Tzvi continued in the traditions of his holy fathers. In particular, he inherited the character and traits of his illustrious grandfather the "Chavat Daat" of Lissa. He wrote many responsa in Halacha to his father the Gaon Reb Elazar, an also to his brother-in-law the Gaon Reb David Dov of Lask, the author of the Responsa of R"DD.

Reb Tzvi Hirsch died in the year 5658 (1898), and his place was inherited by his son-in-law Reb Shlomo Yehuda Leib HaKohen, the son of the old age of the first rabbi of Zgierz, Reb Shalom Tzvi of holy blessed memory.

We found the following article I "Hatzefira" number 249, from the year 1897 (5658) regarding the death of Rabbi Tzvi the son of Rabbi Elazar HaKohen of holy blessed memory, and the coronation of Rabbi Shlomo Leib HaKohen as the rabbi of the city. We cite this article below:

Zgierz (Piotrkow region) - On this past eve of Sukkot, there was weeping and mourning for the people of our city, for the rabbi and head of the rabbinical court, the modest and discreet Gaon Rabbi Tzvi HaKohen of holy blessed memory was suddenly taken from atop our heads. He was the son of the Tzadik and Gaon Rabbi Elazar of holy blessed memory, the head of the rabbinical court of Pultusk. The rabbi was approximately seventy years old when he died. During the final years of his life, he knew terrible sickness, and was oppressed with suffering. However, his suffering was the suffering of love, for there was no abandonment of Torah. His mouth did not desist from learning until his final moment. I described him as modest and discreet, for indeed he excelled greatly in those two good traits, and he was an example in them for those near and far. We can see his great efforts for Torah from the multitude of Torah writings that he left behind as a blessing, bundles of novellae in Halacha and agada (lore), written down, arranged and prepared for publication.

His sudden death frightened all of the cities around our city. Many rabbis, headed by the rabbi and Gaon of Lodz, hastened to come to eulogize and weep for him. Our townsfolk were able to see that they excelled over all of the neighboring cities in peace and truth, for they all put their eyes towards the son-in-law of the rabbi, the Rabbi and Gaon Shlomo Yehuda Leib HaKohen to fill the place of his father-in-law. The leaders of our city immediately asked the rabbi and Gaon of Lodz to give the rabbinic writ to him, and express congratulations to him on behalf of the entire community.

The young man Rabbi Shlomo Yehuda Leib HaKohen, aside from being the son of the rabbi and Gaon Shalom Tzvi HaKohen who sat on the rabbinical seat here and spread Torah for about fifty years, and established many students who sit on the seat of judgements in the cities of Poland, is worthy in his own merit in a sublime fashion to that title. He is great in Torah, and was ordained by the Gaonim of the land. He is wise, knowledgeable in the vernacular, and in all the wisdom that is required of a rabbi of Israel. It has been three years since he passed the test in front of the gathering of examiners, and obtained his certificate of excellence.

Any person, who knows the controversies and disputes that accompany every rabbi at his time of being chosen in a city with Jewish inhabitants, should rejoice at this heartwarming site, for all of the factions were united, and nobody opened his mouth in dispute.

The aforementioned conducted his rabbinate with a high hand. On the Sabbath of the Torah portion of Bereshit [19] he delivered a large sermon before a large crowd, spiced with words of moral instruction, pleasant to the ear who hears words that are acceptable to the heart. On birthday holidays [20] he preached about matters of the day in an appropriate fashion in the

Russian language, and all of the members of the community were glad that their head was such an enlightened rabbi, who was able to serve the dual function of a rabbi of the community and as a representative of the community to the government and his majesty. Our joy was doubled when we saw that he did not rest and was not silent from the time that he ascended the rabbinical seat. From time to time, the heads of the community would call to him to repair breaches and fill gaps regarding communal needs.

Hope delighted him, for many of the people of our town stood at his right to help him whenever possible in accomplishing his desired. And now, honorable rabbi, G-d is with you, go forward with your strength, only be strong and vigorous!

Rabbi Shlomo Yehuda Leib HaKohen of holy blessed memory
May G-d avenge his soul (The final rabbi of Zgierz)
By Rabbi A.Y. Brumberg

Rabbi Shlomo Yehuda Leib was born to his father Rabbi Shalom Tzvi HaKohen in the year 5627 (1867). He was ten years old when his father died, and he was educated, along with his elder brother Reb Yitzchak Menachem, by Rabbi Tzvi Hirsch, the second rabbi of Zgierz.

From his youth he excelled as a genius. He studied with the rabbi of Kutno, the Gaon Rabbi Yisrael Yehoshua Trunk. When he reached majority, Rabbi Tzvi Hirsch took him as a son-in-law, marrying him to his daughter Tzipora. He was supported at his father-in-law's table for about ten years. His father-in-law was like a father and teacher to him, and instructed him in Torah and the fear of heaven.

Following the death of his father-in-law in the year 5658 (1897), the members of the community coronated Reb Shlomo Yehuda Leib as the rabbi to take the place of his holy fathers. Like his father and father-in-law, he endeared himself to the members of his community. He was a wonderful preacher, and his mouth was full of gems. He was an astute and energetic activist in communal matters. He had an honorable place among the Hassidim of Gur, but his set place was in the synagogue of the city.

Rabbi Shlomo Yehuda Leib HaKohen of holy blessed memory

Aside from his vast knowledge in the Babylonian and Jerusalem Talmud, in the early and late responsa, and in the wisdom of Israel, he was also fluent in other books of wisdom, such as the "Guide of the Perplexed" [21], the Abarbanel, the Akeda, the Maharal of Prague [22], and others. He was also an expert in general philosophy, and knew how to debate and answer researchers in matters of thought and deep study.

Regarding the statement of Professor Yechezkel Kaufman about the book of Oswald Spengler "the Destruction of the Land of the West" (published in the "Rimon" anthology of literature, 5682 / 1922 in Berlin), Rabbi Shlomo Leib writes his comment about it, that with regard to relations with Spinoza, Leibnitz and Kant, these matters never enter the mind at all. He places the entire broad and deep philosophy of Kant into a very narrow realm, and restricts them with split words and empty content. He also restricts the concept of "time" into his fundamental bounds, by negating reliance on the researchers who put nails in happenings and events of the eras. When the book of Professor Albert Einstein "The Theory of Relativity" was published in the 1920s, the rabbi expressed his admiration of this philosophy, and also hastened to explain its principals to intelligent people.

With all this, he found time to spread Torah to the masses - especially to young men and youths who attended a regular class in Gemara and Jewish legal decisions with him. Even though he occupied himself with Torah and wisdom day and night, he was also a man of action, involved in all aspects of communal activity. He not only concerned with spiritual matters, but also with day to day physical activities. Therefore, he endeared himself to the masses of people in the city, who saw him as a defender who fought their battles and protected their status and rights.

The Yiddish writer A. Litwin, who visited Zgierz in the year 5672 (1912) wrote an article on Rabbi Shlomo Yehuda Leib entitled: "Jeremiah the Prophet from Zgierz". He called him by this nickname since he witnessed him weeping and lamenting about the national and economic destruction of the Jewish people of that generation. This was not about the ideas and research that were culled from his writings, but rather that which his eyes saw and what took place with him over the previous five or six years. He wrote with the anger of the prophet, and with the blood of his heart: "I am the man who witnessed oppression..." [23]. He wrote page after page with the moan of pain and agony, and came to the terrifying conclusion: "The Jewish people is quickly approaching the time of national and economic destruction". One by one, Rabbi Shlomo Yehuda Leib outlines the tribulations and persecutions that come upon the Jewish people like a thief. Behold electricity, which so to speak came to bring progress and benefit, robbed the livelihood of one hundred Jewish wagon drivers. Zgierz is a city of industry and manufacturing, but almost all of the factory workers were non Jews, rather they were Poles and Germans. Despite this, hundreds of Jewish families earn their livelihood from these workers through their small business and handicrafts. However now came a revolution, and overturned the plate. The workers organized themselves into cooperatives to obtain and market their needs, and they no longer required the services and stores of the Jews. Therefore, all of the Jewish storekeepers and artisans in Zgierz became impoverished, and many of them were forced to take up the wandering staff, to wander afar to find livelihood and sustenance. Only a few storekeepers and peddlers remained, who maintained a hold on their livelihoods with their fingernails. However, even these diminished in number with the passage of time. There was one area which was not oppressed, neither on account of the electricity nor on account of the cooperatives, for they were not able to take away the rights: this is the weavers. However even these people were pushed

301

by their Jewish brethren, the large scale manufacturers, who opened textile factories in Zgierz that pushed aside the small scale weavers.

More from the article of the aforementioned writer: Through the years, there was an organization called "Machzikei Hadat" [24], which was set up by the Orthodox manufacturers. They founded a Yeshiva and supported several dozen youths. The rabbi was invited to the opening celebrations to deliver a lecture to the guests. In his lecture, the rabbi deliberated over the painful question that left him with no rest: the destruction of economic life in the city. He severely blamed the large scale Jewish manufacturers who refused to accept Jewish workers. These words kindled their wrath. They complained to him: "Why does the rabbi become involved in matters that are of no concern to him? He should speak of matters regarding strengthening of faith, and not in matters that are not in his realm". These words hurt him deeply, and he stopped his sermon in the middle.

He would participate in meetings of the communal council on a regular basis, and he would give his opinion on all matters that were open for deliberation. He also appeared at every public event, festive gathering, or protest rally. His words were always presented in a high and fiery fashion.

His regular sermons in the synagogue gave forth an echo within the community. As was the custom, the time of the beginning of the sermon was previously announced in all synagogues. Many people could be seen streaming in to hear the words of the rabbi. Among these, most prominent were the Yeshiva students, Torah scholars, Hassidim, and those scholars with sharp minds, who left the shtibels wearing their silk cloaks and shtreimels on their heads, so that they could also greet the rabbi, and stand within his realm during the time of the sermon. These people came for the most part to hear words of Torah, ideas and words of wisdom regarding sublime matters of Torah and Judaism, and particularly about man - which was a central theme in all of his sermons: man in his battle with his impulses, man with his Divine spark and his desire for completeness, man as the crown of creation, the ways of man in self dedication and sublime traits, etc. He dealt with these topics generally in the latter half of the sermon, and they found favor with those who understood Kabbalah.

Rabbi Shlomo Yehuda Leib did not belong to any faction. He stood above all of the factions on the Jewish street, and therefore was able to reprove them whenever he saw them straying from the straight path and moving towards improper behavior.

In the year 5691 (1931), he succeeded, after great effort, to see his novellae, deliberations and ideas published in the book "Neve Shalom" in Piotrkow. He writes the following in the introduction, among other things:
{Photocopy page 361: The title page of the book "Neve Shalom" ("Dwelling Place of Peace") which was written by Rabbi Shlomo Yehuda Leib Hakohen, the head of the rabbinical court of Zgierz. {*Translator's note: The title indicates that this book includes sermons and explanations by Rabbi Yehuda Leib Hakohen the son of the Tzadik and Gaon Rabbi Shalom Tzvi HaKohen of holy blessed memory, and the son-in-law of Rabbi Tzvi Hakohen, the head of the rabbinical court of Zgierz. It is published in Piotrkow by Chanoch Henech the son of Yeshaya Zeev Falman in 5681 (1921).*}}

"In my work, I include a few of my novel ideas on halacha, points and deliberations to decorate the first fruits [25]. If one can find in them some god thing, it would make the entire book worthwhile. May G-d grant me the merit to publish my novel ideas on Halacha that are with me, to learn and to teach. I called my composition "Neve Shalom" ("Dwelling Place of Peace") dedicated to my father the Gaon, the sign of his generation, the true Tzadik, the Hassid of the Priesthood, the head of the Yeshiva, our honored master and teacher Shalom Tzvi HaKohen of holy blessed memory, who served in the rabbinate here in Zgierz for 54 years. From his Yeshiva went forth hundreds of expert students, and approximately 50 rabbis, including some greats of the Jewish people. I was born to my father of holy blessed memory in his old age. My righteous mother Dvora was the daughter of the Hassid Reuven Yitzchak of blessed memory, who was the son of the holy rabbi Shalom of blessed memory, the head of the rabbinic court of Piatek, who was the son in law of the Gaon Natan of blessed memory, the head of the rabbinical court of Staszow.

I also hereby mention positively my brother the rabbi and sharp Gaon Reb Yitzchak Menachem may he live long, my righteous sister Chaya may she live, and my sister Breina may she live.

Similarly, I mention the kindness of my father-in-law the Rabbi and Gaon Tzvi HaKohen of holy blessed memory, the head of the rabbinical court of Zgierz, who was like a father to me. I was supported at his table for approximately ten years. He was to me a rabbi and teacher. I studied from him all the days of his life. I recognized his righteousness and modesty when I was still living with him. A midnight never came with him asleep. He barely knew the form of a coin, for money was not valuable in his eyes. He distributed his income to charity secretly. He was humble, but nevertheless, he was not embarrassed in front of mockers. Whenever he saw a breech of any form regarding religion, he became like a roaring lion. He did not like fame. He was a holy man, the son of the holy Gaon Reb Avraham of holy blessed memory the head of the rabbinical court of Sochaczew, and the son-in-law of the light of the exile Rabbi Yaakov of Lissa of holy blessed memory, the author of "Chavat Daat". My righteous mother-in-law Sara Blima of blessed memory - was of good heart. The breadth of her wisdom cannot be described. I was peaceful and content in their home. My righteous wife Tzipora may she live, inherited the spiritual riches of her parents of blessed memory.

After the death of my father-in-law of blessed memory, the people of my city of Zgierz, may G-d protect them, chose me to fill the place of my fathers. I have dwelt with them for these 33 years in quiet and contentment. They generously provide all of my needs, and they still recall their love of my parents of blessed memory. There is peace and contentment in my city with the transmission of the traditions of fathers to sons. I thank them and all of the communal administrators, particularly my friend, the well to do man, the head of the community Eliezer Sirkes may G-d bless him, who helped me with his money and the communal coffers to publish my work. May G-d reward them for their generous deeds with bountiful livelihood, life and health, from their young ones to their old ones.

My G-d recall for good my dear and accomplished son, Rabbi Shalom HaKohen, may he live long, and his wife Rivka the daughter of the Torah oriented man Reb Yeshaya, and my baby grandson Tzvi may he live.

As well as my dear daughter Dina may she live, and her husband, my dear and accomplished son-in-law Rabbi David may he live, the son of Rabbi Yosef Pacanowski, the author of the book Pardes Yosef may he live, and my eldest grandson, the baby Shalom Tzvi may he live.

I will also mention my sickly daughter Breina may she live. May G-d send her a complete recovery in the midst of all the sick of Israel. And may I merit to see contentment from her daughter Sara may she live.

Zgierz, 7 Adar 5691 / 1931.

The author- Shlomo Yehuda Leib HaKohen, the head of the rabbinical court of the community of Zgierz."

Reb Shlomo Yehuda Leib did not merit publishing his Torah novellae and novellae of Jewish law. Their lot was the same as the lot of the rich, ancient, and broad rabbinical library of the rabbi - there was one lot for them and for all the cultural and spiritual property of Polish Jewry under the government of the cruel Nazi vandals.

Indeed, just as Jeremiah the prophet prophesied in his time, he also bore the news about what the enemies were doing to his people and his community, in which he served with the rabbinical crown for 41 consecutive years. He saw with his own eyes the synagogue, from which he had preached for all the years about love of Israel and love of one's fellowman - go up in flames and be destroyed. Woe to the eyes that saw such! He wandered around to find a refuge for himself and his family. Thus did he arrive in Warsaw, the capital of Poland. There, in the Warsaw ghetto, he as well as a significant portion of Zgierz Jewry found temporary refuge after the expulsion. Among them, there were some people of means who supported him. The rabbi was taken to Umshlag Platz [26] during the large scale aktions of 5702 (1942). From there he was sent to the Nazi death camps. May G-d avenge his soul. May his soul be bound in the bonds of eternal life.

The First Rabbi of Zgierz (Yiddish)

The organized Jewish community of Zgierz, whose beginning is dated in official documents from the year 1824, already at that time had the need to engage a rabbi.

In a request to the municipal committee that dealt with religious affairs, the dozors (communal leaders) Baruch Sztejnbok and Meir Blumental requested that the Old Believer [27] Rabbi Shalom Hirsch Cohen, for this was the wish of the entire "Parish" [28].

In their request to the authorities, the dozors describe the candidate for rabbi as exemplary in his moral conduct and sincere in his rendering of prayers. Therefore, the communal organizations request that a concession for the office be granted to Rabbi Shalom Hirsch Cohen. His salary would be 60 Polish Zloty.

The confirmation of Rabbi Shalom Hirsch Cohen as rabbi did not come easily. The municipal authorities did not rely on the recommendation of the dozors, but they rather demanded certificates and recommendations regarding his rabbinical capabilities and his person. Manes Kalski and Aba Darenwus gave such recommendations. In their declaration, they asserted that Shalom Hirsch Cohen, the rabbi of the house of prayer and the city of Zgierz, had already in the year 1823 taken the office and performed the function of rabbi in the town of Grabowo (Leczyca region).

Aside from the recommendation, Rabbi Cohen went himself to the office of the mayor of Zgierz and presented his certificate of ordination, which was given to him by the rabbi of Leczyca. The document states as follows:

"I know Shalom Hirsch Cohen, the beloved rabbi of the city of Zgierz, as a fine person, who is intelligent in learning and piety. He conducts himself very well in religious ceremonies. I know that he has a fine manner of speaking, saturated with Talmud, as well as early and latter laws. In debates with him, I find him full of wisdom and piety. All of his deeds are exemplary. In accordance with this, I treat it as an honorable thing to support him with my hand, stating: he should teach and judge, so that mattes should be in accordance with his opinion. To certify this he (Rabbi Shalom Hirsch Cohen) possesses a certificate from the esteemed Strykower Rabbi, Moshe Aharon. Two is indeed better than one (with respects to certificates), and these two testify to the stability of such a virtuous man. These words are stated in honor of his learning and piety.

In Leczyca- on Monday, January 24, 1827.

(Signed) Chaim Ickowicz Auerbach - Leczyca.

In agreement with the original that was presented, I issue my certification - Zgierz, January 27, 1827.

Y. Zymski - judicial translator.

It was issued in the city of Zgierz in February, 1827.

In the office of the mayor of the city of Zgierz, the Old Believer Shalom Hirsch Cohen presented himself, and was qualified as rabbi after giving over the following declaration: "Seeing that he is qualified as a rabbi, as he showed the examination certificate of the rabbi of the community of Leczyca, which is placed before me, he will take on the duties of rabbi in the local (Zgierz) synagogue. As well, the enclosed declaration of the communal leadership demonstrates (that he is fit to take on the office of rabbi), and I issue a concession for that office.

This declaration is signed by Shalom Hirsch Cohen."

At the end it is signed by: Grzegorzewski, mayor of the city of Zgierz.

Reb Shlomo Yehuda Leib HaKohen of holy blessed memory
The last rabbi of Zgierz

Zgierz was known for its great rabbis, which made it famous in the world as a place of Torah and Hassidism.   The first rabbi, Reb Shalom Tzvi HaKohen, known as The Elder Tzadik, was known as a Gaon and genius. Even during his youth he was known as a wonder child.

A considerable number of rabbis who later occupied the rabbinical seats in many places in Poland came from the Yeshiva which he founded in Zgierz. Great rabbis of the world came to him for approbations on their works [29]. He was also the builder of the Great Synagogue of Zgierz. According to the stories told by people, he also worked wonders, such as for example with the case of the grandson of Reb Yitzchak Zylberberg, who was mute.   Reb Shalom Tzvi gave the young boy a pear and told him to recite a blessing. The young boy recited the blessing and began to speak.

The second rabbi after Reb Shalom Tzvi was also called Tzvi. In order to characterize him, it is sufficient to bring down the following fact: when he noticed that one of the residents of Zgierz was building a house on a day of Chol Hamoed, he requested that the man stop building the house and not desecrate Chol Hamoed.   The Jew answered that he already had paid the workers for their work. Then Reb Tzvi invited him home, and took out the sum of money that was required by the workers from a drawer so that the Jew would not suffer any loss.

The final rabbi, Reb Shlomo Yehuda Leib was not only a great scholar, but also a Maskil, who occupied himself with logic and philosophy over and above his Torah learning. Aside from the Jewish philosophical world, and Jewish philosophy from the middle ages and other time, he also thoroughly studied general world philosophy, and was capable of talking about Kant, philosophy. However Reb Shlomo Yehuda Leib was not only involved with Torah. He was also interested in everything that took place in the city. He was concerned about the livelihood of the average Jew of Zgierz, and he fought like a lion against the manufacturers who completely or mostly displaced the Jewish workers from their workshops, due to economic or social reasons. He was a father and provider for everyone. More than once he used his personal situation to interfere with the affairs of the manufacturers - for the benefit of the interests of the workers.

It is interesting to bring down the characterization of the rabbi of Zgierz, according to the description of the Jewish writer A. Litwin, who visited Zgierz in 1912.

"I visited the 'Prophet Jeremiah' of Zgierz who regretted the situation of Jewry in Poland and lamented over their national destruction. The rabbi of Zgierz does not talk in abstract issues. He describes and portrays facts that he had seen. I have seen him sit and write entire scrolls [30], dripping with agony and pain. Here... he blames the construction of the tramway, which came and tore away the livelihood of one hundred Jewish wagon drivers. The factories push away the means of livelihood of the hand workers, almost all of whom are Jews. The gentiles have already become active in business, they set up cooperatives and the Jewish storekeepers must seek their bread in an entirely different manner."

Such was the image of the last rabbi of Zgierz, as he was seen by a foreign tourist.

Alas, Reb Yehuda Leib foresaw, but not in its entirety. He did not imagine that very soon they would not only take the livelihoods away from the Jews, but also their lives. Together with his community - old and young, rich and poor, important Jews and ordinary Jews - all of them were murdered in a cruel fashion. The Christians were left a Judenrein Zgierz. Much, much, more tragic than in the times of Jeremiah the prophet.

May his soul be bound in the bonds of eternal life, and may his name shine among the martyrs of Israel.

The Rabbi and righteous teacher Reb Yechiel Ichel Elberg of holy blessed memory
And his son Reb Avraham Natan by Yehuda Elberg
May G-d avenge his blood
The head of the rabbinical court- Laski and Sanok.

Rabbi Yechiel Ichel Elberg of holy blessed memory

The young Rabbi Ichel was different than other people. The way of people is to breathe into their midst air that bestows upon them the force of life. However for Ichel, the study of Torah was his breath from which he drew his life force. Without it he had no life.

Reb Ichel devoured pages of Gemara at all hours of the day and night. The wick of the lantern was already charred; the light was dwindling, the kerosene running out, and Ichel continued to swallow up the page of Gemara into the breath of his nose. The time passes, but the Torah of G-d exists

309

forever. Every page that he absorbs into his essence is part of the "treasury of life".

The friends of Reb Ichel were already young married men, fathers of children... It was also necessary to enlist in the army. What would become of Torah?

It happened that the rabbi of Zgierz died, and left behind a widow with two orphans. Reb Ichel decided to marry the widowed rebbetzin. The community would certainly concern itself with her livelihood and the livelihood of the children, and he would be able to dedicate himself to the study of Torah; indeed, she was older than he, what does that matter? She would still be able to bear him children and to raise them in Torah and the service of the Creator...

There were some people who demanded that the husband of the rebbetzin fill the place of the deceased rabbi. Yechiel Ichel did not agree. He would agree to issue decisions of Jewish law as they come up, but the rabbinate... is like an "axe" [31]... No, to this he could not agree. Lest you ask, livelihood? Thank G-d, Jews bake bread, bread requires yeast. Give over to the rebbetzin the rights of selling yeast and G-d will help.

Reb Ichel became a "Judge" in Zgierz, and his wife Dvora became known as the "Yeast Rebbetzin" ("Yoven Rebbetzin").

Reb Ichel constructed for himself a lectern from the wood of the boxes of yeast. He hung a kerosene lamp from it, and the members of the household would find him poring over the Gemara, when they were asleep or awake.

The first rabbi of Zgierz was the cousin of the Admor Reb Henech of blessed memory of Aleksandrow. Both of them were relatives of and Hassidim of the Admor of Kock. The Rabbi of Kock requested that the rabbi found a Yeshiva and spread Torah. This Yeshiva was later the "forging vessel" for rabbis and Hassidim who spread out to all of the cities and towns of Poland. The rabbi was great in Torah and sharp. He bestowed these fine traits to his children Yitzchak Mendel and Shlomo Leib, who later basked under the shade of their stepfather Reb Ichel.

The Admor Reb Yechiel of Aleksandrow placed his eye on Yitzhak Mendel, and grabbed him up as a groom for his daughter before he was thirteen years of age. The second son, Shlomo Leib, too the daughter of the new rabbi of Zgierz as a wife, and thus did he later inherit from him the rabbinical seat.

Reb Ichel was greatly pained that his son Natan was small in stature in comparison to his stepbrothers [32]. He felt that the lad suffered from feelings of inferiority. People called him Natale [33], and he, Natale, his head being filled with Talmud and Jewish law, was great in Torah and had his own novel ideas, and his name went forth in the entire country.

When Rabbi Yechezkel Michelzon of Plonsk took Natan as a husband for his daughter, he also concerned himself with coronating him as a rabbi in some community, but Natan refused to accept the rabbinate.

Reb Ichel was surprised and wished to ascertain the reason for this. Even though he himself had refused to accept the yoke of the rabbinate, this was because of his fear of forsaking Torah. However he, Natan, who has time thank G-d also to look into a newspaper, and also... to occupy himself with secular matters... Therefore he wanted to enter him into a position of leadership and to make him fulfil the duty of "honoring one's father". However, the eyes of Natan filled with tears, and his body shriveled even further. The father understood what was in the heart of his son. His small stature was what held him back, and prevented him from succeeding. Reb Ichel made peace with the situation, that he should occupy himself in business. However, even in this area, success was not forthcoming. In the meantime, Reb Natan occupied himself with Torah and Divine service, and he succeeded in enriching the body of rabbinical literature with the books that he authored, such as Bayit Neeman (Faithful House), Beit Avraham, Pinat Habayit, and others, which were received with blessing in religious circles.

` Chavale, Natan's wife, who was used to a life of comfort in the home of her father, did not Heaven forbid complain when things came down to a slice of bread. Reb Ichel saw the situation, and requested a small salary from the community for his wife the rebbetzin who owned the rights. He then transferred the right of the sale of yeast to Natan for his livelihood. Chavale was embarrassed to have Natan occupy himself in this manner, which was beneath his honor, so she herself took on the yoke of the work.

Her father-in-law Reb Ichel saw how she, the small one, dragged the boxes of yeast to the purchasers, and his heart fell within him. This pampered one... and his heard lamented: Chana herself is also small in stature, and these young children, oh, Master of the Universe!... If they would be similar to their father... and he shed tears and supplicated to his Creator, begging that his grandchildren would be people of stature and not be embarrassed like their father to be rabbis of the Jewish people.

His prayers were accepted. The children grew up and became tall. They studied and excelled in Torah. However after the First World War the yeast business declined, and there was great financial pressure in the house. The children began to entertain thoughts of desertion, and began to desist from the study of Torah. Tevil went to work in a weaving factory. Later he began to go around without a beard, and he cut his curly peyos (sidelocks). Eventually he joined the Zionist Chalutzim (pioneers), and prepared to make aliya to the Land of Israel.

Reb Ichel went to supplicate on the graves of his forbears. He wept, supplicated and begged for mercy over the fate of his son Natan and the fate of his grandchildren. In the interim, Reb Natan accepted a rabbinical position in a small town, but Reb Ichel complained that this place was not fit for the honor of such a great scholar as his Natan.

Then the news arrived that Reb Natan was called to an honorable position, to serve in the city of Bielsko. Reb Ichel wept from great joy, and when they brought the rabbi under the canopy to the synagogue [34], Reb Ichel pulled his grandson Yitzchak Yudel to join with his father under the canopy. He was certain that the merit of his late father would stand up for the great-grandchild who bears his name, so that he would dedicate himself to this path, the path of the rabbinate. In the eyes of his spirit, he saw him as a rabbi with a splendid countenance, a full beard, preaching with exactitude in front of the congregation, like his father, grandfather, and the entire dynasty of rabbis of blessed memory. He learned an "a priori" logical deduction from his son. If Natan, who is not of fine stature, merited this greatness, he Yitzchak Yudel would certainly be fitting to stand at the helm of a large congregation, especially if the merit of his father, the Reb Yitzchak Yudel the Tzadik of Kutno, stands up for him.

Yudel wrote his Torah novellae and sent them to his grandfather. The grandfather expressed admiration and emotion, and compared the Torah novellae to raindrops falling onto the sea. The fish that live in the water swallow up with thirst each drop of rain that falls to them from above. Thus are the novellae of Torah to those that study them… Every novel idea is like a raindrop of pleasant rain.

Rabbi Avraham Natan Elberg

One day a Jew of Bielsko came to Zgierz, turned to the Beis Midrash, and related: Yudel left his father's house and went to Lodz.

Reb Ichel was astounded to hear this bad news. He had dedicated his soul on behalf of this grandson, and it was only on his behalf that he made strong efforts so that Natan would accept a rabbinical position, so that he would be in a place of fine greatness, which would be a place for this Yudel to come to his own.

Reb Ichel shed many tears. His stature was bent, and his health weakened. When he tripped on a rock, he took to bed with his leg bound up in a cast, he felt pangs of regret that perhaps he was punished over his lack of faith in G-d. Was it not possible for the son of Natan, who was immersed in Torah, to remain G-d fearing in Lodz?

When he received a letter from Yudel, he hurried to write to him a letter filled with words of Torah. At the beginning he wrote: "In honor of my dear grandson, the rabbi and great in Torah, the sublime lad Reb Yitzchak Yudel may his light shine".

313

His leg healed with difficulty. At the behest of the doctor, they took Reb Ichel to a village in the forest of Dombrowka. The rabbi felt that this fresh air would hasten his recovery. On the Sabbath, people came to him from the city, worshipped with a quorum and read the Torah. During the weekdays, the Jewish people were bound up with the bonds of livelihood. The men returned to the city, and then... five entire days without a quorum, without being able to recite "kedusha", and without answering "amen" [35]....

On one of the days of the week, Reb Ichel woke up his household, and requested that a wagon be summoned to take him back to the city.

The route was long.. he did not have patience, and he did not stop asking "When? When will we reach the city already?"

At home he began to make preparations. He washed up very well, and wrapped himself up with his tallis and tefillin. His prayers were recited silently, without strength, but the silence also reached the ears of his attendant, who realized that Reb Ichel was praying with the tunes of a festival.

After his prayers he made the "shehakol" blessing [36], drank a bit of water, made the "Borei Nefashot" blessing, and continued with his preparations. He once again washed up... and tried to drag himself to his bookcase, but his energy left. He turned to the attendant and said: "There, under the shofar is my kittel, and under the kittel are my shrouds".

Now the attendant became afraid. Reb Ichel ordered him "Be careful! I will be a righteous advocate for..."

Reb Ichel requested that the attendant recite the deathbed confessional with him. After the recital of the final "Al Chet" [37], he hinted to him with his ten fingers that he wished a quorum to be summoned. His lips moved as if he was answering "Amen". His eyes closed, and his breath ceased. With the final "Amen", his soul departed to the other side of the gate of heaven" - said the attendant.

May his merit stand for the entire community of Israel.
(From the works of his grandson, the writer Yehuda Elberg)
Translated into Hebrew by Y. A. Malkieli.

Rabbi Yitzchak Mendel Cohen of holy blessed memory
(Admor and forger of ideas)

One of the prominent and interesting personalities who peered out from the depths of life in Zgierz was without doubt Reb Yitzchak Mendel, the son of the first rabbi of Zgierz Reb Shalom Tzvi, and the brother of the last rabbi, Reb Shlomo Leib.

When the previous rabbi of Zgierz, Reb Shalom Tzvi HaKohen reached his old age, he lost his wife Rachel. Since she left him only daughters and not sons, the matchmakers urged him to marry a wife, and gave him several ideas.

From all of the honorable ones that were presented to him, he chose an eighteen-year-old girl from a fine family. After hesitation, she finally agreed to marry the old, septuagenarian rabbi, after he promised her a male child.

Indeed, she bore two sons to him, who were very similar to each other, Reb Yitzchak Mendel and Reb Shlomo Leib, the final rabbi of Zgierz who perished along with his community during the time of the German occupation.

The eldest son Yitzchak Mendel was created for greatness. He was a genius in his youth, sharp with a brilliant mind. When he reached the age of Bar Mitzvah, the Admor Reb Yechiel of Aleksandrow chose him for his daughter. The wedding was celebrated about two years later with great splendor and glory in nearby Aleksandrow (for the rabbi Rabbi Shalom Tzvi died a short time after the birth of the youngest son). Throngs of Hassidim gathered from near and far. All of the Admorim of the land came together to celebrate in the joyous occasion of the Aleksandrow Rabbi, some for the wedding, and others for the Sheva Brachot [38].

Rabbi Yitzchak Mendel Cohen

315

Yitzchak Mendel spoke for a long time at the sermon at the wedding ceremony. He went from valleys to mountains and from mountain crests to plains. He uprooted mountains and ground them one against the other, until his father-in-law Rabbi Yechiel himself stopped him, and covered the face of the groom with his hands, so that Heaven forbid the evil eye should not take control of him.

After the wedding, he was supported at the table of his father-in-law, who honored him and raised him up. The Hassidim of Aleksandrow saw in him a heir to the dynasty of Aleksandrow after "one hundred and twenty" [39], even though that from among the sons of the Rebbe was Reb Yisrael Yitzchak, the author of "Yismach Yisrael", who would be fitting for that post.

The good and peace of the Rebbe was deprived. For not too long passed, and the anger of the Satan jumped upon him, which danced among the Hassidim and instilled in them the venom of dispute and controversy. Reb Yitzchak Mendel, just like his father the rabbi, was of the faithful of Gur. There was controversy and competition between Gur and Aleksandrow all the days. The dispute continued from the days of Kock and Warka. The war raged throughout all public gathering, and every rabbi, parnas (communal administrator), shochet and any other functionary was involved. In short, it raged in all areas of influence in Jewish communal life.

The Hassidim of Gur suffered greatly and were deeply pained about this great "Gur" soul who defected to the Aleksandrow camp; that walking encyclopedia of Torah and fear of Heaven that disappeared and left their camp. Young Hassidic men, the best friends of Yitzchak Mendel, to whom this matter affected their hearts, decided to take matters into their hands, and to return the "exile" to the camp of Gur. In the darkness of the night, they smuggled him from his room in the fortress of Aleksandrow and brought him with joy and gladness to their Rebbe, the author of the "Sfat Emet". Disappointment and pain prevailed then in the camp of Aleksandrow, but the Hassidim of Gur raised their heads and celebrated their victory with shouting and joy.

The camp of Aleksandrow would perhaps have been prepared to swallow this bitter pill, which touched the innermost parts of their revered Rebbe. However, young Yitzchak Mendel overdid it. He added fuel to the fire when he mocked and disparaged his brothers-in-law, the sons of the Rebbe. When

316

one of them would present a certain novel idea in learning to him, he would turn to him with mocking and denigration: "An ignoramus such as you, for is it not written in such and such a Gemara, on this page… these words are written, so why are you claiming it as a novel idea?"

His brothers-in-law were not able to forgive his behavior, and they did not permit him to sit with them at his father's table. These matters came to arguments and strife, and he finally divorced his wife and returned to Zgierz.

After this deed, he repented and recognized his error. However, as a Cohen, he was not able to fix the matter and remarry his divorced wife [40]. His eyes were opened up now to see that his friends who incited him to this misled him. He decided to distance himself from them.

He stopped worshipping in the shtibel, and distanced himself also from Gur. He went to the Beis Midrash to worship with the "masses", who were far from the tumult and gaiety of the Hassidim.

He married a second time, but again got divorced. Then he remained without a wife.

However, he did not abandon his studies. He read a great deal, and began to take interest in world literature, especially German, and in books of philosophy. He recited poems, songs, and segments of operas that he knew by heart. He philosophized with anyone who was willing to discuss with him these matters that he was attracted to. He would wander around the Beis Midrash for hours and hours, thinking and pondering, with his head in the highest heavens. His discussions were spiced with adages from the Talmud, Kabbalah, and Rambam, and he would transfer over to Aristotle, Schopenhauer, Pascal, and Spencer. He would bring a proof to his words from here, a contradiction to his interlocutor from there, he would build towers and destroy them with his impressive and unique knowledge and sharpness.

Sometimes he would approach his brother the rabbi with a joyous face: he found the correct answer to a question in the Tosafot [41] of a certain Gemara. The rabbi attempted to debate with him and to adjudicate the essence of the discussion, until finally he would agree with him, for there was no other way. After he finished with his brother, he would find someone else, start up with a Hassidic topic, move over to Kabbalah and philosophy, jump to Plato, turn back to Zohar [42], and then return to Hassidic stories, like a spring that is overflowing its banks.

317

In his old age, Reb Yitzchak Mendel merited to find some peace and calm for his stormy soul. The rabbi of Zyrardow, who lived in our city, died without leaving a successor. His orphaned Hassidim decided to coronate Reb Yitzchak Mendel as their Rebbe in his place. The also bought him a "spodek" and silk cloak. Rabbi Yitzchak Mendel led his flock faithfully, and sustained them with a great deal of Torah and knowledge, until the world war broke out and the Jewish world in Poland was turned inside out. Destruction came upon everything. May his memory be a blessing.

The Courts of Admorim

Our city of Zgierz did not merit having its name known in the name of one of the Tzadikim who lived in it, as did nearby Aleksandrow and Strykow - nevertheless it found favor in the eyes of several Admorim who desired it as their place of residence

Indeed, two Admorim lived in the city. One was the Rebbe of Brzeziny who died in the first years of the 20th century. The Hassidim built a canopy for him in the cemetery. The second was the Rebbe of Zyrardow, who was buried under the canopy of the aforementioned after his death. To our sorrow, we were not able to find any other personal details regarding them.

The House of the Admor Reb Shmuel Bornsztejn of holy blessed memory of Sochaczew

He was born in the year 5617 (1857) in Kock to his father the first Admor of the Sochaczew dynasty, the Gaon Reb Avraham Bornsztejn of holy blessed memory, the author of the "Avnei Nezer" and "Eglei Tal", and to his mother the rebbetzin Sara Tzina of blessed memory, the daughter of the Admor of Kock, Rebbe Menachem Mendel Morgensztern of holy blessed memory.

He spent the years of his youth in Parczew and Kroszniewice, where his father the Gaon served as a rabbi. He was an only son to his father, and his father instilled his entire essence into him.

In the year 5629 (1869), his father took him to his own Rebbe the Admor Reb Chanoch Henech HaKohen of Aleksandrow. On their way, they passed through Zgierz and stayed over at the home of the elder rabbi, Reb Shalom

318

Tzvi HaKohen of holy blessed memory, who was an enthusiastic Kocker Hassid. There, he met the two sons of the rabbi: Reb Yitzchak Mendel and the final rabbi of Zgierz, Reb Shlomo Leib, may G-d avenge their blood.

After he married his wife (in the year 5634 - 1874), the daughter of one of the finest of the Kocker Hassidim, Reb Eliezer Lipman, the son-in-law of the Admor of Radomsko, the author of the "Tiferet Shlomo" -he was not supported for long at the table of his father-in-law. Rather, he returned to the place of his father, who in the meantime had become the rabbi of Nasielsk. When the author of the "Avnei Nezer" moved from there to Sochaczew, his final stop in the rabbinate, his son Reb Shmuel followed after him. He lived in a large home in the center of the city, and earned his livelihood from the wine business. However his heart did not go after business, and he spent most of his time with his father, and his hand did not depart from him.

Reb Shmuel of holy blessed memory was also active in communal life. He took a stand regarding the entire problem that came up during that time, even regarding the Zionist movement that was then beginning to develop. All of his days, he wished to make Aliya to the Land of Israel. He visited the Land in the year 5651 (1891) - with the encouragement of his father the Gaon - with the aim of purchasing land there and establishing a Hassidic settlement. The ban that existed at that time from the Turkish authorities regarding the sale of land to the Jews of Russia prevented him from going through with the purchase. At the time of the Balfour declaration, he took a positive stand regarding Orthodox settlement in the land of Israel.

After his wife died in her prime, he married a second wife (in the year 5663 - 1903), Mirel the daughter of the Gaon Reb Moshe Natan Szapira, the head of the rabbinical court of Kozienice and the author of the book "Shemen Lamaor".

(The Rebbetzin of Sochaczew was a known and recognized personality in Zgierz. She continued to live in the Rebbe's "court" even after the death of her husband the Admor, with her sons who were orphaned at a young age, until the Holocaust. She moved to Lodz during the first years of the war, and from there to the Warsaw Ghetto, from where she set out on her final journey with her family to Treblinka, may G-d avenge their blood.)

After the death of his father (in the year 5670 - 1910), Rebbe Shmuel was coronated as the second Admor of the Sochaczew dynasty, and he moved to live in his father's house. At the time of the outbreak of the First World War (5674 - 1914) he was in Germany, and he remained there for convalescence at the medicinal springs. After much effort, he succeeded - along with several other Admorim, to return to Poland. However, he did not return to Sochaczew out of fear of the Russian authorities, and he moved with his family to Lodz.

He continued to lead his flock in Lodz, instilling in them faith and strength to keep and guard all of the principles of Hassidism even during the difficult years of occupation. In the year 5678 (1918) he decided to distance himself from the tumult of the large manufacturing city, and he moved to nearby, quiet Zgierz. However, even there he did not find rest at first. Horodlicka, a great hater of Jews, persecuted him and wished to expel him from his residence. Only in the year 5682 (1929), did he manage to find rest and respite, when he set up his own Beis Midrash and Yeshiva. He placed Reb Mendel Wechsler may G-d avenge his blood, who was an old student of the Gaon Reb Avraham of Sochaczew, and a resident of Zgierz as the head of the Yeshiva. On Sabbaths and festivals, Hassidim came from all corners of Poland, Hassidic students and those who did not know all that much but were nevertheless honorable. They came to listen attentively to the Torah that was spoken by their Rebbe by the table. They turned Zgierz into a city of Hassidim.

Reb Shmuel did not last long in our city. He took ill in 5686 (1926) and was taken to Otwock, where he died on the 24th of Tevet 5686 and was brought to burial, accompanied by a great crowd, in the canopy of his father the author of the Avnei Nezer, of holy blessed memory, in the cemetery of Sochaczew.

After his death, his book "Shem MiShmuel" was published in eight volumes. It included words of Torah and Hassidism ordered by the weekly Torah portions and the festivals, which he was wont to say each Sabbath and festival between the years of 5670 - 5675. The book, which took its place among the classic books of Hassidism, was written in a rich and clear language. Aside from his own ideas and novel thoughts, he brought down many words from his father the author of the "Avnei Nezer", and from his grandfather the Rebbe of Kock of holy blessed memory.

His son, the third Admor of Sochaczew, Rabbi David Bornsztejn of holy blessed memory, who was known as the Rebbe of Wyszogrod, was also a Gaon and giant of Torah. He served as rabbi in Tomaszow and Pabianice. He led his flock for about seventeen years, and died in the Warsaw Ghetto on the 8th of Kislev 5703 (1943). His entire family likewise perished, except for one son, Avraham, who lives in Israel.

The second son of Rebbe Shmuel of holy blessed memory, Reb Henech Bornsztejn of blessed memory, was later coronated as the fourth Rebbe of Sochaczew. He made aliya to Israel in the year 5685 (1915) and lived in Jerusalem. He died there on the 26th of Elul 5725 (1965).

The fifth Admor (the son of Reb Henech) was Rabbi Shlomo Bornsztejn of blessed memory, the rabbi of Yad Eliahu of Tel Aviv. He was killed in an automobile accident (20 Av 5730 1970), in his prime.

One of the sons of the Admor Rebbe Shmuel was the well known Yiddish writer Moshe Bornsztejn of blessed memory (his pen name was M. B. Stein), the author of the play "Heaven and Earth" (Himel un Erd), and many other books. He died in Jerusalem (12 Shvat 5621 - 1961).

One of the sons-in-law of Reb Shmuel was Rabbi Yitzchak Yehuda Trunk, the rabbi of Kutno, one of the founders of Mizrachi in Poland. He was a scholar and warrior.

The children of the Admor Reb Shmuel of holy blessed memory who live today in Israel are:

1. Reb Aharon Yisrael Bornsztejn (the son-in-law of the Admor Reb Yitzchak Zelig Morgensztern of holy blessed memory of Kock, the head of the rabbinical court of Sokolow), who lives with his family in Tel Aviv. His eldest son Shmuel Avraham, who was born in Zgierz, fell in the War of Independence on Lag Baomer, the 18th of Iyar, 5708 (1948) in Tel Adashim. He was 20 years old when he died, may G-d avenge his blood.

2. His daughter Sara (the wife of Shaul) Rapaport and her family, who live in Bayit Vagan in Jerusalem.

(From an article by Chetzroni in "The Book of Sochaczew", and other sources.)

The House of the Admor Reb Menachem Mendel Landau of holy blessed memory of Strykow

The Tzadik Reb Avraham Landau of Czekanow, the founder of the dynasty of Admorim of Strykow, was from among the students of Reb Fishele of Strykow (the student of the Magid of Mezerich and Reb Elimelech [43]). He was born in the small town of Parzenczow near Leczyca to his father Reb Rafael Dobrzinska and his mother Roda, in the year 5549 (1789). (As is known, Reb Avraham adopted his family name Landau as a token of recognition of his father-in-law Reb Dan Landau from the city of Plock). In the year 5579 (1819), he was coronated as the rabbi. Also he was the head of the rabbinical court in the community of Czekanow. He died in the year 5635 (1875) at the age of 86.

The history of the Admor Reb Avraham Landau of holy blessed memory is related in the book of Reb Pinchas Zelig Glicksman, (his father Reb Avraham Hirsch Glicksman was one of the prominent people and activists of the city of Zgierz), which was printed in Lodz in the year 5694 (1934) in the name "Rabbi Zeev Lipshitz" - the City of Ozorkow and its rabbis. There he brings some sections from the letter of the Admor Rabbi Menachem Mendel Chaim Landau of holy blessed memory to P. Z. Glicksman about the history of his grandfather Rabbi Avrahamele of Czekanow.

"… His father Reb Rafael was one of the hidden Tzadikim. He lived in a village near Parzenczow, where he had a liquor store that was leased to him by the head of the village. He dressed as did the farmers. I heard wondrous legends about him that testify to his greatness and holiness.

The mother of my grandfather of holy blessed memory was named Roda. She was a scholarly woman of valor. Her father Reb Moshe of blessed memory died during her childhood, and she was educated on the lap of her maternal grandfather the famous Rabbi and Gaon Reb Zeev Wolf Auerbach of holy blessed memory, the head of the rabbinical court of Leczyca.

Reb Rafael of blessed memory had three sons and two daughters. The first son was my holy grandfather Reb Avraham of holy blessed memory. The second was Rabbi Yitzchak from the city of Bierzwienna, who died during his young adulthood during the times of tribulation. The thirst was the Rabbi, Gaon and Hassid Yisrael of blessed memory, the head of the rabbinical court of Lutomiersk. The daughter Sara Rivka was the wife of the Rabbi, Gaon and Hassid Reb Menachem Zeev HaKohen Jerozalimski of holy blessed memory, who was the head of the rabbinical court of Lodz. Later he was accepted in the city of Janowa, and he was appointed as a rabbi in Kock by order of the holy Reb Menachem Mendel of holy blessed memory, the Kocker Rebbe. There he reposes in honor.

The daughter Rachel Lea was the wife of the Rabbi, Tzadik, Hassid and ascetic Yitzchak Izak of holy blessed memory of Zgierz.

The aforementioned Rebbetzin Sara Rivka of blessed memory was famous for her righteousness, and studied as a man. Torah and wisdom were united in her. She reposes in honor in the city of Zgierz, next to the grave of her pious mother Roda of blessed memory and her pious sister Rachel Lea of blessed memory. After the death of her husband in Kock, she moved her dwelling from Kock to Zgierz, where she earned her livelihood from a spice store. She was known to be always occupied with commandments and good deeds."

It is further related that after the death of Reb Rafael the father of the Admor of Czekanow, his wife Roda moved to Zgierz. They set up for her a liquor store, as she had previously in Parzenczow. Her son the Admor of Czekanow used to visit her annually in Zgierz and spend several days with her, in order to fulfill the commandment of honoring one's mother. She had great joy and contentment to see how the Hassidim streamed to him.

Roda Dobrzinska, as we read, struggled greatly for the rights to live in her house on Sieradzka Street, which was outside of the area of Jewish residency. After a lengthy battle that was conducted with strength and diligence, she received the right to settle there, only until the year 1832, with restrictive conditions. Only Mrs. Dobrzinska and her unmarried children were permitted to live there. No other Jew could live in the house, and it was permitted to rent out to a Christian. A heavy monetary fine would be imposed if the conditions were transgressed.

Her daughter Sara Rivka of blessed memory, who was knows as "The Janower Rebbetzin" died on the day after the holiday of Sukkot in the year 5643 (1884). Her sister Rachel Lea (died on the 5th of Kislev 5637 - 1877) was a widow for many years after the death of her husband, the scholar and Hassid Reb Yitzchak Izak of Rakowice, who reposes in honor in the old cemetery of Lodz. She earned her livelihood from the liquor store that she inherited from her mother Roda of blessed memory. Her husband died on the 20th of Elul 5608 (1848) at the age of 50 in Lodz. He had fled there from Zgierz due to the cholera epidemic that was ravaging Zgierz. Their only son Reb Moshe Bunem, was a scholar and well-known Hassid. He resided in Zgierz, where he reposes in honor. Their son-in-law was the rabbi who was great in Torah and Hassidism, a Hassid of Tzanz, Reb Yitzchak Asher Izak, whose mother-in-law Rachel Lea supported them for many years. Reb Yitzchak Asher Izak made a name for himself as one of the great ones when he published the Laws of Fundamentals of the Torah of the Rambam [44] in a small volume (Warsaw 5624 - 1864) with his two commentaries "Beir Hamelech" and "Archut Hamelech". The rabbi of Zgierz, the Rabbi, Gaon and Tzadik Reb Shalom Tzvi HaKohen wrote about him in his approbation to the book "that he is diligent in the tents of Torah and divine service, and this will merit the many". Reb Yitzchak Izak Kihen went to his eternal world at a young age, when he was 35 years old, around the year 5641 (1881), and reposes in honor in the old cemetery of Lodz, where he lived during his final years.

Tied with family connections to Zgierz, in the year 1920, the Tzadik Reb Menachem Mendel, the son of Reb Dov Berish the Admor of the community of Biala Podlaska and the grandson of Reb Avrahamele of Czekanow, came to live in Zgierz. He died in Otwock on the 19th of Shvat 5696 (1936), where they erected a canopy over his grave. His son Reb Yaakov Yitzchak Dan Landau inherited his seat. He had previously been known as the Kinower Rabbi.

His Hassidim built him a house on the Jewish street. He had a Beis Midrash and Yeshiva, were approximately sixty students gathered, who streamed to him from the entire area. They were supported in the dormitory that was in the house of the rabbi. Some were put up in the rabbi's court and others in rented rooms. The final head of the Yeshiva was Reb Tovia Landau, who was the son-in-law of the Admor of Slonim, who lived in the city of Baranowice.

Hundreds of Hassidim would come to Zgierz for the festivals. Most of them were put up on the Street of the Jews. One of them was a famous prayer leader, Reb Yaakov Doran (Yankel Prager) who conducted services

324

on the High Holy Days. At the outbreak of the war, the Rebbe of Zgierz moved to the Warsaw Ghetto, where he lived in a bunker until the Ghetto uprising. He was ultimately sent away on a "transport" along with his family.

Today, his son the Admor Reb Avraham Landau may he live long serves as the head of the dynasty of Strykow. He conducts a Yeshiva, Yeshivat Strykow "Kol Yaakov" in his home in Tel Aviv.

P. Sirkes.

Reb Avraham Yaakov Weisenfeld of blessed memory
(The lion of the community of Maskilim in Zgierz)

From P. H. Wetsztejn: "The Book of Correspondence between Reb A. Y. Weisenfeld and Sh. Y. R., Mizes, Sh. Z. Ch. H., Keller, Zwiefel, Yaffa, and others" (Krakow 5660, 1900), and from other sources.

Reb Avraham Yaakov Weisenfeld, who was one of the pillars of the life of the spirit in Zgierz during the 19th century, was born in Krakow in the year 5589 (1929) to pure and upright parents, honest with G-d and man. His father Reb Simcha Moshe, a learned man and honest merchant, sustained his household in an honorable albeit greatly restricted fashion. The worries regarding livelihood did not prevent him from toiling with all his soul to raise his son in Torah and religion. At the age of twelve, he studied with the sharp rabbi Reb Leibish, Reb Yoseles Bleicher, who also educated the children of the Gaon Reb Berish Meisels the head of the rabbinical court. About two years later, when he was learning Torah from his second rabbi, Reb Mordechai Blateiz the son-in-law of the Rabbi and Gaon Reb Shlomo HaKohen Bertram the head of the rabbinical court in the city of Szkucin and later in Krakow, he already excelled in the Talmud and its commentaries, didactics and reasoning, and his name went forth throughout all corners of the city as a genius of excellent spirit. When he reached the age of eighteen, he began to round out his knowledge with languages and science, like all of the Maskilim of the old generation, whose inner inclinations awakened in them the deep desire to delve into books of research and knowledge, even though the path was strewn with obstacles placed by the zealots and traditionalists.

Reb A. Y. Weisenfeld delved deeply into the wisdom of Israel, Talmud, Midrash, Jewish lore, Jewish law, scriptures, religion, philosophy, and the history of the Jewish people and its greats. With great concentration and strong consistency, with a refined and truthful spirit, pure from any prejudice, he delved into the depths of the opinions and ideas of the researchers and philosophers of the Jewish people and the nations of the world. He also studied for some years with the great scholar Reb Yitzchak Mizes of blessed memory, who helped him to venture into sublime matters.

It is self evident that the zealots saw him as the one who "peered and was damaged" [45], and they set their tongue and arrows after him to excommunicate him. Weisenfeld was summoned before the court of law of the Gaon Reb Berish Meisels. He, knowing the purity of heart and straightness of the path of Reb A. Y., invited him to his court to calm the storm of the zealots. The Gaon talked to him softly, and strengthened his heart to be one of those who accept embarrassment and not one of those who embarrass, for many of the Maskilim do not sit idly, but rather retort with curses to their detractors.

Still during his youth, Weisenfeld exchanged letters with the Gaon Reb Tzvi Hirsch Chajes and other greats of the spirit. When an impure spirit began to take hold of the hearts of the Maskilim, and the began to make breaches and expose meanings in the Torah that are not in accordance with Jewish law, and that blacken the face of Jewish traditions, Weisenfeld went out in a religious war [46] against the "destroyers and up rooters". He also engaged in a vigorous battle against the group of Hassidim who hatched plans to remove the rabbinate from the Gaon Meisels and replace whim with one of their own group who did not even reach the ankles of the rabbi.

In the year 5620 (1860), Weisenfeld married an intelligent girl from Zgierz. She was the only daughter of an honorable family, who were all knowledgeable in Torah. Her father Reb Yosef Leizer Weilnad was an honorable and dear man, who knew the book and was also an honest merchant.

On the day of his wedding, his friends and pals, people of note from near and far, gave him great honor and feted him with songs and gifts. Rabbi Mizes gave him the book of the Ramchal [47] "Layesharim Tehilla" ("Praise to the Upright"), since this book was a gift similar to the composition that he wrote in honor of the marriage of his friend. Mizes inscribed the following words at the front of the book: "To my dear friend, wise and whole, Reb Avraham Yaakov Weisenfeld, may his light shine. Regarding whom G-d did not grant me the proper endowments, and the poetic talents were not with me to prepare for you the tasty morsels that I love; and as my soul approaches the day of your wedding and joy of your heart, I said that I would give you this dear poem as an eternal souvenir, and this honorable poet will be for me like the song of my mouth, for honor and praise is fitting for you. Things should go well for you al the days of your existence. To your soul like my soul, the soul of your friend who holds you in esteem, Yitzchak HaKohen Mizes, Krakow, Saturday night, the first day of the month of Bul [48] 5660.

Reb Nachman Keller of Tarnow gave him as a gift "The Guide for the Perplexed of the Time" by Ranak [49]. In the cover of his book, he wrote a special poem that he wrote in Weisenfeld's honor for his wedding day. We will bring down here a few stanzas.

You, my friend, are not of the "Perplexed of the Time"
For I brought you this "Guide" on this occasion;
In this foggy land your eyes were opened,
To see clear light and know good reasoning.

Indeed, among many perplexed blind people you are intelligent
You go in a straight path between the lame who limp;
With a glance below, foolishness and lies fly
Then the intelligent person is silent - for nobody is listening!

-- -- -- and now my friend who battles forever

With a strong arm against those who disparage wisdom
To build for you a house, you have now come:
To cleave to your wife and to marry her in faithfulness;

Look upon this "Guide" and gird yourself with strength!

327

This man Krochmal saw toil and anger,

And his spirit did not wear out, the night brightened for him

He worked on many things - and now, you go do so with your strength!

Do and you will succeed, for G-d helps you

And He will bless the fine man on the day of his wedding:

Your wife should be like a fruitful vine in your home

And the angels of G-d shall answer: "Thus shall the man be blessed!"

After his wedding celebration, Weisenfeld set up his home in Zgierz, and lived a life of peace and honor with his wife. His mother-in-law, who was an elderly widow, gave over her business to him, a medicine shop, as well as all the income from her stone house, which provided a large income. In establishing his residence in Zgierz, which was still a small city, where the spirit of enlightenment had not yet shone its light, he pined for Krakow and its people, its scholars and rabbis who were near to him in spirit and ideas. Therefore, he provided joy to his soul by exchanging correspondence with his far off friends, until he became accustomed to the place and found friendship and camaraderie also in Zgierz, with a group of people of Torah and thoughts, who would be faithful with him. Even the Orthodox Hassidim made peace with him, and valued him as a scholar and a Maskil, who was faithful to both his G-d and wisdom.

The rabbi of Zgierz of that time, the Gaon Reb Shalom Tzvi HaKohen of holy blessed memory, the student of Reb Bunem of Przysucha, who headed a large Yeshiva that educated great rabbis, became a friend and a brother to Weisenfeld. Their friendship lasted for seventeen years until his death, as can be seen from his letters, and from the eulogy he wrote about him in "Hatzofeh Lehamagid" (volume 2 from the year 21).

During his travels to Germany, Weisenfeld met with the wise men of the west, including Frankel and Graetz [50]. During his discussions with Graetz, he pointed out some of his errors in relation to various Jewish scholars. Graetz thanked him and promised to fix the errors.

Weisenfeld earned the friendship and camaraderie with many scholars and writers such as Zwiefel, Reifman, Fein, Frischman, Sokolow, Yisrael

Yaffa and others. The writers of articles wrote the following about him: "Reb A. Y. Weisenfeld is like a man who took up his box and went out to the field, found barley and put it in, found wheat and put it in, as well as lentils and beans, and when he came home he sorted out each species. Weisenfeld went out to the field of our literature, to all of its domains and realms, found a word of Torah and set his eye upon it, found a word of secular wisdom and set his heart upon it, as with Midrash and research. When someone would visit him in his home, he would separate each genre, and discuss matters of Torah with a Torah oriented person, matters of wisdom with a Maskil, and matters of research with a researcher. His mind was fine and broad, and his manner of speech was pleasant and refined. His spirit was the spirit of wisdom, etc."

In Nachum Sokolow's eulogy for Weisenfeld ("Hatzefira", issue 272, from the year 1897) he said: "There are wise people who prefer that people not know them face to face, but rather should read and study their books. On the other hand, there are certain exceptional individuals who prefer that everyone knows them only face to face. One such exceptional individual was Weisenfeld. Those who knew him saw him as the symbol of a progressive Maskil, a treasury of knowledge and information, a living monument from the era of splendor and glory of the Haskala of Galicia, a monument forged from the honorable chair of the Ranak [51], the Gshir [51] and other like people. Those who knew him not only honored him with glorious honor but also loved him with a high degree of love, not only for his expertise, knowledge and thinking, but also for his sublime character, beauty of soul, and purity of spirit that warmed the hearts of those near to him. He was enthusiastic about and loved the Torah, literature, and the Hebrew language - with clear fervor, faith, enthusiasm, and emotion, - - - one of the remnants of the old generation of the wise men of Galicia, one of the "early ones", of the generation of those that raised the flag of the Hebrew Haskala in Galicia."

Weisenfeld lived in Zgierz for 33 years, until he was forced to leave. He then returned to his birthplace of Krakow. This exile that was decreed upon him pained him greatly, and he was sad to leave his many friends who "cleaved to him and hung on to him like a flame to a coal", even though many of them set out on the journey to meet him and see him again. Even

329

the fine and important people of Krakow, both Torah oriented and Maskilim, old and young, came to his door daily.

On the 11th of Kislev 5658 (1897) in the 69th year of his live, he was requisitioned by the celestial court. The following words are engraved upon his tombstone.

A sublime man rests in this grave A great scholar, of mighty spirit With great humility, fear of Heaven, and all knowledge He went in the path of faith all of his days Torah was his desire from his youth Day and night he talked about it, and it was all his striving Evening and morning scholars were among his household Their faces became gloomy on the day of his death The scholars ceased, the choirs stopped!

Reb Tovia Lifshitz of blessed memory

Tovia Lifshitz

One of the great luminaries of the city of Zgierz was Reb Tovia Lifshitz of blessed memory. He was born in 1843 in Siadi, of the Kovno region of Lithuania. He studied in the Telshe Yeshiva and excelled with his sharp mind. He was also a student of the Sirvintdai Rabbi, Rabbi Tzvi Shapira, who was nicknamed "Hershel the Crazy" [52] due to the fact that he was always involved with mathematics and astronomy. This Hershel later became known as Professor Herman Shapira of the University of Heidelberg, on of the founders and the directors of the Jewish National Fund.

Reb Tovia Lifshitz arrived in Zgierz around 1868. The poet Yaakov Cohen mentions in his memoirs ("Netiv Chayay" - "Paths of my Life" - in the "Haboker" newspaper) that in his youth, he became close with Reb Tovia Lifshitz, who displayed love toward him and brought him very near.

According to the memoirs of the poet, Reb Tovia Lifshitz was known as the head of the Maskilim of Zgierz after the departure of Mr. Weisenfeld in the year 5653 (1893). Aside from his expertise in the sources of Hebrew culture, he brought with him also knowledge of German. He was conversant with the German classicists and philosophers. He conducted deep research into the Yiddish literature, both secular and religious, and the sources of the Semitic languages.

He participated in "Hamelitz" of Zederbaum [53] as well as in "Hatzefira". He wrote various articles in those periodicals. Along with this, he corresponded with various important personalities and writers such as Y. L. Gordon, Peretz Smolenski, Harkavi, Dr. Feilchenfeld of Posen (Poznan), Professor Hildesheimer [54], Mordechai the son of Hillel HaKohen, Zalman Lebuntin and many others. He also participated in the Odessa committee of "Chovevei Zion", and was the first chairman of the Zionist union in Zgierz.

Reb Tovia Lifshitz was a deep thinker and knew how to present his words in a clear form, sometimes sharp and even a bit sarcastic. For example, in his book "Nitfei Tal" [55] in his commentary on the Torah portion of "Shmot", when the leaders of people in Egypt come to Moses with the complaint "Why did you do evil unto this nation?" [56], Reb Tovia Lifshitz comments: "We hear this complaint even today from the opponents of Zionism. They fear that the political situation will worsen for the nation, and attempt to put an end to its motion. Thus is the manner of those small in faith and mind during all eras. Oh let it be that the end of their complaints during our day will be like the end of their complaints of that era." (Nitfei Tal page 18).

And in another place, he states: "If the people who come up from Egypt will see..." [57] - how difficult is it for those born into slavery to be freemen, - - -"(ibid, page 32).

In the memoirs of the poet Yaakov Cohen, Reb Tovia Lifshitz is presented as a man of average stature, with very handsome grayish eyes, filled with intelligence and the joy of life. He was a broker by occupation. Of the sixteen children that his wife bore him, five sons survived. Of them the poet knew Yitzchak who was the friend of my older sister, and Shimon and Leon, who were students of Katznelson.

Yaakov Cohen relates: "About one month after the Zionist Congress, the Maskilim of the city and the notables were invited to the home of Reb Tovia Lifshitz. The host lectured to them about the Zionist idea and about the duty of the nation to organize in order to give the needed to support to those who speak on behalf of the movement, and to collect the needed means. They decided to found an organization called "Bnei Zion". "I myself proposed the name", writes Yaakov Cohen. The host volunteered to give over the room in which the meeting was held for a certain period as a meeting place for the members of the organization. Thus a faithful core group was founded that used to gather in particular on Sabbath afternoons to read newspapers and Zionist literature, and to hear the discussions of the owner of the house about issues of the movement and his commentaries on the weekly Torah portion, which were also for the most part bound up with ideas relating to the nation, its qualities, and its roots.

In his book "Nitfei Tal" (page 136), the speech that he presented at the founding of this organization is brought down. We will bring down few sections that are worthy of being remembered.

In his logical commentaries on the Midrash in the Torah portion of Vayeitzei [58] regarding Jacob's dream, where in accordance with the Midrash, when G-d showed Jacob the ladder, he was showing him the history of the Jewish people and its spiritual power that would hold it throughout the generations -after an explanation that encompasses the entire Midrash, Reb T. L. states: "My masters, every prophesy that is written was written for the generations, in accordance with the words of our sages of blessed memory. Let us examine the status of Israel during the past thirty years, from when Alexander II opened up the door of freedom before us, how fragmented the Jewish people have become; The Maskilim among us went forward "to the place from where they will not return", for they assimilated, forgot the Rock that forged them, and have become dry bones without the moisture of Judaism, neither religious nor national; on the other hand, the observant and Orthodox people have sequestered themselves into the four ells of the Beis Midrashes, and have become like the Egyptian mummies who would melt into dust if a wind were to blow upon them. Even the Orthodox, the last people who guard the walls of religion and the people, have become fragmented into small groups, dispersed and dry; the Western Jews can be considered as those who dwell in the grave, for they have tasted completely from marriage [59], and have erased any memory and sign even from their prayer books: can we not way as Ezekiel: "Our hope has disappeared - for it has been decreed upon us" [60], four our bones have become dry and they cannot be revived?

However, please see one of the wonders of our chronicles, the wonders of G-d "who stands with us", for thunders came and stripped the crookedness from our hearts. Thunders came to damage the remnants of the house of Israel. However, instead of causing all of the leaves to fall that have become worn out from the tree of Judah, we have seen the opposite, that the worn out leaves have awakened to a new life."

Reb T. L. waxed long in his words, as he analyzes the vision of the prophet with reference to the current times and its course, with emotional words that awaken the national spirit amidst the Jewish youth, who had just previously been lackadaisical and narrow minded. "However the storm winds come, a general wind from the four directions of the heavens, which blow upon the four corners of the earth, and awaken all of those that slumber in the earth. All of them stood up upon their feet, not a scattered flock but rather "a very great crowd" from all factions and groups, from all nations and lands. In all of them one spirit is blown, the spirit of Zionism, "And I brought you into your land", "when I open your graves, oh my nation."

Reb T. L. concludes: "With Zionism, we return to the nationhood of Israel, but it is incumbent upon us also to return to the Torah of Israel and its spirit, as stated by the words of the prophet "And I will place my spirit upon you and you will live, and I will place you upon your Land, so that you will know that I am G-d, who speaks and carries through."

Indeed these fiery words of prophesy delivered more than 65 years ago ("The Bnei Zion group" was founded in the year 5657 / 1897) by Reb Tovia Lifshitz in Zgierz, can be seen today as the words of the living G-d.

Tovia Lifshitz' book includes two compositions: a) commentaries and notes upon the Bible; b) "Nitfei Tal" (T. L. being an acronym for his name), which includes articles, speeches and articles of correspondence which were written by chance, or which were written to mark important events in the Jewish world. The book was published by Krinski in Warsaw (5664 1914).

Lifshitz was one of the most important and honorable men in our town, one of the notables of the city. His influence in cultural and Zionist life in our city was without bound. For a certain time, he also served as the treasurer of the first "Gemilat Chasadim" organization. He donated his rich library to the Hebrew University of Jerusalem.

Reb Tovia Lifshitz died in the year 5676 (1916) at the age of 73, during the time of the First World War. Almost the entire city participated in the funeral. The mayor and wise men of the city eulogized him as a great Jew in his generation, who was faithful to his people.

There is a long epitaph on his gravestone, praising his deeds and activities. It was written in verse by Reb Moshel Eiger with the participation of Isucher Szwarc, and concludes with the old classic statement: "He loved Plato and Aristotle, and truth above all".

May his memory be a blessing, and may his name flourish among the great people of our city.

One of his sons, Arieh (Leon) Lifshitz, was a scholarly and learned man. From him, we obtained the details and main biographical details regarding his father of blessed memory. He was active in the fields of culture and education in Zgierz and later in Lodz. His name is remembered as a well-known pedagogue. He is also known as being the founder and director of the first school for the deaf and the mute in Lodz. Here in the Land of Israel, he was active as a volunteer for the teaching of Hebrew to new immigrants in development towns. For a time during the 1950s, he was on the board of the "Organization of Zgierz Émigrés in Israel", and he donated his portion to the Book of Zgierz by writing an essay on his memories that is published in this book. Earlier he also lived in Gan Shlomo next to Petach Tikva, and later in Upper Nazareth, where he died.

May his soul be bound in the bond of eternal life.

W. P.

Reb Tovia Lifschitz by Aryeh Lifschitz

Reb Tovia Lifshitz was born in Siadi, Lithuania in the year 1849. He remained in Zgierz for 70 years. He died in 1916 during the time of the German rule. He studied in the Telshe Yeshiva, and excelled with his sharp, analytical mind. He became a student of the rabbi of Sirvintdai, Reb Hershel Shapira. (They called him the crazy Hershel because he delved into mathematics and astronomy. Later he became the renowned Professor Shapira of Heidelberg, the creator of the Jewish National Fund).

Lifshitz was heartily involved in studying the Hebrew literature and language. He also explored the Yiddish, world, and religious literature of various hues, and became fluent in the German language, in which he studied the appropriate literature of Judaism and Semitic languages.

The researcher collaborated in and published articles in Zederbaum's "Hamelitz" , and in "Hatzefira" which was edited by Chaim Zelig Slonimski and Nachum Sokolow. He carried on a wide ranging correspondence with great Jewish personalities, such as Yitzchak Leib Gordon, Smolenski, Zederbaum, Harkavi, Dr. Feilchenfeld from Posen (compiler of works on Jewish memorials), Professor Hildesheimer, Mordechai the son of Hillel HaKohen, Zalman Levontin, (the first director of the Palestine Bank).

Lifshitz took part in the Odessa Committee of Chovevei Zion and was the first chairman of the Zionist union in Zgierz.

Reb Tovia Lifshitz left in his well his immense, variegated library, which for the most part consisted of works on Judaism and the wisdom of Israel, to the national library of Jerusalem. It was transferred there shortly after the First World War.

Aryeh Lifshitz

The Writer and Poet David Frischman of blessed memory

Of the Educators and teachers of the generation

David Frischman

Deep in the Heart
Is the land of "Ophir" [61]
Treasures of gold are found therein
There, there are diamonds and emeralds
Memories from the time of youth.
(From the poem- "Ophir".)

Zgierz did not only produce rabbis and great scholars. It was also the birthplace and place of nurturing of scholars and writers, men of renown, who laid the foundations of Modern Hebrew literature and thought. Among these writers was David Frischman.

Frischman was born in Zgierz on the 5th of Tevet 5620 (December 31, 1859). His father Reb Shaul, who was a merchant and a scholar, was known as "a person with both a strong and sharp intellect". Frischman's mother as well, Freda Beila, was, as is described, an intelligent women with a poetic soul. Some of his relatives on his mother's side were renowned artists and sculptors, such as Henryk Glickensztejn, and Shmuel Hirshenberg (a national artist, and also a teacher in "Betzalel" in Jerusalem [62]). David's parents left Zgierz when he was still a child, and moved to nearby Lodz, which had a broader vista both for business and Haskala. Later, David was sent to Zgierz to study Torah, Talmud, and Jewish law from the Judge Reb Moshe Bennet of blessed memory. There he befriended Isucher Szwarc, for study and self-completion.

During his childhood, he was meticulous in the observance of commandments, and he absorbed his Torah from the cheder, the melamed, and also the Beis Midrash of Zgierz. His governess taught him European languages, and also customs and mannerisms that were accepted in the progressive circles. He was very diligent with his books. His power of memory was great, and he also had a good and quick grasp. He was quiet and silent by nature, closed and inwardly focused; he was always thinking, envisioning, and dreaming. During his early youth, he worked greatly on the meanings and concentration in prayer, in order to bring near the end and bring nigh the redemption. Stories of wonders captivated his heart, as well as stories of morality and Kabbalah. These sowed scattered seeds in his fertile mind, and filled his creativity with prose and song.

He wrote poems, stories and articles already during his youth. Aside from writing in Hebrew, he also wrote in German, and he translated from language to language. During his early youth, he translated the first section of "Et Tzavua" ("Colored Pen") of Mapu into German, and also "The Count of Monte Cristo" of Dumas into Hebrew. His first book that became known was "Hamoreh Tzedek" ("The Righteous Teacher"), which was printed in

Hashachar in the year 5638 (1878). Frischman said that it was in honor of his Bar Mitzvah. However, his era of creativity primarily began with the publishing of the story "On Yom Kippur" (printed in "Haboker Or" in the year 5641 - 1881) after he published a small satire "On a Rooster and a Hen" [63].

In the year 5673 (1913) the Hebrew writers celebrated his literary Jubilee (Thirty years), and in honor of the festival, they published the entire writings of David Frischman, and a selection of his translations in 16 volumes (published by "Tushia", Warsaw, 5674). Four volumes of the selected writings of Frischman were already published in the years 5659 -5672 (1899 - 1912). Later, "New Writings" of Frischman were published (published by "Sifro", Warsaw, 5671-5672, 1911-1912) in five volumes.

During the period of his youth, Frischman was attracted to the style of writing of the Maskilim of his era. On the manuscript of the translation of the book "Monte Cristo", "Nakam Veshilem" ("Revenge and Recompense"), Frischman writes: "This fine composition was written by the exalted French writer, Alexandre Dumas in his native tongue, and received acclaim, and now has been translated in to the Hebrew language by myself, the young man David Frischman, who basks in the shadow of his forefathers here in Lodz (volume I), the year 5634 (1874) (that is to say, when he was fourteen years old).

He adds a dedication to his parents on the second page of the manuscript.

"A note of gratitude. In honor of my father, the prince, the intelligent, the dear one, honored and noble, a man of faith, with a dear spirit, pure of heart, sublime and splendid, my Father Shaul Frischman, may his light shine. And in honor of my modest and upright mother, the intelligent dear, honorable princess, may she be blessed over all women in the tents, and she excels over them all, Freda Beila may she be live. From their son the translator." [64]

The era of Frischman's study in Zgierz under the judge Reb Moshe Bennet, left a deep imprint upon his soul, as can be seen. Its signs are evident in his many creations of prose and poetry. He always saw before him the elderly rabbi, and his leadership that decided the life of the community. He delved deeply into the souls and spiritual essence of the elders of Torah in a language filled with signs and symbols that included both reverence and satire together.   The following segment of his poetry is an example that demonstrates the resonance in Frischman's soul regarding his memories of Zgierz:

... And furthermore, I will recall for a second time:
Our rabbis taught!
Myriads of torches of sun, a pillar of grains of gold,
Engraved pillars of light from the wonders of a wondrous world,
Come down through the window and shine upon the Gemara,
And also shine upon my cheeks; on the pages of the half diagonal
And I in the second half - and I am then a young lad,
Sitting before the table of G-d with my page of Gemara.
And from within a bright cloud that sometimes goes and then descends,
It sometimes dips down and disappears, sometimes dips down and appears,
An oval shaped head, flooded in a cloud of curls,
A twisting of gold sparkles - has the Divine Presence descended upon me?

It is possible to learn something regarding the connection of Frischman during his youth with Isucher Szwarc from the letter of Isucher Szwarc to the writer Mr. Getzel Karsel on the eve of Passover, 5685 (1925), in which he passes along a letter of Frischman to him, along with a copy of several of his poems that he wrote at the age of twelve.

"In order to remember!
Men who were very evil - they devoured me, they frightened me,
Wounded me, persecuted me - at the time they were jealous of me,
Or did worse than this, for they also loved me,
In their hearts there was only evil, at the time that goodness was expressed;
And what did I do them do to them that they have surrounded me so?
For they loved me so, they hated me so?
For they have frightened me so and surrounded me so with their entire mouth?
For they shut their ears to me, or did they hear?
Are you yourself one of them perhaps?
My brother! I do not demand that you love my soul
Not friendship nor brotherliness do I request at this time

But only not to do evil to me and not to hate me
Do not create waters of the seas in a place of dry land
In order make me fall, in order to drown me…

"In the multitude of days and in every place where you are, remember these words that come from the depths of my heart, and may these words serve as a testimony for me that I did not ask anything that was not part of the circles of simple life, and remember that these ideas did not come from an abundance of good upon me. Your faithful friend.
D. Frischman"

From this outpouring of Frischman's soul, it is possible to figure out the status of his spirit, and the suspicion that was planted in his heart with regard to his circle of friends, whom he regarded as if they speak one thing with the mouth and another with the heart, without doubt from personal experience. He was seeking complete faithfulness and dedication, honest love.

Szwarc continues in his aforementioned letter, and write among other things: "I send you with this 'The Song of the Wine' that was written by the late man in the year 5631 or 2 (1872), when he was still very young, approximately twelve years old (Frischman was born in Zgierz in the year 5620 - 1860), unlike that which was published in his annals of 5625 (1865). His birth certificate (1860) can be found here in the home of the officials)".

Isucher Szwarc writes the following regarding the family of Frischman:

"I remember from my youth his grandfather Reb Avigdor Frischman, an honorable man in our city, a merchant and a man of Torah. He had a large library with books of religion and research. He took great delight in this grandchild of his, who was a genius in the full sense of the word. He studied diligently the Talmud and its commentaries. He learned Hebrew in Lodz from the Hebrew teacher, the Maskil Tzvi Goldstejn of Piotrkow, who also was involved in the writing of poetry, and translated "Lehakat Hashodedim" ("The Band of Thieves") into Hebrew. His parents moved to Lodz prior to his Bar Mitzvah, and sent David to the city of Zgierz to study from the local judge, Reb Moshe Bennet of blessed memory. Already then, he would read

340

with me the books of Schiller and Goethe.

He wrote me many letters from Breslau (Wroclaw), but they are sitting in some corner, and I cannot find them now.

With greetings of peace, Isucher Szwarc."

In the year 5680 (1920) the year of the war between Poland and Soviet Russia, Frischman left Warsaw and went to Berlin. In the middle of the year 5682 (1922) his gallstone and liver illness worsened. He was operated on in the month of Av that year due to a difficult illness. He died in Berlin on the 10th of Av and was brought to burial there.

Frischman was a complete world of Hebrew literature and its creations. Generations enjoyed his creations with a spiritual, esthetic enjoyment. They served as material for many books and researchers, to read and dissect.

In Zgierz, where he was greatly revered, they decided to honor his memory on the anniversary of his death with a reading in his name in the Jewish public library. That library was called "The David Frischman Jewish Library of Zgierz" until its final day.

His good memory will remain within his nation forever.

Y. A. M.

A rich and wide ranging bibliography on David Frischman and his creations can be found in the Lexicon of Hebrew Literature by Getzel Karsel and in the Lexicon of Jewish Literature by Zalman Reisin.

My Father Isuchar Moshe Szwarc (Schwartz)

Translated by Doubi Szwarc and Jerrold Landau [65]

1949 will mark a decade since the death of the enlightened and renowned Jewish thinker, Isuchar Moshe Szwarc. He was eighty years old when he died in his hometown Zgierz, a day before the deportation.

They burnt his library, which was one of the most well known, important private collections of Jewish books (known as Hebraica in the vernacular). Even his house was completely destroyed.

As can be seen, those murderers were not satisfied with murdering an old

Jew, a drop in the sea of six million that they murdered in a cruel fashion - for their plan was to exterminate the Jewish body of knowledge, along with the Jewish people, by destroying all Jewish books, and even the houses in which such books were found.

In this case, they had no complaints. For Isuchar Szwarc's home in Zgierz was the home of Jewish Haskalah and intelligentsia, writers, scholars, communal leaders and artists - starting with David Friszman and Nachum Sokolow, and ending with Yaakov Cohen, Katzenelson, Nomberg, Glicenstein and others.

The family of Isuchar Szwarc on the occasion of the wedding of Shmuel Schwartz in Odessa in 1914. Standing from left to right: Shmuel, Manya, Dov, Simcha, and Marek- Sitting: Agatha (the bride), Sara and Isuchar Szwarc, Roza, and Yechiel Frenkel- Lying at the bottom Aleksander Szwarc (currently in Canada). [66]

You, my beloved friend, my brother of the Jewish people of Zgierz, have convinced his eldest son to write about his father's great personality. Can indeed a son write without a dose of reverence, for who has any other option than to suspend the objectivity that is needed to write about such an enlightened personality as Isuchar Szwarc?!

Incidentally, I have an additional fault: I write a poor Yiddish, for I have already been away from the home for over 50 years.

Even though one does not forget one's mother tongue, I rarely have the opportunity to write in Yiddish. As long as my father was alive, I corresponded with him in Hebrew, and with my mother in Polish. In truth, we spoke Yiddish at home - in those days it was still referred to as "jargon" - however I never wrote Yiddish.

It is written in Pirke Avot [67]: "Someone who quotes something in the name of the person who originally said it brings redemption to the world." I wish to commence describing the character of my revered father with a quote from one of his original statements, which helped me greatly in my literary work:

First, regarding the origin of the word "Marrano", the term used for the secret Jews of Spain and Portugal. From where does the term "Marrano" originate?

In the Spanish and Portuguese languages, the word "marrano" means a pig, and this case, the term "Marranos" means "pigs". However, this is not correct, for in the entire literature of the inquisition, spanning over 300 years and over 40,000 inquisition trials that can be found today in the Lisbon archives, one does not find the term "Marrano", the term that was and still is used by the masses. They are called "Neo-Christians", or simply "Jews", as well as "meshumadim" [68], and such terms as "hunt" [69]. But the term "Marranos" was unknown there. This proves that the term does not stem from Portugal, and has nothing to do with the Spanish and Portuguese word "marranen" (pig).

According to my father, the term "Marrano" comes from the Hebrew "Lemareh Ayin" [70] that is a Christian only as appears to the eye - and from there arose the term "Marrano".

343

I do not wish to record here all of the statements that my father made in helping me with my work, for I would have to write a book… but one more fact is indeed worthy of repeating:

One of the old tombstones from 1345 that is found in the Jewish museum of Tomar ends with "Nun Bet Tav and he is buried in this grave". What does Nun Bet Tav refer to? My father was able to decipher the inscription: these are the initials of the statement "Nafsho Betov Talin" ("his soul shall rest well"), from Psalms 25, 13.

As I have stated, I am his eldest son. He was only twenty years older then I; we looked more like two brothers. I was born in 1880 in Zgierz, and as I calculate, my revered father was born in 1860 or 1859 (I am not sure which), also in the city of Zgierz. His father was Hersz Ber Szwarc and his mother Miriam (nee Glicksman).

My grandfather Hersz Ber of blessed memory was a wealthy metal trader. My grandmother Miriam of blessed memory was his second wife.

My grandfather had four sons from his first wife, all merchants and metal traders. He had only one son, my father Yissachar Moshe (pronounced Isucher [71]), from his second wife.

My father's house that the Germans destroyed was built in the lifetime of my grandfather Hersz Ber. My mother Sara, also born Glicksman, was very beautiful. She was tall, with blue eyes, black hair, and clear, white skin, milk and blood…

My father was also tall and slender. He was a handsome, delicate young man. From among all his brothers, he was the only one who did not become a businessman. He consecrated his life to studying. Don't think he went to a Gymnasium, Heaven forbid! After some time in cheder, a tutor was brought home to teach him. At first, obviously, it was a tutor who taught him Bible and Talmud. Later, he also studied German, Russian and Polish. Generally speaking, I can say that he was self-educated. The fact that he wore a long kapote cloak did not stop him from delving into the writings of Mendelsohn, Heine, Zunz, Luzzato, or into the works Modern Hebrew writers of the era, such as Yehuda Leib Gordon, Mapu and Smolenski. I also know that he read Frug's Russian poetry in Russian, and "Meir Ezofowicz" by Orzeszkowa in Polish. He was able to read whatever he wanted, and, as it seems, he combined Bible, Talmud, the love of Zion of Mapu, and the Shulchan Aruch

(Code of Jewish Law).

Already at that time he began establishing his library, his book collection, which was as dear to him as his own life.

At a young age, my father married his beautiful and beloved cousin Sara Glicksman. He was a young man of nineteen, and she - a child of sixteen. As was the custom, his father-in-law supported him for a year or two, till he could choose a means of livelihood. Less than a year after his marriage, my grandfather Wolf Glicksman, died. Since mother was the youngest daughter, the beloved mezinka [72], my widowed grandmother did no want to be separated from her. That is why my father lived and was supported at my grandmother's home for eighteen years, as long as my grandmother lived.

In the interim, my Szwarc grandparents died. My grandfather's house was left as an inheritance to my father.

The income from the house enabled my father to educate his children in Gymansias, and to send me, his eldest son, to study in Paris. My father was free of financial worries. He was able to dedicate himself to "Torah Va'Avoda" [73] and to his intellectual aspirations.

As far as I am concerned, my departure for Paris to study always was a miracle, since my father had always wanted me to study to become a rabbi at the Hildesheimer Rabbinical Seminary in Berlin [74].

Although a liberal, my father still wore a long kapote cloak. Discarding it and replacing it with a short coat required a great deal of courage…

This he did in 1892. While visiting St. Petersburg, where he met Jewish leaders, he visited the Imperial library, and befriended the famous poet Yehudah Leib Gordon.

After my father returned from St. Petersburg, he never wore a long coat again.

After the death of my grandmother Zise, my father's financial condition deteriorated considerably. My grandmother's house, where my parents were living, was given to one of my uncles [75] as an inheritance. The period of in-law support ended, and my parents had to move to their own house which they had inherited from my Szwarc grandfather. Since my parents took over the best part of the house for themselves, the income from renting the house decreased, and was not sufficient to provide for their day to day needs.

My father then opened a factory that produced silk ribbon. This enterprise did not last long. The factory burnt down, and my father lost the little money left from the recent inheritance.

At that time, a government school of commerce was opened in Zgierz with all the rights of a Gymnasium, which accepted Jewish children without a percentage quota. Many young Jews arrived in Zgierz from Poland and Lithuania. This created new opportunities for landlords in the town: renting rooms to Jewish students. My father also opened such a hostel, since he had a large multi-room house.

Obviously, the entire burden fell upon my mother's shoulders, but she undertook it lovingly. Father again was free of worries of livelihood, and was once again able to dedicate himself to his books and the like.

At that time, I was a student in Paris. The hostel business continued for several more years, and ended when the regime moved the commerce school to Russia. By that time, I had already graduated as an engineer and was working in Spain and Africa. I already had the financial ability to help my dear parents, and I gradually paid back a part of the large expenses they had spent for my studies.

This enabled my father to provide higher education for almost all of my brothers, to marry off my three dear sisters, and my father himself was able to continue his publicity efforts, in writings and in oral presentations, towards a renaissance of Polish Jewry.

A few Jewish intellectuals were living in Zgierz at the time, and they cooperated with my father in his publicity activities. Two were much older than father, Reb Tovia Lipszicz, a good Hebraist and a picturesque Lithuanian Jew; and the elderly Galician Jew A. Y. Weicenfeld, who was an expert in Jewish and German literature. The third was from Zgierz, still a young man, Moshe Eiger, a grandson of Rabbi Akiva Eiger [76].

They all used to meet every Sabbath afternoon at Mr. Weicenfeld's little one-story house at the market square. I came along many times.

Most of their activities were oral. Only my father used to publish articles from time to time in the "Hatzefirah" newspaper, and later in "Hayom", as well as in the Yiddish journals of Warsaw and Lodz. He wrote under the pseudonym, "Yam Shachor" (Black Sea). The Yod and Mem were the initials of Yissachar Moshe, and Shachor (black) was for Szwarc.

My parents conducted an Orthodox household. My father was tolerant with respect to the greater or lesser religious observance of his children.

On Sabbaths and festivals we all went to the Beis Midrash, since my father did not worship at the Great Synagogue, but at the more democratic Beis Midrash. My mother was more fastidious with regards to her religiosity, and would ask me at times whether I had recited my prayers.

I will never forget my embarrassment when, on my first return from Paris for the summer vacation, mother unpacked my luggage and asked me if I had worshipped every day. "Of course," I replied. She examined by Tefillin bag [77], and took out a gold coin that she had put there before I left for Paris for the first time. You can imagine my shock, shame, and also my disappointment...

My father was a close friend of Nachum Sokolow, and of the native of Zgierz David Friszman, who lived in Lodz. Father used to often visit Warsaw. He went to Lodz almost daily, even before the Zgierz - Lodz tramway was installed.

Transportation was in horse drawn wagons. Most drivers were Jews. The wagon station was on Schule Gasse very close to father's house. There were four seats in a wagon. If a fifth passenger came, he had to climb up with the coachman.

When the driver collected the fees from four or five passengers [78], they set off. The drive to the old city of Lodz was approximately one and a half hours.

In the winter times, when the highway was frozen, the poor, lean horse could not carry the wagon uphill, and the passengers had to go out and push for quite a large part of the way.

My father was very disorganized. It could happen, for example, as he himself would tell us, that he would travel to Lodz, while the whole family was expecting him for lunch. Simply, he met up with a friend who was travelling to Lodz, and he traveled together with him, without contemplating that they might be concerned at home as to why he has not shown up for lunch.

I was familiar with the 10-verst [79] stretch from Zgierz to Lodz like the back of my hand [80]. When the carriage brought us, through the grace of G-d, safely to Siebler's garden (I have no inkling of what it is called today), we would take comfort that we were almost in Valut [81]. That is the same Valut that the Germans converted into a ghetto, and later - into a cemetery.

My father visited me twice in Paris. Once it was completely unexpected. In Paris he met with the famous professor Joseph Ha-Levi, with the Chief

Rabbi Zadok Cohen, and with Max Nordau, Dr. Marmorek and others.

I have forgotten to write that my father was always a Zionist. I can remember how fifty years ago, when Dr. Herzl published his "Judenstadt" ("State of the Jews"), father wrote to me in Paris: "I am for him, and his dreams are mine".

My father did not eat non-kosher food. While he was in Paris, I had to go with him to eat in a kosher restaurant in the Jewish quarter. My mother however, when she arrived in Paris in 1900 for the International Exposition, was not satisfied with the kosher certification of the restaurant, but went into the kitchen herself to make sure personally that the meat was properly rendered kosher in accordance with law and tradition. Father would be satisfied with the sign of certification. He used to say, "If someone's name is Gnendel, we can eat her Kendel [82]". He understood that I could not go daily to eat in the Jewish quarter, a two or three hour journey from the Latin Quarter, where all of the students lived.

My father's life was generally happy. He was somewhat delicate physically. He never complained and never went to a physician. I never remember seeing him ill enough to take to bed. My beloved mother kept him well - and they both lived happily and joyously.

During my youth, my younger brother died in his childhood. However, their first disaster and greatest tragedy was the death of my sister Miriam (Mania). She was only 25 years old. She had gotten married and settled with her husband in Tel Aviv. A few months later, she died of typhus. The sanitary conditions were still very poor in those years.

This did not stop my other sister, Tzipora, who married the famous Zionist leader of Radom, Yechiel Frenkel, from settling in Tel Aviv, nor my brother, the engineer Simcha, from settling in the Land of Israel with his family. They have already been living there for about 20 years. They were the only ones who inherited and fulfilled my father's dream, and his love for the Land of Israel.

My father was also a delegate to the Zionist Congress in Vienna in 1913. I came from Spain to visit with him there.

The biggest disappointment that my parents had from a child was from my brother Mordechai, the famous painter and sculptor, who lives in Paris. It is no longer a secret that he converted from Judaism with his wife and child... One can imagine the terrible chagrin that this caused my poor parents.

Marek (Mordechai) was the best-loved son. He would often come to Poland for exhibitions, and he would paint and sculpt for my parents. He was very attached to our parents, and they loved him very much.

His apostasy was not only a terrible shock to my parents, but also to the entire Jewish world. It took place suddenly and unexpectedly approximately twelve years ago, and nobody can understand the reason until this day.

My father withstood the unexpected catastrophic shock. He tried to persuade his beloved son, whom he always - even after the conversion - referred to as Mordechai the Tzadik, that he was living an error. He would write to him heartfelt and philosophical words. All of the brothers, even myself from my side, wrote to Marek and attempted to convince him that he had committed a terrible travesty, and that his crazy deed was a deathblow for our dear parents. However, it was to no avail.

For my mother, that blow was the most terrible. It shortened and embittered her life. She died suddenly of a heart attack. She was three years younger than my father, and died two years before him, at age 75. She died without having previously been ill, through a kiss of death, as a righteous woman [83]. One can consider it to be lucky that she died before the war, and did not witness how the German murderers killed my dear father. All her life was devoted to her husband, enabling him to live without having to work, so that he could devote himself to the benefit of his people and the benefit of Judaism. She deserves to be remembered as a model mother in Israel. May her holy soul be bound in the bonds of eternal life!

My father died as a Tzadik in sanctification of the name of G-d. The same fate was in store for my brother Hersz-Ber, and my youngest sister Zosia who were killed along with his wife and children in the Warsaw Ghetto [84]. From all the family living in Poland at the time, the only one to survive was the eldest son of my brother Hersz-Ber, David Szwarc, who was saved thanks to a Polish acquaintance, a refined person, Stanislaw Pielka (who lived in Mokotow, Palencka 3). He saved David's life at the risk of his own. I am writing about him here, before the community and congregation, in order to express my best and heartfelt thanks to him. My nephew David is now living in Canada, with my youngest brother, Dr. Aleksander Schwartz.

My brother Dr. Aleksander Szwarc is a famous chemist, a scientist who settled in Canada. He might be successful in becoming a professor, something that my father might have become had he lived in a free country.

I wrote in error that my nephew David Schwartz was the only member of the entire family in Poland who survived. After the war, my brother-in-law, the engineer Kazimierz Lewi, came back from Russia. He was not able to find his wife, my sister Zosia, and his only son, who were gassed and burnt.

My other brother-in-law, Yechiel Frenkel of Tel Aviv [85], is the only one who can be compared to my father. One can state that he was the "alter ego" of my father, with respect to his virtues, Jewish education, and love for Israel, where he has already been working for 20 years.

He translated my writings on the Marranos in Portugal into Hebrew. These were published at "Ha-Yom" (Today) in 1926. I turn to him today, as I used to turn to father, for consultation on difficult Hebrew manuscripts that I find in the local archives.

As for myself, the eldest son, I inherited my Father's love for books, love of Judaism and of the History of the Jewish people. Thanks to this, I undertook my work regarding the Marranos. I published a work on their prayers and customs. Thanks to my research, I was able to rescue an old synagogue from the 15th century, and turn it into a Hebrew museum with the support of the government. I also established a large Hebraica book collection which is found in the museum. This collection was founded by my wife and myself, and will one day be sent to Israel.

I would also like to mention my studies about David Reuveni, Shlomo Molcho, and about anti-Semitism. These have been published here. I thank my revered father for the motivation for this.

All of my brothers, and my brother-in-law Yechiel Frenkel, as has been stated, inherited some of my father's qualities. However, none of us has inherited his golden soul, his exceptional goodness, his great altruism, his extensive knowledge, and his clear mind, May his soul rest in peace.

By the Engineer Shmuel Schwartz

Lisbon, February 15, 1948

Isuchar Moshe Szwarc of blessed memory by Y. A. Malkieli

Translated by Doubi Szwarc and Jerrold Landau [86]

One of the most respected members of the city, and the glory of the Zgierz community, a central figure in the community, a scholar, an erudite thinker, a lofty public activist, one of the old-timers and builders of the community, an outstanding person, an educator of the generation, whose home was a meeting place from which Torah and wisdom was disseminated

350

to the public such was Reb Isuchar Moshe Szwarc of blessed memory.

He was born in Zgierz on the 7th of Adar, 5619 (1859) to his father Reb Hersz Ber Szwarc. His father was a merchant and prominent person, who educated his children in the spirit of Torah and tradition. He studied in cheder during his youth, and later studied Torah from famous rabbis, including the first rabbi of Zgierz, Rabbi Shalom Tzvi HaKohen of holy blessed memory. He became involved with Haskalah at a young age, but he never severed his connection with religion and tradition. He was a childhood friend of his fellow native, the eminent writer David Friszman. They delved into Torah and wisdom together, studying Talmud, Jewish law, language and science. He was a close friend to his educated and erudite friends, Reb Tovia Lipszicz and Reb Moshe Eiger of blessed memory. Together they formed a threefold strand [87], as they disseminated Torah, light and knowledge in our city.

After he married his cousin Sara the daughter of Reb Wolf Glicksman of blessed memory (in the year 5645 - 1885) [88], he opened a factory for silk ribbons, and earned a good livelihood. His Torah and wisdom did not become his profession, but rather remained his main delight for all his days. He dedicated all of his free time to Torah and literature.

Isuchar and Sara Szwarc [89]

He published many articles In "Hashachar", "Hamagid", "Magid Mishneh", "Hatzefirah" and other periodicals on historical and bibliographic topics. In these articles, he demonstrated a deep breadth of knowledge, as he shed light on books, their authors, their time period, their locale and their style. He signed with his real name, and under pseudonyms such as "Yam Shachor", "Shachor Tushiya", and others. He published an important historical survey on Tiberias, its settlement and its rabbis in the weekly

"HaMenora" that was published in Lodz (edited by Reb Moshe Helman). He published articles of research and bibliography on books about Torah, and he also published twelve historical articles in Yiddish under the name "Barimte Kinder" ("Eminent Children"), regarding the Marranos of Spain and Portugal. He also published articles and essays, on a reasonably regular basis, in the Yiddish newspaper "Lodzer Tagblat".

He maintained contact with great leaders of his generation. The poet Y. L. Gordon mentioned him in a positive light in his memoirs. Nachum Sokolow mentions him in his book "Ishim" ("Personalities") as a regular visitor at the literary parties that took place each Monday in Warsaw. The writer Reb Avraham Weicenfeld (author of "Sdeh Chitim" - "Wheat Fields") who lived for a period time in Zgierz, was among his friends. Visitors to his home included David Friszman, Yaakov Cohen, Binyamin Katzenelson ("Binyamini") and his son the poet Yitzchak Katzenelson, H. D. Nomberg (who was for a period of time the tutor of the older sons in his house), his relative the sculptor Chanoch Glicenstein, Nachum Sokolow, and others. The sage Reb Eliezer Tzvi Hakohen Zwiefel contacted him on his visit to Zgierz and corresponded with him by letter. Some of these letters were published in "Haolam" in 1939.

On his visits to St. Petersburg (today Leningrad [90]), he would visit Y. L. Gordon and also, lehavdil [91] also met the Russian priest Johan Kronshtedsky, an advisor to Czar Aleksander III (it was interesting to hear him tell of his impressions of his discussions and debates with the clergyman). He visited the home of the famous Polish writer Eliza Orzeszkowa, a righteous gentile who wrote about Jewish topics in her books, and related to the Jews with great admiration.

His rich library included thousands of valuable books and manuscripts, It is possible to say that it was one of the richest and largest in Poland. Szwarc used to lend books to sages and writers, such as Dr. A. Sh. Poznanski, Sh. P. Rabinowicz, etc. During the time of the Beilis blood libel trial (1913), Dr. Israelsohn, Brodsky's secretary (Brodsky being one of the wealthy men of Russia, who paid the legal fees for the trial) expressed his anguish about the fact that he was missing several books, particularly about the topic of Kabbala, that the anti-Semitic "expert" the priest Franeitis relied upon, as it were, in his accusations against Jews and Judaism. Reb Isuchar Szwarc made haste and promised that he would find for him any book that he was missing, and he fulfilled his promise. Dr. Israelsohn thanked him in public for this ("Hatzefirah" from the year 5673, 1913).

He not only collected books but also studied them day and night. The fruits of his thoughts were written in their margins: explanations, notes with Russian and Greek adages, and other pearls of wisdom and science that gave testimony to his all-encompassing body of knowledge. It was not for naught that he was referred to as "a living encyclopedia". Many secret storehouses were bound up in his closed closet, which could shed light on many issues regarding the Haskalah era, memories of the renaissance of the national idea, etc. It is too bad that this precious storehouse was destroyed by the vandals of the 20th century, for there is no replacement.

Isuchar Szwarc was friendly with different Jewish circles, both in Zgierz and outside of it. He cultivated friendly relationships with the rabbis and Hassidim of Zgierz. Reb Moshe Helman writes in his memoirs (still in manuscript form) that he was once present during a visit in the year 5648 (1888) of Reb Isuchar to the home of Rabbi Eliahu Chaim Meizel of holy blessed memory, the rabbi of Lodz, and the rabbi greeted him with a kiss on the face.

He further relates in his memoirs that, once a month, Reb Isuchar Szwarc would travel to Lodz to join a circle of Maskilim. Once a month, that circle would also meet in his home in Zgierz, and occupy themselves with Torah thoughts and research. The chief spokesman in that circle was, of course, Reb Isuchar Szwarc, who was able to walk comfortably among the old and the new, among life in accordance with the Code of Jewish Law and in the spirit of Haskalah, that is to say, with classical humanistic tolerance.

Mr. Helman relates that during one of these meetings in Zgierz, it was decided to send a delegation to Warsaw to the wedding of David Friszman, and to give him a gift of valuable silver vessels worth approximately 1,000 Rubles. Of course, one of the members of this delegation was Reb Isuchar Szwarc. David Friszman writes the following in his thank you note of 1903: "-- -- -and say to Y. M. Szwarc that I received the letter that accompanied the gift with a great deal of pleasure, and I recognized it as the work of his hands. It is clear to me that this man realized, as he states, that Lodz takes pride in me, and indeed, I can state the opposite with full sincerity, that I take pride in Lodz, and I am proud of it. For at the end, we did not see any deeds such as this in any city other than Lodz, which is the first city to us, and which is a sign to others. Peace and blessings to the friend of my youth, to Szwarc."

Already from the time of his youth, Reb Isuchar Szwarc was a loyal member of Chovevei Zion. He already merited to be accepted as a member of Bnei Moshe, which was established by Echad Ha-Am (he appears in the list of Yehuda Appel, # 1942), and he took pride in it for his entire life. When Zionism arose, he immediately joined its ranks. He was chosen as a delegate to Zionist Congresses in London and Vienna prior to World War I, and he participated in every effort on behalf of the people and the Land.

His personality was a pleasing combination of an old type Halachic Jew and a modern communal activist. He was noble in his virtues, good natured, loved by the public with a distinguished appearance and a splendid visage, which inspired respect and love in all those with whom he came in contact.

He always held a chief position in our city, as a communal leader, as the head of public institutions, as the head of the Zionist organization, and a member of the town council (from 1928 until the outbreak of the war, he served as head of the "Lawnik" division), etc.

On the occasion of his eightieth birthday (in the year 5699 - 1939) the Jewish press all over Poland and also in the Land published articles in his honor, including his photograph. He was honored with the title of Honorary President of the community of Zgierz. For all his life, he desired to make aliya to the Land, but he never merited doing so.

Reb Isuchar Szwarc had five sons and also five daughters [92]: the eldest is the engineer Shmuel Schwartz, who is famous for his activities regarding the Marranos of Portugal and his research into their lives and history; Hersz Ber Szwarc who lived in Lodz; Simcha Szwarc, and engineer who made aliya and died in the Land; the sculptor Marek Szwarc who lived in Paris; and Dr. Aleksander Szwarc, a chemist who today lives in Montreal, Canada. His daughters were Miriam (Manya), who made aliya at age 25, got married and settled in Tel Aviv, and died of typhus a few months later; Tzipora who also made aliya with her husband, the well-known Zionist activist Reb Yechiel Frenkel of Radom who stood at the helm of the veteran Zionist in the Land; and his daughter of his old age Zosia, the wife of the engineer K. Lewi, also from Radom, who perished in the Holocaust with her child.

Destruction came upon the Jews of Zgierz towards the end of his life, with the invasion of Poland by the German army. The Nazi murderers had no mercy upon his home. They pillaged his property, including his one-of-a-kind valuable books and manuscripts, into which he poured all of his energies. When he rose up to defend his library, and all of his pleas had no influence upon the hearts of the enemy, as they pillaged and burnt his library - he collapsed and died of a heart attack. According to the reports that we received, the Red Cross took care of his burial, since there were no available members of the Chevra Kadisha. Nobody from the town came to pay him his final respects. This was on account of the expulsion, for the expulsion of the Jews of Zgierz from the city took place that very day.

Reb Isuchar Moshe Szwarc died on 14th of Tevet 5700 (December 26th, 1939). He was 81 years old when he died. He was one of the earliest residents of Zgierz, and also the last one that stood on guard of its flock until the bitter end. May his soul be bound in the bonds of eternal life.

Some One in the City
(Isuchar Szwarc - as I remember him)

Reb Isuchar Moshe Szwarc was one of the most prominent personalities in our city, and his popularity, his radiant personality grew into the frame of a representative patriarchal family portrait, which his children witnessed and portrayed.

Reb Isuchar Szwarc was the pride and gem of Jewish Zgierz [93]. He was respected and held in esteem by all segments of the Jewish population. This was not only the case with Jews - the Christian population, especially of the older generation, respected him. For many years, he was the only Jewish lawnik - and later also a councilor - on the Zgierz magistrate; where with his high level of intelligence and rich body of general knowledge he was often drawn into involvement with joyous and cultural events in the city. He was, especially in the early years, the head of the standing group of representatives of the Jewish community to various official civic enterprises, particularly for Polish nationalist government celebrations. He often served as the representative along with the rabbi. Both represented the Jewish community of Zgierz with dignity, wearing silk top hats. Also in times of distress and threatening danger, he bravely was the representative to intercede for the good of the wronged Jewish minority.

Isuchar Szwarc as a delegate to the Zionist Congress [94]

In the 1850s, when the first rabbi of Zgierz, Rabbi Shalom Hersz Hakohen of blessed memory, occupied the rabbinical seat, Zgierz became known as a place of Torah and Hassidism in Poland. In the 1870s, after the two well-known Maskilim who were scholars and deeply knowledgeable about Judaica - Reb Avraham Yaakov Weicenfeld of Krakow and Reb Tovia Lipszicz from Kovno - settled in Zgierz, the first kernels of Haskalah began to be appear in Zgierz, and a fruitful field for their pioneering cultural work. A recognizable group of the more progressive and intelligent young people formed who diligently and thirstily studied the ways of education and Haskalah. One of the first of these - together with his friend David Friszman, a student of the old rabbinical judge Rabbi Moshe Bendet -was Isuchar Szwarc. Due to his deep level of knowledge and broad Jewish conception, and the rich baggage of general world images that he had acquired by that time, he became recognized as an important, creative factor in the community. He became the third element of the threefold strand that worked for and sowed the basis of the intellectual environment for the Jewish nationalistic renaissance idea in our city.

With respect to his important service for the Jewish community, it is necessary to especially mention his devoted and tireless work for the spreading and popularizing of the Hebrew language and culture among the youth of Zgierz, and his publicity of the idea of Chovevei Zion at every occasion. Together with his older friends, the aforementioned Reb Avraham Yaakov Weicenfeld and Reb Tovia Lipszicz, he was the most active and important factor in the establishment of the fundamentals of modern Zionism in Zgierz. Firstly, with his bringing of the well-known Maskil and Hebrew writer Reb Binyamin Katzenelson from Warsaw to open and run the first "Cheder Metukan" [95] in the city, he began a new era in the Zgierz Jewish nationalist educational style. Zgierz was known in Poland not only for its "Torah and business", but also for its nationalistic Zionist intelligentsia as well as a center of Haskalah.

The dignified elder (and we remember his as a tall, thin, stately elder) who was known in the Jewish world as a Torah scholar and a Maskil, as a scholar and a commentator, as a writer and a bibliographer, also became, with the passage of time, a dedicated communal activist, and for many years was the elected communal leader. He was the chairman of the "Agudat Hatzionim" ("Union of Zionists") for many years, and was also the "leader" of all of the Zionist events. He was an eminent representative to all of the recognized humanitarian and social institutions in the city.

His large, two-story, brick house on Strykowska and Krotka Streets, which was built by his father Hersz Ber Szwarc - who himself was a determined fighter against the "quarter settling" during the first half of the 1800s [96] - was a veritable gathering place of scholars. With his famous library, containing a large Judaica section, his house was a serious cultural center for the Hebrew-Jewish literary world and Jewish students. Isuchar Szwarc himself was a bibliophile by nature in accordance with the finest definition of the term. It was a veritable pleasure to see him in his large library room, as he caressed each book that he took off the shelves with the tenderness of water.

His characteristic image, his fine mannerism, his majestic, measured gait, all elicited notice. People would look at him - Reb Isuchar Szwarc! This harmonized wonderfully with his natural, sincere modesty and populist simplicity. If a passerby greeted him with a "good morning", he would bow and answer with a grateful smile. He would often stop a child that he encountered and ask him who he is, to whom does he belong, where does he study - and parted from him with a caress on the head... he was a true father to all in the city, and his heart was full with love of his fellow Jew. I still remember with certainty who of us (alas, alas, very few of us can still remember...) how he would often turn to us, the young youth of Zion, with an enlightening discussion or similar conversation, and he would began with the call "Children!" - in the manner of a fatherly educator...

Isuchar Szwarc with his in-law Sh. Barabash at the Zionist Congress in Vienna, 1913 [97]

Reb Isuchar Szwarc was also an exquisite raconteur, and his ordinary conversations, spiced with words, quotes, adages from our sages, and anecdotes, left a deep impression, and were literally like an oral tradition to his various young listeners... Therefore, it is no news that his reports on the Zionist congresses, in which he took part as a delegate, always elicited great interest in Jewish social circles, and simultaneously blew a fresh breath of life into the Zionist groups. I use the term "reports", however, these were really impressions and reflections upon greater and more intellectual experiences. His incomparable encounters and discussions with leading personalities of nationalistic Judaism, and his personal contacts with the ideologues and guides of the world Zionist organization, imparted a special significance and importance to his speeches and deeds, which left a strong and favorable impression upon those gathered together.

His seventieth birthday (in the year 1929) was celebrated in Jewish Zgierz in a valuable and positive manner: with a solemn reception organized in the large "Lutnia" movie theater in honor of the renowned Zionist activist and political leader of Polish Jewry, Sejm deputy Yitzchak Grynbaum - on his visit to Zgierz. The participants who mainly included the city notables and national-social activists - decided, through a special elected committee, to inscribe the "Zionist elder" of Zgierz, Reb Isuchar Moshe Szwarc, in the "Golden Book" [98]. As well, his closest friend, the late Zionist activist Reb Tovia Lipszicz, was inscribed in the "Golden Book" on that occasion (as described in the "Lodzer Tagblat", December 18, 1929).

Unfortunately, in his later years, he did not have a great deal of contentment. In particular, the death of his beloved and dear life partner Sarahshe, the exemplary wife and mother, of whom even age could not efface her prior beauty and refined grace, had such a great effect upon him that he withdrew from all of his societal work and sought solitude and consolation in the books of his library. One could also see him going for a walk from time to time, resting on his cane, on the way to the rabbi's home. There, with his closest friend the scholar Rabbi Shlomo Leib Hakohen, he attempted to rediscover his spiritual balance through their conversations on religion and philosophy.

On the tragic winter day of the expulsion from Zgierz (15th Tevet 5600 - December 27, 1939), when over 5,000 Jews were thrown out of their homes with death and destruction -the great Jew and dignified resident of Zgierz, Reb Isuchar Moshe the son of Hersz Ber Szwarc of blessed memory, was killed, or expired from fright. It is not for us to determine the supernatural equations of those bizarre days of confusion. However, this is clear: he was the last Jew of Zgierz who was buried in the holy earth of the generations old cemetery of his community, with which he was bonded with thousands of bonds. Indeed, he merited having a Jewish burial. Even this is a consolation...

In those dark days, together with the covering of the ground over the grave of Reb Isuchar Moshe Szwarc, the tragic end of the glorious and effervescent history of Zgierz Jewry arrived. How fateful and symbolic... May his soul be bound in the bonds of eternal life.

By Vove Fisher of Tel Aviv

Isuchar Szwarc, drawn by Henry Glicenstein [99]

Song about my Grandfather, Isucher Schwartz of Zgierz by Czajka

(Izabela Gelbard) [100]

{Note from translator: At this point, there is a footnote in the text with a biographical note. There is a Yiddish and Hebrew version, both with different details. They contradict as to the relationship of Gelbard to Isuchar Szwarc. Mary Seeman points out that the Hebrew version is correct - Izabela Gelbard was the great niece of Isuchar Szwarc, not the granddaughter. She is the granddaughter of Isuchar's half brother.}

{Yiddish}
Izabela Gelbard (pen name: Czajka) is a granddaughter of the renowned activist and cultural leader of Zgierz Isuchar Szwarc. She was active in the partisan movement in Poland during the Second World War. She was also the author of several books (in the Polish language), which relate, among other things, to the era of destruction. They were published in Polish under the pen name Czajka. (Related by Aryeh Ben-Menachem.)
{Hebrew}
Izabela (Bella) Gelbard, later Stachowicz (from her second husband) was the daughter of the nephew of Isuchar Szwarc, that is to say, her grandfather was the brother of Isuchar Szwarc. Her first husband was Jerzy Gelbard, an architect by profession. She was a graduate of the academy of arts of Paris. During the Holocaust, she lived in the Otwock ghetto near Warsaw. At the time of the liquidation of the ghetto, she managed to escape and join a group of partisans. Later she joined the Polish army. The name Czajka was her pseudonym during her time in the underground. She published 11 books, including
an anthology called "Songs of the Ghetto". She died in Warsaw in 1969. (Related by Aryeh Ben-Menachem.)

It was He, my grandfather Isuchar, who stood by the side of Moses at that time.
When Moses smote the rock and commanded: "Let the water come forth!"
It was He, together with Jacob, who climbed the rungs of the ladder that reached to the heavens,
Protected from the fate of Sodom, free of sin - G-d kept him away from sin.
He wandered through the pages of the Bible for a thousand years
When He was lost in the desert - the moon led him through the desert night!
When He was hungry - the manna nourished him, and he pleaded towards the ruddy desert heavens:
"Please send us in your mercy, oh Eternal Creator, our daily morsel of bread!"

He forever had these words engraved as prayers in his heart -He, my
grandfather - Isucher Szwarc, the eternal Jew from Zgierz
 Our King David sang his Psalms with a melody for him,
 Waiting for grandfather's praises, for is there enough grace present in those
verses?
And he, grandfather? - His gaze towards heaven, his arms outstretched:
- My King, venerate the eternal God in your heart, rather than in half uttered
words."

{Note from translator: the following section was not in the Yiddish translation in the Yizkor
book, but was provided in

Mary Seeman's translation.}

It was he, my grandfather, who secretly watched Joseph, the son of his late
years
When he in silvery consecration bent his face over the water
Night darkened with envy. The young and victorious
Form of his son he fixed with a penetrating eye:
"A charmed narcissus believes in his beauty
Vanity of vanities- in the passage of a wave
They lose that which is immortal - nothing will save them.

{Note from translator: the Yizkor book provided translation resumes here.
[101]:

... And I - His granddaughter, today sing this song of love, bearing my
grandfather's fate
My body - with his bones is bound, and bonded with his Jewish blood;
My origin is from his thoughts, and I wish it would remain so forever
No storm will break me, and no wide horde will trample me.
Flames of fire will not scorch me, floods of water will not drown me,
Neither murder, nor war, nor burning pillars of fire -
I will be completely protected from slaughter, and withstand the storm like a
mountain;
Not one hair from my head will fall to the ground,
I will overcome everything, like the beams of the first light.
For My grandfather, with his might, mandated me to live.
For me, his bright shadow is like the illumination of an elder prophet
I will bear his great and immortal heart in my bosom
The heart of my grandfather from Zgierz - Isuchar Szwarc.

And now I want to praise and sing to Zgierz, the cradle of my holy forebears
The simple marketplace, lined with white gutters of limestone:
In springtime - the leaves of the chestnut trees softly cling to the glittering panes,
I wish to laud the crooked houses and also the weary fences.

The following two lines are not in the Yiddish translation in the Yizkor book,
but were provided in Mary Seeman's translation.}
Bearded goats amble along the narrow streets
The wind ruffles their beards, they point at the sky with their horns.
{Note from translator: The Yizkor book translation resumes here.}
It is Friday evening- The Sabbath. You can see through the windows silver candlesticks and burning candles.
On the tables - white bearded goats amble along the narrow streets.
tablecloths, bedecked with the fish, challas, and the wine - it sparkles: You can still hear the prayer, and the Sabbath Kiddush still shivers in the still alleys. [102]
Why, with tears in my eyes, do I now mention the world that is no longer?
Where lies the dark secret of my grieving heartfelt lament?
Long ago, long ago, I lost my religious belief
Yet - my heart is full of that world, which was holy and Jewish.

In grandfather's room- Books, books right up to the ceiling
Purple hyacinths blooming from the salon run over the wall;
In the day - white doves, pigeons knocking into the windows
For grandfather scattered little seeds from his outstretched hands.
I still see him still - his holy hands, straight like the pages of a book
Pouring out the little seeds with humility and zeal.
Later -he sits at his writing desk in order to delve into Torah,
Old ledgers, and books full of wisdom , knowledge, and depth.
In solitude, his glowing thoughts wander over starry paths.
He wants to illuminate the haze, to pierce the darkness of black eras,
He is still young, in old age, for everything he searches for a bright solution -
For the spider web of years and time has no control over him.
Day in and day out, he paces through the alleys of Zgierz,
As if fulfilling a holy command, he visits relatives daily -
The distant and the close, in the marketplace of Zgierz. In the vault of things
gone by He sits with us for a long time, the times whisper: "See, without the

363

evil eye, how young he is,

Oh Dear Father [103], grant him in Your mercy long and healthy years."

They bow their heads in prayer - the relatives and neighbors, all pious, utter:

"See, he goes, Isucher Szwarc!" - we still hear the flowing of their lips about.

-- -- -- -- -- -- -- -- -- -- -- -- -- [104]

Until the burning Satan casts his net of murder and death upon the earth, [105]

On all of the Jewish cities, on every settlement, every town that has a prayer hall (kloiz);

A decree of fire and hatred falls, and kith and kin are cut off -

And now only in cinders fly about - my grandfather's tiny, black letters.

From Polish: Yeshayahu Spiegel.

Shmuel Schwartz of blessed memory
The Researcher of the History of the Marranos of Portugal

Shmuel Schwartz. *[106]*

Shmuel Schwartz was born in Zgierz to his father Isuchar Moshe Szwarc and his mother Sara the daughter of Zeev Glicksman. He received a traditional education, studying in cheder, and later on in a modern school that

364

was based upon Torah and haskalah - "LeTorah VelaTeudah", which was located in Lodz and was under the direction of the scholar and scribe Chaim Yaakov Kremer. During his childhood, Shmuel displayed excellent capabilities, and his father, who realized that he was gifted, sent him to Paris to complete his studies, even though the separation from his son was difficult.

After he finished high school, he entered a polytechnic institute, and graduated with an engineering degree. He then entered a specialized scientific university in the faculty of mountain mining. Among his friends in this study hall was the son of the "renowned philanthropist" James Rothschild, who maintained a friendship with him afterwards.

After he finished his studies as a mountain engineer, he went to practice his field of mining mountains in Monta Rosa on the Italian border, and later in Spain and eastern Africa, where he worked in gold mining. His professional work and research are published in several important works.

He was appointed as a member of the Scientific Academy of Madrid on account of his scientific work. He lived in Spain for a few years, and maintained his connection with Paris, where he spent most of the years of his youth.

In 1914, he married the eldest daughter of the renowned banker in Odessa, Shmuel Barabash, one of the earliest Chovevei Zion activists. He was the treasurer of the Odessa committee, and one of the directors of the treasury for Jewish settlement (Colonial Bank) based in London. He was also one of the founders of the Yeshiva in Odessa, along with the poet Chaim Nachman Bialik and others. In this Yeshiva, one of the Talmud lecturers was Rabbi Chaim Chernovitz ("The Young Rabbi"). The matchmakers were Nachum Sokolow and M. Spektor of Warsaw, and the first meeting of the in-laws, the matchmakers, and the bride and groom took place during the eleventh Zionist Congress in Vienna.

The father-in-law Shmuel Barabash promised to give his daughter a dowry of 50,000 rubles, but when he saw the groom speak a clear Hebrew as a living language (which was a very rare thing), he added another 25,000 rubles to the dowry.

This was the year of the outbreak of the world war, and the young couple, who had traveled to honeymoon in the countries of Europe were cut off on their journey in Lisbon, the capital of Portugal, and they remained there. Obviously, all of their money was lost.

In their difficult straits, being trapped in a foreign country, cut off from their city and their country, alone, without a coin in their pockets to maintain themselves, they decided to sell the jewelry of the young woman and use the money to engage in the tin business, a metal that was found in great quantities in Portugal. The business succeeded, and they founded a shareholder-based company with the assistance of well-to-do people in Portugal and England, for the purpose of salvaging the local tin mining industry. The company, which was under the directorship of Shmuel Schwartz, developed well, and took a prominent place among the well-known economic enterprises of Portugal. His rich father-in-law Shmuel Barabash died in the interim in Odessa of hunger and famine, after the Bolsheviks impoverished him and made an example of him as an empty vessel.

Even though Shmuel Schwartz was extremely involved in his professional business, such as salvaging the mining of mountains, and the mining of tin and other metals, his heart was always alert to everything that took place in the Jewish Diaspora, and he dedicated himself full heartedly to helping the poor of his people in every manner possible.

During his travels throughout the Pyrenean Peninsula, Spain and Portugal, the noble images of the Jewish greats of "Golden Age" of Spanish and Portuguese Jewry arose before the eyes of his spirit. He researched the roots and the successors of this Diaspora, and put together a rich amount of historical material regarding the Marranos of Portugal. His book "The Neo Christians in Portugal in the Twentieth Century" (Lisbon, 1925), was translated into all European languages. It was translated into Hebrew by his brother-in-law Yechiel Frenkel in the "Hayom" newspaper of Warsaw.

It was an accepted belief that the remnants of the Marranos had already died out, for they had assimilated among the gentiles. However, during his business travels that took him through the length and breadth of Portugal, Sh. Schwartz came into contact with many Marranos. He examined them carefully and discovered their Jewish spark. His knowledge of languages allowed him to find the key to their closed hearts and to the secret of their double lives, even though this could not be done publicly, due to the fear that had been implanted in them from generation to generation, and the fear of the inquisition that ruled over their conscious. Step by step, with caution, he won their hearts, until they revealed to him their deep seated secrets, which were only clear to themselves in part, for they lived in a spiritual fog.

The stories of how he uncovered Marranos in the mountain mining area of Da-Astrala, as well as in Belmonti, Covilha, Faro, Pondision, Castelo, Branco [107], and in many other places, how he won their friendship to the point where they allowed him to study their secret texts, are most fascinating. He succeeded in collecting an entire anthology of manuscripts of their prayers, in the Spanish and Portuguese languages. He also wrote down the prayers that had been transmitted to them orally as a legacy from their parents and grandparents.

Sh. Schwartz worked hard for the ingathering of the Dispersed of the Jews. He provided two explanations of the term "Marranos". One was, in accordance to his view, given to the Marranos by the Jews, since they loathed pork, which is called "Maran" in Spanish. The second explanation comes from philologist Isuchar Moshe Szwarc, who saw in the name "Maran" a corruption of the Hebrew expression "Mareh Ayin", that is to say, that they were Christians only with regard to external appearance

In his latter days, he published his book of translation "Song of Songs" [108] that completed his research in a praiseworthy manner. Prior to this, he published, in addition to the book that was mentioned above, scientific treatises on "The Archeology of Minerals", "The Judeo

Portuguese Museum of the City of Tomar", an anthology on the topic of anti-Semitism, and other works on Jewish topics. In his last days, he planned to publish a set of books on the history of the modern Sephardic Hebrew community of Lisbon, and he did not know if he would be able to complete this work during his lifetime. In 1952, Sh. Schwartz published a series of articles on Portuguese Jewry in the Yiddish newspapers "Der Tag", and "Forward" of New York.

Sh. Schwartz saw himself as the redeemer of his Marrano brethren. For this reason, when he was in the city of Tomar close to Lisbon, and he found the ancient synagogue there, the only synagogue from the period prior to the expulsion, he purchased it, and transferred it as a gift to the Portuguese government on the condition that a Jewish museum be established there.

The Rabbi of Zgierz, who recognized and honored his activities on behalf of the nation, gave him his portrait as a symbol of thanks and appreciation.

The following is written on the portrait: "To my friend the Engineer Reb Shmuel Schwartz, the son of my friend Reb Isuchar Szwarc. A souvenir with love. I take pride in this unique individual - a native of my city of Zgierz, who was sent by Divine providence to the country of Portugal to return the dispersed Spanish Marranos to their foundation rock. Shlomo Yehuda Leib HaKohen, the Rabbi of Zgierz."

Sh. Schwartz desired to make aliya to the Land with his entire family, and he even publicized this desire. However, he took ill suddenly and did not recover. He died on 28th Sivan 5613 (June 11, 1953), and was gathered unto his people and buried there, prior to actualizing his desire.

The following was stated at his eulogy: "This man is fitting to be remembered forever in the heart of the nation".

From sources given by A. Y. Brzezinski [109] and other sources.

The Shapira Family
Reb Yosef Hersz Kahana Shapira of blessed memory

Reb Yosef Hersz Shapira set up his household in Zgierz during the 1850s, after he left the city of Aleksander. He was a large-scale forestry merchant. All of the forests between Zgierz and Lodz belonged to him. He was a Hassid of the Rebbes of Kotzk, Aleksander, and Gur.

On one occasion, he mentioned his difficult means of livelihood to the Rebbe, Reb Henech of Aleksander. The Rebbe said to him: "It is said of you that you earn on occasion 100,000 Karvonim [110] at one time, and you are still complaining about lack of livelihood?" Reb Yosef Hersz answered him:

"This is indeed the truth, but what can I do if the small change is not available in my hands for my daily sustenance?"... As he was seated around the holy table that Sabbath, the Rebbe began: "I have heard from a Cohen of good lineage that if one earns a large sum of money at one time - even though one's fortune continues to grow - this is not considered sustenance. From this it is possible to learn that we do not do good deeds for the reward, but rather so that the fortune should continue to grow"...

**On the left, Rivka Shapira, the daughter of Rafael Yaakov
On the right, Avraham Yitzchak Shapira**

During the time of the Polish revolt ("Powstania") against the Russian government in the year 1863 (5623), they imprisoned Reb Yosef Tzvi on the pretext that he granted some of his money to the government in order to put down the revolt. They sentenced him to death by hanging. They erected a gallows in the old marketplace of Zgierz and prepared to hang Reb Yosef Tzvi. His granddaughter Hena Glicka accompanied him with tears to the place of execution. At the last moment, the priest of Zgierz came and testified that Reb Yosef Tzvi was forced to give over his money to the government against his will, and thus was he saved from death.

Reb Yosef died on the day after Yom Kippur of the year 5639 (1878). Since he built the canopy over the grave of the elder Rebbe, Reb Shalom Tzvi HaKohen of holy blessed memory with his own money, he merited to be buried next to him.

His children were: Reb Rafael Yaakov, Roiza Eidel the wife of Reb Sender Landau of Krakow, as well as three other sons and two other daughters. Reb Sender Landau was a communal activist, and also the trustee of the Chevra Kadisha (Burial Society). He was buried next to the grave of his father-in-law.

369

The children of Reb Sender Landau were expelled from Zgierz to Austria by the Russian authorities, since they were foreign citizens. The exiles included the Hassidic writer Reb Aharon Markus of blessed memory, the author of the book "Hassidism". He had been living in Zgierz at that time. The great-granddaughter of Reb Sender Landau is the wife of the Admor Reb Yisrael Alter of Gur, may he live long, of Jerusalem.

Reb Rafael Yaakov Shapira of blessed memory

Reb Rafael Yaakov was the expert student of Reb Henech of Aleksander, until the time that the latter was coronated as Admor. His father Reb Yosef Hersz once asked Reb Henech how his son was advancing in his studies, and he answered: "He is absorbing it thoroughly".

Reb Rafael Yaakov was very distraught over the termination of his studies with his Rebbe. When he traveled after the death of the Rebbe to supplicate over his grave, he did not leave a note, in the manner of Hassidim. He said, "I feel myself at home with him, and therefore I do not leave a note at the grave."

A strange event took place to Reb Rafael Yaakov on May 19th, 1894. When he was in Warsaw, he passed in front of the national bank, and due to his sensitivity, he hid one of his sidelocks (peyos) under his hat. (At that time, the Russians punished people with long peyos). A Russian policeman caught him in his disgrace, and fined him five rubles. In the receipt, it was written: "The sum of five rubles was received from Rafael Yaakov Shapiro for the wearing of one peyah (sidelock)"….

Reb Rafael Yaakov used to gather all of the guests and wanderers who remained in the shtibel on Sabbaths into his home, and who were not invited to the homes of other Hassidim for reasons of cleanliness, etc. He would provide them food and drink from all the good of his home.

It is related that in the week that he married off his son, Yosef Hersz, to the daughter of the Radziner Hassid, he opened an iron vault in front of his son and said to him: "Take as much as you want, on the condition that you do not turn to another Rebbe"…

A receipt for the payment of a fine for the bearing of peyos (1894)

Reb Rafael Yaakov died on the 28th of Shvat 5661 (1901) and was buried next to his father Reb Yosef Hersz and his brother-in-law Reb Sender Landau. Due to the shortage of space, his grave is found the distance of 1/2 meter from those two graves. (Had he died in the summer said the men of the Chevra Kadisha - it would have been impossible to bury him between them.)

In exchange for the price of the grave, the Shapira family paid for the first legal eruv (Sabbath boundary) [111]. The arranging of the eruv cost several hundred rubles, and was attached to the telephone wires (of course, with the help of payments to the authorities).

His wife, Rivka Shapira, was known as Roitsha Di Shpirita [112] (the beautiful) [113]. Like her husband, she also excelled at the providing for guests (Hachnasat Orchim), and in the days before Zgierz had a restaurant, wayfarers knew that they would receive good meals at the home of "The Shpirita", without payment, of course. There were guests who got annoyed and pushed her to accept payment, but "The Shpirita" was stubborn, and it was impossible to convince her otherwise.

She bore fifteen children. Their sons include Reb Yosef Hersz, Reb Moshe, and Reb Avraham Yitzchak Shapira. May their memories be blessed.

The Eiger Family
By Engineer Avraham Eiger
(Events from home)

The life and youthful years of my father Reb Moshe Tzvi (Hersh) Eiger of blessed memory were bound up with the life of his uncle Reb Yossel Rubensztejn and his entire family.

Moshe Eiger and his wife Miriam

Moshe Eiger was born in Zgierz on July 18, 1859 (5619). His father Reb Eliezer, who had rabbinical ordination and should have become a rabbi, died young during the time of the cholera epidemic. His mother Zissele and her brother Yossel Rubensztejn brought up Moshele. Our entire family was located in two houses on the Jewish street: the Wagmans, the Lesmans, and the Grynfarbs. Their aunt also lived there, the widow Freida Rachel, a woman of valor who managed a textile manufacturing business. In those times, when many German hand weavers came to Zgierz, there were many small-scale manufacturers from Silesia there, and Aunt Freida Rachel would purchase merchandise for her business from them. The German manufacturers lived mainly on the following streets: Hernstrasse,

Glukstrasse, and others. Jews had access only until the "Szlaban" (city gate). Past that was already German "domain". The German families who later became well known lived there: Ramish, Achert, Binder, Krusche, Lorenz, Mierhoff, Bretshneider, Ernst, and others.

Yossele Rubensztejn was the first in Zgierz to set up two hand workshops with the help of a German who would purchase chemical materials from the Wagman's shop. That same German also informed him about all of the goings on of the weavers' guild, and also familiarized him with the appropriate literature. Rubensztejn quickly became fluent in the German language, and similarly learned the trade thoroughly. He was even in contact with Jewish manufacturers in the Sudeten [114], and became known as a specialist in the textile business. People came to him not only from the nearby cities of Lodz, Ozorkow and other towns, but also from Lithuania, Podolia and other such places. The following master weavers who later became well known were his students: Busak, Heller, Aronson, Pruszinowski, Epsztejn, Sawelson, Horowicz, Gold and others. His was the first Jewish textile school in the region. He took on students for a two-year training period, with full support, with which his wife Malkale was involved. His students included, aside from the aforementioned, his sons Meir and Leizer and his sons-in-law Avraham Zylberszacz and Leizer Sztachelberg, as well as Moshel Eiger.

Moshe Eiger, possessing a certificate from Rubensztejn, was employed as a designer in one of the largest Jewish factories in Lodz, the "Moshe Aharon Wiener" firm. He was 17 years old when he obtained this post, and he quickly became known as a first-class tradesman. He was 22 years old when he married his cousin Miriam. She was a pretty, educated woman who was taught by her father David Fuerszter. David Fuerszter was called the Kaminsker Landowner (Poretz), for he served as an administrator for the best of the Kaminsker and Radomsker Poretzes. His children were educated in the religious spirit, but also with Polish culture. He himself even took part in the Polish uprising in the year 1863, and later was rescued by his peasants. Miriam's older sisters were Mrs. Hendeles, Mrs. Bornsztejn (her husband David Bornsztejn was from Tomaszow) and Mrs. Hamburger from Sosnowiec.

In Zgierz, on account of the work and business relations with the Germans, Jews were mainly educated in the German language, and also in Russian. This was a time when a significant portion of the Poles had almost completely become Germanized, and even took German woman for wives, as did Rudowski, Maczewski (of the beer brewery), Pawinski, Pienkowski and others, who educated their children in the German spirit. These were the original root of the later "Folks German" in Zgierz, as in all of Poland.

After their wedding, Moshe and Miriam Eiger lived in Lodz. However, after an unfortunate fall by their first child, Leizer, who fell from the third floor of the house in which they lived -Moshe Eiger, out of great agony and pain, resigned from his position at Wiener's and returned to his hometown of Zgierz in order to be among his family.

There, he began to work with his own hands and accounts, but fortune did not favor him. At that time, a very honorable commissar lived in Zgierz, Reb Shlomo Sirkes, who came from Podolia. They merged professionally, in the entrepreneurial spirit, with honesty and dedication, and formed the firm "Sirkes and Eiger". The firm grew in a short period of time and they became wealthy. The firm purchased the factory of Philip Margolies in the New Market, and expanded it. It later became the largest Jewish factory in Zgierz, and the firm "Sirkes and Eiger" became famous for its products not only in Poland, but also in the far of lands of Russia of that era.

Now that his existence was secured, Moshel Eiger again found time to occupy himself with his favorite - Hebrew language and literature. Aside from his wide ranging correspondence with the Hebrew writers of that era in Odessa, Petersburg and other places, he himself took to writing and publishing several articles in the Hebrew periodicals. He became friendly with the Maskil who was older than he, Reb Tovia Lifszitz, as well as with Isuchar Szwarc. The three of them were the leaders of the Haskalah and national emancipation in the Zgierz community. In truth, it did not go so straight and smoothly, for the largest segment of the youth came from Hassidic homes, where the tendency toward literacy and knowledge was not even brought to the mouth. Those three arranged get-togethers on Sabbath evenings - "Sabbath discussions", in which a significant portion of the youth participated, paid attention, and were enriched in Torah and in knowledge. These get-togethers took place every Sabbath in the homes of one of these three Maskilim. At the beginning, David Friszman used to take part, until he moved to Warsaw.

To their activities, one must also ascribe the bringing to Zgierz of the Hebrew writer and Maskil Reb Binyamin Katzenelson (father of Yitzchak Katzenelson) who opened a Modern Cheder in Zgierz, which utilized the

"Hebrew in Hebrew" teaching style for Bible and also for higher education. The curriculum consisted of Jewish subjects until noon, and secular subjects (Mathematics, Russian, etc.) in the afternoon, which were taught by H. Wachtel, the teacher of the public school. Among others, the following people studied at the Modern Cheder: Yaakov Kahan, Shmuel Szwarc, Aryeh (Leon) Lifszitz, Avraham Eiger, Weiss, Shlumiel, Fabian Grynberg. At that time, when most of the children from wealthy homes were educated in the assimilationist spirit or under the influence of the anti-Zionist "Assistance Association for German Jews" - the youth of Zgierz from the Jewish middle class congregated around the three aforementioned Zionist activists, through whom the Zionist idea was spread in an organized fashion (obviously discretely, since organized political activity was forbidden in Czarist times).

In the year 1898, the first Russian style business school was founded in Zgierz. As is known, Jews were accepted in Russian government schools based on specified quotas. The newly opened Zgierz business school had all of the rights of a government school, and Jews were accepted there without a quota. Therefore, Jews came there from all parts of European Russia. Only a few of those youth were from Zionist roots. The largest segment of them were Socialists. Even the former directors of that school, such as Siniawski and later Golowodski were left-leaning. Moshel Eiger used to arrange discussions with students in his house every Sabbath (we lived in Eberling's house and had two rooms in the courtyard for that purpose), but this as not very successful. The youth of the school belonged to P. P. S., Bund, S. D., and were not inclined toward Zionism. The activists who later became known, who received their education in the business school, included Czerniochow, Dr. Jakob Eicjner, Ajzensztadt, Weiss, Michel Grynberg, Bryn, Pacanowski and others, who already at that time had begun their work in the domain of the school.

Moshe Eiger was chosen as a delegate to the Second Zionist Congress in Basle in 1898. He gave a speech there.

He was also among the founders of the so-called "Eiger Association" (families who stemmed from Rabbi Akiva Eiger [115]). At the get-together in Berlin in 1913, Moshel Eiger gave a toast speech in Hebrew, which was well received by the 700 members of the Eiger family.

After the First World War, Eiger prepared to travel to the Land of Israel. However, he later gave up this plan (under the influence of Dr. Nordau, who believed that the Land of Israel requires "muscular Jews"). With his cooperation, the important manufacturer and Zionist, Wolf Reichert traveled from Zgierz to the Land of Israel in 1921. He was the director of the first completely automated textile factory of several Zgierz factories (among them was also the "Sirkes Brothers" firm).

In later years, after the death of his wife in 1930, Moshel Eiger moved to his daughter's home in Lodz. He continued to play an active role in Zionist institutions and the national funds (Keren Hayesod and Keren Kayemet) in Zgierz.

He published a collection of songs in Hebrew and Yiddish in 1913, called "Leben Lebat" (To the Son and the Daughter) (an anthology of songs by Moshe Tzvi Eiger). This provided a window into the soul of that great Jew Reb Moshe Tzvi Eiger.

His refined soul departed in 1935. He was buried in the Lodz cemetery near to his dear life partner Miriam.

May their souls be bound in the bonds of eternal life.

Engineer Avraham Eiger

Reb Moshel Eiger, the speaker at the 20th year anniversary celebration of the Maccabee group.

(Remark: I found the need to add to the "The Eiger Family" article a short family description and a letter from Karol Eiger. Translated and adapted by V. Fiszer.)

His children: Engineer Avraham Eiger of blessed memory; Dr. Salomon (Shlomo) Eiger of blessed memory - he was a member of the directors of "O.R.T.".

He was involved with the social Zionist path. He was killed in the Warsaw Ghetto. His wife Dr. Charlotta Eiger was murdered in Auschwitz;

Karol (Akiva) Eiger of blessed memory, a social activist. The founding and existence of the Maccabee Sporting organization in Zgierz is bound up with his name. He died in Tel Aviv; His daughter Rosalia Levenson-Eiger of blessed memory - murdered in Auschwitz;

His daughter Rota Eiger lives in America

Avraham Eiger of blessed memory

A few words about Avraham Eiger of blessed memory:

The writer of the article about his experiences, Engineer Avraham Eiger, was the oldest son of Reb Moshel Eiger. He was born on May 14, 1886 in

Zgierz. He studied in cheder, and later in the Modern Cheder of Reb Binyamin Katzenelson. In 1898, he moved from there to the newly founded business school where the Jewish students (who were also from Polish provincial cities and even from Lithuania) who enjoyed the liberal attitude toward them by the Judeophile director Golowocki. A. Eiger graduated from that school in 1905.

He traveled to Moscow in 1906 to attend the "Imperatorskaya Moskovskaya Technitsheskaya Utshilishtshe", from which he graduated in 1910 with a diploma as an engineer-technologist. He worked there as an operator in a textile business. He returned to Zgierz at the time of the outbreak of the First World War in 1914.

He went to Lodz in 1921, where he married Masha (Elania) Rozental, a daughter of the well-known Lodzer cloth manufacturer and social activist Yankel (Julius) Rozental. He came to Israel via Romania in 1942.

Avraham Eiger had a warm feeling for the Zgierz society, and later, for the Holocaust survivors. He also served for a certain time on the committee of the Organization of Zgierz Natives in Israel.

He died on June 21, 1970. May his memory be an honor.

The Industrialist - the Poet

Lines about the person of Reb Moshel Eiger of blessed memory
"When I thought about from where the spirit came to me to wade through verse, I remembered that the place is the factor, for Zgierz is a city that produces poets." (from his letter to Avraham Chaim Michelson)

Among the people who were graced with extra spirit, who spiced up the atmosphere of Zgierz and raised the honor of the city, one person excelled. He was short in stature but great in spirit, the well-known Zionist industrialist Reb Moshe Tzvi, known locally as Reb Moshel Eiger.

He was born in Zgierz in the year 5619 (July 18, 1859), and was orphaned from his father at a young age. His father Reb Eliezer Eiger, who was a candidate for the rabbinical seat of Zgierz, died in the cholera epidemic that ravaged through the country of Poland. The orphan Moshele was educated by his mother Zissele, under the supervision and guidance of his uncle, his mother's brother Reb Yossel Rubensztejn, who was a diligent man of action. He was the first one to set up a hand-run weaving machine in

Zgierz. He founded a school for textile studies, and served as a teacher and mentor for the expert weavers in Zgierz and the region.

Young Moshele, who was the sixth generation from his great-great-great-grandfather, the Rabbi of Posen Rabbi Akiva Eiger of holy blessed memory, grew up and was educated under the guidance of his uncle, who concerned himself especially with his spiritual education and his competence in Judaism and in secular knowledge. When he took note of his unique diligence and wonderful talents that were beyond his age, he decided also to teach him the textile business in his school.

As can be seen, the Eiger family was not only blessed with wisdom and Torah, but also with the knowledge and competence to succeed in matters of livelihood. Moshele quickly absorbed the field of weaving and textile creation. After his uncle gave him his professional diploma, he was appointed as an expert and fashioner in the well-known textile firm in Lodz "Moshe Aharon Wiener". He also married his cousin Miriam.

Several years later, Reb Moshel returned to Zgierz, with his name preceding him. He was already known as a first class expert in the textile industry. He then entered into partnership with one of the known textile professionals of the city, Reb Shlomo Sirkes. The well-known firm "Sirkes and Eiger" was founded, which was known throughout the world, and was the largest firm in Zgierz. His unique prominence was not only on account of his status within the textile industry that flourished in our city, and made Zgierz famous in the markets of Poland and wide Russia. He had unique characteristics that were stamped upon his spiritual personality that raised him to the heights and placed him in one line with the eminent personalities that lit up the horizon of the Jewish community of Zgierz, whose shine reached afar. He was interwoven with the threefold thread that included Tovia Lifszitz and Isuchar Szwarc, who raised the flag of the national Jewish revival movement in our city with strength and pride.

Reb Moshel Eiger exuded grace and mercy from his essence. As he was once described by I. Szwarc, Moshel was a lover of his fellow Jew on par with Reb Moshe Leib of Sasow. He not only had an "exemplary" personality in the narrow sense of the term, but his noble way of conduct displayed his aristocratic face as if through a lens. This was particularly true with respect to his personal relationships, for he enchanted and attracted the attention of everybody.

His mannerisms and interpersonal relationships set him up as an example for the public, who saw him as a splendid descendent of that Gaon and halachic decisor of Posen, whose portrait decorated the walls of the home of every Jew who was an enthusiast of Torah throughout Poland. His relations with people were generous, blessed and upright. He had on his office desk a small marble plaque on which was engraved the verse from the Book of Proverbs, "Anger rests in the bosom of fools", in order to protect himself so that he would not let down his guard during his hectic business dealings.

Indeed, Moshel Eiger was known as a scholar and wise man. The wonder was that during those years when his work machines worked without stop to expand the output of textile production in order to supply the merchandise needed for the hungry markets throughout the expanses of Russia; the weaving machines let out their exhaust day and night, and thousands of workers were hitched to machines to produce products - when the entire city was bustling with the great symphony of work, who could imagine that one of the great manufacturers of the city, short Reb Moshel Eiger, turned aside from his large-scale business to write poems and chapters of verse. He was a diligent manufacturer and also a poet, and this does not make sense. These two characteristics do not blend together from a logical, practical standpoint.

Yaakov Kahan relates to us in his memoirs (Haboker, January 23, 1953), the following from the year 5655 (1895):

"At the end of Kislev 5655, there were general exams in the upper classes of our school, and on one evening of Chanukah there was a festive concluding celebration of the oral exams in the presence of the invented parents. I recall that I was examined on Isaiah and on general and Russian history. I read Pushkin's ballad, "The Song of Oleg the Wise" by heart. My aunt sat beside my father, and both of their faces were beaming. I won the nicest prize: The Choicest Poems of Yehuda Halevi, published by "Achiasaf" in a splendid volume.

One moment remains in my memory from that evening. One of the parents of the students, of the Maskilim of the city, and incidentally a descendent of Rabbi Akiva Eiger, found it appropriate to compose a poem in honor of the event and to read it before the students after the conclusion of the exams. This poem was connected to historical memories of the holiday of Chanukah, and was composed for the younger generation."

Indeed, Reb Moshel Eiger wrote poems at every opportunity that presented itself -on the occasion of festivals, on memorial days, for communal and family celebrations, or for each New Year. These poems were written partly in Hebrew and partly in Yiddish. Some of them were a blend of the two languages, in the form of unruly art. Some of these poems were published in a small book in the year 5684 (1924) called: "To the Son and Daughter, a Collection of Poems by Moshe Tzvi Eiger". On the title page was the following dedication: "To my dear and precious son Avraham Eiger, this compilation is given as a memento from your father Moshe Tzvi Eiger, Lodz, 24 Nissan 5685."

We will bring down two poems from his poetic treasury, from which we can understand the soul of their author:

In one poem that he wrote to greet the new year of 5683, he questions the character of the upcoming year, and asks:

"Tell me, whose daughter are you, oh New Year, are you the daughter of Heaven or Hell?
Will you bring good news, or send upon us difficulties, and what will drop from your lips, gall or nectar?
With what group will you come to us, with the vale of weeping, accompanied by angels of peace, or angels of destruction?
Do you bring a cup of comfort, a cup of blessing, or a cup of wrath and curse?
Your sister 5682 - was an accursed and castigated year, that filled us with bitterness, only evil and anguish;
And we went down and cannot arise, will G-d curse? Was it not enough?"

In another poem that he wrote in Lodz in 5655, he curses and agonizes over his dwelling in the Diaspora. The title of the poem is: "A Voice Calls unto me…"

"And now, what is there for me, to freeze in the cold, without air to breathe, without sun and light?
Living with fear and terror around, you were like thorns for your neighbor, for denigration and hate…
And there is no hope that the wrath will let up and pass, so why should I dwell hear, old and without reason?
It is enough! There have already been seven dirges and lamentations… take up your stick and your bundle, and go to your Land!"

381

Here, the manufacturer-poet apparently struggles with himself. He left "lines of thought" with an empty line, and concludes in astonishment and agony:

"Year after year passes, and in my place
I am still sitting, and dreaming my dreams..."

In a letter to Mr. Avraham Chaim Michelson that was written in Lodz on the second day of Chanukah, 5682 (1922), he writes:

"In honor of the Torah person, who studies and learns, a basket filled with Sifra [116], Mishna and Gemara; a communal activist, well-known for praise, the trustee of the charitable organization. He can do anything difficult, Reb Avraham Chaim the son of Michel;

I wrote these verses last Saturday night, for I wanted to travel to you in Zgierz for the Keren Kayemet celebration, to read them at the time of the lighting of the candles. The Satan intervened, and the trip did not work out for me, and the song remains without "rectification". However, since the time has not yet passed, I am sending them to you. Perhaps you will have the opportunity and desire to read them before the young people of our city, so that they will know what the people hope from the pioneers of the People of Israel, and especially from the natives of Zgierz, that faithful bastion of Zionism.

When I thought about from where the spirit came to me to wade through verse, I remembered that the place is the factor, for Zgierz is a city that produces poets. From it came forth David Friszman, Yaakov Kahan, Yitzchak Katzenelson, and I the least of them -like the galbanum in the incense [117]."

In the margins of the letter, he greets all of his acquaintances, particularly Isuchar Szwarc and Yosef Meir Harun.

At the end of his life, his spirit fell for he felt that all of the work of his hands was completely worthless. Even his desire that he longed for, for Zion, failed him.

In his words "to the son and daughter", he writes the following at the end of his work of poetry (in Sivan 5684 - 1924):

"... At the time of my old age, when I have performed a brief inventory of my life, I see to my great anguish that all of my travail was carried away

382

by the wind. The world war and also the general depression that followed it consumed almost all of my effort and wealth. My only consolation is that during your childhood and youth, I hired for you Hebrew teachers so that you could study the Hebrew language and the history of our people. However even that did not fill me up satisfactorily, For on the day that you stood up under their own permission, you forfeited everything, and this Torah was almost forgotten from your hearts. Therefore I said that I will compile into a book all of the remnants of my poetry that is still with me. If it will come to pass that you, my children and dear grandchildren, ask about the meaning of the book, you will say to them: "This small collection of poems that your grandfather wrote at various times - you should attempt to study it in our Holy Land, and this will be my small reward. Your father, Moshe"

In the preface to these poems, a number of lines are written in pencil, which is a type of will to those that come after. He wrote:

"Indeed I am neither a poet nor the son of a poet, I was busy in my factory, and I had a great deal of interaction with the workers, for I myself was the master and director. Nevertheless I wrote a great deal in Hebrew and also in Yiddish, whenever I found the time. Now that I am old and the time has come to make a small accounting, what benefit did I get of all the travail that I worked throughout all the days of my life?

I already have written my first testament, and from that time, my fortune has increased further... I realized then that it was from G-d that I am able to leave to my children after me. However currently, the last war from 1914-1918 has put an end to my toil and fortune, and only very little is left in my hands to leave to my children after me. Nothing is left of all my property. From all my hopes, and all of my enterprises... nothing is left, only one comfort, that I conducted business faithfully, and did not..."

(This introduction was copied by Mr. Zev Fiszer. In the places where there are lacunae, the text was written in a cryptic fashion and it was not possible to interpret.)

He was a special person. His body passed away, his great material achievements was as if they were naught, but his spirit remained whole. That, he did bestow upon his children after him and also upon the natives of his city.

Reb Moshe Tzvi Eiger died with a good name in Lodz in 1935. He was brought to rest there next to his partner Miriam.

May his memory be blessed- Z. Fiszer and Y. A. Michaeli

Akiva (Karol) Eiger of blessed memory

Akiva, the youngest son of the manufacturer and Maskil Reb Moshel Eiger, was one of the most popular personalities in the Jewish societal life of Zgierz. From his earliest youth, he displayed a tendency toward societal work, including in the nationalist youth groups.

As a son of a warm, Zionist father, and a student of the Hebrew writer and teacher Binyamin Yaakov Katzenelson, the feeling for Jewish self-identity, along with the idea for a national Jewish emancipation, awakened in him early. When he later became a student of the business school, he had the opportunity to overhear the discussions of the older students - among them also his older brothers Avraham and Salomon, on topics that were of utmost importance to the Jewish youth in Eastern Europe at that time. Akiva did not pay attention to the fact that the greatest portion of his school colleagues belonged and agitated for various Socialist, leftist groups on the Jewish street, and was not influenced by their slogans. On the contrary, the idea that his father had implanted in his consciousness became more timely - the idea of the renaissance of the nation, of the Jewish national awakening.

Akiva (Karol) Eiger of blessed memory as an officer in Anders' army
[118]

It was already clear to the Zionist cultural activist that alongside the revival of the Jewish spirit, must also come the rebirth or reshaping of the Jewish corpus, that had been neglected over the generations. A young, healthy and sturdily built Jew with a dignified head and muscular body; brave, bold with heroic deeds for his people and his land - according tot he Zionist educators, that was a necessity for the building up of the homeland.

Reb Moshel Eiger, Akiva's father, was the prototype of those that were found in ancient Jewish history - at the time of the Maccabees. Indeed, in all of his speeches, he would elucidate with great enthusiasm on the heroic stories of the dynasty of the Hasmonaim in order to demonstrate that it was that type of Jew that we must have in order to build up our Land, and become a nation with national equality.

That ideal, which the father instilled in the young Akiva, gave him no rest, and he fulfilled it at the first opportunity. With the assistance of a few friends, including the energetic and fiery Zionist Leon Rusinow, he created the first Jewish sports club in the years before the First World War. It was a branch of the cultural organization "Hazamir", in which he was also an active member. With a generous hand, he provided all the needs of such a tournament organization. With his organizational skills and disciplined character, with great might and boundless dedication, he succeeded in creating a healthy and resolute backbone of a modern sports organization, that quickly developed and grew into a wide-branched Jewish tournament and sports organization and obtained a prominent name among Jewish sportsmen in Poland. After it joined the Maccabee Jewish world sports organization, the Zgierz tournament organization became an educational focal point for the larger portion of the youth of Zgierz. This was not only for physical culture, but also to a greater degree for the spiritual, national-Jewish culture. Thus did Akiva attain the possibility, albeit partial, to develop the ideas of his father.

Akiva Eiger was greatly beloved by the Zgierz youth. Paying no heed to his status, he became a friend and close pal of his tournament brothers, and helped many of them with their needs. He was a true and dedicated patron of his creation - the Maccabee Jewish tournament organization. He served as its president until the destruction of Zgierz.

Akiva was also the president of the Jewish manufacturers union and the founder of the Jewish bank. The small businessmen and craftsmen found him to be a good intercessor for their needs in the tax offices, in matters of credit, or with bank loans.

Akiva-Karol Eiger was a proud Jew and an exemplary citizen. During the time of the First World War, he joined the civic militia in order to maintain order in the city. Years later, he joined the fire-fighting commando. He encouraged others to emulate him in both roles. Aside from everything, he demonstrated to the local Poles and Germans that Jews do not stand apart from others, and that they do fulfil their civic duties.

After the occupation of Zgierz by Hitler's Germans, Akiva was arrested and sent to the concentration camp in Radogoszcz, where he endured difficult physical and spiritual afflictions. Miraculously, he succeeded in sneaking out from there, and he arrived in Romania after a series of dangerous detours. From there, he went to Cyprus. There, he enlisted in General Ander's army, where he became part of the Third Carpathian Brigade of General Kopanski, as an officer in the cultural and educational office. From Cyprus, he went to Tabruk, where he took part in the battle against Rommel's army. After the battle, while on leave, he went to the Land of Israel along with the brigade. Then he continued on the Iraqi desert where he enlisted several Zgierz natives into the army. Together with his close friend, the former secretary of the Zgierz Maccabee, Moshe Yaakov Grand (incidentally, who will later give us over details of A. Eiger in Ander's army in his own memoirs), he participated in further battles, until he reached Monte Cassino.

As a lecturer about Jewish matters in the Near East in the second department of Ander's army in which there were (until their arrival in the Land of Israel) approximately 5,000 Jews, Akiva did a great deal to improve their specific situation with respect to the large camp of Poles, so that no anti-Semitism would be experienced. Similarly, honor and praise is due to him for the efforts he put forth in order to ensure that the army leadership would issue an order that permitted and authorized Jews under Christian names to officially revert to their Jewish names and Jewish belief, - an act of the highest form of idealistic Jewish patriotism, which is not yet well enough known and appreciated.

After the war, in approximately 1952, Akiva Eiger returned to Israel - this time in order to settle there. He took great interest in the Zgierzers in the Land, and volunteered for the committee Zgierz Organization in Israel. However, a serious illness suddenly laid him up. He never recovered. He died on the 19th of Kislev 5714 (November 26, 1953) in his 63rd year of life.

From his sickbed, he wrote a few words for the Zgierz Memorial Day, dedicated to the destruction of Zgierz:

"I regret that I cannot be with you as you sanctify the memory of our murdered fellow natives; however my heart is with you. Let this memorial gathering unite us with brotherly relations and mutual help among our survivors, as we recall their memory. Be strong!"

Thus did Akiva Eiger bid farewell to the survivors of Zgierz.

Y. L. Weinsztejn, V. Fiszer

Reb Yaakov Binyamin and his son Yitzchak Kacelenson
Reb Yaakov Binyamin Katzenelson

Our father Reb Yaakov Binyamin Katzenelson was born in Kopyl, and moved as a child with his parents to Bobruisk, one of the largest cities in the Minsker Gubernia. Bobruisk is the cradle of our large family, which gave rise to the famous Buki the son of Yagli [119] (Dr. Katzenelson), and our cousin the Israeli leader Berl Katzenelson. Furthermore, Yitzchak Tabenkin, the leader of Achdut Haavoda (the Union of Workers), is also the son of our father's sister.

As one of the finest Yeshiva students in Volozhin, father received his rabbinical ordination even before his Bar Mitzvah.

During his early youth, he took interest in Russian language and literature. He arrived at the Haskalah path of Jewish life along with the rest of his contemporaries.

He joined the Chovevei Zion and Chovevei Sfat Ever movements. At the founding of the Haeshkol Hebrew Journal, he was invited to Warsaw as one of the important editorial workers.

He left his post and became a teacher on account of differences of opinion over the methods of the editor Nachum Sokolow. A few well-known Maskilim and householders of Zgierz (Isuchar Szwarc, Tovia Lifszitz) invited him to direct a modern cheder.

This took place at the end of the 19th century, when Zgierz was still considered as older than Lodz, which had first become an industrial center.

As a Modern Hebrew teacher in Zgierz, father had two famous students: the poet Yaakov Kahan and his own son. He was honored and loved by everyone who esteemed his national educational work

We settled in Zgierz immediately after the High Holidays of 1884, at the beginning of the term. The important men of the city were already waiting impatiently for the famous Maskil Binyamin Yaakov Katzenelson, who was to start a new, modern era in Jewish nationalist education in the boundaries of Poland. From among the householders, the erudite Isuchar Szwarc took special interest in the cheder. He was the father of the famous painter Marek Szwarc and the scientific researcher into the history of the Marranos in Portugal, Engineer Shmuel Szwarc.

The finest families, included several from nearby Lodz, sent their children to the Zgierz modern cheder of Reb Katzenelson. However, he did not spend more than two years in Zgierz. He was attracted to the growing industrial metropolis [120], that had already absorbed the nearby
villages, and into which flowed streams of Jews, who streamed in from all of Poland and wide Russia.

Father became closer to "jargon" [121] and wrote a few poems in Yiddish about the bloody Petlura pogroms after the First World War.

Aside from his work "Olelot Efraim" (published in 1889), he also wrote "Chazon Ben-Yamini", "Yehuda Maccabee", and "Gedalia Drag". His literary pseudonym was "Ben-Yamini".

Yitzchak Katzenelson

When his family came to Zgierz from Karelitz in 1894, Yitzchak was not yet eight years old.

Zgierz, the prosaic, smoky from the factory chimneys, had a bright shine in Yitzchak's life. The only good thing that he used to mention about Zgierz was that it was the birthplace of his poetic talent. Perhaps he was influenced thus by his older friend and student from Father's cheder, the poet Yaakov Kahan, whose Hebrew poems evoked wonder from the Hebrew circles and pride from our father.

Right: Binyamin Katzenelson. Left: Yitzchak Katzenelson

The ambitious Yitzchakl, looked at the success of his friend, who at the age of ten wrote his first Hebrew, juvenile, yet juicy, charming song that penetrated all the readers, and became a classic song in the kindergartens:

"On the window, on the window

Stands a pretty bird", etc.

In 1896, the Katzenelson family moved from Zgierz to Lodz, where his father opened a modern cheder. However, Yitzchak returned to Zgierz nine years later, this time, in order to learn a trade as a master weaver with his uncle (his mother's brother) Mordechai Gershon Horowicz, a textile manufacturer. This was in 1905, the year of the first Russian revolution. There, Yitzchak found the height of revolutionary activity, strikes and demonstrations. The uncle did not like the fact that his nephew befriended the "Achdut people", and also feared serious consequences, so he sent Yitzchak back to his parents.

Yitzchak Katzenelson was very popular and beloved in Zgierz. When he arranged the children's costumes for his Hebrew school theater in Lodz, many Zionist oriented young people from Zgierz traveled to witness his accomplishment. Katzenelson came to Zgierz often, when he was invited by cultural institutions when they held their lectures on Hebrew literature and art.

An excerpt from the book "Yitzchak Katzenelson" by Tzipora Katzenelson-Nachumov- published in Buenos Aires, 1948.

The Poet Yaakov Kahan

Yaakov Kahan

Yaakov Kahan was born in Slutzk Byelorussia, on the 1st of Tammuz, 5641 (1881). He moved with his parents to Zgierz when he was still a baby. How did the family end up in Zgierz? The poet himself tells us about this in his writings:

"This city (Lodz) always attracted to itself and to several nearby towns that developed as manufacturing cities in its wake, new alert powers from other areas of Jewish settlement in Russia. They slowly expanded their business with all provinces of Russia through their networking and vigilance, and they even reached to Siberia and Bukhara. It is important to point out that almost all of the commissioners and "comiviasors" (traveling merchants) were Jews from Lithuania and other areas.

My father, who had a wonderful handwriting and was knowledgeable in bookkeeping, also tried his luck and turned to this endeavor that had many opportunities. In one of the towns, he had a relative from his father's side, Reb Shlomo Horowicz. He found an opportunity to study the ways of business with him. Slowly but surely, he became a bookkeeper and correspondent for his brokerage business. Despite this, his salary was not sufficient to bring his wife to him. She remained in her parents' home with their firstborn daughter, and he would only visit her at the time of the major festivals of Passover and Sukkot. Only five years later, one year after he went into his own business, did my mother come with their two children to the dwelling that he had prepared for them in that town, which is Zgierz. I was a child of a year and a quarter."

In his memoirs, Yaakov Kahan writes that his father was of a good lineage, which included the names of the great Gaonim of Israel. His great-uncle was Reb Yomtov Lipman HaKohen, the rabbi of the community of Zambrow and the region. The first who lives in the memory of the family was Reb Moshe Kahan of Slutsk, who was both an expert in Torah and a wealthy man. He was the brother-in-law of the author of the "Or Chadash", and also wrote an approbation for that book.

Yaakov's grandfather married Esther the daughter of Reb Zelig, the son of the rabbi of Dolhinov. Reb Zelig was an intelligent man who served as a regional official. He was in charge of the collection of the excise on liquor, which was leased from Count Jozel Gincberg. He was also an excelled violin player. He was especially a great scholar. He earned his livelihood in a meager fashion, albeit honorably.

He had four sons. The eldest Michael was the cantor in the Zeichev Synagogue in Kiev. The second, Yaakov Hirsch owned a weaving factory in Rozhava of the Minsk region. The third, Binyamin (born on the 27th of Iyar 5616 -1856), was the father of Yaakov. The fourth was Shmuel Aharon.

Yaakov's father was religiously observant and careful about the observance of commandments. Simultaneously, he possessed secular knowledge. Yaakov entered the cheder of Katriel, and elderly Lithuanian teacher, when he was six-year-old. The teacher apparently did not draw near the heart of the boy, who felt himself as if he was in jail. Nevertheless, apparently, the rabbi instilled many of the foundations of Judaism into him, which were absorbed by his soul, and served as a sure foundation for the future. After studying in this cheder for three years, he transferred to the modern cheder of Binyamin Katzenelson.

Binyamin Katzenelson was a native of Kopyl, and was educated in the Yeshivas of Volozhin. He received his rabbinical ordination. However, like many others who were caught up in the current of the Haskalah, he involved himself in the study of Hebrew and became a teacher. He worked for a time at the Eshkol institution of Sokolow, and also published a book "Olelot Efraim" (in the name of Y. Ben-Yamini). This was a book of verse, written in the spirit of those times, at the beginning of Chovevei Zion, that stood as a symbol of the revolution of the Haskalah movement, intermixed with romantic longings for tradition.

Yaakov Binyamin Katzenelson was brought to Zgierz from the city of Karelitz of Lithuania (the city from which Reb Yaakov Milichowcki hails from) through the efforts of Isuchar Szwarc, who met him in the circles of the writers and Maskilim in Warsaw. His first efforts in Zgierz were difficult. There were few students, and he was there alone, without his family. Slowly, the modern cheder expanded. In the fourth year, Katzenelson moved to a large premises, and brought his wife and two children, as well as an assistant to help him with the lower grades of the cheder, that had grown significantly.

Yaakov spread his wings in that cheder. He learned well Hebrew, grammar and Bible. He also studied Russian, arithmetic and other subjects from a special teacher who taught in the modern cheder. Yaakov excelled in all of his subjects, which brought joy to his father, who took pride in his son and saw to it to educate him in the path that he saw as correct, in accordance with family tradition. He was particularly insistent that he join him in prayers at the synagogue. This synagogue experience on festivals enriched the soul of Yaakov, and set his sprit to the future poetry.

The dwelling of the Kahan family was in the home of Reb Avraham Yaakov Weizenfeld. This closeness with Weizenfeld served as a strong influence in enriching the spirit of Yaakov. Weizenfeld's home was a gathering place of writers and Maskilim, and the young boy stood at their feet, and absorbed everything that he could at his age.

392

Yaakov's mother

Yaakov's mother Pesia was born on the 15th of Elul, 5616 (1855) [122]. As opposed to the custom of the times, she studied Torah as one of the boys, and was the only girl in the cheder among the other boys. She did this without the knowledge of her parents. She studied everything except for Talmud. Nevertheless, she absorbed words of the sages that were always upon her mouth, together with verses of Proverbs, chapters of literature, and pearls of journalism. She took interest in every discussion and in every group. She was more careful than his father was in matters of religion and the fulfillment of commandments.

Yaakov loved his mother very much. "A flood of memories and painful longings for my mother, who was taken from me at an early age" - writes Yaakov Kahan in his memoirs "prevents me from even beginning to write about all the good that I received from her during those few years that I had the privilege to flourish in the light of her eyes. - - -My relation to her is filled with feelings of love and an endless embrace. I revered and feared my father, and there was always somewhat of an aloofness between us that was hard to overcome. There was no division at all between Mother and I. Her goodness was always bestowed upon me with open hands. He commands were given with a bright face, and even her words of chastisement were calm. She knew how to spice them with verses of Bible, statements of the sages, and at times even a story."

His mother's death spread a spirit of depression upon young Yaakov, and he was immersed in deep sorrow. He exerted himself over the upper spheres and "eternal questions". In the meantime, he found the "Hamelitz" newspaper of Chovevei Zion in his father's bookshelf, bound in fifteen large volumes, dating from the early 1880s. He also received volumes 1 and 2 of Hapardes from the Maskil Reb Tovia Lipszitz, which included the works of Achad Haam.. There was much therein to enthuse the heart of the proud youth, whose heart was filled to the brim with the national spirit and zealousness for the honor of Israel.

He was invited by his sister to Bialystok in his seventeenth year. He went there for a few weeks [123]. There, he gave lessons as a teacher of German to beginners. At that time, the famous rabbi of the city, Reb Shmuel Mohilever died (18th of Sivan 5658 - 1898), and the house of the rabbi turned into a gathering place bearing his name "Beit Shmuel". Yaakov often visited that house, listened to the lectures, and took part in the cultural activities.

Yaakov Kahan writes the following about his sojourn in Bialystok, "The main value of my sojourn in Bialystok was that I breathed a different spirit. I saw new people, a new environment, and even attained a certain level of independence for the first time. All of this was without doubt a catalyst for my maturing, even though within my spirit there still rested a bit of the solitude of the child who watches the stormy sea from opposite, and still is not able to take part in it, and he finds some salvation from his own pain of longing by pouring himself into the agony of the entire nation. The poem "To the poet" (written in three stanzas) gives over the spirit of those days to some degree."

Yaakov returned to Zgierz when he heard that a seven-level business school was about to open. His intention was to enter the seventh level after preparing for the exams of the six levels. He also received a letter from his father informing him that he was asked to appear before a military evaluation committee to establish his age, since his birth certificate had been lost. His plan to enter the business school was not realized, since only five levels were opened. He also found a surprise at home. When he returned home on the eve of Passover of 5658 (1899), he found a new one-year-old brother Yosef, who was born to his father's second wife.

Awakening to Poetry

In the meantime, a strong change overtook Yaakov. His spirit was filled with poetry, and this general feeling was expressed in the poem "Thoughts of Spring", in which he expressed the vision of his spirit and his longing for the spring of the national renaissance:

"The awakening of the national feelings in the nation", states Yaakov Kahan, "the blossoming of the national hopes with the appearance of Herzl,

394

the spark of new powers in Hebrew literature, gladdens me and strengthens in me the multi-faceted vision of national revival, all of these enthuse in me the poetic spirit; all of these penetrate into me, and at times I find myself in a spirit of drunken dreaminess. My communion with nature was deep and decisive.

He wrote the first poems, including "In the Garden", "Night Darkness", "In the Heart of the Forest", "The End of all Flesh", "Visions of G-d", "Sunset", etc. The latter was also the first that was published in Hashiloach, edited by Klozner. The poem "A Meditation in Memory of Judah Maccabee" was also printed in the "Yearbook", edited by Sokolow in the year 5660 (1900).

The taste of freedom that he felt in Bialystok encouraged him to find a source of income. At the beginning of the year 5660 (1899), he accepted some classes in Hebrew. His first students were the young children of Isuchar Szwarc. At the same time, he also tried his hand in publishing articles on the new style of literature. These were published in Hashavua of London.

Yaakov moved to Lodz at the beginning of 5661. This city always enchanted him with its splendor. During those years, he was put up by his aunts (his mother's sisters) and almost all of his mother's brothers. He enjoyed these experiences of being close with these families and being their guest. At this time, with his thirst for the variegated life of art and its splendor, his desire for complete independence that grew stronger, along with youthful feelings of love -all of these attracted him to the large city. He would come to Zgierz as a "Sabbath guest". He would also spend the summer months, vacations and festivals there.

"It was pleasant for me to rest there (in Zgierz) from the hustle and bustle of the large city" said Yaakov Kahan - "to return and visit my forests around it, and to have solitude with my soul. Indeed, most of what I wrote during the two years that I was in Lodz (from the autumn of 5661 until the autumn of 5663) was written in Zgierz.

On the Ascent of the Mountain

During his stay in Lodz, Yaakov had the opportunity to meet his fellow native David Friszman. They were friends from their youth, and very close. He was the editor of "Hador", and gladly accepted one poem, and later another poem authored by Kahan. He was also effusive in his praise of his poems that were published in "Olam Katan" and in "Luach Achiasaf". His feeling of debt to such a strong inquirer and stickler as Friszman encouraged Kahan to continue in his creative work with greater strength. He appreciated his closeness and friendship with the writer and editor, and knew how to relate to him with reverence and approval.

After his poem that he wrote at the age of ten about the death of his mother, he continued to write about his impressions. In the year 5660 (1899), his first poem ("A Meditation in Memory of Judah Maccabee") was published in the "Yearbook" edited by Nachum Sokolow. In the summer of 5662 (1902), his first anthology of poetry was published ("A Book of Poems", published by Tushia in Warsaw) after a long wait, much thought and editing. He left for Switzerland in 1903 to complete his studies. Six years later, in the year 5668 (1909), Yaakov received his Doctorate of Philosophy degree from the University of Berne, for his work on "A Critique on the Concept of Pride".

From the First Zionist Congress, Kahan dedicated himself to national-cultural activities. He was one of the founders of the Ivriya Zionist student's organization, and its director in the year 5666 (1906). From the year 5670 (1910) until the First World War, he worked for the strengthening of the status of Hebrew in his role as head of the "Organization for Hebrew Language and Culture" in Berlin. He published Hebrew manuscripts, including the "New Hebrew" (5672) that set up in a forum befitting of the Shiloach of Achad Haam. During the years 5676-5678 (1916-1918) he served as a teacher of Hebrew literature in the high school in Lodz. In the year 5678 (1918), he began his activities as the editor of Hatkufa, published by Shtibel in Moscow, and later also in Warsaw, along with Y. P. Lachower. Later, he himself was the editor of a fine section on literature in Hatekufa.

In the year 5684 (1924), he accepted a position of supervisor of Hebrew studies in the bilingual schools of Poland. In the years 5687-5993 (1927-1933), he lectured on Hebrew literature in the Institute of Jewish Wisdom in Warsaw. He made aliya to the Land in 5684 (1934), and settled in Tel Aviv.

From 5684 and on, he edited the anthologies of Knesset together with Y. P., renewed Hatekufa, and edited volumes 28 and 29. Two years later, in the year 5689 (1938), his creation, the dramatic symphony "At the Pyramids" won the Bialik Prize. The Massada publication published his poems under the auspices of "The Committee for the Publication of the Manuscripts of Yaakov Kahan". In the year 5703 (1942), he was chosen as the chairman of the literary board that was affiliated with the Bialik Institute.

Again in the year 5706 (1946), he won the Chernikovsky Prize for exemplary translations, for his translation of Faust and Goethe. He also published an anthology of children's poetry called Birchat Boker.

He was honored with the Israel Prize twice, once in 5713 (1953) and a second time in 5718 (1958). He also won the Chernikovsky Prize for a second time, one year before that (1957) for his achievements in the field of Hebrew translation (for additional works on Heine and Goethe" [124]). That year, the publication of all of his letters in ten volumes was completed by the jubilee committee.

The works of Kahan were published in a variety of forms. The twelve-volume Jubilee edition was published in the year 5705, 5716. In the year 5724 (1964) a two volume edition was published [125]. In his latter years, he began to publish his memoirs in the Haboker newspaper (29 Elul 5712 / September 19, 1962) under the title of "Paths of my Life". This continued week by week. In these, he dedicated several fine chapters full of appreciation for Zgierz, and its life.

Yaakov Kahan died in Tel Aviv at the age of 80 on the 1st of Kislev 5621 (November 20, 1960), and was buried in Jerusalem in accordance with his will.

His memory will be preserved in our hearts for praise and appreciation.
Y. E. M.

The Poet Yaakov Kahan

It is possible that the struggle between "young" and "old" in our literature is nothing more than a happy joke, about which who knows when it began and whether it will end sometime. That thought swims around with me when I take it upon myself to write about the writer who is already over 75 years old: Yaakov Kahan. He has perhaps already three times more the years of literary activity than the entire lives of other younger writers.

Bialik greeted Yaakov Kahan with a Shehecheyanu blessing [126] over 50 years ago, after he read his first anthology of poems. Then Bialik wrote his famous article "Our Young Poet" in which he very warmly portrayed the three young ones - Yaakov Kahan, Zalman Shneur and Yaakov Steinberg. In each of the three, Bialik detected the "life juices" that fermented "like new wine in a jug, like boiling blood and lively flesh". In each of thee he found, "beauty, strength, and wholeness". He declared the following about Yaakov Kahan, "He is all silk in the morning wind".

"Silk in the morning wind"… is indeed the seal of the gentle lyrics that flow out from most of Yaakov Kahan's creations. He concerned himself with the dove and the shmeterling [127], the silver swan that swims out from the blue azure and about water streams that flow out of fountains. His eye joined together playful wonder-stars and prayerful trees in the pale night. His heart twisted when he saw an orphaned flower tread under foot. His heart expanded with the spreading out of the morning dew.

From the very beginning, Yaakov Kahan was the poet of unification with eternal spring, the poet of gentleness and intimacy, the poet of crystallized life and of a lifelong holiday. "The herald of the beautify world", called him one literary scientist.

However the poet and lyricist was a son of a people who were not created so idealistically so as to be able to look out and have pleasure from G-d's fine world. With time, the "herald of beauty" became the printer of agony and desire for redemption of his people. His song was crowded with agony and pain, and with strong protest against the strong people of the word and against the boot-lickers of his own people.

The poet of silk became a punisher, a sermonizer, and a warner in playful lines about leaves and grass. His songs went far off, until the "Song of Iron" - "The silent iron, which pushes up in revenge. For when a world is enveloped in darkness - for it has in it here a comfort, there a sureness, and finally, hidden hope." The day came with the gentle poet sent us pastoral, nationalist songs that called to a battle, to rebellion, to the conquest of the Land.

In his sixty years of literary activity, Yaakov Kahan was involved with various branches and genres of literary creation - from songs to drama. He recently said about this, "From time to time, I feel the inclination toward an other genre - like a tree that always gives forth new branches."

Indeed, the canvas of his creations is very wide and full of various themes and motives. However, in all of his meanderings from one form to another over all of the branches of literature, he remains - it seems to me - a "big child". Perhaps it was for such a big child that he wrote his superb, "Legends for Big Children" - "That which preserves in him the pureness and wholeness of the childhood days, despite the fact that they strongly attacked and ruined the streams of life."

When you ask him which of his works he loves best, he answers: always the last work - like a mother who lover all of her children, but the youngest brings her more joy in all of her limbs. Aside from this - from her first steps until today, Yaakov Kahan wrote ballads and dramas, visions and great novels (all, "aside from a great novel", as he himself said, "but never should a small poem be compared to great dramas").

As in all of his incarnations - Yaakov Kahan was anchored in his lyrics, in the small joys and sufferings of human life.

Yaakov Kahan was born in the city of Slutsk in White Russia. However, when he was still a child, his family moved to Zgierz, the industrial and business city near Lodz, where David Friszman was also born. Nevertheless, very little of the business spirit of his childhood city rubbed off on the poet. Once, at a social gathering here in the land, the poet heard from a person who came from "those places" [128] that the large forests in the region of Zgierz were destroyed during the war. The poet signed with pain: "... my forests". Those gathered wondered: until then they did not know that the poet possessed forests - until it became clear to them that the poet was not talking about a material possession, but rather about a possession of lyrical youthful life.

Regarding his sensitive-lyrical nature, the following fact can give testimony. Yaakov Kahan attained much higher education in German universities, where he studied philosophy and history - completely "dry" subjects, in which he attained the title of Doctor - however his "home" was always in the fine literature, particularly poetry. He invested his best desire and feeling into it. Friends and other curious people often asked: what was the purpose of so much study? He used to answer: "Only to mystify my fields". -and his fields remained: storytelling, poetry, legends, drama...

Y. Aviyashuv, "Last report", Tel Aviv, January 25, 1957, for the poet's seventy-fifth birthday

Reb Mordechai Shmuel Cudkowicz

From among the residents in the house where we lived, I remember one couple who occupied a small dwelling on the ground floor, connected to a store that opened onto the courtyard. It was a store that sold hides, shoes, and other leather objects, from which the owner earned his living. They called him Shmuel Chasid (The Pious) due to his generous traits, that included sublime piety, modest demeanor, and self-abnegation. He was indeed a modest, humble and quiet man, who restrained himself from any extra comfort. He distanced himself from the communal debates and from anything that had the taint of evil talk or embarrassment to another person.

It is especially worthy to point out the wonderful relationship that Shmuel Chasid had with Rodel his wife. She was also modest and quiet, restraining herself from any excess conversation and from injuring the honor of any person. Apparently, she learned from the traits of her husband, and received a great deal from him, both from her love and reverence to him and also from her appreciation of his exemplary behavior toward her. It was a pleasure to see the peace, confidence, and refinement in the relationship between this couple, especially after ten years had passed since their marriage, and she had not yet given birth. Her husband had the permission based on Jewish law to divorce her, but twelve years passed, fifteen years passed, and more, and he never acted upon his privilege. Of course, there was no shortage of whispers, hints, and even reproof from friends and important people. He listened and was silent.

Indeed, Rodel did not forego any effort to find a way out of her predicament. She traveled to a Tzadik, asked doctors, and employed all sorts of remedies. Once, a day or two after the festival of Sukkot, my mother sent me to get her Etrog that was promised to her, so that she could use it for the potion that she was preparing. The woman took the Etrog, and before she gave it to me, she closed her eyes, whispered something, bit of the pitam [129] and swallowed it. This was strange to me, and I told it to my mother. My mother laughed and said: "Indeed it is a proven remedy". She told me that the pure woman saw in the swallowing of the pitam a portent for the birth of a male child.

The fine life of this couple fluttered before my eyes as I wrote "Peretz and Naomi" many years later. Perhaps it was from them that I received the

400

first impetus to write any poem.

Aside from his work in religious education, Reb Mordechai Shmuel was known as the author and distributor of the general annual calendar that was used throughout Poland.

Yaakov Kahan (from his memoirs "The Paths of my Life")

The Sirkes Family

The Sirkes family - Reb Shlomo and his wife Sara

The Sirkes family is numbered among the Hassidic families whose influence was noticeable in our city throughout fifty years, from the 1880s until the 1930s, in economic, communal and religious life.

Reb Shlomo Sirkes of blessed memory

The father of the family, Reb Shlomo Sirkes, was born in the year 5620 (1860) in Yaryshev, out side of Mohilov-Podolsk. His father Reb Eliezer, a Hassid of Sadigora, died when he was five years old. He was educated by his grandfather Reb Daniel, and was regarded as a genius. His grandfather always took him to the Admors of Zenkov and Medzhibozh, the grandsons of

401

the Admor of Opatow, the author of "Ohev Yisrael".

After his marriage to Sara, the daughter of the philanthropist Reb Mordechai Helman of Dinowicz, he came with his father-in-law to Lodz and set up his home in Zgierz. He established a factory of fine woven goods along with Mr. Moshe Eiger. This firm, "Sirkes and Eiger" became famous in Poland and throughout the breadth of Russia.

Reb Shlomo was known in public as an upright and faithful man, who conducted business honorably. Thanks to the trust that he gained in the world of business, along with his great energy that he placed into the business, he did well, and became wealthy.

Despite his occupation in multi-branched business, he dedicated a great deal of his time and also money to daily difficulties and people in difficult circumstances. His donations to charity and good deeds were famous. He gave his money with a generous hand and a good eye, for the most part, more than he was asked. He did not speak about his kind works, which were his daily custom, in front of his wife and family. These things always became known to them incidentally, from the outside [130].

Reb Shlomo was involved in communal affairs. He was the chief of the founders of the Yagdil Torah Yeshiva in Zgierz, which existed until the outbreak of the First World War (1914), and was also a member of the communal council of Zgierz for many years. As a member of the council, he represented the Jewish community and was a member of various delegations. During the time of the First World War, he participated in the Jewish delegation that stood before the Russian army commander Otomanov in Vilna that presented a request to rescind the command of expulsion of myriads of Jews who were residents of the regions that were adjacent to the front.

With the closing of the Russian markets and the confiscation of its merchandise by the German occupiers, the firm Sirkes and Eiger disbanded and ceased existence. Reb Shlomo left the world of business and manufacturing, and devoted the rest of his days to Torah, religion and communal activism.

He remained an upright man of solid character for all of his days. His garments were clean and his soul was pure. He was a scion of the family of the Bach (Reb Yoel Sirkes, the author of the Bayit Chadash commentary on the Shulchan Aruch), of the Schorr and Margolios families, a descendent of the Gaon Reb Tzvi Hirsch Schorr (the father of the author of Torat Chayim) and of the Gaon Reb Avraham Horowitz (the author of Emek Habrachah, the father of the holy Shla).

His wife Sara was also a charitable woman, who was known in our city as an energetic, wise person. She bore five sons to Reb Shlomo: Eliezer, Daniel, Tzvi, Peretz and Pinchas.

She died in Warsaw on the 29th f Cheshvan 5688 1928) and is buried there.

Reb Shlomo made aliya to the Land in the year 5694 (1934) and settled in Petach Tikva at first. He spent his last years in Jerusalem, involved with Torah and worship.

He died at an old age on the 18th of Cheshvan, 5702 (1943) and is buried on the Mount of Olives. May his soul be bound in the bonds of eternal life.

Reb Eliezer Sirkes of blessed memory

Eliezer Sirkes

Reb Eliezer Sirkes was born in the year 5640 (1880) to his father Reb Shlomo Sirkes of blessed memory, and his mother Sara, the daughter of Reb

Mordechai (Motia) Helman of Lodz (the father of the well-known activist Reb Moshe Helman of blessed memory), of a family that was related to the Admor Reb Yehoshua Heshel of Opatow, the author of Ohev Yisrael. His parents arrived in Zgierz when he was three years old. He excelled as a person of blessed abilities, with a quick grasp of his studies already from a young age. He married Chaya (the daughter of Reb Chaim Rotenberg of Skryhiczyn) when he was eighteen. She was a descendant of the Gra (Gaon) of Vilna of blessed memory, and of well placed families in Poland.

After he finished being supported at the table of his father-in-law, he returned to Zgierz and opened the textile factory "Sirkes and Sirkes" with his brother Daniel. It developed well until the outbreak of the First World War. The Admor of Gur, the author of the Sfat Emet of blessed memory gave them his blessing and commanded them to study together every morning. This factory stood out in that it hired only Jewish workers, and closed down two days a week, on Saturday and Sunday, as well as, obviously, on Jewish Holidays.

Along with his work in the factory, Reb Eliezer found time to be involved in communal matters, even when he was young. His seal is stamped upon the life of Zgierz. He served as a member of the communal council and its president for nearly 25 years, from 1910-1935, with a small break in the years 1918-1924. He was elected as a member of communal council for a period of approximately 20 years, from 1916-1935. He was also a member of various civic committees, the valuation committee, the regional government, etc. He was the president of Agudas Yisroel in Zgierz, and a member of the leadership committee of Agudas Yisroel of Poland. He was a delegate to the large convention of the Aguda, etc. He was elected as a delegate to the Polish parliament (Sejm) from 1922-1927 on account of his party, in a block of national minorities.

His home was always open to the downtrodden and needy. Small-scale merchants and workshop owners came to him house to pour out their bitterness of heart to him, and to request his help before the tax collecting committees that imposed upon them taxes beyond their means. He would put aside his private business and run to the mayor, the valuation committee or other authority to obtain the leniency that was requested.

Reb Yehoshua Berliner-Baniel tells that Reb Eliezer once went at his request to intercede on his behalf for a reduction in the income tax that was imposed upon him. In order to meet with the appropriate official, Reb Eliezer worshipped in the first minyan in the synagogue on the day of Hoshana Rabba (his shtibel worshiped later) in order to have sufficient time to fulfil the request. When he returned, he informed him that his mission was successful. This was one incident out of many.

Like his father Reb Shlomo of blessed memory, he was numbered among the Hassidim of Gur and one of the faithful followers of that group. In his own faction (Agudas Yisroel) he was always among those who looked approvingly upon the Land of Israel and participating in its up building. In 1919, he joined with his brother Reb Daniel in sending weaving machines and looms to the Land of Israel, an activity that was organized by the Zionist Mr. Zeev Reichert of blessed memory. As is known, these machines arrived in the Land, but they were not used, and they remained in huts exposed to the sun, and rusted. Only during the last war, when there was business with such machines in the land, and years of prosperity arrived, did these machines find their use in the factories of "Tzena" (utility in the vernacular), obviously, by others...

In 1924, he went to the Land of Israel with a delegation of Aguda (the Admor of Gur of blessed memory joined this delegation) in order to invest money there and to fund factories. He returned full of enthusiasm for the idea of settling the land, and made a strong decision to settle there.

Reb Eliezer had a weakness for the printed word, and he use to collect all daily newspapers starting from 1924, and bind them into volumes. He brought them to the Land, but they rotted in some cellar in Jerusalem after his death. He also brought "Pinkas Zgierz" with him, and the copy remained in Zgierz. His book collection was famous in our city. His collection included valuable first editions, which he would willingly lend out to the scholars of the city such as Rabbi Chanoch Henech Ehrsohn, Rabbi Nathan Elberg, and others. Reb Eliezer brought this valuable collection to the Land, and grew it to 15,000 volumes (including some rare collections of responsa, prayer books, Passover Haggadas, Hassidic books, and reference and study books). Toward the end of his life, he donated this collection to the Sfat Emet

405

Yeshiva in Jerusalem. This library is open to anyone who wants, and is called by his name "Ginzei Eliezer" (Eliezer's collection).

Reb Eliezer excelled in the entertaining of guests, and made sure to have a guest at his table on Sabbaths and festivals. It is especially worthwhile to point out one incident. Once, on the eve of the festival of Sukkot of 1920, when the war between Bolshevik Russia and Poland had not yet finished, a group of Jewish Russian soldiers who had been taken prisoner came to the shtibel of Gur, with torn clothes and rags on their feet. They were surrounded by an armed guard of Polish soldiers, and waited for invitations to the houses of the worshipers. Nobody came to their rescue. The Hassidim were afraid to take them home, lest they be suspected of having connections with the Communist enemy. Reb Eliezer was the only one who had the braveness of heart, and he took them all (more than ten Jewish soldiers) to his home. He fed them and gave them to drink, and did not deprive the Polish guard either.

That year (1920) in the midst of the war, soldiers of Haller's army (they were called Hallerczes) and began to attack the Jews of Zgierz on the roads of the city, cutting off beards and pulling off peyos. A pall of fear fell upon the Jews of the city, who closed themselves into their homes. When this became known to Reb Eliezer, he endangered himself, hurried to Mayor Szwircz, and succeeded in arrested the perpetrators.

Reb Eliezer succeeded in actualizing his goal at the beginning of 1935. He arrived in the Land with his wife and party of his family. He never saw his love of the Land as contradictory to his Hassidic world. His father Reb Shlomo made aliya before him. Two of his sons were in the Land, and his brother Reb Daniel was already a resident of Tel Aviv. He saw himself as reborn. He toured the land and enjoyed its sights. He lived in Tel Aviv at first. He quickly moved to the holy city of Jerusalem, purchased a dwelling and settled there.

He did not abandon his communal work even in Jerusalem. He found a place in the Aguda circles, and was numbered among those dedicated to the movement. He participated in a delegation to the High Commission, and in all other important activities of his movement. He was appointed as the director of the bank "Loan Cassa of the Orthodox People of Poland". He was chosen as a member of the directorship of the Shaarei Tzedek and Bikur Cholim hospitals, Rabbi Meir Baal Haness, and other organizations. He endeared himself to anyone who came in contact with him, whether in his communal life or his personal life, thanks to his spiritual nobility and personal refinement.

Reb Eliezer merited witnessing the birth of the State. His children and grandchildren participated in the War of Independence, and he prayed that they would return healthy and whole. His prayers were answered.

Reb Eliezer died in Jerusalem on the 25th of Elul 5712 (1952) and is buried on Har Menuchot.

His wife Chaya was a pious woman, modest in all her deeds. She discretely occupied herself in communal affairs both in Zgierz and Jerusalem. She was conversant in all the chapters of Psalms. She was an expert in Tzena Urena [131] and also the legends of the Talmud. She died in Jerusalem on the 25th of Sivan 5722 (1962) and is buried beside her husband.

Five of the sons of Reb Eliezer and Chaya Sirkes of blessed memory perished in the Holocaust with their families. Six of their remaining sons live with us in the Land.

Reb Daniel Sirkes of blessed memory

Daniel Sirkes

Reb Daniel Sirkes was born in the year 5642 (1882) to his father Reb Shlomo Sirkes and his mother Sara, the daughter of Reb Mordechai Helman of Lodz. His wife Nechama was the daughter of Reb Yaakov Blass of Warsaw (the daughter of Reb Itza Blass, who was related by marriage to the Rebbe of Kock.)

He was modest in his manner, and had a personality that made an impression and arose honor. He was a scholar and a man of deeds, who spoke little, did charitable acts in secret, and was a man of spiritual completeness.

He was one of the chief activists of Zgierz and in Poland in general. He was at the head of the G-d fearing people in the Orthodox camp in Poland. He helped establish an Orthodox organization in Zgierz, and served as its chairman. However, his love for Zion and for the building of the Land took hold of him quickly, and he turned his back on Aguda that rejected, in his opinion, the building of the Holy Land, and dedicated most of its energy to matters of Diaspora Judaism. He joined the Mizrachi and was one of the flag bearers of that movement, as it waged war upon all opponents of Zionism from the right and the left. He was true to his heart and his inclination, and he decided to make aliya to the Land and to actualize the aim of Zionism with his body. Even though he was busy in Poland with many important matters in the real of education and communal activism, as the chairman of the Beit Ulpana (girl's school) in the city (1917-1918), the chairman of Mizrachi, the chairman of the communal council (1918-1924) and active in the highest echelons of the national movement - he abandoned all these, liquidated his factory in Zgierz, forfeited much of his property, burned his bridges behind him and made aliya in 1925 with all of his family. He purchased a house and settled in it.

Even though he was used to a life of comfort and luxury in Zgierz, he did not find it constricting to live in a dwelling of two small rooms with his wife and eight children in the Bukharian Quarter of Jerusalem. There, he educated his sons and daughters to love modesty, work, and a life of dedication. He did a great deal to even the temperament of his family, and he found a common language with the young, pioneering generation.

Reb Daniel stood up against stains that arose in communal life in Israel. He wrote articles on issues of the day in the Hatzofeh newspaper, of which he was a founder. His ideas drew closer to revisionist Zionism. As the chairman of the communal council of Tel Aviv, he led the community without playing favorites. He was also vice-chairman of the Mizrachi Bank, a member of the leadership committee of HaPoel Hatzioni, a member of the directorate of the Jewish National Fund, and a representative to Zionist congresses. He was one of the signers of the Declaration of Independence, and was very happy when he merited in this.

At first, Reb Daniel settled in Haifa. From there, he moved to Tel Aviv. With the transfer of the authority of the Jewish community to the city council of Tel Aviv, he decided to settle in Jerusalem.

In his book "With an Upright Posture", that included an anthology of his ideas and saying, he spoke out against several ideas that were going through the Land, which he saw as contradictory to pure Zionism. He was always careful and cautious to speak the truth, and he did not refrain from lashing out at the time of need even toward the activists of his own party, if he saw them tilting toward national or communal themes that were not fitting with his ideas of the unity of the nation and the approaching of the redemption of the nation and the Land. Reb Daniel Sirkes dedicated his final years to the Yeshiva of Rav Kook of blessed memory, in which he saw as a blessed means of sublimely educating the nation and repairing its spirituality.

**Representatives of the Zionist groups at a joint meeting -
In the center - Reb Daniel Sirkes**

Reb Daniel was fortunate to have all of his sons and daughters in the Land during the time of the Holocaust, and he saw a fourth generation in the Land.

Reb Daniel died of old age on the 9th of Adar 5724 (1965) and is buried in the family plot on Har Menuchot. He left of his fortune to charity and institutions.

His wife Nechama Matel was intelligent, refined, and charitable. She died on the 16th of Adar 5629 (1969 in Jerusalem. She left a large family that is rooted in the Land.

A street in Jerusalem is named for Reb Daniel Sirkes.

Leibel Sirkes of blessed memory

He was born in the year 1899 to his father Reb Eliezer Sirkes.

In his youth, it was clear that he was created for greatness. He was considered to be a genius, as a pit that does not lose a drop [132]. At the age of 12, he published his novellae in the Shaarei Torah monthly that was published in Warsaw.

He joined the Zionist movement in 1917, and was active in it until 1939.

He was always full of humor. He reacted to incidents in our city with pleasant rhymes and jokes. He wrote a number of books that were left to the shredder. The tragedy that overtook him in the year 1920 (when he served in the Polish army in the war against the Bolsheviks, was injured in a battle and lost a hand) did not affect his spirit and his commitment to communal life in the city. He loved his friends very much. They were always happy to greet him, and they sang together the songs that he composed.

He married Chana the daughter of Binyamin Fogel of Zgierz. They had one daughter, Sara.

He fled with his family to Warsaw in 1940. As is told, he encouraged all of his acquaintances and family members with his words that were always laced with humor and sharpness, even n those difficult days.

The fate of the Jews of the Warsaw Ghetto did not pass over him and his family.

His memory shall remain as a blessing among his friends and acquaintances.

P. Abba

The Boaz Family by Avraham Boaz
(A wide-branched Zgierz family)

The Boaz family was one of the largest Jewish families in Zgierz.

The founder of that family along with the Aharonson family was Reb Yisrael, or as he was called, Yisraelche. He was the son of Reb Avraham, one of the first residents of Zgierz, who settled in the city in the first half of the nineteenth century

The only son who remained in Zgierz was Yisrael of blessed memory, the father of the so-called "Boaz Brothers", the owners of the factory for woolen men's articles in Zgierz.

The "Boaz Brothers" firm had a name in mercantile circles in the cities and towns of Poland as a solid manufacturer of fine woolen merchandise. The Boaz brothers excelled at charitable endeavors. One of them, Reb Chaim, was a representative in the Jewish community council, and the other, Reb Avraham was a councilor on the town council.

At the time of the outbreak of the war in 1939, the large Boaz family, including their children and grandchildren, numbered almost one hundred souls. The largest portion lived in Zgierz - a situation which continued for approximately one hundred years.

Reb Yisrael Boaz and his wife Rivka died in Zgierz.

In 1927, a branch of the family, the children of Moshe and Shifra Aharonson, their brother-in law Yitzchak Mintz and son Avraham Aharonson founded a large textile factory. It was also for woolen articles, and had the name, "Mintz and Aharonson". The factory and stockyard were located on the main Pilsudski Street 45.

In 1938, the business revenue of the firm reached 5 million Zloty. At that time, this was a colossal sum.

The Boaz family, as well as the Mintz and Aharonson families, were known as Hassidic Jews, with their customary garb. They were also very charitable. Yitzchak Mintz was active as vice president of the merchant's union.

Another chapter about which it is worthwhile to write is the issue of employing Hassidic young men in the textile factory of the Mintz and Aharonson firm. Sine Jewish businesses were boycotted by the Polish population in the decade previous to the outbreak of the Second World War; many Jewish businesses were compelled to close. Hassidic Jews, formerly merchants and business employees, wished to work in the factories. Mintz and Aharonson were the first to take in Hassidic youths and young men into their large textile factory. They gave them employment and livelihood.

In the walls of the factory, one could see Hassidic weavers and shearers - with long tzitzit, beards and peyos. This was a new thing in Zgierz.

The Mintz and Aharonson firm was not plundered by the civilian population at the time of the invasion of the German army into Zgierz on September 7, 1939. The owners continued to operate the factory for a few weeks, until the military commander ordered the confiscation of all Jewish businesses and enterprises in the city.

The confiscation was enacted, and a Zgierz German was installed as commissar of the factory. The Jewish owners had to give over everything - merchandise, yarn, money - and leave the business with empty hands.

During the time of occupation, from the end of 1939 until 1943, the Mintz and Aharonson families resided in the Warsaw Ghetto. Afterward, the family succeeded in leaving Warsaw and moving to Vitel [133] France, where the renowned poet from Lodz, Yitzchak Kacenelson, was located. Their objective was to cross from there to Switzerland. A secret provocative denunciation to the Gestapo put an end to the plans of the Mintz and Aharonson families, as well as to the plans of the poet Yitzchak Kacenelson.

Early one morning, they were all arrested and sent to Auschwitz, from which they never returned.

And now, I will describe the murder of Fela Trocki (Boaz) and her child Ilana in Nieswiez (White Russia) in the year 1942.

The war-blizzard drove several families of Zgierz to Nieswiez. These included members of the intelligentsia in particular, such as the Horowicz brothers, Bolek and Fela Trocki and their daughter Ilana, Dr. Joszek Cohen, his sister and other Jews of Zgierz. At the outbreak of the German-Soviet war, this circle held together. With the arrival of the Nazi hordes in Nieswiez in June 1941, the entire Jewish population felt the blows of the Nazis.

Fela Trocki was yellow-blonde with blue eyes, and she was able to make the impression of an "Aryan". She was able to be hidden with her child by a Christian. A White Russian anti-Semite knew about them, and informed the Gestapo. Fela and her daughter were shot in the middle of the market, as a warning to the non-Jewish population that they should not hide Jews.

Avraham Boaz

The Greenberg Family

My uncle Gedalia Yedidya Zwikelski was doubly connected to our family. He was the husband of my father's sister, as well as my father's cousin. He, my uncle, was one of the best students of the first Sochaczewer Rebbe, Reb Avrahamele. He was sharp, knew how to learn well, and was known in the city as an intelligent man to whom people went to ask advice when one reached a crossroads and did not know which route to choose. He was a steadfast, rigid character. He could not remain in his office for long as a Chevra Kadisha Gabbai (trustee of the burial society). He was a city councilor for a long period of time.

He was cold and sedate, the opposite of my second uncle Noach Trocki, the husband of my father's youngest sister, who was impulsive and impetuous when he dealt with communal matters, in which he took great interest. He was a disciplined Zionist; he deserved to be elected as a member of the communal council from the Zionist organization. Unfortunately, he did not serve as a representative for long. He died young after an operation in 1928. He was buried in the Zgierz cemetery.

My great grandfather Yosef Zwikelski was bound to the land. He was a "farmer" as one calls it today. At the time, Jews were not yet owners of land. He leased the land from the poretz (landowner) of the city Proboszczewice, not far from Zgierz. My great grandfather built an oil press in Proboszczewice. The pure product was sold to the German factories in Lodz, and to the pioneers of the Lodz textile industry. His oil products were also sold in various parts of Poland
and Russia. This was in the first decade of the nineteenth century.

His daughter Chana, my grandmother, married my grandfather Binyamin Greenberg in Sochaczew. They settled in Zgierz and opened a lumber business. Strangely, and I do not know the reason, Jews considered that line of business to be honorable. Sholem Asch describes this in one of his works.

My father Gedalia was also a lumber and forestry merchant. He was a sedate, peaceful and reasonable man, with an inclination toward philosophical thoughts, as a result of his intensive studies in his youth. In that time, he strongly felt the destruction of Zion, and therefore arose at midnight to recite the Tikkun Chatzot [134]. He changed under the influence Haskalah stream, through Mendelsohn's German commentary on the Torah. For him, modern philosophy took the place of the old books.

413

Fela Greenberg of blessed memory

My good Jewish mother, Feigele, came from Kalisz. However, she became bound with our city. She was deeply involved in philanthropic activity, and was also active in the affairs of the Dvora women's Zionist organization.

By Fabian Greenberg, America

Fabian Greenberg

There were personalities in Zgierz who excelled in communal activity, and stood out in the community as expert intercessors and communal representatives, due to their personal virtues and honorable appearance, which imbued a suggestive influence upon those with whom they came in contact.

414

One of these bright activists was without doubt Fabian Greenberg, today the last Mohawk of our communal activists.

He was born in Zgierz in the year 5653 (1893). His father, Reb Gedalia Greenberg, was a Maskil, a scholar and great philanthropist. He would delve into the content of the prayers, the hymns and psalms, and research their origins, eras, and authors. His home was an exemplary Zionist home. When Fabian, at age nine, was asked what his father did, that is to say, what is his occupation, he answered with childhood innocence, "He is a Zionist".

From among the documents that remain from those days, we find written in the memorial book of the Chevra Kadisha, "As a token of thanks to Reb Gedaliahu the son of the late Reb Binyamin Greenberg of blessed memory, for the kindness that he bestowed upon the people of our community regarding the debt due to him from people of our community, of a value of approximately 2,000 silver rubles, we have decided to appoint him as an honorary member of the local Chevra Kadisha." The document is dated "Saturday night of Parashat Shmot, 5669". It is signed by Shlomo Yehuda Leib HaKohen, the rabbi and head of the rabbinical court, Shalom Zandberg, Mendel Finkelsztejn, Michel Prinz, Mordechai Shmuel Zudkowicz, Binyamin Szaransky and Yosef Hirsch Szapira. Gedalia Greenberg concludes the list of signatories.

Reb Gedaliahu Greenberg was also appointed by the rabbi of the city as the head of the committee for improving and repair of the Mikva (ritual bath) in the year 5669 (1909). The other members of this committee were Reb Mordechai Shmuel Zudkowicz, Reb Yisrael Frugel, Reb Zeev Reichert, Reb Binyamin Szaransky, and Reb Aharon Yosef Berger.

In his childhood, Fabian studied in the cheder of Reb Wolf Leib Haltrecht, who was one of the most progressive teachers in the city. He completed his studies at the business school in Zgierz, and continued his studies in the business academy of St. Gallen, Switzerland.

The following people of the group of young people of Zgierz signed the letter of friends that was sent to him to Germany: Menachem Berliner (the founder of the group), Menashe Swarcbard, Aharon Cincinatus, Mordechai Szapszowicz, Yosel Krasnopolski, Yehoshua Raveh (today the writer Yehoshua Manoach, a founder and resident of Degania Aleph), Asher Klorfeld, Meir Preiz, Yehuda Weisbaum, Yechezkel Kojawski, Fishel Leczyski, Leibel (Leon) Rusinow, Michel Szidlowski, Yaakov Hirsch

415

Waldman, Asher Goszdzyk, Chaimel Lerer (the grandson of the Admor of Brzeziny) and others.

Fabian traveled to Westphalia, Germany to meet his family two days before the outbreak of the First World War in 1914. He was kept there in confinement as a citizen of an enemy country until August 1915. There, he continued to maintain correspondence with his friends, and took interest in what was happening in his city. From there, he also sent articles to the Polish newspaper that was published in Berlin, Dziennik Berlinski.

Fabian Greenberg absorbed the Zionist atmosphere from the home of his parents and from the Zionist literature. His Zionism was particularly forged by the Polish anti-Semitism. In his memoirs, he writes that the prayer "Hineni Heani Mimaas" ("Here I am, poor in worthy deeds") that the prayer leader recites prior to the Musaf service on the High Holy Days, penetrated to his soul, was absorbed therein, and served as a "compass" for him in his communal work throughout his life.

His first contact with Zionist activity was in 1908, at the illegal meeting that took place on the fourth memorial day of the passing of Dr. Herzl. He came with his father to this meeting in the "Gemilut Chasadim" hall. From then, he often participated in meetings and gatherings. He stood out in discussions, and was elected to the committee of the Zionist chapter and later as the chairman of the "Agudat Tzionim". During this period of time, he gave a great deal toward the raising of the stature and influence of this honorable organization, until it became the center of the general Zionist movement in our city.

It is a natural phenomenon that when one stands out in activism and effort, additional tasks are placed upon him. With the expanding of communal activity in Zgierz, and as he spread himself into different realms, civic, philanthropic, cultural, etc., Fabian Greenberg bore this yoke, and quickly found himself in the center of all facets of active life in the city.

The demands of the life of activity took their toll. He had to conduct a continuous struggle in the social and communal realms against the theories of the Bund, and also against the Aguda camp. These were the days of the Balfour Declaration, and Greenberg did much to win over souls for the fortification of Zionism in the city.

He was elected by the communal factions as a member of the city council, and was very active on it. He was appointed as chairman of the cooperative union that took care of distributing food from the city council, and stood on guard to prevent shortages and deprivation in the distribution of food to the Jewish population during the first years following the First World War. The Jews of the city saw him as the protector of their interests, and would stop him on the street to ask for his assistance. He never refused anyone. His success on behalf of his fans encouraged him to continue along his path, and through this, he neglected his personal, affairs.

From the city council, he stood on guard for the Jews of our city. When an anti-Semitic member of the city council delivered a venomous speech against the Jews - he would receive an appropriate response from him. During the time of the pogrom of Przytyk, rumor spread in Zgierz that the Endeks (an extreme right wing party) were preparing to conduct hooliganism, and also have some "fun" in Zgierz. The Jewish community took these rumors seriously, and decided to turn to the police superintendent to avert the evil. Unfortunately, the superintendent was not present. He was on vacation in the village of Dombrowk, and it was forbidden to disturb him. Isucher Szwarc and Fabian Greenberg took the initiative and traveled to Dombrowk. The police superintendent listened to them, and the peace of the city was not disturbed.

For many years, Fabian served as the representative of the Jewish population in the civic court of the justice of the peace, and he stood on guard for cases that affected Jews, making sure that they would be conducted in a fitting, objective manner. The sittings would often proceed for entire days. Nevertheless, he dedicated all of his time to the Jewish community, without expectation of reward. He was also the impetus behind the plan for the creation of a civic council that would centralize and direct all communal work, in which all of the organizations would participate. His plan was well accepted by the community, but the plan did not come to fruition due to communal divisiveness.

It is important to point out in particular, with regards to his efforts in the fields of education and culture, the establishment of the first Jewish institution for the for the dissemination of knowledge and enlightenment to wide segments of the population -the Hebrew library, which raised the cultural level and enriched the spirit of the masses of the youth with the treasures of literary creations, original and translated. Greenberg, who was of the first founders of the library, which was later called by the name of David Frischman, worked greatly for it, and dedicated special attention to it, to

417

develop, strengthen, and broaden it. This activity stood at the head of all of his communal work.

Fabian Greenberg was also one of the founders of the "Kinderheim" children's institution, that later became the orphanage. He dedicated him to this institution along with his wife Regina (the daughter of Reb Hershschel Kohn, an intelligent man, one of the city notables) with fatherly, dedicated care. They imbued the children with a warm family feeling, with concern, drawing near, and love. The few children who survived, today as adults remember their patron with gratitude and reverence.

A special chapter in his communal activities for Zgierz Jewry was his dedicated work for the survivors after the Holocaust, and especially his interest and dedication to the "Book of Zgierz". Immediately after the conclusion of the war, when the Zgierz natives organized themselves in America, his requests for appropriate assistance for the refugees of our city were not answered generously. He did not hesitate to leave the organization with a reprimand against the stubborn committee. Yaakov Grand and others left the organization with him.

Greenberg remained in constant connection with us in the Land. Thanks to his wonderful memory, he enriched the Zgierz book with his interesting memoirs and other interesting documentary material, which added historical and cultural value to the book. Even in his country of residence, the United States, he from time to time published articles in the American Yiddish newspapers on social topics, including memories of his birthplace of Zgierz. Despite the distance in time and place, he today remains the Zgierz activist who works on behalf of the Holocaust survivors with love and dedication.

When he visited Israel in 1959, the Organization of Zgierz Natives in Israel arranged a festive reception in his honor.

Z. Fisher

The Reichert House - The First Zionists of the City

By Zeev Eliahu Reichert

Zeev Eliahu was one of the dear ones of Zgierz, and one of its first Zionist activists.

He was born in Ozorkow in the year 1882, to his father, the wealthy Hassid Reb Eliezer Chaim Reichert, who was generous and pursued justice, and was one of the pioneers of textile manufacturing in our city. His mother was Ruchama the daughter of Chanoch Kriszk, one of the wealthy, honorable people of Ozorkow. His father's family was very wide-branched, of the descendent of the Maharal of Prague [135]. One of the early patriarchs of this family was the generous Re Leib Koszmirak, of the same generation of Sir Moses Montefiore, who began to redeem the land of the Jericho valley already ninety years ago. To this end, he transferred 100,000 rubles to Jerusalem, to the hands of Rabbi Meir Auerbach, which was not effective.

Zeev Reichert was educated in the Cheder, the Beis Midrash and the Yeshiva. He obtained general education from private teachers, and gained great expertise in old and new Hebrew literature, as well as world literature. He took particular interest in Jewish history, which attracted his heart. This delving into the history of his people brought him to a love of Zion. When Herzl appeared on the stage of Zionism, he was one of the first to join the ranks of active Zionism. He became one of its dedicated fighters.

When he was still young, he married his relative Machla, the daughter of the scholar and Maskil Reb Moshe, who owned an estate in the village of Dronzwa, in the Makow region. He was known as being very hospitable, and honored among his acquaintances. He was chosen as an arbitrator to the Russian Duma in the Ostrolenka region.

He settled in Zgierz after his marriage. Along with his brother-in-law Reb Zeev Michel Reichert, he founded a textile factory there in 1905. This was one of the largest factories that was established in Zgierz. That factory was engaged in the cleaning and dyeing of wool. Approximately fifty workers, all gentiles, worked in that factory. The Polish worker's union opposed Jews working in manufacturing. After the First World War, Jewish workers worked in the factory despite this fact - especially those who came from Russia in an illegal fashion, and pioneers who were preparing to make Aliya to the Land of Israel. There were many female Jewish workers.

He stood out as an enthusiastic activist and Zionist immediately after his arrival in Zgierz. The well-known scholar and lover of Zion, Reb Isuchar Szwarc, was among his friends who remained in close contact with him.
After he gave himself over to the service of the Zionist movement, was one of the founders of the Zionist union of Zgierz, and was even elected as its chairman, he subsequently was one of those who laid the foundation stone for Mizrachi of Zgierz. He was always one of the greatest donors and canvassers of the Zionist funds. He was also one of the distributors of shares for the "Treasury for Jewish Settlement". He did not spare his time, money or

efforts. The fact that he was a traditional Jew and worshipped regularly at the Shtibel of the Hassidim of Ger who did not look favorably upon his Zionism, did not distract him from working diligently on Zionist matters. He attracted many of his opponents due to his complete and convincing personality, and he acquired souls for Zion both publicly and privately, even from within the shtibel.

Ezra Reichert

Zeev Eliahu and Mahla Reichert

His home was imbued with a strong Zionist spirit. He gave his children a Zionist education, and taught them to speak Hebrew. Most of the Jewish enterprises such as Hendeles' spinning mill, the weaving factories of the Boaz brothers, Leczyski, Kaufman, Haron and others were located in his courtyard, as well as most of the Zionist organizations in the city, including the Zionist union, and the Dvora women's organization, of which his wife was the life spirit and chairwoman. The Hebrew scouting group Hashomer Hatzair, the Maccabee organization, the public library and the first Hebrew kindergarten, which was supervised by his wife, were also located there. All of these institutions and organizations that were centered within the precincts of Reichert's courtyard gave the place a special government status both among the Jews of Zgierz and among the Poles, who looked at all that was transpiring with an eye of indignation. Not infrequently, the children of the shkotzim [136] threw stones into the courtyard, and engraved the word "Palestyna" upon the words of the sanctification of the moon that was on the

420

gate of the house [137]. Indeed, this was the nickname that was generally given to that Zionist fortress, "Palestyna"

The Reichert house, "Palesztynka" in Zgierz

Zeev Eliahu actualized his love for Zion by making aliya himself. He made his first visit alreadyin 1906. In the diary that he left after him, he wrote that in those days, he felt a need to see with his own eyes the Land of Israel about which he had always dreamed. This trip was a fulfillment of his dream. He went there with a group of four people, including his two brothers-in law Zeev Michael Reichert and Tzvi Tenenbaum. Despite the fact that the details of the journey were kept secret so that the plan would not be disturbed, news of the journey spread in the community within a few days. There homes began to bustle with visitors. The people of Zgierz literally became overexcited, for in those days, the arranging of a trip to the Land was a great event. Hundreds of people surrounded him, wishing to know about the itinerary, about the possibilities of investing money in the Land, and about whether such an adventure was not dangerous, etc. There were also those who gave him notes to place into the cracks of the Western Wall and Rachel's Tomb.

Many came to the Lodz train station to take leave of him - family members, friends, Zionist, and communal activists. Among them was the Hebrew writer Ezra Golden.

The group traveled to Odessa, and from there set sail to Jaffa. In Odessa, they met Menachem Ussishkin as well as A. Droyanov, the secretary of the Odessa committee of Chovevei Zion. Zeev Eliahu consulted with him about the plans for the trips and the possibilities of investing money in the Land.

The trip to the Land of Israel lasted approximately four months. They crossed the length and breadth of the country on a stage-coach, on a horse drawn carriage, on the saddle of a donkey, and also by foot. They were strongly influenced by the beauty and charm of the Land.

Zeev Eliahu made plans to acquire plots of land, to set up a factory, etc. However his plans were not actualized as he had wished.

In 1910, he tried to establish, along with his two aforementioned brothers-in-law, the first factory for the cleaning of wool in Rishon Letzion. Through the intermediary of Zeev Gluskin, Baron Benjamin Rothschild rented them a place for this enterprise in the buildings of the winery, and also agreed to provide them with steam from the engines of the winery. Due to the inappropriateness of this wool for textile manufacturing in Poland, it was difficult to sell the cleaned wool, as he had planned.

The second plan of Zeev Reichert to establish local textile manufacturing and to use the wool of the Land also did not work out well due to Turkish tax regulations, which did not protect local products at all. This hindered the progress in this area, and the enterprise closed.

His wife Machla and sister Eida, the wife of Michael Zeev Reichert, also joined him on his tour of the Land. They wished to check out the situation with regard to the plan of settling the Land. The First World War that broke out in 1914 thwarted all plans. There was also a plan to set up a garden city on the shore of the Sea of Galilee. Through the efforts of Reichert, a group of Jews from Zgierz and Lodz purchased plots from "The Organization of Preparation of Settlement", and the plan reached the threshold of fulfillment. The war that broke out dried up all plans, and left everything to naught.

A strong national movement was awakened in Zgierz in the wake of this journey. Many made aliya on account of its influence, and no small numbers were helped by him. Thanks to the efforts and influence of the Reichert family, Menachem Berliner of blessed memory made aliya. He was one of the first of the dedicated workers of the Land, and met his death by yellow fever. As well Yehoshua Manoach, one of the founders of Degania who served as a Hebrew teacher in the Reichert home, was led to aliya by the spirit that he drew from that home.

Reichert not only worked in the Zionist movement. He also fought for the local rights of his fellow townsfolk. He was a member of the city council of Zgierz, and the Jewish community council. He concerned himself with the needs of the locals.

During his free time, he would take a book into his hands. He would also occupy himself with scientific work. In his large library, various books on Jewish subjects stood out. He also translated "The Wars of the Jews" of Josephus (Joseph ben Matityahu) into Hebrew, published articles in the Jewish newspapers, corresponded with researchers of Hebrew history, and wrote a book on the life of the Jewish during the time of the Second Temple, which was not published.

After the First World War, fate turned against him. In the year 1919, his dedicated wife, the great lover of Zion who always assisted him, took ill and died, after much suffering. She was a young woman of 39. Her longing and love for the Land did not dissipate even as she lay on her sickbed. A few days before her death, she asked her husband to transfer her remains to the land of Israel. She was buried in a wooden casket. Her funeral was one of the biggest that the city of Zgeirz had ever witnessed. Thousands of people followed her casket. The concerns of the times and the opposition of the rabbis to disinterring her casket from the grave prevented the fulfillment of the wishes of the deceased. This crushed the spirit of Zeev Eliahu and left him in sadness. Many Jews of Zgierz and family members planted a grove of trees in the Herzl forest in her memory.

At the end of 1918, Zeev Eliahu was chosen as a delegate to the national convention of Polish Jewry that convened in Warsaw. At this meeting, it was decided to found a high national political organization that would stand on guard for the interests of Polish Jewry. Participants would include the powerful people of the various parties, communities and institutions from all parts of Poland. When he returned, he presented a detailed accounting of the proceedings of the convention in the Zionist hall of Zgierz, on January 9th, 1919.

In 1921, the children of Zeev Eliahu along with the family of his brother-in-law Zeev Reichert, made aliya to the Land. They brought with them a complete array of new machinery for the textile factory. His brother-in-law remained in the Land to direct the factory, which was perhaps the first one in the textile field, and paved the way for others. He, Zeev Eliahu, remained in Poland to liquidate the property that he had in Zgierz.

Zeev Michael Reichert   **Yehudit Reichert**

In 1925, Zeev Eliahu made aliya to the Land once again, and remained there for over a year. His intention at that time was to set himself up in the Land and firm up the well-being of the factory. When he returned to Poland to liquidate the remainder of his affairs, the general economic depression in Poland overtook him. He lost his fortune and his situation became desperate.

At the outbreak of the Second World War, he was brought low along with the rest of his people by the flames of the terrible Holocaust that engulfed them from all sides. As his family found out, he wandered from Zgierz to Lodz and from there to Czestochowa and Warsaw. The last communication from him was received by the Red Cross in Sweden in 1944, which contained the following plea, "Save me! Take me out of the vale of murder!" From then, nothing more was heard. He met his bitter end along with 6,000,000 of his brethren, prisoners of the inferno, who were murdered and burnt in the gas chambers.

This was the peculiar end to the man whose lot was great within the Zionist renaissance movement and the personal actualization of the return to Zion. May his soul be bound in the bonds of the eternal life of our nation, which he so faithfully guarded.

Machla Reichert of blessed memory

Mrs. Machla Reichert, the wife of Zeev Eliahu Reichert was a native of the village of Dronzwa in the Lomza region, where her grandfather had an estate.

As a pretty, intelligent, and talented girl, she married her cousin Zeev Eliahu at a young age, and moved to Zgierz. There her husband and his brother-in-law set up a factory for the dyeing and manufactory of wool. Her life was harmonious and full of content. She assisted her husband in Zionist activities, as well as in his scientific and literary pursuits. She gave birth to six children. She was a pleasant and splendid woman in her externals as well as in her behavior. Despite her weak health, she was dedicated completely to communal matters, and did not spare any toil.

She founded the Dvora women's Zionist hall along with her sister Aida, and stood at its head. She also founded the first kindergarten in Zgierz. She gathered money and jewelry on behalf of the Jewish National Fund. She also excelled in her proper expression, and spoke with talent and grace at many meetings.

A certain winter's day is remembered by the family. A meeting of the organization was supposed to take place. She suddenly disappeared beforehand. They found her in the same room that was set aside for the gathering place. She was exerting herself to light the oven, despite the fact that she was not supposed to exert herself.

Her soul desired to settle in the Land of Israel throughout her short life. She always dreamed of setting up her home on the banks of the Sea of Galilee, so that she could swim with her children upon its blue waves. Despite the fact that she visited Israel twice, she did not merit reaching the shore of her desire. After the war, her illness worsened. She returned her spirit to upon high when she already owned a passport for the land of Israel. Her request that her remains be brought to the Holy Land was not fulfilled. She was buried in the Zgierz cemetery.

Her resting place was destroyed by the enemies. The gravestones were used to pave the streets of the city.

In the Lodzer daily "Lodzer Tagblatt", of January 26th, 1920, an account of the memorial evening was published. This evening was dedicated to the late Mrs. Machla Reichert, the founder and directory of the Dvora Zionist women's organization. Isuchar Szwarc and the chief cantor of Lodz, H.

Alterman, participated. Dr. Sterman portrayed the refined personality of the deceased, and her activities for the Zionist idea and the Zionist "Prevl School" in our city.

May her soul be bound in the bonds of eternal life.

Eida the daughter of Moshe Reichert of blessed memory

Eida Reichert, the wife of Zeev Michael, was born on her parents' estate in Dronzwa, in the region of Lomza. She was a refined woman, and following the leader of the family, she married her uncle Zeev Michael. Her family moved to Zgierz along with the family of her sister. She was very talented, pleasant and energetic. She founded the Dvora hall for Zionist women along with her sister Machla. She collected money and jewelry for the Jewish National Fund. She was a delegate to the Zionist Congress on two occasions. She was an excellent orator. She worked on behalf of the Land of Israel with enthusiasm and love. After the First World War, in 1931 [138], she took her family and the family of her sister Machla of blessed memory and traveled to Israel. Her two sons were among the first employees of the electric company.

She was not too involved in communal work in the land, since her diabetes that she contracted at a young age distracted her. He house was open to everyone, and the extended family would gather in her house on every holiday and festival. He house served as a refuge to many when they arrived in the Land. May her soul be bound in the bonds of eternal life.

Ezra Reichert of blessed memory

Ezra Reichert was born in Zgierz to his parents Reb Zeev Eliahu and Machla Reichert. He received his early education in the traditional cheder, as was customary in those days, as well as from a private teacher, Mr. Yehoshua Manoach may he live and be well, a member of Kibbutz Degania Aleph. Ezra continued his studies in the Yavneh Gymnasium of Lodz.

His father Reb Zeev Eliahu, one of the first active Zionists of Zgierz, toured the Land of Israel prior to the First World War, and also purchased a lot with the intention of settling in the Land with his family. His desire did not materialize, however his children, Ezra included, made aliya to the Land of Israel in 1921.

In 1923, Ezra was accepted as a student to the agricultural Mikve Yisrael School. There, in the variegated community of students and activists imbued with vision, the youth Ezra tried his hand at writing poems. After that, he began to publish articles in the monthly student newspaper regarding research into the topic of improving the security and life situation in the institution. His writings were esteemed and revered by the community of students. They exposed his spirit, his proper outlook, and his alertness to all that took place in his environment, despite his personal modest and retiring demeanor. Ezra frequently toured the Land, and he described his experiences with great talent. He sent the fruits of his pen on many topics to various venues. Readers in the Land and in the Diaspora benefited from no small number of his writings. He also wrote greatly about his impressions of the travels of daring explorers, who wrote of their experiences and adventures in books that are in the annals world literature.

During the Second World War, he served as a librarian in the periodical section of the Massada library. Later, he served in the Ohel Shem Library in Tel Aviv for seventeen consecutive years, until his final illness laid him low.

One can learn about his feelings during his final days from a segment of his writings that was written before his death, in which he bares the stirrings of his soul and his unfulfilled desires.

He died on the 4th of Cheshvan 5729 (1969), and was buried in the area of the graves of the Reichert and Tenenbaum-Arzi families in Kiryat Shaul. May his soul be bound in the bonds of eternal life, and may his memory be for a blessing.

Yehudit Reichert

She was the daughter of Wolf Reichert. She was born in Zgierz. She was a well-known artist and teacher. She made aliya to the Land in 1936.

She regularly participated in the exhibitions of the organizations of artists and sculptors in the land. She also set up five solo exhibitions in the Land and also several exhibitions in the Diaspora, in Sweden, Paris, etc. between the years 1958-1966.

By Tamar Itinzon-Reichert

Zeev Michael Reichert of blessed memory

Zeev Michael Reichert the son of Avraham Gershon was born in Kodkow near Krosniewice in 1861. (According to written and oral information, he was a descendent of the Maharal of Prague.)

From his early youth, he wandered around his father's estate in Dronzwa and dreamed of the land of Israel. He married the daughter of his sister, Eida the daughter of Moshe Reichert (the sister of Machla Reichert). They moved to Zgierz after a short time. There, he and his brother-in law Zeev Eliahu Reichert established a factory for dyeing and wool manufacturing. In 1919, along with his brother-in-law Zeev Eliahu, he founded a textile company in Zgierz with the aim of transferring it to Israel. He was the emissary to set up the operation of this factory. He moved with his family to Tel Aviv in 1921, and established a factory for the sewing and weaving of cotton. He worked on it with dedication until his old age, despite the difficulties in operations and in livelihood. He would arise each morning and direct his enterprise. His children urged him to sell the enterprise and rest from his work. With difficulty, he acceded to the wishes of his children. He was a man of action, and without activity, he was depressed and broken. He died at the age of 92.

Grandfather Reb Fishel Bunim Hollander, the Shochet of blessed memory

[139] Reb Fishel Bunim Shochet - or has he was simply called, Reb Fishel Bunim - was without doubt one of the honorable people of the city, and also one of the most popular personalities in the former Jewish life in our city. His patriarchal gait and mannerisms of importance evoked respect and confidence. He was one of those few people who grew together with the city, shared its birth pangs, and also made frequent efforts to formulate the religious life of the young Jewish settlement. As a student of the first Zgierz rabbi, the "Old Tzadik" , may his virtue stand us in good stead, he was one of the first of the young people who absorbed not only Torah and Hassidism, but also good character and love of Israel. He related to his job as a highly responsible mission, like holy work. He interacted pleasantly with his fellow, and was greatly beloved by the members of the community. Among other things, Reb Fishel Bunim was known for leading services in the synagogue on the High Holy Days. With is unique, loud voice, in the old Jewish prayer

style, his prayers moved every Jewish heart and left the worshippers with a deep impression for a long time. His house on the Jewish street was known in the entire city. It was imbued with Torah, Hassidism and fine Judaism.

We bring here a memorial in words for a respected grandfather, written by his grandson Reb David Wechsler (today in America), which he writes with reverence and love. He reminisces about a piece of life from a time that is now relegated to eternity.

V. F.

My grandfather Reb Fishel Bunim, aside from being a great scholar and fearer of Heaven which were once the primary qualifications to be a shochet in a city - also personified a slice of history of Jewish Zgierz of two or three generations ago. His father's arrival from the large and old city Leczyca to tiny Zgierz which was just beginning to be built - was bound with the Hassidic ways that were so characteristic of those times.

I remember what my mother of blessed memory told me about him:

My great-grandfather Reb Leizer (Reb Fishel Bunim's father) was once held over in Kock, and was unable to return home for the Kocker Rebbe did not bid him farewell for several weeks. Indeed, what Hassid would go home without being bidden farewell by the Rebbe? He waited. One day, his door opened suddenly - and the Rebbe came in. Reb Leizer was there. At the leave-taking, the Rebbe told him: "In Zgierz, they need a Shochet. Go there and be successful". Generally, one first goes alone. One must get to know the people and set up contact with the community. At first, Reb Leizer lodged in the Kocker Shtibel. When the matter became known, there was a din in the town - is it a small matter? The Kocker Rebbe himself sent a Shochet! He was immediately accepted as the Shochet of Zgierz, and asked to bring his family. There were no trains at that time. They traveled for several days with horse and buggy - this was in the middle of winter - until they finally arrived in Zgierz. This was in the year 5607 (1847). Since a house was not yet prepared for them, the Hassidim set them up temporarily in a side room of the Shtibel until a home could be found. Thus began the life of our family in Zgierz.

Already from his youth, Fishel Bunim exhibited great diligence in learning, and became a genius. He studied in the famous Yeshiva of the first rabbi of Zgierz, Reb Shalom Hirsch HaKohen of holy blessed memory, which was known throughout Poland. Simultaneously, he studied the laws of Shechita (ritual slaughter), and after the death of his father, the city took him on as a slaughterer in his father's place. At that time, he got married to the daughter of a resident of Zgierz, Reb David Mordechai. Her name was Keila (that was our grandmother Keila of blessed memory). They purchased a house on the Jewish Street, where Jewish life was concentrated in our city. This was in close proximity to the synagogue and Beis Midrash, whose highest window overlooked grandfather's court. I still recall the days of summer, when one could always here the melodies of Torah and prayer from the open window.

Grandmother and grandfather had eight children.

It is superfluous to state that their children received an upbringing in careful observance of Judaism. Their sons and sons-in-law were all known as scholars and sharp Hassidim. Our grandfather used to travel to Chidushei Harim, and later to Reb Henech of Aleksandrow, the Sfas Emet and to his son Reb Avraham Mordechai, all of blessed memory. He would always take a son along on every trip in order to educate them in Hassidism. The daughters were also permeated with the observant Jewish spirit, and were considered to be righteous women in the city. They paid no attention to the various spirits of the times that went through Grandfather's home with its growing family. Respect for parents was always on the highest pinnacle, and a word from the parents was treated as a command. It is difficult to think of anything that the children did not do in accordance with the will of their parents -and it was all with sincere dedication. Even later, when they themselves had grown children and were householders with daily concerns, it was not difficult for them to bestow goodness and love upon their parents.

Grandfather's custom was that when a daughter of his got married, he would support her with her husband and children for three years in his house. During that time, the son-in-law would find his means of livelihood and then would vacate the dwelling for another daughter. When my mother got married, Grandfather built a dwelling for them in the large yard of his house. They lived there for thirty years.

The personality of my Grandfather is etched in my mind when I saw him as a prayer leader in the synagogue or the Beis Midrash on Rosh Hashanah and Yom Kippur. He stood at the bimah wearing his white kittel, adorned with his tallis with a silver band over his head. His face was flaming and his white beard trembling - apparently out of fear. He began with a prayerful voice, and then the Hamelech [140]. A shudder went through the bones, and the congregation appeared flustered. One could hear a lament from the

430

women's section, and Fishel the Shamash would bang his hands on the table and shout, "Sha Sha!" Thus did Grandfather worship.

After Grandmother Keila died, Grandfather lived with his youngest daughter Glika, his son-in law Chaim Yaakov and two grandchildren Avraham Mordechai and Shmuel Leizer. Later, when he retired, he sat day and night and learned.

Grandfather felt that his time was nearing. He summoned several of his relatives who were members of the Chevra Kadisha (burial society), and told them his wish. Since an unused plot was still available next to the old Tzadik, he would like, as his student, to lie next to his Rebbe.

On the seventh of Shvat 5683 (1923), Grandfather died. A snowstorm raged that day. The trains were not running normally, and the Lodz-Zgierz tramway stopped completely. Therefore, all of the grandchildren from Lodz came by foot to Zgierz in order to pay last respects to their grandfather. The funeral was delayed until evening for another reason. The children of Reb Yisraeltche Boaz claimed that the plot that was near their father's grave should belong to them. A rabbinical judgement was solicited from the Zgierzer Rav, Rabbi Shlomo Leib HaKohen, at which it was decided that the land belongs to Grandfather. The funeral took place from the Beis Midrash in which Grandfather had been the prayer leader for many years. My father Reb Mendel Wechsler was the first eulogizer. From the Beis Midrash, they took him to the synagogue courtyard where he was eulogized by the Zgierzer Rav. This did I bid farewell to our illustrious grandfather, who graced the entire family with his good name.

Woe regarding those who have departed and are not forgotten.

David Wechsler

Rabbi Mendel Wechsler may his blood be avenged

Rabbi Mendel Wechsler, a scion of illustrious forbears, of the descendents of the Maharal of Prague, was born in the city of Zawiercie in the year 5641 (1880) to his father Reb Yitzchak Wechsler. His grandfather Rabbi Leibe Hirsch and great-grandfather Rabbi David Dayan all served in the rabbinate in the city of Czestochowa, Poland.

Reb Mendel stood out as a genius in his youth. He studied in the Yeshiva of the Rabbi of Amstrow, and from there he transferred to the Yeshiva of the Admor Reb Avraham of holy blessed memory of Sochaczew the author of the Avnei Nezer and Eglei Tal. He was one of his finest students. After his marriage to Chana Sara the daughter of Reb Fishel Bunim the Hassid, the veteran Shochet of Zgierz, he moved to Zgierz (in 1900) and was supported for several years at the table of his father-in-law. He was known in town as Reb Mendel Fishel Bunim's.

On account of his diligence in his studies, he gave lessons to the students of the Yagdil Torah Yeshiva. The students considered it to their merit of they attended a class of his. A few years before the First World War, he acquired the rights for the sale of salt from the Hassid Reb David Bendekowski. When a competitor schemed against him and disturbed his peace with threats, Reb Mendel turned to his Rebbe from Sochaczew and poured out his worries and anguish to him. The Rebbe promised him Divine assistance. The situation ended with Reb Mendel on top, and his tormentor going bankrupt.

With the invasion of the Germans to Zgierz in 1914 and the closing of sources of livelihood, the end of the salt rights of Reb Mendel also came. Having no recourse, he began to earn his livelihood from teaching. At that time, the modern cheder called "The School for Torah and the Ways of the World" was established. Reb Mendel joined this institution as the teacher of the upper grade. Among his students were Pinchas Sirkes, the brothers Yitzchak and Meir Szaransky, Tebil Elberg (all of them today in Israel), and, from among those who perished in the Holocaust: Avraham Aronson, Yaakov Szapira, David Baum, Shimshon Szabszowicz, Avraham Yaakov Celnik, and others.

The children of the Admor of Sochaczew, Reb Shmuel of blessed memory, the author of Shem Mishmuel, studied Torah from him in a private lesson. One of them was Reb Aharon Yisrael Bornsztejn lives today in Israel, and another was his brother Rabbi Avraham the Rabbi of Kutno, may G-d avenge his blood.

On Sabbaths and festivals, many people streamed over to the Beis Midrash to hear Torah lessons from him. He never stopped studying. He dedicated his entire life to the study and teaching of Torah.

From the year 5680 (1920), he served as the head of the Yeshiva in the largest Yeshivas of Poland: Yeshivat Beit Avraham of Lodz, Yeshiva Beit Avraham of Kalisz, and between 1929 and 1939 (5689-5699) at the large Yeshiva Beit Meir founded by Reb Meir Rappaport in Krakow. There, he found a wide field for his work. Several of his students survived the Holocaust and serve today as rabbis and Yeshiva heads in Jewish communities in the Diaspora and also in Israel.

Reb Mendel loved his fellow Jews. He pursued peace, inspired peace, and drew hearts near. He was of the students of Hillel [141]. His ways were ways of pleasantness. He behaved nobly, and served as a fine example of a Hassidic Jew and scholar.

At the time of the Holocaust, he was exiled from Krakow to the city of Wolbrom. From there, he was brought to a concentration came in the city of Stryj, Galicia. When he was called to meet his fate, he refused to look into the face of the enemy, and turned his face from them. They then shot him in the back and he fell, holding a Bible to his heart. May G-d avenge his blood. May his soul be bound in the bonds of the eternal life of our people.

David Wechsler

As a student of our teacher Reb Mendel Wechsler, from whom I studied for about four years, first at the Beit Ulpana and then at Yesodei Hatorah, and after that also in Yeshivat Beit Avraham in Lodz, I see it as my pleasant obligation to dedicate a few words to his personality.

His style of teaching was didactic and sharp. He was sharp, and an "up rooter of mountains" [142]. He would present his lesson and bring us to the point where we would come up with questions on the difficulties of the Maharsha, the Pnei Yehoshua, and other commentators. He would express his joy when one of the young students would come up himself with the words of the master of didactics. He would take out his notebook, the book of "marks", and write a praiseworthy note about the student. He had great prowess also in Hebrew and grammar. He would encourage us and assist us in progressing. He would recommend books of study, and offer his comments.

His face was always bright, with a smile. He was one of the veteran students of Ger, under the influence of his father-in-law. At first, it was difficult for him to travel to Ger, as he was a student of the Avnei Ezer, the prince of Torah, so why would he need Ger. However, when he finally went to Ger, something novel was exposed to him there, and he continued to travel there.

P. Sirkes

From the words of his students in Krakow: Rabbi Kopel Zylberberg of Jerusalem, Reb Moshe Zylberberg of Bnei Brak, Reb Simcha Szklarcyk, Reb Moshe Sheinfeld, Reb Dov Englard of Tel Aviv.

Even though more than twenty-five years have passed, and many things were forgotten or erased by the Holocaust, we are duty-bound to offer some impressions and outline some notes about the noble personality of one of the unique people and bright personalities of that generation, who departed from us and is no longer here.

Reb Mendel Wechsler sent out his splendor to the people of the generation, and his name went before him everywhere that he went. When he was in Krakow, a city of scholars and writers, a center of giants of Torah and fear of Heaven, he was always the first one to whom all of the institutions of Torah and education turned to honor and involve in every event and festive occasion. If a guest passed through Krakow, he would immediately feast his eyes upon the name of Reb Mendel Wechsler who graced the headlines of the newsletters of the Torah institutions on occasions of his appearances and lectures. He was also an examiner in the Beis Yaakov teacher's seminary, and the living spirit in the Torah atmosphere of the city. May his memory and activities be blessed forever!

Reb Aharon Yosef Berger by Z. Ben Shimon

Reb Aharon Yosef Berger

Reb Aharon Yosef the son of Reb Yechezkel Berger was numbered among the honorable people of the city and the people of deeds. Reb Aharon

434

Yosef Berger of blessed memory His name went before him as a faithful man of the community, to whom the good of the public and the foundations of social justice were always his guiding light, to which he dedicated his efforts and strength.

Reb Aharon Yosef was born in the city of Podamwice [143] in the year 1878. He grew up and was educated upon the knees of his maternal grandfather, the holy Rabbi Yitzchak Yaakov Kaufman of blessed memory, the head of the rabbinical court of the holy community of Podamwice. When he was still young, at eighteen years old, he arrived in Zgierz, to his uncle the manufacturer Reb Mendel Kaufman, who was one of the important householders of the city.

Aharon Yosef quickly acclimatized himself to the unique atmosphere of Zgierz, to its culture and industry, and went from success to success. As a man of pleasant mannerisms, he acquired a good name in the community of merchants and manufacturers. People had faith in him and valued his rightness and levelheaded opinions, even though he knew how to stand strong and defend his ideas when he saw them as correct. He also had a charming appearance, and the people of Zgierz related to him with appreciation and politeness.

His name was first mentioned as a communal activist in the year 5669 (1909), when the rabbi of the city, Rabbi Shlomo Leib of holy blessed memory, appointed him as a member of the committee for the community Mikva (ritual bath). The institution of the Mikva was one of those institutions upon which Jewish life in the communities of the towns was based in those days. The rabbi therefore made sure that the heads of this institution would be responsible people, G-d fearing, proper, and acceptable to the public. Members of this community included Reb Gedalia Greenberg, Reb Mordechai Shmuel Cudkowicz, Reb Yisrael Frugel, Reb Zeev Reichert, Reb Binyamin Szaranski, and Reb Yosef Berger, the youngest in this committee - all of them were prominent people.

He became especially close with the rabbi, who recognized him as a generous man, and understood his serious relationship to the values of Judaism. Without doubt, he also took note of his rabbinical origins. They had a friendly and understanding relationship throughout the years. In the years of 1910-1912, when the rabbi was involved in a serious battle against the powerful manufacturers over the issue of hiring Jews in the Jewish factories (an issue that was fraught with certain difficulties) Aharon Yosef stood at the right side of the rabbi in his battle, along with the well-known just, upright manufacturer Reb Moshel Eiger. The first people who transferred all of their work in their factories to Jewish hands were the manufacturers Moshe Hendeles and Eliezer Shlumiel.

During and also after the years of the First World War, Reb Aharon Yosef stood in the communal field for the benefit of the Jews of the city. This was true especially at the outset of the war, with the destruction of manufacturing and an alarming economic situation, when illness and hunger pervaded among the residents and there was a need for special measures to organize communal life and relieve the pressure. He was a member of the important committee, the financial and taxation committee, which was chosen at the first meeting of the communal council that took place on August 1, 1915. At the beginning of 1918, he was elected to the communal council in accordance with the official electoral law, along with Messrs. Daniel Sirkes, Isuchar Szwarc and Zeev Eliahu Reichert. From then, he could be found on almost all of the important committees that were chosen by the community for various communal and national purposes.

Aside from his work on the communal council, Reb Aharon Yosef also played an active role in other communal institutions of the city. He signed a certificate dated June 30, 1926 as the chairman of the "Jewish Union of Manufacturers and Merchants in Zgierz". Similarly, he was among the founders of the Bikur Cholim of Zgierz, and was also active in the field of traditional education. He did a great deal of work on behalf of the national funds for the Land of Israel.

He died on the twenty-ninth of Kislev 5684 (1934) at the age of 56.
Honor to his memory.
Zeev the son of Shimon

Reb Fishel Rus

Reb Fishel Rus

Zgierz had many "fine Jews" and also many Torah scholars. However, people did not have too much time to dedicate to the study of Torah, for they general were preoccupied with worries of livelihood.

Reb Fishel Rus was certainly a fine character of an Aleksandrow Hassid and scholar. He was well-known by every Jew of Zgierz on account of his sweet prayers on the High Holy Day Musafs in the city Beis Midrash.

Reb Fishel Rus, a scholarly Jew, would sit in his dyeing workshop with a book in his hand. He was not a communal activist or an opinion giver in the city. He had no airs about him.

Fishel's discussions of Torah were intelligent and matter-of-fact, calm and peaceful. Everyone around him had to perk up their ears in order not to miss a word of his. His every word was like a precious pearl sliding out of his mouth.

He was so straightforward and honorable in his dyeing shop, with matters of selling and regarding the dyes - so straightforward was he with his Torah discussions. He did not hold himself high. He did not show off his knowledge. On the contrary, he made efforts to understand others.

With Fishel Rus, the bookshelves did not stand orphaned as they did with other wealthy people of Zgierz, who had lovely bookshelves with glass doors, where the Vilna Shas [144] stood forlorn, like a mere decoration. With him, the bookshelves had a proper use. They were often opened by the hands of the scholar in order to take out a book.

When Fishel, the Aleksandrow Hassid, would come to worship Mincha and Maariv in the Gerrer Shtibel, it was a joyous occasion there. The learners derived pleasure from having a conversation with him about significant matters. At such a moment, they forgot about the divide between Gur and Aleksandrow.

May his memory be blessed. Yitzchak Szaransky

Reb Avraham Klorfeld of blessed memory

He arrived in Zgierz from Kamenetz-Podolsk. He worked as an employee in the weaving factory, and was quickly exposed as a visionary, who had great influence upon the younger generation. He encouraged those who rebelled against and despised the life in the exile, who struggled for "renewal". Incidentally, he struck fear into the hearts of the fathers who were unhappy with their children turning to deviation, to Zionism, from whence a whiff of danger to Judaism emanated. He joined forces with the Hebrew teacher in order to instill the language to those who wished to learn it. He himself fulfilled his own preaching, and sent his son and daughter to the Land of Israel when they got older.

He himself prepared daily for aliya, and set times for the study of Torah. His home was a meeting place for Zionism. Menachem Berliner of blessed memory, and may he live, Yehoshua Manoach, today of Degania, could be found in that house. In that house, it was always possible to find a Hebrew book, the Hatzefira newspaper, and to hear the latest news from the "colonies" in the Land of Israel.

During the time of the "kulturkampf", money for assistance was collected in that meeting place. At the end of the First World War, he actualized his desire and made aliya to the Land with his family. Despite his advancing age, he was not adverse to difficult physical labor. He loaded zifzif (coarse sand) onto the backs of camels and dragged bags of sand. He did this all with love.

In his latter years, he merited to see children and grandchildren working the fields and vineyards in the State of Israel, something that he did not do himself even though he dreamed of this for all of his days. His memory will not depart from us. May his soul be bound in the bonds of eternal life.

Yoav Katz - ("Davar", May 25, 1958, the day of the death of A. Klorfeld.)

Zalman Feldscher

Zalman Grondwald, even though he was only a feldscher [145], indeed a Starshi [146] feldscher, with three brass plates over his entrance - was known in the city, and furthermore in the surrounding villages as a great professor. His face, with a pointed gray beard, always shone with a splendorous friendliness, as if born to heal and calm the ill.

On occasion, a carriage or horse drawn coach would come from far off villages to take the feldscher Grondwald to a farmer or an ailing landowner. The farmer's wife would wring her hands and murmur that Grondwald could not help, that the priest must come to administer the last rights to the sick.

He was a renowned person in the city. Jews and Christians knew that Zalman Feldscher understood medicine more than the doctors to whom one removes one's hat if they actually come to a sick person in the house.

Zalman Feldscher did not only use cupping glasses, leeches, administer an enema or excise wild flesh. He also wrote prescriptions that were tolerated by the Christian pharmacists in the city.

For complex diseases, when the doctors decided to convene a conference, they would invite Zalman Feldscher as one of the consultants, and they would take his opinion into account.

When Zalman Feldscher came to the home of a Jewish ill person, he acted joyously. His simple Yiddish discussion with the sick person, and his calming of the family greatly lightened the illness, and lessened the somber mood of those around.

If there was an epidemic in town, Zalman Feldscher would run from one sick person to another without tiring. He would write prescriptions and administer massages. He would literally give of himself, and, unlike the other doctors, he was not afraid of catching the illness.

Zalman would demonstrate his deep humanity to poor Jews. Not only would he not take money for the visit, but he would also give money to purchase the prescription. His memory should be honored.

Yitzchak Szaransky

Yaakov Berliner-Baniel of blessed memory
(The researcher and philosopher)

Yaakov Berliner-Baniel

Yaakov Berliner (Baniel) was born on the 9th of Kislev 5642 (1882) in Zgierz, to his parents David Aryeh and Ruchama. This was a pious family of good lineage, a scion of the family of Rabbi Yom Tov Lipman Heller, the author of Tosafot Yom Tov. Yaakov was the third son of the family, which consisted of six sons and two daughters.

From his youth, Yaakov excelled in his studies, and even became known as a genius and diligent studier. When he was nine years old, he moved from the cheder to the Beis Midrash to study Torah along with the adult attendees of the Beis Midrash. At the age of fourteen, he studied Torah from the rabbi of the city, and also began to complement his education with foreign languages, mathematics and business. This later became his path in life, to mix Torah and tradition along with general knowledge. These two areas complemented each other with him, and made peace with each other.

"The foundation for his spiritual and cultural development arose from the unique atmosphere of his native city of Zgierz - which has two meanings: the

440

clear and healthy air of the expanses of the fields and forests, and the sharp atmosphere of the unique Jewish community." (Y. D. Beit-Halevi: Yaakov Baniel (Berliner), the researcher and philosopher, Nivim, the Cooperative Center, 5717 / 1957, Tel Aviv).

When he accepted upon himself the family yoke, he moved to Lodz, and began to work as an accounting manager. In his free time, he gave lessons in Greek and Latin. His command of those languages was phenomenal. Aside from Hebrew, Yiddish, and classical languages, he knew Armenian, Polish, Russian, English, French and German.

Despite his many concerns, Baniel found time to work for Zionism. He was greatly troubled that his brother Menachem preceded him in aliya in the year 5671 (1911), even before the First World War. Menachem, who gained expertise and a diligent agricultural worker and as a brave guard, was one of the first settlers of Atarot (Kalandia), and later one of the founders of Gan Shmuel. He was a man of work and Torah, in accordance with the traditions of the family. After a hard day at work, he would find time to teach Hebrew to the new immigrants. He was loved and revered by all who knew him. At the time of the First World War, he contracted Yellow Fever, from which he died.

Yaakov made aliya in the year 5686 (1926) in the wake of the Fourth Aliya, along with his family of six. However, he was not able to secure his livelihood, for the great depression that pervaded in the Land at that time overtook him. This depression caused many to leave the Land. His broad intellect stood for him during his time of tribulation, and he succeeded in obtaining half-day work in the cooperative committee affiliated with the city council of Tel Aviv, as a leader and accounting auditor of the cooperatives.

The all-encompassing knowledge and talents of Yaakov Baniel began to bear fruit. He related to the bookkeeping profession not as a mechanical task of combining numbers and auditing accounts, but as a science, bound by specific rules. He demanded that people of this profession study and review the internal meaning and content of the numbers. "Life and death is in the hands of numbers", he used to say. He did a great deal to teach this profession too many, in the manner that he regarded it as a science.

However, as has been stated, Yaakov Baniel was not merely an accountant. He delved into the depths of the professional regimen. He never stopped studying, and conducted a great deal of research. The fruits of his research were published in various manuscripts in "Leshoneinu" - an organ for the expression of the linguistic committee; in the Tarbitz quarterly that was published by the Hebrew University; in the Sinai monthly published by Mossad Harav Kook, and also in various daily and weekly newspapers. From time to time, he also gave lectures on the topics of his research. He lectured on the topic of "Patterns of the verb in the Hebrew language" at the world convention of Jewish scientists that took place under the auspices of the Hebrew University in Jerusalem in the summer of 5607 (1947). Several of his research articles were published in his book Nivim, in the section of translations. In one of them, he delved deeply into a wonderful discussion in the Jerusalem Talmud, which he dedicated to the memory of Reb Isuchar Moshe Szwarc of blessed memory, whom he described as the "Splendor of the Jewish community of Zgierz, my native city."

He was diligent in the fundamental understanding of Bible, and researched deeply into the Talmud and Midrash. He had great satisfaction when he succeeded in understanding a difficult issue. He then immediately tried to impart his new ideas to the public, and to spread from his well outward. A large part of the progress of Yaakov is related to his dedicated and faithful wife Pessa Elisheva, the daughter of Reb Leibel Herzon of Zgierz, who supported him and encouraged him.

His home, which was a gathering place for scholars, was pervaded with Torah and research. His work room was covered with covered with shelves of books from floor to ceiling. Despite the fact that he was accepted in the intelligentsia circles in the Land, he did not grant himself rest as an expert scientist, whose profession was Torah. He conducted himself modesty, and did not aggrandize himself over the richness of his knowledge. He distanced himself from all hyperbole and did not act in a grand manner. Rather, he delved into Torah as a scholar who bestowed merit upon the masses. He never kept his novel ideas to himself. If he discovered some idea, he would make haste to present it in public in his own unique fashion, calmly and with full explanation, without negating the opinions of others. His ideas were always listened to with great attention.

He observed and valued the traditions of his fathers. He fulfilled the practical commandments and the interpersonal commandments with a unique graceful manner. He was always in good spirits with his family and people who came into his house. He taught well and fulfilled well.

Yaakov Baniel was modest and discreet, despite the fact that he was great in Torah and wisdom. He was comfortable with philosophical sciences. He published research articles on issues of Judaism, Hebrew language and grammar, and fundamental linguistic creations based on comparisons and logic. Even more than what he published, there remained with him many manuscripts that did not see the light of day. Even during the time of his difficult illness, he lectured to his relatives and friends about his deep, organized research ideas, which were ready for compilation and publication, something that he would do when he would regain his health...

However, he did not regain his health. His malignant illness was strong, cruel, and merciless. He fought it strongly, attempted to ignore it, and hoped for the future with his literary plans, even though his situation was extremely serious, as he was lying on his sickbed.

On the Sabbath of the 19th of Kislev 5710 (1951), he fell asleep in his suffering and did not arise again. May his soul be bound in the bonds of eternal life.

(From Y. D. Beit-Halevi in the book Nivim, and other sources.)

Menachem Berliner

Zgierz, even though I was only there for a small period, is guarded in a warm area of my heart. It was the last stop during my life in the exile. From there, I made aliya to the Land, and there my Zionism ripened.

I came to the Reichert house as a teacher to Zelig. I stress "melamed", and not "moreh" [147]. The house was jointly owned by Zeev Michael and his wife Eida, and Zeev Eliahu and his wife Machla. The wives were sisters and the husbands cousins. When I arrived there more than sixty years ago, the first family had already visited the Land twice, and the second one, once. The brother of Zeev Eliahu, Yisrael Yitzchak (known today as professor

Reichert), studied in a teacher's seminary in Jerusalem. His daughter Tamar studied in a public school in Rechovot. They were Zionist Jews who observed the commandments. Their suitcases were effectively packed. Indeed, t hey made aliya immediately after the First World War.

Menachem Berliner

It is impossible for me not to describe my first dinner in the Reichert house. The memory of that meal will always be with me. We washed our hands, and recited the Hamotzie blessing. On the table were black olives, which I was seeing for the first time in my life. The mistress of the house urged me to try the olives. I agreed, took one and put it in my mouth. The taste was bitter and unpleasant, and I was about to take it out to throw it out. However, when I saw that the eyes of all of those gathered at dinner were looking at me in anticipation, I understood the situation. I chewed it, swallowed it, and took a second one. They broke out in laughter, and I joined in with them. However, once I got used to them, I would eat dozens of them. I recall how they would hurry to remove them from the table - for it was an expensive food. I received an important lesson in the economy of the Land, where black and green olives are a course in every meal.

How did I come to meet the people of Zgierz? How did we come in contact for the first time? I do not recall at all. For the first part, I was a teacher of Zelig Reichert, as I mentioned, and for the second part for the Koretz family. I forgot all of the details. However, I recall very well the family of Avraham Klorfeld. I would visit their house and I was friends with their older children Asher and Lea. This family made aliya. I also recall the head of the family, a weaver by trade, who when he first made aliya worked for some time in transporting building materials by camel. They presented a unique image of a Jewish family of that time, which changed its external appearance and way of life completely. They attempted to acclimatize themselves to the landscape of the Land, and planted themselves there in the most extreme fashion. I often thought about this family, the son and the daughter. For some reason, I did not remain in contact with them in the land. This is a mystery that I cannot solve. However, their memory is guarded with me as one of the finest.

I remember Reb Isuchar Szwarc, whose house I visited often. He provided me with a letter to Dr. Kaminka, who lived in the metropolis of Vienna at the time, that he should help me with my aliya. He was pleasant in his manners, and always cheerful. He was a scholarly Jew and a friend of many writers, including Nachum Sokolov. The Land of Israel was always a topic of conversation among us.

Everything is like in a fog. I do not remember even how I met Menachem Berliner, with whom I was connected and whom I later met several times in the Land. However, the appearance of his face stands as if alive before my eyes. His prominent chin exuded strength, power, and internal confidence. He was born on the 14th of Av 5651 (1891). H received a Torah oriented Jewish education, and was dedicated to work in the Zionist movement from his youth. He founded a library, established courses in Hebrew, and organized groups of youths for Zionist work.

He fled Zgierz with one ruble in his pocket. He crossed the border to Germany through Kalisz. One of his brothers chased after him. Menachem saw him in Kalisz, but the brother did not see him. He wandered greatly along the way. He experienced many adventures until he arrived. He was delayed in Berlin, Vienna, and later in Trieste. He danced for joy like a young child as he climbed the mountains of Trieste. He would shortly be in the land. Here is a letter from him from Trieste.
"Sunday, 10:00 a.m.

I am traveling from here in two hours. I have to go to the seashore. Before I take leave of the bitter exile, I raise my hands in an oath: I swear in the name of our people who have suffered for 2,00 years; I swear by the blood of our brethren that was spilled as water; I swear by the broken sword of Yochanan and Bar Kochba; I swear by the souls of our fathers who were killed in sanctification of the Divine name; I swear by the new Hasmonaeans who arose for us after the exile of 2,00 years; I swear by my brave brothers in the Land of Israel; I swear by the renaissance of the People of Israel on our land - that I will never return to the Diaspora, and I will fight for our people and our land until my last drop of blood, on the mountains of Zion and Jerusalem."

This is a pure and wondrous innocence. From where did this spirit come? From where did this internal flame come? It is impossible to read this letter without emotion. A warm feeling envelops you, and you are captivated by it. These are the sparks that arose from the field of the renaissance of our nation. Isolated and scattered, one here and one there -but they joined together and were attracted here by a power that is hard to define. To here, to here, the shore of the blue sea. More than sixty years have passed since then. It seems to me that he was one of the first that made aliya from Zgierz.

From Jaffa, he went to Petach Tikva. He remained there for about six weeks, and then went to Rechovot, a nine hour journey. He remained there until he moved to Gan Shmuel. He was among the ten people who were summoned there to work and guard the orchard, to expand the place, to improve it and build it up.

I still have dozens of letters that he wrote while on the journey to the Land, on his experiences in the Land and his work. All of them form one long sequence of events, deeds, meetings, visits, and festivities. They all exude a good spirit, boundless faith, and unblemished warmth. He was good hearted, and a faithful and dedicated friend. His hand was outstretched to offer help without any hesitation. His hand was open and his heart was good.

"Not infrequently, he paid the debts of friends in a store, and shared his possessions with his friends" - writes A. M. Kolar of blessed memory, who worked with him in Gan Shmuel, in "Davar"" (9th Nisan 5700 / 1940), on the 25th anniversary of his death.

He donated 20 Francs to the fund for the printing of Hapoel Hatzair. In those days, that was a huge sum for a day worker. (Incidentally, he wrote to his relatives in the Diaspora and advised them to donate as well, and send money to that fund.)

446

He sent many letters to friends and acquaintances in order to urge them to make aliya. When his brothers pointed out to him the cost of the stamps, he answered that he believes that his letters will exert influence, for "words that come from the heart enter the heart". Therefore, it was forbidden for him not to write. (Incidentally, in all his letters, he asked that the address be written only in Hebrew, with the addition of "Palestine".)

"I go to work with joy and diligence" - he writes in one of his letters. "I got used to the spade. My friends are surprised as to how my face has improved, since I was pale when I arrived.". In another letter, he writes, "I am happy with my lot here. I was created for the Land."

It is appropriate to dedicate a few words to the work with which Menachem was occupied.

He writes and tells a great deal about the work with the hoe and the spade. Those who became attached to this type of work do not forget it. The back pains, the blisters on the hand and the general fatigue that accompany any beginner, pass quickly. There is something about this type of work, the work with the hoe and the spade. During the time that one stands so bent over, digging furrows around trees or turning over the entire area of the orchard with the spade (known as 'tachmir') - there is a feeling of self-transcendence that blows internal confidence and self-worth into one's being: behold, you have become a worker in the Land of Israel; behold, you have become accustomed to the work and earn your livelihood from the toil of your hand; behold I am fulfilling the obligation of "conquest of the work", and the Arab labor is becoming Hebrew labor. Was this not the reason that we made aliya to the Land!

Our Menachem, with his boundless energy and initiative, quickly became one of the expert workers of the spade, and earned the title of king, King of Spades. His eye was open to anything new that took place in the area that he was working, and his hand was outstretched in guidance assistance for anyone who was faltering. If anyone did not complete his quota of furrows around trees, or if there was a suspicion that someone would be pushed out of his rank by Arabs -Menachem would immediately jump in and set to work with the spade or the hoe, quickly and diligently to avert the problem, and then return to his place.

447

Menachem always was able to save. His energy was with him. From where did this weaver of Zgierz get such energy? He had the will, the strong will of a Jew, to take over the work and turn it into Hebrew work, to prove that a Jew is able to work at any difficult labor. He was always enthusiastic and diligent, without any compromise with himself. He worked and was successful. He conquered himself. As has been mentioned, he knew how to share his bread with others. His hand was open and his heart was proper. The conditions at that time were different. There was no organization as there is today. Mutual assistance organizations were not yet founded. However, there were warm hearts infused with truth, and Menachem was one of the best.

Menachem Berliner as a guard

448

He was himself as duty bound to participate in any activity that raised the status of Hebrew work and the Jewish worker, the love of the Land and the people of Israel. Therefore, he went and became a guard in the vineyards of Rechovot in the summer of 5672 (1912) (we will still speak about the guard duty). He was passionate about the strength that he was imparting to Jews against the Arabs. When he was summoned in the winter of 5674 to go to Gan Shmuel, a place afflicted with malaria, where the work was being renewed by a group of workers from Rechovot, and he had private reasons not to go (his bride Rachel was about to arrive) - Menachem went. Was it possible to be otherwise? When he went, he went with a full heart. Thus does A. M. Kolar write about him in the aforementioned work.

"In the winter of that year 95674) Gan Shmuel was settled by a group of workers, most of them were guards who worked with "Hashomer" in Rechovot, who had left the settlement with him. Menachem was called by the members to join the group. He answered the call, since young, dedicated, diligent workers were needed. He gave himself over to the work with the entire warmth of his heart and strength. He quickly became an important force in the farm. In his letters to his family from that era, filled with enthusiasm and joy, he describes at length the life of the group, which was not a life of renewal and happiness. 'One the one hand', he writes, 'the war was dragging on, and there were endless victims, and on the other hand, Hebrew life is growing out of all those graves. I live with the work and with nature, with every flower and tree.'

Many tribulations afflicted the group in Gan Shmuel during its first year. The afflictions were genuine. Malaria often afflicted him, and he swallowed a great amount of chinin [148]. As with the rest of the members, he was not concerned about the situation: if the fever dropped, they would get out of bed and go to work. He was completely immersed in the work and in the farm.

He would quickly tell his brothers about any thing new in the place; about any new animal or bird; about the building of new homes; about the gaining of new members; about the upcoming harvest; and about how happy he was 'in our small world'. However his soul knew no rest, and he dreamed about traveling to the Galilee to conquer new areas.

As an experienced guard, he took active part in guard duty and the defense of Gan Shmuel. The first months of the group were filled with clashes with the Arab neighbors, who would often pillage the area. More than once, they hatched plots to break through the fence at night and steal. Menachem performed his guard duties with full seriousness and a watchful eye. One night, when the neighbors attempted to break into the orchard, they attacked him and his fellow guard. He fought against the intruders, and they were forced to flee after one of them was wounded in the hand."

One could depend on Menachem. His responsibility surpassed all bounds. Before I conclude, allow me to tell about my meeting with him.

He knew about my coming, but he did not come to the ship. I was quite surprised. However, later I found out that he had been bitten by a mad jackal. Since there was not yet a Pasteur institute in the Land, he was taken to Cairo in order to receive anti-rabies shots. His letters from Cairo display a unique side of our Menachem's personality. He did not have the means to stay in a proper location. He also did not have sufficient food. He managed. He slept where he sat and ate what he could obtain from the soup kitchen - in cheap and unsanitary places.

I obtained work in the vineyards of Rishon Letzion, and awaited his arrival. He found out about my arrival and my place of work as he arrived by boat to Jaffa. However, he did not go to Rishon Letzion so that we could get together, but rather hurried to guard duty in Rechovot, despite the jaguar bite. Weeks passed before we designated the day that I would come to him in Rechovot, one Friday afternoon after work.

Yehuda Gorodiski, a farmer from Rechovot, waited for me until I changed my clothes. I took the pillow and blankets that I brought to Menachem from his parents, and we set out to Rechovot in a horse drawn carriage. Rather than traveling through the shortest and most direct route through Nes Tziona, the farmer traveled through Beer Yaakov, since he was interested in the route.

I left the pillow and blankets with the farmer (incidentally, he never came to take them), and set out to see the chief guard of the Moshava, so I would be able to find out the place where Menachem was guarding. This is a long story, which I will not tell here. Mendel Portugali of blessed memory, one of the chief guards, showed me the way that I should go to arrive at the vineyard which Menachem was guarding. I set out in that direction. I met a guard after my first steps, who transferred me to his neighbor, and the neighbor transferred me to his own neighbor. Thus I passed from hand to hand until I reached Menachem's vineyard. But Menachem was not there. Where was he? He would come immediately. I heard the guards whispering among themselves, as if they were keeping a secret from me. I looked somewhat strange to them. I was wearing a white suite, white shoes, and a straw hat. They were wary of me. Who knows what type of a covert visitor this guard might be expecting? They left me and continued on their guard duty.

It was a moonlit night. There are no words to describe the moon as it lit up the fields of almonds and grapes. The nighttime silence enveloped me, and I was engrossed in it. No wind was blowing. No leaf rustled. For the first time in my life I felt this sort of eternal feeling, which bound me up. I stood in one place, paying complete attention. This wondrous silence spoke to the heart. The calm and silence were like wings to the imagination. Suddenly, the howl of jackals. I contracted. A shudder passed over my entire body. I never heard such a howl, which, as it passed through the wide fields and reached every ear - sounded similar to the heart-rending cries of children, the shrieks of the weary and suffering, the voices calling for help and demanding it was such immediacy that it could not be put off for a thousandth of a second.

I will never forget that night. I was young. These were among my first steps in my old-new homeland. All the history of my people, all of the suffering and weeping that they endured, passed quickly through my memory. This howl told and retold a story. I forgot myself and my surroundings, as I paid complete attention. More than 59 years have passed since that moment, however, I remember that night as if it was taking place now. Behold, here I am listening and paying attention...

I got tired. I ascended the ladder of Menachem's guard booth, took out a squashed mattress, shook it out, and sat down upon it. After that, I lay down, with my eyes pointed to the sky, peering at the bright stars, the stars of the Land of Israel. Obviously, sleep overtook me. Suddenly: Bang! Bang! Bang! Three shots of a revolver rang out close to my ears. I obviously awoke and jumped up in a start. As I jumped up, I fell into Menachem's arms. He hugged and kissed me, with a bright, smiling face.

Where had he been? He went to meet me in Nes Ziona. He stood on the route and waited for me. Another guard went with him. The guards of the area, when they heard that Menachem's friend from his native city was coming, and was arriving from Rishon Letzion, made an agreement among themselves not to let anyone know about his travel and his leaving of his guard post. They would not let any visitor know of his whereabouts, and they would divide the Menachem's guard duty among themselves until he returned. As I mentioned, I had traveled through Beer Yaakov, and he waited in vain. He waited for a long time, for he could not imagine that I would not come, and he was concerned that I got lost on the route, and that if he would go, I would suddenly appear?

He told me about his internal struggle between his guard duty and his concern for me. He thought that he would return at the beginning of the night, and permitted himself the misdeed of leaving his guard post. Had he known that this would have happened, he would not have gone. He had pangs of conscience over his deeds which had a taint of dishonesty. It was a "miracle' that on that night, no visitor, rider, or guard came until he returned, since everything was clean externally. He was not caught. However, the incident bothered Menachem's heart.

He came late, and his neighboring guards began to worry about him. What happened? Why was he not returning? The route was long. It was an hour and a half or two hours. However, when he arrived at the first guard in the vineyards of Rechovot, in the direction of Nes Tziona, the guard told him that someone was waiting for him near his tent. He crouched down, saw my face, became excited, and shot three shots, as I have mentioned.

The joy was great. We embraced as we walked the route of his guard duty and chatted. We discussed and poured out our hearts. More accurately: Menachem talked and poured out his heart. He had already been in the Land for three quarters of a year! He had what to talk about! He talked very little of himself. He talked about events that were taking place, on what was to come and what had passed. On occasion he forgot that he was on guard duty and raised his voice too high. Thus did we pass the time until morning.

This was my first meeting in the Land with Menachem Berliner. We were young. We were the same age. More than 59 years have passed since then. I am alive, and he, Menachem, where is he?

Let us once again see what A. M. Kolar writes about Menachem's end.

"One day, at he beginning of Adar 5675 (1915), Menachem returned from work in the middle of the day with a high fever. He was immediately taken to the hospital in Hadera. He lay there for a few days, and the symptoms of yellow fever were quickly recognized. He was transferred the care of Dr. Hillel Yaffa in the hospital of Zichron Yaakov, a dedicated physician who was an expert in the care of fevers. However his faithful care was for naught. Menachem bore his illness in silence. He did not complain, and did not speak much. He greeted his friends from the group, who came to visit him, pleasantly, as was his usual fashion. He did not cease to take interest in what was going on in Gan Shmuel. His strong body build finally gave in, and on Friday afternoon, 19th of Adar 5675, he gave up his pure soul at the age of 23 ½."

I was told that he fought with death for three days and three nights. His strong heart stood against it, and did not let it overtake him. Dr. Yaffa was excited at the strength of his heart, and he was not able to forget this sick person for quite a while, to whom life was so sweet and pleasant such that he did not want to part from it. Dr. Yaffa mourned for him especially.

We are separated from him, from Menachem. He belongs to those who are connected to the chain of generations of our people, the People of Israel. He is folded into the great gloom of our people, about which the Scripture says: "And he expired, and was gathered unto his people" (Genesis 49, 33).

May his memory be a blessing.

He is buried in the cemetery of Zichron Yaakov.

Yehoshua Manoach, Degania Aleph

The following is the text on the gravestone of Menachem Berliner in the cemetery of Zichron Yaakov :

Here rests the young man Menachem the son of David Berliner Who died of yellow fever on 19th of Adar, 5675 To a dear friend - a memorial from the group of Gan Shmuel May his soul be bound in the bonds of eternal life

Rabbi Chanoch Henich Ehrsohn

He was a scholar and author of books. He was known in our town as "The yellow Henich". He was married to Elka the owner of the butcher shop (Elka the butcher), an honorable woman, who was known as a generous and charitable woman. He was one of the honorable Hassidim of Ger. Yeshiva students would come to him each Sabbath to be examined. He served as principal of the Yesodei Hatorah School in 5778-5779 (1918-1919). He died in the early 1920s.

The following are his books that were published before the First World War: 1) Chanukat Hatorah, 2) Kol Eliahu (about the Vilna Gaon), 3) Minchat Chanoch, 4) Gan Raveh (on the Torah), 5) Motza Mayim (about variations in versions).

Reb Yosef Bialystoki of blessed memory

He was known by his name, Yosef Shmuel Chassid's, that is to say, the son-in-law of Reb Shmuel Chassid.

He was also a zealous Hassid of Ger. He occupied himself with Torah and Hassidism for all his days, and watched over the younger generation with a vigilant eye, that they should go in the paths of the fathers and not wander into strange fields.

His book, short in length but great in quality is called "Mesora Gedola" It is on the tractate Chagiga [149], and includes "the words of our rabbis from various places in similar language forms, by conjoining words and innuendoes in accordance with the commentators" (from the preface). It was published in Piotrkow in the year 5693. Aside from the approbation of the rabbi of the city Rabbi Shlomo Yehuda Hakohen and his brother Yitzchak Menachem Hakohen, it also contains approbations from the Admorim of Ger, Sochaczew, Sokolow, Strykow, Rabbi M. Shapira of Lublin, Rabbi Menachem Zemba of Prague, and others.

He died during the Holocaust. May G-d avenge his blood.

Avraham Chaim Michelson of blessed memory

He was born in the year 5646 (1886) to his father the Hassidic bibliograph Rabbi Tzvi Yechezkel Michelson, the rabbi of Plonsk and Warsaw. He was the son-in-law of Reb Baruch Nekricz of our city.

During his youth, he followed the path of his father and also worked on the annals, stories and words of Torah of the rabbis and Admorim. He wrote about the rabbinical greats of their time.

He served as secretary of the community in our city for a number of years. He was one of the intelligentsia, and a lover of the Hebrew book. He was blessed with a sense of humor. His adages made their way around the city.

His books include: "Shemen Hatov" (5665 - 1905), a monograph about Rabbi Shmelke Horowitz the rabbi of Nikolsburg and his brother Rabbi Pinchas Horowitz, the rabbi of Frankfurt am Main; "Dover Shalom" (5671 - 1911) about the Admor Rabbi Shalom of Belz and his son Rabbi Yehoshua; "Ohel Elimelech" on the Admor Rabbi Elimelech of Lizhensk; "Ohel Rebbe" about the Admor Rabbi Yaakov Yitzchak Horowitz, the Chozeh of Lublin; "Ateret Menachem", and "Ohel Naftali" (written in Zgierz).

He died during the Holocaust. May G-d avenge his death.

Avraham Morgensztern

Every city and town in Poland had people who felt more than others the intolerable plight of the poor people, the circumscribed rights of the citizens of means, and considered it to be a deep insult that Jews were classified as second class citizens of the country and state, without full rights. These people came to the conclusion that in the atmosphere of hate and oppression, the only way of existence was to fend for oneself - the way of organization. They formed corporations that were able to speak and take great measures, demand more rights, struggle against anti-Semitism, take part n the broadening of legislation, in which the organizations took interest in supporting the treasuries of the Jewish past, and forge onward with the golden chain. These specific ideas were the call of the times.

Large organizations were founded in Warsaw whose purpose was to organize the Jewish people throughout the entire country. To that end, they required people who were interested in opening local branches.

We had such a person in our city. His name was Avraham Morgensztern. He was short, and he had the nature, as if to compensate, to invest a great deal of energy in organizational activities. He was represented in all local Jewish institutions - as founder, chairman or vice-chairman.

If a controversy arose, as is wont to occur in social institutions, he would appear on behalf of a specific organization. He would feel an inner push, a need to create something and bring help to another segment of the Jewish population of Zgierz.

The youth also had a friend in him. He was the founder of the touring organization. Thereby, he did not neglect the cultural interests of a portion of the Jewish population of our city. The "Hazamir" displayed a strong activity for a period of time. The choir sang Hebrew and Jewish songs. Readings took place with the participation of renowned writers such as Hillel Cejtlin, Yitzchak Kacenelson, Dr. Mokdoni, the editor Y. Unger and others.

Avraham Morgensztern knew Jewish life in Zgierz very well. His activity of many years' duration as councilor in the city council provided him with material to conduct correspondence regarding Jewish and general life in Zgierz in the Lodzer Tagblatt under the pseudonym "Amen".

The aforementioned section presents picture of a person who gave his entire life over to the Jewish society of Zgierz, often neglecting his private interests.

His name should be engraved in an esteemed fashion upon the monument of Zgierz Jewry.

Fabian Greenberg-Green

Reb Yehuda Leib Szaransky

Reb Yehuda Leib Szaransky

Reb Yehuda Leib (Leibl) Szaransky was born in 1886 in Zgierz. His father was Reb Binyamin the son of Reb Yitzchak, who was a native of Lithuania and came to Zgierz from the city of Kovno with a stream of Lithuanian Jews who was attracted to economic opportunities in the manufacturing region of Lodz. Reb Yitzchak, who was known locally as Reb Itche Kovner, was a scholarly, Hassidic Jew, formerly a follower of Kock and later of Ger. He was the grandson of Reb Zecharia Mendel of Jaroslawow and a scion of the Gaon of Vilna.

Even though Leib was nurtured in the world of Hassidism, he always had a tendency to "lateral" thinking and research. He displayed tendencies to activism and struggle. He jumped with warmth and enthusiasm into the Mizrachi camp, even though the world around him, in the Shtibel and with the Rebbe, waged a holy war from the camp of Agudas Yisroel against Mizrachi, and steadfastly opposed its ideas and activities.

Leib Szaransky also stood out in his activities within the Jewish community of Warsaw, which played the central position in the life of the Jews of Poland. The inter-factional relationships and their struggle within the Jewish street took place in full force in the capital of the country. The community of Warsaw served as a guide and example for the Jewish community of Poland.

Leib moved to Warsaw on the eve of the outbreak of the First World War, and worked in business there. During the First War (1914) he began to become involved in communal affairs,
and took a position within the central organization of Mizrachi. There he displayed his talents in polemics and controversy, with fiery, emotional speeches. Thus did he forge himself a position within the Jewish community, of which he was one of its outstanding representatives. He was active in the electoral procedures of the Polish Sejm, and also in the elections to the Zionist congress. In the year 5681 (1921) he was selected as a representative to the congress in Basle, and continued on this role as a representative of Mizrachi in later congresses. In 1933, he was chosen to fill the position of a member of the Jewish Agency, and at the last congress in August 1939, the eve of the Holocaust, he stood out among the dynamic representatives. He was the right hand of Hershel Farbsztejn, the leader of Mizrachi in Poland.

**The Certificate of a Fighter Against the Nazis
of Yehuda Leib Szaransky [150]**

From time to time, he published articles on questions of the time. His articles always excelled in logic and clarity. His steadfast character earned him the name of a fighter and struggler within his party. His Hassidic affiliation often served him as a fence for his factional position. There were times when he struggled not only with fellows in the party, but also with himself - with his own opinion that was at times divided, rigid and uncompromising.

During the times of tribulation in the Warsaw Ghetto, he was one of those who preached revolt and uprising. In a meeting that took place in the house of the Rebbe of Sochaczew, in which the community notables participates, most of those gathered were of the opinion that they should restrain themselves, with faith in G-d, and not revolt against the powerful government that is subduing the entire world. A revolt might hasten the end, and one should await Divine salvation. Leib responded strongly to them: "I am a good Jew like you, who believes with perfect faith in Divine providence, but the Jews of Poland are given over to a death trap, with the partnership of the Nazis and the Poles, for the destruction of Israel - that is decisive. We should at least die in honor."

He placed himself at the disposal of the activists of the revolt. He established ties with the underground Polish Workers' faction, who apparently decided to join the efforts, but did not provide weapons.

Anielewicz [151] and his friends were at first wary to accept him into their confidence. He was an aging Jew, with a large beard, from a group of people who do not like uprisings. How would he fit into the camp of fighters that was mainly composed of young men and women? Leib threw himself into the work diligently. He quickly became an expert in weaponry, and often took dangerous tasks upon himself. He once shot and killed two Germans, and his hand was badly injured in the exchange of fire.

When the "aktions" started, he hastened from place to place to warn the mislead Jews about the true purpose of the emissaries, and he wept at their shortsightedness. His anger was very great at the wealthy people in the ghetto whose hearts still misled them to believe in their life, so that they hid bundles of money and precious stones in their clothing. Szaransky asked them to give over everything that they had, gold, diamonds, and the rest, for the purchase of weapons for anywhere available. It was possible to obtain weapons from the Poles for an exorbitant price. He also used force to request them to turn over their money, and more than once, he came face to face with death on account of this.

He was finally captured by an S.S. man Szaransky succeeded in throwing a hand grenade at him, but the activity did not succeed, and he blew himself up.

His wife Dvora, who was the daughter of the Hassid Reb Mendel Blausztcjn of Zyrardow, also perished later, along with his three daughters. (From the book "Eileh Ezkera" by Hillel Zeidman)

459

Rabbi Meir Szaransky of blessed memory

Rabbi Meir Szaransky

Rabbi Meir Szaransky, the principal of the Beis Yaakov seminary in Tel Aviv, was born in Zgierz in 5665 (1905) to his father Reb Binyamin Szaransky of blessed memory, the six in the male line from the Vilna Gaon of holy blessed memory.

His father Reb Binyamin was born in Kovno, the capital of Lithuania, and was the son of the Gaon and Hassid Reb Yitzchak, who was the son of Reb Mordechai, the son of Reb Avraham, the eldest son of the Gaon of Vilna.

Reb Yitzchak married off all of his sons into prominent and renowned families of Hassidic Poland, and made sure that they would move from Lithuania, the land of the "Misnagdim" to Poland, which was influenced by Hassidism. His son Reb Moshe was the head of the community of Lublin, and Reb Shlomo was the head of the community of Siedlic. Reb Binyamin, the youngest of the sons, married Chava, the daughter of the Hassid Reb Nota Heinsdorf. Reb Nota was one of the greatest Hassidim of Kock, and the head of the Hassidim of Zgierz.

Reb Binyamin, the father of Reb Meir, was a scholar about who it could be said, "He is fitting and his mantle is fitting" [152]. He excelled in his traits and mannerisms, and was splendid in his garb. During his youth, Meir

460

was one of the activists in the Agudas Yisroel movement, whose main concern was Orthodox education in the city. He served as chairman of "Agudas Yisroel Youth" and was among the founders of the Beis Yaakov religious girls' school in Zgierz. He was very dedicated to its development and also served as its principal.

When the Aguda movement gave the approval for aliya to the Land, and many of the Agudas Yisroel activists began to set out to the Holy Land, Meir also girded his loins and made aliya to the Land with his family in the year 5633 (1933). Here, he continued his activities on behalf of religious education, and was among the first to found a Beis Yaakov school for girls. He was also the energy behind the establishment of the wide network of such schools in other places in the Land. He also founded a seminary for kindergarten teachers and teachers of the Beis Yaakov network, from which came religious educators throughout the breadth of the Land.

He founded the first Beis Yaakov School in Tel Aviv in a room in his dwelling (which consisted of two rooms and a small kitchen) for the first five girls. He served as secretary, principal, teacher, and fundraiser of this "institution". After a period of suffering and difficulties, when he nurtured the institution and grew it with dedication and diligence, the number of classes increased and a fitting premises was rented. Later, new branches were opened. Then he began to dedicate himself to the founding of the first Beis Yaakov seminary for kindergarten teachers and teachers.

After he attained great milestones in the field of religious education, he was granted a token of recognition for his educational work in an impressive public gathering of the 'Dinar" annual convention.

Rabbi Szaransky excelled also as a fruitful author. His books on the field of education and the topic of Hassidism, especially his unique history books on the subject of religious education, were widely disseminated. They imparted wide-ranging and useful knowledge to the religious youth, especially to the observant girls.

The chief of his literary activities can be seen in his creation of the eight volume "Haever Hayisraeli", encompassing Jewish history and to a significant degree also general history, written in accordance to the Orthodox outlook. As Orthodox critics describe these books, "they describe all of the historical events from a religious perspective, in accordance with our sages and the greats of Israel throughout the generation. It answers a professional and pedagogical need, for we need these books to teach this refined subject."

Reb Meir Szaransky was also active in Agudas Yisroel and its institutions, and was a member of leadership of the Chevra Kadisha (Burial Society) in Tel Aviv, and in other institutions.

He died in Tel Aviv at the conclusion of the Sabbath, the thirtieth of Tishrei 5633 (1973). May his soul be bound in the bonds of eternal life.

(From the newspapers.)

Reb Yitzchak Menachem Bornsztejn of blessed memory.

He was one of the rare personalities in the Hassidic world of Zgierz, a remnant of the old generation, whose name preceded him. He was not only renowned among the Hassidim of Sochaczew, but all other Hassidic groups in Poland knew his by the name "Reb Mendel Siedlicer". When he was young, he received a Torah and Hassidic oriented education from his grandfather the Gaon Rabbi Zeev Nachum, the rabbi of Biala (an in-law of the rabbi of Kock), the author of "Agudas Ezov". His diligence in his learning and his talents were known the many, and he quickly became known as a "diligent learner".

From the time of his youth, he exhibited a special love for books. He acquired them at any opportunity, and with the passage of time, he amassed a large library of he best Torah works. However, during the time of the First World War, during the well-known battle on the Wisla River when almost the entire town of Sochaczew, his place of residence at the time, turned into ruins - his books were burned. He agonized over this for all his life, and mourned over them as if he was mourning for a dead person.

After his marriage, he moved to Siedlic. There he occupied himself in business and also studied Torah day and night. He received his ordination, but he distanced himself from the rabbinate and did not accept the urgings from various places to sit on the rabbinical seat.

During the time of his residence in Sochaczew, he served as the head of the Yeshiva along with the Gaon Reb Tzvi Aryeh Frumer of blessed memory, who at the end of his days was the head of the Yeshiva of Chachmei Lublin. Survivors of the students of this Yeshiva are with us today in the Land and remember the name of their illustrious teacher with reverence. He not only served as head of the Yeshiva. He was faithful to the Sochaczew dynasty even already during the first Admor of this dynasty, Reb Avraham Bornsztejn of holy blessed memory, the son-in-law of the Admor of Kock. The editing

462

and redaction of the books "Eglei Tal" and "Avnei Nezer" of the Admor Reb Avraham of holy blessed memory and "Shem Mishmuel" of the Admor Reb Shmuel of holy blessed memory was given over to Reb Mendel. He himself also wrote novellae of Torah, but he never was able to publish them.

Reb Mendel was greatly beloved among the community of Hassidim of Sochaczew and the admirers of this renowned dynasty who came to bask in the shade of the Admor. He earned special appreciation for his various statements and Hassidic stories, with which he enchanted the hearts of his listeners.

During the days of the First World War, when he was forced to leave Sochaczew on account of the battles, he moved to Warsaw, where he lived for a few years. He maintained friendly ties with all circles of Hassidim and studiers of Torah. After the ceasefire, he moved to Zgierz, and later to Lodz. With the outbreak of the war in 1939 and the conquest of Lodz by the Nazis, he

was imprisoned in the ghetto where he died on the thirteenth of Ehul 5603 (1943). Prior to the termination of the period of mourning for him, his wife and two daughters, Miriam and Margalit, were sent to Auschwitz where they perished. May G-d avenge their blood.

David Eisenberg in Haboker, February 28, 1946

Those who are familiar with Kabbalah, particularly Hassidim, will certainly recall that in Lodz there was a venerable scholar, an expert student of the Avnei Nezer, named Reb Mendele Bornsztejn, may G-d avenge his blood. This Reb Mendele, a relative of the Shem Mishmuel and one of those who sat first at his table, lived in the Lodz Ghetto under the direst of circumstances, when a slice of bread was nothing more than a dream... He sat and studied day and night. A difficult question was going through his mind. When will be after my death? Those around him did not know the answer to the matter that was bothering him.

After his death, his neighbors on 24 Zgierska Street found an answer to this question. A will was found in one of the drawers of his house that bore the date of the day after Yom Kippur, 5701 (1942). Among everything else, the will stated, "The hairs of my white beard, which I cut on account of the wrath of the tormentors, I hid in tractate Baba Batra, in the middle of the chapter "Chezkat Habatim". I wish that the hairs of my beard, along with my

463

"Chovot Halevavot" [153] should be buried in my grave..." A special court of law constituting three judges, sat and decided, "It is a commandment to fulfil the words of the deceased". The will of Reb Mendele was fulfilled in full.

Elimelech HaKohen Schwartz, Los Angeles

"Digleinu", Nisan 5625 (1965)

Rabbi Moshe Goldberg of blessed memory

Rabbi Moshe Goldberg

He was one of the most enlightened people from among the young leaders and activists in Zgierz. He was born in Lodz in 1898 to an Orthodox Hassidic family. He excelled in his talents and pleasant mannerisms already as a youth. The heads of the Yeshivas in which he studied and his teachers of general studies prophesied a bright future for him. He did not betray their vision. He succeeded well at his studies and was ordained as a rabbi at the age of 20.

He quickly became a blessed and talented leader of the Hapoel Hamizrachi Orthodox youth organization, and a member in the central organization of Mizrachi in Poland. He was a wonderful orator. He was invited to cities and towns throughout Poland. Through his rhetorical prowess, he was able to present his words, full of content, in a simple manner that was understandable to the masses of people from all strata that came to listen to his speeches and presentations on various political and cultural issues.

He was accepted as the principal of the Hebrew school of Zgierz in 1919, and quickly won the faith and admiration of the residents of our city. There, he met Chaya Bornsztejn. They married in 1921 and set up residents in Zgierz. Many from among the intelligentsia of our city were numbered among their friends, and their home became a meeting place of scholars.

M. Goldberg was active in almost all of the cultural, communal and Zionist organizations in our city, such as Mizrachi, Keren Kayemet, Keren Hayesod, the Office of the Land of Israel, and others.

The Goldberg family, along with their 5 year old daughter Hadassah, immigrated to the United States in 1928, where Goldberg's parents lived. He immediately became known, and was accepted as a rabbi in one of the synagogues of Oakland, California. At that time, he began to attend the University of Berkeley. His desire was to become a lawyer, and later to make aliya and settle in the Land of Israel. However, this fine dream was not actualized. He was killed in a severe car accident when he was only 31 years old.

During the time of his brief sojourn in America, he acquired many friends from all strata, who still remember the great loss to this day.

Chaya Bornsztejn-Goldberg

She was the eldest daughter of Reb Yitzchak Menachem Bornsztejn (Reb Mendel Siedlicer). After the sudden, tragic death of her husband Rabbi Moshe Goldberg of blessed memory, she continued living in California, guarded his memory in hear heart forever, and remained a widow until her final day.

She possessed broad general knowledge and deeply rooted Jewish knowledge. She earned her living from teaching Hebrew in Hebrew schools, and English to new immigrants. During the Second World War, she was

465

accepted, on account of her wide knowledge and command of various languages - as a senior official in the civic censor office of the United States. Along with this, she continued to teach and broaden her knowledge in many areas of study.

Her path was not paved in roses, and she raised their young daughter who came with them from Poland under difficult economic conditions. After time, her daughter married Professor Ralph Kramer, today a guest lecturer at the Hebrew University of Jerusalem.

About a half a year before her death, she went with her daughter and son-in-law to Israel, and lived in Tel Aviv. This was her fifth visit to the State of Israel. As a veteran communal activist, she quickly became involved here in communal and cultural life. She became active in the Organization Against Air Pollution, and gave classes in English to those of limited means. All of this was voluntary, without any expectation of reward.

She planned to finalize her move to the State of Israel, but a brief illness put an end to all of her desires. She died on the 16th of Adar 5731 (1971). She is buried in Holon, in the native Land, the desire of her soul from her early youth.

Y. Lavie "Hatzofeh", March 23, 1971

Aharon Cincinatus of blessed memory

He was born in Zgierz, Poland in the year 1895. At the end of his studies in the Gymnasium, he traveled to Vilna, where he studied at university and graduated from the faculty of law. His wide ranging communal and Zionist activities began in Vilna, where he served as chairman of the Organization of Jewish Students.

Aharon Cincinatus

He edited the Vilna Zionist newspaper "Di Zeit", and represented the Jews of Vilna in the city council. He was also a writer from the Zionist Newspaper "Heint" of Warsaw, a member of the central Zionist organization of Warsaw, and an activist in the Keren Hakayemet and Keren Hayesod.

His wife and two daughters were killed in the Holocaust during the Second World War. After the war, he rebuilt his life with his new wife, and returned to communal activities. He served as the head of the Zionist movement in Poland, the editor of "Unzer Vort" Zionist newspaper, and a representative to the first post-war Zionist Congress in Basle. He moved from Poland to France, and served as one of the important assistants of the French "Unzer Vort". He made aliya to the Land in 1950.

He died on April 29, 1961 and is buried in the Kiryat Shaul Cemetery.
(From the book, "Happenings of Three Years, 1958-1961, by Shmuel Shachor, published by the archives of "Haaretz".}

My Brother Aharon

He was born in Zgierz and graduated from the local Gymnasium. He was a teacher in the Jewish People's School of Zgierz. Later, he studied in the University of Vilna, and graduated from the faculty of law. He married Rosa Berman when he was a student. Aside from his private work as a jurist, he was active in social organizations, particularly with Zionist tendencies. Aharon was the chairman of the Jewish students' organization. He worked in the "Yekapa" law offices. Later, we find him in the responsible position as editor of the daily Jewish newspaper of Vilna, "Di Zeit". With his talented pen, he fought strongly against Communism among the Jews, and therefore later suffered from sharp tribulations after the year 1939, when the Soviets occupied Vilna.

During the time of Polish rule until the Second World War, Aharon was the Zionist representative in the Vilna city council, and also the Vilna correspondent of the "Heint" of Warsaw. His articles were also published in "Davar" of the land of Israel. He was a representative to the Zionist Central Committee of Poland and an instructor for the Keren Kayamet and Keren Hayesod.

In 1941, when the German murderers ruled Vilna, his wife and two daughters were murdered in the communal grave on "Polygon". Her brothers and relatives were killed along with her. After the war, Aharon lived in Lodz with his second wife, Sonia. He again became active as a journalist. He was the editor of the Zionist "Unzer Vort". He was the Polish delegate to the renewed Zionist congress that took place in Basle in 1946, the first after the great destruction.

The fifth grade of the elementary school (1918) with the teacher Aharon Cincinatus

He remained for a while in France while on the way to Israel. He worked on the local Zionist newspaper "Unzer Vort". In 1950, he and his wife made aliya to Israel.

Aharon Cincinatus was active in the Zionist workers movement for all his years - in "Hitachdut". He was a witty and talented speaker and writer. He used this talent to give over the Zionist ideal. When he arrived in the Land, he had a difficult time acclimatizing. Those difficulties and his difficult experiences during the war years took a serious toll on the sparkling personality of Aharon Cincinatus. He gave up his soul on April 29, 1961.

The Jews of Poland in general, and in particularly those of Zgierz, Vilna and their vicinities who live in Israel and knew, heard or read Cincinatus - will also remember positively that interesting personality.

May his memory be blessed!

Tola Cincinatus of Tel Aviv

Reb Yoshka Lewin of blessed memory

Yoshka Lewin

Yoshka was a known personality in the city. He was a scholarly Jew, who cared for children.

There was no kiosk for Jewish newspapers in the city, for two reasons. First, one would need a special permit from the magistrate, and mainly - a kiosk would cost a few thousand Zloty. Reb Yoshka did not have available such a sum.

He took over the newspaper distribution from David Gotheiner, who had a printing press on Pilsudski Street. At that time, many Maskilim would come to the front of his store to purchase a newspaper and to snatch a conversation about Zionism or politics.

Yoshka was the only person who sold reading material in the city. On a Friday or the eve of a festival, his home hummed like a beehive - for who would want to be without a newspaper on the Sabbath or festival?

Yoshka, a Hassidic Jew who sat and studied in the Aleksandrow Shtibel every evening, simultaneously knew how to distribute, aside from the "Heint" and "Moment", also Alter Katzizne's "My speaking film", the "Jude" of the Aguda, and the Sabbath "Folks Zeitung".

He worked hard, summer in the heat and winter in the cold. He carried the bundles of newspapers, and concerned himself that everyone in town

470

should have reading material. He supported his wife and children modestly and honestly. May his memory be a blessing.

Y. Sh.

Machla Wronski (the Heaven Gazer}

Machla was known as an honest and energetic woman who headed a growing family, in whom she instilled Torah and Judaism. She earned her livelihood from a large spice store in the old market, where there was always a lot of bustle. The farmers from the surrounding villages would gladly purchase, for the "Machlowa" is "Pobozna" (religious) and honest. She also had an open hand for the poor and needy. When her husband Moshe looked heavenward, Machla would look around to see if there was in some house a poor woman in labor, a sick person without someone to tend to, or just a suffering widow who did not have anything for the Sabbath. She would then fill a large bag with paper bags of rice, cereal, kasha, flour, and sugar, and hide it under the table. Later, women such as Chava Ita, Reitza the yellow Yosef's, Mindel Rivka and others would come and take the sacks to where they were needed.

Machla also occupied with other good deeds. For example, for 40 years, she would light the candles in the burial canopy of rabbis and Rebbes, every Sabbath and festival eve, summer and winter.

She was a trustee of the women of the Chevra Kadisha (Burial Society), and would occupy herself with those matters particularly on festivals, if a tragic event were to happen. She bore in mind the poorest people of the city. She considered this to be a special good deed.

Machla merited coming to the Holy Land, where she died - as was told by a grandchild - at the age of 110.

Chava-Itta by Yitzchak Szaransky

Chava-Itta

Who did not know Chava-Itta, the Tzadeket (righteous woman) of Zgierz, the wife of Shalom Henech Bomes? Her equal with regard to modesty and dedication to giving help to the ill or the needy - did not exist in the city.

Herself sickly and week, she had a family with five children. Livelihood was very meager, yet she still concerned herself with making soup for a poor person, a sick person, or a woman in labor who concealed her poverty.

She went to people of means, not to speak evil talk or to spread city gossip, but rather regarding soup with a wing for a poor sick person, but to ask that they include the feet as well.

Chava-Itta did not wait until someone came to tell her that someone or other is lying sick or needs help. Rather, she went to seek them out. When she found such a sick person, she did not rest, but rather ran straight to make something for him.

Her second good deed was to concern herself with Jewish prisoners who were incarcerated in the Zgierz "koze" before arrest. She provided them with

472

some warm food and cigarettes. She would often put in a good word, requesting that the prisoner not be treated badly.

Chava-Itta began her activity sometime before Passover. She did not rest as she searched out Zgierz Jews who were not able to make Passover. She would go to the city administrators and request that they provide those Jews with matzos, potatoes and eggs for Passover.

Her husband, Shalom Henech the coal dealer would remain in the Kloiz for a long time on winter evenings after Mincha and Maariv. During that time Chava-Itta would provide a poor woman with a sack of coal for free. She knew that without coal, the poor woman would not have anything with which to heat her cold house.

Honor to her memory.

Yitzchak S.

Yisrael Weinik

(Murdered in the Warsaw Ghetto on August 19, 1942.)

He was born in Zgierz, near Lodz, Poland, and completed higher education. He came to Warsaw at the beginning of the 1920s, and became a teacher. He was the manager of summer colonies for Jewish teachers. He was politically active n the Bund. Later in the Warsaw Ghetto, he became active with "Oneg Shabbat" and the underground Ringelbaum archive.

Until 1939, he published articles, portraits, and travel columns in the "Folks Zeitung" of Warsaw. Later, he wrote reports of ghetto life. A report from 1941 was found in the Ringelbaum archive, called "Leib Demkowski's Departure", published in the anthology, "Between Life and Death", Warsaw, 1955, pages 20-23. He was murdered at the time of the first liquidation of the Warsaw Ghetto.

"The Lexicon of the New Yiddish Literature". (Bible.) Y. H., Our time, August 1943; B. Mark, Murdered Writers in the Ghettos and Camps, Warsaw, 1954, pages 56, 67, 109, 129; and "Between Life and Death", Warsaw, 1955.

Weinik was the husband of the teacher Fela Lindeman. She was born in Zgierz around 1899. She was bound up with the entire school circle in Zgierz. She was the administrator of summer colonies for Jewish teachers. She was involved in other scientific undertakings of the "Culture League".

473

She was killed in the Warsaw Ghetto.
The Teacher's Yizkor Book. New York, 1952-1954. Page 149.

Pinchas Bizberg

Pinchas Bizberg

He was born in Zgierz, on July 20, 1898. He studied in cheder and yeshivas. He went to Germany in 1918, and completed the Gymnasium in Zonenberg and Tiringen. He studied in the universities of Cologne and Bonn. He received a degree in agronomy in 1923. He practiced in Germany, Denmark and France. In 1927, he was sent by Y"Y"K" as an agronomist for the Argentinean Jewish colonies. He was active in the Jewish agrarian bank. He was the founder of a colony near Buenos Aires. He was the technical secretary of the YIVO in Buenos Aires, and the director of Jewish schools. After the First World War, he became the German correspondent of the Warsaw "Heint". In Argentina, he published stories and articles in the Jewish newspaper, Der Shpigel, Das Neie Leiben, Ofsnei, Pnimer and Pnimlech, and the Colonist Cooperative. For a year, he was the editor of the Neie Tzeit, the Poale Zion organ in Buenos Aires. For three years, he was the co-editor of the Jewish newspaper. He was a member of the editor's college "Argentinean Yivo Writers", the co-editor of Educational Problems, a member of the Inainem Editor's College (the anthology book of the cultural congress), the

474

editor of Das Yiddishe Vort. He published the following in books: Neie Heimen (New Homes), Buenos Aires, 1939, 278 pages; Miguel Sacharov, Buenos Aires, 1940, 280 pages; Sabbath and Festival Jews, Buenos Aires, 1940, 180 pages; he wrote with a monograph about Dr. Yarchi, Buenos Aires, 1943, 1623 pages; Levi Yitzchak Berditchever, Folksshpil, Buenos Aires, 1952, Chana Senesh, a Jewish Heroin, published in Buenos Aires June 1948. In 1950, he published the play "When Forests Burn" in Buenos Aires, and the dramatization of Yehuda Elberg's story "Agent 838". In 1948, he produced the drama "Night in the Nurenberger Ghetto". He lived in Santiago, Chile since 1935

From "Lexicon of the New Jewish Literature".. Botashanski, Mother-Yiddish; Sh. Rozanski, The Yiddish Printed Word in Argentina, Buenos Aires, 1941; Anthology of the Jewish Literature in Argentina, Buenos Aires, 1944.

Pinchas Bizberg - the Writer and the Man
(On the occasion of his 70th birthday.)

P. Bizberg entered Jewish literature with the baggage of higher education, with knowledge of language and literature, laden with deep Jewish knowledge, a master of the old and new Jewish literature, and laden with Hassidic spirit and zeal, with burning enthusiasm. However, more than anything, he brought into Jewish literature his rich bounty and his great command of the Yiddish language, as a supplement to his literary talent.

As almost any beginner, Pinchas Bizberg took his first steps as a writer in poetry. However, these were weak and helpless steps. His poems were barely poetic and greatly narrative, so that they could not be published as appropriate in his youthful mood.

Fortunately, Bizberg soon chanced upon his appropriate genre, which was his true niche within Yiddish literature, for which he as born - prose. He became quickly known in Argentina as a talented writer - as the Argentinean Jewish writer.

Bizberg settled in Argentina in 1927, and he became known as the writer and portrayer of the Jewish colonies in Argentina, which were then in their full bloom.

Bizberg began writing already in Poland, but he became fully engaged in Yiddish literature when he was in Argentina. Aside from his dozens and dozens of professional articles on agronomy, articles about cultural and social problems, essays and satires portraying colonial life, Bizberg produced significant fictional works in the form of narratives that appeared in book form, under the name of "New Home" in 1939. P. Bizberg is also the author of several dramas, including "Hannah Senesh", which were performed on the Yiddish stage in Buenos Aires. His monograph about the legendary Dr. Yarchi brought to light the generation of Jewish pioneers in the Argentinean "Pampes" (steppes). Bizberg's splendid novel about the autobiographical character "Sabbath and Festival Jews" was published by request of the central committee of Polish Jews in Argentina.

Sabbath and Festival Jews is not only the chant of a generation, as is claimed in the subtitle of the book, but is also the chant of Pinchas Bizberg himself, the chant of his soul and life. It reads as a long chant, a song of life, written in prose. In that work, without doubt, Bizberg reaches the zenith, the pinnacle of his creativity.

Bizberg's subject matter was broad and realistic. His sharp eye penetrated into many hidden corners of life in general and of the individual in particular. Jewish colonization in Argentina was the healthy base of the Jewish community in that land, and the colonial writers were the ground-layers and columns for Jewish literature in Argentina. Bizberg's name is inscribed in the literary and cultural history of Jewish Argentina, together with the names of Mordechai Alperson and Baruch Benderski, with the caveat that Bizberg's place in the literature is broader.

P. Bizberg displayed with his first, strong and fundamental narrative entitled "Under Entreriaser Heavens" in the provincial publication "Entreriaser Grandstand", a narrative with which he later opens his first book, "New Skies". This is an ode to the early Argentinean land, which received the wandering and harassed Jews into her arms and bosom. Soon Bizberg became known and was published in all the best newspapers and publications in Jewish Argentina.

Bizberg toiled hard and bitterly through his life. Bizberg was an employee of "Ika" as an agronomist. There, he was a colonist on his own account, a

476

teacher, and a cultural activist. He became a cultural creator, and went on to become a ripe and fruitful writer.

Bizberg's lineage was from Hassidic nobility and spiritual aristocracy. His grandfather's legacy included a washbasin in which the Gerrer Rebbe washed his hands. His father, Shabtai Nachum's, the Hassidic silken young man, lived for a period of time without doing anything for the world, he was not given over and not bowed under the yoke of livelihood, and he did not let himself be restricted within the four walls of a store. Later, he even took up the pen, and called himself Sawelinomowicz. Later, he served Shabtai Nachum's. When he came from his far-off business trips, he would quickly cast off the "German" and put on the silken kapote of his own "self".

I met P. Bizberg in 1954 when he moved from Argentina to Chile to edit the new edition of "Dos Yiddishe Vort", which began to appear twice a week.

From the first day of our working together, I followed Bizberg's every step with devotion. Above all, he was new in Chile, and I had been a resident there for 30 years. He valued my sincerity to him, and treated me with comradely trust and good friendship.

Bizberg was stricken by a hard blow in 1956 - an illness made it impossible for him to work. For the past 12 years, the ill writer has lived in Israel in oblivion. At first, he lived for a decade in Kibbutz Ein Hashlosha, and for the last two years, he lived in Jerusalem.

Yaakov Pilowski, "Latest News", Tel Aviv, December 6, 1968.

Riches is not the Main Thing

An intimate, friendly, and heartfelt letter to a friend from P. Bizberg. It characterizes well the later writer.

Oveshaneda, April 3, 1949

Vove Fisher, my cordial friend of my youth!

Your letter was indeed touching, infused with so much nice happenings. I do not know to whom, but I believe that Zgierz was a wonderfully aromatic town, where we all lived our own peculiar fine lives.

This is already years ago, and we already exchanged the first fifty [154]. The dainty childhood years remain in memory. I know a body of water, a forest, a garden, a girl - and herewith stands a bloody sea of millions of martyrs. Personally, we dispersed ourselves so early. I went away to Germany in 1918, studied agronomy, went to Holland, Denmark, Belgium, Switzerland practiced, worked, later had a possession in France. In 1927, I came to Argentina in the administration of the Baron Hirsch colonies, later became a colonist, had a large tract of my own land, and machines. For fifteen years I was with the colonies, and then finally ended up in the city. I was with the locust infested, dryness, aridity, and various other plagues from which a worker of the land suffers. I lost my means, became a pauper, and lived again in the city, despite the fact that I do not like the city. I experienced a great deal in life. Now I am a bit of a teacher, a bit of a writer, a bit of a dramatist, and now I am trying to be a bit of a merchant. In the meantime, I have not made any America here in America. Many Jews here, generally very coarse Jews, are very wealthy people, millionaires. But I am a writer among Israel (I am reckoned among the best storytellers of the Argentinean Jewish writers, G-d should not punish me for boasting). Lately, I have specialized in dramatic writing, and not with meager success. The critics extol me. But I must do other tasks daily that have no connection to writing. I work 14 to 16 hours daily so that I can write a few hours a week. Thus, the few years have already passed by. I have already published two books. When I received samples of the books, I will send them to you. The book "Sabbath and Festival Jews" which, is partly a reminiscence of my youth, childhood, Zgierz, Lodz, and my small journeys to Polish shtetls, will appear in a few months. You need not ask, for I will certainly send it to you. In six weeks, my new play "When Forests Burn", will be performed. This work is dedicated to Janusz Korczak, the martyr who was murdered in the Warsaw Ghetto. I have a wife and a child, a daughter Chemda who is fifteen years old. When I have an opportunity, I will send you a photograph. With regard to livelihood, I get by, riches is not the main thing. The main thing is life.

Regarding the book, I have started to do something. Firstly, I have sent a notice regarding do not know if I will have success with my announcement, for if the Zgierzers have no written material or documents, there is nothing I can do about it. I will later send a sample of my book, in which Zgierz is portrayed in fictional form under the name Miechow. Regarding this matter, you must also notify the North American Jewish press. There, there are many Zgierzers. Here there is not a unique Zgierz organization, but only a Lodzer organization, to which the Zgierzers belong.

And you, what are you doing, dear friend? What do you work on? I believe that your father of blessed memory was a contractor for road building. You were a bit of a poet. You wrote short songs with such a fine handwriting - do you still write? From your letter, I see a considerable feeling for writing, and also talent. Write me more about yourself.

My heartfelt thanks to you, regarding the birth certificate. If it costs money, I will reimburse you. In any case, thank you very much.

I intend to travel to Israel. I intend to do so a year from now, because one has to expend a great deal of money for this. We are so far, far apart, for an airplane ride to the Land via Europe is a three to four day event, not more - however, we wish to travel by ship. However this will take a year and a half. One must be in Israel, to help build the land, where social justice will be.

With heartfelt greetings, dear friend, from me, my wife, and daughter,
Pinchas Bizberg

Lazo Waszasz-Szaransky
(Born 1900, murdered 1942)

After she completed the Beis Yaakov women's seminary in Krakow, she became a teacher. She published songs and articles about education, which were translated into Polish as well, in the Beis Yaakov Journal and in other periodicals of Agudas Yisroel.

She was murdered in the Polish death camps.
{"Celestial Lodz", Ch. L. Fuchs.}

Shia Zaklikowski

Few people in Zgierz knew Shia's family name - Zaklikowski.

His nickname "Sok", was inherited from his father, who was called Yosef Sokolower (because he came from Sokolow).

Yosef belonged to the old-time Kocker Hassidim. He was a scholarly Jew, but poor. He put a positive spin on his poverty: "Poverty is fitting for Israel", he would say.

The only thing that Shia inherited from his father was... poverty.

As a young lad, Shia had to stop his studying and start working in order to help his old father relieve his need.

479

In 1905, Shia already belonged to the "Achdut" revolutionaries. Zgierz manufacturers trembled at his words. Everyone knew that Shia had a "Shpeier" (revolver) in his pocket. Nobody should issue a decision against Achdut, or else Shia might show what he could do…

When Shia Sok got married, many hoped that he would become a "static" (well-poised person). This hope was not realized. Shia remained a revolutionary, worked in the professional union, agitated the workers and reproved every rich person and his grandfather [155].

In his latter years, Shia Sok used to come every Sunday to the "berze" near the Gmina [156] and preach justice and fairness, thereby getting even with the communal "meddlers".

Shia had a great deal of contentment from his children. They followed in his path and became active Communists. However, all of them were killed in their "fatherland" Russia. One daughter was saved and is today in Israel.

Y. A.

Yaakov Aharon the Water Carrier
Our sincere common people - a memorial

The water carrier was always the lively nerve of the town, and, as a typical expression of the Jewish manner of that time in the region, he often also served as a popular theme for the creations of the Jewish writers and poets.

The memory of Yaakov Aharon remains in my memory from among the water carriers of the old city of Zgierz. He was a small, thin, lively Jew, with a fiery, ragged face, replete with a black-gray beard and a long disheveled hair under his hat. He knew everybody in the city, and they all knew him, for he was a part of the landscape of the city.

He was not written up in the chronicles, but rather people said of him that he was born orphaned from his father, and when his poor mother died, the community gave him to Fishel of the poorhouse to raise him. The community also paid his Talmud Torah tuition for him, and Yaakov Aharon studied Hebrew. Soon, he started working around the wagon drivers and porters. Thus did he earn his daily livelihood.

Days and years past, until there was a tumult in town: the cholera epidemics, Heaven preserve us, that swept through Poland at the time, also afflicted Zgierz, and took a great toll in the homes. As the situation became very grave, the utilized the last means - the well-known remedy against epidemics: arranging a marriage between two round, unmarried orphans, placing the chupa on "good ground" and -the epidemic ends... Thus did the short Yaakov Aharon obtain a wife, along with a present from the community: a new koromisel (shanges) [157] with a pair of wooden water cans. Thus did Yaakov Aharon, with good fortune, became a water carrier in town.

Industrious and agile in his work, he bore his burden with responsibility. His bakers were never late with their baked good, and his "madames" were never left embarrassed in the middle of a wash. He served everybody honorably and efficiently. Therefore, he also quickly started making the rounds to the wealthy houses of the old city, and later, when Moshe the water carrier gave up his buckets from old age, Yaakov Aharon became the ruler of the marketplace pumps. If someone was blocking the way to the pump for a while and Yaakov Aharon had to wait, the heavens opened up! The voice from the small Jew projected through the entire market and surrounding lanes. He would curse and cause uproar as he walked with the full cans of water. Things would often come to blows, especially on a market day, when a strange gentile farmer attempted to give his horse to drink. The gentile could not understand how such a small "Zhydek" told off him, the Pole - and then slapped him over the face. However, as quick as lightning, Yaakov Aharon grabbed the pole with iron chains and swung them, like the blade of a windmill, over the farmer's head. The farmer grabbed his head and uttered a bloodcurdling scream, "O, Je-zu!". A stampede ensued, and Jews were afraid of what was going on around them, a pogrom, Heaven forbid. Soon an official from the magistrate ran out waving a sword to disperse those running: "Ras-cha-di-i-i-s!" When Yaakov Aharon later walked along the street with the water cans, he stopped everyone: "Did you see how I slapped that Esau?!" [158] He knew nothing of fear. Those in the market wondered: from where does he get such strength, such nerve? Old Jews worried and murmured amongst themselves, "He will cause us to be sent into exile, this Yaakov Aharon". Only Yisachar Mendele the blind Shmuel's used to stick up for Yaakov Aharon. He would later slap him playfully on the back, "Molodiec Yaakov Aharon, Molodiec!" [159].

Despite the fact that Yaakov Aharon came into many houses and knew what was going on with everybody, he was considered as different, outside the community, for all his days.   His face was always sullen, and he would barely answer a friendly "Good morning". He would even barely talk to his neighbors in the Beis Midrash behind the oven, and he would not answer at all Uncle Falik's jokes.

The handiwork of the raffia sculptor Baruch Meirentz:
"The Water Drawer"

Thus did Yaakov Aharon pass his years, summer in the heat, winter in the frost, day after day, from dawn until late at night. When one could hear a tired, weary yawn over the empty market, the women on the steps knew that Yaakov Aharon is ending his day" work - it is already time to go to sleep.

When Yaakov Aharon reached old age, he remained alone, like a stone. He was without a wife and without a child. When his last energy gave out, he hung the buckets on the wall. Then, the Gabbai of a Hassidic Shtibel took him on as an assistant Shamash. He filled the sink with water, lit the candles, went on errands, and did other such tasks. On winter days, he would stoke the stove, take a nap, or shuffle through the Yiddish pages of a large book of Psalms. Often, he would sit on the bench with both hands in the pockets of his creased overcoat, looking out the window and thinking. Perhaps in his tired head, he was thinking about "practicality", about his loneliness after such a bustling, life of toil?

One day, a rumor spread through the old city that Yaakov Aharon the water carrier had ordered a monument, and it was already ready for "when the time will come".

Nobody believed this. What? A monument during one's lifetime? However, when the community went out the cemetery on the eve of Yom

482

Kippur to petition for a good year, Yaakov Aharon was already standing at the open gate with a large paper sack of cut up honey cake and poured a drink to anyone whom Aharon-Yitzchak (Chemia Itzel) called over to see the monument. Silver letters were already engraved upon it, which said in Hebrew:

Here is buried a straightforward and upright man, who earned his living for all his days through the toil of his hands, Reb Yaakov Aharon..." -- etc. The Jews shook their heads in astonishment, took their glasses and wished Yaakov Aharon a long life and many other blessings.

When Yaakov Aharon remained alone, he went to the monument, looked at the letters and at his name that glistened with gold, and, with an exquisite gentleness, touched the stone and the letters with his toil-weary fingers. A smile of inner joy shined on his disheveled, always cloudy face... and this was the only smile that ever lit up the face of Yaakov Aharon.

Yoav Katz of blessed memory

Yoav Katz

He joined the Hebrew scouting movement in his native city of Zgierz when he was still very young, and was active in all youth activities on behalf of the Keren Kayemet (Jewish National Fund) and the Land of Israel. His love of the Land was fundamental, soulful, and ingrained in his blood. At the end of the First World War, he uprooted himself with force from the city, despite the difficulties that stood in his way, and went wandering along the paths of Europe in order to reach his destination - the Promised Land.

Yoav was not deterred or broken from all of the difficulties and setbacks that he met along his journey. After a half year of wandering on land and sea, he arrived with the well-known Group 105 to the Land.

As one of the first pioneers, the pioneers of the Third Aliya, ingrained with the spirit of work and sacrifice, he went through all of the tribulations of acclimatizing and settling down. He worked in farming, guarding, drying of swamps, and paving roads, from the north to the south, from Ruchama until Degania and the Galilee.

Yoav was one of the first activists who worked at the port. He was one of the first of the Jewish tax workers at the port of Jaffa, and served as the chairman of their union for many years, as well as a member of the business association.

He was an active member in the Haganah and was involved in communal activism. He had pleasant mannerisms, was a good friend, and excelled in his uprightness and dedication.

He was also gifted with the writer's pen, and brought forth the memory of known personalities of our city in newspapers here and in the Land.

He especially excelled in his founding the organization of Zgierz natives, and was one of the heads of the "Committee for the Zgierz Book" until his last day.

He died in Tel Aviv on the 18th of Sivan 5729 (June 4, 1969), at the age of 69. May his memory be blessed.

Zgierz natives building up the Land of Israel. Klorfeld, Kuperman, and Yoav Katz paving the road from Tiberias to Tzemach (1920) (They are the second, sixth, and seventh from the right, in the upper row.)

From the Diary of Yoav Katz of blessed memory:

"The strong desire to make aliya to the Land of Israel burned within me already from the time of childhood, at the threshold of the first decade of my life. The songs of Zion that I sang with the rest of the boys at the modern cheder of my Lithuanian teacher, always served as fuel for the "fire of Zion" that burned in my heart. How jealous was I of my neighbors the Klorfelds who traveled to Israel. My jealousy was particularly ignited for Menachem Berliner, whom I saw as an angel who went before me to show me the way. At my urging, he sent me a detailed description of his travels in the Land. I decided to follow in his footsteps no matter what.

The First World War that broke out thwarted my plans, but I was able to fulfil my vow and arrange my trip immediately at the conclusion of the war. Indeed, in November, 1918, when the Germans vacated Poland, I immediately arranged a group of youths of my age and planned the journey to Israel. We cast lots regarding the day that we would setout. On this day, November 15, 1919, seven youths set out on our unknown journey.

We met our first bitter obstacle when we arrived in Vienna. The Zionist institutions did not permit us to continue our journey. When I asked my eldest brother Yosef, who was a member of the Zionist organization of the city, for help, he showed me the palm of his hand - that is to say, when hair grows here...

We were persistent and continued on our journey. We met obstacles at every step along the way. This was the situation in Zagreb, one of our stops on the way, as well as in Rome. In Italy, groups of clandestine immigrants from all corners of Poland sat and waited. We organized a protest march at the Italian parliament, submitted petitions, but nothing helped.

A ship that sailed from Italy to Egypt, transporting freed soldiers, fulfilled the objective of our hearts. After several mishaps with other ships that came before, we succeeded in boarding the ship through the intercession of Dr. Vigdorchik, who drew us near to him. However, when we arrived in Alexandria, the British refused to give us visas for the land. Only after waiting for several months in Egypt did we finally succeed in boarding a transport wagon, and with the help of G-d, we arrived at the object of our desire, prepared to greet the hardships that would come in the beloved Land."

Menachem Mendel Zakon of blessed memory

Menachem Mendel Zakon was born in the year 5664 (1904). His father, Reb Aharon HaKohen was a learned man and an enthusiastic Hassid of Aleksandrow. His mother Tzipora was the daughter of the shochet Reb Yisrael Yitzchak Gad, an honorable man of the community.

Menachem was educated in an Orthodox home that took pride in its lineage, and placed stringent fences upon him regarding any appearance or event that was not fitting to the spirit of the home. Even though Menachem was very faithful to tradition and cleaved to Hassidism, he always chose to go in his direction without worrying about the opinion of others, even of those who would distribute honor. He was straight in his path, with a strong, powerful personality. He fought valiantly for his opinions when he decided to do something. He would grind down mountains that stood in his path, and was not deterred by any obstacle.

He was one of the founders and activists of the Mizrachi youth of Zgierz, and was dedicated to the national religious movement with all the warmth of his soul. He also participated in collections of money and other activities for the Land of Israel and the Jewish National Fund.

Menachem Mendel Zakon of blessed memory

486

He made aliya to the land in the year 5689 (1929) along with his fiancée Chaya Feiga, who bore with him the lot of their joint life with great strength. Even here, in the land, he was dedicated to communal work that was close to his heart, through many difficulties and struggles. His life in the land was not simple. Aside from the difficulties of absorption and concerns about livelihood, he was afflicted with lack of understanding from within his family, which caused difficulties for the life of the couple.

Menachem worked at a regular job in the city council of Tel Aviv, and dedicated his energies to the Mizrachi movement, to religious education, to the founding of a neighborhood for employees of the city council in Yad Eliahu, and especially to the founding of a synagogue in the neighborhood. Despite his meager means, through his energy and faith he succeeded in actualizing his vision - the establishment of the Ramah Synagogue named after Rabbi Menachem Mendel Hager of blessed memory [160], whose memory as a leader of the movement he bore with reverence. He was diligent regarding the establishment of the synagogue; he concerned himself with establishing a charitable fund, and did not desist from anything that he felt effective and worthwhile.

Menachem was also one of the founders of the Organization of Zgierz Émigrés in Israel, and a member of the committee of the organization. He worked very hard for he Yizkor book of the community of Zgierz.

He died on the thirtieth of Shivat 5629 (February 18, 1969). May his soul be bound in the bonds of eternal life.

Leon Rubenstein

Our member Leon Rubenstein is also already in the club of septuagenarians. His prime activity - despite the fact that he was bound up and involved with all other activities of the movement -was and remains with the education of Jewish children in the nationalist Zionist spirit. This was a great merit, but Rubenstein's merits were greater due to his "chutzpa" and "aggressiveness". Who knows how many children have received a good Jewish education with us because Rubenstein "threw them" into our schools with all the zeal that he could muster.

Leon Rubenstein

The Zionist Worker's Movement - mainly from the former Poale Zion and Tzeirei Zion, which were included in the Jewish National Worker's Union -gathered together, here in America members from all corners of Eastern Europe. One can indeed say that the vast majority of them, the first ones, came from the Russian and Lithuanian regions, or at least from the "outlying regions". Few of them stemmed from central Poland, and absorbed the unique, Polish-Jewish zest. Our member Leon Rubenstein, a native of Zgierz, was one of the exceptional ones. Through the "medium" of Poale Zion, he came very early and took a central place. As the editor of the periodical publication "Farn Folk" (the organ of Tzeirei Zion), he was a co-worker with two such Chaims as Chaim Arlozoroff and Chaim Greenberg, may the later live long. This was in the 1920s. However, Rubenstein later devoted his journalistic career to the benefit of educational and cultural activity. To this he dedicated his fire, passion, and even became impatient; and here, in this area that is often considered as a stepchild, he - with the characteristic manner of a Polish Jew - he did not push it down into some forgotten corner... even when this is what people wanted.

The member Rubenstein has already lived on the American Continent for exactly fifty years. He is one of the activists in the Zionist-pioneering camp. He is a central person, not only in the real of education and culture, but also in all other areas of movement life. Everywhere, he would utilize his strength

488

to exclaim the highest 'no' when he did not like something; and to express the courage to give a bang on the table and demand justice -even when important great and important people are present. The movement even often had need of his "sheigetzvaten" [161] temperament --- in the style of Polish Jews; particularly when they had to send a representative to other "tables"... Member Rubenstein was also on occasion the teacher and guide whom did not give in or bend.

For more than fifty years, member Rubenstein accumulated a great many roles in the movement and its various institutions. Certainly, his close friends can attest to this. I, from our time, wish only to publish the best wishes to the jubilee honoree an wish him, together with others, that he will maintain his concern for all good deeds for many years to come, and also that he will not let others rest; that he shall be able to very soon realize his literary plans that he has already nurtured for a number of years. Until a hundred and twenty.

Mordechai Streliger ("Yiddisher Kempfer", New York)

Various people have all sorts of passions in their life. Some concentrate on fame, others on wealth. Certain people have a passion for drinking and card playing, and still others seek a career in social status. Leon Rubenstein has two passions - Zionism and Jewish child rearing.

His Zionism stems from his earliest youth. At the end of 1918, immediately after the First World War, he left his native city of Zgierz and traveled to the land of Israel, as one of a group of leaders and pioneers of Jewish scouting. He arrived in Israel as one of the first of 105 pioneers who were the vanguard of the Second Aliya.

Unfortunately, he was only to remain in Israel for a short time, about a year and a half. He became ill with tetanus, a fatal disease, in the Gan Shmuel group in which he worked. He remained alive through a miracle. He was forced to leave the Land of Israel to go to a land with a colder climate. He arrived in Canada in 1920, and began there a new career as a Jewish educator. He gave himself over completely to the efforts to develop a new school system, where Yiddish and Hebrew would be the languages of instruction. He became known as a teacher in the Jewish People's School of Montreal, and later as the director of the Y. L. Peretz School and the general director of the Jewish People's Schools of the Zionist Workers' Movement in America.

Rubenstein brought an unbounded measure of enthusiasm and pedagogical knowledge to all of those positions.

489

It is characteristic of Leon Rubenstein that his societal activities went hand in hand with his educational work. School and society were one with him, also - Zionism and Jewish education. It is rare that a Jewish educator finds so much time to be involved in Jewish educational life, as was Leon Rubenstein. He was also active in the Tzeirei Zion movement and one of its founders in Canada. He helped oversee its unification with Poale Zion.

Rubenstein was a delegate to Zionist congresses, a representative of the Zionist Action Committee and vice president of the national fund in the United States. If you do not believe me, Rubenstein spent time and energy to serve as a dynamo for all purposes in which he sends his warm heart as well as his brain, full of plans and ideas.

Dr. Sh. Margoshes ("Der Tag", February 22, 1967, New York.)

Rabbi Yechiel Zeltzer

I had opportunity to look in the book "Ner Lameah", which was written by Rabbi Yisrael Zeltzer, a native of Zgierz who today lives in the United States.

The parents of Reb Yisrael Zeltzer were the Hassid and scholar Reb Tzvi Yehuda (Reb Hershel), and Chana Leah the daughter of the Hassid, one of the elders of the city, Reb Yosef Ber Lewkowicz.

I remember the Sabbath days, when the students of the Yeshiva Yagdil Torah, myself included, would come to Reb Hershel to be examined on the weekly lesson. He would always greet us pleasantly, and relate to us with love and desire. As such, he reduced the natural anxiety that preceded the exam. We always succeeded in obtaining high marks and words of praise. A warm, Jewish family atmosphere pervaded in his home.

It seems that their son Yerachmiel continued to weave the entire Jewish tradition into his life, with all of its detail. We see that he was not only diligent in his Jewish studies, but he also labored and delved into the depths of Halacha, and dug trenches into the discussions of the Talmud and the halachic decisors. His book "Ner Lameah" on the topic of Chanukah, dedicated to the memory of his parents who died in the Auschwitz camp, testifies to the level of toil and effort that Rabbi Yechiel Zeltzer put into the tents of Torah.

This book is filled to the brim with novellae and citations from the experts of Halacha, and encompasses all of the ideas, expositions of law,

490

responsa and customs associated with the Festival of Lights and its commandments. It contains approbations from the rabbinical greats. One of its approbations, signed by Rabbi Yitzchak Eizik Liebes, the head of the rabbinical court of Grinding, states: "I see a man who hastens in his work and sits before angels (who are the angels, the rabbis), that is my friend the sharp rabbi, who is expert in Torah and the fear of the pure G-d, our rabbi and teacher Rabbi Yerachmiel Zeltzer may he live long, one of the important people of the city of New York, may the Lord preserve it well. In his dear book "Ner Lameah" on the matters of Chanukah, the pure man gathered diligently and expertly material that is full of splendor and exudes glory. No secret is hidden in it. He gathered from all that was brought down by the greats of the generation and the giants of spirit. The aforementioned rabbi continued to add shoots and flowers to our holy Torah, with good taste and proper ideas. May his well flow outside, and may G-d be with him. May he be granted great success, and may it be G-d's will that he succeed in enlightening the eyes of scholars and their students with his candle, so that many will benefit, and knowledge will increase."

Indeed, Rabbi Yerachmiel is diligent with Torah and Divine service. It is a wonder, after all that he endured in the death camps, that such a man can still have undiminished spiritual strength to grind down mountains and flatten valleys in the wide world of Talmud.

Pinchas A. Sirkes

He was born in Zgierz, near Lodz, Poland in the year 1907. He was the son of the Aguda deputy in the Polish parliament, Eliezer Sirkes. He studied in cheder, Yeshivas and with private teachers. From his youth, he was active in the Orthodox youth movement, and one of its first activists, which preached pioneering of the Land of Israel. He settled in the Land of Israel in 1933. He was the founder of Hassidic agricultural colonies.

His first poems were published in the collection "Unzer Treibkraft", Lodz 1926. Since then, he took part in: "Der Flaker", "Der Yiddisher Arbieter", "Beis Yaakov" Journal, "Undzer Lebn" (as editor) - all in Lodz; "Der Jud", "Das Yudishe Tagblatt", "Orthodoxishe Yugent Bleter", "Darcheinu", "Dgaleinu", and others in Warsaw; "Dos Vort", Vilna; "Hamodia", "Shearim", "Eretz Yisrael", and others. In book form (Under the name P.

Sirski) - "Gilgulim", a Hassidic drama in three acts, Piotrkow, 1929, 144 pages.

"Lexicon of the new Jewish Literature". Sources: Ch. L. Fuchs, Literary pages, Warsaw, March 15, 1929, New Folksblatt, Lodz, May 12, 1930, in Z. M. B. from the recent past, page 3, New York, 1957, search note; information from Y. Fridenson, New York.

Yehuda Elberg

He was born on May 15, 1912 in Zgierz, near Lodz, Poland. His father, Avraham Natan of blessed memory, was a rabbi in Sanok and in Blaszki; his mother's father, Tzvi Yechezkel Michelzon, was a rabbi in Warsaw. Elberg received a religious education. From 1934, he studied as a textile engineer in Lodz, where he worked as a master weaver until the Second World War. He was in Warsaw from 1940 until 1943. He participated in the Warsaw Ghetto uprising. He was a founder of the first Jewish committee in Lublin (1944), and one of the initiators and cofounders of the Jewish Press Agency (Y. Y. P. A.) in Lodz, from the Historical Commission (later the Historical Institute), and in the Lodzer Newspaper "Das Neie Leben" (The New Life), of which he served as the editorial secretary from May 1944 until the end of 1945. He wrote correspondences for the "Davar" in Tel Aviv and for "Morgen Journal" in New York. He moved to France at the end of 1946, where he was the editorial secretary of the editorial journal "Kiyum" since its founding in Paris in 1947. He went to New York in 1948 as a delegate to the first convention of the World Jewish Culture Congress. He was a collaborator of the "Histadrut" since 1951. He made his debut as a writer with a story ("Der Lep") in the Lodzer Folks Blat", 1932. After that, he published stories, reports, articles and correspondences in "Das Neie Lebn", "Yiddishe Shriftn" - Lodz; "Morgen Journal", "Di Zukunft", "Yiddisher Kempfer", New York; "Kiyum", Paris; "Davar", Tel Aviv, and others.

He published the following in book form: "Unter Kuperne Himlen" ("Under Copper Skies"), a
story that was published by the Central Organization of Polish Jews in Argentina, with the help of David Ignatof-Fand in Yew York; by the publishing house "Polish Jewry", Buenos Aires, 1951, 252 pages (premiered in 1951 from the Jewish Culture Congress in Brazil). The story "873" from

the book "Unter Kuperne Himlen" was also made into a play by the writer Pinchas Bizberg and performed by the Young Yiddish Theater in Buenos Aires.

In the collection "Unter Kuperne Himlen", the artist-chronicler deals with the influence of his painful past in the artistic form of his style. However, apart from dealing with his own self, these are artistic chronicles. They are important in that in them one finds a key to the young writer's leitmotif (Sh. Neiger).

Elberg was active for many years in the Zionist Worker's Movement. He visited Argentina in 1960 on a mission from the "Jewish Histadrut Campaign". He wrote also under the pseudonyms
Y. Bergel, Y. L. Berg. He lives in Montreal, Canada.

(Lexicon of the New Yiddish Literature". A rich bibliography, beginning from Y. Rappaport, Australian News, Melbourne, June 27, 1947 - From Dr. Y. Shatzki in Jewish Bookland, New York, May 1952 - from Ch. Grade, A. Leieles, Ch. L. Fuchs and others - from (in English) Whose Who in World Jewry, New York, 1955, page 177.

D. The Holocaust

A Dirge for my Nation…! By Yoav Katz of blessed memory

By the rivers of the Tiber, Vistula, Rhine, and Dnieper, where we sat for years and years, generations and generations, and wept for Zion [1].

Our heart went out for that beautiful and good land that was bestowed upon our fathers, and from where we were exiled due to a decree from the Most High, who became strange to us, and hid his face from us.

Behold, how bitter is our lot in this generation, that at the time of our return to our land and the renaissance of our people from slavery to freedom and servitude to liberty, this was decreed upon us, Oh… That we should sit by our rivers - the rivers of our land that has been shaken out of its desolation and lowliness, and here, in particular here, in the midst of our redeemed land and lament, weep and eulogize the many myriads of our brethren who were destroyed and annihilated in all of the lands of the Diaspora in which members of our nation found themselves.

How great and scalding is the pain over this breech that took place to our nation on the threshold of the renewal of its national life.

My heart, my heart goes out to the multitudes of our brethren, giants of spirit and thought, great in Torah and piety, great in fine deeds, entire communities, filled with the human flocks, our brethren of the House of Israel, upright and pure people, who ate their bread through the toil of their hands, visionaries and poets, believers and scribes, teachers and cheder students who never tasted the taste of sin.

Oh… Zgierz, my bereaved city of Zgierz, it is not for you that we await with our pining and longing… You became strange to us, a cruel mother, a darkened land. Our heart goes out, beats, and pines with our entire being for the myriads of our relatives who had their graves dug in your midst, upon your fields and your forests.

Our parents, brothers, sisters, and all who were dear to us who were turned to dung upon the face of your fields, to fertilize your plantations and crops. We will never forget them forever!

494

Pillaged Zgierz along with all of your sisters, the cities of Poland, your sisters in murder and annihilation, fortunate is he who will repay you when your day comes, and the blood will be avenged.

In One Day by W. F.

(Wednesday the fifteenth of Shvat 5700, December 27, 1939)

Thirty-five years have passed since that dark day when shots were fired, and the entire Jewish population left their hometown of Zgierz.

On that day, confusion and terror enveloped the big and the small, the poor and the rich. Children lost their parents and parents searched for their children. The weeping and screaming could be heard on all of the streets.

Driven to the old marketplace, with their packs over their shoulders, the Jews of Zgierz fled into the forests with the fear of death that only the eyes that saw could believe. The largest group of them fled to Lodz, a smaller group went to Glowno, and only a very few set out and arrived in Warsaw. In their despair, the unfortunate souls could not imagine that all of the roads were leading to a strange ending, to death.

Thus in one day did end the flourishing Jewish community of Zgierz, which numbered 5,000 souls and was bound up with the city throughout the 200 year history with intertwined work for its growth and development. It ended -for not only were our holy shrines burnt, but the despicable people even desecrated the 150 year old cemetery and covered it over with earth, so that there would not remain even a memory of Jewish life on Zgierz soil.

For us, the survivors, lies the great and holy duty to observe this Memorial Day and perpetuate it forever. This should be a day of memory and warning - for us and for our children.

Just as we light the memorial candles for our martyrs, we also must not forget the curse and the eternal hate for the disgusting criminals and murderers of the Jewish people.

We who remain in sorrow should find comfort in the work for those close to us, and in the work to perpetuate the memory of our martyrs - our parents, our brothers and sisters, relatives and friends - and the entire community of Zgierz. May their memory be blessed!

Jews of Zgierz under the German Occupation of Terror
By Danuta Dombrowski and
Avraham Wein of Jerusalem

The Tribulations Began During the First Days of the War

On the eve of the Second World War, there were approximately 4,800 Jews in Zgierz, out of a general population of 25-30 thousand residents of the city.

Already during the first days of the war, refugees began to stream into Zgierz, both Jews and Poles, from the towns of the border regions that had been immediately occupied by the Germans. The German air bombardment of the city began on September third 1939 it lasted for three days until September 6th. For the most part this took place during the day; one could breath a bit easier at night. The bombardment, which was directed at the train station as well as the outskirts, cased fires and destroyed houses. There were also casualties. The bombardment was very strong on Tuesday, September 5th. It hit houses in the center of the city. The evangelical church was destroyed, as was the German Theater on Pilsudski Street. There were also victims from among the children. The following Jews were wounded from a bomb that fell in the neighborhood of Narutowicza and Dabrowskiego Streets: Leibel Librach the son of Asher, his wife Esther who was the daughter of Yitzchak Meir Zylberberg, and their only daughter Sara.

The Jewish population, as well the Polish population, started to panic and began to flee en masse to the surrounding cities: Lodz, Strykow, Ozorkow, Piatek, and even Warsaw. The tramways that connected Lodz with the nearby towns ceased their usual routes. The trains were full of Polish soldiers and officials were being evacuated along with their institutions. The refugees filled up all the routes.

In the meantime, the Nazi soldiers approached the city. On September 6th, the evacuation of the Polish authorities took place as the culmination point: the police, the firemen, and the officials of the magistrate headed by the mayor all left the city in haste. Chaos prevailed. There were no electric lights in the city, and the streets were dark. The Polish riffraff began to rob the Jewish businesses.

On Thursday, September 7th, the city was taken over by the German military. The first German soldiers were seen at 10:00 a.m.

According to the testimony of several eyewitnesses, the German soldiers, prior to their entry into Zgierz, murdered in a bestial fashion five Jewish refugees who were on their way from Zgierz to Strykow. The Zgierz merchant Zusman was among them. The soldiers robbed the refugees and then murdered them in a cruel fashion.

(Another version relates the story in the following way: Gershon Zusman was on his way to Dombrowka with his children when the Germans captured him and shot him. According to this version, the victims were forced to dig a grave for themselves prior to their death.)

On the next day, September 8th, on the second day of the marching in of the Germans, the soldiers began to rampage in the city. They captured Jews in the streets and also took them from their houses. The several hundred captured men were rounded up in the old marketplace, in front of the building of the magistrate and were surrounded by guards. A few Poles and local Germans were included among the arrested. They took everything from the Jews, including money and jewelry. After that, the arrested people were taken to the Catholic church, where nearby lay a few dead German soldiers who fell during the battle. In the presence of the fallen, they announced to those arrested that they would be held responsible for every German soldier who might be killed in the city and region. The few arrested Germans were freed. The Poles were still held, but separate from the Jews. (According to one witness, the arrested Jews included: Mendel Gibralter, the pharmacist Rosenberg, Nachum Kaminski, Moshe Itzkowicz, Berl Helman (the undertaker), Avraham Yaakov Rodzinek, and several others who I no longer remember.) The Germans lined the Jews up into two rows, and had to remain standing for hours with machine guns pointed at them. A few times, a German functionary came to them and threatened that shortly the church would be torn down or burnt. The Germans constantly beat the Jews with deathblows, and a few Jews had half of their beards burnt off.

On the first day, they allowed the prisoners to go out to attend to their physical needs, but on the second day, they even forbade that. The prisoners were not given food or drink. The Zgierz Jews intervened when it was possible. Apparently after they gave bribes, the Germans permitted giving a little bit of food and water to the prisoners (once in three days). Yehuda Borkowski's wife brought the food. Among the guards that watched over the prisoners, there were a few Austrians who had some compassion for the

497

prisoners. Quietly, so that their German friends would not see, they brought a drink of water to the Jews from time to time.

On the morning of the Sabbath (according to a few eyewitnesses, it was Sunday), the Germans took out two Jews from the church - Fishel Grynsztejn and Mordechai Zelmanowicz. People were afraid that they were going to shoot them. However, they shortly returned, and it became clear that the Germans summoned them to transport the corpses of Dr. Zygmunt Kaltgard and his sister Kama, who had committed suicide, to the cemetery. They had poisoned themselves. A large group of Zgierz Jews, who were lucky enough not to find themselves among the prisoners, attended the funeral.

This case of suicide was not a unique occurrence in Zgierz. There were other Jews who were psychologically unable to bear the indignities and persecutions of the first days of occupation. Two young women who came from Przemysl and worked as druggists in Rosenberg's drugstore also committed suicide.

The prisoners were freed on Sunday, September 10th. One of the local Germans, the scribe of the magistrate's office, lectured them and warned them that in the future, they must be loyal to the German authorities. By a stroke of good fortune, the rabbi of Zgierz, Rabbi Shlomo Yehuda Leib HaKohen of holy blessed memory, was not among the prisoners. It is told that on the second day of the occupation of Zgierz, a German officer came to him and asked to visit his house. He spoke politely to the rabbi and explained that a difficult period was coming for the Jews. He made the pretence, perhaps even with sincerity, that he had compassion for the Jews. When the rabbi remarked that the Germans are known as a people of culture, and that they certainly would not deal treacherously with innocent people, the officer was silent.

The local Germans, that is to say the Volksdeutschen [2], who were on good terms with the Jews prior to the war, completely ended their relations with the Jews very shortly after the marching in of the Wehrmacht. They began to cause trouble for the Jews, who were their acquaintances and neighbors. The Jews suffered in particular from the Volksdeutsche Strobach, who at that time became the mayor (Bergenmeister) of the city. Not far behind him in demonstrated hatred and persecution for the Jews were two other Volksdeutschen: the aforementioned official Mille, and Kerner.

Constant persecutions against the Jews of Zgierz began. The soldiers, the S.S. members, and the local Germans beat and tortured Jews on the streets, organized lapankes [3], conducted searches and robbed Jewish houses. Daily, various anti-Semitic ordinances and decrees were issued. A curfew was declared for the Jews between 5:00 p.m. and 8:00 a.m. They were forbidden to gather together for public prayer. The synagogue, Beis Midrash, and shtibels were closed. The ban was applicable even to prayer quorums (minyans) in private houses. The Germans threatened severe punishments, including the death penalty, for any Jew who disobeyed the ordinances. With a heavy heart, the rabbi was forced to declare to the Jews that they should not organize private minyans on the eve of Yom Kippur.

No small amount of fear was awakened in the Jews when the decree was issued that the entire Jewish population (according to another version -only the men), must register. The Germans imposed the duty to conduct the registration upon the community itself.

The Jews suffered a great deal of vexation from the local Polish population. The tribulations from the Polish anti-Semites were especially difficult with respect to attempts to obtain food. There was a shortage of food during the first weeks of the German occupation. When long lines formed outside the bakeries in the evenings, the anti-Semites, or the ordinary hooligans, threw the Jews from the "kolejkes" [4]; it also happened that they turned over Jews into the hand of the Germans. Indeed, the nightly attempts to obtain a morsel of bread were fraught with mortal

danger. On more than one occasion, the attempt of someone to obtain a bit of food for his family would end with a beating or even death blows.

As has previously been mentioned, there were incidents of robbing from Jews by the riff-raff already in the first days of confusion at the beginning of the war. After that, when the Germans took over the city, the robbery became widespread. On the Sabbath of September 9th, the Germans perpetrated a massive pogrom upon the Jewish stores on Pilsudski Street. They pillaged and destroyed the businesses of Mandel, Korcacz, Bechler, Spiewak, Yitzchak Grand and others. The owners were cruelly beaten. They did not even spare women.

Many Jewish merchants closed their businesses during the first days of the occupation for fear of robbery. However the mayor (bergenmeister) Strobach strongly warned that people must keep the businesses open, and threatened severe penalties for those who did not.

A series of searches in Jewish homes began on September 10th. The pretext was that Jews held arms, and that they were engaged in food speculation, an activity that carried with it the death penalty. During this opportunity, money, jewelry, food, clothing, linens and furniture were removed from the Jewish homes. During the searches, the Germans and their assistants sadistically destroyed the Jewish homes: they tore apart the floors, destroyed the ovens, pillaged the cellars, and simply made mayhem.

In the following weeks of the occupation, the new civic authorities granted the robbery a stamp of "legality" so to speak through their ordinances: all Jewish stores, enterprises and factories were requisitioned. The factories were provided with German commissars (Treihender), who oversaw their operations. Rosenbaum's pharmacy was also requisitioned. The Germans issued ordinances that required the Jews to register their gold, silver, jewelry and other items of value, including their furs.

As in other places under German occupation, the Jews of Zgierz were permitted to possess 2,000 marks of ready cash. The remainder had to be deposited in a "spare account", which for all practical purposes meant that the money was taken from them.

Another form of theft was the contributions that the Germans imposed upon the Jews. They required the Jews to pay two contributions. The witnesses related the following sums: 10,000 Zloty, 50,000 Zloty, 100,000 Zloty and even 250,000 Zloty; it is difficult to establish the exact amount.

The first contribution was imposed right after Sukkot 5700 (1939) [5]. Three weeks later, the Germans suddenly arrested twenty prominent citizens as hostages, among them the rabbi, the dozor and communal head Aharon Hersch Kompel as well as several Jewish manufacturers and merchants or their wives (Mrs. Poznerson, and Mrs. Aranson). After a few hours, German Functionaries came to the hostages and ordered them to produce detailed lists of their assets. Afterwards, the Germans demanded a new contribution from the Jews and forced the hostages to underwrite an obligation that they would pay it the next day by ten o'clock. The hostages were freed from arrest once they underwrote the obligation. The contribution was paid according to the set terms; it was given over to the aforementioned functionary.
Slavery, Humiliation and Torture

Jews were conscripted for work, for the most part hard and dirty labor, already in the first days of the occupation. The Volksdeutschen and police grabbed Jews as individuals or in groups. Those who succeeded in hiding were tracked down and chased in the homes, and dragged out of their hiding places. During the time of their labor, the Jews were beaten with deathblows, tortured, and degraded. The women were told to remove their dresses. Wearing only their shirts, they had to wash the floors of the offices and barracks with their dresses. They were forced to clean latrines with their bare hands. In such a manner, for example, the Volksdeutsche Brand went into the home of the Grand family and grabbed two women -Guta Grand (today Fein) and Chava Zylberberg - beat them and then forced them to wash the corridors of the magistrate. A day later, that same German brought a group of women - Gittel Grand and Waks (dentists), Glowinska (from the iron works in the old market), and Fela Boaz -into the building of the seminary near the train station, and forced them to wash the windows with broken panes for an entire day, without food or a drink of water.

A short time later, the Germans, over and above the wild Lapankes [6], set up forced labor for the Jews of Zgierz. They forced the community to provide daily a large contingent of Jews for the work (one witness mentioned the number as 200). The Jews were employed by various enterprises in town, including in military positions. Work groups gathered together each day in front of the communal building, and from there they were led to their work under a guard consisting of police and Volksdeutschen. The Jews suffered from the seven fires of hell on their way to and from work, and also while at work. They were beaten, chicaned and mocked before the eyes of the masses. A group of rich Jews was able to elude the fate of the slave laborers; they hired proxies from among the destitute people who had lost all means of livelihood.

The Git Lusmieci [7] was a steady place of hard work for the Jews. About forty men were employed there in unloading the garbage and in dragging (four Jews were harnessed to one wagon). One day, one of the workers, a young boy by the name of Skosowski (Zalman Feldscher's grandson) did not wish to laugh when a soldier of the guard played a joke on another Jew. For that, that young boy was shot on the spot. Similar attacks were a common occurrence during the time of work.

At the work place not far from "Lustgarten" on Piotkowska Street, where the Jews worked with the stodoles [6], a soldier noticed a watch on Hershel Kaliski, and asked him to give it to
him. When Kaliski refused, the solder shot him.

Murder came to Jews at every occasion, and for the smallest pretexts. Only a small number of the names of the victims are known. For example, Wolf Szietonski was severely wounded. Shimon Zusman's brother Gershon

501

was shot. Prior to his execution, the murderers forced him to dig a grave for himself. The Zgierz Jew Leibel Librach was shot in Strykow. In the cellar of Meir Szwarc's house, under Rosenberg's pharmacy, the Germans set up an inquisition room, where they tortured and flogged Jews. Among others, the coal exporter Dubin was interrogated there.

If the above mentioned murders had "accidental" characteristics, the sending (in November 1939) of Jewish notables and party activists to the Radogoszcz Concentration Camp near Lodz was already an organization aktion with the aim of killing members of the Jewish intelligentsia and cultural activists. Like other cities in Warthegau (the Polish western realm, under occupation of the Reich; to which Zgierz belonged) and first and foremost in Lodz, in November 1939, there were arrests and expulsions of Jews as well as the Polish intelligentsia to Radogoszcz. The following names are known from among the Zgierz Jews who were arrested and sent there: Karol Eiger (the president of the Maccabi, the son of the well-known Zionist activist Moshel Eiger), Avigdor Roszalski, Avraham Zylbersztejn, Leibush Srebnik, and Yosef Pantel. The same fate overtook several Polish personalities in the city, including the previous mayor Szwiercz, the director of the gymnasia, and others.

From the first days of the occupation, the Germans conducted anti-Jewish propaganda efforts directed towards the Polish population in Zgierz. Placards were posted in the streets that incited the Poles against the Jews and promoted rumors that Jews were speculating with food, causing difficulty in obtaining approvals. The Hitlerists placed anti-Jewish slogans, caricatures, etc. in the windows of various Jewish premises. For example, the window of Moshe Sidlowski's requisitioned manufacturing enterprise was always decorated with "Der Stuermer" with the large type headline of its articles: "The Jews are our enemies", "The Jews are warmongers", etc.

Along with the anti-Jewish incitement propaganda, the Hitlerists conducted activities that mocked the Jewish religion and denigrated the national honor of the Jews. For example, they forced Jews, at the time of their forced labor, to wash floor, trash bins, and lavatories with tallises and parochets [8]. During the time of the searches, the removed Torah scrolls, tefillin, tallises, and mezuzas from the Jews, and they beat their owners in a bloody fashion. Pages of books were desecrated, torn into pieces and burnt in the marketplace, along with other holy objects.

A beloved activity of the Hitlerists and their accomplices was the shaving off of the beards and peyos of Jews. The shaving was more tearing, plucking and burning than shaving. On one occasion, the Germans forced the victim to eat the shorn hair. Despite all this, G-d fearing Jews did not want to part with their Divine image, and bound their faces with kerchiefs under the pretext of being in pain, so that their beards and peyos would not be noticed by the murderers. Once, the German police brought the rabbi to the barber's chair and bid him to have his beard and peyos cut. Then, they brought the rabbi to the dozor Kompel and ordered him to pay for the rabbi's shave.

Almost every Sunday, and sometimes on weekdays, the Volksdeutschen along with the Wehrmacht soldiers organization large scale plays in which the victims were Jews. They grabbed Jews, forced them to don tallises and tefillin or women's clothing, put women's hats, wigs, or ordinary pail on their heads. The victims held Chinese lanterns or brooms in their hands. Then, they forced the Jews to sing "Hatikva", "Das Shtetele Belz", or Russian songs. The Jewish actors had to shout the slogans: "All Jews are swine", "We Jews are responsible for the war", etc. The participants in such a performance then had to perform gymnastics, jump, crawl on the ground, dance, and drag the fireman's wagon. Not infrequently, hundreds of Jews would take part in such a performance - and the jeering lasted for a long time. The witnesses mention the following people among other tortured Jews of Zgierz: The lawyer Jochwet (Eliezer Shlumiel's brother-in-law), Mordechai Srobka, the dozor Kompel, David Dawidowicz, Shimon Zusman, Mordechai Jakubowicz, and others. On one Sunday, the Germans forced a few hundred Jews into the new marketplace and from there to the fire station, where they were told to lie with their faces in the dirt, as they were beaten with death blows. As the witnesses relate, Shlomo Bialystocki and Yechiel Kompel were among the wounded who died later.

On another occasion (probably in November), the German dragged Shabtai Itzkowicz, Reichmanen and Mrs. Gitel Grand to the building of the Polish school, and asked them to tear down the cross from the wall and throw it on the street. When the Jews absolutely refused to do this, the murderers beat them and threw them in jail.

The culmination point of the violation of the sanctity of Israel was the burning of the synagogue and Beis Midrash. The first attempt to burn down both buildings (apparently, this took place on October 27, 1939) did not succeed, for the neighboring Jews succeeded in extinguishing the fire and saving the Torah scrolls, which were later transferred to canopies in the cemetery. The Hitlerists quickly found "the guilty party". The arrested the tinsmith David Gotlieb, who lived close to the Beis Midrash. They accused him of setting the building on fire. Gotlieb spent six weeks in jail. One month later (apparently on November 24, 1939), the Germans set the synagogue and Beis Midrash on fire for a second time, and this time, they succeeded. Both buildings were completely burnt down. On that critical night, when the synagogue was still in flames, a group of German soldiers, Volksdeutschen and firemen came to the rabbi and demanded of him a payment of 250 Zloty as payment for "their effort in saving the Jewish homes from the fire". According to another version of the story, they demanded the sum in payment for the benzene that they needed in order to ignite the buildings. The rabbi asked that they wait until the next day so that he could collect the money. However, they requested that he immediately go to the dozors of the community to collect the money. Along the way, they forced the rabbi to stand and look at the fire for a long time. Other witnesses relate that they brought the rabbi to the magistrate, and forced him to write a declaration that the Jews alone (or himself alone) ignited the school and the Beis Midrash.

They also destroyed or demolished all of the shtibels in Zgierz - the Gerer, Sochaczewer, Strykower, and Aleksandrer. It is not clear if this happened during the first months of the occupation, or after the expulsion of the Jews of Zgierz.

They also desecrated the Jewish cemetery. The Polish population played an active role in this. On one occasion, on a Saturday morning, the Poles broke the large wooden fence of the cemetery and began to steal the boards. One Jew, together with Berl Helman the undertaker, ran to the magistrate and requested intervention. They were told that the police would become involved, but in fact, they did nothing. A few hours after the deed, two policemen came, but there was not even a remnant of the fence left. Some time later, after the expulsion of the Jews from Zgierz, they removed all of the tombstones and broke down the canopies that covered the graves of the rabbis. They paved streets with the stones, and they uprooted the very old pine trees to use for lumber. Finally, the Germans ploughed over the Zgierz cemetery and covered it with earth.

The Jews of Zgierz had to persevere many other persecutions and vexations that the Germans perpetrated against the Jews, as in other places.

Thus, in November 1939, the command was issued for Jews to wear a yellow band on the sleeve of their outer garments. One month later, an ordinance was issued, exactly as in other places in Warthegau, that the Jews of Zgierz must wear a yellow Star of David on the breast and shoulder of their outer garments.

A ghetto was not created in Zgierz, but the Jews suffered no small amount of tribulation from the constant evictions from the choicest dwellings. At the time of an eviction, they were not allowed to take anything with them. Thus, for example, did they evict all of the Jewish residents of Tauber's house on Pilsudski Street within one hour. Included among those evicted was the textile manufacturer Yaakov Meir Kupfer, who was kicked out of his dwelling without anything. He went to live in the house of Yosef Meir Haron (the owner of the dyeing factory), however not too long thereafter, the Germans also evicted all of the Jewish residents of that house as well.

The number of Jews in Zgierz began to decline during the months of September-December, 1939 for many Jews "voluntarily" left the city during the time of the battle, and also thereafter, in an attempt to flee the Hitlerist persecutions. A group of them fled to Lodz, but the majority fled to the cities under the Generalgouvernement (the central authority of occupied Poland). A number of Jews of Zgierz succeeded in stealing across the borders and arriving in areas that were administered by the Soviets. From among those who fled to those areas, a large number of Zgierz residents fell into the hands of the Germans, and were murdered very quickly at the time of the beginning of the Soviet-German war; a few perished due to the tribulations of hunger, cold, illness, and hard labor, and a larger number succeeded in surviving there until the liberation. Most of the refugees (aside from the youth) were from the upper classes; most of the Jews of modest means remained in the place, for they did not have the means to pay for travel. In total, approximately 2,000 Jews were left Zgierz in this manner, that is to say, close to a half of the Jewish population of Zgierz.

The Beginning of the End

The liquidation of the Zgierz community took place at the end of December 1939. On Tuesday, December 26 (14 Tevet 5700) the Germans issued an order that all Jews must leave Zgierz. They threatened the death penalty to anyone who transgressed this order. The Jews were to gather together at 7:00 a.m. in the Sokol sports arena. They had a baggage limit of

505

25 kilograms and a cash limit of 50 Zloty per person. Prior to the execution of the order, those who had the means (and only a few Jews had the means) left the city on their own volition and brought with them a few of their belongings. Already in their first steps out of the city, the Germans and Poles robbed those Jews, and did not spare them beatings and persecution. The majority of the Jews, about 2,500 people, gathered together the next day at the specified gathering point. There, the Germans doled out cruel beatings right and left. They stole the money and baggage from some of the Jews. After this introduction, they were driven towards Glowno, which belong to the Generalgouvernement. Along the way, the German guards threatened the Jews with shots if they would find money or other items of value on them. The terrified Jews quietly tossed away the rest of their belongings along the way.

Yissachar Szwarc was "fortunate" - he was spared the torment of exile. He died one day prior to the expulsion, and the Jews brought him by a hand wagon to a Jewish grave in the Zgierz cemetery.

A few Jewish families remained in Zgierz. For the most part, they were tradesmen, shoemakers and tailors, with their families. The Germans were in need of their vocations. A few names of those that remained are known: Dawidowicz, Blanket, Ziskind, the two Waller shoemakers, Wroclawski and others.

Emanuel Ringelblum, in his notes written in the Warsaw Ghetto, provides some incomplete information about the Jews in Zgierz. On October 4, 1940, he writes that he heard about the expulsion of the Jews of Zgierz. Ringelblum does not mention the date of the expulsion. It is possible that the news of the expulsion of December 1939 reached him late. It is also possible that he was writing of a new expulsion of Jews, who arrived in Zgierz from other places during the course of 1940. In those notes, Ringelblum further writes that the Jews of Zgierz (he does not give the number of those remaining Jews) had the right to live in the surrounding villages, but the Germans permitted the peasants to sell the Jews only limited amounts of food. From that note, we can deduce that the Jews were forbidden from living in the city itself.

A later bit of information about the group of Jews in Zgierz comes from a German document from the beginning of September 1941. According to the document, there were 81 Jews in Zgierz (22 men, 30 women, 22 children, and 7 elderly). These were tradesmen who were needed by the Germans, and their families. On January 12, 1942, that group, now numbering 84 or 85 people, was transferred to the Lodzer Ghetto. The Jews were transported to Lodz in wagons with all of their belongings, even with relatively large reserves of food and wooden materials.

Prior to the transport, there was a long correspondence between the government president Eibelher, the Lodzer Ghetto authorities, and the mayor (bergenmeister) of Zgierz. As a result of this correspondence, the government president gave his approval on September 5, 1941 for the transport, which was to take place, as mentioned, four months later. The reason for this is not clear. It is worthwhile to note that the transfer of the group of Zgierz Jews to Lodz was probably tied up with the general German plan of creating a central concentration point of all the Jews of Warthegau in the Lodzer Ghetto.

The fate of the expelled Zgierz Jews was exactly the same as the fate of the other residents of the Lodzer Ghetto. Both the earlier refugees, and the Jews driven out of Zgierz, suffered the tragic fate of the settlements to which they came.

Approximately 350 Zgierz Jews survived the war. A few of them survived the hell of the German concentration or work camps. A few came back from Soviet Russia. In the first postwar years, about 60 Jews of Zgierz lived in Poland. Most lived in Lodz or in Lower Silesia. A small number returned to Zgierz: Gittel Grand-Fein, her brother Avraham David, Aharon Zeidel and his wife, Ketler, Chaim Szulcz, Yitzchak Zelgaw, Przedworski, Jakubowicz, Grynbaum, the two Feldman brothers, Honigstok, and others.

The survivors did not remain for long amongst the ruins of the Jewish community of Zgierz, and they gradually left the city.

List of Sources

The Central Archives in Jerusalem: S. 26, No. 1208 – Komisja dla Spraw zydow Polskich, Jerozolima, kwiecen 1941 (protkol zeznania zlozonego w Zjednoczonym Komiticie Pomocy dla Zydow Polskich w Jerosolimie, dnia 28.8.1940)

The Yad Vashem Archives in Jerusalem: Historical questionnaire number 536.

Eyewitnesses (in the archives of the editor of the Yizkor book)
1. from Leib Gelbard
2. from Gittel Fein-Grand
3. from Yakor Blosztejn and Shaul Blanket
4. from Chaim Zalman Roses
5. from L. Weinsztejn
6. from W. Fiszer
7. Avraham and Esther Gotthelf
8. Fishel Feldon   and others

Publications

S. Huberband: Kiddush Hashem (Sanctification of the Divine Name), Tel Aviv, 1969.

M. Zanin: Over Stones and Sticks.

E. Ringelblum: Writings from the Ghetto, volume 1, Warsaw, 1952.

A. W. Jasni: The History of Jews in Lodz During the Years of the German Extermination of the Jews: Volume 1, Tel Aviv, 1960.

"Davar" 41.1.1940 [9].

1. Eisenbach: Geto Lodzkie, Warszawa, 1946.

T. Berenstein, A Rutkowski: Przesladowania Iudnosci zydowskiej w okresie hitlerowskiej administracji wojskowej na okupowanych ziemiach polskich ("Biuletyn Zydowskiego Instytutu Historycznego" 196, No 39-39).

D. Dabrowska: Zaglada skupisk zydowskich "Kraju Warty" w okresie okupacji hitlerowskiej ("Biuletyn Zydowskiego Instytutu Historycznego" 1955, No 13-14).

Kronika getta Lodzkiego vol 1, Lodz 1965.

The collected knowledge, eye witness reports and other information for this article was expounded upon (when possible) and amended – W. Fisher

The Synagogue is Burning! By Chaim Zalman Rus

From Sunday September 3rd until Wednesday September 6th 1939, German bombs fell on Zgierz, especially in the afternoon and evening hours. Only during the night was it quiet. On Thursday, September 7th, around 10:00 a.m., the first German soldiers were seen on the streets of Zgierz. Throughout the entire day, the sounds of gunshots and the crackle of machine guns could be heard. Nevertheless, a few Jews ventured out of their hiding places.

On the next day, Friday, throughout the entire morning, they grabbed Jews from their homes and streets and locked them in the local church. From time to time, people thought that they would tear down or burn the church. For three whole days, until Sunday, the unfortunate ones were help in very cramped conditions, without food or drink. They were all freed that afternoon.

I do not remember if there were any Jewish casualties from the bombardment, but I do know that some Jews were wounded. On Sunday morning, the murderers set the synagogue on fire; however the surrounding neighbors succeeded in saving the Torah scrolls. The Germans set the synagogue on fire a second time, and that time, it was burnt down completely. This took place on the 14th of Cheshvan, 27th October, 1940. That same day, I organized a minyan (prayer quorum) in the home of my eldest brother-in-law Yechiel Meir Kotek of blessed memory, with whom I lived, for that day was the yahrzeit of my father Fishel, may G-d remember him, who died in the year 5697 (1936) [10].

In the midst of the prayers, a few Poles who worked in the same courtyard came in and informed us that the synagogue was on fire, and had been completely destroyed. With weeping and screaming, Yankel Himel arose stood up and called out:

"Woe Jews, how can I pray when our holy synagogue is burning?!..."

He removed his tallis and tefillin and wanted to run there. It took time for us to calm him down and remind him that he is needed for the minyan, and he should remain until the prayers are finished.

On the Sabbath of November 18th, 1939, Jews were ordered under the threat of death to wear the yellow badge. The next day, on Sunday afternoon, the murderers drove several hundred Jews into the new market place and into the fire station, and forced them to lie down with their faces to the ground, which was wet and muddy. The unfortunate people were goaded and beaten, and there were a few casualties. As far as I remember, Shlomo Bialystocki and Yechiel Kompel were killed that day.

On Monday, November 20th, I decided to leave Zgierz. I went to Lodz on the tramway. In those times, such a journey was fraught with the peril of death. The walls of the tramcars were sprinkled with blood - and the conductor told me that one-day earlier, a few Jews were killed there…

Jews of Zgierz in the Warsaw Ghetto (from a letter to Wolf Fisher) by Mary Fisher-Fishman of Montreal

… With regard to a Zgierz "Landsmanschaft" [11] - such did not exist at all. Furthermore, there were not a large number of Zgierz Jews there. Most of them went to Lodz or the Warsaw area. I cannot remember the name of the town, which was not overtaken by the "Reich". There, from Zgierz, there was the Boaz family, the father of Genia of blessed memory. Tears welled up in his eyes when I brought him on Purim… a spirited little something. At the end of the deportation, he was held in a cellar, full of mice. Hid daughter told me that at the time of the aktion that grabbed older people… There, there was also the sister of Boaz-Tracki - Andzia. Her son was run over in the Ghetto.

Kohn with the long beard from the mill (he was also run over on the street) was in the Warsaw Ghetto, as was Gincberg with his wife and son, of blessed memory. He died from typhus in Radom. Jeszik Gross and Falcza with their child were killed during the deportations. Falcza Braun, the daughter of Herman Braun of Warsaw, was a well-known singer in the Ghetto. She composed and wrote the well-known song "Through walls, through holes, and through fences". I believe that I am the only one who remembers and knows the melody. It is difficult for me to write about the Siedlowskis (Moshele and his wife). They literally died of hunger. I kept them alive as long as it was possible to move about in the city. Same with the Dawidowiczs - I brought them bread and potatoes. I did this in memory of their children - Ali and the others, and also in memory of the devotion of these people to me when I was treated as one of them in their home.

Do you know what Zgierz Jews did in the Ghetto? --They died of hunger! Only one, Yaakov Albersztejn acted deplorably. He once stated: "I fear that this war will end". He turned me over to the police when he caught

510

me. He gorged himself, and was happy. What overcame that person - nobody knew. The Haron family was also in Warsaw, and had what to survive. They ate in the same kitchen as the Dawidowiczs, as long as they could move about and pay. The fate of the Zylberberg (Genia) family, Itzik of blessed memory's wife, was tragic. The children and parents fell like flies. The large family had no recourse. Only Genia herself had where to eat. The Dawidowicz, Itzik's children and myself, young and capable, with a bit of an entrepreneurial spirit, sold coupons on Gensze Street. I had brought them from Warsaw in great amounts and stored in the cellar, thereby risking my life. Later, when Piniush of blessed memory returned from the Russian side, he took part as well. Unfortunately, there was no longer any merchandise.

We could still own gold and jewelry - and I had an idea. We also smuggled old items, and Poles would come into the Ghetto and exchange them for a piece of bread or butter.

On Meizels Street # 3, where we lived along with our uncles the Bergers, one of our neighbors was the Zgierzer Rabbi, who lived at # 7. Once, my brother-in-law of blessed memory took me along to the rabbi, and brought him a few Zlotys for Passover. He introduced me to his daughter-in-law. The rabbi blessed me, and talked about my father, Shimon Fiszer of blessed memory.

As I have already written, the Zgierzers in Warsaw were not organized. I was culturally active as long as it was possible, while we still had what to eat. I found myself together with H. Wynik, as far as I remember. I spoke to him twice. At that time, I was still in contact with the historian Dr. Emanuel Ringelblum. From that time, I lost track of him.

I transcribed my poem "Yom Kippur" from memory. I also wrote a poem about Zgierz, leaving out almost nothing that is important to perpetuate. I wrote it only for myself, in Polish, not for the Yizkor book.

I wrote a great deal, but not what you requested. As I myself know, my head is full of a strange chaos, and a rush toward memory, when I think about those terrible days - and in the end, nothing comes out. Therefore, Passover is not the time for this. Indeed, I wanted to answer you earlier.

This Must Also Be Written... by W. Ben Shimon of Tel Aviv
(A diary from that dark time)

End of November, 1939

It was already daybreak when the peasant took us with his wagon to the agreed upon place, after a night journey full of terror. Without saying a word, he pointed us with his whip in the direction of an isolated country cottage, and immediately started his return journey along the same dirt road.

We were eight people, including two women. We wished to go over the Bug River to the Soviet side. We did not have any large packs with us. We had just left our homes, saying: until the storm shall pass. We threw knapsacks on our shoulders and, with great caution, like mute shadows so that one dog would not disturb the next, we arrived at the cottage of the "Przewodnik" (guide) - which was not far from the riverbank.

Around, it was deathly quiet. On the right, between the willows of the riverbank, there was from time to time a glitter from the surface of the river. We had just traveled, and we were edgy from the night journey. We speedily went into the cottage. By its side, there was an overturned boat.

Suddenly, a shout cut through the air:

"Stop! Stand still!"

We stood frozen. Our hearts paused. Unexpectedly, we were met by a German border patrol with pointed guns who greeted us with shots. The deathly danger immediately brought us back to consciousness: We were caught! And we were only about twenty meters from the Bug... at the threshold of rescue...

They took us in an opposite direction - over ploughed fields and roundabout ways. Finally, they let us off at a footpath that led straight into the woods. Our thoughts and feelings are easy to imagine. At that time, we already knew very well about the robbery, murder, and sadistic torture perpetrated by the guards when they caught Jews sneaking across the border. (Incidentally, this is a separate, horrible chapter, which should be written as an integral part of our Holocaust history.)

At that time, there was another dark thought that was drilled into our brains: nobody would know what became of our remains... The women sobbed out loud. The oldest of the patrols, apparently not yet completely poisoned, had a humane conscience. He understood our thoughts and tried to

512

calm us, primarily the women, by telling us that we were being taken to the border commandant

A large, wooden building stood at the entrance to the forest. They brought us to a large hall with a bench in the corner, where we were to wait for the arrival of the commandant. He would interrogate us. We sat with our heads bent down as if we were doomed, each with our own thoughts, in which we conducted a painful stocktaking of our lives...

The commandant arrived. The mood of the soldiers became more serious. Our hearts started to beat faster -shortly, it would begin... It was not long until they took us, the entire group, with our packs in our hands, into the office of the commandant. He sat by the table - a firmly built man in his fifties - and seriously considered each one of us. The manner in which he conducted the inquest took us by surprise, and we were completely confounded -he talked to us like humans! And we... we were at that time officially known as thieves, bandits, parasites; as guilty for the war; as the greatest enemies of the German Reich and their Fuehrer; as enemies whom every scoundrel and sadist felt it was their patriotic duty to humiliate, beat, shoot or sentence to death...

After the regular questions: Who are you? From where do you come? Where are you going? etc. - looking over documents, he asked more personal questions regarding our professions and employment, about our families, about the reasons for our flight, and our prospects in the Soviet Union. Instinct prompted us that we should tell him the entire terrible and murderous truth. A feeling arose in our hearts that here sits and officer in whom, beneath his uniform, beats a humane heart, and also treats us like humans. We opened up our hearts and portrayed to him our tragic situation; that we went out from our homes, tore ourselves away from our families in order to flee with the fear of death so that we can find a refuge until the storm calms.

The commandant listened attentively to our confession. He went over to the women who were sitting down and weeping, and soothed them, telling them that nothing bad would happen to us. The soldier who was searching for "contraband" in our sacks throughout all this was told to repack the sacks and return them to us.

"They are all free, they can go!"

As we were thanking him for his extraordinary consideration of us, one of the women, completely unintentionally, asked something about the dangers of crossing the river. He caught on to this, and he asked about which

513

danger she is talking. Then we told him about the robbery and murder defenseless Jews who cross the forests and rivers in the dark of night in order to cross the border. The organized gangs utilize the opportunity to get rich during the night, without risking legal proceedings or a punishment.

The commandant asked the name of our "Przewodnik", but we did not know his name. We were only able to describe the place from which we were captured.

As we returned along the road through the fields, we did not say any word to each other. We were in a deep shock. One of us murmured: A miracle! A miracle!

The sun was high in the sky. It was already the height of the day when we approached the yard of the "Przewodnik". Suddenly, we heard the sound of a galloping horse behind us. Who was chasing us? Our hearts were throbbing... We cleared the route for the approaching rider and... we recognized that he was the commandant!

We looked about and did not understand what was taking place. Our astonishment was great. We then saw the commandant engaged in a conversation with a tall person, in whose hands, as we were later to discover, rested our fate. Seeing us, the commandant said that we could be completely calm. He made the person personally responsible to insure that each of us would be transferred... The commandant also would make sure to send two soldiers at the designated time to be present as we were transferred over the Bug.

When the eldest of our group, the engineer Kazimierz Lewi (Isucher Szwarc's son-in-law) thanked him for his humane deed at such an extraordinary moment for us, the commandant said that he does not deserve any thanks, for it is every person's duty to help his fellow man during a time of difficulty. Then, he spoke to us freely and intimately - he never believed what they were writing about the Jews; he himself is from Vienna and often came in contact with Jews; he himself played sports with people from the "Hakoach" team of Vienna; he believes that we are doing the correct thing by going over the border; he had left a wife with children at home; we do not know what tomorrow might bring and when freedom might come. He greeted us with a handshake and bade us farewell. Then he mounted his horse and galloped away...

The sun had set, and it was getting darker and darker. A damp, autumn chill hung over the river. On the other side there was a gigantic forest -black

514

and silent -that was shrouded in mystery. Around, there was a thick calm. We could hear the swaying of the river willows. It was uncanny and frightening. What awaited us, alone and forlorn, on that strange soil in such a stormy time? Would we find there the asylum we craved, or "the night of the long dagger"?

I glanced backwards. The sounds of the tips of the willows made a soft sound, like an evening prayer. Perhaps they were sending us their blessing on the threshold of our new, involuntary, and unknown journey... There was also a silent and warm prayer on our own lips...

We noticed at first, there among the willows, two silhouettes of armed soldiers - reclining motionless on the tree stumps. Yes, he kept his word, the German commandant, regarding the border guard. Honestly, and with true self sacrifice...

When, many years later, I visited the forest of the "Righteous Gentiles" in Jerusalem, I knew very well how to evaluate the deep humanitarian meaning of the great, worthy and historical project. I thought about that officer in the uniform of the "Reichswehr" (Reich Army) who personally helped the forlorn and persecuted Jews - we were most certainly not the only ones whom he helped escape from the talons of the devouring Hitler-beast. Yes, without doubt he deserves to be mentioned here with full honor. Where can we obtain his name, and who knows if he might have paid with his life for his humanitarian and courageous heart?

Let these lines serve as a modest monument for eternal praise and gratitude in memory of all righteous gentiles, so that their deeds - often bound up with self-sacrifice - and their names shall be remembered.

The Way of Martyrdom for a Jew of Zgierz by Adasz Rozenstrauch of blessed memory

Adasz Rozenstrauch

Adasz [12], the author of the following written experiences from the Second World War, was the son of Daya and Shalom Rozenstrauch, grandson of the notable householder and communal activist Reb Natan Ader, and the great-grandson of Leib Parizer - an uncommon character from the old generation of Hassidim, who himself traveled to the Trisker Maggid, the Magen Avraham of holy blessed memory.

Adasz was beloved in his family. When the war broke out in 1939, he was a 9th year student in the Lodz Hebrew Gymnasia. He went through the war with all of its tribulations. The sole compensation for his hellish suffering was possibly that he merited to witness with his own eyes the downfall of his tormentors.

Adasz lost his family in the German death camps. A year after the war, his own young life was lost after an illness, on German soil. May this mention serve as a good remembrance.

The First Bombardment

Long, incessant whistling of sirens - an air raid alarm. Thus began the repeated and already loathsome daily game of "hiding oneself". But what can one make of it? It was the beginning of the war. There were readily issued threats and penalties. Without recourse, we would leave everything in the house and hide in the cellar among the firewood. Only grandfather remains in his post as the commandant of the block of houses for air-protection, and also as the emissary. The streets are empty, as a shudder passes through. Suddenly, we hear the noise of airplanes. I left up my head. We already see the steel birds in the skies. It is beautiful - yet at the same time frightful. The seconds pass, the noise approaches and becomes louder and louder. They are already over our heads. Doors open and some long objects fall out. A terrifying whistling of air takes away the breath. Then -a deafening explosion. One, two, three, four... a loud "Shema Yisrael" [13] from my grandfather brings me back to consciousness. Then I understood that the situation is serious. War has been etched in my thoughts. This was not a practice alarm. The minutes pass endlessly. I want to be with my parents and my beloved brothers. However, this is impossible. With the airplanes are flying low over the town, they would surely shoot me. I must therefore wait. The first hour of the war seemed to last for an eternity.

Finally, I heard the whistling of sirens - the air raid ended. I ran back to the garden in one breath. Thank G-d, everyone was alive and well. As well, the city did not suffer much destruction. We were all greatly shaken up, including grandfather who always was always a paragon of boldness and self-assurance. With a feeling of relief, we together took the packages and returned home.

In the evening, after "Dziennik Wieczorny" (the nightly news), we discussed the events of the day.

Monday September 4th was completely calm. On Tuesday there was another air raid. We ran to the garden, but this time I did not leave the family. We lay under a large linden tree, pressed one against the other. This time, the air raid was frightful. A bomb fell in the neighboring garden and made a huge pit. The earth flew up into the air and was stirred it so much that it became dark. With great effort, I succeeded in calming the women, for they

517

were certain that this was a gas bomb. A few minutes later, everything became still, and the air became clear. We lay there and waited until the cessation of the explosions convinced us that the airplanes had moved on. The sirens gave the signal that the air attack had concluded, and we were relieved. However, this air raid caused a nervous shock for my mother and grandmother. The city was bombarded heavily. Many houses collapsed, burying many victims underneath. The house of one of our cousins was completely destroyed, however they and their family survived.

In Lodz

After hearing that the day had been calm in Lodz, we decided to go there. We left Zgierz at ten o'clock with the last train. When we arrived at the Baluter Rynek, we realized that the situation was not that happy. Military divisions and regiments from the Polish army that was defeated at the Warta River were retreating in disarray through Brzeziny, in the direction of Warsaw. It was terrible, but there was nothing we could do. Sorely frightened, we went to our uncle. The living quarters were not good. Ten people occupied a small room. We lay down on the floor and quickly fell asleep.

At 5:00 a.m., I got up and ran out into the street. That which I saw caused me to despair. Together with the troops, the police, and following them the P. W. "Przysposobienie Wojskowe" [14]), a few organization, civilians, women and children were marching along. By an order issued over the radio from Pulkownik (Colonel) Umiastowski, they were all leaving Lodz in order... to defend Warsaw. I ran back to my parents and told them what I had seen. They became very nervous, and nobody knew what to do: to leave town or to remain. There was a struggle between two opinions - but grandfather decided: we will remain.

For the Lodzer residents, leaving the town, as was to become obvious later, was a fatal error. The tragedy that took place on the Lodz-Brzeziny-Warsaw highway will certainly be written about in the history books. Pulkownik Umiastowski was certainly a German spy, and with his appeal to leave Lodz, he intended for the civilian people to block the way of the retreating military regiments, who would have great difficulty passing through the masses of refugees. The German aviators took advantage of this

518

situation. They flew low and opened a hurricane of fire with machine guns. There is no need for me to write about the outcome. There was a mangled mass of corpses, intermingled with killed horses and overturned wagons. Many people, seeing this bloody slaughter, returned along the way. Only a small number arrived in Warsaw. Afterwards, there were two calm days in Lodz.

On Friday, what we had feared took place. The greatest tragedy in the history of European Jewry had begun. At around 5:00 p.m., the first group of the Hitlerist Storm Troopers began to appear in the Plac Wolnosci (Freedom Square). A half an hour later, the city officially surrendered. I was an eyewitness to this. From that moment, the Jews were no longer free people. **Our fate was sealed.**

In the morning, pogroms and pillaging of Jewish businesses and homes began. Conscription for work and beatings became a daily, normal occurrence. This went on for days and weeks, during which time the morale of the Jews sunk, and they became physically downtrodden. We heard and saw things which makes the blood in the veins curdle.

Realizing that living in such conditions would bring a complete breakdown of morale, and seeing what was taking place in the Hitlerian hell, I decided to flee at any cost. I tried to convince my parents to sneak across to the Soviet territory, but my mother did not wish to leave her parents under any circumstances. I was not behind the times, though, and they thought that it was not reasonable that we should go away. When my parents realized that they could not convince me, they proposed a compromise: we would go to the Generalgouvernement - Warsaw would be our destination. We packed the most necessary belongings and sent them away with a Christian acquaintance. We left Lodz on December 25th. They inspected us from head to toe at the border. Fortunately, we had given over our jewelry to the acquaintance.

In Warsaw

The difference between Lodz and Warsaw was great. Here, there was business, and a great deal of movement and commotion, like before the time of the war. As previously, the Gensa and Nalewki were the centers of commerce, speculation, and high earnings. The unusually low prices of food products provided good opportunities for earning a livelihood. In such a situation, there was not yet talk of traveling on. I was dedicated to the will of my parents. Father earned well, and we lacked nothing. For a half year, I ate, drank, and enjoyed myself. At the beginning of June, I decided to become somewhat independent, and to work in a military enterprise. I had little means other than what I earned from the official service, so I was very satisfied with the work. I believed that one must have a profession to be able to coexist with the Germans. To that end, after three months of work, I had saved a little money, so I registered for a locksmith course with the Jewish community. I completed the course after six months with good results. Then, I had to search for appropriate work. Thanks to the contacts of my grandfather, I found work as an assistant machinist in the military mechanical workshop. I worked there until the outbreak of the war between Germany and Russia. Work in our workplace stopped when the Germans ceased claiming the finished products. I was again left without employment. At that time, the situation in Warsaw became extremely critical. Hunger, want, and epidemics were prevalent. I also became ill with dysentery, but I regained my health, since I had been robust previously. However, I did not have the means to support myself.

I Search for Field Work

In the middle of the month of July, the "Topserol" agricultural organization organized a work expedition to the Lublin countryside at the time of the wheat harvest. I volunteered, however the health commissioner rejected me because I had been greatly weakened. I did not resign myself to this, and I sought out 'protektsia' [15]. At the end, I was given permission to travel. Even though it was difficult to part from my parents at such a hard time, I went so that I could lighten the situation and send products.

I traveled to Lublin with a group of 120 people. From there, they sent us to Bukowa, from where the work office sent us to the neighboring villages and put us up in peasant's huts. As is usual at harvest time, the work was difficult, especially for me, for I was not used to it. I had no day or night. I was always compelled to work. However, the good food strengthened me.

After the wheat harvest, the peasants stopped the work and we had to leave. I returned with a heavy heart, for we had heard terrible news about epidemics that claim hundreds of victims daily. I purchased flour and shortening on the way, which I hid very well. The journey went peacefully, as did the search upon entering the Warsaw ghetto. I arrived at night on the eve of Rosh Hashanah.

In the Warsaw Ghetto

I will never forget the welcome I received from my parents. They simply did not recognize me. I left the city pale and emaciated, and I returned tanned and filled out. When I told them about life in the country, they were astonished that life was so good. When I unpacked the sticks of shortening and butter, their astonishment knew no bounds. They made a feast in the middle of the night - the first time in a long while that they ate to satiation.

A few days after my return, I contemplated our situation and determined that no manna from heaven would fall in the ghetto. I should again go to work. This time as well, grandfather assisted. I worked as a polisher of molded aluminum spoons. Now that I was a metal worker, I learned the trade very quickly. I worked at night, and helped my father as much as possible during the day. I did not have the good fortune to work there for very long. The electric power was cut off at night, so the foundry had to shut down.

I again began to search for work. This time, my uncle registered me on the list of the egg workers, which led to employment in one of the best workplaces of Warsaw. Now I began to earn a living in an excellent fashion. The work was on the Aryan side. I smuggled various items of merchandise there, and brought products back in return. From these, I ate fifteen eggs daily raw or in other forms (eggnog, with coffee or with borscht). The work was not difficult; therefore I was able to renew my strength. However, this did not last for long.

Wednesday, July 22nd, a day that no Warsaw Jew will forget, was the day that the "liquidation" began (an unfortunate term coined by the refined German murderers). The Judenrat received an ordinance that they must give over 7,000 Jews daily to be settled in the newly occupied eastern regions and to be employed in various enterprises. They were promised good wages and food. Families who present themselves voluntarily would not be separated. Each person would receive 3 kilos of bread and a kilo of marmalade for the journey. Given the need and hunger that prevailed in thousands of homes, it is no wonder that a large number volunteered. This went on for 5-6 days. Then, the number of people [16] shrank, and they began to capture people on the streets, the poor, ragged and emaciated people, and the residents of the so-called "points". When this "reservoir" was also depleted, groups of Lithuanians and Ukrainians were sent into the ghetto. These people (if you can indeed call them humans) broke into house after house and grabbed anyone who lacked a work permit. During such an aktion on August 3rd they took my grandfather - and I never saw him again. My father and I had our documents in order, so my mother and brother were able to be hidden temporarily. In order to be able to grab a greater number of victims, the German authorities ordered that all certified enterprises provide special blocks of housing for their workers. Therefore, I had to be separated from my parents. They lived in the block of the "Schilling" firm, and my fellow workers and I were on Zamenhof Street in the ghetto. During the time of the aktions, thanks to my locations, I was fortunate not to be a witness to the terrible scenes that took place in the Jewish quarter. The shrieking and weeping could rouse stones - but not the stone hearts of the German murderers and their helpers, the Ukrainians and the Lithuanians.

I was never sure that when I would come home from work, I would still see someone from my family. The required quota of deportees was raised to 12,000, and the number of people was shrinking. My heart would palpitate when I arrived home after work: would I still find my parents there? This was the only question that always tormented me.

In the ghetto, the starving people would not let us pass by. They wanted to purchase everything that we had succeeded in smuggling in from the Aryan side. They did not inquire about prices. Money was not important. I would pass quickly through at the side, running like a fool, as I wished to see my dear ones.

Alas, I was not fortunate for long. On August 14th, I received a terrible blow. On that day, they set up a blockade around the "Schilling" area. My father was at work when my mother and brother were in a warehouse of cooked goods and wood scraps. I do not know how this took place. They discovered my mother and shot her. Due to her strong constitution, she survived for about 20 minutes. Then, a second group of murderers arrived who had pity on her, and shot her twice more. Thus, ended the life of my 38-

year-old mother. Indeed, she had prayed for such a death, rather than being shipped in a wagon to the gas chambers.

At Umschlag Platz [17]

I was completely broken for the first days. Finally I regained my composure, and father also pulled himself together. He did not change in any recognizable fashion. I began to work again. An ominous spirit came over me and told me that "this is not the last misfortune". Indeed: on

Friday, August 28th, they stopped everyone at the entrance to the workplace and conducted a selection. Twenty percent were freed. I, along with a majority of the workers, was set off to a side, certainly for evil. We waited on Leszno Street until 8:00 p.m., when the last group of workers came from their places. They ordered a march (better called - a run) to Umschlag Platz. Those who had knapsacks with belongings had no option, they threw off their bags, and those who came after fell over them and blocked the way. Those who followed, driven and beaten by the wild Ukrainians, trampled over the fallen. The murderers beat those who did not stand up in time with the butts of their rifles and poked them with bayonets. They shot over our heads along the entire route in order to cause a commotion. The shots flew over our heads. The run went on for a full half-hour, until we reached Umschlag Platz. We spent that night together under the clear sky, quaking in terror that they would load us on wagons at any moment.

The first day was relatively calm. People searched for acquaintances from the "Ordnungs Dienst" (the cleaning service), who, for a large sum of money, along with the Ukrainians, would take people into the ghetto. It went on like this for a second and third day. People came and went. Five Jews from our living place were freed, after each paying 6,000 Zlotys. I was there for five days, until Wednesday, when, for 2,000 Zlotys, I was placed among the freed workers of the "Avia" workplace, and taken back from the Umschlag Platz. At home they were certain that they would not see me again. Spending five days at Umschlag Platz and not being sent off -that was indeed a miracle. The miracle was indeed the dearth of train wagons.

It was not for long that I was able to catch my breath among the survivors. On September 6th, the A. G. "Kessel" was formed. Those who lived outside of the ghetto had to present themselves at the mill for a

523

selection, so that "those who can remain alive" could be enumerated... After hearing about this ordinance, I immediately went to father, packed all of the belongings, and went with him and my brother to a dwelling to hide from their selection. Our block on the Koszarowa was excluded from the ordinance in the meantime. I succeeded in holding them in my house with great difficulty, for it was forbidden to hide people who were not employed in our place of work.

They conducted the selection in the afternoon. I saw it very well from my window. Parents who wished to save their children placed them in knapsacks, and appeared before the selection as such. Older children were immediately placed on the wagons along with their parents.

Father wished to obtain a number, in order to be in compliance with the ordinance. I tried to dissuade him from this at all costs, for I felt that it posed a great hazard. Unfortunately, he did not desist from trying to arrange this. I only managed to persuade him regarding the children, seeing what it would come to. Therefore, he decided to leave my brother with me, and take him back upon his return.

The next day, September 7th, despite all of my pleas, father did not desist from making arrangements, and went out the gathering depot. He went out, and he never came back. My brother and I were left as orphans.

I found out a week later that they collected 2,000 healthy people, including my father and cousin, and sent them to work in the Lublin countryside. Now, I had to come to terms with the bitter fate, and not loose my bearings. I was the sole guardian of my brother.

The aktion ended three days later. All of those who remained sighed with relief. From July 22nd, there was not one day that did not claim victims. The authorities normalized movement and work, as if nothing had taken place. Only the beating of Jewish hearts had lost their rhythm. Since going out to the placowka [18] had become more difficult, I began to work in a group that cleaned the former area of the ghetto. I found many items of value, which I sold to people from the Placzowka or exchanged for products. My brother assisted in this business. He cleaned the dwelling and cooked food. In the evenings, I would visit my neighbor Madza, who interested me very much. In time, we became good friends. However, I was not destined to live with her. Our friendship did not last long.

A new misfortune came on January 18th. The second liquidation took place, which lasted for almost a week. Again, there were thousands of victims. Life returned to a semblance of normalcy after the aktion, even though we were awaiting a complete liquidation of Warsaw. Therefore, we began to build bunkers, so that we would be able to hide when the time came.

Underground Activity in the Ghetto

At the end of February, the large enterprise "Schultz and Tiebens", which employed thousands of Jews, moved their workshop to Poniatow. They asked the Jews to move there voluntarily with their families and belongings. At the outset, everything proceeded in an orderly fashion, but when people began to hide, they began to capture them in the Ghetto. Then, Jews began to organize and arm themselves. The story of Treblinka, where they burned thousands of people, was known by everyone. There was nothing to lose. The partisan activity began in the hours of the night, and many Germans fell. The Ghetto was surrounded by soldiers, police, Ukrainians, and S. S. officials. An extinct city - that is how they referred to the ghetto, but it was not extinct, since thousands of Jewish hearts beat in underground bunkers, waiting impatiently for the night, when they could come out and deliver their blows to the Hitlerists.

On Thursday, April 25th, we were awakened by powerful detonations. The Germans blew up house after house. Parts of neighborhoods of the ghetto collapsed, burying thousands of victims underneath. The misfortune drew closer with each minute. While sitting in the bunker on Saturday afternoon, we heard footsteps, and then, the wild shouting of the Ukrainians. They warned us to come out, for they were going to burn down the house. When nobody came out, they got down to work. At a certain moment, the murderers fell upon the house beneath which our bunker was located. They searched every room. We held our breath and nervously waited. I felt my brother huddling up against me on one side, and Madza and her sister on the other side. On occasion, we heard hard knocks on the floor. The murderers were searching for an empty resonance, a sign that there was a bunker underneath. Fear took away our breath, for the knocks were coming closer to us. A minute later, everything was hopeless. We were discovered. There was silence, and then - a powerful explosion. We noticed that the light bulb went out and that the air had become heavier. A frightful truth - we felt the lack of air. We decided to open the door and look out at the "world". Then we realized the terrible situation. Puffs of smoke penetrated our bunker. A panic ensued. Everyone stormed for the exit, for the wires had become ignited, and were live. I did not leave. My brother made his way out first. Later, I exited via the window. The fresh air intoxicated me. A terrible picture appeared before my eyes: we were surrounded on all sides by fire, and the houses were burning. There was nowhere to escape. What could we do? Finally, we decided that we had to surrender. Simply - to go out in the street and to give ourselves over to our fate. That is indeed what we did. We opened the doors, and a crowd of approximately 250 people went out. We were quickly surrounded by the S. S., who searched us. They then divided us up into five groups, and marched us off to Umschlag Platz with raised hands. Night fell, and our fate was still unknown. Rumors spread that they would send us to Poniatow. The next morning, they began to chase us. Along the way stood Ukrainians, who endlessly beat the Jews with their rifles. I grabbed my brother and pushed him down with one jump, so that he would not receive a blow.

In the yard, they divided us into groups of five, and marched us to the wagons. The Lithuanians calmed us, saying that we were not being sent to Treblinka, but rather to Poniatow. At first, when they divided us up, placing 70 people in a wagon, and gave us each a half-kilogram of bread, we were calmed. The trip lasted for an entire day. A deathly silence pervaded in the wagons. A glimmer of hope existed in our hearts.

In Majdanek

We remained for a half day in Lublin as they unloaded us. Order was kept by Jews, prisoners of war from the Polish army, who treated us with exceptional severity. Then the segregation began: tailors, shoemakers, hat makers, and furriers were placed together. Then they again loaded us in wagons. My brother and I were placed in the group of locksmiths, electricians, technicians and engineers.

We continued on. The journey lasted for approximately one hour, and we approached a lit up area where we saw barbed wire and buildings. There were watchtowers with machine guns on all four sides. There were guard booths near the towers. There were strong, blinding reflector lights on all sides. Inside, there were rows of wooden barracks. A deathly silence and calm pervaded. We were taken to the so-called "Koiln Platz", where men and women were placed separately. The men were taken for a march through the

526

entire camp. This march lasted a good three hours. Afterward, we were led back to Koiln Platz. The women thought that they would not see us again. Unfortunately, we were not reunited for long.

After all these events, I lay on the ground and soon fell asleep. At 6:00 a.m. a new guard arrived. He commanded us to line up, and began with a new selection. The handicapped and old people did not pass through. The others were led to a bath. During the march, they captured my brother. I was helpless. We managed to catch a glance for the last time. Until my death, I will never forget his sweet blue eyes and blond head of hear, and the way he smiled at me for the last time. I was left alone.

I continued marching. They led us to the bath. They beat us with sticks and drove us into a hall. When we appeared before the camp commandant, the put three chests in front of us, and everyone had to put their money, gold and valuables into them. There was a special place for clothing and other items. From there we went to the barber, and then came the selection. "Left" or "right" was the only words that the camp commandant said. Later we found out that "left" meant - the gas chamber. I went "right" into the bath. Then they prodded us naked through a field to a second building with wooden steps, inscribed with the letters K. L. (Konzentrations Lager). There we received underwear, clothing and belts. I simply could not climb the first pair of steps, for I had turned around. When I saw my friends, I laughed and cried. We looked like circus clowns.

When we had all gotten dressed, they took us to a barrack on the third punishment field, in one of the large concentration camps not far from Majdanek - in Majdan Tatarski. They wrote down our details, and we were given small numberplates, tied with a wire around our necks. From that time, I was prisoner number 981. The camp commandant informed us of the regime of the camp, and after the speech we all realized - that we had been sentenced to death.

I went into block number 8, where the block master was a Jew, one of the greatest murderers in Majdanek. Already at the first encounter, I received 25 lashes. Then, I received a brief lecture about restraining myself. In the afternoon, I went under the supervision of a kapo to my first stop, for a medical examination. Standing in line, I recognized my cousin who was sent away together with my father. I wanted to run to him, however fear took away my strength, and I was not able to stir. As he passed by me, he told me that father had been together with him, and he died in the middle of January.

527

The next day, we were placed into groups and assigned work places. I worked for the first two days at the railway grounds with a group of 100 people. The kapo was a Jew from Vienna who arrived a few days before us. As time went on, he learned from his friends their sadistic methods, and our life became hell. Every day brought with it beatings. In order to save ourselves from the massacre, we had to sell our daily bread ticket (referred to as the "peike"), and one of us would give the kapo 1,000 Zlotys each week. Thereby, our situation improved slightly. Nevertheless, the work was very difficult.

Two weeks later, I went to the A. G. "Sheiss-Commande". There, I was able to catch my breath a little. A few times a day I went out to the field where women worked. I met many acquaintances, to whom I transferred over letters, at great risk. Thereby, I received some food, so that I would note waste away from hunger. The only problem was that I had to present myself at each excursion, and I received beatings.

In Skarzysko

One July day, after roll call, they conducted a selection and selected 1,000 young and healthy men and 500 women. The transport went out, and we had no idea what this was about. Two weeks later another selection took place. This time, I was also placed in the transport to Skarzysko. There, I saw people from the previous transport. In Skarzysko, there were three camps near the "Hasag" ammunition factory. As a locksmith, I was fortunate to remain in camp A, where the conditions were the best. I began to work in the infantry division. Life in this camp was different. There was a lighter discipline, a calmer work, and freedom after work. Anyone who had money - did not feel any lack. The food and living conditions were better than in Majdanek, but one did not really feel it. We exchanged ideas. However, the earlier workers did not receive us well. They oppressed us at every opportunity, which had a bad impact upon us.

Aside from all of the difficulties, I had a diseased foot, and there was no opportunity to heal it.

At the beginning of February, the Hasag firm opened a branch in Czestochowa. Due to a dearth of professionals, they selected a few people for each job type and sent them to Czestochowa. I was also one of this group. One March 27, I along with 200 people traveled to work in "Wartawerk". At the outset, the conditions and food were better than in Skarzysko.

528

After working for a few months, I became ill and went to the hospital for six weeks. A faulty injection infected the veins in the flesh of my hand, and as a result, I was not able to bend my arm. I had to again recover for a month. After recovering, I began work in the "Hauf Kolone", whose task was to keep the camp clean. I was occupied with this work until noon. I searched for some sort of job to do after that. Thereby, I came in contact with the kitchen. We had to concern ourselves with bringing coal and provisions from the warehouse. As a reward, we received 3-4 soups twice a day. For the most part, I sold mine, and therefore obtained other necessities. Now, I was not able to complain. I was able to take care of my appearance, purchase a few things, and obtain a different perspective on life. Moreover, good news began to arrive from the fronts. Hope reawakened.

A page from the diary of Adasz Rozenstrauch, written in Polish

529

At the end of November, they liquidated our "Hauf Kolone" and the people were sent to the new enterprise "Zicherung -Hilzn" (grenade detonators). The new work required a great deal of exactitude, the quotas were large, and there was not one minute to rest. I was a robot. I was not away from the machine for twelve hours, for we had to manufacture the 2,700 detonators. This was our quota.

The sole incentive that gave us the strength to work was the news from the front, and the steady approach of the Red Army, which seemed like our only redeeming angel from our Hitlerian tyranny. The camp continued on until the first day of January, when a transport of Jews was sent to Germany. From then on, we were able to navigate. We counted the days until our liberation and then news came. In the factory, the proprietors made new lists of those who were selected to travel on. Our despair had no bounds. Five years of being crushed under the Nazi yoke - and now, at the final moments, death. No, this must not be.

The Liberation

On January 14, the situation became extremely tense. The Russians pushed onward. Our factory was occupied by the S. S. They began to perpetrate all kinds of sabotage. At the same time, they selected 1,000 people for deportation. We were not allowed to work any more, in order to cut off any contact with the city. On January 17th, the Red Army completed their encirclement of the city. The German army retreated in a disorderly fashion. When the camp commandant fled, his deputy ordered us to line up so that 150 persons can be taken to the place where there were machine guns. We were so near to rescue that we acted crazily. The minutes were decisive. Airplanes bombarded, fire was all around, the Katyushas played their "music", and there was nothing to loose. We fell upon the Ukrainians who guarded us. They quickly fled. We were now in control of the situation. There was no trace of the Germans. Whoever had arms went out on the street. After a long time, our people returned and told us that they had met Soviet patrols who advised us to return to the camp for our own safety and wait until the morning. This is what we indeed did. When the people heard this news, they broke out in dances, with shouting and kisses. We waited for this minute for six years.

Unfortunately, not very many lived to see this…

(Translated from Polish: D. Sh.)

From Skierniewice to Monte Cassino by Moshe Yaakov Grand
(The experiences of a Jewish officer in the Second World War)

A.

I was enlisted three days before the outbreak of the Second World War. At the time, I led the weaver's school in Lodz. When I was drafter, I informed my brother's son in Zgierz (today in Israel) who was studying with me. My father and brother came to see me. I also saw my only daughter. I never saw them again.

I sat in a train and went to Skierniewice. When I arrived, the second reservist brigade was marching by at the time. I quickly began to seek out acquaintances, and indeed I found the Zgierzer Herman Rozenzweig and the tall Yokel, my sister's son.

A few days passed before we were issued uniforms. On Thursday, I and another Jewish officer were called up to guard a group, to be constantly on watch and shoot person who approached. Suddenly, I heard the noise of motors. This was the first time that we encountered the Luftwaffe (I would later call them as "Binen" [19]). Two bombs fell upon the building in which we ate, and one bomb fell at the gate. My eyes only saw a great deal of blood and dismembered limbs. The screaming was terrible. An order came:

"March to Warsaw!"

Our march delayed because of the civilians who occupied all of the roads, and, in the meantime, the "binen" delivered death from above. We hid in the potato fields, but very many did not come out of there. Our military unit ceased to exist.

Along the way, a Jewish soldier, a reservist from Lodz, came to me, and we went on the way together. We arrived in Warsaw in the evening. After crossing the Prager Bridge, we went to a military point, and received the order to go to Garwolin.

We arrived in the afternoon, and along the way, we met some people from our unit. We continued traveling, and the "binen" continued to fly over our heads. We, a small group of four officers, arrived in Tursk, and there we fell into Russian hands.

If I am not mistaken, this was the eve of Yom Kippur of 1939. They brought us to Szepetowka in loaded wagons. They registered us at once, and whatever we had, they took from us. The next day, they gave us a bit of freedom and we traveled further. Not far from Lemberg, we had to build an expressway to Kiev. We widened the highway by a meter and a half on each side. I had to go to a doctor, since I was weakened by the hard work. The doctor, a Jew, gave me a certificate of exemption, and I traveled to Lemberg. From there, I went to Bialystok, where I found many Zgierzer "biezszeniec" (refugees). Knowing that there was an empty cellar on Pierackiego Street, I put myself up there.

B.

Refugees from the German side arrived via Malkinia. They were murderously beaten, and all their possessions had been taken from them. There were some Zgierzers among them. Balek Trocki came from Lemberg. There, he had worked at an airfield. He assisted us a little. With his help, I obtained work.

Once, while sitting in the evening in our cellar, our door opened, and Leon Rusianow of Zgierz entered. He portrayed for us a frightful drama of his experiences. As soon as the Germans occupied Lodz, four Germans went into the Astoria coffee house. One of them shot at the ceiling with an automatic rifle and shouted: "Do not move!" Then, they confiscated everybody's documents and ordered them to present themselves in the morning at a designated place, where soldiers with transport trucks were waiting. They collected the Jews from all sides and transported them to a forest outside of Lodz, where they were commanded to dig pits. The rows of pits became more numerous. After driving the Jews into the pits, they shot them with automatic rifles. Then, more trucks came with Jews. The Germans drove them into the pits that were still empty and shot them. Leon remained alive, as he "worked" in covering over the pits. They told him to come the next day to retrieve his document. When he came to retrieve his document, he found many women who came to find out about the fate of their husbands. They answered the women that their husbands had been arrested, and they would be freed for ransom money. The women ran to bring the ransom money for their murdered husbands. Leon explained that that situation was written about sufficiently, and was sent from Poland to America [20].

Yaakov Grand on the Italian front in 1944

C.

Election Day came in Bialystok. They forcibly ordered us to enter automobiles to go to vote. They drove us to a polling station, gave us each a printed piece of paper to put in an enveloped and throw into the voting box.

At that time, thousands registered for work in Russia in accordance with their trades. However, their disappointment was quick in coming - a tailor was sent to construction work; a weaver to saw trees in the forest, etc.

An order was issued that every "biezszeniec" (refugee) must obtain a Soviet passport. Many Zgierzers indeed obtained such passports. On a certain evening, a Russian in civilian clothing came and said: "Passporta, Pazalusta!" Those who did not yet have passports (including myself) were told to follow him. This arrest took place in May of 1940. They took us to rooms that were guarded by soldiers. Each of us was told to sign a document in Russian, which we did not understand. Afterwards, they loaded us on trucks and drove us to the Bialystok jail. We were 600 people. Each day, we received a portion of bread with water. After registering us, photographing us, and cutting our hair, they loaded us onto trucks. There, I met Yume's eldest son. He gave us each 100 rubles, 25 for each of the Zgierz people, for we were not allowed to carry more than that on us.

They loaded us in a train, which went as fast as a bow from an arrow, until it arrived in... Kotlas [21]. The N.K.V.D. counted us. Only shadows remained of all of us. They put us in a camp, surrounded by barbed wire. On another day, they took me and other Jews to the river. Guarded by the N. K. V. D., we were taken onto a barge, where we received some bread and a little herring. This made us thirsty, but they did not give us any water. We arrived

533

to a camp on the banks of the Dvina. There, I went to the doctor to obtain something for a headache. The doctor, also a deportee, was a very fine person. He told me that healthy people do not come out of the camp. Most of the deportees die.

Once at mealtime, I noticed an unusual face among the Russians. He came to me and asked if Jews are coming. I explained to him that we were Jews from Poland. He greeted me with a 'shalom aleichem' [22] and told me that he was in a government position, and that he works and lives in Odessa. He is a Hebrew writer and poet. His works were published outside of the country, and his honorarium came in dollars. They arrested him for receiving dollars from outside of the country, and sentenced him to sixteen years. He requested of me that if anyone is able to leave, they tell about him. His readers would certainly remember his name - he wrote under the pseudonym of Yellin.

Two days later, they again called me up, and I heard the "zoftik" [23] Russian language. We traveled on further and came to camp number eighteen, in Komi-A.S.S.R. [24]. There was not any time to rest after the journey. They divided us up into brigades during the journey. I met some Zgierz Jews in the camp. However, they did not belong to my brigade, and I was not able to communicate with them. We had to get up at 4:00 a.m. We received 300 grams of clay-like bread and a little water with cabbage leaves. Then, with genuine Russian curses, we were driven twelve kilometers to the workplace. The work consisted of sawing trees. Naiman became ill, did not receive any medical care, and died. The regulation was that we could be sent out to work only if it was above 50 degrees of frost [25]. However, even if it was 50 degrees of frost, the official would warm up the thermometer with his sleeve to show 48 degrees, and would send us out. If we did not wish to go out to work, he would consider it as sabotage. After work, Rosenberg lay down in the "pritshe" and did not get up again [26]. I was very upset after his death. A beam fell on my hands during work, and they become swollen. I was only able to work at 30 percent of the normal speed. They threw me in the dungeon as a punishment.

For six weeks it was only day, for Komi was above the Arctic Circle. The nerves were very strained. More than one person was crushed by a falling tree during work and was thereby redeemed from labor. We were jealous of such people - better death than the dog's life...

D.

An ordinance was issued that we "Zapadnikes" (from the western regions, from Poland) would be sent to the eighteenth camp, and from there we would be freed. After my liberation, I presented myself to the Polish group, and after a great deal of difficulty, they accepted me into the Polish (Alternative) army [27]. I removed the rags which I had been wearing for two years, and dressed myself up in the woolen clothing and leather shoes that I received.

We traveled to Uzbekistan on April 10th 1942. On May 5th, we arrived in Gozar, where we were examined by a medical commissar the next day. I was certified, and received a military uniform. On August 13th, we traveled from Gozar to the port of Krasnovodsk. We sailed on the decks of freight ships to Pahlavi, on the Persian side of the Caspian Sea. After an additional five days of travel in cars, through Teheran, we arrived in Iraq.

I was assigned to the 7th Polish division of light artillery, where I found 34 Jews. It was the eve of Yom Kippur. An order was issued that the Jews should go to the synagogue for Kol Nidre. As I was entering the synagogue, I met Akiva Eiger. He was about 50 years old. He served in the third Carpathian Brigage, which was formed in Cyprus. He had taken part in the battle of Tabruk against Rommel's army, in North Africa. We remained together.

We went through intensive training the winter of 1942-1943. We arrived in the Land of Israel before Rosh Hashanah 5704 (1943) for a respite. There, I met many people of Zgierz. I and Karol Eiger [28] decided to fight against the Germans - until their defeat.

We traveled to Alexandria and from there to the front. We landed in Taranto, Italy at the end of January, 1944. At the beginning of March, we traveled to the front in order to assist an American artillery division near the mountain of Monte Marrone (Brown Mountain), which was greater than 2,000 meters in height. We descended into a valley. Opposite Monte Marrone, to the right, was a second mountain; everything was in order, and there were even telephones laid out there. We were shot at by German grenades, one cannonball after the other. Shrapnel fell on the command center of the second division, and everything was wiped out. My group belonged to the second artillery group. According to the order of the general, we changed positions a kilometer to the right. In the night, there was a

German assault. The entire artillery opened fire and cut off the way. The cannonballs fell for five hours. First they sent us to the "right" positions, opposite the monastery of Monte Cassino. I remained there with my battery until April 12th, 1944.

One offensive after another, one attack after a counter-attack, that was the way things were.

E.

Finally, on May 18th, 1944 in the morning, I saw through my field glasses the Polish flag fluttering atop the monastery of Monte Cassino. We shot in all directions - eight cannons shot 30,000 shots during that time. For the first time, on May 26th, we went away from that position.

I arrived in Bari on the Adriatic Sea, where Karol Eiger was together with the censor division. There, I slept in the Jewish brigade club.

I went again to the Poles. The Polish army, which pursued the Germans by the Adriatic Sea, halted for a while, and they were in need of artillery. We began to pursue the Germans. My officer fell past Ancona. I endured all of the battles until Firenze.

On the second day of Passover, we received an order to conduct an offensive by the Siena River. The Germans had become entrenched there, and it was a difficult piece of work. With great difficulty, and indeed with many victims, we held our own, and the Germans were driven away from there.

Bologna then fell. We marched in, and at first took up positions on the Piechota. To the left, the Americans marched in.

That was our final battle against the Germans.

A Few Words about Yaakov Grand of blessed memory, the Author of "From Skierniewice To Monte Cassino"

Yaakov Grand

Moshe Yaakov the son of Reb Henech Grand of blessed memory was one of the few Zgierzers in the Alternative Army, which played an active part in the battle against the enemy, and thereby enhanced the national pride of the Jewish warriors. He did not believed that he reached his objective with his arrival in the Land of Israel, and that he would be able to enjoy personal security and peace. On the contrary, when a friend counseled him to "desist" and take it easy, he asked with astonishment: "What? Now, where there are twenty 'iron fists' that are reaching backward?"

Together with his old friend of over fifty year's duration, Karol Eiger, he endured the march on the front that flared up in Italy.

Many years later, when Grand visited Israel with his wife, he became acquainted with our activities on the Zgierz Yizkor Book. He felt an inner urge to tell over his own war experiences, which are filled with dramatic

tension and terrible situations. He undertook the task with zeal and diligence. I received an express delivery that contained a written description of his experiences. These formed a very bright canvas, and could have been a book unto itself. The
editor had to distill out its main ideas and principles, for various formal and matter-of-fact reasons. With no small amount of regret, she had to shorten the long narrative to its current form, making sure to transmit the most important of his memories.

Moshe Yaakov Grand also was committed with great dedication to the action towards the Zgierz book. His donations were always given with fondness and responsibility towards this great endeavor.

His premature death was a painful and great loss, not only for his family, but also for the activists and doers of the Zgierz Yizkor Book.
With honor and memory!
V. Fisher

Hershel - One of the First Victims of the Nazi Murder
By Abu Aryeh

He came from a poor family. His father died when he was still suckling from his mother's breast.

A double yoke fell upon his mother: to raise the young orphan and to toil to earn a livelihood. The widow toiled for sixteen hours a day. Later, she sent him to the best teachers in town and dressed him respectably, so that he need not be ashamed in front of the more well-to-do children with whom he studied in cheder.

At age fourteen, he went to study in the Beis Midrash. He studied Gemara with people who were significantly older than him. He was not beneath them, in fact, he was above them.

Living in poverty, and seeing how his mother worked hard and bitter to maintain the home, encouraged him to study a trade. He qualified as a barber at age eighteen, and he did not permit his mother to work anymore.

"Mother", he said, "You have toiled for eighteen years to support me. Now the time has come for me to repay the debt."

He had also a second debt to pay, to a completely different character: this took place on the first day of September, 1939. The Nazi troops searched the streets of Zgierz for Jews in order to torture them. When the encountered

538

Jews, they immediately cut off their beards along with a bit of chin, and beat their lungs [29]. Hershel also encountered a Nazi in the street who ordered him: "Jude, get over here". Hershel refused. The Nazi responded with a strong beating, so that Hershel's blood began to flow from his mouth, nose and ears. Hershel did not let it go; he beat the Nazi in return. The German took his revolver and immediately shot the unarmed Hershel, who remained dead on the street.

He was one of the first victims of Zgierz, who fell in a struggle with the Nazi murderers.

Honor to his memory!

Drops of Agony from the Sea of Destruction by Hela Goldberg-Finkelstein

"… And only I escaped to relate…" (Job 1, 15)
I was the only one from my family who remained, alone… everyone else perished and died… My father Leib Goldberg of blessed memory, a native of Lowicz, was a G-d fearing Jew. Simultaneously, he was educated and progressive, wise, and possessing of a good heart. He ran a dye shop, but he had to give it up on account of his protracted illness.

He devoted the best of his time and energy to communal and social work. In 1924, when Eliezer Sirkis served as the head of the community, he served as his deputy. My mother Freida, the granddaughter of Avraham Konski the pioneer of the thread dyeing industry in the city, was a woman of valor. She imbued our home with a warm and hearty atmosphere. I grew up in this home along with my sisters Manya, Sala, and Etka, and my brother Moshe.

I remember my father when he was transferred with my mother to the concentration point in Opatow-Kielecki in October 1942. He attempted to encourage and strengthen my mother's spirit. Immediately on September 1, 1939, at the outbreak of the war, the persecutions and frights began. I ran by foot from Lodz to Zgierz along with my late husband Avraham Kanarcuker, for the electricity was no longer working. The entire way was lit up in a frightful manner by the flames that arose from the thunderous bombardment. We transferred father, mother, our brother Moshe, his wife and two children (Bronya and Czesia), our sister Manya who was pregnant, her husband Geniek Milgram, Sala and Etka, to our home in Lodz on Magistracka Street #15. We left all their belongings to the Polish neighbors. The men then immediately began to flee in the direction of Warsaw. This was a tragic flight, for many of the fleeing masses died and were killed along the way.

During the fracas of the events that took place, we later fled to Lowicz, and there we were thrown into hell. They put the men to work under frightful conditions at the Bzura River. We had to sell all of our jewelry and belongings that we owned in order to sustain ourselves. When we were expelled to Warsaw along with all of the Jews in the outlying towns, we began to experience hunger in all its aspects. With the assistance of my friend Aharon Atner, I received a permit to live in Opatow-Kielecki, and to find there along with Avrahamek bread and refuge. However, it was difficult for me to swallow the food knowing that the family I had left behind was dying of hunger. I worked to amass a sum of money to bring, with his assistance; to my family (I recall that mother transported it in a jar of salted fish). At that time, I worked in a hospital, and I contracted typhus. Dear Mrs. Anter looked after me and my family with dedication. When I regained my strength, I received a small room to live in. I slept in it on boards, and Etka also joined me in this "home".

At that point, the family broke up. Moshe, his wife Esther and their children went to her parents in Zadonska Wola. He perished in a tragic manner already in 1941 in a camp near Posen (Poznan). We heard that they would beat the prisoners in that camp until death. I do not know how my sister-in-law Esther and her two beautiful daughters died. Sala, who remained in Warsaw, lived with the Harun family (cousins of my mother). She perished in Treblinka.

I lived and worked in Opatow until 1942. On Yom Kippur, we persuaded father to fast and to entreat G-d to come to our aid and to redeem us from our straits. In the midst of this holy day, all of the Jews of the region were expelled to Treblinka. I asked father a painful question, which I regret to this day. His answer was strained and perplexed. That month, my poor father and the entire family went on their final journey to that death camp.

It is difficult for me to explain the secret of how I was saved. Perhaps it was by some coincidence. My friend helped me a lot. I was saved during the time of the expulsion of the remnant of the Jews from Sandomierz. I came to Avramek in Skarzysko. He was the only one of my family left alive. We lived together in the camp and suffered from pressure and tribulations. To our ill luck, we were separated one day prior to the liberation. With the approach of the Russians to Czestochowa, where we were imprisoned, the Germans succeeded in removing the men. Avrahemk was shot on the route from

Buchenwald to southern Germany, literally in the final hours before the approach of the Americans. It was told that he was shot for the "sin" of extending his hand to take a potato. My friends Aryeh and Stefan Atner, who were like brothers to me during the years of suffering, also perished there. There are no words in my mouth, or on the lips of mankind, to describe the tribulations and torture that we endured during the dark years of our lives, between 1939 and 1945.

Thirteen! I was bereaved of thirteen members of my family, and I was left alone. My husband's family also perished, and the end came to a traditional, wide branched family, as happened to myriads of other families of our people. When my time comes, the last shoot will also disappear, without a remnant and a memory... how painful and heartbreaking!

Translated from Polish: A. Wien

The Destruction of Zgierz by Rabbi Shimon Huberbrand

Footnote at the bottom of the page: From his unpublished writings, transcribed by W. Fisher, with the permission of Yad Vashem which obtained the material from the Jewish Historical Institute of Warsaw, number 108/1 (from the Ringelblum archive).

... They arrived in Zgierz on Thursday; September seventh in the year 1939.They stabbed a transient to death. They encountered the well-to-do man from Zgierz H. Zusman, who was coming to Zgierz along with four Jews from the nearby village of Strykow, after fleeing from the bombardment. They took everything that the Jews had on them. They took 600 gold dollars from H. Zusman. Afterwards, they literally cut the five Jews into pieces, limb by limb, and threw them into the water. Later, the Jews collected some of their limbs and buried them in Zgierz. (Editor's remark: this case is not known to us.)

That same Thursday, they arrested all of the Jewish men and imprisoned them in the Catholic Church. A few thousand people were arrested. There, those arrested were beaten with death blows, and not given any food or drink. It was not permitted for their wives to bring them even a drop of water. They were not permitted to attend to their personal needs. Every hour, people came in and declared to them that they should be prepared to be shot. On Saturday, September 9, 1939, the prisoners were freed.

On Friday the 8th, a young German came to the rabbi. He presented himself as a low ranking officer who came from Nuremberg. He expressed the desire to become acquainted with a Jewish rabbi and a rabbinical home. Prior to leaving, he expressed his gratitude for his visit with the elderly Jewish rabbi. "Indeed, Jews will be at peace here!". The rabbi expressed his doubt about this, for Germans, as bearers of culture, would certainly not conduct themselves badly with innocent people [30]. No answer came to the rabbi's remark.

On Sunday the 10th, searches began among all the Jews with the purpose of finding arms and ammunition. Naturally, they did not find any arms among the Jews, however they took everything that the Jews had - money, belongings, gold, silver, products, bedding, clothing, and furniture. They took everything that they were able to.

During the searches, they also took from the Jews Torah scrolls, tefillin (phylacteries), mezuzas, tallises (prayer shawls), and ordinary books. Bitter and anguished were those Jews in whose homes they found some of the abovementioned items that were connected to Judaism. They would beat the owner with deathblows. The Torah scrolls wee cut up and torn, and afterwards burnt in the middle of the market along with the other books, tefillin, and mezuzas.

That same Sunday, they began to capture Jews, both men and women, for work. The men were terribly beaten at work, and they were tortured in a terrifying fashion. They were forced to make somersaults in the middle of the streets while dressed with kittels [31] and tallises - and they were afflicted with other tortures. They were given tallises, small tallises [32], and parochets
[33] to clean up the filth. Women were forced to remove their dresses, and to wash the floors of the German barracks and offices with their dresses while dressed in their underwear. They commanded Jewish women to clean toilets with their hands, and they were given - along with the men - tallises for that job.

As much as possible, people tried to hide, but there was not the opportunity to do so. They conducted operations, and the men and women were removed from their hiding places. Women also were enlisted to cook for them. When Yom Kippur arrived, some of the Jews wished to form minyanim (prayer quorums) in their own homes in order to conduct the public prayer service. However the rabbi warned them that he was issuing a ban against worshipping in public [34].

Immediately after Sukkot, they imposed a contribution of 10,000 zloty on the Jews, due immediately.

Three weeks after Sukkot, they suddenly arrested twenty prominent Jews of the city, including the rabbi. After several hours of nervous suspense, the commandant and commissar came into the room, and asked each of the prisoners to given an accounting of his means. After taking care of this, they decided to impose a contribution of 250,000 zloty upon the Jews. This must be paid by the next morning at 10:00 a.m., and the prisoners must sign for this. All of the prisoners signed for this.

Since it was past the curfew, each Jew was accompanied to his home by a soldier. The sum was paid the next day by the deadline.

Over and above the payment of the contribution, further searches were conducted daily on the Jews. They tore up floors, dismantled ovens, dug up cellars, and took everything from the Jews.

Eight days after the payment of the contribution, at approximately midnight, the synagogue was set on fire and completely burnt down with all of its contents, with the exception of the Torah scrolls, which were rescued in time and hidden in the canopies of the cemetery.

At 3:00 in the morning they knocked on the rabbi's door. Numerous soldiers, volksdeutschen and firemen entered the house. They declared the following to the rabbi: Since a fire broke out in the Jewish synagogue, they were required to rescue the entire street so that it would not burn down, for there was a threat that the houses would burn down because of the fire in the synagogue. Therefore, he must pay 250 Zloty in return for their efforts.

The rabbi did not have that amount of money, and begged that they wait until the next morning, when he would collect the required sum. They did not wish to hear about that proposal. Rather, they insisted that he go together with them to the head of the community. Even though there was a different route to the home of the head of the community, they led the rabbi to the burning synagogue, and forced him to remain there for a long time, watching the synagogue burn. The head of the community paid the sum on the spot.

The next day, they set fire to the Beis Midrash and once again, they were required to pay 100 Zloty in return for their efforts. A Jewish tin worker by the name of David Gotlieb lived in the Beis Midrash. He was arrested after the fire in the Beis Midrash on the pretext that he had set fire to the synagogue. Afterward, he was set to a concentration camp, where he was imprisoned for six weeks.

They removed all of the monuments from the cemetery and flattened all of the canopies. The cemetery was ploughed over and turned in to pastureland for cattle.

From time to time, Jews were expelled from certain houses. The Jews had to leave their dwellings, leaving everything behind.

On Tuesday, December 26th, 1939, a soldier came from Krakow and ordered all men, women and children to assemble at Sokol Platz on the next day, Wednesday, the 27th. Each person was permitted to bring 25 kilo of belongings, and 50 Zloty.

Rich people attempted to escape from the town that same day, taking with them whatever was possible. However, not everyone succeeded in doing so, since for the most part, they grabbed people on the route, administering cruel beatings.

The poorer members of the Jewish population assembled at the designated place at the required time. There, they took everything from the Jews, included the permitted 25 kilo and 50 Zloty. Then they were murderously beaten. Even the baby strollers that mothers used to transport their young children were taken. The mothers were forced to carry them by hand.

The entire Jewish population of Zgierz was expelled to Glowno at one time. They beat them murderously along the way. The guards informed them along the way that if more than the permitted amount was found upon any Jew along the way, he would be immediately shot. Those Jews who succeeded in smuggling items such as gold and jewels out through various tricks during the time of the search threw everything away along the way.

544

An impoverished, downtrodden, tortured camp of hungry Jews arrived in Glowno.

The Germans of Zgierz Showed their Faces
By Yaakov

… Everything that I am now going to tell over about Zgierz, I saw with my own eyes. Zgierz suffered an air raid already in the first days of the war. It was particularly strong on the fifth and sixth of September in the afternoons. My parents fled to Lodz, abandoning everything. They only took a bit of jewelry. The next day, the Germans entered Lodz. That very day, towards evening, the S. S. men went from house to house on Pilsudski Street, taking gold, silver and money from Jews. They took everything that my parents had, and beat my father as well. The next day, on Thursday, my parents returned to Zgierz.

The Germans of Zgierz, who had always lived in peace with the Jews, began to show their true face towards their Jewish neighbors shortly after the Nazis occupied the city. They became the de facto rulers over the downtrodden Jewish population. The Jewish of Zgierz suffered great tribulations from the local Germans: Straubach, Miele, Kerner and others, who robbed and tormented. Many Jews were driven out of their homes. They drove out all of the Jewish tenants of Taubert's home in Pilsudskiego with one hour's notice, without permitting them to take anything. Yaakov Meir Kupfer, one of the largest and richest textile manufacturers, was evicted from his dwelling, and then went to live with Yosef Meir Harun. Later, they drove everyone out from Harun's house. Karol Eiger, the chairman of Maccabi and the son of the prominent Zionist Activist; as well as Yosef Pantel and Leibish Srebnik (the Revisionist [35]) were sent to the Radogoszcz Concentration Camp.

… The well-known lawyer Jochwed (the son-in-law of Eliezer Shlumiel) was dressed up with a dress, a wig on his head, and a broom in his hand, and was paraded through the streets of the city in that manner. At every intersection, he had to sing Russian songs and dance.

Dr. Kaltgrad and his sister committed suicide, not being able to bear the oppression. Almost all of the Jews of Zgierz participated in their funeral.

545

The two Freilins (from Przemysl) who worked in Rozenberg's drugstore also committed suicide. Rozenberg's drugstore was taken over.

Many of the youth of Zgierz fled. The greater number fled eastward and went to Russia. It is not possible to tell everything over in a letter. The catastrophe was so great that one remains dumbfounded.

... Only thing did I forget to bring down: the synagogue and the Beis Midrash were set on fire by the Germans, and were burnt down completely. The Rabbi of Zgierz was compelled by the barbarians to pay 250 Marks for the firefighters. They threatened him that he would be sent to a concentration camp if he does not pay.

Shimon Zusman's brother (who owned a colonial store on Piantker Street) was forced by the Germans to dig a grave for himself. Then, he was shot.

(Morgen Journal, New York, March 12, 1940)

Jumping from the Death Wagon that was Traveling to Treblinka by Mordechai Grand

After my father and older brother Berl (Dov) left their home in Zgierz in haste for Bialystok [36], Russia, the Germans issued completely new ordinances almost every day in order to make the lives of the Jews more difficult.

At the end of December 1939, the Jews of Zgierz were driven from the town towards the "Protectorate". The border was between Strykow and Glowno. Lowicz, Skierniewice and other places were already full of uprooted Jews. Our aunt Leah, mother's younger sister (nee Sperling), reminded us that we had a cousin in the town of Laszkowice who was a tailor. We all set out from Lowicz on a frosty day, on a wagon hired out from peasants, with a few meager belongings that we managed to take from home. We rented a room in the town with the help of our cousin. We were not able to remain there for long. It was a very difficult winter at that time. We lost our means of livelihood, and the persecutions and restrictions imposed by the Poles and Germans increased. In this manner, we wandered for a year between the towns of Laszkowice, Skierniewice, Lowicz, Glowno, and Lask.

Only 400 Jews remained in Zgierz. These were various workers whom the Germans needed. I remained in Zgierz at the time, at the home of my

546

grandfather Reb Avraham Grand and grandmother Hodel, near the castle in the old market. They secretly returned home from Lodz after the expulsion. There, I ran into some people. Since other means of livelihood were lost, and in the house we had hidden a little jewelry and dollars in an iron safe under the wooden floor, we decided who among us should enter the sealed home.

During the time that my younger brother Adam served as a shepherd with a farmer in Lask, and my sister Sara, my youngest brother Shimon, and Aunt Leah remained in Laszkowice, my mother and I succeeded in sneaking into Lodz, and from there to Zgierz, to my grandparents. At their home, we planned out how to "break in" to our house, which had been sealed up by the Germans.

On a frosty evening, during the time of the curfew when it was forbidden to go out on the streets, I sneaked out of grandfather's house, accompanied by my mother's blessing and fear. The streets were empty. I crawled through yards and fences. At the beginning of Leczyza Street, near the "Lutnia" cinema, an armed German gendarme was wandering around - in and out of doors. During a time when the German was inside, I quickly ran past. He shot at me in a perfunctory fashion when he noticed me. I went into the house on Piatkowska Street 11, which bordered on the yard of our house.

I went through the fruit orchard, crawled over a high fence, and was already in our yard. was concerned that our neighbor, the Pole Tomczak, should not recognize me. I decided to wait on the porch of the house on Leczyza Street, even until the middle of the night. Full of terror, hungry, trembling and cold, I counted the hours that were chimed by the courthouse clock.

Realizing that Tomczak was certainly asleep, I went along the fence crawling on all fours, so that the frozen snow would not squeak.

As I crawled by the neighbor's window, I heard his loud snoring. This gave me courage. Finally, I stood by the sealed door of the house in which I had spent my childhood and had grown up - a childhood that was so cruelly torn away. Today, I was already an "adult" with many life experiences; I already knew how to avoid people who can be worse than animals in a forest - I was already 15 years old…

There was a small shelter around the door, and over that, an attic hole through which I crawled like a cat. I went down from attic with the stairs. I was now standing next to the sealed door of my house. Unfortunately, I did not have the necessary utensils to break in, so I had to leave empty-handed and return back along the same terrifying route. I had to wait in the house on Leczyza 8 until 8:00 a.m. when the curfew finished. These hours passed like years. My dear mother as well as my grandmother and grandfather did not sleep for the entire night, for they were waiting for my return with fear. Finally, I fell into mother's arms…

b)

A while later, with mother's help, I procured a few tools from a Jewish shoemaker on Krotka Street: a hammer, pliers, and a screwdriver. Once again, on a dark night, I set out along the terrifying route, until I came to the door of my house. Perking up my ears to ensure that not a rustle would be heard, I lit a match, pulled out some nails, and succeeded in opening the door with the screwdriver. I lit a small light, looked around, and only G-d knows what was going on at that time in my heart. My language is too poor to write it down! The portraits of my parents were looking down at me from the walls over their beds. I saw the clothes wardrobe that was carved from oak. On the left was the sofa and on the right the covered oven, which was now so cold and strange to me…

I quickly got down to work. I removed two boards from the floor of the kitchen. I reached the safe, opened it, and took everything out. I closed it again and replaced the boards. I placed the treasure in the "bandages" that my mother prepared for me, and I wound them around my body. As I was doing this, I noticed that someone had already paid a visit here, for the Singer sewing machine and other small items were missing. The place was already in disorder, for someone had ransacked it. Afterward, I returned along the same frightful path. Mother and my grandparents were waiting for me.

Later, we returned to Lodz. I smuggled meat from Zgierz to Lodz for a certain period of time. On one occasion, I almost paid with my life - then mother did not allow me to go anymore. Entering and leaving the Lodz Ghetto was becoming increasingly difficult. In order not to remain locked up in the ghetto, mother decided to return to Skierniewice. This was a dangerous route. Grandfather and grandmother remained in Lodz with the remainder of the family. They all died there - whether from hunger or disease.

c)

Treblinka and other death camps were already operating with full strength. From time to time, the German barbarians conducted aktions in the towns between Lodz and Warsaw. They compelled the Jews to concentrate themselves in the ghettos of both large cities. We all went to the Warsaw

Ghetto and lived on Ogrodowa 13. This was a period of difficult struggle for existence. The Germans conducted aktions very often, and the ghetto was being liquidated. One time, during a "Lapanka", they captured and imprisoned our dear and refined mother in "Pawiak". Miraculously, she left there after two weeks.

In October 1942, the murderers drove out tens out thousands of "unproductive" Jews from the ghetto - men, women, children, and the elderly. Our lot was to be among them. The barbarians drove us out by foot onto the Warsaw-Mordi highway. A transport truck with S. S. men drove by. They began to shoot at the Jews with machine guns. This was like an angry dream. I sunk down into a faint. When I opened my eyes, I saw a horrific picture. First, I was bereft of my mother and Sara. They both lay shot, wallowing in puddles of blood. I realized that I was left alone. In the turmoil, I lost my young brother Shimon, who was 12 years old. I could not even find his body. I later met both Adams, my brother and my cousin Rozszalski, in Siedlce. Other martyrs were not even brought to a Jewish burial.

Remaining alive after the slaughter, I decided to avoid large settlements. For a period of time, I lived like a wild animal, wandering around. Later, when the three of us met in Siedlce, we worked together in a German camp, which was completely unguarded. One day, the Germans took us by surprise, loaded us like sardines onto transport wagons, and drove us away with a train that was pulled by two locomotives with a great speed, so that nobody could jump out. I remember that it was evening. Here and there, I noticed that there was snow. I was there with both Adams. It is hard for me to write about what was taking place in the wagon. People looked like specters. Some of them had already given up on life. It was obvious that we were been taken to Treblinka. Young people jumped out of the windows, putting on white shirts over their clothes so that they would not be noticed as they fell into the snow. It was no easy matter to reach the small windows. For a certain time, I was overcome by weakness, and fell asleep from fatigue. When I awoke, I decided to save myself, my brother and my cousin. They were very afraid that people would shoot at those that jumped from the outside. I was compelled to be the first one to do so. We decided upon a point of jumping that was near a farm of a Pole for whom all three of us had worked at one point.

I chose an appropriate moment to jump. Between us, we found a locksmith who was requested to open the inside door. I remember the words he spoke at that time: "This is my last wish, save yourselves if you can. You are young. I am already old and I have nobody in the world. If you survive, I beg of you, remember me."

The train continued onward to the death camp. I jumped. Then I heard a series of shots. A Ukrainian guard shot at me. I remained lying on my back, and quickly turned myself over. I saw another jumper approach me, who was shouting loudly that he had been wounded in the stomach. However, I was helpless. I could not help him at all. I had jumped into the ditch beside the railway line, and I found there a group of young people who had jumped before I did. We spent the entire night in a barn. In the morning, everyone went on their way. I set out for the designated spot, traveling through fields and forests, in the snow and frost. It was a long way, which seemed endless.

d)

The place at which I jumped from the train was approximately 5 or 10 kilometers from Treblinka. As I have said, after jumping, we were to meet at a farm in the region of Lask owned by a good Pole. I, my brother Adam Grand, and our cousin Adam Roszalski worked there some time previously. At the time there was a lot of frost and snow. The journey took about 10 days, as I went by back routes. Along the way I encountered a Jewish woman from the same transport who also succeeded in jumping. She confided in me that she has a large sum of money, and proposed that we go together to Mezherich [37], where her husband was working in a German brush factory. We were very tired and hungry. It was night. We knocked on the door of a farmer, who gave us potatoes with red borscht, and let us spend the night, obviously for payment.

Having fear of hiding Jews, the son of the farmer told us the next day that on the other side of the highway there was a work camp for Jews. I already knew very well the meaning of a work camp, and was not about to be convinced to go there. My endeavors to talk the woman out of going there were not successful. She set out for the camp.

It was evening, and I was not able to remain there, for it was dangerous for me as well as for the farmer. Having no choice, I set out in the direction of the camp. As I neared the place, I heard a shot. With fear, I returned to the farmer and sneaked into his barn, obviously without being noticed. I spent the night there and covered myself with straw to protect myself from the great cold. In the morning, the farmer noticed me as I was sleeping. He gave me some bread and ordered me to leave. Incidentally, he told me that the woman had been shot by the Germans.

I arrived at the farm after a few days of traveling. However, my brother and cousin were not there. Most probably, the youths did not jump from the train, and were murdered in Treblinka, at the ages of 12 and 13.

e)

I arrived at the Mezherich Ghetto during my further wanderings. At that time, it was already after the fourth aktion. I do not have the ability and energy to write about the hell in the ghetto. It is sufficient to state that I endured the fifth, sixth and seventh aktions - until the ghetto was liquidated. I succeeded in fleeing from there with my dear friend Simcha (I do not remember his family name), a butcher from Janow Podlaski. After a long period of wandering, we arrived at the partisans on Shavuot [38] 1943. We joined the group of Vladimir Mikhalovich Sinotov [39]. We conducted numerous diverse actions against the Germans in the regions of Brest Litovsk, Terespol, Janow Podlaski, Sarne, Mardi and Lask. Our division consisted mainly of Jews and Russians.

Thus did I take revenge against the Germans. I was liberated by the Red Army at the end of June 1944 in the region of Lublin.

The furnaces of Majdanek near Lublin, photographed after the liberation in 1944. {Translator's note: the errata add "with the permission of The Ghetto Fighter's Headquarters (Beit Lochme Hagetaot).}

My Child... My Child... by W. Ben Shimon

A small monument in memory of our dear, kosher children who were devoured by the Nazi man-beasts - at the time that their fathers, who were sent to the taigas of the white "sever" in
Russia, were overcome with grief and longing for them.

When a silent lament rips through in the heart: My child, my
child

A fright shudders through my lonely bones: My child, where are
you now?

When the day breaks, so dull, so sorry My child, my
child...

When the sun sets hotly in the west My child, where
are you now?!

On the desolate bed, during sleepless nights, My child, my
child...

Chopping in an ancient forest, a tree is knocked down My child, where are
you now?!

When a flower flutters on a path in the forest, My child, my
child...

When one feels like a sparrow after the hunt and capture My child, where are
you now?!

With a wooden spoon, when the hand shakes My child, my
child..

Tearing oneself into pieces... Beating
one's head against the wall My child, my
child! Where are you now?!

Written in a labor camp in Komi A.S.S.R., 1940. [40]

The Miracle with My Child by Tamar (Tala) Cincinatus

During the sorrowful Hitlerian war, having already been through the cruelest ghettos in Polish Ukraine, we succeeded in obtaining "Aryan" documents. The initiators and providers of these documents were my two brothers Avraham and Motek. However, they are no longer here - and I was left in that dark time with a young child. We succeeded, as "Aryans" in leaving Poland, together with the Poles with whom we were among. We traveled to Germany for compulsory labor. Along the way, I went through numerous medical checkups. Even though we had to strip naked for these exams, I hid my Witold from the doctors.

He hid under the luggage for eight hours in Dachau. I spent some time in Dachau, and from there our group was sent all over Germany. My child and I were sent to Munich, where I began to work in a brick factory for twelve hours a day. My seven-year-old Witold became our provider who conducted our business. He would go to purchase everything, clean the barracks and cook for us.

The following is one of the countless awful episodes:
On a certain day when I was at work, a man in military uniform turned to me and asked:

"Are you the mother of the child? Of Witold Wieczorek? My wagon broke one of his feet."

Is there a limit to Jewish tribulations? In short: my Witold ended up in a German "sick house" in Munich. They wished to wash him before placing him in a bed. However, he did not let anyone undress him. He held strongly with his hands and did not allow this [41]. He had his full faculties - however I did not. At first when I saw his large, Jewish, terrified eyes, I remembered where I was holding in the world...

I turned to the nurse.

"Allow me to wash him myself. He is a difficult child, with complexes. His chief complex is that he is ashamed."

Thus it was. I washed the uppermost parts of his body, took off his long hospital gown and then finished by washing the lower parts of his body. His foot was swollen, and therefore was placed between two boards. Thus did he lie in the hospital for two weeks. He was very popular there. He was

553

considered to be an abnormal child, for he would not let anyone approach him. Each time when I came to him, he would assure me:

"I remember, I remember during the day and night. I do not forget!"

During one of the countless, terrifying air raids on Munich, when it seemed that the world was doomed, I realized that Nusbau Strasse was burning. The hospital in which my child was laid up was on that street. There was no means of communication in such a case. I ran to my child by foot, a good ten kilometers.

In the hospital, there was full-scale chaos. They had to free up beds in order to accommodate the wounded from the air raids that had just taken place. People were dragged from bunker to bunker, back and forth. I realized that this was the appropriate day for my son's cast to be removed. I went to the chief doctor and categorically requested that his cast be removed that very day -and he agreed. The took him to an operating room. A doctor and a nurse were present.

I remained there with my head pressed against the door of the operating room. At one point, I got the impression that they were arguing and wrestling with my son. I heard a raised voice. When I took away my son with his cast replaced, I felt as if a Divine providence existed.

My son told me that he did not allow them to lift up his shirt. Then the nurse requested to the doctor that he leave him be, for this is an abnormal child.

That same day, I brought my Witold back to my barrack, where he laid with his case for seven weeks.

Today, my son Witold-Avigdor is in Israel. He completed university in Jerusalem, and is a high school teacher.

My Two Friends from Zgierz in the Warsaw Ghetto by Hirsch Wasser of Tel Aviv

Yisrael Weinik

My memories of Yisrael Weinik center on activities and programs that are connected to the "Oneg Shabbat" ("Sabbath Celebration") - the underground ghetto archives that were founded by Dr. Emanuel Ringelblum of blessed memory.

The fact of the founding of the ghetto archives gives testimony to two things: first to the efforts and rebellious flame of Y. Weinik; second, to the trust that the leadership of "Oneg Shabbat" placed in the collaborators. For collaborating with the underground archives was fraught with mortal danger, in a literal sense.

Yisrael Weinik, a functionary of the Jewish Socialist Self-Assistance and an inspector of several refugee points [42], had direct contact with the worst of the terrible war-induced poverty in the Warsaw Ghetto. It is no wonder that a person with a social conscience and warm Jewish heart found a reason and a rectification in helping the uprooted Jews whose weeks and days were numbered. Here is not the place to describe the details of the refugee activities, but one thing can be stated: only someone very strong in spirit and ideas can take on the duties of caring for and worrying bout those in need - robbed of their means and hopes.

Given that, among other things, "Oneg Shabbat" collected material about the refugee points, Yisrael Weinik set out to work. He was a man who was not able to merely witness was taking place in the centers of need, but who also had the capability to write down the facts, from which he was able to separate the obvious and the primary points.

Yisrael Weinik's work regarding the refugee points excelled with precision, adequacy, and solid sociological foundations. One could detect the hand of an expert.

I often went to meet with my friend Yisrael Weinik (I was the secretary of Dr. Ringelblum), and we planned a great deal of work in the activities for the Jewish Social Self-Assistance and at the refugee points. We prepared the foundations and the points. However, the commencement of the liquidation aktion (July 22, 1942) put an end to the preparation.

Yisrael Weinik was taken away to the gas chambers of Treblinka along with the rest of Warsaw Jewry.

Leibel Rosenberg

Leibel Rosenberg was a struggler, in accordance with his disposition and upbringing. He would always claim that his Jewish nourishment came from the revisionist path. A toiler with broad shoulders, a resolute stance and an encouraging glance, Rosenberg quickly stood up for his oppressed fellow natives. The activity in the landsmanschaft [11] had a thoroughly Jewish character - the delegates received no payment from the Jew. Socialist self-assistance was certainly not from his own empty account.

I was the secretary of the umbrella organization of the approximately 100 landsmanschafts in Warsaw, and had daily contact with the delegates from the various landsmanschafts. Thus, I would meet with Rosenberg. He did not pay attention to the ideological differences between both of us, and we were friends - possible due to his honorableness, open-heartedness, love of his fellow Jew, and dedication to the saving of Jews from hunger and doom. He dreamed of resistance and struggle.

The realities were indeed cruel to him. He himself, and later his wife, became ill with typhus. After that, the gradual, yet constant, decline began for them both.

I saw Rosenberg when he would come to see the people who were doomed for death. Despite his slow decline, he did not lose his humanity and idealism.

It can be stated without exaggeration that the man of the people Leibel Rosenberg, the righteous intercessor for his fellow natives - went to his death like the rest of them. The Nazi occupiers made sure that hunger, illness and the difficult conditions would oppress their victims until the point that they give up their souls in sanctification of the Divine Name.

The last time we met together, at my dwelling on Moranowska 6, and at his dwelling on Nowolipia 36, he talked incessantly of rebellion and battle. Perhaps that is the reason that his portrait is etched in my memory. Perhaps that is why I have preserved a bright memory of him. Perhaps that is why I searched and found the means of living on, and I have taken the anonymous forgotten ones and brought them to a Jewish grave [43] with the help of the written word.

Our Family and Other Jews Were Saved
By Shalom Tzvi Laskier of Paris

After the Germans entered Paris, I fled to Grenoble in the so-called free zone that was under the rule of the Petain regime [44]. After a brief time, and thanks to my financial situation, I was able to purchase good relations with the police prefects in Grenoble. Those contacts enabled me to help and save hundreds of Jews who, just like me, had fled from occupied Paris to seek out a place of refuge in the free zone.

The Jews who came to the new place first had to declare themselves. Then there was a question of food cards, a dwelling and other elementary needs. Each day at 9:00 a.m., the prefect collected many of such unfortunate brothers who were in need of help. Since I frequented the Vichy police office, I succeeded in accommodating all of their needs, and I thereby enabled the Jews to immigrate. Among them were a succession of esteemed personalities from the present Jewish community of Paris, such as Mr. Aharon Shvartog who was the president of "Chesed VeEmet", Mr. Shmelke Kahan with his family, and others.

I recall how a Jewish communist, for whom I obtained the required papers, wished to express his appreciation and told me that "when the Russians will come into Paris, you will become a great man". My answer was, half humorous and half ironic, "I have already grown big enough"...

I was fortunate that even during those difficult times, Jews such as Maurice Schwartzman and the aforementioned Shmelke Kahan entrusted me with their estates, and placed absolute trust in me.

On a certain day when I was in the prefect's office, I heard a knock on the door. The police commissioner told me that the Germans have come to take down the addresses of the Jews who were in Grenoble. I quickly grabbed as many files with addresses such as mine as my hands could hold. Those addresses never fell into German hands.

If the Jews knew about my contact with the police, it is most certain that this was also known by some Vichy policemen [45]. A few of them, presenting themselves as Gestapo agents, knocked on the door of my villa on a certain evening, issued threats and demanded money. I realized that they were Frenchmen, and did not pay attention to their terrorizing. I indeed gave them a bit of money, and then rid myself of these unwelcome guests.

A high French military award for Shalom Tzvi Laskier - recognizing him for his service during the Nazi occupation of France in the Second World War. - Translator's note, dated in 1966

The next day, when I came to the prefect office, they warned me that my situation was serious, and they threatened me with arrest. I had to hide. Now I was a persecuted person myself. One night, the police indeed searched for me in my dwelling, but they found only my wife there, who was in her eighth month of pregnancy. This did not prevent the murderers from hitting her when she answered that I was not there, and that she did not know where I was. She even claimed that her husband was lost...

I myself had fled to the villages in Barbizon.

A while later, my wife succeeded in sending both children to me, each separately. She placed my fourteen-year-old son Maurice in a crate, and loaded him on a truck that transported such crates. Then, a second shipment awaited me. In the same manner, but in a different time, my eleven-year-old

558

son Charles arrived. Some time later, when my wife along with Mrs. Schwartzman wished to come to me, they were stopped at the border at Bordeaux and sent to a camp. Mrs. Schwartzman was subsequently deported. On the other hand, my wife succeeded, after difficult endeavors from my side, to be reunited with the entire family.

However, our luck did not last long. In 1943, the German murderers entered Barbizon. We had to once again take the wandering stick into our hands and flee. We found out that higher up in the mountains, it was possible to assure a more certain refuge for a persecuted Jew such as myself. It was difficult to leave the warm home of the secretary of the mayor of Barbizon, who took us in to his house based on a letter of recommendation from the prefect of Grenoble. However, this did not help, and we fled into the mountains.

I will never forget this image: when we gathered together at the heights, at Notre Dame, we ran into two Jewish families who decided to leave Notre Dame and set themselves up in... Grenoble. Later we found out that on a certain day, the order all of the residents to gather together in the market place. The murderers declared that if the Jews do not gather together voluntarily, or the population themselves do not bring over the Jews, everyone will be killed. Those two families were subsequently shot.

Finally, we merited to witness the day of liberation. Our family set out for Paris. The city itself was indeed whole, but almost all of the Jewish homes were occupied by French people. A series of processes to get back the dwellings began. For us, this was relatively easy. After meeting with the police commissar of our arrondisement, I persuaded him that he himself should approach the Christians who occupied Jewish homes and convince them to leave, in order to avoid unnecessary processes and dragging out the situation -for he indeed knows that the law gives the Jews the rights to return to their dwellings. He indeed did this. Thanks to this, many Jews were able to avoid legal proceedings and other difficulties in order to regain the roof over their heads.

A new life began - and I am happy that now, even in my old age, it is possible to perpetuate in our Yizkor Book the experiences of a Jew from Zgierz, who during those difficult times did not forget the Divine image and was able to quietly and modestly help save our Jewish brethren from the Nazi talons.

559

I believe that this is thanks to Jewish Zgierz, and the years of my childhood and youth in that city, where I studied in a Yeshiva for eighteen years.

Recorded by D. Sh.

With The Germans and Russians, and in Postwar Poland by Dov Grand of Jerusalem

It was August 1939. It was a glorious summer. I was already an older youth. I recall: I had jut returned home in the middle of the day from a walk in the Dabrowski Forest with my two friends, Meir Grinwald (perished) and may he live, Shlomo Slotkowicz. I found my mother in the kitchen. My father had closed the butcher shop and came home in the middle of the day. Something was hanging in the air. We were talking very openly about a war. We all sat by the table. My dear, unforgettable sister wished to eat. She looked at the faces of our parents as if they would be able to read into her.

Mother and father discussed among themselves that which we children did not understand. An oppressive mood pervaded in the street.

Various rumors were circulating around. We heard the Polish Foreign Minister Bek on the radio. Groups of people were standing around everywhere and talking of war. The minister assured us with emotion that "we will drown the Germans in their blood". Then we heard Hitler thundering: if they do not give him Danzig with the corridor, he will turn Europe into a cemetery.

Friday, September 1 arrived. That same day, German airplanes were seen over Zgierz, heading in the direction of Warsaw. This was the last normal Sabbath eve for us, with the silver candelabrum on the table, with challas, with tasty fish and delicacies. That same Friday night, we already did not sleep with our usually worry-free sleep. The frequent air raid sirens chased us out of bed.

Airplanes flew over constantly, but the Poles were certain that these were "our birds". The next day, Sunday, "our birds" dropped bombs also on Zgierz. A panic ensued. People thought that the Germans would destroy the city in accordance with "Boruta-Works". Therefore, many residents fled to the surrounding villages.

Father took us all together, and we fled to a farmer we knew in the village of Rudnik. There, we spent a few days and sleepless nights. On Monday night going into Tuesday, we survived an exchange of severe artillery fire from both sides. Our village with in the middle. As this went on for days, the farmer kept his silence as the Polish positions were being disrupted.

Day and night, refugees streamed onto the highway from the village and headed eastward, as the German airplanes mercilessly bombarded them with machine gun fire. Our Polish hosts, formerly good friends, showed their true faces and unambiguously made us understand that the Germans were already in Zgierz, and that they were going to issue ordinances regarding the Jews.

That same day, Wednesday, September 6 at noon, we left the village. We encountered German motorized columns along the way, which at that time did not have time to bother us.

As we neared the city, my mother gave me the key to the house. I quickly set out and was the first to arrive home. I fell down on the porch and kissed it. I began to get all choked up, and I began to weep silently. I felt that difficult times were ensuing. I opened the shutters and windows and dried my tears, for I was ashamed to be seen with a weeping face.

Then we were all here. Mother, paying no heed to her tiredness, began to prepare lunch [46]. In the butcher shop, father found that everything had been stolen. Someone broke into our butcher shop during our absence, as happened in other Jewish stores. Everything was taken.

The new authorities attempted to open the businesses. They even to operate the weaving plants. This was all done in order to confiscate Jewish property.

b)

The Germans issued new ordinances and decrees every day. They placed a commissar from amongst the Volksdeutschen [47] in every Jewish business, who became the bosses. People began to be conscripted to forced labor, replete with oppression and anguish. The barbarians set the synagogue and Beis Midrash on fire on the eve of Rosh Hashanah. The rabbi of Zgierz was ordered to pay a fine of 250 marks for the fire.

The ordinance that required the wearing of the yellow armband was issued. The Jewish youth began to flee to the Russian side. One day, I found out from a Polish official in the town council that the Germans had collated a list of 500 Jews whom they were going to shoot in Lagiewniki. My father was on the list. A few days prior to this, two Zgierzer Germans came to the home of my uncle Avigdor Roszalski, may G-d avenge his blood, and took him away to the Radogoszcz torture camp. A bitter weeping broke out, and we were all in despair. After these events, a few butchers came into the dwelling of Wolf Szmietanski on Piatkowska Street near us. We decided to flee to Bialystok.

At literally the last minute, mother dressed me up with a few pair of underwear and sent me with father. It was already night, and we bade farewell with weeping. We silently made our way to Leczycka Street. From there, we traveled with the tramway to Lodz. As we drove through the Jewish street, we still caught a glimpse of the burnt synagogue, and our hearts were filled with deep sorrow. We all felt that difficult happenings were awaiting us. However, nobody had any idea as the extent that the Germans would permit things to go. Consequently, everyone would say: "until the storm passes"… we believed that we were leaving our home temporarily.

We spent the night in Lodz with a family on the Balut, and the next day we traveled by train to Warsaw. We arrived just before the curfew hour, which began at 8:00 p.m., anyone the Germans would find on the street after that time would be shot without warning. We had nowhere to go. A Jew who noticed that we were seeking shelter took us to a half-destroyed synagogue. It was already the end of November. We spent a sleepless night. Our teeth were chattering from cold and fear. A dead body without a head was lying at the entrance of the synagogue. A stray bullet killed him.

Early the next morning, we saw what the German barbarians had done with Poland's capital. Half of Warsaw was already destroyed by that time. Our group was taken in by a family on Swietojanska Street. Three days later, we waited for a train that was going to Malkinia. A few Jews of Zgierz joined us in Warsaw.

It was not so easy to find the means of traveling by horse drawn cab to the eastern station in Praga. German gendarmes circulated around the Kierbedz Bridge and conscripted Jews for forced labor. From our group, they captured Grand. They first administered to him a pair of enthusiastic beatings, and then forced him to clean latrines. To our luck, they let him go after some time and packed us all in transport wagons. The train started to move. Late in the evening we heard shots mixed in with the horse, drunken voices of the Germans. "Jews left, Poles right".

They drove all of us, numbering approximately 500, off the train and began to lead us in the darkness through a forest. We were accompanied by Germans with malicious dogs, which tore pieces off of us. There was also no shortage of Poles who assisted in the torture. It became obvious that they were preparing to liquidate us in the forest. Many Jews recited their confession. We arrived at a lit up house. There we received the full share of beatings. A cousin of mine was with us, and the Germans broke a thick stick over his head. It was made out of metal, and the German had it hidden. My cousin returned home and later died.

c)

We spent three terrifying days and nights at the border crossing near Malkinia, before we crossed the Russian border. We went by foot through Zareby Koscielne and Czyzewo, and we arrived in Bialystok alive. The city was full of refugees. We found a temporary place in a Beis Midrash on Piwna Street number 4. Most of the Jews there were from Zgierz. Later we went on to Dzika, past Bialystok. This was a summer colony. We spent the winter there. It was difficult. When the snow got deep, we returned to Bialystok and remained there until the Russians took all of the refugees and held them for a few days with the N.K.V.D. Then they packed them onto cattle cars and sent them off. After six weeks of suffering, we arrived in the far north, in Komi A.S.S.R.

They had forest work for us. Uncle Yisrael Yitzchak was taken separately, with "loafers", and placed in a "correctional" camp. Yaakov was also in one of the camps in Komi.

After Hitler's invasion of Russia, all of the former Polish citizens were freed. At that time, my father and I worked in a slaughterhouse in the village of Kortkeros, 80 kilometers from Syktyvkar. Things were relatively good for us.

One day in Syktyvkar, father ran into Uncle Yisrael Yitzchak by chance. This was a very touching encounter. When both brothers met in Kortkeros, I was very happy. My uncle soon became a butcher. Our cousin Yaakov was wandering around at that time. He was on his way to mobilize in General Anders' Army. Yaakov did not remain very long with us, and soon set out on his way.

This good did not last long, however. With the speedy forward march of the Nazi soldiers, the Russians mobilized us in the work battalion ("Trod Armia"), They sent us, hundreds of Jews and thousands of Russians, to another region in Komi - Zheshert. There, we had a very difficult time. During the course of 11 months, 40% died from the hard work, poor sanitation conditions, hunger and cold. Uncle Yisrael Yitzchak took ill with dysentery. He died alone in the hospital in Syktyvkar.

d)

In the summer of 1944 all of us former Polish citizens were evacuated to Ukraine, into areas that the Germans had recently evacuated. Father and I came to the Sovkhoz "Petrovka", in the region of Chernigov. There I worked for approximately two years. The so-called repatriation took place in February 1946, and we returned to Poland.

Shortly after we crossed the border at the Chelm depot, which was at one time a major Jewish center, we received a "warm" greeting. A Pole shouted out: "See now, some Zydes! Did Hitler not stew them all?"

We traveled further and ended up in the new Jewish center of Dzierzoniow (Richbach) in Lower Silesia. I quickly began to search for relatives at the local Jewish committee. Wherever it was possible, I wrote, asked and researched. Wherever I gave the names, they did not show up on the lists. Then I met a young man who had been in Zgierz a short while ago. He lived there with Avraham David, who had recently been freed by the Polish army. Avraham David's son Hertzke was still in Zgierz. I wrote them a letter. At the same time, my brother Mordechai, whom I no longer believed was still alive, returned to Zgierz from Altstein, East Prussia on a short furlough from the Polish army, with the hope of meeting father and I. He also did not believe that I was alive. Mordechai saw my letter there with great joy. Having obtained our address, he set out for Richbach and immediately went to the Jewish committee. There he met a well-known Jew who took him to our address. Mordechai did not tell the Jew whom he was, but only for whom he was searching. They met along the route - Mordechai and father. At first glance they did not recognize each other. The six years had taken their toll. Father had aged greatly and Mordechai had grown up. Moreover, Mordechai was wearing the uniform of a Polish officer. One word followed the next - and they fell into each other's arms... I was at home alone at the same time. Together they came to me. Father waited outside. As he entered, the Jew said "good morning", and a Polish officer followed after him. At first I had no idea who he was. He asked me in Polish: "How are you? Are you content with your dwelling?" I answered him: "We have recently returned from Russia, Mr. Porucznik". At that moment, he fell upon my neck, started kissing me and weeping. I was confused. He told me in Yiddish: "Do you not recognize me, Berl?" Then father entered. None of us

564

could control our weeping. It seemed as if our source of tears would not end. Even the well-known Jew wept with us. He himself was left alone, having lost his dear ones in the war.

We slowly regained our composure. Mordechai began to tell us of his experiences. It is impossible to write everything down on paper, for we would have to write a book of several hundred pages.

e)

Father became ill after our return. He spent some time in the "Oza" Hospital in Rybak. Shortly after the frightful pogrom in Kielce where 44 Jews who had not been beaten by the Nazis were killed, already in the socialist republic of post-war Poland, we decided to flee to the Land of Israel. I came with my sick father to Austria at the end of July, 1946. There, he spent the entire time in hospitals. In that camp of despair, the son shone upon my bitter life -I met my mate, whom I had already known in Swidnik, Poland. We got married n Linz in August, 1948. My ill father was not able to be present at the wedding.

We started making aliya in November 1949, my wife my father and I. In Italy, my father's health took a turn for the worse. After spending two weeks in the hospital in Bartletta in the region of Bari, father died at the age of 56 years. I gave him a Jewish burial in Trani.

I arrived in Israel with my wife in December, 1949. A few weeks later our son Moshe Zvi was born, who was named after my father.

The storm was over. However, it had torn away our beloved ones. Our town of Zgierz was left without Jews.

Encounters with Zgierzers in Russia
By Yitzchak Gotthelf of Ramat Gan

I, Avraham Gotthelf, was born in 1899. I left Zgierz in December 1939 with my wife Esther, nee Ziprowi, and our daughter Miriam. Fleeing the city was the cause of my arrest. They arrested me and accused me with placing a placard in the Town Square on November 11 upon which was written: "Down with Hitler!" When I succeeded in being released from arrest, I left Zgierz and went to Bialystok.

I was sent together with my family to the Archangelsk Oblast Kargapolskaya region, "Lespunkt" Pervomayskiy.

After the liberation, we were brought with a troop transport to central

565

Asia, in Karaganda. Weinberg was also with us. Wachs traveled to Tashkent.

After returning to Poland, I found my family in Kokand, working in a hospital where the tailor Rotenberg from Zgierz died. I also found Baum there (I do not recall his first name). He was formerly a master craftsman with Eiger, and lived in the New City. After the liberation in Russia, while traveling with the troop convoy to central Asia, we stopped over in Turkestan. When I went out of the station and went into the large waiting area, I saw someone dressed in rags, who was calling my name. When I approached him, I recognized Mr. Wachs, Glicksman's son-in-law. He told me that he had already gone for three days without bread. With Weinberg, we tool two loaves of bread from the wagon and gave them to Mr. Wachs. He told us that he had been working in the magistrate in Grodno, and had a good position. He showed us letters with photographs that he had kept from his wife. She wrote to him that the family had been able to take the children from Paris through the Red Cross. They were evacuated when the Soviet-German war broke out. At a certain station, when the train was stopped, a group of hooligans opened the door and took everything from the wagon. The people were left naked. Therefore he remained in the station wrapped in a blanket. When we first opened the wagon, we realized our blunder. We had to take him with us, in our wagon. This took place in October, 1941 [48]. I arrived in Israel in 1958.

Sad Memories by Esther Gotthelf of Ramat Gan

As I was going home from my Uncle Nachum Glowinski with my young daughter (today grown up and living in Akko) through Strikower Street, I was afraid as I went through the market. I noticed that the Gestapo was standing in front of the home of the rabbi. I quickly went up on a porch.

A short time later, the Gestapo took out the rabbi. I quickly went home - I lived on Pilsudskiego 14. I noticed that they were taking him to the New City. A German named Reich lived in our house. I give him five Zlotys and asked him to go find out where they were taking the rabbi. The German later told me that they took the rabbi to the barbershop. He said: "Mrs. Gotthelf, what they were doing with the rabbi - it was difficult to figure out".

After a long while later they brought the rabbi back and compelled him to pay for the cutting off of the hair of his head and beard.

One night, they gathered up about one hundred Jews, headed by the lawyer Jochwed. The Germans conducted a "masquerade". The lawyer Jochwed was dressed up with a tallis, and held a lamp in his hand. As far as I remember, Motek Szrowka was there, dressed in a woman's housecoat. They were forced to shout out: "Jews are great swines!". They took them to the magistrate. What they did with them there - I do not know.

In My Destroyed Home by Fabian Greenberg of New York
Memories and reflections from a visit to Zgierz in 1959

Fabian Greenberg

1)

Here I am, standing once again on in the old market of my hometown that I had left 20 years previously. This particular point gives me the spiritual longing (and to a certain degree - also physical) to embrace the entire city, especially the Judaism in it, that has forever passed away.

The houses stand sorrowful - poor, dilapidated, like orphans. Sorrow overtakes me. How can it be that my grandfather's house, built like a fortress, stands intact? The plaster was cared for and clean. This is a sign that

567

the Christian who now lives in the house is a very good homeowner. I wished that this house had appeared bitter and black, damaged like the other Jewish homes in the city.

My grandmother had told me that the post office was in their house. Wagons drawn by four horses would carry mail and passengers to the surrounding villages. As the wagons coming from the directions of Ozorkow approached the civic garden, one of the drivers would sound a trumpet - the mail is coming. The horses realized that their home was nearby. At the end of the trip, they would run into grandfather's yard in order to rest for a day. This house also had an eminent resident. The Maskilim of Zgierz of that time brought in the

Hebrew-Yiddish poet Yaakov Binyamin (Ben-Yamini) Katzenelson in order to open up a modern cheder for their children. His son, the later poet-martyr Yitzchak, wrote his first Hebrew poems in that house. One of Ben-Yamini's students later opened up a cheder near the fish market, in a long yard. This cheder was always left neglected, until it had to be shown to a school inspector. The Rebbe did not observe the ordinances of the Lodz school trustees. Mordechai Szwarc and I were among the youths who were happy to have a day off. He, Marek Szwarc did not absorb enough Judaism from that cheder to last him an entire lifetime…

I will most probably not see my grandfather's home again during my life. I want to take another glance. A happy moment comes to my memory: Purim with my grandfather. The entire family is gathered around the table. It was before the Purim feast. The door opens up and the Purim players push themselves in. The "repertoire" changed every year. This time it is about "the binding of Isaac". The players were hand weavers, craftsmen, and students. Their acting was not bad. Perhaps they felt that this was the last time. Therefore they indeed paid attention to the roast turkey that was sitting in the roasting pan in the kitchen window. "Let them come!", grandmother said.

Yes, they were correct. This was the last time. An era ended. Revolutionary winds began to blow along the Jewish street, and blew away several traditional Jewish customs.

2)

Here is not far away from the Jewish street. There, the synagogue and the Beis Midrash stood. My parents worshipped there on the High Holy Days. My father, a Maskil and a scholar, regarded many prayers as literary creations. He analyzed piyutim of the Rosh Hashanah and Yom Kippur Shmone Esrei [49] along with his neighbor on the eastern wall of the Beis Midrash. They figured out what century the particular piyut was written. The prayer "Hineni Heani Mimaas" [50] made the greatest impression upon me. That prayer was for me the theme of all my later societal activity in the municipal institutions, where I became the speaker for the rights of the Jewish community of Zgierz.

Thinking about the burned holy buildings, I walked along the alley upon which my father, still a young man, was carried to his eternal rest. His son has now come from a far away land to visit the graves of his ancestors. I found a few broken monuments in the cemetery. This ground upon which the barbarian enemies uprooted our holiness has become a wasteland - very fresh green grass for cattle grows here.

The houses standing around the market did not have any luck. They did not awaken any memories, with the exception of Zalman Feldscher's (Grynwald's) house. The famous poet Yaakov Cohen spent his youth in that house. One day, I came to that house along with my father of blessed memory. As we traversed the market, we saw Leon Rosinow standing near the entrance. He reproached us as to why we had not taken the sidewalk around the market. The official of the Russian Police, Stanislavski, lived in the second house, and the meeting of the

Gemilut Chassadim [51] on the second floor was illegal. There was a fear that the police would arrest all who gathered together for that memorial evening on the fourth yahrzeit [52] of Dr. Herzl.

That meeting was conducted with the Zgierz Zionists and with my latter longstanding friend Leon Rusinow of blessed memory. He was a very impulsive, energetic man who was imbued with fire during a discussion with political opponents. He was as sober as a Litvak [53], goodhearted and sentimental. His heart was as soft as butter when it came to dealing with Jewish needs.

The societal work kept us very busy. I remember that during an enthusiastic speech delivered by Yitzchak Nissenbaum in Lodz to acquaintances, we were both so overcome by emotion that we were not embarrassed to weep, despite the fact that we were both known as young Zionist revolutionaries.

3)

Our old wellspring was also of interest. We studied Ein Yaakov [54] privately with Reb Wolf Leib Haltricht, in order to bind the golden past with the gray struggle, so as to create a bright future in the land of our dreams. He, Leon, was not destined to see the Land. He perished in the Holocaust [55].

This was the time when the Jewish press in Poland grew and made inroads among the broad masses. Our Zionist circle gained new people. Among others, this included the enthusiastic member Menachem Berliner, with his hoarse voice. He impressed the youth with his unshakable belief, deep persuasion, logical thinking and fascinating example. He made aliya to Zion, worked hard, and wrote spirited letters. He came back after some time. However, he was not able to remain long in Zgierz. The Land called him. He was lacking his hands [56]. Menachem was not of those who go halfway. He again found himself among the pioneers who were drying up the malarial swamps.

In the midst of the First World War, the sad news arrived that our fellow died of that terrible disease.

4)

... A house stood not far from the place where I find myself -and it is not there. The Germans took over this house and simply tore it up. This brick house belonged to Isuchar Szwarc. This house housed the Jewish library, where our meetings took place, where books were collected and later purchased. There, a library of several thousand Jewish and Hebrew books grew.

Isuchar Szwarc loved the youth. He would come in with a smile on his pleasant face. He had a majestic presence. He would admire the first sculpture work of his son, tell a story, and encourage us in our further work. He was the admirer and important activist. He was a delegate to the First Zionist Congress. He was a scholar, and wrote articles in Hebrew periodicals under the pseudonym "Yam Shachor" (Black Sea). He was known far from the borders of our city. His eldest son was no embarrassment to the Szwarc family. He was famous as the researcher of the Marranos in Portugal. He left behind a manuscript in French regarding his life's work. This manuscript found its way to the editor of the New York "Teg", Aharon Alperin - and began to be published. His son Mordechele became Marek Szwarc, a well-known painter and sculptor found an interesting sculpture by him in the French Institute in London.

The Jewish library, which bore the name of our fellow native, the writer David Frischman, played an important role in Zgierz. It increased the cultural achievements of the Jewish population, especially of the youth. We wished to include the Beis Midrash students in our circles. At that time, that element was under the influence of the anti-Zionist religious leadership. By becoming a reader in the library, the boy would come a bit closer to Zionism.

Aside from the Zionist literature, the atmosphere was Zionistic, and we developed an audience for Zionist readings. As well, the Hebrew courses at the library were a laboratory for preparing the appropriate human resources for the benefit of the ideal that occupied us. The image remains in my memory of Wolf Fiszer and his friends dressed in clean Jewish hats and long kapotes, coming for the first time in the library. They remained on the doorstep somewhat ashamed, for they had not yet completely decided to "cross the Rubicon".

That element later helped us attain a greater position in those institutions that had a relationship to the religious needs of the Jewish population.

Our friend Menashe Szwarcbard was among the founders of the library. He was a man of the people with a fine sense of humor, and was close to the Jewish masses. As a former Beis Midrash student, he took advantage of the opportunity to influence the youth from religious homes and to bring them into the library circles. He often held readings for the youth.

We became friends, and worked together in the library and in the Zionist organization. He also realized his ideal and immigrated to the Land of Israel. They encountered unfavorable conditions, and he returned with his family, and died. I honor his memory.

I can also mention that among those who took an interest in the founding of the library was Aharon Cincinatus, who died in Israel. He left the city and went to Vilna, where he later became the Vilna correspondent for the Warsaw "Heint".

5)

The First World War broke out and completely ended the entire social, cultural and political activity of the Jewish community of Poland. The parties began their competition, and a general mobilization of the youth commenced. Who would dominate? For the future of the Jewish Land, it was important that the greatest Jewish community should for the most part be on the side of

our agents and leaders who prepare the terrain for great and important happenings. We realized that each city and town is important. With youthful fire and zeal, we placed the Zionist stamp on all Jewish institutions in the city.

If leaders were lacking, one member would take on several positions. If we had no understanding at all of philanthropy, it was important that the activists in the philanthropic institutions should be our friends. If it was crowded for us in the clean house of the Jewish organization, which was bounded solely by religious needs, we knew that when the census of communal activists who belong to the Zionist camp would take place, our society would belong to them. We broke the Orthodox stronghold. We transferred the leadership of the community to the religious wing of our organization, and the victory would be acknowledged in the entire region, for it was bound up with a struggle within the Sirkes family. They were a typical example of well-known Hassidic families who were cracked on the route to the Jewish renaissance. This was a political and religious struggle between two brothers. The Orthodox chairman of the community, Eliezer Sirkes, was forced to leave his post. The Mizrachi man Daniel Sirkes became the head of the community.

The communal councils of surrounding cities, Such as Strykow, Glowno and others desired the same inclination as we conducted and won the election struggle. We sent our members to those places (Yitzchak Glicksman of blessed memory and others) - and the communal councils of the entire region became dominated by Zionists.

As one position was conquered, we went over to a second. It was time to demonstrate to the world that we desire to save our people -that we are searching for a refuge for them. Our leaders wished to conduct a referendum. This would help their endeavors to maintain the Balfour Declaration. We did this thoroughly, so that no Jewish home would be passed over. I shudder with excitement to this day as I recall entering a Jewish house where I requested a signature for the declaration. The Orthodox young man answered me: "No, we have a different way". The answer that our members had was satisfactory. We had a wonderful, knowledgeable youth, and every action in the city was conducted with national discipline and responsibility.

572

6)

... After everything, I am still standing in the old market immersed in thoughts. For me - the city hall, the magistrate. I entered there in 1919 as a young councilman in the first elected city council of Zgierz in free Poland. The united Jewish list was led by three councilmen; Eliezer Sirkes (from the Orthodox), Avraham Morgensztern (independent), and Fabian Greenberg (from the entire Zionist spectrum).

Eliezer Sirkes was a factional Orthodox activist. He founded various institutions in the city, such as "Hazamir" and the orphanage, and he was a co-founder of the touring organization [57], etc. However, not having a backbone behind him - an organization or a party, it always happened that either the institution disappeared after a certain time, or the leadership was given over to other hands. In this manner, he was not able to immediately create a new organization.

Our task in the city council was twofold: defending the rights of the Jewish population and stressing at every opportunity that Jews are citizens of the land with equal rights. We were representatives on all of the commissions, which took up a great deal of time. Each of us was required to serve as a member of different commissions.

A characteristic situation must be pointed out here. It was shortly after the First World War. The population was in need. The industrial enterprises, primarily the textile factories, were waiting for the calm to prevail outside the country in order to set the weaving looms in motion, which provided a livelihood for the majority of the population. A shipment of old dresses from the United States arrived at the city council, for the impoverished Christian population of Zgierz. The Jewish caucus felt the need also to have a representative in the distribution committee in order to demonstrate that we Jews also participate in the management of the city. We had to go from house to house to determine who has the right to receive these old clothes. On the day of the division of the items, it became obvious that there would not be enough for all those who have the right to receive help. The crowds were raging and were on the verge of demolishing the entire office. The socialist councilors understood that the first victim would be the Jewish councilor - and they let me go out through the back door...

I can see here the window of the large meeting hall of the magistrate, where for 20 years, the entire length of time that Poland was an independent republic; we wrangled with those who hated us, who wished through various

573

means to tear away the piece of bread from the Jews. We defended the right of the Jewish population to receive subsidies for their philanthropic and cultural institutions. The efforts and endeavors of the Jewish councilors in intervening with the local authorities to prevent a malevolent official from mistreating a Jew were very difficult. It should be stated here that they counted on us Jewish councilors. The makeup of the city council was such that in many cases, our votes were decisive. Now I am standing in front of the city hall as a broken person, and I call out with pain in my heart: where are my constituents, what happened to them?

7)

I come from the State of Israel. I circulate around the splendid buildings of the University of Jerusalem [58]. But here I hear the resounding applause from the hall of the nearby "Luna" theater. The enthusiasm is for the founding, in 1925, of the University on Mount Scopus. The following people speak: the editor Y. Ungar of Lodz, and the Zionist councilor. Representatives of all of the nationalist groups in Zgierz bring their greetings as well. The feelings of the gathering are raised. One can hear the waving of the wings of the redemption, as the speakers call out that the university is a step forward along the difficult path to a Jewish independent state. There were two things that we could not know at the time: that the realization of the hopes would cost so much blood, and the buildings of the university on Mount Scopus would remain
empty and orphaned [59].

But enough of these thoughts. Come, my dear readers, dear Zgierz Jews. We will move from this place, and go around the city through the main street of the city. There were Jewish shops on both sides of the street. They did business. However, the shops had to close at 2:00 p.m. Not even one shop remained open. The synagogue was crowded. The call to protest the Kristalnacht pogrom in Germany had a sharp echo. The president of the city, Jan Szjercz gave me permission to close the stores. He was not an anti-Semite. At that time, that was a great accomplishment. We entered the corner where the building of Mottel Margolies stood. The communal offices were on the first floor, and the Gerrer Hassidim worshipped underneath. This caused a constant war. Everything was so new. Stretch out the hand -and the shtibel can be taken over by the communal council. We were dragged along the way many times. I remember the disgrace that the two Reichert brothers-in-law had to endure when they worshipped in that synagogue. They were Zionists, Heaven forbid!

This was also the case with our friend, the Mizrachi member Manes Engel. Not adventurists, but rather Hassidic youths knocked him down in the shtibel, beat him, and tore up and threw away his kapote. He did not go to the Polish court, but a religious judgement granted him a sum of money. He took the money, and made aliya with his family to the Land of Israel. We kissed each other in his own house in Pardes Chana.

I stand and observe the window of the communal office, and my heart throbs with pain: there I participate in all political actions, local and national, relating to the city council or the Sejm during the 20 years of the existence of the Polish state. There we extended a helping hand to the refugees of Zgierz who were driven away to Zbaszyn by the Germans [60].

During the time of the Russian-Polish war in 1920, when many soldiers passed through Zgierz, we made an effort to host all Jewish soldiers during Rosh Hashanah and Yom Kippur. The Jewish population demonstrated a wonderful display of solidarity. Rich and poor took in the Jewish soldiers. An embarrassed Jewish daughter came to my writing table and gave me a note from her father: "I apologize many times, but we unfortunately cannot take in Jewish soldiers. It will be a sad holiday. We have no livelihood."

Our youth, from all parties, conducted this activity with great responsibility. They did not ignore one Jewish household.

8)

The economic situation of the Jews of Zgierz was generally better than that of other Jewish cities and towns. The textile industry, which was concentrated in the hands of a few Jewish and non-Jewish firms prior to the First World War, underwent a great metamorphosis. It was transferred to the hands of people who had no involvement with that industry, such as small-scale craftsmen who rose to a higher rung on the financial and economic ladder during the time of the war. At that time, the old manufacturers, who suffered greatly from the Bolshevik revolution whose former customers in Russia had their means confiscated, and also suffered from the German confiscations - were not able to conduct their businesses in the same scope due to capital pressure. Several liquidated their businesses, and the rest strongly felt the competition of the numerous newly arrived, small manufacturers. They ensured that a greater number of people would be employed by the mechanized weaving operations and the various auxiliary occupations.

The rabbi of Zgierz was concerned to ensure that Jewish workers would also find employment. It is worthwhile to stress that he was a rabbi who not only took interest in religious affairs, but also in social affairs. The number of Jewish weavers increased. However, they could not find employment in the city. With the initiative of the rabbi, a meeting of all Jewish manufacturers was called. He demanded simply that all Jewish manufacturers must employ 10% Jewish weavers. From that day on, the unemployment of the Jewish weavers ceased.

... Enough of standing here. It is futile to look around.

Jews would stand and converse in the center of the city. Good news and bad news would be shared. A commissioner with a merchant appeared. One had to run home. They did not wish to lose the ransom.

A group of Jewish porters stood there and waited patiently from someone to ask them to carry some merchandise or yarn for the weaving plant. Among them, was "the Bielas", blond, angry, with a strange face. At his side - his sister, like two drops of water, figuring like a classic tragic comedy. Looking at them, it was possible that it was necessary to repeat that a person is created in the image of G-d. However, it was possible to admire the warm feeling of family solidarity which always pervaded between them, and the concern of one for the other.

It is possible that Yosef Meir Haran would also come out from the alley. He was a good friend, the last chairman of the Zionist organization in Zgierz. The tenants of his house were the Zionist office and the Jewish library.

The mind works, the realities are sad - and with such a mood I go further around the city. At its summit, at the so-called new part of the city stands a large factory building, the former property of the well-known textile firm "Sirkes and Eiger". The partner of the firm, Moshe Eiger was a Jew who was a Maskil. He was a calm, peaceful, feeling, poetic soul, who published a collection of poems in Hebrew and Yiddish. We young people did not see him among us. However later, in his old age, he drew nearer to us. We had the impression that he believed that money can be lost, but the extra soul remains forever. He became very active in Zionist and societal life, as if he was rectifying and paying back for the previously neglected time.
9)

Before the walk ends, I want to tell not only of what took place in that

576

Garden of Eden, but also about that which surely did not bring honor to Jewish Zgierz. Enough water flowed into the Bzura River of Zgierz since two "nice youths" were disgraced in our city: they were out of jail and we then saw them go forth again with chains on their hands, under a police guard. They were thieves and extortionists. They tortured the poorest of the poor, Jewish servant girls from whom they demanded redemption money. Those who did not comply with their request were beaten and threatened with rape. Zamele somehow was able to detach himself from hell, for he later got married and earned his piece of bread honestly as a tailor. Itchele left Zgierz, apparently across the ocean.

Of the approximately 5,000 Jewish souls, a miniscule percent were lawbreakers.

10)

I leave you, my old city. Presently, "old city" is not a rhetorical term. Digging under the earth below the foundation of the large "Boruta" chemical factory, stone and iron items were found. The vases with relief drawing were from a much earlier time. Historians estimate that there was already a human population here from the 3rd century. About 70 years ago, one could see Swedish trenches around Zgierz from the Swedish-Polish war. Jews lived in Zgierz for approximately 250 years. A small corner of the Polish-Jewish settlement bound and connected with it and with the entire Jewish population of the wide world.

Three Jews remained in Zgierz. A patio saved them. I rejoiced with them in Israel.

On that day when I set out on my far journey, I saw one of the pioneers (chalutzim) who underwent their Hachsharah with us in the city. When he found out where I was going, his eyes opened wide and he asked:

"Why not to the land of Israel?"

It was hard for me to answer him. However, his question has been ringing in my ears for all these years. I could not find him in Israel. Who knows if he came to the Land? However, hen I came to the Organization of Zgierz émigrés, a soldier woman came to me, hands pressed together, and told me that it was because of me that she was here in the Land. I knew that she was not the only one, and I also had helped carry a few bricks for the rebuilding of our land.

I know also that that chalutz, if he is still alive, still hold his eyes open -

and perhaps asks the same question...

**The Bielases - a brother and a sister (covering her face), the most well
known porters in the town**

.

For My Birthplace Zgierz by Yisrael Asher Malchieli

Memorial bricks
To a Jewish community
That was pushed away
And is no more...
1)
"My birthplace"? - - Indeed? - This is not the true meaning of the words,
Your language is foreign to me, with it can I not express thoughts;
Not in you did mother's birth pangs frighten me, to the air of the world did I

hasten,

Not in you did my nursing mother satiate me, on the breasts of peace did I clasp my fists;

To walk on two, already with a "name", I already learned proper things,

I became familiar with the Lithuanian language, my mother tongue, and I chattered in it;

I differentiated, and discerned between the hugs of mother and embraces of grandmother,

In the courtyards, I played together frequently with children of my age,

"There", in the city in Lithuania, which dwelt in strength from a time ago,

As a Divine cloud from the tents of Jacob, in the spirit of the Gra [61];

The voices of "Sinai" echoed, and filled the entire Kloiz,

Every common person there knew Torah, and the masses - Gemara.

2)

And I - when I came to Zgierz, I was big, I was already five years old,

I studied Chumash and Rashi, and my steps were encouraged with the Scriptures;

The prayers were fluent on my lips, and I also studied chapters of Talmud,

"I ploughed" in "These are the found objects", and in "The ox that gored the cow" [62]...

On my student desk, among older people, I was never embarrassed of their friendship,

And the queries of the rabbi and his riddles, I answered easily, before everyone.

Indeed, I was already older when I came,

This five-year-old was not a small mater,

And I knew well how to differentiate,

Between that which was forbidden and permitted...

3)

But to you, my city of Zgierz, where I took my first proper steps,

But you were new to me, my youth rejoiced in you;

The tumult of your streets and their crowds, and various childhood pursuits

Made me forget my memories from "there", slowly slowly they were stored away and were no longer; Even though my complaints were many, I did not know pleasure and enjoyment I found what was to be found for my age, and my cup was filled to abundance; From your clear autumn days, did not caress me in the summer with my guile

And in the civic "pleasure garden", my feet never trod upon,
I also, in my manner, enjoyed my life at that time,
I strengthened myself with walks, and my soul ascended to the clouds.

4)
On Sabbath and festival days, when I went out together with my father
Outside of the city, to the fields, there, to the railroad bridge,
Then my soul was filled with joy. All sadness distanced itself from me,
I moved my legs like rams, and I skipped along without stopping.
As usual, Reb Isucher Szwarc or his brother Shmuel joined us,
Both of blessed memory, may their soul dwell with G-d;
Also Reb Wolf Leib, the wonderful prayer leader, whose melodies I so
enjoyed,
He was also an expert mohel, and he busied himself with watches in his
corner,
In that small store, the likeness of which I can still see in my dreams,
However his portrait, the mohel, is very much etched in my memory…
For he always would visit us, and he would also join us for meals,
On the long Sabbath evenings, or at the conclusion of the day of rest,
His palate enjoyed the appetizers, or the taste of raisins and plums,
He would always say that the raisins were the best…
And once on a Rosh Hashanah evening, I remember, when he came to us
He brought a small bunch of grapes for the Shehecheyanu blessing [63];
I asked "Is this from the Land of Israel?" - What a forlorn question;

-       "From where did you think?" - was the answer that shot out,
        And three small grapes, that I so desired to chew and swallow,
        I tasted the taste of delicacies that I will forever never forget - - -
5)
As I talk about "prayer leaders", other cantors come to memory,
Reb Fishel Bunim, with his yellow beard, who lead prayers on the Sabbaths
of the year,
And Reb Fishel Rus, who sang nicely, and his prayers cut open into the
heavens,
He called together all of the angels of high, and even arose the dead to life;
On Rosh Hashanah and the fast of Yom Kippur, he stood like a "rock for his
nation,

Like the sharpest attorney, there was none more successful than he in his
task,
All of them like the cedars of Lebanon, mighty in prayer and song,
They died, passed away and are no longer, and their melodies have ended.
We are speaking of Fishel, and I remember one more, who would sit in the
tents of study,
He stood on Holy guard, and he was not a cantor or a mohel;
Reb Fishel the well-known shamash, who kept his post without problems,
At the Great Synagogue and also at the cemetery for those who dwelt in the
graves,
Where his family were slaughtered like sheep, and his own life was crushed
to the ground,

During the time of the evil murderers, by whose iniquity suspicion was
aroused in his community.
6)
I surely remember you, Zgierz, your poor and your noble ones,
I remember your elite, and also your dross;
The open street of the Jews, where your beloved ones were centered,
There the synagogue and the Beis Midrash stood as the main places
and centers for your flock;
The Beis Midrash! Where I worshiped daily and also studied Gemara,
Along with my older friends, who also set aside times to study Torah there;
If I am not mistaken, even the rabbi of the city also stood to assist his
dwelling,
From atop that public oven, which was very crowded before Passover;
There we baked matzos together; we kneaded and rolled the dough,
We poured the "mayim shelanu" [64], we divided up the pieces,
There are the round, large matzos, which we carried on the shoulders with a
sheet,
And I waited to greet Passover night - the time to dispense with bread…
For the matzo was dear to me, together with the four cups of wine,
I waited with joy in my heart, and the festival was tied to me with
bonds - -
7)
I mentioned the rabbi of the city,
His image is still before me,
As he lectured before his flock,

With words so saturated with sadness;
I was crowded among his listeners,
Who included sons with fathers,
And I listened to the flames in his words -
To his voice that hewed flames;
Sometimes he would raise his voice in a roar,
As he preached his message and his discipline,
The faces of his audience fell and froze,
They were filled with worry;
I heard him on Shabbat Hagadol [65]
Where he talked about the days of yore,
Also on Shabbat Shuva and Chazon [66]
When he discoursed upon the "Hiding of the Face" [67]
And in the gatherings of the masses, at times of joy and sorrow,
The rabbi preached his words before all of the elderly and youth;
He was a merciful father to his community,
And a strength for the downtrodden and those who toiled,
To bring bread to their homes,
And to take out the curse [68] from the uncircumcised ones.
8)
Yes, this was the bustling street of the Jews, where living Judaism was nurtured,
And to separate with the boring "Lutnia", and with him also "Trzeciego Maja",
We also lived on these streets, I saw in them suffering and hope,
On them I played, studied, worshipped, and also accompanied to the Mikva [69]
Father of blessed memory, I was always joined him on his paths,
To his friends and the homes of his acquaintances, I was bound with bonds of yearning;
For he delivered lessons to private people outside of the hours of cheder,
To good students, of good fortune, who were born to the homes of the wealthy;
I accompanied him of my own desire, and perhaps also to his command...
That I should not waste my time, and that he would bestow of his Torah also to me;
I enjoyed these visits, for aside from the fact that they prepared treats for me,

582

On occasion I would also find some boys and girls there,
Especially at the home of Richert, where there were young people and games,
And I was able to slip out into the yard at times;
For I loved the garden of Berger, I tasted his fruits on occasion,
Also at the home of P. my friend, where I became close with his sisters,
They were beautiful girls, and I always desired their friendship,
With a Gemara open before me, more than once I placed their face before me...

9)
And "Stary Rynek", this is the market, I remember it on Mondays and Thursdays,
(Also, as usual, on the following day, Friday, the eve of the Sabbath),
The bustling of selling and buying, where all of the villagers gathered,
With their wagons laden with all good things, they placed their bounty before the Jews;
They hated and were jealous of the Jews, but they removed their hats to receive their money, And the Jews did business and purchased, enjoyed and ate to their satiation. There, in the east side of the square, the flag of the "magistrate" fluttered, That place of strange government, which I would pass by slowly, As I thought about the "evil eye" of the guard standing in the gate, (In the exile, I was afraid of police, always, when I was young). And to the left of that building, as I walked with my friend to his father's home, We passed in front of a mighty building, with a tower and gate around, That cast its heavy shadow, and its heavy bells tolled That "Kosciol" was a deterrent, in my imagination - the home of the demons, As I passed by - my hair bristled, I was afraid, and I hid my steps, My heart pounded fearfully, I was covered with strangeness and frights.

10)
I will recall further the market square, with its water wells at its belly,
Where I would visit in the mornings with pails, every day or two;
Then, with Tzirel Poiznerson, a widow, a woman of means,
Who stood at the entry gate, and raised the fee every year;
This Tzirel, who educated [70] her children, and she was so strong and wonderful
The fate so darkened her face, weariness was always with her.
Chaim Pinchas her eldest - his name was like fine oil,

He was observant and followed the Torah, he was upright and faithful to his people -

He was also a Maskil and knowledgeable, an activist and enthusiastic Zionist,

He went out barefoot, cut off, towards the Heavens in mourning for this father,

On the day that the weeping was bitter, and his agony spilled outward - -

11)

I will no longer wax great with words, and it is best that I run to the "Blotene" [71]:

This is "Ulica Blotna", the street upon which I grew up,

I worked at every hard task, and I also toiled in my studies,

Then the world war broke out, and the bread - Oh! It disappeared from the market,

I forgot previously to mention the farm of the gentile "Kaczok".

She was a Pole, crafty, conceited, who spoke Yiddish as a Jew,

However, her mouth only spoke sycophancy, and we were not admired in her eyes...

There were many good neighbors there, to my sorrow I do not remember their names,

Except for the families of Librach and Blatt, and this...Moshe Yosel who remains in my memory from among their children. Those were difficult years, laden with much suffering and fear, We endured famine and horror, and all the misfortunes came upon us together.

12)

However, from the midst of the clouds of agony, the stars gaze down and wink,

Bright lights in the darkness, which broke through and peeked from the clouds;

A that time, I toiled greatly in Torah, and I increased my wisdom and knowledge,

For in this father fattened me up, as much as his hand was able;

Then, many students streamed to father's cheder,

Including the children of the poor and struggling, but the vast majority from the well off,

These broke the famine in our home, and enabled us to provide our needs and food,

They studied, became wise and knowledgeable in the words and vision of the

Nation of Israel. These were the sons of Richert, Wader, the Katzes, and many others like them, To my sorrow I am not able to remember and name everyone by name, Also the children of Haron and Berger, and including Meir Mendzicki.

13)

From here, we will turn aside to another street, and go over to "Marshal Pilsudski". That is where Jews desired to live, among gentiles and the upper class;
There, the magnates were known to the poor, and every woman honored her husband.
We had lived on this street previously, when we first arrived in the city,
I was still young at the time, a boy, very, very young...
We lived in the large courtyard of that fat Szymanski,
A gentile, who blessed aloud, and also answered Amen to curses.
There, across from us what the "Zgoda", that building of great proportions,
The dwelling of the money powers, and the fortress of the reservoirs of "the futures"...
Jews mixed with gentiles there, and competed in the making of money,
Until the end approached, and they ere annihilated and lost with the multitudes
And, to differentiate, I will also mention the "tower of Richert", the source of all action and deeds, Where Zionism was commanded and nurtured, and the hearts were prepared for Redemption: There, the youth saw their home, and there they suckled strength and power, To fight the battles of their nation, to approach the inheriting of the Land; There "Hatzofim" conducted its activities, students came with teachers, This was an exemplary house, as a sign for generations to come.

14)

There were youth in Zgierz, young and very active Zionists, Mizrachists, Agudists, students of the Beis Midrash, scouts, Maccabeans; Even those on the margins and assimilationists whose entire life was based on false hopes, Destruction overtook them all, together we were judged for annihilation, Aside from the few, free people, whose soul yearned for redemption, They made haste and made aliya to the Land, and broke through even as it was locked; I will remember these in trembling, as they entered into Richert's home at night, As they walked in the shade on the streets, with energy and might as people of valor; They were accompanied by marching songs, as they

opened their mouths in song, And the voice of the leader shouting:
"Forward, left, right!" At the head of the marchers I remember, a lad,
intelligent and good, I do not know who was in the ranks, here my memory is
weak, But I recall the head of the marchers: It was Yoav Katz the drummer.
15)
I had counted your streets, from the market to the new city,
Walking and marching forward, towards "The New City".
There, there are gay and lovely houses, clean streets, polished,
There is no trace of the poverty of the poor, and old houses are no longer
seen;
There riches rule, and a new life turns over,
There a Jew walks with pride, walking as a man among men;
Near here, also the "tram", the king and pride of transportation,
Moving to and fro, going to Lodz and its crowds. From the time I departed
from the "tram station", many many years passed And I do not know what it
was doing during the days of Hitler, whether it to brought people to the
furnaces - -
16)
Oh remember! I will remember Zgierz, your residents and Hassidim
decorated,
With beards and clothing, peyos and splendid kapotes,
The Jews of the Sabbath and festivals, and the Jews of all the days of the
year,
Imbued with faith and awe, and also the "progressives" and those weak in
faith,
Manufacturers, men of commerce, and practitioners of all skilled crafts,
Men of initiative and deeds, and also those eat the bread of sadness;
From the "Tolaat Yaakov" store, I would bring goods for my mother
And from "Tzofe Shamayim" in the square - salted fish and bagels;
And Aharon Yitzchak, that is "Nechemia Itzel" who would "donate" [72]
greatly to charity, He would speak quietly and calmly, and he would bear all
depressing burdens on his shoulders; He was always wandering the streets, I
never knew where he lived, His image still stands with me, as his spittle ran
down his beard.
17)
From where did I purchase fruit and vegetables? This was from "Tzadok
Hatzahov" [73] Whose store was filled to the brim with the fat of the land He

had good merchandise, well preserved and set out He was assisted by the woman of valor, his wife Menucha. I loved his pickled cucumbers, and I especially purchased his radishes, (For my father loved radishes and he saw in them wondrous benefits, for those who suffered maladies of the liver and intestines, and other types of illnesses.) I did not purchase apples and pears, and this astonished his customers Until at one time he embarrassed me. In front of all the woman customers, As he saw me, he called out "Here he is, the radish lover!..." [74]

18)

I will also recall Kaszikoc the worker, a Jew who wove linens,
At the edge of the city, close to his farm, and here I will also recall the pitchers -
Pitchers of bubbling milk, that I brought to our home each day,
We loved this drink, which was our chief beverage,
Warm, fresh milk - I watched over the milking,
At "Frau Peltenberg", of Mielno, a quiet and dear family,
There were Germans, proper and good gentiles,
They did not pursue gain and honor, and they were not gluttons and drunkards,
Their son Ervin was calm and peaceful, and he was called "Charvona" [75] by us.
He also had an older sister, modest and refined;
Who would have possibly imagined that when the Hitlerist storm arrived,
That these would also turn into Volksdeutsche, and would let lose and behave wildly,
These too - Woe! - they took a rope, in the cruel hunt for Jews,
To rob them, frighten them and beat them, hang them and bring them to the skillets.

19)

There are many more people of Zgierz whom I feel obligated to mention,
Including Reb Rafael Henech Blausztejn, may G-d remember him for good,
Who taught us Gemara with Tosafot [76]. He was a "Sinai" and an "Up rooter of   Mountains' [77],
He fed our spirit with his didactics, and tied them into bundles;
He even prepared our lectures for Bar Mitzvah. How he toiled to impart to us, I   Remember,
The days were short at the time, and we studied by candlelight.

587

He was an exacting teacher. He was meticulous, he came to class seriously,
To impart his Torah that was his merchandise, and to spread from his
wellspring outward,
The sons of Sirkes, Szapira, Szternski, also Tevil the grandson of the judge;
I cannot remember them all, for the bed is too short to spread out,
There were many diligent lads, I walked with them all as a friend.
And my friend, David Abramowicz, who was an artist and a sculptor
together.
Who made aliya with me to the Land, and returned to the Diaspora out of
fear,
Lest he want for bread in the Land, and there he was torn apart,
I do not know what his fate was, did he perish in a furnace and was burnt?
And Yitzchak Weisbaum, who was pleasant, how pleasant was his friendship
to me,
We were good friends, and he was uprooted and disappeared with his wife.
I forgot Zalman the medic, he was a feldscher who could do everything
He was the chief sorcerer for any illness, from the head and heart to the liver
and spleen,
He was a redeeming angel to the suffering, and an expert craftsman for all
wounds,
He would extract teeth magically, and present medicine at the spur of a
moment.
I still have to obligation
To recall with blessing and good
Zodekowicz, Reb Mordechai Shmuel
Who waited and pined daily for the coming of the redeemer
He was a wise man who possessed nobility,
Who worked me hard in studying the calendar
He taught me the mathematics of "Iyb Tshzag" [79]
To determine the start of the month and the date of the festival - -
20)
Where are they, the Hassidim of Gur, the faithful of Strykow and
Sochaczew, fine people?
Destruction overtook them; they were cast upon the fields like dung!
Men of Torah and Divine service, experts in prayer and Kabbalah,
They were sacrificed to the demons; the angels of destruction trampled and
crushed them;
Your afflicted and shriveled bodies were torn up by the human beasts,

You did not come to rest in the grave, and your blood was not covered by the dust -

He will pass judgement on the nations, and it will be filled

with corpses [80] - the children of Israel who fertilized the

fields,

Who were pilled up dead and alive, in pits dug by the enemy.

May their names and memories be blotted out, may Amalek be destroyed forever!

And may the redeemer come to Zion, and the exile be swallowed up forever!!!

My soul weeps for you, woe! - Zgierz, what became of all your Jews?!

All of you left, and are no longer! - - not one will return to you;

Strangers devoured their hosts, and they applauded loudly your castaways;

We will erase the memory of your builders from you, the voice of

those that speak finely is silent,

All of it in the days of darkness, it was turned to dust and ashes

   And nothing is left of the nation except for a memory in a book - -

E. Eternal Lights

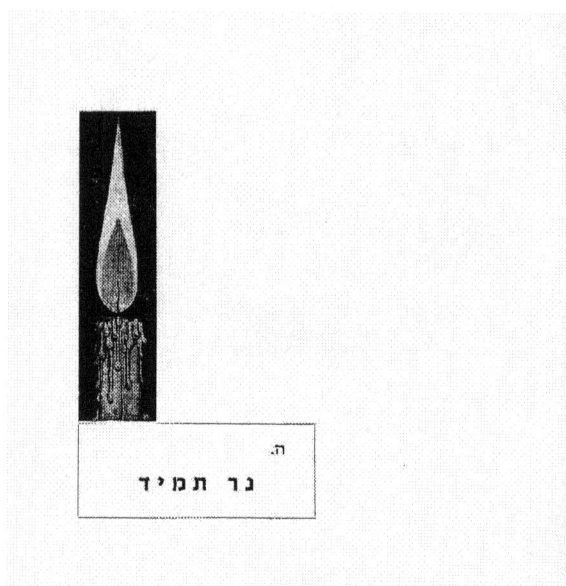

נר תמיד
.ה

Yizkor - May we remember

The natives of Zgierz - men, women, and children who were tortured and murdered in sanctification of the Name of G-d by the German enemy and their assistants, may their names be blotted out. May G-d remember them for good, may their souls be bound in the bonds of life, may their eternal response be under the wings of the Divine Presence with all of the holy martyrs of Israel. For the Avenger of blood will remember them, and He will not forget the cries of the oppressed

[Psalms 9:13. Also part of the Av Harachamim prayer recited on Sabbaths in memory of martyrs.]

With deep feeling, we memorialize all of the Jews of Zgierz who were cut off along with their families, without leaving anyone to remember and perpetuate their names.

In glorious memory of our teacher and rabbi
Rabbi Shlomo Yehuda Leib HaCohen of holy blessed memory, the head of the rabbinical court of
Zgierz, the son of the pious Gaon Rabbi Shalom Tzvi HaCohen of blessed memory.

He died in the holocaust in the year 5702.

The Zgierz rabbi, Rabbi Shlomo Yehuda Leib

the son of Shalom Tzvi Cohen of holy blessed memory, the outstanding preacher of peace, friendship and proper living. Rounded up in the Warsaw Ghetto at Umshlag Platz in 1942, and sent to Treblinka.

A memorial candle to the Ader family

Nathan and Esther Malka

My father Reb Nathan Ader the son of Shlomo David of Kalisz
My mother Esther Malka Ader the daughter of Aryeh Leib Prizer - they died
in the Warsaw ghetto
My brother Shmuel Ader, his wife Dvora the daughter of Tovia Kopel and
Yocheved Bumes,
And their two year old daughter Chana - they were killed in the Glowno
ghetto
My sister Dacha Daya, her husband Shalom Zigmund Rosenstrauch,
Their eight year old son Ulesh - killed in the Warsaw ghetto,
And their son Avraham Adash, 22 years old, who died after the war in
Germany in 1945.

Daya and Zigmund Rosenstrauch, Shmuel Ader

Perpetuated by their son and Brother Yaakov Ader and his family

In Eternal Memory

My father Reb Avraham Yitzchak the son of Reb Yosef Akerman, who died
in the city of Radom
My mother Esther Golda the daughter of Naftali Hertzke Gruzworcel, who
was murdered in the Radom ghetto
The wife of my youth Perl Akerman, the daughter of Moshe Eliezer Hofstein
My sons Avraham Yitzchak, 15 years old Shlomo, 12 years old
My daughter Chaya, 9 years old
My sisters: Perl Zigman (nee Akerman) and her husband Shmuel, with their
three sons and one daughter
Zisel Zaonce (nee Akerman), with her 2 daughters and son
Tzipora Friedman (nee Akerman), her husband Nachum and daughter
Sara Erlichman (nee Akerman) and her two sons
Her husband Reuven Erlichman who died in the United States
Chaya Weisman, her husband Shalom and her three children

All of them perished in the holocaust.

May their souls be bound in the bonds of eternal life.

Perpetuated by Moshe Meir Akerman

A memorial page to our dear ones:

Reb Hershel Tzvi Itzkowitz, who died before the war in Zgierz Glika Itzkowitz, who died in her old age in Tel Aviv

Their hands were open to all in need. Their sons and daughters

Freda and Azriel Klichman, their children Mindza, Yeshayahu, Moshe, and Rachel Leah killed in the holocaust
Shabtai and Leah Itzkowitz - died in the United States
Sarah and Shabtai Itzkowitz, their children Mindel, Leibish, and Moshe - killed in the holocaust
Shabtai and Rivka Itzkowitz, their children Mindel, Yona and Mendel - killed in the holocaust [2]
Yitzchak and Keila Itzkowitz, their children Mindel, Manya and Golda - killed in the holocaust
Leah and Shmulik Kuperman, their children David and Mindel - killed in the holocaust
Golda and Avraham Korzec, their children Dvora, Yona, and Hershel - killed in the holocaust
Frimet and Yehuda Rosenstrauch and their son Tzvi - killed in the holocaust
Moshe Itzkowitz - died in Israel
Their son-in-law Yosef Orvi - died in Israel

Moshe Itzkowitz

May their memories be blessed forever!

Perpetuated by Chana Globitzower and family, Paula and Refael Katz and family, Batia Orvi and family of the family of Zelig and Zisha Itzkowitz.

In memory of our dear parents

Our father Reb Yerachmiel Bornstein of blessed memory {photo upper right}, the son of Rabbi Avraham of holy blessed memory, the head of the rabbinical court of the holy community of Rawa.

Our mother Mrs. Freda Bornsten of blessed memory {photo to left}, the daughter of Reb Akiva Frenkel (who was known as Akiva Lerer - the teacher} of blessed memory. They perished in the Lodz ghetto

Our sister Rachel Bornstein (photo lower right} Perpetuated by Miriam Leah Bornstein of Milwaukee, United States And by Avraham Mordechai Bornstein of Bat Yam, Ramat Yosef

In memory of our aunts Dova and Esther Frenkel (the daughters of Reb Akiva Frenkel of blessed memory) our uncle Reb Yitzchak and Mrs. Beila (Frenkel) Weitzman, and their daughters Sarah, Chana, and Golda

A monument to the souls of our parents and sisters.

Our father Reb Yitzchak Menachem Bornstein (Reb Mendel Shelditzer), {photo upper right}, who died in the Lodz ghetto on the 17th of Elul, 5603 (1943)
Our mother Elka Bornstein (nee Wolf) {photo upper left}, killed in Auschwitz, 1943
Our sister Miriam {photo lower right}, killed in Auschwitz, 1943
Our sister Margalit {photo lower left}, killed in Auschwitz, 1943
Perpetuated by Sarah Lavie (died in Israel, 1974), Rachel Rader, Chava Liberman, Aharon Bornstein.

In memory of the Blanket family

My father Moshe Blanket the son of Menachem and Chana Liba - perished in
the Zosinki camp
My mother Sheindel blanket the daughter of Yitzchak and Rivka-Rachel
Rozalski - perished in the holocaust
My sisters Esther Hadasa (born in 1915)
Chana Liba (born in 1921)
Sara Hinda (born in 1922)
Rivka (born in 1929)
My brothers: Shlomo (born in 1926)Yitzchak (born in 1931) - all of
them perished in the Ghetto

**Standing: Shlomo, Chana Liba, Hadasa and Rivka. Sitting in the
center: the father Moshe Blanket**

Perpetuated by Shaul and Chava Blanket and their family

**In memory of my uncle and Aunt Avigdor Rozalski and his wife
Golda (nee Sperling)**

And their children Chana, Sara, and Adam - all of whom perished in the
holocaust.

My uncle and aunt Wolf Schmitanski - died after the war
His wife Bela Schmitanski (nee Rozalski)
Their daughters: Bluma, Chana and Adzia
All of whom perished in the holocaust

Perpetuated by Shaul Blanket

In memory of my dear grandfather and grandmother

Yeshayahu Flam
Chaya Freda Flam (nee Mintz)
Died before the war in Zgierz, in 1933

Perpetuated by Chava Blanket

Mrs. Feiga Berliner of blessed memory

Feiga Berliner of blessed memory, born on the 4th of Av 5655 (1895), died on 24 Adar I, 5719 (1959)

Fifteen years have passed from the bitter day when our dear mother Feiga of blessed memory was taken so suddenly from us. She was the wife of Rabbi Aharon David Berliner may he live long.

When we asked our mother to rest a bit from her journey, she would say that after 120 years, it would be possible to rest; however as long as man lives on earth, he has to toil and toil, whether it be in the doing of good deeds or in other matters that the Torah commands us, with our bodies or our money.

She would always find a "downtrodden widow" whom she could comfort and assist.

She learned her manner of education from her father, Rabbi Binyamin Sczaranski, and from her renowned Hassidic grandfather Rabbi Nota Heisdorf of holy blessed memory, as well as from her mother-in-law the Rebbetzin of Janow of blessed memory.

She not only succeeded in educating children, but also in educating adults. She arranged "Sabbath celebrations" for the adults. Every Sabbath, she would invite important men and women to lecture to the women about matters of Judaism, the Sabbath, etc.

She lived with a good name, and died with a good name.

May her memory be blessed, and may she intercede for the good for her family and the entire house of Israel.

May her soul be bound in the bonds of everlasting life. Perpetuated by her husband Aharon David Berliner Her daughters Chava Stein and Hadasa Orstein Her son Binyamin Berliner And her grandchildren

An eternal flame in memory of our family

Our father Baruch Baruch the son of Avraham Yitzchak and Zisel - perished in the holocaust. Our mother Feiga Lea Baruch the daughter of Aharon Yosef and Sheina Liba Borkowski Our sisters Bracha Baruch - who perished together with mother in the Lodz ghetto And Golda Rachel Baruch - who died in Auschwitz
Our uncles Yisrael Yehuda Borkowski, his wife and their three children. And Shalom Hirsch Borkowski, his wife and their children Moshe and Rivka All of whom died in the holocaust

The Borkowski-Baruch family in 1938 in Zgierz, next to the grave of Aharon Yosef Borkowski
May their memories be a blessing!
Perpetuated by Chaim Zalman and Ziskind Baruch and their families.

In memory of

My parents Izak and Lea Blank
My wife Esther Blank
My son Avraham Blank, 5 years old
My sisters Hinda, her husband Yitzchak Rosenblum and their 10 year old son
Esther Blank
Chana Blank

All of whom perished in the holocaust

Perpetuated by Baruch Blank of blessed memory.

In eternal memory

My father Binyamin the son of Yaakov Yitzchak HaCohen Bekerspiegel
My mother Yenta the daughter of Sender Gelbard
Brother Avraham the son of Binyamin
His wife Gittel and their child
My sisters Rhoda, Blima, Rachel, Rivka, Miriam and Esther
All of them killed in 1942 near Staszow

My grandmother Golda Goldberg, killed in the Lodz ghetto

Perpetuated by daughter Dvora Lempel of New York.

In eternal memory
Of my parents
David Brandt of blessed memory
Leah Brandt (nee Zusman) of blessed memory
Murdered by the Nazis in sanctification of the Divine name.

The murdered aunts and uncles
On my father's side Yochanan Brandt and his sister Esther Chaya of blessed
memory
On my mother's side Gershon Zusman of blessed memory, Shimon and
Melech Zusman of blessed memory

Perpetuated by Shlomo Brand of New York

In memory
Of our dear unforgettable parents
David the son of Mordechai
Hinda Esther the daughter of Yaakov
And our sister Gittel the daughter of David

Murdered by the German murderers

Perpetuated by Hirsch Leib Gross of Brooklyn, New York,
And Moshe Gross of Israel

In memory of our dear

My father Yoel Goldberg - died in Tel Aviv, 28 Tevet 5714 (1954)
My mother Tzila Zvia Goldberg (nee Dnishevski) died in Tel Aviv,
July 11, 1957

My sister Esther Erica Roter the daughter of Yoel and Tzila Goldberg

Died in Tel Aviv August 28, 1967

Perpetuated by Vela (nee Goldberg) and Yaakov Eshel

An eternal Candle to my dear ones

Sala, Ganek Milgrom, Minia, Esther, Moshe Goldberg, Hala and Avramek Kanerzuker, Bronia the daughter of Moshe, Aba Leibel, Esther, and mother Freda Goldberg.

My father Leibel the son of Eliezer Goldberg

My mother Freda Goldberg (nee Konski) - perished in Treblinka, 1942

My brother Moshe Eliezer - died in the Pozen camp

His wife Esther (nee Gershonowitz) and their daughters Bronia and Tzasia - perished in
Treblinka, 1942

My sister Mania Miriam, her husband Ganek Milgrom, and their daughters Bronia and Gina,
perished in Treblinka, 1942

My sister Sara Sala - perished in Treblinka

My sister Esther Etka - perished in Treblinka, 1942

May their souls be bound in the bonds of eternal life

Perpetuated by the daughter and sister

Hala Goldberg-Finkelstein, the only one who survived.

In memory of

My husband Avraham Kanerzuker the son of Yitzchak - perished in Buchenwald

My only son Yizik Kanerzuker - died in Lodz at the time of the outbreak of the war

My mother-in-law Shrpintza Kanerzuker - perished in the holocaust

My sister-in-law Frania Neuhaus and her husband - perished in the forests of Poland

My sister-in-law Chana Kanerzuker - perished in the forests of Poland

My brother-in-law Alter Kanerzuker - died in Russia

Perpetuated by Hala Goldberg-Finkelstein

In memory of my only son

Yosef the son of Shmuel and Mina Gotthelf

Born on June 10, 1937
Died during the holocaust

Yosef

Perpetuated by Shmuel Gotthelf

In eternal memory

Janek, Sara, father Chanoch and mother Esther Goldstein
Our father Chanoch Goldstein the son of Refael Asher (from Lancica)
Our mother Esther Goldstein, the daughter of Aharon and Chaya Kolski of
Podmiesce - perished
in Chelmno on April 10, 1943

Our sister Sara, her husband Yisrael Yehoshua Trunk the son of the rabbi of
Kutno, and their son
Refael-Raffi
(Sara and her son Raffi perished in Chelmno on April 10, 1943, her husband
Yisrael Yehoshua
perished in Russia.)
Our brother Yaakov - Janek - perished in the Vilna ghetto
Uncle and Aunt Menashe Sheiniak and his wife Lea (nee Kolski) - perished
in the Warsaw ghetto
Their daughter Sara and her husband Zelig Rosenzweig - died in the
holocaust
Their son Anshel Alec who was a soldier in the Polish army, died in 1947
after the war
Our uncle and aunt Yisrael Lencicki and his wife Tova (nee Kolski)
Their daughters Regina and Chana-Hanka - all of them perished in the
Warsaw ghetto

Perpetuated by the sons Peretz Goldstein and his family, and David
Goldstein-Di-Zahav and his
family

In memory of the Gornicki family

My wife and our beloved mother Raizel Gornicki (nee Freistadt)
My daughter and our sister Ruth Gornicki - perished in the Kaliski ghetto
My son and our brother Asher Gornicki, who fell in the War of Independence
in Ein Shemer

Perpetuated by Yosef Gornicki and the daughters Rivka Katz and Paula
Hinenberg

The Gornicki family - Reizel and Yosef, and their children Rivka, Asher,
Paula, and Ruth.

After the Germans captured our city, my father, sister Rivka, and brother
Asher fled to Russia.

After great suffering, they arrived in the city of Brisk on the Bog River.
After a short period, they were exiled to Siberia, where the worked in the
forests. My sister Ruth, my mother and myself remained in Zgierz. After
some time, the Germans separated us. My mother and sister were expelled
from the city. I succeeded in returning to Zgierz, however only for a very
short period.

At the same time, the Cohen family was together with me (they were related
to the Wachs family, the dentist), Tonia, Genia, and their elderly mother. We
became quite close. They received small packets from Leon Cohen of
France. The Cohen mother never forgot to give me something to taste.

One day, Tonia took ill, and the situation became serious. I and another
Jewish girl went to a German doctor who lived in the new houses outside of
the city. We requested that he come to the sick person, whose brother in
France is also a doctor. He refused and said: "Let her die!" Tonia died the
next day, holding in her hand a sugar cube that her brother had sent from
France. Her last word was "Leon?"

My mother and sister spent some time with a Christian woman in some
village, however my mother was captured by the Germans. My sister
received an identity paper from Polish friends. It had the name of Janina
Dominiak. She looked like a Pole, and succeeded in spending some time
with a Christian women in the town of Kaliska. One day, she went to visit
some of her friends in the ghetto. There the Germans captured her. I know

608

this from the testimony of a Jew whom I met by chance after the war. The expelled me from Zgierz to Lodz. There I worked in a laundromat. When the ghetto was liquidated, the sent me in a transport to Auschwitz, then to Freiburg, and finally to Mauthausen. I was liberated in May 1945, and after a difficult illness, I traveled to Poland. In the interim, my sister, brother, and father returned from Russia. We felt that there was not our place. We traveled to Germany, and from there we all made our way to the Land of Israel. My brother Asher came to Israel as a foreign army enlistee (Gachal). He fell in the War of Independence at Ein Shemer.

A memorial monument to the Glazer family

My dear parents Reb Eliahu Yaakov Glazer the son of Reb Eliezer of blessed memory, from Lodz
Dova Glazer the daughter of Mordechai Cohen of blessed memory
My father was the nephew of the renowned rabbi, the head of the rabbinical court of Zgierz,
Rabbi shalom Hirsch HaCohen of blessed memory.

They were murdered in Treblinka by the German enemy, may they be blotted out.

May G-d avenge their blood!

Perpetuated by Mordechai Glazer of Holon

My brother Eliezer the son of Eliahu Yaakov Glazer of blessed memory
His wife Genia (nee Rubin) of Lodz and their children
My sister Sara Segal the daughter of Eliahu Yaakov Glazer of blessed memory
My brother-in-law Mendel Segal the son of Yeshayahu Henech and their two children

All of them were murdered by the Nazi murderers.
Perpetuated by the brother and brother-in-law Mordechai Glazer of Holon

In eternal memory

My Uncle Reb Moshe Meir Brin of blessed memory from Sieradz
My aunt Pessa Brin (of the family of Mordechai Cohen) of blessed memory
The niece of the righteous Rabbi Shalom Tzvi HaCohen, of holy blessed
memory, the head of the
rabbinical court of Zgierz
Their son Mordechai Brin with his wife and two children
Their daughter Male Rosenberg (nee Brin) and her husband Michael of
blessed memory
Who perished in the holocaust.

Perpetuated by Mordechai Glazer of Holon

In memory of my wife and our dear mother

Sonia Glazer of the family of David Lebow of blessed memory
Died on the 5th of Iyar 5630 (1970) in Israel

Her parents David the son of Izak of blessed memory (from Kiev) and Leah
(Lula) Lebow,
Perished in the holocaust

May their memory be a blessing!

Perpetuated by her husband Mordechai Glazer
And the children David and Eli Glazer

In eternal memory of my parents

Right photo - **Shimshon Wolf**
Reb Shimshon Wolf Glicksman
The son of Reb Efraim Fishel And Rivka Ita Glicksman
left photo
Chana Rachel Birenstock, Dvora Glicksman

My sisters
Dvora, Freda Perl, Miriam, Yocheved

My brother Efraim Fishel

My mother-in-law Chana Rachel Birenstock

May their souls be bound in the bonds of eternal life

All of them were killed in sanctification of the Divine name in Tomaszow
Mazowiecki in the
years 1942-1943 - they were victims of Hitler's murders.

Perpetuated by Shlomo Glicksman of New York

611

In eternal memory

Of our unforgettable parents
Henech the son of Dov and Yocheved Grand

Our dear Sister and Brother
Bluma Leah and Dov

Killed in the Lodz ghetto

Miriam Rachel and her husband Isser the son of Eliezer Goldberg
And their children Zvia, Pese and Efraim Dov
Chaim Leib and his wife Miriam and son Yosef
Murdered in Auschwitz by the German murderers

May their souls be bound in the bonds of eternal life

Perpetuated by
Avraham David Grand of Israel
Guta Grand-Fein of Israel
Moshe Yaakov Grand of New York

In memory of my only child

Miriam Rachele Grand
The daughter of Sonia Antignes and Moshe Yaakov Grand

Perpetuated by Moshe Yaakov Grand of New York

In memory of

The family of Gedalia Goldberg
And the family of Tzvi Cohen

Perpetuated by Fabian Greenberg and his wife Regina the daughter of Tzvi
Cohen (United States)

In eternal memory

Of our uncle Chaim Baruch Gibralter

Our aunt Bella Gibralter the daughter of Chava and Meir Leib Zucker
who died before the war

Their adopted son
Meir Leib Rosenberg the son of Bracha and Isser
His wife Adela Rosenberg (nee Wrobel)
Their daughter Leah Rosenberg - all of them perished in the holocaust

Perpetuated by Chava Machtinger-Botzinski

In memory of my dear husband and father

Aharon Davidowitz

The son of Moshe and Tauba Goldstein
Born in Zgierz died in Tel Aviv on the 18th of Adar 5731 (1971)

Perpetuated by his wife Chana and daughter Lili Davidowitz

In memory of

Roza Davidowitz (nee Shmuelewitz)
The first wife of Aharon Davidowitz who perished in the holocaust

Moshe Otek Davidowitz the son of Roza and Aharon
Who was killed in the holocaust at age 15

Yechiel Chilek Davidowitz the son of Roza and Aharon
who died on the route from Teheran to Israel, age 6

Perpetuated by Lili Davidowitz

In eternal memory

Father Reb Nachum the son of Moshe Aharon Domnakowitz of Ozorkow
Died on 26th of Shvat 5686 (1936)

Mother Leah the daughter of Yaakov Lisner

My sisters Chana Rivka and her husband, Esther, Kreindel

My brothers Chaim Eliezer, Yosef Meir, Yaakov Zeev, his wife Reizel
(nee Fisher), two daughters Miriam and Beila and son Yosef Meir

All of them perished in the holocaust

My wife Tona (nee Jacob) Domnakowitz, died in Israel on 16th of
Nissan, 5622 (1962)

My son Menachem Domnakowitz the son of Avraham Nissan and
Tona, died in Israel at age 11,

11 Av 5703 (1943)

Perpetuated by Avraham Domnakowitz

In eternal memory

My father Moshe Eliezer Hofstein, perished in the Lodz ghetto
My mother Roiza the daughter of Naftali Hertzke Gruzworcel, perished in the
Lodz ghetto

My brother Avraham, his wife Chava the daughter of Bendet
And their daughters Pese (18 years old), Leah (16 years old)
Their sons Yosef (15 years old), Wolf (13 Years old) and
Leibish (11 years old)

All of them killed by the German murderers

My sister Esther and her husband Gedalia, the son of Berl Weisbaum

Murdered in Auschwitz, to where they were deported from Holland

My brother Yechiel Hofstein, died in Israel
His wife Sima Hofstein (nee Basiok)
Their two sons Yosef and Yisrael, and daughter Rivka

All of them murdered by Hitler's murderers

Perpetuated by the daughter and sister Chaya Hofstein of Holland

Tova Bliman Honigstock of blessed memory

The first days of 1939 already caused deep pain for the Honigstock family. Roza Honigstock, the mother of four daughters Yente, Paula, Tova and Rivka, died at age 46. The father Ber took full responsibility for the education of his two young daughters, Tova (14 years old) and Rivka (12 years old). The family had not even had a chance to recover from the tragedy of the loss of their mother when the Second World War broke out, which separated the family. Ber Honigstock fled to Lodz with Paula, Tova and Rivka. Yenta fled eastward to Russia.

The Honigstock family lived in inhuman conditions in the Lodz ghetto. The father and Paula worked in a leather factory, Tova in shoe workshop, and Rivka took care of the home. In August 1944, when the ghetto was liquidated by the German murderers, the Honigstock family was sent to Auschwitz. Only Tova survived this death camp. After many tribulations, she was liberated from Auschwitz in May 1945. She returned to Zgierz along with other survivors, hoping for a miracle - to meet members of her family. Perhaps there would be signs of life from Yenta from far-off, freezing Siberia, as well as Paula and Rivka. However there were only false hopes. Life continued on, and one had to prepare for the future.

Tova married Leopold Bliman in November, 1945. Even after founding her own family, she did not cut off her connection with the Zgierz natives. In particular, she kept in touch with the Fogel, Ber, Feldon, Freistadt, and Rotafel families.

She made aliya to Israel in 1957 with her husband and two children. There were the usual difficulties of acclimatizing; however there was the hope in the heart that everything would work out. Indeed, by the beginning of the 1970s, things were looking positive toward a good future. The son finished his engineering studies, and the daughter was studying in high school. However, a sudden illness overtook her, and on December 3, 1971 (15 Kislev 5732), our dear Tova went to her eternal rest, leaving behind pain and agony in the family, who loved and respected her so much. The last remnant of the Honigstock family passed on.

May her memory be blessed!

Perpetuated by her husband Leopold Bliman, son Dov of blessed memory, and daughter Irit

617

An eternal flame to the Honigstock family

Paula, father Ber, Tova, Rivka, mother Roza, and Yenta

{Lower right photo}
Tova Bliman (nee Honigstock), died on December 3, 1971
{lower left photo}
Dov Bliman the son of Tova and Leopold, who fell in the Golan Heights during the Yom Kippur war.

Perpetuated by husband Leopold Bliman and daughter Irit Bliman

An eternal memory to our dear grandfather and grandmother

Reb Yehuda Aryeh (Leibel) the son of Yitzchak Haron
Of blessed memory

Reb Yehuda Aryeh (Leibel) the son of Yitzchak Haron of blessed memory
And Feiga Rivka Haron the daughter of Reb Avraham Konski of blessed
memory
Who bestowed to us in our youth a great deal of love and dedication.

They passed away before the war in Zgierz

May their souls be bound in the bonds of eternal life.

Perpetuated by the granddaughters Chaya Halperin and Rachel Shapira

In memory

**Yosef Meir Haron the son of Reb Leibel
Roiza Haron (nee Bikowski)
Sara (Sarka) Haron**

Perished in the holocaust

Perpetuated by the family

In memory of my dear father

Avraham Haron

The son of Yosef Meir and Roiza
Born in Zgierz in 1909
Died in Tel Aviv on 1st Nissan, 5723 (1963)

Perpetuated by his daughter Elana Haron-Bar Chaim and their family

A memorial candle to my dear family
My father Avraham the son of Moshe Himelfarb, perished during the war in
Russia
My mother Tauba Himelfarb (nee Winogron)
My brother Yosef Himelfarb
My sister Hinda Rivka Himelfarb - perished in the Warsaw ghetto

Aunt and uncle Kasriel the son of Moshe Himelfarb and his wife Gella
Their son Chaim and daughters Necha and Hinda - perished in the holocaust

Aunt and Uncle Chaim Hirsch the son of Moshe Himelfarb, his wife, sons,
and daughters -
perished in the holocaust.

Aunt and uncle Shlomo and Dvora Fisher the daughter of Moshe Himelfarb -
perished in the
holocaust

Yissachar Mendel Lifschitz and his wife - perished in the holocaust

Asher Lifschitz and his wife - perished in the holocaust

Perpetuated by Moshe the son of Avraham Himelfarb and family

In memory of our dear family

Our father Reb Shaul Wizonski the son of Kopel and Feiga, perished in the
Abramkovo camp in
Russia, 1940
Our mother Reila Wizonski the daughter of Yeshayahu Hillel Bialostocki,
perished in the
Treblinka camp, 1940
Our sister Malka Mala Wizonski, perished in the Warsaw ghetto, 1942
Our brother Kopel Wizonski, perished in the Treblinka camp, 1940

Perpetuated by Chaya Wizonski, the daughter of Shaul and Reila
And Yechezkel Wizonski, the son of Shaul and Reila

In memory of our grandfather Reb Yeshayahu Hillel Bialostocki,
died in Zgierz prior to the war
Our uncle Reb Yitzchak Meir Bialostocki the son of Yechezkel, died prior to
the war
His wife Charna - perished in the Lodz ghetto
Their children Yechezkel Bialostocki, his wife Sonia (nee Bahrir) and their
two children -
perished in the Lodz ghetto
Eliezer Bialostocki - killed after the war in Lodz in a traffic accident
Berel Bialostocki - killed after the war in Lodz

Reb Shmuel Pinchewski, his wife Sonia Sara the daughter of Yeshayahu
Hillel Bialostocki and
their children - perished in the holocaust

Reb Yehuda Leibish Wyszogrodski - died in Israel
His wife Ita the daughter of Yeshayahu Hillel Bialostocki and their children -
perished in the
holocaust

Perpetuated by Chaya Wisonski the daughter of Shaul and Reila
And Yechezkel Wizonski, the son of Shaul and Reila

622

In Memory of

Our grandfather Yosef Mendel Wrozelowski, died before the war in Zgierz
Our grandmother Pese Wrozelowski, died in Canada, 1968

Our aunt Foigel Kolski (nee Wrozelowski), her husband, three daughters and
two sons, perished in the holocaust

Pessa Wrozelowski

Perpetuated by the family

In memory of

My parents Mordechai the son of Mendel and Frimet Wrozelowski
My sisters Sara, Rachel and Dina
All of whom perished in the Lodz ghetto

Perpetuated by the son and brother Yitzchak Wrozelowski

623

In memory of

My parents Yaakov Wrozelowski the son of Mendel, his wife Mira
Wrozelowski (nee Podmaska)
My sisters Sara Rachel and Hinda
My brothers Gershon Binyamin and Chaim Hirsch

All of whom perished in the holocaust

{A Polish poem, written by Dina, follows.}

Perpetuated by the daughter and sister Dina Wrozelowski-Borochowski and
family

Skąd niema powrotu...

Druty kolczaste prądem nasycone,
Więzili, pętali miliony ludzi.
Do drutów szli swe głowy przytulić
Aby się nigdy już, nigdy się zbudzić.
Komory gazowe... ognia czerwone języki,
Obojętnie tłumiły ludzkie okrzyki.
Władczy jak Niemcy, bez serca i duszy,
Naszych najdroższych na popiół kruszył — —
A ogień potężny, złowrogi w swej mocy
Wciąż głodny był ofiar, w dzień i w nocy. — —

Wy, ludzie-heftlingi; wy, ludzie-numerki!
Nie zapomnijcie tej poniewierki!..
Pomścicie ojców, dzieci i żony —
Zemsty wołają ofiar miliony.

DINA

In memory of

my father Avraham Wiczocki the son of Mordechai and Hinda, died in Lodz
after
the war, in 1947
My mother Chaya Sina Wiczocki the daughter of Mendel Wrozelowski
My sisters Rozka and Sara - all of whom died in Treblinka
My brother Yechezkel - died in the Polish army, 1938

Perpetuated by the son and brother Tzvi and Sara Wiczocki

In memory of

My father Oren-Zalman Wiczocki the son of Mordechai
My mother Sheindel Wiczocki (nee Moszkowicz)
Riva Woczocki, my father's second wife
My sisters Leah-Lula and Hindele
My brother Yechezkel

Perpetuated by the daughter and sister Alta Sara Wiczocki-Kaftan and family

In memory of

Our father Reb Shalom the son of Yosef of blessed memory Weinstein,
perished in the holocaust
Our mother Leah the daughter of Reb Yehuda of blessed memory Tamerzon,
died before the war
Our sister Altshe Swartzbard (nee Weinstein)
Our brother-in-law Menashe the son of Eliahu of blessed memory Swartzbard
Aliza the daughter of Menashe of blessed memory Swartzbard
All of whom perished in the holocaust
May their souls be bound in the bonds of eternal life
Perpetuated by Yehuda Leib Weinstein and Yosef Weinstein

625

In eternal memory of our dear ones

Our parents Rabbi Yaakov Mendel the son of Reb Yitzchak of blessed
memory Wechsler, the
head of the Beis Meir Yeshiva of Krakow *{photo of Yaakov Mendel on left}*
Chana Sara Wechsler the daughter of Reb Fishel Bunem of blessed memory
Hollander, a ritual slaughterer in Zgierz *(photo of Chana Sara on right}*

Our sister Freidel the daughter of Reb Yaakov Mendel of blessed memory
Izbitzki of Lodz
Our brother-in-law Yaakov Shimon the son of Reb Avraham of blessed
memory Izbitzki of Lodz
Their daughter Keila the daughter of Reb Yaakov Shimon of blessed memory
Izbitzki of Lodz
Their son Fishel Bunem the son of Reb Yaakov Shimon of blessed memory
Izbitzki of Lodz
Who were murdered by the Nazi murderers and their assistants in Belzec,
Stryj and Lodz, Polandin the year 5603 - 1943
May their souls be bound in the bonds of eternal life

Perpetuated by David Wechsler of New York
Yocheved Meltzer and Yehuda Wechsler of Israel

626

In eternal memory of
Our dear husband, father and brother
Leizer the son of Reb Menachem Mendel of blessed memory Wechsler

Who died in New York on 20th Tevet 5624 (December 25, 1964)

May his soul be bound in the bonds of eternal life

Perpetuated by the family:
Esther, Morris, Victor, and David Wechsler of the United States
Yehuda Wechsler and Yocheved Meltzer of Israel

In eternal memory of our beloved wife, daughter and mother

Feigele Wechsler the daughter of Reb Hirsch of blessed memory Wagman
Keila Yocheved the daughter of Reb David Wechsler

Who were murdered by the Nazi murderers and their assistants,
May G-d avenge their blood
In Belzec, Poland in the year 5703 (1943)

May their souls be bound in the bonds of eternal life

Perpetuated by David Wechsler of New York, Golda Rappaport
of New York.

627

In eternal memory of our dear parents

Our father Reb Hershel the son of Reb Shmuel Fishel of blessed memory
Wagman
Our mother Esther the daughter of Reb Fishel Bunem of blessed memory
Hollander, a ritual
slaughterer in Zgierz
Who were murdered by the Nazi murderers and their assistants
May G-d avenge their blood
In Belzec, Poland, 5603 (1943)May their souls be bound in the bonds of
eternal life

Perpetuated by Shmuel and Shlomo Wagman of New York

In eternal memory of our dear family

Our uncle Reb Chaim Yaakov Eisenschmidt the son of Reb Moshe David of
blessed memory
Our aunt Glika Eisenschmidt the daughter of Reb Fishel Bunem of blessed
memory Hollander, a
ritual slaughterer in Zgierz
Their son Avraham Mordechai the son of Reb Chaim Yaakov Eisenschmidt
of blessed memory,
his wife Freda, and their daughter
Their son Shmuel Leizer the son of Reb Chaim Yaakov Eisenschmidt of
blessed memory and his wife

Who were murdered by the Nazi murderers and their assistants
May G-d avenge their blood
In Belzec and Kielce, Poland, in the year 5703 (1943)

May their souls be bound in the bonds of eternal life

Perpetuated by the Wagman Family of New York and Israel
And the Wechsler family of New York and Israel

628

In eternal memory of the Warshawski family

Reb Menachem Mendel the son of Reb Fishel Warshawski of blessed
memory {photo}, died in
Zgierz in the year 5688 (1928)

His wife Gella (nee Kowalski), died in 5687 (1927)

Their sons
Reb Binyamin Meir the son of Reb Menachem and his wife Zelda and their
children, who
perished in the holocaust
Reb Moshe Yaakov the son of Reb Menachem, his wife and children who
died during the war

Their daughters
Chana Kriza, her husband and children Adolf and Regina
Baltsha Lidzworski - perished in the holocaust
Machtza and her husband Refael Feiner - perished in the holocaust
Gitla Fuchs - died in France

May their memories be a blessing

Perpetuated by Yaakov Fuchs of Nancy, France.

In eternal memory of the Warshawski family

Reb Menachem Mendel the son of Reb Fishel Warshawski of blessed memory *{photo}*, died in
Zgierz in the year 5688 (1928)

His wife Gella (nee Kowalski), died in 5687 (1927)

Their sons
Reb Binyamin Meir the son of Reb Menachem and his wife Zelda and their children, who perished in the holocaust
Reb Moshe Yaakov the son of Reb Menachem, his wife and children who died during the war

Their daughters
Chana Kriza, her husband and children Adolf and Regina
Baltsha Lidzworski - perished in the holocaust
Machtza and her husband Refael Feiner - perished in the holocaust
Gitla Fuchs - died in France

May their memories be a blessing

**Machla Wronski (upper right photo}, died on 17 Av 5710 (1950),
in Tel Aviv, age 110.**

**Eliahu Wronski (upper left photo) the son of Yaakov Moshe and
Machla, died in Israel on 28th
Iyar 5609 (1949)**
Perpetuated by Batya Orvi-Wronski and family

**Yosef Orvi-Wronski the son of Zeev and Feiga Lea {lower photo}
Died in Tel Aviv, 1974, on the 12th of Tevet 5734, aged 62.**

Perpetuated by his wife Batya, children Shay and Yaakov, and their families

In memory of

Reb Zeev Wronski the son of Yaakov Moshe and Machla
His wife Feiga Leah (nee Domkowitz)
Their daughter Miriam and her husband Yitzchak Weil and their children
Their daughters Rachel and Chaya

**Chaya, the father Zeev, Rachel, Yitzchak Weil the groom, Miriam the
bride, and the mother Feiga Leah
Their son Yaakov Moshe {*flower photo*}
All of whom perished in the holocaust**

Perpetuated by Batya Orvi-Wronski and family

In eternal memory of my unforgettable

Parents Reb Yitzchak Meir and Rachel Zilberberg, daughter of Reb Yosef
Konski
Brother Yehuda Leib Zilber, his wife Chaya and nine children
Sisters Sarah with her husband Wolf Zsimnawoda and children
Esther with her husband Leib Librach and daughter Sara
Genia with her husband Yitzchak Davidowitz
Chaya Eva, Golda, and Itka Yehudit

All of whom were killed by the Nazi murderers in the Warsaw ghetto

Perpetuated by Bronia Yora-Zilberberg of New York

In eternal memory of

Reb Mordechai Nathan Kuperstock
Rivka Kuperstock the daughter of Yosef Konski
Avraham Kuperstock, his wife and children Tovka,
Yoash, Genia, Chava, Chaya, Roiza Rozka,
and Yosef Kuperstock
All of whom perished during the time of the
holocaust on the Russian side
May their souls be bound in the bonds of eternal life
Perpetuated by the family

In eternal memory of

Our father Reb Yehoshua (Shia) the son
of Reb Yosef Konski
Our mother Rivka Rachel Konski the daughter
of Chaim Knig of Lodz
Our brothers and sisters Sara, Chaya and Avraham Konski
All of whom perished in the holocaust
May their souls be bound in the bonds of eternal life

Perpetuated by their sons and brothers Yehuda and Shlomo Konski and
families

An eternal flame to our dear

Father Aharon Zeidel the son of David and Rachel Leah (nee Haron), died in Israel on the 10th of Tamuz 5731 (1971) {upper left photo}
Mother Dina Zeidel the daughter of Yaakov Weingort, died in Israel on the 12th of Adar II , 5733 (1973) {upper right photo}

My brother David Zeidel the son of Aharon and Dina who perished in the Warsaw ghetto on Yom Kippur 5703 (1942) {lower photo}
May their memories be a blessing!

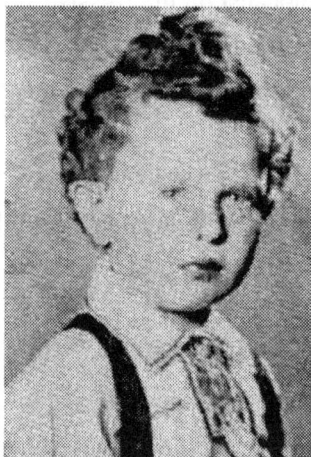

Perpetuated by their children Aryeh and Yaakov Zeidel

634

In memory of the Zilberberg family

Standing: Duvtzu and Fishek. Sitting: Rivka, the father Yitzchak Meir and mother Fela Zilberberg.

My father Reb Yitzchak Meir Zilberberg
My mother Feiga (Fela) Zilberberg (nee Koren)
My brother Fishel (Fishek) Zilberberg
My sister Rivka, and her husband and children
My brother David (Duvtzu) Zilberberg

All of whom perished in the holocaust

May their memories be a blessing!

Perpetuated by their son and Brother Yehuda Zilberberg and family of Tel Aviv, the only survivor of the entire family

An eternal flame

My aunt Rachla Lencicki
Her children Danial Lencicki and his wife
Yisrael Lencicki, his wife and two children
Fishek Lencicki and his wife
Fela Lencicki
Karola Lencicki
Mania, her husband and children

My aunt and uncle Reb Yosef Bialostocki, Mania Bialostocki (nee Koren)
and their children

All of whom perished in the holocaust

May their memories be a blessing!

Perpetuated by Yehuda Zilberberg

An eternal flame in memory of

My father Yehoshua David Zakelikowski the son of Yosef and Masha, died
on the eve of
Shavuot, 1939
My mother Freda Zakelikowski the daughter of Yitzchak and Malka
Torunczik, perished in the
holocaust
My eldest brother Yitzchak Yosef, who fought in World War II and was last
seen in 1945 in
Russia
My brother Hirsch Leib (Leibek) - perished in the holocaust
My sister Malka - perished in the holocaust
My grandmother Masha Zakelikowski (nee Kirshbaum) - died before the war

Perpetuated by Leah Zakelikowski-Lavie and family

In memory of our dear family

Our father Moshe Torunczik
Our mother Zelda Torunczik (the daughter of Reb Hershel Tzegelhof)
Our sister Dvora Torunczik
Our brother Shmuel Torunczik, all of whom perished in the holocaust
Our brother Binyamin Wolf Torunczik - fell in battle against the Nazis in 1944
Our brother Avraham Torunczik - died in 1951 in Germany

Their memory will not leave us forever

Perpetuated by Esther Lichtman and family
And Chaim Torunczik and family.

In memory of the Chaimowitz family

Our father Reb David Chaimowitz the son of Fishel
Our mother Dina Chaimowitz the daughter of Eliezer Korzerj - both of whom perished in the
Warsaw ghetto
Our sister Dvorale the daughter of David
Our brothers Velvele-Zeev the son of David
And Shmuel-Zalman the son of David - their place of burial is unknown

May their memories be a blessing!

Perpetuated by Yisrael, Fishel and Yaakov Chaimowitz and family

In eternal memory

Of my dear ones, who were victims of the Hitlerian murders during the years
1939-1945

My father Nachum Kaminski
My mother Sima Kaminski (Zilberg)
My sister Hela Kaminski
Her husband Shlomo Zilberg
And their son David Zilberg

Perpetuated by Yosef Kaminski

Who went through the camps during the years of the war.
After the war, he was liberated in Brussels, Belgium.
Now he lives in the United States.
Nobody else survived from the family.

In eternal memory of my dear family

My father Reb Mendel Togendreich the son of Moshe Leib and Roda -
perished in the Lodz ghetto in 1942 My mother Esther Chaya Togendreich
the daughter of Malka and Yaakov Moshe Wronski My brothers and sisters:
Yaakov Meir, Roiza Mindel, Feiga, Baruch Ozer, Tauba, Yisrael Wolf - all
of whom perished in the Auschwitz
My mother Esther Chaya Togendreich

My brother

May their souls be bound in the bonds of eternal life

Perpetuated by Rachel Haber (nee Togendreich) and family
The sole survivor of the family

A memorial candle to my family

My father Nachman Yechiel Yakir, aged 65
My mother Leah Yakir, aged 60
My sister Miriam Yakir, her husband and their children
My brother Mordechai Leib Yakir, his wife and their children
My sister Fradel Yakir, her husband Yisrael and their children Yitzchak and
Moshe

All of them perished in the holocaust.

May their memories be a blessing!

Perpetuated by Naomi Feitzuntka-Yakir

In eternal memory of

Our parents Reb Nathan David the son of Yosef Shaul Katz
And Tova the daughter of Moshe Shmuel Frankel
Our brothers Yoav, Menachem and Nachman
Our sister Rivka and her husband Yitzchak Tamerlin

May their memories be a blessing!

Perpetuated by the Katz brothers and sisters, and their families

In memory of

Zalman Weinstein (a weaver - he worked for the Jakubowitz's)

His wife Roiza (nee Diament) from Zadnoska-Wola

And their five children

All of whom perished in the holocaust

May their souls be bound in the bonds of eternal life

In eternal memory of my parents

Zeinwel and Tila (nee Hershkowitz) Cohen
My sisters Feiga, Dvora Gittel and Sara Cohen
Perished in the Warsaw ghetto in 1943
Perpetuated Chaya Jozefowitz-Cohen

In eternal memory of our parents

Daniel Gershon Jozefowitz, murdered in the Lodz ghetto
And Esther Malka Jozefowitz (nee Weisberg), perished in Auschwitz
My brother Yaakov Jozefowitz, perished in Russia, 1942

Perpetuated by the brother and sister Roza and Yosef Zelik Jozefowitz

In eternal memory of my parents

Shia Mendel and Chaya Freda Flam
My sisters Blima Rivka and Esther

Perpetuated by the daughter and sister Luba Jozefowitz-Flam

In memory of

My husband Leon Jalazni, who perished in Slonim, 1941
My beloved only daughter Halina, three years old, who perished in the
Warsaw [2] ghetto, 1942

Perpetuated by Dora Ber

In memory of the Segal family

Our Aunt and Uncle Chanoch Segal and his wife Keila (nee Ber)

Their daughter Leah, her husband Moshe Prashker, and daughters Henia and Mania

Their son Chaim-Yitzchak Segal, his wife Dora (nee Prashker) and three children: Moshe, Esther, and Frania Their son David Segal, his wife Sima (nee Weinzimmer), and children Dorka and Meir

Their son Mendel Segal, his wife Sala (nee Glazer) and two children

All of whom perished in the Warsaw ghetto

Perpetuated by Dora Ber and Esther Krol

In eternal memory of the Jozefowitz family

My father Mendel Jozefowitz the son of Zelig and Miriam, died prior to the war

My mother Dvora Jozefowitz-Kalski (nee Zaonce), perished in the Warsaw ghetto, 1943

My brother Chanina-Chuna Jozefowitz

His wife Hela (nee Jasczamska)

Their ten year old daughter Zosia

Perished in Majdanek, 1943

Dvora Jozefowitz-Kolski

Perpetuated by Chaim Jozefowitz and family

In memory of my wife and mother Zisa-Zosia Jozefowitz (nee Gledner) *{lower photo}*

My son and brother Mendel-Moshe Jozefowitz, 4 years old who perished in Auschwitz, 1942.

Perpetuated by Chaim Jozefowitz and Chana Jozefowitz-Alish

642

A memorial candle to the Jakubowicz family

My father Reb Mendel Jakubowicz the son of the scribe Hershel - died in
Zgierz prior to the war
My mother Machla Jakubowicz nee Ber - died in the Lodz ghetto in 1941
My sister Sheindel and her husband Breitberg [1] and their sons Mendel and
Shmuel
My sisters Ava
And Rosa - who was a member of Hashomer Hatzair and later of the
communist party. She spent
a year in jail for organizing a strike in the Petria chocolate factory.

My sister Bronia - who was a member of Hashomer Hatzair

All of them perished in the Warsaw ghetto in 1941

**Photo on right} Sheindel Jakubowicz Breitbard} {photo on left} Rosa
Jakubowicz}**

Perpetuated by Dora Ber-Jakubowicz
Esther Krol-Jakubowicz
and their families.

In memory

My only son Eliahu-Elias the son of Mendel Jakubowicz. Born on
September 18, 1936. Died in the Lodz ghetto in 1944.
My husband Mendel the son of Yisrael Hirsch Jakubowicz. An engineer of
machinery and textiles. Born in 1899 - died in the holocaust.

{Photo on left of Mendel} {Photo on right of Eliahu-Elias}

Reb Hirsch and Yenta Jakubowicz (He ran the Parizer Shtibel in his home
and cared for it for the sake of the mitzvah.)

Their daughters
Esther and her husband Mordechai Brafman and their three children
Miriam and her husband Moshe Bzozowski and their two children
Leah and her husband Nachum Rosenstrauch and their two children
Sima and her husband Leon Topolski

All of them perished in the holocaust - may their memories be for blessing!

Perpetuated by Malka Jakubowicz-Gothelf

An eternal flame in memory of the Librach family

Reb Eliahu Asher the son of Reb Meir Librach - perished in the Warsaw ghetto
His wife Nechama Blima Librach (nee Shapira) - died at the outbreak of the war
Berish Librach
His wife Natsha (nee Shapira) and their daughter Sarah - perished in the holocaust
Shmuel Leib and his wife Esther (nee Zilberberg) - perished in the Lodz ghetto
Their daughter Sara and son Izak - perished in the Warsaw ghetto

May their souls be bound in the bonds of eternal life.

Perpetuated by the daughters Yehudit Weinstein-Librach and family
And Naomi Czaranikowski-Librach and family

In memory of the Liberman family

My father Shimon the son of Yaakov Liberman
My mother Rachel Leah Liberman, the daughter of Shaul Dan Ginzburg - they perished in
Treblinka in 1942
My brother Eliezer the son of Shimon Liberman
My brother Nathan-Nota the son of Shimon Liberman
My sister Chana the daughter of Shimon Liberman

My aunt and uncle Roiza (nee Liberman), her husband Velvel Kaufman and son Yaakov
My aunt and uncle Mordechai Liberman, his wife, and daughter Feiga
My aunt and uncle Boaz and Masha Liberman, and their children Yaakov and Moshe
Yitzchak Liberman, his wife Mindel (nee Shteier) and son Yaakov

All of whom perished in the holocaust

May their souls be bound in the bonds of eternal life

Perpetuated by Yehuda Leibish the son of Shimon Liberman

In eternal memory

Of my unforgettable parents, brothers, and sisters, who were murdered in sanctification of the
Divine name - they were victims of the Hitlerian murders, and did not die a natural death.

My father Reb Mendel Lasker of blessed memory was a Strikover Hassid. He frequently visited
the Strikover Rebbe. We were seven children: four sons and three daughters. My father died on
the 11th of Iyar 5678 (1919), at age 57. May his memory be a blessing!
My mother Hinda of blessed memory. She was known as a righteous woman in our town. The
Germans, may their names be blotted out, took her to Strykow and she died there.

My eldest brother Fishel Lozer studied Torah up to the time of his wedding. Then Rabbi
Treistman took him as a faithful staff member of the slaughterhouse. Fishel Lozer was killed
under tragic circumstances. During the first world war, on a Sabbath night, when he went to
pray the Mincha (afternoon) service in the Vilker synagogue on Zachondia Street in Lodz, attired
in his silk frock and velvet hat, an armed German who was leading a deserter approached.
Suddenly, the deserter began to flee and the soldier began to shoot. However, the bullet hit
Fishel Lozer, who fell to the ground all covered in blood. His death shook up the entire town.

My brother Yitzchak, may G-d avenge his blood, did business with small objects in Zgierz, like
my father of blessed memory. He was murdered in the crematoria [3] by the Nazi murderers, may
their names be blotted out.
My brother Henech studied for a time in Otwock, where he made a name for himself in his
studies in the Beis Midrash. He died at the outbreak of the Second World War.

My eldest sister Sara-Blima, the wife of the manufacturer Yisrael Judkawicz, died in Pabianice
prior to the war.

My sister Gnedel, may G-d avenge her blood, the wife of Yehuda Leib Korczej, may he live long.
She was killed with her five children by the Hitlerist murderers, may their names be blotted out.
My sister Frumet, may G-d avenge her blood, the wife of Malenberg [1] of Lodz - murdered by
the German murderers, may their names be blotted out.

May these words serve as an eternal candle for the unknown graves.

Perpetuated by Shalom Tzvi Lasker of Paris, the only survivor, son and brother of the dear Lasker
family.

A memorial candle to my family

My father Reb Shmuel the son of Hershel and Zisel Landau - died in Zgierz
before the war
My mother Esther Malka the daughter of Yechezkel and Rachel Rosenbaum
My sisters Paula-Perl, her husband Yaakov Walman and their children
Chava and her husband
Tzisia (Tzipa) Ziskind, her husband and two children
Sara
Rivka
My brothers Moshe
Yechiel, his wife and two children

All of whom perished in the holocaust
May their souls be bound in the bonds of eternal life.

Perpetuated by Dvora Landau-Kratigner and family
The only survivor of the family. She was in Israel with her family from
1926.

A candle to the souls and the memory!

Our father Reb Yisrael Meir Mandelman the son of Yaakov and Rachel
Our mother Chana Mandel the daughter of Avraham Leibish and Necha
Bluma
Our sister Rachel Blima Mandelman
Our brother Eliezer Leizer Mandelman - all of whom perished in Treblinka
Our Uncle Reb Yosef Mandelman the son of Yaakov and Rachel - murdered
in Auschwitz
Our Aunt Rachel Leah Mandelman the daughter of Avraham and Sara
Kuperman - died before
the war, in 1935
Their children: Rechel and her husband Moshe Kinris and their six children
Leibel Mandelman, his wife and three children
Moshe Mandelman, his wife Rechel and their two children
Dvora, her husband Hirsch Leib Itzkowitz and their son
Netanel-Sana Mandelman
Dina Mandelman
All of whom perished in the holocaust
May their souls be bound in the bonds of eternal life.

Perpetuated by Refael and Nachum Mandelman, the sons of Yisrael Meir

648

In memory of my dear parents

My father Tzvi Aryeh Landau the son of Reb Pesach - perished in the Lodz
ghetto on 19th of
Sivan, 5702 (1942)
My mother Hadasa Aida Landau the daughter of Aharon Eliezer and Dina
Rubinstein of Lodz
Perished in the holocaust in 5705 (1945)

Tzvi Aryeh and Hadasa

The gravestone of Tzvi Aryeh and Hadasa Landau in the Lodz cemetery
{Hebrew inscription: Here is buried Tzvi Yehuda [4] the son of Pesach
Landau, died on 19th Sivan 5702. Polish inscription: Pamieci ukochanej
matki Idesy Landau Ktora Zginela z Rak Hitlerowskich, Corka Zieci
Whuczna. (In memory of our beloved mother Idesy Landau who perished at
the hands of Hitler, by the daughter, children and grandchildren.)
Perpetuated by their daughter Dvora Landau-Frugel and family.

In their memories

{Upper left photo} My grandfather Reb Yechiel Meir Mankita of blessed memory, who perished in the holocaust

{upper right photo} My grandmother Mrs. Chana Mankita of blessed memory, nee Korzerj, who perished in the holocaust

{Lower left photo} My uncle Avraham Mankita of blessed memory, who perished in the holocaust

{Lower right photo} My aunt Chava Mankita of blessed memory, my aunt Tauba (Yona) Korzerj of blessed memory (nee Mantika), and her daughter, who perished in the holocaust [5]

Perpetuated by Naomi Mankita

650

Reb Menachem Mankita, in his memory

Menachem Mankita} [6]

Oh how I loved to hear the stories of my dear father, Reb Menachem Mankita of blessed memory, about his life in Zgierz and the household of his father, my grandfather, who was known as a warm Jew. He was Reb Yechiel Meir of blessed memory. His wife, my grandmother, was Chana Reizel of blessed memory. On many occasions, I saw in the eyes of my spirit that town, with its houses, gardens, houses of study and Jews, who were such colorful characters in their traditional Jewish dress and with their fundamental righteousness. The town was known for its Jews and its unique righteousness.

The Korzerj family, with its many branches, many children and well-known strength, was known by the nickname "Kurziklech", which means chicks in the language of opposites [7], to accentuate their great strength. The father, my father's maternal grandmother, the father of Chana Reizel of blessed memory, was Reb Eliezer Korzerj of blessed memory. He was a well-known scholar, with a long beard flowing over his cloak. Many in the town studied Torah from his mouth, and everyone knew him for his praiseworthy

651

character. He conducted a traditional Jewish home, good and open t o help others. Nobody would ever leave his home hungry. There were always pots of hot food on the oven, which his righteous wife Zisel of blessed memory prepared, and the joy would be great. Reb Eliezer of blessed memory had fourteen sons and daughters, and there would always be many grandchildren running around his house, including my father Menachem of blessed memory, his twin sister Tauba of blessed memory, his sister Chava of blessed memory, and his brother Avrahamel of blessed memory. The joy would be particularly great on festivals, when the teacher would not instill fear upon the students. This would be so

even with Reb Yitzchak the teacher, a unique person, who attempted to "instill" Torah and commandments into the brains of his stubborn students, whose hearts tugged at them to go outside for a game of basketball (a game played with a unique ball, made of rags). When does one play basketball? - Please mention it silently! -Basketball in the home of an Orthodox Jew?...

My grandfather, the revered father Reb Yechiel Meir of blessed memory, educated his children to fear G-d and love their fellowman. He was a well-known activist in Agudas Yisrael

[8] in the town and was prepared to struggle for his ideas -but nevertheless he was a pure, upright, popular Jew. He was beloved by his fellowman. Thus, between the home of the grandfather Reb Eliezer Korzerj of blessed memory and the home of the father Reb Yechiel Meir of blessed memory, the youthful Menachem - my father, grew up, absorbing the goodness and light from both homes.

Time passed, and he was already a young man, dressed in the traditional Jewish garb of a dark cloak and a black Jewish hat, a special type of "kaskat" with small flaps. He wore the hat always even when he tended toward coquettishness, the one vice he permitted himself in the society of Orthodox Jews. His shoes were so shiny - he was a scholar, and his clothes must not have any patches. He began working in a profession that would earn him a livelihood. He did not forget about his studies in the Beis Midrash, however at this point he wished to learn a trade. Since it was known that there was a clothing factory in Zgierz, he began to study weaving with great diligence. In the meantime, he got married. His bride was also from Zgierz, the daughter of Reb Shalom Hirsch Shevach of blessed memory and his pious wife Chava Rachel of blessed memory. His bride, my dear mother Tzipora, may she live long, expressed her desire to marry my father of blessed memory, however she insisted on only one condition: that they build their faithful Jewish home only in the Land of Israel, which was known as Palestine at the time. He agreed to this, and, thus, six weeks after their marriage, the young couple set out for the Land of our Fathers. They were accompanied by the young brother of my mother, my Uncle Shmuel, may he live long. They already had some family in Israel, the brother of my mother, my Uncle Avraham may he live long, who made aliya to the Land in 1925 as a pioneer and settled in Jerusalem.

Thus the three of them made aliya: my father of blessed memory, and, may they live long, my mother and her young brother Shmuel. Only her sister Perl Dina of blessed memory remained with her parents. This was in the year 1935. Of course, they decided to settle in Jerusalem, near to the eldest brother Avraham Shevach, who was already established in the Land. The times were difficult and the Jewish community was small. Earning a livelihood was very difficult; however they never entertained any thoughts of returning to Poland, where the large family could help and sustenance could easily be obtained. The letters "home" to Zgierz were filled with descriptions of the good life in our homeland which was being built, and about the good sustenance which could be found...

The Second World War broke out, which brought with it the destruction of the Jews of Europe. The dire fate did not pass over the town of Zgierz, with its dear Jews. The communication with the family was severed, however there was still the hope that the situation would return to its former state, and that the ill fate would not affect our dear ones...

Here in the Land, several years passed. Since the livelihood was scarce in Jerusalem, the members of the small Mantika family decided to move to Tel Aviv. My father of blessed memory worked for many years as a weaver, the field in which he was an expert from his youth. He never aspired to greatness. He conducted a warm and faithful Jewish home, in the true sense of the word. Even though earning his livelihood absorbed most of his time, he did not forget the life of the "spirit". He spent his spare time inside the synagogue, among Jews who were as pious as he was, studying Talmud and Mishna. His voice was particularly good. He loved to lead the prayers and to sing pleasantly in front of the congregation who loved his prayers. He served as the prayer leader on the High Holy Days, not in order to receive a reward, but because of the exaltedness of his spirit.

Thus, time passed, until the bitter day arrived - the 28th of Cheshvan 5629 (November 20th 1968). My dear father felt ill and within a few moments returned his pure soul to his creator. He was only 57 years old. May his soul be bound in the bonds of eternal life, and may his memory be blessed!

Perpetuated by Mrs. Tzipora Mankita and his daughter Naomi Mankita

In eternal memory of my dear family

My father Moshe Meir Skosowski - died in Zgierz prior to the war
My mother Sara Hinda (nee Zucker) - perished in the holocaust at age 74
My sister Resha, her husband Chanoch Waldman and five children - perished
in the holocaust
My brother Yeshayahu, his wife Tzesia (nee Lewkowitz) and their sons
Aryeh and Yitzchak -
perished in the holocaust
My brother Avraham and his wife - died in Israel
My brother Yaakov - died in Paris
My brother David - died in the United States
My brother Baruch and his wife - perished in the holocaust
My brother Noach - perished in the holocaust
May their souls be bound in the bonds of eternal life!

Perpetuated by Zeev and Bella Skosowski of Israel

In memory of

Our uncle Wolf Slodkowitz
Our Aunt Mina Slodkowitz, the daughter of Avraham Leibish and Necha
Blima Michowitz
Their son Refael Slodkowitz and his wife
Their son Eli David Slodkowitz
Our Uncle Refael Michowitz the son of Avraham Leibish and Necha Blima
Our aunt Tzipa Michowitz
Their daughter Necha Nechtzia - all of whom perished in the holocaust
Our grandfather Avraham Leibish Michowitz - died of hunger in the Lodz
ghetto

Perpetuated by Refael and Nachum Mandelman
And Meir and Chana - the children of Yisrael

A memory candle in memory of

My father Nathan Dov Liberman the son of Yaakov and Golda
My mother Sara Feiga Liberman, the daughter of Gershon and Yehudit
Dersler
Who perished in the holocaust
My brother Gershon Liberman the son of Nathan Dov - died in Russia, 1942
My sister Leah Trauanowski the daughter of Nathan Dov Liberman and her
son Chaim - perished
in the holocaust
My sister Chana Liberman - died before the war in 1938

May their souls be bound in the bonds of eternal life.

Perpetuated by Leibish Liberman and family

A memorial candle in memory of

My dear family members who were murdered by the Germans in the
Treblinka death camp
My father Emanuel the son of Yisrael Milinarski, 44 years old
My mother Rivka the daughter of Yedidya Milinarski, 42 years old
My brother Avraham the son of Emanuel Milinarski, 14 years old
My sister Reizel the daughter of Emanuel Milinarski, 4 years old
May their souls be bound in the bonds of eternal life.

Perpetuated by Yedidya Milinarski and family

In the merit of the souls of our dear parents of blessed memory

Our grandfather Reb Shlomo the son of Eliezer Sirkes - died in Jerusalem on
the Sabbath, 18th of
Cheshvan 5702 (1941)
Our grandmother Mrs. Sara Sirkes the daughter of Mordechai Helman - died
in Warsaw on the
29th of Cheshvan 5688 (1928)
Our father Reb Eliezer the son of Reb Shlomo Sirkes - died in Jerusalem on
the 25th of Elul 5712
(1952)
Our mother Chaya the daughter of Reb Chaim Rotenberg - died in Jerusalem
on the 25th of
Sivan 5722 (1962)
In memory of our brothers and sisters who were victims of the holocaust,
may G-d avenge their
blood

Leibel Sirkes, his wife Chana the daughter of Reb Binyamin Fogel and their
daughter Sara
Ita, her husband Yosef Rotenberg the son of Reb Mordechai Kalman and
their daughter Sara
Hena, her husband Moshe Strykowski the son of Reb Lipman and their

656

children Mindel and
Daniel
Mirel, her husband Yaakov Bhareir the son of Reb Moshe Yehoshua and
their son Chaim
Mordechai Sirkes, his wife Chana the daughter of Reb Menachem and their
children Moshe
Mendel and Chaim
Fela the daughter of Reb Tzadok Strykowski (the wife of our brother
Avraham, may he live long)
and their son Chaim

May the earth not cover up their blood!

Perpetuated by Yehudit, Pinchas, Avraham, Peretz, Shmuel and Miriam

In their memory!

Reb Shlomo the son of Eliezer Sirkes - died on the holy Sabbath, 18th
Cheshvan 5702 (1941)
Sara Sirkes the daughter of Reb Mordechai Helman - died on the 28th of
Cheshvan 5688 (1928)
Reb Daniel the son of Shlomo Sirkes - died on the holy Sabbath, 9th of Adar
II, 5725 (1965)
Nechama Sirkes the daughter of Yaakov Aviezer Blas - died on 16th of Adar
5729 (1969)
Yaakov Aviezer the son of Daniel Sirkes - died on 9th of Tishrei, 5707
(1947)
Mordechai the son of Daniel Sirkes - died on 28th of Adar 5724 (1964)
Rachel the daughter of Daniel Sirkes - died on 9th of Tevet 5696 (1936)

May their souls be bound in the bonds of eternal life!

657

The farewell with the family. Mrs. Chaya Sirkes takes leave of her sons and daughters in Poland, Kolumna, 1938.

Upper row: Dvosia, Reb Refael Henech Blostein, Pinia, Leibel and Ita Sirkes. In the middle row: Pinchas, Tzvi and Daniel Sirkes, Yehoshua Kaufman. In the bottom row: Reizel Kaufman, Sara, Nechama and Chaya Sirkes. (Photographs in 1915).

An eternal candle in memory of the family of Shimon Sribnik

Reb Shimon the son of Nathan Nota, the son of Reb Leibish Sribnik of
blessed memory (who
was known as Reb Leibish Bialer)
Sheindel Sribnik the daughter of Reb Moshe Yaakov Kopel of blessed
memory, from the city of
Pabianice
They were murdered in the Warsaw ghetto on the 13th of Av 5702 (July 27,
1942)

Their son Leibish Melech Sribnik, murdered in the Pawiak jail during the
Warsaw ghetto uprising
in 1943
His wife Guta the daughter of Reb Tovia Kopel Bumes - perished in the
Warsaw ghetto

Leibish Melech a communal grave of the Sribnik family - details cannot
be made out

Sabina (nee Sribnik) and her husband Meir (Max) Witekowski from
Kutno. They were sent along with their son David Nota to a death camp
where they perished at the hands of the German murderers.

David Nota (Right)

Leah (Lausha) Sribnik and her husband Shraga (Pawek) Rosenman. They perished in Zoludek (Byelorussia) on the 24th of Iyar 5702 (May 11, 1942).

The young girl Mindel Chaya the daughter of Shimon Sribnik
Our dedicated teacher will also remain in our memory: Rivka the daughter of Reb Yosef Kirsh of
Strykow, who perished along with my parents in the Warsaw ghetto
Perpetuated by Moshe Yaakov Sribnik and family, the only survivor

A memorial page to Reb Shimon Landau of blessed memory

Reb Shimon Landau (known as Reb Shimon Annower) was one of the honorable residents of the city of Annow. He owned much property, forests, and a sawmill.

Reb Shimon Landau had family connections to Zgierz. His two sons and daughter married people from Zgierz. His eldest daughter Leah (Lehka) married the scholar Reb Leibish Sribnik, the son of Rabbi Nathan Nota of holy blessed memory who was the Rabbi of Biala and the brother of the renowned Hassid and scholar Reb Noach of holy blessed memory. Reb Noach was the rabbi of Pieczenia (he was known as Reb Noach Pieczener). His second daughter Perl married Reb Yosef (Yosel) Librach, the son of a distinguished family which was rooted in Zgierz. Reb Shimon's son, Hirsch Leib, was the father of the brothers Pesach and Eliezer Landau, a well-known family of merchants and manufacturers in our town. Since Reb Shimon Landau was connected to Zgierz and its Jews, he donated four gigantic thick trunked trees to the synagogue. These trees were the best trees of his forest. They were to be used for the support pillars in front of the sanctuary. These were splendid pillars, in classic Corinthian style, which with their height and beauty blended in harmoniously with the monumental holy ark, also made out of wood. They were rich in Renaissance style etchings and decorations, and they added an air of majesty and splendor to the house of G-d.

Dedicated by Moshe Yaakov the son of Reb Shimon Sribnik (a descendent of Reb Shimon Landau).

In eternal memory of the dear

Shimon Henech Sribnik the son of Leibish of blessed memory
Rivka Sribnik (nee Warshawski)
Their sons: Noach, his wife and two children
Baruch, his wife (nee Berkowitz) and two children - all of whom were killed
by the Hitlerist murderers
Moshe - died before the war
Perpetuated by the son and brother Leibish-Leon Sribnik and family of New York

662

In memory of the Kaufman family
My father Abba Kaufman
My mother Tsharna Kaufman (nee Sribnik)
My sisters Rachel and Golda
My brothers Velvel and Shimon
All of whom were murdered by the German murderers
Aryeh - died in Russia
Perpetuated by the daughter and sister Sara Kaufman-Sribnik of New York

An eternal flame to our dear parents

Reb Leizer Akbia the son of Mordechai and Gnendel Esther Malka
Akbia the daughter of Baruch and Nechama Podmaski Perished during
the holocaust in Konin

Leizer and Esther Malka

Their memories will not depart from our hearts
Perpetuated by the daughters Mira Akbia-Stopai and family in Israel
Leah Akbia-Shprei and family of the United States

An eternal flame to their memories

Our grandfather Leib Feldon the son of Moshe and Gittel {upper right photo}
He was born in Zgierz, and died in 1935, before the war.
Our grandmother Sara Feldon the daughter of Chaim and Mirel Bornstein {upper left photo} -
perished in the holocaust in Glowno
Our uncle David Podmaski - died in Russia
His wife Sheva and their sons Baruch and Sender - perished in the holocaust

May their souls be bound in the bonds of eternal life

Perpetuated by Mira Akbia-Stopai and Leah Akbia-Shprei

An eternal flame

To Reb Yaakov Fuchs (photo}
the son of Avraham and Sara - died in the 22nd of Elul 5734
(September 9, 1974) in France

Perpetuated by his wife Freda Fuchs

In memory of

My father Wolf Slodkowitz the son of Moshe Aharon of Zgierz
My mother Freda Rachel Slodkowitz the daughter of Yisrael Shmidniakow of
Liskowica
My sisters Yocheved, aged 16; Masha, aged 14; Chana, aged 12; and my
brother Meir, aged 9
My uncle Yitzchak Slodkowitz with his wife and children

All of whom perished in the holocaust

My aunt and uncle Nachum Slodkowitz and his wife Mania (nee Sperling)
and their two sons
My aunt and uncle Tovtzia Slodkowitz, her husband and their children
My aunt and uncle Tovtzia Slodkowitz, her husband and child [9]

Perpetuated by Shmuel Slodkowitz and family

665

An eternal candle to my dear family

My father Reb Avraham the son of Reb Dov Fuchs of blessed memory -
perished in the holocaust

My mother Sara the daughter of Reb Shlomo Yitzchak Laslau - died in the
Warsaw ghetto

My brother Moshe the son of Reb Avraham Fuchs of blessed memory - died
in the Polish army in
the year 5679 (1919)

My brother Yosef the son of Reb Avraham Fuchs of blessed memory, his
wife and their children -
perished in the holocaust

My brother Dov (Berl) the son of Reb Avraham Fuchs of blessed memory,
his wife and their
children - perished in the holocaust

May their memories be a blessing!

Perpetuated by Yaakov Fuchs of Nancy

My father Reb Avraham Petachia Finkelstein the son of Mendel and Dvora -
died in Zgierz, 1932

My mother Freidel Finkelstein (nee Offenheim) -- perished in Majdanek

My brother Leibel Finkelstein, his wife Frania, and their son Avraham

My brother Eliahu Finkelstein and his wife Rozka

My sister Esther Malka, her husband Avraham Yaakov Zelnick and their
daughter - perished in
the holocaust

My uncle Yisrael Finkelstein the son of Mendel and Dvora - died in Russia

My aunt Mania Finkelstein (nee Itzkowitz) - perished in the holocaust

Their son Mendel - died in Russia

Their daughter Dvora

Their daughter Rivka-Roda

Their son Leibish - all of whom perished in the holocaust

My uncle Reb Yoel Kauawski and his wife Paula (nee Finkelstein) - perished
in the holocaust

May their souls be bound in the bonds of eternal life

Perpetuated by Sara Bernstein-Finkelstein, Rachel Weisbrot-Finkelstein, and
Rivka Eichler-
Finkelstein of the United States

666

In eternal memory of our beloved dear ones

Our father, modest and discreet, of a fine soul and pure heart, Reb Shimon the son of Shlomo
(Zalman) Fisher of blessed memory - died on 27th Tevet 5691 (1931)
Our mother, who dedicated her soul in love to the welfare of her children, Chana the daughter of
Reb Moshe Yaakov Kopel of blessed memory (of Pabianice) - perished in the Lodz ghetto, 13th of Cheshvan 5702 (1941)
Our sister, the lovely girl, who was cut off in her youth, Sheina Malka the daughter of Shimon Fisher - died on 5671 (1911)
Our good and boundlessly dedicated sister Bina the daughter of Reb Shimon Fisher - perished at
the hands of the German murderers during the holocaust, may G-d avenge her blood.
Bina, our dear beloved sister, we always mention your name with tears.

May their souls be bound in the bonds of eternal life.

Perpetuated by Wolf Fisher of Israel, Tzasha Rosenblum Fisher of Montreal, Yaakov Fisher of
Israel, Mary Fishman Fisher of Montreal

A memorial candle to

Rota the daughter of Reb Yaakov and Celina Fisher of blessed memory -
perished in the Lodz ghetto in the year 5702 (1942)
Our beautiful and unforgettable daughter Celinka who was cut off by the
hands of the German murderers in the Lodz ghetto in the year 5702 (1942)
May their memories be blessed and their souls enjoy the Garden of Eden
Perpetuated by Zeev Fisher

A memorial candle to

My uncle and father-in-law Reb Yakov the son of Zalman Fisher of blessed
memory of Lodz [10]
And his eldest son Shlomo (Salo) Fisher
Who perished in the holocaust, may G-d avenge their souls

Perpetuated by Zeev Wolf Fisher of Israel

A memorial candle to the family of Reb Zalman Fisher

Reb Shlomo Zalman the son of Reb Zeev (who was known as Reb Wolf
Toshiner) Fisher of
blessed memory.
One of the honorable citizens of the city of Kutno. He was a generous
person, a merchant of
forest products, and the owner of the profintzia [11] in the reagion of Kutno.
In his latter years,
he moved to Warsaw and their he died.

His wife Tzipora of blessed memory (of the Librach family of Ozorkow)

Their sons:
Reb Leib Fisher and his wife Zisa Reizel of blessed memory (nee Katz), of
Kalisz
Reb Moshe (Moritz) Fisher and his wife Mina of blessed memory (nee
Monitz) of Warsaw
Reb Wolf (Vovtshe) Fisher and his wife Guta of blessed memory (nee
Pinkus) of Lodz
Reb Feivish Fisher and his wife Golda of blessed memory (nee Robenlicht)
of Lodz
Reb Mordechai Fisher and his wife Esther of blessed memory of Ozorkow
Reb Shimon Fisher and his wife Chana of blessed memory (nee Kopel) of
Zgierz
Reb Yaakov Fisher and his wife Celina of blessed memory (nee Wishlicki) of
Lodz

Their daughters:
Riva the wife of Reb Avraham Perla of New York
Leah the wife of Reb Leib Eizenrobicz of Piotrkow
Gella the wife of Reb Yudel Librach of Lodz
Mania the wife of Reb Yitzchak (Izak) Berger of Warsaw
Riva the wife of Reb Avraham Perla of New York

May their souls be bound in the bonds of eternal life

Perpetuated by the grandchildren:
Marila Mandelzon (nee Fisher) of Israel
Zeev Wolf Fisher
Yaakov Fisher of Israel
Tzasha Fisher Rosenblum (nee Fisher) of Canada
Mary Fishman (nee Fisher) of Canada

A memorial candle to the family of Reb Moshe Yaakov Kopel

Reb Moshe Yaakov the son of Reb Elimelech of blessed memory Kopel
A scholar in both religious and secular studies, a proud Jew, one of the
honorable citizens of the
city of Pabianice.
His wife Bina the son of Reb Shimshon Poznanski of blessed memory

Their daughters:
Mindel, her husband Reb Eliahu Hirschberg of blessed memory of Zadonska
Wola
Chana, her husband Reb Shimon Fisher of blessed memory of Zgierz
Sheindel, her husband Reb Shimon Sribnik of blessed memory of Zgierz
Hinda, her husband Reb Menachem (Max) Prinz of blessed memory of Lodz
Malka, her husband Reb Baruch (Bronek) Walman of blessed memory of
Lodz

Their sons:
Yehuda Kopel and his wife Sala of blessed memory (nee Donsky) of
Radomsko
Shimshon Kopel, and his wife of blessed memory of Sosnowiec

May their souls be bound in the bonds of eternal life

Perpetuated by their grandchildren:
Zeev Fisher of Israel
Yaakov Fisher of Israel
Tzasha Rosenblum-Fisher of Canada
Mary Fishman-Fisher of Canada
Yeshayahu Hirschberg of Holland
Moshe Yaakov Sribnik of Israel
Chava Gomolinski-Hirshberg of Poland
Aryeh the son of Menachem Prinz of Israel

A memorial candle to

Yehuda Leib Waldman of blessed memory
The son of Asher Anshel and Liba (nee Warshawski) Waldman of blessed
memory
Of a long-time honorable family of Zgierz
Murdered by the Nazi murderers on the 28th of Shvat 5703, February 3, 1943

Our dear and wonderful children
Shimon, born on the 2nd of Iyar 5795 (May 5 1934)
Aliza born on the 21st of Sivan 5699 (June 8, 1939)
Perished in the holocaust on the 30th of Av 5703 (1943)

May their souls be bound in the bonds of eternal life

Perpetuated by Tzasha Waldman-Rosenblum (nee Fisher) of Montreal

An eternal candle for the Davidowitz family

Reb Shmuel Davidowitz of blessed memory, an honorable citizen of Zgierz
His wife Riva (nee Poznaczowski) Davidowitz of blessed memory
Who perished in the holocaust

And their children:
Pinchas the son of Reb Shmuel and Riva Davidowitz of blessed memory -
perished in the
Majdanek death camp
Yitzchak the son of Reb Shmuel and Riva Davidowitz of blessed memory -
perished in the
Majdanek death camp
And his wife Genia Davidowitz (nee Zilberberg) - perished in the holocaust

May their souls be bound in the bonds of eternal life

In eternal memory of my dear parents

Reb Yitzchak Fishman of blessed memory
Frania (nee Kwat) Fishman of blessed memory

And my brothers and sisters: Tuya Fishman, Leon Fishman, Bluma Fishman,
Shlomek Fishman,
Bella Fishman (all born in Radom)
All of whom were murdered in the holocaust at the hands of the German
murderers

May G-d avenge their blood!

Perpetuated by the survivor Morris Fishman of Montreal

In eternal memory!

My father Binyamin Feldon the son of Wolf - died before the war
My mother Sara Feldon (nee Kalisz) - perished in the Borzecin ghetto
My sister Roiza Gitel, her husband Zalman Kosiash and ten children -
perished in the Borzecin ghetto
My sister Rivka Rachel, her husband Aharon Abramowitz and two children -
perished in the ghetto
My brother Shmuel Yosef Feldon, his wife Roza (nee Fuchs), and five
children
My brother Yisrael Yitzchak Feldon, his wife Feiga (nee Zelanzi) and child -
perished in the Lodz
ghetto
My uncle David Yosef Feldon, his wife Tsharna - died before the war
Their daughter Rachel Leah and family, their son Getzel and family -
perished in the Lodz ghetto
Perpetuated by the only survivor, the son and brother Fishel Feldon and
family

671

In memory of our families of Zgierz

Who were killed by the German murderers, may their names
be blotted out, in sanctification of the Divine name between the years of
1939-1945 - our parents

Nachum Feldman and our mother Pesa of blessed memory
Leibel Jakubowitz and mother Roda of blessed memory
Sister Seitel Jakubowitz

Perpetuated by the surviving children
Wolf Feldman and wife of New York
Feiga Rachel Jakubowitz-Feldman - of New York
Moshe and Mendel Jakubowitz of Glasgow, Scotland

A yahrzeit candle for the family of Avraham Pzedworski of blessed memory

Father Reb Avraham the son of Shimon Pzedworski *{upper right photo}* - perished in Lodz on the 19th of Adar 5702 (March 18, 1942)
Sister Chaya Rachel and her husband Yisrael Leib Baum *{upper left photo}* -perished in the Lodz ghetto, 25 Iyar 5702 (1942)
Mother Chava the daughter of Eliahu Shraga - perished in the Lodz ghetto in Sivan 5702 (1942)
Sister Rivka, her husband Yitzchak Neiman and three children - perished in Auschwitz, Passover
5701 (1941)
Brother Eliahu Shraga, his wife and two children - perished in Lodz, 20th Tammuz 1942
Sister Yocheved - perished on 1st of Tishrei [12] 5704 (1943)

Sister Dvora {lower right photo} - perished on 20th of Kislev 5701 (1940)
Brother Shimon {lower center photo} - perished on 5th of Shvat 5704 (1944)
Brother Yitzchak (lower left photo} - perished on 29th of Tevet, 5702 (1942)

Perpetuated by Shlomo David and Fishel Bunim Pzedworski, Gittel Goldwasser, Esther Keila Russ of New York

In eternal memory

It is over thirty years since the end of the Hitlerian violence - and still today, I can see before my eyes all of their refined methods of murder which they used to kill our people. Like the rest of us, my close relatives were murdered by the German beasts.

My dear father, Shmuel Freundlich, died in Zgierz in 1929. My dearly beloved mother Eidel Freundlich (nee Grinfarb) was murdered in the Lodz ghetto in 1941. My dear and beloved brother Avraham Yaakov Freundlich was murdered in the Lodz ghetto in 1942. My dear and beloved sister Rivka Poznanski, her husband Yechezkel and two children were killed in 1942. My dear and beloved sisters Chele, Masha and Hodes were murdered by the German murderers.

My dear wife Aida (nee Jakubowicz) and delightful children Estusha and Shmuel. My wife's parents, my father-in-law and mother-in-law Itche and Rivka Jakubowicz with their daughters Natasha, Esther, and Paula.My dear uncles: Shulem Hirsch Goldfarb, with his wife and two children; Isser Dszaliski with his wife (nee Grinfarb) and their daughter Chele Eisen, and Chele's husband Lozer and their two children; Harry Grinfarb, a sincere Jew, died in America in 1973.

My dear and beloved aunt Rachel Rubin (nee Grinfarb) died in America in 1971.

My sisters-in-law Ita Bracha Mindele, Rivkale and their brother Efraim were murdered in the Lodz ghetto.

I will remember my near and dear relatives, victims of the Hitlerian murders, until the end of my life.

We must never forgive the murderers of our people.

Perpetuated by Yosef Freundlich of Haifa, the only survivor, son and brother.

In eternal memory!

Our father Reb Yisrael Frugel the son of Mordechai Leib {upper right photo - died in Israel on the seventh day of Passover 5711 (1951)
[13]
Our mother Chana Sara Frugel (nee Krimlowski) {upper left photo} - died in Israel on the 23rd of Iyar 5713 (1953)

Our sisters: Esther, her husband Wolf Sziwicz and their son - perished in the Lodz ghetto

Malka Frugel

Our brothers Betzalel Frugel, his wife and two children - perished in the Lodz ghetto

Moshe Frugel, his wife and son - perished in Posen (Poznan)

May their souls be bound in the bonds of eternal life.

Perpetuated by Aryeh Frugel and family, Yeshayahu and Dvora Frugel and family.

A few words about my family

My father, the last Jewish guild master in Zgierz was born in the village of Wolia Jankowa in the area of Radomsko. He settled in Zgierz, according to my estimation, sometime between 1890 and 1892. My mother was born in Zgierz. She was from the Wigdorowicz family.None of my family was in town on the day of the expulsion from Zgierz. My father had been arrested by the Nazis and was in Radagoszcz. My mother and two sisters Mania and Rozka were in Warsaw. I and my three brothers, Yeshayahu, Avraham and Mordechai were on the other side of the Bug, in the Soviet region. Yeshayahu was killed in the Vilna ghetto. Hirsch was with the partisans, and fell at the end of 1943.Avraham and Mordechai, along with my sister Tola and her son, had obtained Aryan documents. They were all together for a certain amount of time. However, they had to separate for the group was too large. My sister Tola and her son survived and live today in Israel. Avraham and Mordechai were murdered by the murderers. My parents and sisters Mania and Rozka perished in the Warsaw ghetto.

Perpetuated by Yaakov Cincinatus

The Frugel family prior to the aliya of Yisrael and Chana Sara Frugel to the Land of Israel in 1936

In memory of
Our father Feibish Preshker the son of Yehuda
Our mother Rachel Preshker (nee Zichelinski)
Perished in the holocaust
Our brother Meir Preshker - died before the war at age 12

Perpetuated by Shalom Preshker and family
Esther Preshker-Grussman and family

In eternal memory of

Our father Emanuel the son of Alter and Frumet Fridman - died before the
war
Our mother Reizel Fridman, the daughter of Bina and David Waltman
Our sister Malka Gittel (Manya) Fridman - perished in the holocaust

{Right photo} Grandfather David Waltman
{left photo} Malka Gittel Fridman

Our grandfather Reb David Waltman - perished in the holocaust
Our grandmother Bina Waltman - died before the War in Zgierz
Our uncle Avraham Waltman, his wife Rachel (nee Buczan) and their sons
Binem and Lipman

Our aunt Hinda, her husband Hillel Czizinski and their three children Bina
Leah, Avraham
Yisrael and Esther Rachel (cont)

Our aunt Pessa, her husband Ziskind Mendelewicz and their children Bina
and Moshe
Our cousin Masha the daughter of Shlomo and Tzipora Waltman - all of
whom perished in the
holocaust

Our grandfather and grandmother Alter Fridman and his wife Frimet (nee
Wadowski) - died
before the war
Our aunt Dvora Gittel, her husband Yaakov Wadowski and their four
children Alta Chaya, Beila
Mindel, Mirele and their son Moshe - perished in the holocaust
Our uncle Noach Waltman, his wife Frania (nee Buczan) and their children
Bina, Moshe and Leib

May their souls be bound in the bonds of eternal life

Perpetuated by Rachel Fridman-Rotkowski
Avraham Yaakov and Moshe Fridman
The children of Reizel and Emanuel Fridman

In memory of

My father Yitzchak Freistadt - perished in the Bialystok ghetto
My mother Gittel Freistadt (nee Rubenstein) - a righteous woman who helped
everyone who was in need - died before the war in 1935
My brother David Freistadt - perished in the Bialystok ghetto
My sister Rivka Freistadt - perished in a camp with 1,000 woman
My sister Roiza Freistadt - perished in a camp with 1,000 woman
My brother Melech Freistadt
Manya Freistadt (nee Rafaelowicz), the second wife of my father and their
young daughter Sarale they left the ghetto in an unknown direction.

May their souls be bound in the bonds of eternal life

Perpetuated by Peretz Freistadt and family

In memory of our beloved

{Photo} Standing: Mordechai, Rozka, Avraham, Hirsch, Mania.
Sitting: Father Shlomo, Mother Sara, Shaya Cincinatus

Parents Reb Shlomo Cincinatus the son of Aharon
Sara Cincinatus (nee Wigdorowicz)

Sisters Miriam Mania Cincinatus
Rachel Rozka Cincinatus

Brothers Yeshayahu Shaya Cincinatus
Tzvi Hirsch Cincinatus
Avraham Cincinatus
Mordechai Cincinatus - all of whom perished in the holocaust
Aharon Cincinatus - died in Israel in 1961
His wife Roza and daughters Leah and Dina - perished during the holocaust
in Vilna

Perpetuated by Tola Efron-Cincinatus and family
Yaakov Cincinatus and family of Israel

A memorial candle to the Zelgow family

My father Yosef Zelgow
My mother Reizel Zelgow (nee Brzezinski) - they died before the war
My sister Paula Zelgow - died in Samarkand, Russia [14]
My brother Avraham Zelgow and his two children - were murdered in the
Chelmno ghetto
My brother Yitzhak Zelgow, his wife Bronia (nee Turczinski) and their child
- were murdered in Buczacz
My sister Chava and her husband Motek Epstein and their child - perished
during the war
My brother Yisrael Zelgow - died in Israel on 3rd of Av, 5621 (1961)

Perpetuated by Esther Zelgow-Traub
Moshe Zelgow Ben-Yosef

680

In memory of my dear wife

Chana Zelgow (nee Zeidenwurm)
And my only son Yossi, aged 3 ½
Who were murdered in the Warsaw ghetto

(Photo) Chana & Yossi

Perpetuated by Moshe Ben-Yosef (Zelgow)

An eternal candle to my family

Our father Berel Zelnik the son of Avraham Yaakov, one of the old timers of
Zgierz {*left photo*}
Our mother Chaya Gnendel Zelnik the daughter of Shlomo Eliezer
Lemkowicz of Lodz {*right
photo}* - they perished in Chelmno
Our brothers Avraham Yaakov Zelnik, his wife Mania (nee Finkelstein) and
their daughter -
perished in the Glowno ghetto
Lemel Zelnik and his wife Dora - murdered in the Chelmno camp
Eliezer Zelnik, a partisan - fell near the Oder River
Our sisters Tzipora and her husband Chanan Lerner - perished in the Warsaw
ghetto

May their memories be a blessing!

Perpetuated by their daughter and sister Tzila Harpazi (nee Zelnik) and
family
Their son and brother Nachum Zelnik and family

In eternal memory!

My father Reb Pinchas Zelnik the son of David, secretary of the Jewish community of Zgierz
killed in Siedlec
My mother Chaya Blima Zelnik, the daughter of Reb Binyamin Sczaranski - born in Zgierz,
perished in the Warsaw ghetto on January 13, 1943 (7 Shvat)
My sister Gittel Hendel Zelnik - born in Zgierz in 1926, murdered in Siedlec
My sister Sara Leah Zelnik - born in Zgierz in 1927, murdered in the Warsaw ghetto
My brother Binyamin Zelnik - born in Zgierz in 1929, murdered in Siedlec
My brother Nota Zelnik - born in Zgierz in 1935, murdered in the Warsaw ghetto

Perpetuated by Chava Tusk-Zelnik of New York

In eternal memory

Reb Eliezer the son of Yaakov of blessed memory {photo}

683

And his wife Zisel Korzerj

They died at an old age before the Second World War

Reb Eliezer was known in the town as a Hassid, a scholar, with a broad Jewish heart. Their
home was always open to anyone who was needy. He himself worked hard and honestly to
support their large family, which was blessed with children.

May their souls be bound in the bonds of eternal life

Perpetuated by Yosef Korzerj, Paris, their only surviving son

Reb Michel Kuperman of blessed memory

Michel, the grandson of Reb Yaakov Kuperman of blessed memory, was a descendent of the Alexander dynasty, and a Hassid of the Alexander Hassidim in Zgierz.

He was diligent in Torah, learned, and a master of all the good traits that the sages attributed to a whole person. He was the paradigm of righteousness, honesty, love of one's fellowman and fear of heaven. His prayers were quiet and from the depths of the soul.

His father Mendel Kuperman did not merit to make aliya to the Land, for he died suddenly. However, he bequeathed his dream to his children, who made aliya to the Land as pioneers about fifty years ago and occupied themselves with its upbuilding.

He was active in the Zionist movement, and was a member of the Mizrachi organization of Zgierz. His home always had a warm Zionist atmosphere, and in this atmosphere he educated his daughter Adela, who followed the path of her father.

At the time of the Nazi conquest, he was active in helping those who were suffering and in need. He extended help to people who were in dire straits, even at the risk of his life. People who arrived in the Land after the holocaust told a great deal about his activities during these critical times. He did not lose his ideals even at the most difficult moments, when the people of Zgierz were pursued to the neck and were expelled to the Balot ghetto in Lodz. Even though he himself was oppressed and persecuted, he always made sure to extend whatever help was possible to his fellow. Since he was related to the owner of the bakery, he was generally able to help those in need by providing bread. His family was expelled along with the Jews of Zgierz in 1941 to the ghetto, and from their they were sent to extermination, and all traces of them were lost. A splendid family was murdered. May the memory of the family be blessed forever.

{Photo} Standing: Chaim and Golda Cohen, Sara Kuperman. Sitting, the grandfather Reb
Yaakov Kuperman, Reb Michel Kuperman and his children Meir, Chana, Menachem and Adela

A memorial candle to pure souls

My grandfather and grandmother Yaakov and Hinda Kuperman
My father Mendel the son of Yaakov and Hinda Kuperman
My mother Chana Gittel (Andza) Kuperman, the daughter of Michel and
Chaya Golda
Lichtenstein of Plotzk
My brother Michael (Mechel) Kuperman, his wife Sara, their daughter Adla
and her husband, his
son Menachem Mendel, his son Meir, and his daughter Chana.
Who perished in the holocaust

May their memories be blessed!

Perpetuated by Yaffa (Sheina Eidel) Rakocz, the daughter of Mendel and
Chana, and family
Moshe Nachshon Kuperman, the son of Mendel and Chana, and family

In memory of

Yosef Jawaski (a baker)
His wife Chaya (nee Itzkowicz)
And their three children Yitzchak, Mendel and Rachel

All of them perished in the holocaust

Meir Kolski, his wife Tamar, children and grandchildren
Lived in Zgierz on B. Jaselewicza Street.
They were murdered in sanctification of the Divine name during the years
1939-1945

Perpetuated by their daughter Chana Fuchs of New York

686

Moshe Rosenzweit (Oleinik)
His wife Dvora (nee Zaonce)
They owned a store on Sradaska Street
And their seven children

All of whom perished in the holocaust

In memory of

Avigdor the son of Moshe Reichert
His wife Ava (nee Milstein)
Their sons Moshe and Ezra

All of whom perished in the holocaust

In eternal memory of

Our uncle and aunt Leizer and Yachtshe Shtachelberg of blessed memory
And their children Binyamin Shtachelberg of blessed memory and Chavtsha
Shtachelberg-
Gibralter of blessed memory

Who were murdered during the years 1939-1945

Perpetuated by Frania (Rubenstein) Levitt of Montreal
Leib Leon Rubenstein
Dr. Yosef Rubenstein of New York
Michael Rubenstein of Montreal
Shlomo Rubenstein of New York

The children of Leizer and Baltsha Rubenstein of blessed memory
Grandchildren of Yosef and Malkale Rubenstein of blessed memory

687

In memory of my dear family

Father Avraham Yehuda Schwartz and mother Pessa Gittel of blessed
memory
Father-in-law Yaakov Ring and his wife Baltsha, and three children
Brothers Yisrael Yitzchak and wife Rasha
Kaufman, his wife Sally, and daughter Leahle
Brother Yosef, his wife and young son
Lola's husband Alter, and children Avraham and Rachele
The two children of my younger sister Yehuda and Avraham
Who were killed in sanctification of the Divine name

Perpetuated by Baruch Schwartz

In memory of my beloved parents, brothers and sisters, may G-d avenge their blood, who perished in the holocaust

My father Reb Kalman Baruch the son of Yitzchak Shmuel Rosenblatt
He was born in the city of Bendzin, Poland. He was a G-d fearing and
scholarly Jew. He loved his fellowman and assisted those in need. He was a
Hassid of the rabbi of Sokolow and a member of his inner circle. He was cut
off by the Nazi enemy, may their names be blotted out, in 1940 at age 53.

My mother Rivka Rosenblatt the daughter of Itta and Yechezkel Gotschal
She was born in Pradla, Poland. She was a righteous women who engaged in
immeasurable,discreet giving of charity and extending of assistance. She
perished in the Auschwitz death camp in 1944, at age 51.

My eldest brother Yitzchak Shmuel the son of Kalman Baruch
He was taken to a work camp in Russia, and there he perished in 1942 at age
33.
His wife Lea Ronia (nee Erlich) of Radomsk - perished in a death camp
Their daughter Michla, who perished at age 8
My brother Yisrael Wolf the son of Kalman Baruch - perished in the Warsaw
ghetto in 1942 at
age 31

His wife Dvora (of the Levi family of Alexandrow, near Lodz) - perished in a death camp

Their daughter Ruth - perished at age 6.

Their son who was born at the time of the outbreak of the war, whose name I do not remember

My sister Lula the daughter of Kalman Baruch and Rivka Rosenblatt -taken along with father and perished in 1940, at age 20

My brother Refael Mendel the son of Kalman Baruch and Rivka Rosenblatt - perished in the Auschwitz death camp in 1944 at age 22.

Their memories shall be eternally etched upon my heart.

Perpetuated by Fela the daughter of Kalman Baruch and Rivka Rosenblatt-Gotlieb, their

daughter and sister who survived the death camps of Auschwitz and Bergen-Belsen

In their memory

{Upper right photo} Reb Kalman Rosenblatt {upper left photo} Lula Rosenblatt

{Lower right photo} Leah Ronia, Michla and Yitzchak Shmuel Rosenblatt {lower left photo} Yisrael Wolf Rosenblatt

690

In their memory!

{Upper right photo} Avraham Dov Rothkopf
{upper left photo} Mindel Rothkopf

My father Avraham Dov the son of Yaakov and Esther Ita Rothkopf
My mother Mindel the daughter of Avraham Yaakov and Frumet Zelnik
My sisters: Rachel Rothkopf
Tzipora, her husband Hirsch Gelbard and their daughter Frimet
Rivka Leah (Regina), {lower photo}, her husband Yechiel Shevach and
their daughter

All of whom perished in the holocaust
My uncle and aunt Shaul Rosenstrauch and his wife Miriam (nee Zelnik) -
died before the war
Their son Nachum Rosenstrauch, his wife Chana the daughter of Tanchum
and Liba Bigeleisen
and their daughter - perished in the holocaust

691

My aunt Sheindel Grinberg (nee Rothkopf) - died before the war
My uncle Hershel Grinberg, their daughter Ita, her husband and daughter -
perished in the
holocaust

My uncle and aunt Mordechai Zelnik and his wife Leah (nee Weinberg) -
died before the war
Their daughter Feiga, her husband and their children
Their daughter Tzipora, her husband and children
Their son Shlomo Shimon Zelnik, his wife and children
Their son Simcha Zelnik, his wife and children

All of whom perished in the holocaust

May their souls be bound in the bonds of eternal life

In eternal memory of
Perpetuated by Shmuel Asher Rothkopf -Rothkowski

My father Reb Fishel Rus and his wife Perel
My sister Chana Rachel and her husband Yechiel Meir Katek with their eight
children
My sister Ita Feiga, her husband Yisrael Pruski and their four children
My sister Chaya Roiza, her husband Meir Rosen and their seven children
My sister Miriam Dreizel, her husband Avraham Gurfinkel and their three
children
My sister Zise Esther, her husband Berish Frida and their children
My brother Moshe Nechemia - died at a young age
My brother-in-law Yisrael Yitzchak Weichselfisch and his five children

All of whom perished in the holocaust

May their souls be bound in the bonds of eternal life

Perpetuated by Chaim Zalman Rus, Berlin

In memory of our dear family

Our father Gedalia Rozman the son of Meir - perished in the holocaust
Our mother Pessa Roznam (nee Schneps) - perished in the holocaust

Our sister Rozka, her husband Ben-Tzion Lifschitz and their daughter
Mira - perished in Slonim

Our brother Yaakov Rus, his wife and children - perished in Paris
May their memories be blessed for ever!
Our aunt and uncle Malka and Yitzchak Buczan
And their children Fela and Rivka
Freda and her husband Waltman and children
Rachel and her husband Waltman and children
Leon Buczan, his wife and children
Reuven Buczan

Who perished in the holocaust

Perpetuated by Regina Bialostocki-Rozman and family
Mordechai Rozman and family
Pinchas Rozman

In eternal memory of my parents

Leib and Reizen Rosenberg of blessed memory
Sister Mania, her husband Mordechai and two children
Sisters Zisel, Feiga and Pessa Leah and her husband Shmuel
Aunt Freda
Brother Shmuel

All of whom perished in the Lodz ghetto

Perpetuated by Hirsch Rosenzweig, New York

In eternal memory of my family

Mother Chaya
Brother Eliezer (son of Yerachmiel), his wife Malka and children Shmuel,
Zalman and
Yerachmiel
Murdered in August, 1944

Sisters Naomi and Tova
Brother Nathan (son of Yerachmiel), his wife Esther Rachel and children
Yerachmiel, Avraham,
Efraim, and Chaimel
Murdered by the Nazi murderers in the Lodz ghetto in 1942

Perpetuated by Chaim Itche Shaiak of New York

In memory of

{Photo}**Our father Reb Shalom Tzvi Shevach** of blessed memory, the son of Yaakov and Rivla of blessed memory - perished in the holocaust
Our mother Chava Rachel Shevach of blessed memory (nee Holtzman) - perished in Treblinka
Our sister Perl Dina of blessed memory - perished in Treblinka
Perpetuated by Avraham Shevach and family, Tzipora Mankita (nee Shevach) and family, Shmuel Shevach and family

{photo} Surrounding the gravestone are standing, from right to left: Reb Mendel Shevach of blessed memory, Reb Lipman Shevach of blessed memory, Mrs. Rivla Shevach of blessed memory, Mrs. Leahle Radzinski of blessed memory, Mrs. Radzinski of blessed memory. Sitting from right to left: Reb Shalom Tzvi Shevach of blessed memory, Reb Vove Wolf Shevach of blessed memory.

695

In memory of

Our grandfather Reb Yaakov Shevach of blessed memory, and our grandmother Mrs. Rivla
Shevach of blessed memory - died before the war

Our uncle Reb Wolf Shevach of blessed memory and his wife Simaleh of blessed memory
Our uncle Reb Lipman Shevach of blessed memory and his wife Mrs. Esther of blessed memory
Our aunt Reb Mendel Shevach and his wife of blessed memory
Our aunt Mrs. Leah of blessed memory (nee Shevach) and her husband Reb Aharon Radzinski of
blessed memory and children
Our aunt Rachle of blessed memory (nee Shevach) and her husband

Who perished in the holocaust

In memory of

Mrs. Chana Shevach of blessed memory (nee Zimmerman) {photo}

My dear wife and our dear mother, unforgettable, who died in Jerusalem on
11th of Shvat 5734
(1974) and was brought to her eternal rest on Har Menuchot in Jerusalem
May her memory be blessed!
Perpetuated by her husband Avraham Shevach, and her daughters Esther
Shachar and family,

Rina Gazit and family, Nili Kaminer and family

An eternal flame to my dear family

My father Moshe Asher the son of Yisrael Siedlowski {upper right photo} - perished in theWarsaw ghetto

My mother Ratza Siedlowski (nee Sorzon) {upper left photo} - perished in Treblinka

My brother Shmuel (Salek) Siedlowski {lower right photo} - died after the war in Warsaw, Poland

My sister Miriam (Marishka) Siedlowski {lower left photo} - perished in Treblinka

{Photo - Max}

My uncle Max the son of Yisrael Siedlowski - died after the war in Zgierz
My uncle Michael the son of Yisrael Siedlowski
My aunt Rozia Siedlowski and her husband
My aunt Mania Siedlowski and her husband
My aunt Fela Siedlowski and her husband Brzezinski
And their children Sala, Ala, and Chilek

All of whom perished in the holocaust

May their memories be blessed!

Perpetuated by Bella Gutman-Siedlowski (the daughter of Moshe and Ratza)

An eternal flame to the Sheps family

Reb Menachem Mendel the son of Moshe Yaakov Sheps, one of the honorable old-timers of Zgierz
He was born in Zgierz in 1870. He moved to Lodz in 1903. There he was one of the founders of the well-known Hebrew gymnasia. He owned a chemical factory. He gave a Hebrew, Zionist education to his sons.

His wife Rivka, the daughter of Reb Yisrael Moshe Schwartzman, an expert in secular and Torah knowledge, from the city of Turk. He died in 1938.

Dr. Yosef the son of Menachem Mendel Sheps. He died in Zgierz in 1898. He was a well- known physician in Zgierz. He was a donor to Jewish causes and Zionist funds. In his capacity of Captain in the Polish army, he was killed in forests of Katin, along with hundreds of other Jewish doctors of Poland.

Genia Glasstein the daughter of Menachem Mendel Sheps. She was born in Zgierz in 1901. She attained higher education. She perished along with her husband Zalman and two children Bolek and Miriam in the Lodz ghetto, 1943.

Engineer Simcha the son of Moshe Yaakov Sheps. Born in Zgierz. He was a professor of
Chemistry in the polytechnic institute of Baku, Russia. He perished in the holocaust.

Dr. Saltza Avrahmowicz the daughter of Moshe Yaakov Sheps. He was born in Zgierz. He served as a physician in Leningrad. He perished in the holocaust.

Yosef the son of Moshe Yaakov Sheps. Born in Zgierz in 1903. He immigrated to Basle. There he founded a silk factory and set up a foundation to help those who fled from eastern Europe. He was a long-time Zionist. He died in 1943.

Perpetuated by the children of Reb Menachem Mendel and Rivka Sheps, Tel Aviv
Dr. Shmuel Sheps, Geneva
Zofia Moskowicz (nee Sheps).

700

In memory of our dear parents

**Reb Aharon Sperling the son of Reb Avigdor Meir and Tuna of Lodz
{right photo}**
He died at a very young age in Lodz.

**Glicka (Genia) Sperling the daughter of Reb Leibel and Feiga Rivka
Haron {left photo}**
She was born in Zgierz and died at a ripe old age in Tel Aviv on the 26th of
Tammuz 5728
(1968).

Our beloved and noble mother remained a widow and she dedicated her
entire life to educating
her daughters in the spirit of Zionism and the love of the land of Israel.

May their souls be bound in the bonds of eternal life

Perpetuated by the daughters Chaya Halpern and family, Rachel Shapira and
family

701

In eternal memory of our dear family

{right photo} Chaya Sarkowiak
{left photo} Rivka Rachel Sarkowiak

Our grandfather Reb Yaakov Yitzchak Sarkowiak of blessed memory
Our grandmother Tzirel (nee Bialostocki) - they perished in the Warsaw
ghetto
Our father Reb Avigdor Yechezkel Sarkowiak the son of Reb Yaakov
Yitzchak and Tzirel
Our mother Rivka Rachel (nee Kolbert) - perished in the Warsaw ghetto
Our brother Avraham - died before the war
Our brother Berel Dov - perished in the Warsaw ghetto
Our sister Chaya - perished in the Warsaw ghetto
Our brother Menachem Mendel - perished in the Warsaw ghetto

May their souls be bound in the bonds of eternal life.

Perpetuated by Simcha Binem and Eliakim Noach Sarkowiak

In memory of

Our uncle and aunt Fishel Sarkowiak the son of Yaakov Yitzchak and Tzirel
Malka
Their children Mala, Sara, and Leah
All of whom perished in the Warsaw ghetto

Our uncle and aunt Leibish Sarkowiak - died in the Lodz ghetto
Leah (nee Blank)
Their daughters Hinda and her husband, Aida, Sara and her husband Moshe
Cohen
Their son Fishel Sarkowiak, his wife Chana Rivka and their son Moshe
All of whom perished in the holocaust

Our uncle and aunt Avraham Moshe Reisman
Perel (nee Sarkowiak)
Their daughters Feiga and her husband, Chaya and her husband, Fruma,
Tzirel
All of whom perished in the Lewicz ghetto of a typhus epidemic

May their souls be bound in the bonds of eternal life.

Perpetuated by Simcha Binem and Eliakim Noach Sarkowiak
The sons of Avigdor Yechezkel and Rivka Rachel

In memory of the Shimshowicz family

Father Yosef Shimshowicz, the son of Moshe and Mirel -born in Zgierz,
perished in the Lodz
ghetto
Mother Masha Shimshowicz - born in Lask, perished in the Lodz ghetto
Sisters Esther, Feiga, Chana Rivka and her husband Fishel Sarkowiak (from
Zgierz)
And their son Moshe - Chana and Moshe perished in Auschwitz, Fishel in
the Lodz ghetto
Ita and her husband Hirsch Mordechai Gembiczki (of Zgierz) - Ita perished in
Treblinka, Hirsch
Mordechai in the Warsaw ghetto
Brother Yisrael Yitzchak and his two children Moshe and Reizele - Yisrael
perished in
Auschwitz, the children in the Lodz ghetto.

Perpetuated by Moshe and Rachel Shimshowicz of Israel.

Natives of Zgierz who Fell in the Wars of Israel

Captain David Aloni

704

David Aloni was the son of Yaakov and Esther (nee Katz). He was born on the 13th of Cheshvan 5696 (November 9, 1935) in Tel Adashim in the Jezreel Valley.

He was educated in a school for the children of workers. Later he studied in the "Shalva" high school of Tel Aviv, where he was considered one of the best students. He joined the Israel Defense Forces and took an officer's course. Afterward he returned to his studies, and in 1963, he received a degree in agriculture from the University in Rechovot. He continued with his doctoral studies. He returned to his paratrooper unit at the outbreak of the Six Day War, as a captain of intelligence and operations. From the battles of Sinai he moved over to the Syrian front. His armored truck overturned during the ascent to the crest of the Golan Heights, and he was badly wounded.

He died on the 12th of Sivan 5727 (June 20, 1967), after a valiant ten day battle to save his life.

He left behind a wife and two daughters.

May his memory be a blessing!

Shmuel Avraham Bornstein

He was born on the 4th of Adar 5688 (1928) to his parents Aharon Yisrael and Rivka Bornstein. He was a descendent of the Kotzk Hassidic dynasty, a grandson of the Admors of Sochaczew and Sokolow. He was educated in the Bilu School and the Moria high school. He joined the Haganah at age 14.

Just as he was about to fulfil one of his objectives, which included a trip for educational purposes to the United States, the War of Independence broke out. He gave up on his plans without hesitation and hurried to volunteer with the fighters. He fill on the hills of Nazareth on Lag Baomer (18th of Iyar) 5708 (1948).

May his memory be a blessing!

Sargent Dov Bliman

Dov Bliman of blessed memory, the son of Leopold and Tova (nee Honigstock), was born in 1947, and made aliya to Israel in 1957. He finished high school, and in 1972 received his bachelor's degree in Electrical Engineering from the Technion. The Yom Kippur War broke out while he was in the midst of his studies for his Master's degree. He fell on the Golan Heights on the fifth day of the war. He left behind a wife and son. May his memory be blessed!

Oded Ben-Yamin (Sczaranski)

The son of Reb Moshe Sczaranski of Zgierz, he was born on the 13th of Kislev 5683 (December 12, 1923) [14] in Tel Aviv. He excelled in his studies and finished his studies successfully at the Herzlia high school.

He enlisted for the army at the beginning of the world war. After his release, he studied natural sciences at university. He made a name for himself as a genius in mathematics and physics. He was called up for service at the time of the declaration of the state, and he dedicated himself faithfully to all of his missions to which he was assigned. On the 5th of Shvat 5708 (1943), when he made haste with the 35th division to bring assistance to Gush Ezion, he fell in the mountains of Hebron along with his friends. May his memory be a blessing!

Asher Gornicki

Asher Gornicki, the son of Yosef and Reizel, was born on April 11, 1924 in Zgierz. He finished public school and a few grades of high school.(cont)

At the outbreak of the war, he escaped with his father to Russia, where he was enlisted for hard labor in the forests of Siberia. He returned to Poland in May, 1946, however he was not able to remain their in the atmosphere that pervaded after the murder of the members of his people, including his mother and sister.

He left Germany and enlisted in Gachal[15] at the outbreak of the War of Independence. After two months of army service, he fell in the line of duty at Ein Shemer on October 28, 1948. He was considered to be lost in battle, and when the found his body, he was brought to burial on August 9, 1949 in the military cemetery of Afula.

May his memory be a blessing!

Sergeant Motti Katz

Motti Katz was born to Moshe and Tzipora (Fela) Katz on December 3, 1944, 17 th Kislev 5705, in Tel Aviv. He studied in a new high school and was a member of the "Machanot Haolim" youth movement. After his matriculation examinations, he enlisted in Nachal [16] and joined the "Reim" group in the Negev. He was a communications sergeant in the paratrooper battalion. He fell in battle on the Syrian border on the 28th of Av, 5724 (August 6, 1964). He left behind poems which were published after his death in an anthology called "Im Bo Hashemesh" ("At Sunset"). Nathan Alterman wrote the preface.

May his memory be blessed!

Staff Sergeant Menachem Katz

Menachem was the son of Tzipora and Yoav Katz. He was born on April 34d, 1938 in Tel Aviv. He studied in the Tzafon school, and the Shalva high school. He was an alumnus of Hashomer Hatzair, in the Yami group. He participated in sailing competitions and was the national champion twice.

He moved on from Nachal to the regular army, and served as a paratrooper. He served in armored division 11 in the Six Day War.

He fell in Bloza on the 4th day of the Yom Kippur war. He had volunteered, and was hurrying to save a truck that had veered off the road and had gone onto a road that led to the 3rd Egyptian Army.

He was married, and the father of three children.

May his memory be a blessing!

Major Yaakov Shiloh (Shilek)

Yaakov was the son of Morris and Janina Shilek. He was born in Kalisz on November 15, 1935. He moved to Zgierz with his family at age 3. He went through all the trials and tribulations of the war during his childhood. He made aliya at age 13 with the Youth Aliya and joined Kibbutz Gan Shmuel. He continued his studies at the Shevach School. At age 17, he enlisted in the army and joined the paratroopers, where he served as a teacher and a guide. He participated in various battles, including the Sinai Campaign. After he was wounded badly in an accident, he joined the communications division. During the Six Day War, he volunteered for a special role in Group 37. During his duty as an army airplane navigator, he was killed by an enemy bullet during the battle at Shechem (Nablus) on the fourth day of the war, 28th Iyar 5727 (June 7, 1967). He had served in a praiseworthy fashion, and was promoted in rank after his death.

He left behind a wife and a daughter.

May his memory be a blessing!

F. The Survivors of Zgierz

Our Fellow Townsmen after the Holocaust by W. Fisher

(A survey)
The Desolate Hometown

When the meager remnants of the Zgierz survivors, liberated from the death camps, dragged themselves alive to their native city - they could no longer find a home there. There was not one trace left of Jewish life; sections of the Jewish neighborhoods lay in ruins or were completely torn down; the synagogue and Beis Midrash - the central holy sites for the Jewish community - had been burnt by the Germans; the earth upon which they had once stood so reverently - now lay in shame, ploughed up and destroyed in accordance with the lament of the prophet: "Zion will be ploughed like a field"... (Jeremiah 26:18). The cemetery that had for generations so closely bound up the current generation with their forbears had been completely covered over with earth it was no more. A cold strangeness blew from the houses, streets and alleyways. The former Jewish windows, from which the peaceful joy of the Sabbath and festivals would shine in former times, now grieve over the destruction.

How would it be possible, people thought to themselves: is it possible to continue Jewish life here, on this soil?

From time to time, old images appear on the street... The survivors for the most part were ill, physically broken and spiritually spent. They were living scraps. They were desperately in need of assistance -medical, social, moral. The refugees who had returned from Russia were in a somewhat better state. There as well, Zgierz lost a significant portion of its Jews. Therefore it was natural that it was from those repatriations that the first temporary Jewish assistance committees in Zgierz were formed.

I wish to mention here the open and warm home of Aharon and Dina Zeidel -who were themselves saved in a bunker on the Aryan side, near Warsaw. They were among the first to return to Zgierz. Many refugees enjoyed a meal and a warm bed at their home. During the first days and weeks, this house was a center for visits and meetings. Who did not visit there at the time? The committee was set up in that house, and Mrs. Zeidel served as a secretary. The following people also belonged to the committee:

A. D. Grand (chairman), Itshe Zelgow, Feivish Moszkowicz, Gershon Benet, Yosef Korczej, Grynbaum (of Riga), Shlomo Przedworski, Mrs. Jakubowicz, the writer of these lines, and others.

The tasks of the committee were dictated by the needs of the moment. A two room dwelling in Taubert's house was restored for the new arrivals. A second place was set up as a communal free kitchen. The kashruth was supervised by the Hassidic youths Yosef Korczej and Shlomo Przedworski. Clothing that we obtained from the Lodzer regional committee, as well as food parcels, were provided to those in need.

Naturally, the ill were given first priority in the assistance activities. The city physician Wansowicz, who was put at our disposal, displayed a great deal of sympathy and took interest in his former patients. Many ill people were restored to health by him.

An important area of activity of the committee was assisting those who attempted to repossess their former dwellings. Through our connections with the city administration, the generally complex process was made easier. The committee also assisted in those areas that were now once again under control of the Polish authorities.

The committee set up a prayer hall in another home. This meant that, despite everything, we continued in the ways of our fathers, and bound ourselves, from the distance, with the lot of our people. The memorial gatherings and anniversary of the expulsion from Zgierz were also conducted in that prayer hall. Zgierzers from Lodz and other places would come to such events.

Within a brief period of time, approximately 30-40 refugee families succeeded in obtaining employment in various workplaces in Zgierz or Lodz. Mention should be made of the initiative of some weaving guilds to set up a weaving cooperative in Zgierz, which developed well and served as a source of livelihood for several families.

Already in the first year after returning to the devastated home, the majority of the returnees had succeeded in finding employment in various enterprises, albeit in a temporary fashion. I say temporary because, despite the spontaneous and natural joy of remaining alive, many of the survivors nurtured hopes of better times, and the majority of them did not believe that a Jewish community could be set up on that blood soaked earth and deathly hateful surroundings. That pessimistic thought was painfully strengthened in the Jewish frame of mind after the murderous pogrom in Kielce [1].

712

Suddenly, things once again seemed lawless and insecure, especially in the smaller cities. There were terrifying shadows in the evenings... Anyone who was able to do so moved to Lodz, which was at the time the "metropolis" of the survivors of Polish Jewry. Those of the destroyed cities and towns who survived began there to seek each other out and form "Landsmanschaftn" [2], so that they could maintain their communal existence, even symbolically.

The Landsmanschaft in Poland

Since the majority of Zgierz Jews found their place of refuge in Lodz and reestablished their lives there, it became clear that Lodz should be the center of communal and social assistance activity for the benefit of the Jews of Zgierz. They occupied themselves particularly with the dozens of repatriated families who moved along with the Russian troops straight to Lower Silesia - to the cities of Dzierzoniow, Walbrzych, Wroclaw and others - and were in need of immediate assistance.

In January 1947, the founding meeting of the Zgierz Landsmanschaft in Poland took place in one of the rooms of the Lodz Jewish regional committee. After the stirring memorial for the four and a half thousand murdered Jews of Zgierz, the discussion focused upon the current situation and our severe problems, which required immediate solutions. A committee was chosen, consisting of: L. Weinstein (chairman), Engineer H. Gibralter (vice-chairman), Mrs. Dora Frogel and V. Fiszer (secreteries), Bialystocki (treasurer), Szerakowski, Z. Fogel, M. Akerman, M. Srebnik, Y. Cincinatus and M. Glazer.

אפעל

צו אלע זגערזשער לאנדסלייט!

דאָס ערינג פון אונדזערע רויכמיקסטע אויפּגאַבּן, וועלכע מיר
האָבּן זיך פאָרגענומען צו פאַרווירקלעכן, איז דאָס שאַפן און אַרויס־
געבּן א **פּנקס**, וואָס זאָל, אײַסער דעם זכּור־טײַל, אױך איבּערגעבּן
אַן אַלגעמײ־היסטאָרישן איבּערבּליק איבּער דעם ייִדישן ישוב אין
זגערזש פון זײַן אָנהײבּ ביז זײַן גרויזאַמער פאַרניכטונג,
ד. ה. בּיז צום שרעקלעכן מיירוש־געערזש, דעם 24־טן דעצעמבּער 1939
יאָר.

דער **פּנקס** דאַרף, אַלזאָ, אַפשפּיגלען דאָס גאַנצע שאַפּנעריקע
ייִדישער לעבּן אין אונדזער שטאָטעלע אַרײַ־ אַלע אירע בּ— זײַ־
מיטן די אום... קולטורעלע, שאַפּ...לן ווי אויפן רעליגיעזן, דערצ...
ערישן, די אַרויסן גע...טעל סאַמעלסֿובּן. דער **פּנקס** דאַרף אַרויסבּרענגען
פון דער מאַ... אין שאַ...רישע ל...בּליק אָלע די, הער...לכע האָבּן
מיט זייער פערזאָנלעכן קיום, געטאָגרגיע, אַרבּעטס־סֿליס און קולוּמוּד,
אויסגעבּויאיעדעם דעם גײַסטיקן פאַרמאָג־אַער פונם זגערזשער ייִדנטום
און אים, אַרויסגעהויבּן העַיֶ איבּער די גרענעצן פון זַוין שטאָט,
רשם לחומאַרה.

מיר קאַנען ניטא מאַרבּ־יע, ניטשט דעראָמאַנענדיק דאָ, דעם
איניציע־ פון יענע ה—רלכע... גשטונטאַלטן, וואָס אונזער שטאָמן דאָם
בּעגנבּ... דער ייִדישער העלט, בּ—טלבּע גאַונים, שריפטשטעלֿער און
געלערנטע, ווי דער ערשטער... רואַ דאַתרא (בּאַקלאַנע אַלֿס גלאֶ־
שהכנר צדיק), דער לעבּעדער זגערזשער רבּ (מחבּר פון "ספֿר
המצוות"), דוד פּרישמאַן, יעקב קאַהן, צבּות לישאָף (בּ—ל הטֿ—
טל), אַוּעכַּבּ ויעלביע בּ—ונסטו־קקנסטלער. ווי
מיסכאֶ אירוּנדער און מים. פיר. אַנדערע, וואָס האָבּ... פֿאַ... וידער גיטֿ...
און קֿ—דשער מ—שאַ... בּ—ונוּאַ גיוּוֹ... בּלוּ... פֿ—יען... געפֿ—יער ... צ...
אַוּך אַיֿף אַיֿ... א גאַר גֿוּוֹסן טי—ל ... פון ... אַ ירדֹנֿום.

דער **פּנקס** דאַרף, לֿסֿף, דיעןֿ... אַלֿס ... סֿ—וּוּ ... פֿ...
פֿ... דעם אֿמאֶ... ... פֿ... ... אֿרבּ—גֿ... אֿין ... ...
שֿ—... ... יֿ... ... בּ...ֿ...ֿ... ...

לייֿ... מֿאַרֿ— ... מֿ—... נֿ—... ... ...
וֿילֿ... וֿ—ֿ... ... ...

דאָס דער שמֿ—טֿ... ... ...
שמֿאֶ—ֿ... ... ...
... ...
דעֿווֿ... ... ...
... ...
... ...
לֿאָזֿ... ... ...

העלֿפֿט אונז אין אונזער
פֿאַרֿאַנֿטֿוֿאָרטֿלֿעֿכער, אֿבּער אֿוֿי וֿיֿכֿטֿיֿקֿער
אֿרֿבֿעֿטֿ!

שֿיֿקֿט אֿרֿיֿן אֿיֿן אֿוֿנֿזֿעֿר אֿרֿכֿיֿוֿ:

Sz. Frogel, Łódź, Gdańska 44 m. 14

צֿאֿלֿעֿרֿ—ֿ... מֿאֿטֿעֿרֿיֿאֿל, וֿאָס הֿאָטֿ אֿ בֿ—ֿצֿ—ֿ... צֿ... ...
אֿיֿן זֿגֿעֿרֿזֿש... ... ...

... ...

גֿיֿטֿ יֿעֿדֿעֿר צֿוֿשֿטֿ—ֿ... אֿ—ֿטֿ—ֿר צֿ—ֿלֿ צֿוֿם
בֿ—ֿטֿ—ֿן דֿעֿם בֿ—ֿדֿ—ֿמֿאֿ—ֿ... ... לֿ—ֿכֿ—ֿן דֿעֿם
אֿ—ֿ—ֿ... זֿגֿעֿרֿזֿשֿ—ֿ יֿ—ֿדֿ—ֿטֿ—ֿם.

לֿאָדֿזֿש, סֿעֿפֿטֿעֿמֿבֿ—ֿר 1947.

די פֿאַרוואַלטונג
פֿון דער זגערזשער לאנדסמאנשאפֿט
אין פּוילן

A call to the natives of Zgierz that appeared in Lodz in 1947, regarding
the collection of material for a memorial book to the community of
Zgierz. As follows :}

APPEAL
To All Zgierz Natives!

One of our important tasks that we have taken on is to create and publish
a book that, aside from the memorial segment, will serve as a general
historical overview of the Jewish community in Zgierz from its inception
until its cruel destruction, that is until the terrible expulsion from Zgierz on

December 24, 1939.

This book will display the entire creative Jewish live of our city in all of its manifestations: economic and cultural, social and religions, educational and communal. This book rescue from forgetfulness and oblivion all of those who, with their foresight, energy, industriousness and culture, forged the spiritual character of Zgierz Jewry, and caused it to spread out far beyond the borders of the city in a glorious and exemplary fashion.

We cannot neglect to mention here at least some of those noble personalities that our city gave to the Jewish world. These include such Gaonim, writers and scholars such as: the first rabbi of the city (known to everyone as the "Alter Tzadik"), the last rabbi of Zgierz (the author of "Sefer Hatchuna"), David Friszman, Yaakov Kahn, Tovia Lipszitz (the author of "Nitfei Tal"). As well, there were such unique people as: [3], Moshel Eiger and many, many others, who, with their spirit and culture, influenced not only the community of Zgierz, but also a great part of Polish Jewry.

Finally, the book must serve as a symbolic mass grave for the former pulsating, industrious and culturally creative life of our thriving community, which was so mercilessly destroyed and annihilated by the Hitlerist murderers.

Unfortunately, we do not have the appropriate material that is needed to conduct that task. We also realize that the city archives were severely damaged during the occupation, to the point that no documents or chronological data about the Jewish settlement in Zgierz can be obtained from there. As well, all of the Jewish libraries, communal archives and private collections of documents have been plundered. Even the gravestones were broken and carried off by the despicable people. Therefore, our work is quite difficult. We must start anew.

We therefore turn to you, natives of Zgierz, wherever you are found, with our warm appeal:

Help us in our difficult, responsible, and very important task!

715

Send to our address:
Sz. Frogel, Lodz, Gdanska 44 m. 14

All kinds of material that is related to the Jewish life in Zgierz, such as: notices, documents, statistics, information about important events, memories, articles, photographs, etc. Inform us about Zgierz personalities in the Zionist movement, workers' movements, as well as in the Hassidic and scholarly world. Write us about organizations; institutions; groups; unions; clubs, kloizes; dramatic, musical and artistic circles - even those which did not exist in the latter period, such as "Hazamar"; the Yagdil Torah Yeshiva, and others. Write about a slice in time in Zgierz culture, social, industrial, factional, communal and sport life that is known to you.

Give every contribution and brick to build the literary monument in memory of the destroyed Jewry of Zgierz.

Lodz, October 1947:

The committee of the Zgierz Landsmanschaft in Poland

The first meeting of the Zgierz Natives after the liberation, in Lodz, January 1947

From among the important decisions that were taken at that time, two were of ethical-moral and social significance: a) to recognize and uphold the day of the expulsion of Zgierz (15th of Tevet) as the day of mourning and memorial for all of those who came from Zgierz; b) to publish a book that will perpetuate the memory of the exterminated Jewish community.

The committee understood the full seriousness and great responsibility needed to conduct all of their difficult tasks under exceptional circumstances and abnormal times. However, everyone at the time felt and attempted to fulfil their fateful duty with their full heart and dedication. Thanks to this, almost all of the decisions and tasks were able to be realized during the years of 1947-1949. We only mention a few:

A group of women would participate willingly and intensively on the day of the various communal events and assistance activities -headed by the indefatigable and industrious Dora Frogel.

A Chanukah party for the Organization of Zgierz natives, which took place in Lodz, 1947, at the home of A. Boaz

In order to encourage and cheer up the gloomy mood, from time to time a gathering or party was organized in private homes over a glass of tea, sometimes in Lodz and sometimes in Zgierz. The survivors would tell over their miracles of being saved from death, and others would sing songs from former days that would evoke tears, and at times also joy and hope. Some of

717

these gatherings were arranged around special occasions, such as festivals or other days of celebration. At such times, the significance of the day would also be discusses.

A particularly difficult albeit important job was the returning of the gravestones to the cemetery. Engineer Henryk Gibralter was particularly involved with this. In the name of the managing committee, he arranged that the plastered over gravestones be taken from the civic places and brought back to their former place. This effort lasted for several weeks, and was performed by youth of Zgierz industriously and with goodwill, as a holy task.

The chief task of the committee in those years was the fencing of the cemetery - a responsible and costly job. It was the warm and devoted desire of the surviving Zgierz Jews that the place that was sanctified for generations should be fenced in and protected from desecration by barbarians. The committee selected a special commission to conduct the work as quickly as possible. The contributions to this end were intensive and made with goodwill. Various appeals and fundraising events were also conducted.

After a year of strenuous work, the day of the reconsecration of the fenced in Zgierz cemetery took place. It was Sunday, 22nd of Elul, the first day of Selichot [4] 5607 (September 7, 1947). This event was combined with a general memorial service for the martyrs of Zgierz. The powerful, emotional speech by Aharon Cincinatus left an unforgettable mark upon all of the participants. This was a historic day for the Holocaust survivors of Zgierz, who gathered together from all over Poland for the first time after the war.

Holocaust survivors are re-erecting gravestones in the cemetery. The Germans had used these gravestones to pave sidewalks in Zgierz

The Committee of Zgierz Natives in Poland after the liberation. From right: Z. Fogel, V. Fiszer, M. Glazer, Y. L. Weinstein, Mrs. Dora Frogel, Bialystocki, H. Gibralter, M. Sribnik, Sczaranski, Y. Cincinatus

Re-fencing the cemetery of Zgierz after the liberation (22 Elul, 5607, September 7, 1947)

The Beginning of the Yizkor Book

One of the most important tasks that was begun at that time, but was not able to be acted upon for various reasons was the preparations for publication of the Yizkor Book. We managed only to collect material that was related to the history and development of the Zgierz Jewish community. We searched in the archives of Zgierz and the Lodz civic archives for any document that was related to Jewish Zgierz. The fruits of that effort, which went on for several months, were bountiful.

In that year (1948), Poland was already blowing with the malicious winds of the Stalinist regime. All communal efforts, particular Jewish ones, including charitable efforts, came under political control. We heard about searches of the residences of communal or political activists, which cast a pall over the already terrified Jews. We distanced ourselves from open communal work, and we even removed from our houses any material or document that could be seen as connected to communal or Zionist activity. Thus did the record collecting activity of the Zgierz Holocaust survivors go up in smoke... At the same time, the rumors and the hazy information about the creation of a Jewish state in the Land of Israel began to crystallize - the 2,000 year dream of the return to Zion. Here is not the place to discuss the stormy feelings of the Holocaust survivors when the independent Jewish State in our old homeland was established. Youths who had so recently returned from the death camps, the Siberian taigas or from the Polish military units, went to help the people against the Arab invaders by any possible means. Jews once again started up along their way - for how many times already?

בשנת 41 – 1940

בית-הקברות שלנו, שמתקיים
120 שנה, נהדס עד היסוד
על ידי הרוצחים הנאציים,
הקברים הוללו על ידם,
המצבות השצבורו ובהן נרצפו
רחובות העיר.

בשנת 1947

יהודי זגירז', מעאירית הפליטה,
גררו את בית-הקברות בגדה
אספו את המצבות שהתגוללו
ברחובות העיד וחדשו את
קדושת בית-הקברות.

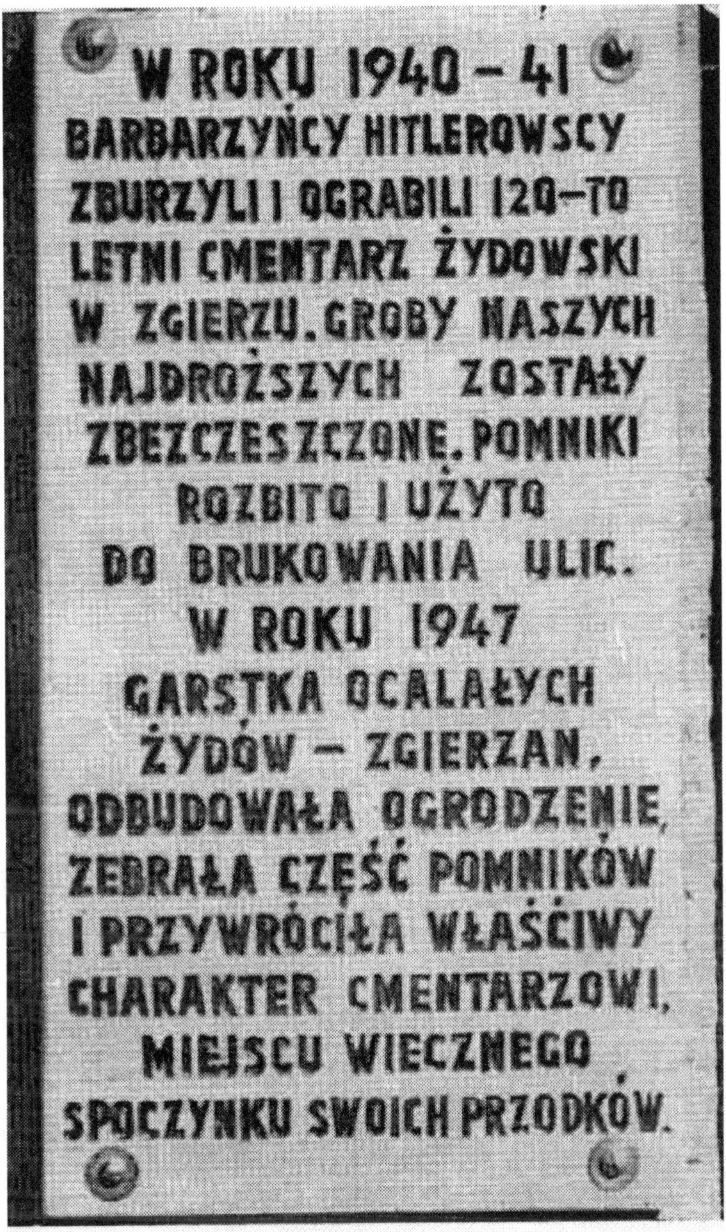

W ROKU 1940 – 41
BARBARZYŃCY HITLEROWSCY
ZBURZYLI I OGRABILI 120-TO
LETNI CMENTARZ ŻYDOWSKI
W ZGIERZU. GROBY NASZYCH
NAJDROŻSZYCH ZOSTAŁY
ZBEZCZESZCZONE. POMNIKI
ROZBITO I UŻYTO
DO BRUKOWANIA ULIC.
W ROKU 1947
GARSTKA OCALAŁYCH
ŻYDÓW – ZGIERZAN,
ODBUDOWAŁA OGRODZENIE,
ZEBRAŁA CZĘŚĆ POMNIKÓW
I PRZYWRÓCIŁA WŁAŚCIWY
CHARAKTER CMENTARZOWI,
MIEJSCU WIECZNEGO
SPOCZYNKU SWOICH PRZODKÓW.

Marble tables on the gate pillars of the cemetery that was reconsecrated and re-fenced by the holocaust survivors. The inscriptions are in Hebrew and Polish.

723

The inscription reads as follows:

In the years 1940-41
Our cemetery, which had existed for
120 years, was razed to the foundations
By the Nazi murderers
The graves were desecrated by their hands
The gravestones were broken and used to pave
The streets of the city.

In the year 1947
The Jews of Zgierz, Holocaust survivors
Enclosed the cemetery with a fence,
Gathered the gravestones that had been taken
To the streets of the city and renewed
The sanctity of the cemetery

Like the vast majority of Jews, the Zgierzers ran to the offices to obtain papers and passports. The family of the chairman of the Zgierz Landsmanschaft in Poland, H. Leibish Weinstein, with his wife and son, were among the first Zgierz families to set out from Lodz to the Land of Israel (via Paris). For that occasion, and also to mark the era of Zionist activity in Zgierz, the committee arranged a warm farewell evening for him.

Jewish communal activity in post-war Poland came to a standstill. Many prepared to emigrate. New problems and challenges arose. However, even given our preoccupation with our "old" life, we did not forget the over 200 typewritten pages about the history of the Jewish community of Zgierz. As some of us went to Israel, we brought with us the basis for a Yizkor book about a vibrant, creative Jewish life that had been so cruelly annihilated.

724

Zgierz Natives in Israel

The remnant of the community of Zgierz, who remained alive after the terrible destruction, came to Israel with the mass-aliya of the Holocaust survivors of Poland in the years 1950-1952. The absorption of the new immigrants in the first years of the State of Israel was particularly difficult by all accounts. The path to economic independence in the Land would have been hopeless for many immigrants without the assistance of the communal organizations and benefactors. Many immigrants, who did not have friends or relatives here in the Land, did not even have any address to which to turn for guidance and advice, and they certainly had no means of support and help.

Only in the year 1952, after a difficult and tiring task of explanation, was it possible to convince the veteran Zgierz natives of the great value of an organized body, which would concern itself with all of the perplexing problems that arose after the war, in the general realm of assisting those natives of our city who came to the land as soldiers of Ander's army and as new immigrants after surviving the Holocaust.

At a special meeting of the former communal activists that took place in the home of L. Weinstein, the following important objectives were set for the coming committee that would be chosen from among the Zgierz natives:

a) To help with advice and deeds the new immigrants from Zgierz, so that they could acclimatize in the Land and to ease their absorption difficulties.

b) To mark the anniversary of the destruction of Zgierz with a general gathering, at which the Zgierz natives would unite themselves with the memory of the martyrs. This Memorial Day would be observed every year.

c) To energetically continue with the work that had been started in Poland - the task of publishing a book that will perpetuate in an honorable fashion Zgierz and its Jews, their deeds and way of life, for generations to come. This book serves as an eternal testimony to the terrible murder and the Holocaust of our people.

d) To choose a temporary committee that would actualize the decisions and arrange the general gathering that would convene for a memorial ceremony.

e) The name of the organization will be the Organization of Zgierz

Natives in Israel.

The founding meeting of the organization took place on Saturday night, January 5, 1952, in the home of Nathan Nekricz. A temporary committee was selected from among those gathered, consisting of Yoav Katz, Nathan Nekricz (treasurer), Leibish Weinstein (chairman), Menachem Zakon, Yitzchak Glowinski, Aryeh Tenenbaum and Zeev Fiszer (secretary).

The First Memorial Gathering

The first memorial gathering of the Jews of Zgierz in Israel, convened by the "committee", took place on the 7th of Shvat 5712 (February 3rd, 1952) in Beit Hachalutzot in Tel Aviv. It was a spontaneous demonstration of an awakening feeling of brotherhood and closeness among the Zgierz natives in the Land. Zgierz natives who had been in the Land for 20 to 30 years, and who had practically forgotten their origins in the far-off Diaspora, came. Forgotten powers, which stormed into their soul with the memory of their forgotten birthplace in which they had spent the years of their youth, with all of their experiences and memories, were awakened in them. The frightening realization dawned on them that the entire old world, the world of their youth, was burnt and went up in smoke, along with their relatives, friends and brothers - the Jews of the community of Zgierz had passed away from the world in the flood of blood and tribulations - they were destroyed and were no longer!

All of these things awakened the slumbering spirit of the natives of Zgierz toward their birthplace, and they all came to the great gathering, from near and far. The meetings of Zgierz natives, who now met face to face and fell into each others arms, were particularly emotional. There were many tears of agony, pain, and joy, intermingled with the embracing of brothers and sisters at that gathering.

The feelings of the community that gathered reached their pinnacle with the communal recital of Kaddish and Yizkor, in a choked and emotional voice that broke forth from the depths of the soul. It is no wonder: for a large portion of those gathered were connected with family ties to the victims that perished in the great destruction.

726

The Selection of the Committee

This gathering obviously served as an impetus to all those people who planned to realize in Israel the objectives that were thwarted from realization in the land from which they came. These tasks were assigned at the meeting, and responsibility was transferred to the new committee, consisting of Yoav Katz, L. Weinstein, M. Zakon, A. Cincinatus, A. Michowicz, L. Tenenbaum, and W. Fiszer - with the hope that they would come to full fruition speedily.

However, for various subjective and other reasons, the tempo of the work and practical accomplishments of the committee were, to our dismay, not in accordance with the faith and hope that we put in the organization. Furthermore, youthful temperament and power of actualization were lacking. Nevertheless, it is appropriate to mention that in the first year of its founding, the fundamentals of the organization were created, its secretaries did all that was in their power to disseminate the knowledge of the existence of the organization to the public, and to forge many connections among Zgierzers in the Land and in the Diaspora.

The Paths of Activity

As we come to summarize the work of the organization throughout the first ten years of its existence, it was primarily in the area of broad based social assistance in the economic and social realms. First of all, it created an address to which one could turn in case of need. In truth, the financial means that the committee had at its disposal were very limited. Therefore, a great deal of good came from the charitable fund, founded under the initiative of L. Weinstein, N. Nekricz, L. Tenenbaum, and Michowicz and directed by M. Zakon and L. Zylberberg. It was the first actual assistance-offering institution for the absorption of many Zgierz immigrants in the Land. First and foremost, it succeeded in setting up those families who were in the weaving profession. These families received direction and advice from the organization, and found work in their profession in the Land. Loans from the fund of the sum of 7,000 Israeli Lira per year, with liberal repayment conditions, assisted many people in establishing sources of livelihood, obtaining dwellings, etc. Similarly, the secretariat of the organization helped

Zgierz natives with the obtaining of documents, permits, and all administrative matters.

The organization offered a great deal of assistance in the restoration of ties between families that were separated and scattered during the time of the war. The organization did a great deal of work in searching for relatives who had become separated from each other, by establishing connections with various institutions in Israel and the Diaspora, and by publishing notices, producing documents and verifying information. At this opportunity, it is worthwhile to mention the role of the our fellow native Shmuel Slodkewicz and his tailor workshop on Lilienblum 20 in Tel Aviv, which served as an information center and meeting place for all Zgierz natives who wished to maintain contact with their fellow natives. This small shop was a fortress for new immigrants from Zgierz. There, the new immigrants found out all the information needed to set up contact with Zgierz natives and to organize themselves in the land. There they forged their contact with the organization, and the map of the Land opened before them. New immigrants and those who had served in Ander's army who were searching for relatives and friends, all those for whom the path of life in the Land was not smooth, went through their first acclimatization course in that place.

Slowly but surely, the work of our organization continued along its course. It broadened and in the committee, and according to their level of dedication and ability. The activities of the committee were focused upon the main gathering of Zgierz Jews in the Land that was connected with the annual memorial day. With the passage of time, these gatherings became a main focal point of the communal life of the Zgierz Jews on an annual basis. There, the committees of the organization were selected, and tasks and directives were issued for their coming work. There, not only did Zgierz veterans in the Land intermingle with new immigrants, but also with Zgierz natives who were scattered across the globe, in all cities and communities. This was also the venue for Zgierz natives to come every year to unite themselves with the souls of their holy, dear martyrs.

זכרון עולם
לקהלת זגירז
על בניה – אנשים, נשים וטף
שהומתו והושמדו
על קדוש השם והאומה
בידי הרוצחים הנאציים ימ"ש
בשנות תרצ"ט – תש"ה

תהיינה נפשותיהם
צרורות בצרור החיים
וזכרונם לברכה ישאר לנצח

שרידי קהלת זגירז, פולין

The memorial tablet in the Holocaust Cellar in Jerusalem.

AN ETERNAL MEMORY
TO THE COMMUNITY OF ZGIERZ

To its people - men, women and children
Who were murdered and exterminated
In sanctification of the Divine Name and the nation
By the Nazi murderers, may their names be blotted out
In the years 5699-5705.

May their souls
Be bound in the bonds of life
And may their blessed memories remain forever

From the Survivors of the community of Zgierz, Poland.

Jerusalem, Mount Zion   3 Elul, 5719

729

We cannot pretend that we were able to offer every kind of assistance to all who were in need. We were unable to reach every downtrodden and bitter soul throughout the Land, to participate in every joyous occasion of our fellow natives, to take part in their sad and sorrowful events; for indeed, the lot of most of the people in the Land was not always good, and everyone was immersed in their own matters and worries. However, the little that we did was done with the best of intentions and enthusiastic participation, with faithful brotherly feelings. We were unable to do much, for we did not have the required means. Lack of financial resources always troubled us, and prevented us from actualizing all of our proper and good intentions toward those in need.

Contact with the Zgierz Natives in the United States

Immediately from the time of the founding organization, we turned with a heartfelt request to the Zgierz Landsmanschaft in America. We informed them of the situation of the Holocaust survivors who had come to the Land, and requested their financial help to support those in need. Unfortunately, the leadership there was not attuned to the holy task of that fateful period of time. They also did not answer the frequent letters requesting help in publishing the Book of Zgierz. Later, we heard that the Landsmanschaft had completely disbanded and ceased to exist.

Special Events in the Life of the Organization

The leadership of the organization was very successful in its annual meetings. It also attempted to arrange get-togethers and social events with a pleasant, family atmosphere. One of the events that was quite successful was the large party in 1959 that took place in the Maksim hall in Tel Aviv, with a full program. The income from this party was designated for the fund to assist the natives of our city. Another gathering of that year, of a different sort, that remains in my memory, was the gathering on Mount Zion in Jerusalem to dedicate the marble tablet in the "Holocaust Cellar" in memory of the of the community of Zgierz. This ceremony of the dedication of the tablet, that took place with the participation of a large number of Zgierzers, was quite moving. That memorial tablet was a gift from the Zgierz native Avraham the son of Shalom Tzvi of blessed memory Szewach.

In general, the year 1959 - the 20th anniversary of the expulsion from Zgierz - excelled as an active year for the Zgierz natives.

The visit to Israel of the well-known communal activist, known to all of the Zgierz natives in Israel, Mr. Fabian Grynberg and his wife, was an important event in the family of Zgierz natives in Israel. The committee organized a friendly gathering with important guests, over a glass of tea, in the hall of "Beit Lissin". The guests were greeted with speeches of welcome by Yosef Katz, W. Fiszer and others.

Some Words about the Book

The social activities of the organization did not remove the matter of a Yizkor Book from the order of the day. This was one of the main objectives of the organization, and the book was the main theme at every gathering and meeting. However, life made its demands, and the assistance efforts for the immigrants from Zgierz who were suffering from need always took first place. Nevertheless, several members of the committee dedicated themselves to the matter of the book immediately upon arriving in the Land, and dedicated all of their time after a day of work. They did this with complete dedication to their personal responsibility, without requesting assistance from anyone. They went to the archives, perused books, notebooks, and newspapers, collecting any article or statement that might serve as material for the book. These were the years of gathering and preparation for the task to come.

Zgierz natives at the unveiling ceremony of the memorial tablet in the Holocaust Cellar in Jeusalem, 1959

A Purim celebration of the Committee of Zgierz Natives in Israel, 1959. Here are three mothers, who have been in Israel for a long time: Misses G. Sperling, G. Itzkowicz, and T. Katz

When he first came to the Land, on occasion doubts about the idea of the book stole into the heart of the writer of these lines, as he surveyed the social and cultural conditions that prevailed in the Land, and he had doubts about the success of the project. Nevertheless, after my visit in Jerusalem to the former Sejm deputy, chairman of the Aguda and long time chairman of the Zgierz communal council Reb Eliezer Sirkes of blessed memory, and after a long discussion with him, it became clear to me that the perpetuation of Zgierz is not only a question of emotion and insight, but above all - a matter of historical, communal and moral requirements. Mr. Sirkes also promised me material for the book (in the form of the minute book of the Jewish community, which we later acquired through his son Avraham; these minutes indeed occupy an important place in the book). During my second visit to Jerusalem, I heard warm words of encouragement from the well-known activist, founder and chairman of Mizrachi in Zgierz, who was one of the best known scholars in the city, and whose family was well-rooted and prominent in the community of Zgierz - Reb Yisrael Frogel of blessed memory. One of his relatives, Reb Hirsch Frogel, was one of the first Jews who built up the Jewish street in Zgierz.

"It is forbidden for a city such as Zgierz to be forgotten from the history of the people of Israel", Reb Yisrael told me. In his words, I felt the pain and anguish that filled his heart. He continued, "Upon you, the Holocaust survivors, rests the duty to tell, to write about what once was and is no longer, as the verse states: 'write this down as a memory in a book' [5]. This is not only a personal, ethical duty - but also a national one."

It was evident that we were not alone in working toward this objective. The task of gathering material continued with greater strength, but the chief burden of the work rested on one or two people - until a public call to all natives of Zgierz to come to the assistance of this project was issued in 1962 . One year later, we were able to enter into negotiations with Editor A. Wolf-Jasni about the editing of the book. In 1963, the prospectus of the book was distributed in Israel and the Diaspora. At this time, we asked people to provide us with the required material. In the interim, A. Wolf-Jasni prepared the translated and edited material (from Polish) that we had brought with us from Poland - approximately 200 units copied from the civic archives of Zgierz and Lodz regarding the history of the Jewish settlement in Zgierz.

It then became clear that the pressure of the communal work on behalf of the immigrants, which was undertaken by the committee, impeded the progress of the preparation of the book. The need to separate the responsibilities and establish a special committee that would be solely dedicated to the matters of the book became obvious. Therefore, at the memorial gathering in 1964, a "Committee for the Book of Zgierz" was selected, and "Keren Hasefer" fund was set up.

Had things progressed smoothly, there is no doubt that the Book of Zgierz would have already found its place on the bookshelves of the Zgierz natives, but everything is dependent on luck. Our fortune took a turn for the worse when, the editor Jasni took ill just as he had commenced his work with our approval. His death caused us great anguish, for his heart was very close to the matter of Zgierz, as a former workers' activist in Lodz. He was connected to our city with warm memories.

The Committee for the book in the United States: L. Rubinstein, F. Greenberg, and D. Wechsler

734

Here is not the place to detail all of the disturbances, tribulations, and feelings of frustration that were our lot during the time that we progressed with our work. However, feelings of despair never entered our hearts. Our gaze was always focused toward the desired goal with diligence and without stopping. (If a researcher would even want to study the methodology of creation of a Yizkor Book, without doubt, he would find interesting material in our archives.)

This would not be a full description of our work for the book if we failed to mention the important and valuable work of one of our lofty people, the scion of the lofty people who grace our book. We refer here to our friend Fabian Greenberg. This friend of ours remained in close contact with us, as he supported us with words and with material. He created a special committee along with Leon Rubinstein and David Wechsler, and remained in constant contact. They visited Israel a few times, became closely acquainted with our work, and greatly assisted us in bearing the burden of the actualization of the endeavor.

As we write these lines, we feel relieved that the burdens of creation are already behind us. Along with the editor of the book, Mr. David Stockfish, we are approaching the goal.

Thus have we, the survivors of the Holocaust, fulfilled our duty of relating, remembering, and perpetuating Jewish Zgierz, which passed from existence. To the extent that we could, we also involve and draw nigh the descendents of the natives of our city to the hometown where their forbears were born and raised, and where they forged the vision of the generations.

As we speak about the "organization" as the active force in the Zgierz family in Israel, we must give thanks to all members of the committee who participated and took interest in the work of the organization throughout the entire era - from its founding until today.

Y. Katz, Y. Weinstein, Z. Fiszer, N. Nekritz, Y. Michowicz, A. Tenenbaum, Ch. Halperin-Sperling, Y. Zylberberg, A. Szewach, R. Katz, A. and P. Sirkes, Y. Lewin, T. Shif-Kirstein, A. Abramowicz, D. Frogel, Sh. Slodkewicz, B. Ber, Sh. Szapszowicz, and others.

Permit me, at the end of this survey, to express my feelings of gratitude and esteem to all of those who helped us through any means in actualizing this endeavor. I especially wish to thank the "Book Committee", whose members traveled the long route together with us, fraught with difficulties and bumps. Double thanks go to the editorial committee, who did their work with diligence and dedication, each in accordance to his task. Special thanks go to Mrs. Chaya Halperin-Sperling for her untiring, dedicated work in publishing the Book of Zgierz. She served as an example to us and a source of encouragement in difficult hours of despair.

We also remember with grief all of those Zgierz Jews who hoped to see the memorial book of their city, and did not merit to do so. Among those are the following members of the committee: Avraham Eiger, Aryeh Lipshitz, Menachem Zakon, Yoav Katz, Menachem Engel, Moshe-Yaakov Grand (America), and Aharon Cincinatus - may all their memories be a blessing.

Members of the Book Committee

Yehuda Weinstein, Yosef Katz, Avraham Szewach, Dvora and Yeshayahu Frogel, Yehuda Zylberberg, Frania Abramowicz-Szapszowicz, Avraham Boaz, Baruch Ziskind, Mordechai Rozman, Avraham Bornstein.

Editorial Committee

Rafael Katz, Mrs. Halperin-Sperling, Zeev Wolf Fiszer, Pinchas Sirkes, Yitzchak Szaranski, Yisrael Asher Malkieli

Translators Footnotes - Section A

1. This is a part of a verse of the Torah which commands the writing down of the history of the battle with Amalek so that it will not be forgotten by the Jewish people.
2. The Yiddish word is 'luftmentchen', a word that is hard to translate. It literally means 'people of the air'. It refers to people who have no definite employment, generally due to them having independent financial means.
3. In the Yiddish text only, the following footnote appears: The source "Polish Cities throughout One Thousand Years" completely diminishes and ignores the role of the Jewish people in the development of the city. Even the tragic destruction of the Jews during the years of the Hitlerian occupation is barely mentioned in the above-mentioned book. This is typical of the majority of the publications that appeared in Eastern Europe after the Second World War. (The Editor).
4. This paragraph and the next were omitted from the Hebrew section, and only appear in the Yiddish. My suspicion is that the Hebrew was translated from the Yiddish. These two paragraphs deal with post war history, and it is quite possible that the Hebrew translator felt them to be irrelevant and perhaps even felt it was degrading to even make note of the post World War Two development of the city.

5. This is a part of a verse of the Torah which commands the writing down of the history of the battle with Amalek so that it will not be forgotten by the Jewish people.
6. The Yiddish word is 'luftmentchen', a word that is hard to translate. It literally means 'people of the air'. It refers to people who have no definite employment, generally due to them having independent financial means.
7. In the Yiddish text only, the following footnote appears: The source "Polish Cities throughout One Thousand Years" completely diminishes and ignores the role of the Jewish people in the development of the city. Even the tragic destruction of the Jews during the years of the Hitlerian occupation is barely mentioned in the above-mentioned book. This is typical of the majority of the publications that appeared in Eastern Europe after the Second World War. (The Editor).
8. This paragraph and the next were omitted from the Hebrew section, and only appear in the Yiddish. My suspicion is that the Hebrew was translated from the Yiddish. These two paragraphs deal with post war history, and it is quite possible that the Hebrew translator felt them to be irrelevant, and perhaps even felt it was degrading to even make note of

the post World War Two development of the city.

9. A specific type of stone is referred to here: Kzszemien stone. I am not sure what this is.

10. Curiously, the term used here is "the Christian Passover".

11. The number seems low. I suspect that these refer to multi-family dwellings, where the owner earns his living from the rent.

12. Meaning by giving measures of produce in lieu of money.

13. Kreiz Stadt, a main city of a region.

14. The term is very strange, literally meaning 'Old Believers'. It apparently means 'Jews', as believers of the 'old' religion. From a later footnote in the text, it comes from the Polish word "Starozakonny").

15. From the term 'bergermeister', this means mayor.

16. A footnote at this point in the text reads as follows: "The Old Believer (Starozakonny) Rafael Dobrzynski is the father of the later eminent Admor Reb Avrahamele of Czeczanow, the founder of the Strikower rabbinical dynasty. Later, after the father's death, he took on the name Roda, or Rafaelowa. For further about this, see the article about the Strikower Rebbe in the chapter on personalities (from the editor)."

17. Groszy is a small unit of Polish money. The connotation here is having to live off of small coins.

18. This expression contains a diminutive, with a slightly derogatory undertone.

19. In Yiddish, the word for glassmaker is 'glezer', which is the same as the surname.

20. Literally "Muddy".

21. Literally, the birthright.

22. I am not sure of the meaning of this phrase.

23. It is not clear to what this refers. The question mark is in the text itself, indicating that the original document must be unclear. All question marks that I include in this section were transcribed from the original text.

24. monczaszes:possibly sellers of flour, kreiczasces: possibly cloth cutters

25. It is not clear to what this refers.

26. It is not clear if this is a repeat of the statement of the previous paragraph, or an additional fine.

27. There is a footnote in the text here that reads as follows: "As can be seen from this paragraph, Grynberg, by virtue of his position that was certified by the burmistrz of Zgierz, made mention of the synagogue to which he belonged, at a time prior to it being authorized by the authorities."

28. An "eruv" is a partition erected around dwellings, streets, or even entire cities, which converts an open area into a "private domain" according to Jewish law, thereby enabling the carrying of objects within that domain. The carrying of objects in an open domain would normally be forbidden on the Sabbath. The laws of eruv are extremely complex, and beyond the

scope of this footnote. An eruv can be constructed from posts and wires. In modern cities, the telephone and hydro poles and wires are often used to form a major part of an eruv. Bans on constructing an eruv are often an indication of anti-Semitism.

29. The Yiddish word here is 'feldscher', which according to Uriel Weinreich's Yiddish Dictionary is 'an old time barber-surgeon'. This vocation evidently entails some form of medical expertise, and seems to be a form of a physician's aide.

30. Here it is spelled Libaniecki, but in all other places it is spelled Lubraniecki.

31. The question mark appears in the text.

32. A footnote in the text appears here, as follows: In the request of Zalewski, Sadokerski was mentioned with the first name David, and in hisown request, his nameis given as Jakob. In anycase, according to his own submitted requestin which he describes himself a homeowner in the Jewish quarter, it is clear that this is the same person.

33. I am not sure of the connotation of this word. It may be a first name, but is unlikely, due to the presence of the definite article.

34. The Polish nobility.

35. Peasants in Congress Poland till 1864 were considered personal property of the landowner.

36. Yiddish word is.konfektzia', konfekcja means clothes in Polish.

37. I could not verify two of these terms, which I placed in quotes.

38. I suspect that the words 'wool, textile' his entry are erroneous, as they appear in the next row as well. In term of the term 'dealers' on the first two items of this table, vs. merchants on the remainder of the items, I suspect 'dealers' refers to wholesalers or middlemen.

39. An interesting term 'dorfgeiers' - village goers. I suspect it refers to those who peddle their wares in the villages of the countryside.

40. In the preceding table, the saloonkeepers seem to be included in the general number of dealers and merchants (the number of which in 1828 - 24 - is equivalent in this table and the preceding table).

41. I am not sure of the meaning of this term.

42. It is not clear what this means. It seems to refer to the official transferring of the permits to the synagogue from the city to the community.

43. Money to bribe the authorities to overlook a situation.

44. The Sabbath boundary whose purpose is to permit carrying outdoors on the Sabbath. The legal technicalities of the eruv are beyond the scope of this footnote.

45. The footnote at the bottom of the page is as follows: In the agreement between the regime of the Kingdom of Poland and between the German colonialists regarding their conditions for settling in newly developed areas.

46. I have used the word 'synagogue dozors' throughout, which bears the equivalent meaning of the term used in the previous historical section. Here the word 'shul' is always given in Yiddish, whereas in the previous section, was given in Polish translation (boznicki). I expect that it does not literally refer to the synagogue itself here, but rather to the religiouscommunity. There is some confusion in this current sentence, as theword 'shul' can mean both synagogue and school. However, I believe it is referring to the same group of communal leaders here.

47. The literal term here is "The last of the men of the Great Assembly", a term taken from the Mishnaic tractate of Pirke Avot. It refers to the last of the group of the Great Assembly, the group of the latter prophets and sages who codified much of Jewish ritual. Here, it refers to the last remnants of an earlier generation of scholars.

48. Szwarc (Schwartz) being Yiddish / German for black.

49. The term Hazamir in Hebrew means 'the choralist', or 'the singer'.

50. I expect that this refers to strikes, but the Yiddish word (bunt) has more of the sense of mutiny or rebellion.

51. The word for Rabbinical here is 'Rabbiner', which has the connotation of a Reform rabbi.

52. According to Torah law, it is forbidden to carry objects in a public domain on the Sabbath. In some cases (the technicalities of which are too intricate to discuss here), it is possible to erect a boundary around a community, thus converting it into a 'private domain' and making it permissible for people to carry objects within the boundary on the Sabbath. Such a boundary is called an 'eruv'.

53. In the corresponding Yiddish section (page 141), there is a footnote here: "August 1, 1915 was the first anniversary of the outbreak of the First World War. Was it a coincidence that the Communal Council had a meeting specifically on that day?"

54. The text appears to be in error following this point, as it does not mention the educational committee, but rather repeats the first line of the preceding sentence 'For the educational committee:'. In the equivalent Yiddish section, page 141, the educational committee is listed with three members: Zwykielski, Strykowski, and Miechowski.

55. The Torah is divided into 54 portions, one of which is read each Sabbath. A Jewish year has anywhere either 50/51 or 54/55 Sabbaths, depending upon whether the year is a leap year (which occurs seven times in nineteen years, and is intercalated with an additional lunar month). In addition, if a Sabbath coincides with a major festival (and this must happen at least twice a year due to Passover and Sukkot, but can occur as much as five times in a year depending on how the calendar falls out), the

regular portion is not read. Thus, there are certain portions that are doubled up to insure that the Torah reading cycle finishes at the appropriate time, on Simchat Torah.

56. Vayigash is the week following Miketz.

57. A milliard is the European term for a billion.

58. "Our hands did not spill this blood" is a quote from the book of Deuteronomy regarding the commandment of the 'Eglah Arufa' (the calf whose neck is broken). If a corpse is found in the open area between cities, the Sanhedrin (the main court of law) is supposed to measure the distance to the nearest city. Then the elders of the nearest city are enjoined to conduct a ceremony, which includes breaking the neck of a calf at a riverbank, washing their hands, and declaring "Our hands did not spill this blood".

59. The Sabbath prior to the new moon, when a prayer for the upcoming month is said. This is often considered a time for a cantorial display.

Translators Footnotes - Section B

1. Modeh Ani (I give thanks), is the first prayer recited upon arising each morning, and is one of the first prayers taught to young children.
2. On the festival of Purim, a large meal is taken in the late afternoon. Purim players often make the rounds from house to house, dressed up in costume, in order to collect charity. A white shroud is the clothing that the dead are buried in, thus this Purim player would have looked like a walking corpse.
3. According to Jewish law, all new utensils that are to be used for food preparation or eating, and were purchased from a non-Jew, must be immersed in a mikva (ritual bath) or flowing body of water.
4. A sukka, the tabernacle in which meals are eaten on the holiday of Sukkot, must be made of a thatched roof constructed of foliage. Often, a retractable solid roof is put on top to protect the sukka to protect it in the event of rain. It is retracted during the times that the sukka is in use.
5. Volozhin was the most prominent of the Lithuanian Yeshivas. Rabbi Berlin was the father of Rabbi Meir Bar-Ilan, after whom Bar Ilan University is named. Rabbi Yitzchak Elchanan Spector, the Rabbi of Kovno, is the namesake of the rabbinical school of Yeshiva University in New York, known as the Rabbi Yitzchak Elchanan Theological Seminary.
6. A misnaged is an opponent of Hassidism.
7. The voice of Jacob refers to the blessing of Isaac, when Jacob was

dressed up as his brother Esau. Isaac said that the voice was the voice of Jacob, and the hands the hands of Esau. Homiletically, the voice of Jacob refers to the voice of the Jewish people studying Torah.

8. The Talmud consists of the Mishnah, the older, terser code of law, and the much longer, more elaborate commentary of the Gemarah.

9. Tallit katan is a four-cornered fringed undergarment, worn to constantly fulfill the commandment to wear a fringed garment.

10. A more organized cheder for older children.

11. The prophetic section of the bible is divided into the early prophets, the books of which are narrative in style (Joshua, Judges, Samuel I and II, Kings I and II), and the latter prophets, the books of which are poetic in style (Isaiah, Jeremiah, Ezekiel, the Twelve Minor Prophets).

12. This is a reference to the different pronunciation styles of the Jews of Lithuania and the Jews of Poland. The references here are to the various vowels, which are signified in Hebrew by dots and dashes under the consonant letters. Kametz hasa short a or o sound, shurukhas a u sound, chirik has a long e sound, tzerei hasan ay sound, patach has a shorta sound.

13. Rosh Chodesh, the first day of a Jewish month (also the last day of any month, which is of 30 days) is considered to be a minor festival.

14. Zgierz Brings Honor to the Jewish Entrepreneurial Spirit by A. Litwin

15. This sentence is very convoluted. I did not translate it literally. Literally, it would read something like, "Zgierz does not glance at Lodz in the eye after a customer".

16. The word shtibel may here mean small house or hovel rather than its usual connotation of a prayer room.

17. Part of the first verse of the third chapter of Lamentations (Eicha).

18. Mariawites were a religious faction that renounced Catholicism.

19. When constructing a new house, it is customary to leave a small area unpainted as a "remembrance of the destruction of the Temple" ("Zecher Lechurban"). The same term is used here.

20. Eicha is the Book of Lamentations, traditionally ascribed to the prophet Jeremiah. The third chapter of Eicha commences "I am the man...", in which the author described his own personal experiences of the destruction.

21. There is a footnote in the text at this point, as follows: "The archives of the Jewish Historical Institute of Warsaw, number 108/ 1 (from the plundered Ringelblum Archive). The destruction of the synagogues, Beis Midrashes and cemeteries, volume 2, transcribed from a manuscript by V. P. with the permission of Yad Vashem."

22. I assume that this term refers to firms of very high (million) value.

23. The Yiddish word here is 'operator' or 'opretor'. I am not sure of the exact meaning. I translated as 'operator' due to the closeness to English.

It is evidently some form of professional associated with the weaving process. There are several terms for weaving professionals used in this article - not all of them could be readily identified.

24. The Yiddish word here is 'woof', which is part of a loom. This word, and several other technical weaving terms used here, are not in my Yiddish-English dictionary, and were unknown to the Yiddish native speaker whom I consult on these matters. I use the word 'woof' for 'ket', and 'warp' for 'shus'.
25. Literally: 'rags'.
26. Here the word 'kibbutzim' refers to Zionist pioneering preparation camps.
27. I am not sure of the difference between these two terms in Yiddish (basheftn, and anshteln). Evidently two different forms of engaging workers are meant - the former probably means employees, and the second may be something akin to hired contractors.
28. I am not sure of the identity of this profession.
29. The term in the text is guilder, which translates into Polish as Zloty. In most other places of the text, Zloty is written directly as such.
30. The Yiddish word is eintzirn, which would mean 'people who pull in'. I am not sure of the exact meaning here.
31. The term here refers to a workshop or farm where people prepare for aliya.
32. Seemingly a device on a loom to protect the user from danger. I am not sure of the translation of the Yiddish term given right after - it is seemingly a colloquial term for the same thing.
33. The Yiddish word is 'barst' - I am not sure of the exact translation.
34. There seems to be a contradiction in this paragraph.
35. A quote from a phrase of Pirke Avot (Ethics of the Fathers), that the way of Torah is to eat bread with salt, sleep on the floor, and to toil in Torah (i.e. to minimize physical comforts).
36. An anthology of the Aggadaic (stories as opposed to legal discussions) of the Talmud.
37. Various books of Jewish philosophy. The Kuzari was written by Rabbi Yehuda Halevi, and outlines a discussion between the king of the Khazars with a Jew, a Moslem and a Christian as he tries to ascertain the truth of religion. Moreh Nevuchim is the Guide of the Perplexed of Maimonides.
38. Farber means 'dyer'.
39. From Balut.
40. Simchat Beit Shoeva (literally: rejoicing of the water drawing) is a celebration held on the nights of Sukkot, reminiscent of the rejoicing that accompanied the water drawing ceremony in the Holy Temple. For a full description of the ceremony in temple times, see Mishna Sukka, 5th chapter.

41. I am not sure of the meaning of this here.
42. The statue of Jesus.
43. Probably has the connotation of 'sky'.
44. The seventh day of Passover marks the day of the crossing of the Red Sea.
45. The eighth day of Sukkot, a full festival day, followed by Simchat Torah.
46. The middle part of this paragraph is in transliterated Russian.
47. A reference to the World to Come.
48. Ein Yaakov is a compendium of legends of the Talmud. It is often studied regularly between Mincha and Maariv by hardworking, non-scholarly Jews, who wish to include a bit of Torah learning in their day.
49. Psalms 1,1.
50. An early summer month.
51. A derogatory term for gentile women.
52. 'Galer', probably barbers.
53. Possible meaning, goldfinch.
54. Kneidlech are matzo balls, kremzelach are pancakes made of matzo meal, and matzo brei is matzo fried with eggs.
55. Kasher is to render kosher. All utensils that are used during the year must be kashered for Passover. Kashering is accomplished by boiling water in a vessel, pouring boiling water in a vessel, purging the vessel by fire, etc., depending on the situation.
56. I believe this refers to a child who has become old enough to have his own wine goblet at the Seder.
57. Matzo shmura (literally: guarded matzo) is matzo prepared with extra stringency, used for the Seders, and by some for the entire Passover.
58. Maos Chittin (literally: money for wheat - i.e. for matzo) is charity given before Passover to enable the poor to celebrate Passover.
59. The ceremonial burning of chometz (leavened bread) takes place in the morning of the eve of Passover.
60. Four cups of wine are drunk at the Passover seder.
61. The Carmel Wine company, centered in Rishon Letzion, started in the late 1800s and is still functioning today.
62. Reminiscent of the cluster of grapes brought back on a stick by the spies in the book of Numbers.
63. It is customary not to eat matzo on the eve of Passover, in order to eat it with an appetite at the Seder. It is also customary not to eat a full-fledged meal that day.
64. Oneofthefour sections oftheCodeofJewish Law (Shulchan Aruch), which deals with thelaws ofthefestivals, among other things.
65. The section of the Talmud dealing with the laws of Passover.
66. A quote from Psalms 114, forming part of the Hallel service.
67. The pseudonym of one of the Gerrer Rebbes.
68. The latter chapters of the book of Leviticus describes the laws of the

Canaanite servant, who is 'owned' by his Jewish master.

69. In Yiddish 'gelt-shmelt'. Gelt means money. Repeating the word and replacing the first consonant with 'sh' implies a derogatory, dismissive attitude to the concept.

70. The three weeks between the fast days of the 17th of Tammuz and Tisha Beov (this period falling anywhere from late June to mid August) is the period of mourning for the destruction of the Temples, and the tragedies that befell the Jewish people through out the centuries. On the latter portion of this period, from the 1st of Av to Tisha Beov (9th of Av), it is forbidden to eat meat and drink wine, with the exception of the Sabbath. This period is known as the Nine Days.

71. Elul is the month after Av, falling in August or September. I believe that this obscure sentence means that during the summer, the homes and windows might have fallen into disrepair, and as the autumn approaches, the housewives need to ensure that there is adequate heating.

72. Haazinu Hashamayim is the Torah portion of Haazinu, consisting of the poetic song recited at the end of Moses' life. This Torah portion is read either on theSabbath prior to or following Yom Kippur. Koheletis the book of Ecclesiastes, read on Sukkot. These sections would be studied in the cheders during the weeks preceding the High Holy Days.

73. I am not sure of the meaning of the phrase used here 'fort a bissel rabin'.

74. The mikva is the ritual bath. Hassidic Jews would immerse in a mikva on frequent occasions, especially on the eve of the Sabbath.

75. A blessing made on a flame after the Sabbath as part of the Havdalah service.

76. I expect that there is an erroneous negative in this sentence.

77. In the Yiddish, Germans are 'Deitschen', and whips are 'beitschen', so the phrases rhyme.

78. Perhaps a kaleidoscope.

79. Yeke is Yiddish slang for a German, primarily a Jewish German, but here seemingly a German in general. In the previous phrase, 'bursch' is German for 'young lad'.

80. During Elul, the month preceding Rosh Hashanah, the shofar is blown each weekday. Elul is a month of repentance and awe that precedes the High Holy Days.

81. Kreutzdonnerwerter literally means 'Lower back thunder weather'. It translates roughly as 'pain in the butt', although it has the literal connotation of passing wind. 'Wir sind ja im krieg' means "We're in a war, after all". I am not sure what the last word or expression means, but the word 'kreutz' (lower back / buttocks) is obviously there.

82. The word used for filthy is 'drekiker', which has scatological connotations.

83. A term for Prussians.

84. A Stychic process is a natural or dynamic process. Upon searching the

web for the word 'Stychic' one finds it used almost exclusively regarding Zionist theory. For example, see the website http://www.angelfire.com/il2/borochov/eretz.html.

85. Metzitza is an element of the circumcision ceremony where the circumcisor (mohel) sucks the wound with his mouth. In modern times, this is done in most cases using a pipette for hygienic reasons, yet it is considered an integral part of the circumcision ceremony. Chalitza is the ceremony of drawing off of the shoe and spitting when a levirate marriage is rejected. The four cornered garment refers to the four cornered fringed garment (arba kanfos) worn beneath the clothing in fulfillment of the biblical commandment to place fringes upon one's garments.

86. Polish expression: describing young solder sent to certain death for sake of military sucess.

87. The Yiddish word here means 'non-kosher slaughterer'.

88. First words of a well known Polish patriotic song.

89. Before setting out for the synagogue at the beginning of Yom Kippur, parents bless their children.

90. The Yiddish word is 'balabusta' which does not translate well into English. It means the 'woman of the house', but has deep connotations of loving, caring, and perhaps a touch of excess.

91. The text includes the word 'not', here, which I suspect is an error.

92. The Polish word for orphanage is Sierociniec, close to the given word. Ochranke means "Secure Place".

93. The Joint Distribution Committee, and international Jewish charitable organization based in America, that concerned itself with disadvantaged Jews.

94. There seems to be something wrong with this number, as the photo on this page from 1921 shows far more than 7 children (unless the number 7 refers to full time boarders).

95. The first chapter in the tractate of Kiddushin, dealing with how the marriage ceremony is transacted. "Haisha Niknet" means "The wife is acquired".

96. This statement is taken from theCode of Jewish Law, with regard to the new crop of grain, which is forbidden unti lthe offering of the Omer sacrifice on the second day of Passover (after thedestruction of the Temple, it is debatable if such is still forbidden, but there are many opinions that hold that new grain is forbidden until after the second day of Passover). This statement has been taken by some to refer to any 'innovations' in Judaism.

97. The word 'shituk' (paralysis) has been used twice so far. I suspect it refers to a stroke.

98. Bein Hazmanim refers to traditional Yeshiva or cheder breaks between terms. These include the time from Yom Kippur until after Sukkot, a

time period surrounding Passover, and the time from after Tisha BeAv until Rosh Chodesh Elul.

99. These Torah portions occur a few weeks before Passover, when the days are already getting longer.
100. The Talmudic tractate dealing with the laws of sacrifices.
101. 'Ach' is a Yiddish pluralization.
102. A section of the code of Jewish law dealing with the laws of kashruth and other ritual matters - the mastery of which is considered essential in order to be able to receive rabbinical ordination.
103. This could render a chicken non-kosher.
104. A question of whether certain menstrual stains render a woman into a niddah - a state of ritual impurity. These laws are very complex.
105. The Vilna Gaon.
106. Tosafot is the main commentary (actually a compendium of several commentaries) that is printed on a folio of Talmud.
107. Prophetic portion read in the synagogue after the Sabbath and festival Torah reading.
108. I am not sure of the reference here.
109. A shiviti is an artistic drawing, upon which the phrase "Shiviti hashem lenegdi tamid" ("I place G-d before me at all times") is inscribed.
110. Artistic renditions of various segments of the prayer service.
111. The word Pension seemingly refers to a small, informal dormitory in a private home for the students.
112. An anti-Semitic political party.
113. A quote from Deuteronomy 7, 26, referring to the abhorrence of idol worship.
114. Derogatory term for a gentile.
115. It is a commandment to count each of the 49 days from the second day of Passover until Shavuot. This counting takes place at night, and is called 'Sefira' (literally - counting).
116. Treifa is a word for non-kosher meat (specific types of non-kosher meat - however the term has taken on a general meaning), and Pasul is a term for a ritual object that has become invalid for use. Here, the terms are referring to secular books.
117. A reference to a beggar's collection sack.
118. This day corresponds to the last day of Passover, however the holiday would have concluded by the evening.
119. I believe that this refers to 'volunteer organizations'.
120. Cousins who were also brothers-in-law.
121. The Jewish National Fund maintains a Golden Book in which people can be inscribed for honorary occasions.
122. Literally "independent powers"
123. Ru is 'rest' in Yiddish, and 'manoach' comes from the root 'nach' meaning rest in Hebrew.

124. I am not sure of the identity of this town.
125. A document formally selling the business to a non-Jew for the duration of the Sabbath each week (with the obvious understanding that it would be repurchased after the Sabbath). This type of document enabled the Jew to continue running the business on the Sabbath through the labor of non-Jews. It seems as if the Orthodox employers therefore preferred to hire non-Jews.
126. As an act of protest.
127. In the text, the name of the institution is given as Yesodei Hatorah. I am not sure why it is different in the photo caption. (In both the Hebrew and English captions, it is listed as Yesod Hatorah.)

Translators Footnotes - Section C

1. The acronym of Rabbi Israel Baal Shem Tov, the founder of Hassidism.
2. The Seer of Lublin.

3. Pronounced Pshischa, as it is known in Jewish Hassidic literature.
4. This is the traditional text of Jewish ordination: "Yoreh Yoreh" means "he shall surely teach", and "Yadin Yadin" means "he shall surely judge".
5. The pseudonym of one of the Gerrer Rebbes (many famous rabbis are known by the name of their magnum opus).
6. In Hebrew "Isur veHeter" - referring to areas of Jewish law where a decision is needed if something is forbidden or permitted.
7. The Taz is the Turei Zahav, and the Shach is the Siftei Kohen, the pseudonyms of the two main commentators on the Code of Jewish Law.
8. Whiskey and other fermented grain products (as well as all leavened products), are forbidden on Passover. The prohibition begins from mid-morning on the eve of Passover.
9. The "Psalms Jew".
10. This refers to a Jewish law regarding the Sabbath. There are various labors forbidden by Torah law on the Sabbath. However, they are only forbidden by Torah law if done in a positive manner. If done in a destructive manner, they are only forbidden by rabbinic law. An example would be the prohibition of tearing cloth. This is forbidden by Torah law if done for the purpose of sewing, but forbidden by rabbinic law (i.e. exempt from the penalty) if done for destructive purposes.
11. He who creates the fruit of the tree - the benediction to be recited prior to eating fruit.
12. He accepted Reb Henech as his own Rebbe.
13. The Chevra Kadisha is the burial society. A Cohen (Jew of the priestly caste) is forbidden to be in contact with a dead body, and therefore does

not enter the room of a dying person.

14. It is a Jewish law that a first born male son, who is not the son of a Cohen mother or father, must be redeemed for the value of 5 silver coins from a Cohen. The rabbi, being a Cohen, was often the officiant at this ceremony, and therefore received the 5 coins each time. This ceremony is called "Pidyon Haben", "The Redemption of the Firstborn".
15. Around the end of the Hebrew month of Av, in late summer.
16. A quote from the Mishnaic tractate of Pirke Avot.
17. Chol Hamoed is the intermediate days of the festivals of Passover and Sukkot. These are semi-festival days, where work is permitted, however unnecessary work is to be avoided.
18. It is customary to study Gemara with a singsong chant.
19. The week after Simchat Torah.
20. National holidays, such as the birthday of the czar.
21. Maimonides' main philosophical work.
22. Rabbi Yehuda Loew of Prague, to whom the story of the Golem is attributed.
23. A quote from Lamentations, 3:1. The Book of Lamentations is attributed to the prophet Jeremiah.
24. The Upholders of the Faith.
25. There is a Torah commandment to bring the first fruits up to the Temple in Jerusalem. These were decorated with extra fruits. The reference here is to an enhancement or an embellishment of a fundamental idea.
26. The area in Warsaw that was used to round up Jews for deportation to death camps.
27. Apparently a Polish term for Jew "Believer in the Old Religion".
28. The term here means Jewish community.
29. When writing a book on a Torah topic, it is customary to solicit approbations from well-known This term has been used extensively earlier in the book. It is rabbis, which are then printed at the front of the book.
30. The Hebrew term 'Megilla' is literally a scroll, more specifically one of the five Megillot of the bible: Esther, Lamentations, Song of Songs, Ecclesiastes (Kohelet), and Ruth. Colloquially, the term refers to a long written discourse.
31. A reference to a statement in the Mishnaic tractate of Pirke Avot that one should not make Torah a spade to dig with - i.e. that one should not use Torah to earn one's living.
32. The word is 'step brothers', but I expect it means 'half brothers' here.
33. A diminutive form of the name.
34. Apparently, the installation ceremony.
35. A quorum (minyan) is a gathering of 10 adult Jewish males needed to conduct a formal prayer service. On can recite the prayer service privately without a minyan, but certain important segments of the

prayers, such as the recital of 'kedusha' (the sanctification), kaddish, and answering amen after the repetition of various parts of the prayer, can only take place with a minyan.

36. A blessing recited before eating various kinds of food, that are not bread, grains, wine, fruits or vegetables. After such eating, the Borei Nefashot blessing is made.

37. Al Chet is part of the confessional recited on Yom Kippur, and also recited if possible as part of the final confessional before death.

38. The 'Seven Blessings', the week of post marriage festivities.

39. 120 years is considered the fullest possible lifespan, and the term is used when talking about realities that will be after the death of someone, but without wishing to imply that one is wishing for that person's death.

40. According to Jewish law, a Cohen (person of the priestly caste) is not allowed to marry a divorcee - not even one's own former wife. Incidentally, no man is allowed to remarry his former wife if the wife has been married, and then either divorced again or widowed, in the interim.

41. Tosafot (literally glosses) is a compendium of commentaries, mainly written by the grandchildren of Rashi, that appear on a Talmudic folio.

42. Zohar is a segment of Kabbalah.

43. Two of the early Hassidic leaders. Reb Elimelech refers to Reb Elimelech of Lizhensk (Lezajsk). For full detail, refer to the Lezajsk Yizkor Book on www.jewishgen.org

44. This is the first book of 14 Volume compendium of Jewish law (Yad Hachazakah) of Maimonides (Rambam). ,

45. A reference to a Talmudic story describing four rabbis who 'peered' into the 'orchard' (a Talmudic euphemism for mystical realms). Rabbi Akiva came out whole, Rabbi Elisha ben Avuya was damaged (i.e. became a heretic), Ben Zoma went mad, and Ben Azzai died. The reference here was to the one who became a heretic.

46. Literally 'milchemet mitzvah', a 'commanded war', referring to the situation in Jewish law where a war is mandated.

47. Rabbi Moshe Chaim Luzzatto, a well-known 18th century Jewish philosopher.

48. Bul is a biblical name for the month of Cheshvan.

49. Rabbi Nachman Krochmal, a 19th century writer and philosopher.

50. Graetz is one of the greatest Jewish historians.

51. I am not who this acronym stands for.

52. Hersh or Hershel is the Yiddish version of the Hebrew name Tzvi.

53. For a short on-line biography on Alexander Ossipovitch Zederbaum, see http://www.jewishencyclopedia.com/view.jsp?artid=76&letter=Z .

54. Rabbi Ezriel Hildesheimer was the founder of a rabbinical seminary in Berlin that taught traditional Torah in a traditional Orthodox style, along with secular studies.

55. Literally, "The Drippings of Dew" - however "Tal" - dew, is also the

acronym for Tovia Lifshitz, so it would mean "The Drippings of Tovia Lifshitz".

56. Shmot is the first Torah portion of the book of Exodus. After Moses and Aaron first attempt to speak to Pharaoh, the slavery is worsened in that the Jews were no longer given straw to bake bricks, yet their quota of labor remained the same. The leaders then ask Moses and Aaron "Why did you do evil unto this nation?"

57. From the book of Numbers, where the 40 wandering is declared upon the Jewish people. G-d states, that it won't happen that "one man of those who went up from Egypt will see the Land".

58. Vayeitzei is a Torah portion from the middle of Genesis, opening with Jacob's dream, and dealing with Jacob's sojourn with Laban, his marriage to Laban's daughters, the birth of his children, and his disputes with Laban.

59. I assume that this refers to intermarriage.

60. A verse from Ezekiel's vision of the dry bones.

61. Ophir is a land mentioned in the bible as the source of many of the precious stones and metals that were used for the building of Solomon's palace and temple. Its identity is unknown, and it has been surmised that it might perhaps be somewhere on the Somali or Omani coast.

62. The Betzalel Academy is a very famous Jerusalem arts academy.

63. There is a footnote in the text at this point, which reads as follows "He wrote many stories on the subject of the landscape of his birthplace of Zgierz, including 'Tikun Leil Shavuot' ('The Order of Shavuot Eve'), 'Kiddush Levana' ('The Sanctification of the Moon'), 'He Died', the poem 'Ophir', 'Three Who Ate', and many others." Note: most of these story titles have references to areas of Jewish ritual.

64. This dedication is replete with biblical innuendoes.

65. Selections of this section were translated from Yiddish to Hebrew by Emek (Emanuel) Frenkel, 1991, and then to English by Doubi Szwarc, 1999. These selections dealt primarily with the paragraphs that dealt with the family itself, and omitted those that dealt with more general issues. Doubi Szwarc is Isuchar's great-grandson, and Emek Frenkel is his grandson. Jerrold Landau, in the context of translating the Zgierz Yizkor book, worked from Doubi's translation, editing it and filling in the missing portions.

66. I translated the caption as it appears in the text (with the exception of omitting the question mark that appears after Roza's name). Mary Seeman, the daughter of Aleksander Szwarc, provides the following elaboration of the caption: "On page 393 - the occasion was Samuel's marriage to Agatha Barabash in Odessa. In the back row from the left: Samuel (Shmuel), Manya, Henryk (Hersz Ber, Berus, Dov in Hebrew, the grandfather of Doubi Szwarc), Szymek (Simcha), Marek. Middle row from the left: Agatha (the bride); Sura (Salomea), Isucher, Roza

(Szymek's first wife); Jechiel Frenkel, a son-in-law (Cesia -- Tzipora, his wife, is not in the picture because she was giving birth at the time). Front row: Aleksander (Oles)."

67. The Mishnaic Tractate "Chapters of the Fathers", that deals primarily with ethical adages.
68. Meshumadim is the Hebrew word for apostates.
69. Dogs in Yiddish.
70. Lemareh Ayin means "to the appearance of the eye". The "Le" is an introductory preposition, and if it is dropped, the phrase "mareh ayin" does indeed sound like Marrano.
71. Pronounced with the accent on the second syllable.
72. An endearing Yiddish term for the youngest daughter.
73. The term literally means "Torah and Work", but here the implication is "Torah and Divine Service".
74. At the time, a progressive Orthodox rabbinical seminary, which believed in the value of secular knowledge as well as Torah knowledge.
75. Miriam Seeman points out that this would have been one of Mordechai's Glicksman uncles (i.e. his mother's brother).
76. A famous rabbi (1768-1838), who wrote commentaries on the Code of Jewish Law and the Talmud.
77. The bag used to store the phylacteries (Tefillin) which are worn by males for the weekday prayers.
78. There is an error in the text here. It says "four or four passengers".
79. A verst is a now obsolete Russian unit of distance, equal to about 2/3 of a mile (according to the Weinreich Yiddish /English dictionary).
80. Literally "like my ten fingers".
81. Valut refers to the area of Baluty, mainly forested at that time, on the outskirts of Lodz.   This was where many Jews were exterminated in the first months after the Nazi invasion. It later became part of the Lodz ghetto.
82. A Kendel is a 'dipper', i.e. soup ladel.
83. The kiss of death is a reference to the death of Moses, who died through a divine "kiss", so to speak. Such a sudden, painless death, without suffering, is considered to be a sign of divine favor.
84. Mary Seeman points out that Hersz-Ber and his wife and son Wladek and Zosia and her son Rysio died in the Warsaw ghetto. David, Hersz-Ber's son mentioned in the next sentence, is Doubi's father. Aleksander Szwarc, mentioned at the bottom of the paragraph, is Mary Seeman's father.
85. Mary Seeman points out that Yechiel Frenkel is Emek Frenkel's father.
86. Translated from Hebrew by Doubi Szwarc. Edited by Jerrold Landau. Once again, there were several missing sections in Doubi's translation, which were filled in by Jerrold Landau.
87. A reference to a verse in Kohelet (Ecclesiastes) that indicates that a

threefold strand is not easily severed.

88. The family. Mary Seeman confirms that they were married in 1879.
89. Mary Seeman, points out that this photo was taken in front of the home of Isuchar and Sara (Salomea) Szwarc.
90. This comment in the text is obviously now obsolete.
91. A Hebrew expression meaning "to differentiate", used when moving from a more holy topic to a profane one - here to differentiate between the Jewish writer and the Christian clergyman - to avoid mentioning them in one breath.
92. Mary Seeman points out that he actually had six sons and four daughters.
93. There is a footnote in the text at this point, which reads as follows:
    "Indeed, that is how he was described by the Zgierz scholar, linguist and cooperation-theoretician Reb Yaakov Baniel (Berliner) of blessed memory in the book 'Nivim' ('Expressions'), chapters on cooperation and language, Tel Aviv, 5617 (1957), page 122 - where he dedicates one of his articles 'to the memory of Reb Isuchar Szwarc of blessed memory, a leader of the Jewish community of Zgierz, Poland, my native city.'"
94. Mary Seeman points out that this was in Vienna.
95. Modern style cheder.
96. The story of Hersz Ber's fight against the ghettoizing of the Jews in the mid 1800s is recorded in the early historical sections of the Yizkor book.
97. Mary Seeman points out that Barabash was from Odessa, and was the father of Agatha, Shmuel's wife.
98. The Golden Book is a book maintained by the Jewish National Fund for the registration of honorable events. It still is maintained today, and many people are inscribed in it on significant life occasions (of course, after making a significant donation).
99. Mary Seeman points out that this drawing was by Henryk Glicenstein who was a famous Polish Jewish artist related by marriage to her family.
100. Mary Seeman identifies the poem as follows: "From a book of poems called Mourning Songs from the Ghetto By Izabela Gelbard (pen name Czajka), Publishing House: Julian Wyderka, Katowice, 1946, (Last Poem in the book) pp55-59. Mary Seeman translated this poem directly from the Polish version. Jerrold Landau compared Mary's translation with the Yiddish translation in the Yizkor book. Minor divergences were glossed over (and the choice was made to translate in accordance with the Yizkor book). Major lacunae are pointed out in footnotes - especially the major divergence in the latter part of the poem.
101. Perhaps the three dots in the Yiddish translation preceding the next sentence is indicative of this lacuna.
102. Kiddush (literally: sanctification) is the prayer recited prior to the Sabbath and festival meals over a cup of wine.
103. Referring to G-d.

104.   These marks are in the text, perhaps hinting to a lacuna.

105.   From a point about 15 lines up until the end, Mary Seeman's translation of the original diverges significantly from the translation of the original. Before that point, there were smaller divergences. Except for the two lacunae I pointed out, I gave precedence to the Yizkor book translation over Mary's translations, and have not pointed them out. These divergences were minor in general. The point of major divergence, about 15 lines up: Mary Seeman speculates that there were probably several editions of this poem, in different forms. The following is Mary's translation from

As Satan rushed to do battle, rape, savagery and murder flourish
Destruction rips apart the capital, the country and towns and cities
And fire from the sky itself grills and chokes - cruel death
Force was used, used to the shame of the enemy

Never again will those greenest of green chestnut trees enfold You
Never again will those sweetest-scented hyacinths embrace you
The terrible deeds of the human heart, sad and terrible!
How the sun's rays dance on the crooked fences…

The screems of victorious soldiers. The sound of mines, the groans of
the murdered
The last judgement. The victory of Satan on earth
Death alone is not enough…Agony is needed too
Let the black earth redden with pale blood
Beastliness has been let loose, to, slaughter, wailing
"Not enough death, more death. Let death conquer.

Amid the red pigeons, calmly near the window
Stood my elderly Grandfather - he is not thinking of war.
And he is not thinking of death - because he is ready
The yellowed leaves of the chestnut trees groaned
Books, manuscripts, texts, and documents ……
Covered in cotton, in leather, in velvet
Books were closest to his heart, faithful companions
Said adieu and moaned (even now I hear their moans)
Clouds float by on the hill…time passes, time flies
"Where are the grandchildren…where are the great
grandchildren…where are my children?"
-They love you; we love you…when the curtain falls
A person is alone with death and dies alone
Do you hear the uproar on the stairs? The echo of deaf footsteps
They're coming…they're already coming... He automatically grips the
nearest book

A book covered in leather, with golden edges
"The Song of Songs" - it speaks with longing of eternal love
He held it in front of him in his tremulous aged palm
With a book of love my Grandfather protected himself, like a shield
Doors battered down. The gang fell upon him with a howl and hollering
The quiet house was filled with obscenity and screaming
"Jude Verflute Alte" He lifted and aimed a bloody dog's fist
Look! Suddenly he retreated, dropped his fist…Why did he not hit him?
The book fell from his grasp. Do you hear…It fell with a clatter
The white head of the old man slowly slumped onto his chest
His seeing eyes focused on a distant nothingness
Before the German could strike………. His life faded away.
I, granddaughter of your blood, bones, your flesh
Have withstood the battle with the enemy….so far I have overcome
The year is forty-three…the war is not over
In flight…in the forest….in hiding……circling an extending net
Grandfather - I promise you I will survive. Revenge - holy revenge
Will be the task of all those in unnamed tombs
I promise You Victory. Your blood flows in my veins.
Soplicow December 1943

106. Mary Seeman believes that Marek Szwarc, the famous artist and sculptor, Shmuel's brother made this drawing.
107. I identified all of these locations on a map of Portugal in the National Geographic Atlas of the World, with the exception of Da-Astrala and Pondision.
108. Mary Seeman points out that this book is a translation of the Biblical Song of Songs (Shir Hashirim).
109. A. Y. Brzezinski is Mary Seeman's maternal grandfather. He was a noted scholar who wrote the definitive biography of the rabbi of Lodz, Rabbi Maizel.
110. Evidently some unit of money. I am not familiar with the term.
111. See footnote in the historical sections of the translation of this book for a full definition of eruv.
112. Shpirita seems to be a play on the name "Shapira". While the name Shapira most probably arises from the Jewish community of Speyer, Germany, it is quite similar to the Hebrew word Shapir
113. (Beautiful).
114. The German areas of the areas that later became Czechoslovakia.
115. A renowned rabbi in Posen Germany (1761-1837).
116. Sifra is a commentary on Leviticus from the Mishnaic era.
117. Galbanum (chelvona) is the one spice in the incense compound of the temple that had an offensive smell.
118. The Polish army in exile, that played a major role in the fight against the allies.

119. Buki the son of Yagli was the Prince of the tribe of Dan, listed in Numbers 34, 22. I am not sure what the reference means here. However, in the list of leaders, the word 'Nasi' (Prince or leader) is not appended to the first few names - Buki the son of Yagli si the first to whom the term is used.
120. Evidently referring to Lodz.
121. A term used by Hebraists for Yiddish.
122. There is a discrepancy of one year between the English and Hebrew here.
123. Evidently, his stay was extended.
124. I was not able to make out the works of these, which are brought down here: "Manginot Ivriyot" of Heine, and "Afigia Batauris" of Goethe.
125. A footnote appears in the text here, as follows: "A detailed bibliography of Yaakov Kahan and his works can be found in the "Lexicon of Hebrew Literature of the Later Generations" by G. Karsal, published by the Poalim Library."
126. A blessing of thanksgiving for reaching a certain occasion.
127. A type of bird.
128. Apparently, a euphemism for the concentration camps.
129. The Etrog is the citron used in the Sukkot ceremonies. The pitam is the prominent wooden stamen of the Etrog.
130. Thereis a long footnotein thetexthere. Itreads as follows: RabbiBromberg, in his book"TheGreats ofHassidism" writes that two veteran Hassidim lived in Zgierz, Reb Nota Heindsdorf and Reb Leibish Pozner, who had business connections with Reb Sh. Sirkes. Once, Reb Leibish came to him and told him of the difficult circumstances of one of the leading Hassidim in Zgierz, who needed 10,000 rubles in order to extricate himself from his straits. He gave him a list of ten industrialists, including his name. After Reb Shlomo looked at the list, he took out 4,000 rubles and give them to Reb Leibish, to cover three names whom he was doubtful would give their share. The astonished Reb Leibish made haste to tell his brother-in-law Reb Nota, and they decided to tell this to their rabbi, the author of the Sfat Emet. The Admor of Gur answered briefly, "May my lot be with him". They did not rest until they brought Reb Shlomo to their rabbi. He indeed became a dedicated Hassid of the Rebbe. After the Rebbe's death, he maintained his faith with his successor, and was counted among his Hassidim and faithful friends.
131. A Yiddish commentary on the Torah, designed especially for women.
132. A Mishnaic adage describing someone with a phenomenal memory.
133. This is the name of a transport camp in France.
134. A midnight service, non-obligatory and generally only recited by particularly pious people, in which one laments the destruction of Zion.
135. Maharal is the acronym for Rabbi Judah Loew of Prague, 1525-1609.

136. A derogatory term for gentiles.
137. The sanctification of the moon is a blessing recited outdoors each month a few days after the sighting of the new moon. Given that it is recited outdoors, the text was engraved on a tablet outside the home.
138. I believe that this is a typo, and 1921 is intended.
139. This introductory section, in smaller font, was written by Vove Fisher, the editor of the book. The article itself is written by Reb Fishel Bunim's grandson.
140. The opening word of the Rosh Hashanah and Yom Kippur morning service, following Psukei Dezimrah.
141. A reference to the Talmudic sage Hillel, who was known for his fine character.
142. A Talmudic term for one who delves deeply into his studies.
143. Perhaps Poddebice.
144. A set of Talmuds.
145. A barber-medic.
146. I am not sure of the meaning of this.
147. Both words connote teacher - although Melamed connotes the more traditional, cheder style, elementary teacher.
148. An anti-malarial agent.
149. The Talmudic section dealing with festival offerings in the temple.
150. Dated 27 Nissan 5627 (Yom Hashoah), May 7, 1967 - an award issued by the State of Israel.
151. Mordechai Anielewicz, 1919-1943, was the leader of the Warsaw Ghetto Uprising.
152. I.e. his essence and his exterior are both fitting.
153. Duties of the Heart - a book on Jewish belief written by Rabbi Moshe Chaim Luzatto.
154. I am not entirely sure, but I believe this is a reference to the first 50 years of the 1900s ending imminently.
155. Evidently, a form of expression - as in English: everybody and his mother.
156. The Berze is a bourse or exchange. The Gmina seems to be the Jewish Community Office.
157. A water carrying set consisting of a pole with two attached pails.
158. A reference to the Biblical Esau, considered in Jewish tradition to be the nemesis of the Jewish people.
159. A Russian term for 'brave young man', used as a compliment.
160. The name Ramah would come from the first letters of Rav Menachem Hager.
161. Gentile-like - although it uses the term 'sheigetz', this is a more derogatory term for gentile.

Translators Footnotes - Section D

1. This is a play on the first verse of Psalm 137, the famous Psalm that begins "By the Rivers of Babylon...". This section contains many snippets of biblical verses and elegies (Kinot) of Tisha Beov.
2. A term used for ethnic Germans in Poland.
3. an organized action of seizing people off the street in order to imprison them.
4. The Polish word for 'queues'.
5. Sukkot concluded on October 6 in 1939.
6. I am not sure of the meaning of this term.
7. From the context, it seems as if this is the trash collection. Smiec is the Polish word for trash.
8. A tallis (tallit) is a ritual prayer shawl worn by Jewish males during prayer. A parochet is the ornamental covering of the holy ark in the synagogue. Tefillin are the phylacteries worn by Jewish men during weekday morning prayers in accordance with a biblical command. Mezuzas are specific sections of the Torah, written on parchment, often encased in an ornamental casing and affixed upon doorposts in keeping with a biblical command.
9. There is something wrong with this date.
10. On the day of the yahrzeit (anniversary of death) of a parent, is proper to recite the daily services with a prayer quorum, and to recite the Kaddish prayer. A prayer quorum (minyan) consists of 10 males over the age of 13.
11. This word usually connotes an organization of emigres from a certain place in a new country (such as the Zgierz Landsmanschaft in the United States or in Israel).
12. The following four paragraphs, written in small type around the photo, is obviously a biographical section, and not authored by Rozenstrauch himself.
13. "Hear, Oh Israel..." - the confession of faith recited daily during the prayers, and also to be recited as death approaches.
14. Paramilitary teaching - a form of basic military teaching at the high school level.
15. A hard to translate word, also used in Modern Hebrew, meaning to utilize influence towards people in power, contacts in high places, etc., to get one's way.
16. Presumably, volunteers.
17. Umschlag Platz was the area in Warsaw where Jews were gathered for deportation. In German, the term means a place of facility where goods (sic) are moved from one transportation vehicle to another.
18. Outpost.
19. "Binen" means bees - seemingly a nickname for airplanes.
20. This sentence is rather cryptic. It probably is a hint to early

information of mass murder of Jews during the war being sent to America.

21. Kotlas is a city about 500 miles northeast of Moscow, towards the Arctic Ocean. It is the site of several 'gulag' style camps.
22. A Jewish greeting of welcome.
23. A Yiddish term for sweet or succulent - here most likely used as sarcasm.
24. An autonomous Soviet Socialist Republic, several hundred miles northeast of Kotlas (in fact, Kotlas is about halfway between Moscow and Komi A.S.S.R.) It is adjacent to the Europe Asian border at the Ural Mountains, not far south of the Arctic Ocean.
25. Seemingly 50 degrees below zero, but it is not clear which measurement scale was being used.
26. "pritshe" means. the bed in a prison cell.
27. Seemingly, and army in exile.
28. Probably the Polish name of the aforementioned Akiva.
29. Probably a way of saying "beat them in the chests", or "beat the wind out of them".
30. There seems to be an error in this sentence.
31. Kittel is the white ritual garment worn by Jewish men on Yom Kippur and the Pesach Seder, and worn by the prayer leader on some other occasions (such as Rosh Hashanah, the prayer for rain on Shemini Atzeret, the prayer for dew on Passover, and Hoshanah Rabba).
32. The tallis is the ritually fringed prayer shawl worn by Jewish men during prayer. The tallis katan (small prayer shawl) is a fringed undergarment worn by Jewish males at all times.
33. The parochet is the cloth decorative cover of the Holy Ark in the synagogue.
34. Out of concern for the safety of the Jews, presumably.
35. A member of the Revisionist Zionist faction - i.e. the right wing Zionist group that followed Zeev (Vladimir) Jabotinsky.
36. Although Bialystok is in Poland, it was in the area under Russian control at the time.
37. Mezherich is a well-known city in Ukraine, however, it is probably here referring to the town of either Mezhirech"ye (Miedzyrzec Podlaski) or Maziarze in Poland.
38. The Feast of Weeks or Pentecost, in late May or early June.
39. I chose the Russian spelling here, due to the information regarding the composition of the group a few sentences later.
40. An autonomous region in Russia near the Arctic Ocean and bordering on the European side of the Ural Mountains.
41. Obviously, this was to hide his circumcision.7. I assume that this refers to points of gathering or points of concentration.

42. A society of fellow natives.
43. Figuratively obviously.
44. Henri-Philippe Petain was the ruler of the Vichy regime.
45. Laskier evidently had contact with the local police force, who were different than the official Vichy police which was evidently more closely connected with the German authorities.
46. Literally, "prepare for noon".
47. The term for German nationals in Poland.
48. There are seemingly some inconsistencies in the dates of this story. Perhaps the 'liberation' referred to here is the liberation from the camp in Arkhangelsk.
49. Shmone Esrei (literally eighteen, from the eighteen benedictions of the weekday prayer service) is the central part of the daily prayer services. In fact it has nineteen benedictions, as one was added later, but it still retained its name. Even though on Sabbaths and festivals there are only seven benedictions (except for Rosh Hashanah Mussaf where there are nine), the name Shmone Esrei still sticks. A piyut (plural: piyutim) is a poetic addition to the prayers. The High Holiday prayers have a large number of piyutim.
50. Literally "Here I am, poor in worthy deeds", the prayer recited by the prayer leader prior to the commencement of the Rosh Hashanah and Yom Kippur Mussaf service. In this prayer, the prayer leader confesses his unworthiness for his task, and asks that the congregation not be blamed for his failings.
51. Charitable organization.
52. Yahrzeit is the anniversary of death. Herzl died in 1904, so this story took place in 1908.
53. Lithuanian Jews (Litvaks) are known as being very level headed.
54. A compendium of the aggadaic (stories or legends) from the Talmud.
55. Literally: He was destroyed.
56. Probably meaning: He was lacking the work of his hands.
57. Turen farein, which I expect means touring organization, as strange as that sounds here.
58. He must be referring to the Hebrew University.
59. 11.   Between 1948 and 1967, the territory surrounding the Hebrew University campus on Mount Scopus was in Jordanian hands. The area of the campus itself was an Israeli enclave surrounded by Jordanian territory, but was effectively inaccessible. After the 1967 war, the Mount Scopus campus again began to function. In the interim, the functioning
60.   Hebrew University campus was in Givat Ram.
61. Zbaszyn is a town on the former Polish-German border. In the pre-war Nazi years, Polish Jews in Germany were deported back to

Poland through that town.

62. The Gra is the acronym for the Gaon Reb Eliahu, otherwise known as the Vilna Gaon.
63. These are names of chapters of Talmud.
64. The Shehecheyanu blessing is a blessing thanking G-d for keeping us alive, which is recited on special occasions, including all festivals. On the second night of Rosh Hashanah, it is customary to also eat a new fruit at the time of the Shehecheyanu blessing.
65. Water that has been left out in the open all night, which is used for the baking of matzos.
66. The Sabbath prior to Passover.
67. Shabbat Shuva is the Sabbath between Rosh Hashanah and Yom Kippur, and Shabbat Chazon is the Sabbath preceding Tisha Beov.
68. The hiding of the face of G-d, so to speak, when evil befalls the world.
69. Literally, Bilaam - whose curses turned into blessings.
70. Ritual bath.
71. The root 'sh k l', could mean to educate, but it can also mean to lose one's children, or even to miscarry. I chose the first meaning here, but it is not clear that the second is not intended.
72. "Muddy", here referring to the Muddy Road, referred to several times in this book.
73. The odd reflexive form here "Hitrim" has the connotation as to take in donations rather than donate.
74. Tzadok the yellow.
75. Does not translate well into English, literally: "He of the multitude of radishes".
76. Charvona was one of the servants of Achashverosh in the Book of Esther, who interceded on behalf of the Jews.
77. Tosafot is a prime commentary on the Talmud (Gemara).
78. The Talmud records a dispute as to whether it is better for a scholar to have a vast repository of knowledge, or to be able to delve deeply into a topic. The term for the scholar with the vast repository of knowledge is "Sinai", reminiscent of the entireTorah given on MountSinai, and the termfor thescholar with theability to delve deeplyinto atopicis"Uprooter of Mountains".
79. Numerical mnemonics used in the derivations of the Jewish calendar.
80. A quote from the memorial to martyrs recited on Sabbath mornings in the synagogue.
81.

Translators Footnotes - Section E

1. Husband's first name not given.
2. The word here is Warta, which is the name of a river in Poland, but I assume it is a typographical error.
3. Obviously a euphemism for a death in one of the death camps, such as Auschwitz. People were not killed in the crematoria, but rather in the gas chambers.
4. Note that the second name on the gravestone 'Yehuda' is different from that given in the text 'Aryeh'.
5. The photo does not include the daughter.
6. This yizkor box extends over three pages.
7. The language of opposites (Sagi-Nahor, an Aramaic word, literally meaning 'a lot of light' but used as a term for a blind person) is a common literary technique in Jewish tradition which uses an opposite term to describe something. The basis of this is, so to speak, to avert the evil eye.
8. A prominent Orthodox movement, still in existence today as a main lobby group of Orthodox Judaism.
9. This repetition is obviously an error.
10. He obviously married his first cousin.
11. I am not sure of the meaning of this word.
12. Rosh Hashanah.
13. The Hebrew date given here is 5701, which corresponds to the English date is 1941. The same discrepancy of ten years exists in the next entry, for the mother. I arbitrarily chose the English date as being accurate, but that is not definitive.
14. The Hebrew and English years do not match here, as December 1923 would correspond to 5684.
15. Gachal is a pre-military corps.
16. Nachal is an army division for recent immigrants.

Translators Footnotes - Section F

1. A pogrom was perpetrated against the Jews of Kielce in 1946.
2. Organizations or clubs for people from the same hometown.
3. The name is faded in the photocopy here and cannot be made out.
4. The daily penitential services conducted from the Sunday immediately prior to Rosh Hashanah (or if Rosh Hashanah falls early in the week, from two Sundays prior) until Yom Kippur.
5. A verse from Exodus, commanding the Jews never to forget the memory of Amalek.

www.ingramcontent.com/pod-product-compliance
Lightning Source LLC
Chambersburg PA
CBHW050234270326
41914CB00033BB/1906/J